HISTORIC DRESS
IN AMERICA

REIGN OF JAMES II

1685

FRONTISPIECE (FIGURE 1).—This plate represents a soft brocade gown which was brought from England to the Barbadoes Colony in 1685 and has been lent to the writer by a direct descendant of the owner. It is looped back over a satin petticoat, originally white, but mellowed by time into a rich ivory tint, and trimmed with two flounces of lace. The sleeves of the low-cut bodice are short and finished with a fringed gimp of the prevailing soft red colour of the brocade. The stomacher is trimmed with graduated bows of ribbon in the fashion called "échelles." The undersleeves of fine lawn are finished with lace ruffles to correspond with the falling band or collar. The skirt of the gown is quite long in the back and is looped at the hips with knots of ribbon; it is laid in plaits around the waist and sewed to the bodice which is fitted close to the figure. At that period the hair was drawn back softly from the face and two curls hung down on the shoulders from the knot at the back.

HISTORIC DRESS IN AMERICA

1607=1870

ELISABETH McCLELLAN

Illustrations by
SOPHIE B. STEEL & CECIL W. TROUT

Two volumes in one
Volume One   1607-1800

PUBLISHED BY BENJAMIN BLOM, INC.
NEW YORK AND LONDON

"Fashion wears out more apparel than the man," and happily for us some relics of by-gone days have been preserved intact and placed in our hands for the preparation of this book—veritable documents of history on the subject of Dress in America, which should teach you "the nice fashion of your country," and help you "to construe things after their fashion."

For these interesting old garments and also for the valuable portraits and family papers most generously entrusted to us for our work I take this opportunity to express, in behalf of Miss Steel and myself, our appreciation and sincere thanks.

ELISABETH McCLELLAN.

PHILADELPHIA, *October*, 1904.

First Published 1904-10
Reissued 1969 by
Benjamin Blom, Inc. Bronx, New York 10452
and 56 Doughty Street, London, W.C. I

Library of Congress Catalog Card Number 70-81515

Printed in the United States of America

Historic Dress in America was reissued in 1937 in an unaltered reprint
as *History of American Costume 1607-1870.*

Introduction to Present Edition

We all know there is much history in costume and yet at the time this work was begun there were many books to be had describing the furniture, silver, houses, churches, meeting-houses, school-buildings and even the coaching inns frequented by the people of colonial days in America, but of the dress of the colonists, little or nothing had been put into book form. Occasionally some contemporary biographer would describe the costumes worn at festivities in the larger towns of the colonies, and by their help we could easily picture to ourselves a lady of that time adjusting her lace ruffles before a Chippendale mirror, or a gentleman studying the graceful use of his snuff box with the aid of his reflection. But of the every day clothes of these same people worn during the busy hours of those stirring times, the dress of the merchants, the artisans, the farmers and their families, there was absolutely no book to be found on the shelves of the libraries. Before the Revolution many a ship load of immigrants, wearing the costume of the country of their birth, landed in our ports, lending a variety and contrast to the appearance of the people. Much research was necessary to collect the material for this book, but Miss Steel and I found that our interest grew as we worked. We are much gratified to know that a new edition has been called for, proving that the earlier one filled a demand and has been of use to authors, artists, playwrights and students of history, for whose benefit it was undertaken.

Elisabeth McClellan.

June, 1917.

CONTENTS
Volume One

INTRODUCTORY CHAPTER

PAGE

The Spaniards in Florida and California, 1565–1764................ 25
The French Settlements in Louisiana and the Mississippi Valley,
1680–1764 32

PART I. THE SEVENTEENTH CENTURY

The English Colonies in Virginia, Maryland, the Barbadoes, and
the Carolinas, 1607–1700.. 39
The English Colonies in Massachusetts, Connecticut, New Hamp-
shire, Maine, and Rhode Island, 1620–1700 79
The Dutch and English in New York, Long Island, the Jerseys,
Delaware, and Pennsylvania, 1621–1700 117

PART II. THE EIGHTEENTH CENTURY

Women's Dress, 1700–1800... 173
    Reign of Queen Anne....................................... 181
    Reign of George I... 190
    Reign of George II.. 193
    Reign of George III 202
    After the Revolution...................................... 255
Children's Garments, 1700–1800................................... 279
Men's Apparel, 1700–1800 295
    Reigns of Queen Anne and George I......................... 299
    Reign of George II.. 307
    Reign of George III....................................... 316
    After the Revolution...................................... 328
    Legal Dress in the Eighteenth Century..................... 335
    Uniforms in America, 1775–1800............................ 340

Glossary 381
Index 397
Authorities Consulted.. 405

ILLUSTRATIONS
Volume One

For this edition all illustrations
are reproduced in black and white

FIGURE PAGE
1. (In colours) Gown of red brocade worn in the Barbadoes Colony about 1685. Lent by Mrs. Rachel St. Clair Miller.................*Frontispiece.*
2. (Initial) Spanish galleon 25
3. Spanish gentleman, end of sixteenth century......................... 26
4. Spanish soldiers with rapiers and arquebuses, middle of sixteenth century 27
5. Fernando De Soto, in Spanish armour of the sixteenth century.......... 29
6. Sieur de La Salle, in French costume of 1680........................ 29
7. Pedro Menendez de Aviles, in Spanish dress, 1565.................... 29
8. Sir Francis Drake, in the dress of an English sea-captain, 1586......... 29
9. French peasant women.. 34
10. Jesuit missionaries 35
11. (Initial) Sir Walter Raleigh.. 43
12. Captain John Smith, 1616... 44
13. Sir Edwyn Sandys, 1607... 45
14. George Sandys, Secretary of the Virginia Colony, reign of Charles I...... 45
15. Sir Isaac Pennington, reign of Charles I............................. 45
16. Sir John Pennington, reign of Charles I............................. 45
17. A farthingale, 1607.. 47
18. Ordinary dress of a boy, 1602–1676................................. 47
19. Dress of a colonial governor, reign of Charles I.................... 49
20. Dress of a colonial lady, reign of Charles I....................... 49
21. Costume of a planter's wife, reign of James I...................... 49
22. Costume of a gentleman planter, reign of James I................... 49
23. Ordinary dress of a little girl, 1602–1676......................... 52
24. English mariner, 1650 and after.................................... 53
25. Countryman in doublet, 1660 and after.............................. 54
26. Soldier in cuirass and morion, seventeenth century................. 55
27. Silver frontlet worn by the Queen of the Pamunkeys................. 57
28. Silver mace, used in the House of Burgesses, Virginia.............. 57
29. George Percy, second governor of Virginia......................... 57
30. Steel vambrace dug up near Jamestown.............................. 57
31. Doublet worn in the reign of James I.............................. 59
32. Indoor dress of an English gentlewoman, reign of Charles I......... 65

FIGURE   PAGE

33. Outdoor summer costume of an English lady, reign of Charles I......... 65
34. Back view of outdoor dress, reign of Charles I........................ 68
35. English lady in hood and apron, reign of Charles I.................... 69
36. English gentlewoman in winter dress, furs and mask, reign of Charles I.. 69
37. A peddler, from an old print 73
37½. Monmouth cap 74
38. (In colours) Lady of quality in the fashionable dress of William and Mary's
        reign... 75
39. (In colours) Typical dress of a child in the seventeenth century.......... 75
40. (In colours) Outdoor dress of a tradeswoman, end of the seventeenth cen-
        tury 75
41. (In colours) Workingman, end of seventeenth century.................. 75
42. (In colours) A gentleman in the reign of William and Mary............. 75
43. (Initial) A Puritan dame... 83
44. Mandillion of black silk, 1620 and after.............................. 85
45. Photograph of a doublet, reign of Charles I 87
46. Photograph of a doublet, reign of James I............................ 87
47. Typical winter costume of a lady, 1640............................... 90
48. Boy's doublet of white linen embroidered with gold silk, reign of Charles I 91
49. Bodice of white satin, reign of Charles I 91
50, 51, 52, 53, 54. Boots, 1595–1660 94
55, 56, 57. Boots, 1660–1690... 95
58, 59, 60, 61, 62, 63, 64, 65. Shoes, 1610–1695 96
66. Puritan colonist of the Massachusetts Bay Company................... 97
67. Puritan woman of the Massachusetts Bay Company.................... 97
68. An English gentleman of about 1666................................. 97
69. A lady of the same date (1666) in walking hood and fur tippet.......... 97
70, 71. Cannons or breeches fastenings, 1650 99
72. Lady's glove with embroidered cuff, seventeenth century.............. 101
73. Head, after Hollar, showing fashionable style of hair-dressing, reigns of
        Charles I and II 101
74, 75, 76, 77. Gloves worn in the seventeenth century.................... 101
78. Man in buff coat and bandolier, 1620–1660 103
79, 80. Points with aiglets, 1650–1660.................................. 104
81. Samuel Sewall, Governor and Judge of Massachusetts Colony 105
82. Sir John Leverett, Governor of Massachusetts 105
83, 84, 85, 86, 87. Various forms of the buff coat........................ 107
88, 89, 90. Gorgets, 1620–1645... 108
91. John Winthrop the second, 1640..................................... 111
92. Sir John Leverett, about 1680 111
93. John Winthrop, Governor of Massachusetts Colony in 1629 111
94. Edward Winslow, Governor of Plymouth Colony, 1644................. 111

FIGURE PAGE

95. (Initial) Dutch colonist in New Amsterdam 121
96. Peter Stuyvesant, Governor of New York Colony, 1647 123
97. Sir Edmond Andros, Colonial Governor of New York, 1674–1681..... 123
98. Henry Hudson, 1609... 123
99. Sir William Keith, Governor of the Province of Pennsylvania, 1717 ... 123
100. Dutch woman in working dress, seventeenth century................. 126
101. (In colours) Dutch lady of New Amsterdam, about 1640............. 127
102. (In colours) Patroon, about 1640................................. 127
103. (In colours) Dutch lady, about 1660.............................. 127
104. (In colours) English gentleman, end of reign of Charles II............. 127
105. Dutchman in working dress, about 1650............................ 129
106. Dutch girl in fur cap and fur-trimmed jacket, 1641.................... 131
107. Dutch lady, hair arranged in puffs at the side, 1645.................. 131
108. Little Dutch girl, middle of seventeenth century...................... 131
109. Little Dutch boy, same period..................................... 131
110. Dutch lady in fur cap and mantle, 1644............................ 131
111. Swedish lady in pointed fur cap and ruff, 1640...................... 131
112, 113, 114, 115, 116, 117, 118, 119, 120. Hats, 1606–1692................ 135
121. Coif of a Dutch matron, late seventeenth century.................... 136
122. Dress of an English gentlewoman, 1640............................ 137
123. Swedish woman in clogs, 1640.................................... 137
124. Dutch lady in outdoor dress, 1640................................. 137
125. English lady in house dress, 1640................................. 137
126. Dutch lady in wide-brimmed hat and ruff, 1645..................... 141
127. English lawyer, seventeenth century................................ 141
128. English woman in silk hood and tippet, 1640........................ 141
129. Dutch lady in fur tippet and hood, middle of seventeenth century 141
130. Boy in periwig, about 1680....................................... 141
131. English woman in coif and kerchief, 1640.......................... 141
132. Portrait of little girls in seventeenth century, reign of Charles I 145
133. Portrait of two Dutch boys, middle of seventeenth century............. 145
134. Periwig of Charles II, 1660....................................... 147
135. Periwig of William III, 1690...................................... 147
136. Campaign wig, 1684... 147
137. Coat and full breeches of buff brocade, 1681........................ 149
138. Coat and full breeches of dark red flowered silk, 1681................ 149
139. Coat and breeches of silk trimmed with fancy braid, reign of James II... 149
140. Jeremias Van Rensselaer, end of seventeenth century................. 153
141. Kiliaen Van Rensselaer, first patroon of New Amsterdam, 1695........ 153
142. Sergeant-at-law, reign of Charles II............................... 156
143. Quaker gentleman, 1682.. 157
144. Quaker lady, 1682 157

FIGURE	PAGE
145. Huguenot lady, 1686	157
146. Huguenot gentleman, 1686	157
147. Sergeant-at-law, reign of James II	159
148. Count Zinzendorf in preacher's robe	161
149. Simon Bradstreet in judge's robe, about 1670	161
150. Lady Fenwick, in widow's mourning, reign of William and Mary	161
151. Elisabeth Boehler, Moravian lady in Pennsylvania, 1787	161
152. Moravian coif	164
153. Reticule of white silk embroidered in crêpe flowers	165
154. Waistcoat of Count Lemcke, about 1798	165
155, 156. White silk pocket cases embroidered in colours, about 1790	165
157, 158. Moravian cap of lawn worn over a coif	167
159. Specimens of colonial silver, seventeenth century	169
160. Specimens of pewter ware, carved knife boards, etc., seventeenth century	169
161. (Initial) Lady in sacque, early eighteenth century	177
162. (In colours) Colonial costume of 1711, of buff chiné silk, from an original gown lent by Mrs. Rachel St. Clair Miller	179
163. (In colours) Gentleman in costume of 1702–1720, reign of Queen Anne	179
164. (In colours) Colonial costume of reign of George I, from an original gown lent by Mrs. Samuel Chew	179
165. (In colours) Man in dress of a gentleman in the reign of George I	179
166, 167. Colonial fashion baby, 1720	183
168, 169. Camlet hood, taken from an original garment of about 1702	185
170. Short sacque, early eighteenth century	187
171. Colonial dress, worn in Pennsylvania in the reign of George I	191
172. White satin wedding gown, 1760	191
173. Lutestring gown worn in Philadelphia in 1760	191
174. Colonial dress of buff chiné silk worn in the Barbadoes Colony in reign of Queen Anne	191
175. Lady in a cardinal, early eighteenth century	194
176, 177, 178, 179, 180, 181. Caps, 1744–1745	195
182. Man in a Roquelaure, reign of Queen Anne	197
183. Back view of a yellow damask gown, reign of George I	197
184. Green brocade gown, worn in Massachusetts Colony, reign of George I	197
185. Back view of gentleman's dress, reign of George I	197
186, 187. Hooped petticoats, 1721–1750	199
188. Pair of stays, about 1770. Lent by Miss Sarah Bache Hodge	200
189. Clog, eighteenth century	201
190. Patten, eighteenth century	201
191. Riding hat of fawn-coloured felt, reigns of George II and III	202
192. Colonial gown of kincob brocade, worn in Massachusetts about 1735. Lent by Miss Archie Newlin	203

FIGURE	PAGE
193. Colonial gown worn in Virginia, about 1775	203
194. Riding mask, eighteenth century	205
195. (In colours) Colonial gown of camlet, worn in the Massachusetts Colony, 1725. Lent by Mrs. Charles Hacker	207
196. (In colours) Gown of kincob brocade, time of George II	207
197. (In colours) Young gallant in full dress, 1740	207
198. (In colours) Colonial gown of green taffeta, worn by Mrs. Wilimina Weemys Moore, about 1740. Lent by Miss Sarah Brinton	207
199. House-maid in sacque, apron and clogs, middle of eighteenth century	209
200. Mrs. Catharine Van Rensselaer in the popular style of cap, about 1770	211
201. Mrs. Nathaniel Appleton in an every-day dress. From photograph lent by Mrs. Cutter	211
202. Mrs. Nathaniel Appleton, Jr., showing a peculiar cap of 1784. From photograph lent by Mrs. Cutter	211
203. Mrs. Mary Faneuil of Boston, about 1750	211
204. A Watteau gown of fawn-coloured silk brocaded with coloured flowers worn in Pennsylvania about 1752. Lent by Mrs. William Bacon Stevens	215
205. Crimson brocade gown worn by Mrs. Faithful Hubbard of the Massachusetts Colony, 1750. From a photograph lent by Mrs. Cutter	215
206. Another view of the green kincob gown over a white satin skirt with apron and stomacher of white silk embroidered in colours	215
207. Back view of the kincob gown showing the Watteau plaits	215
208. Lady's silk shoe, about 1775	217
209, 210, 211. Diagram of white satin gown worn by Mrs. St. Clair about 1760	218
212. (In colours) Wedding gown of a New England Quaker lady, about 1750. Lent by Mrs. Charles Hacker	219
213. (In colours) Gown of rich brocade worn by Mrs. Michael Gratz about 1750. Lent by Miss Miriam Mordecai	219
214. (In colours) Suit of uncut velvet worn by Robert Livingston of Clermont, reign of George II. Lent by Mrs. David E. Dallam	219
215. (In colours) Back view of Watteau gown of fawn-coloured silk	219
216. Beaver hat and short cloak, middle of eighteenth century	221
217. Back view of suit of uncut velvet worn by Robert Livingston of Clermont. Lent by Miss Anna Griffith	223
218. Back view of white satin wedding gown of Mrs. St. Clair	223
219. Everyday costume of a young lady, flowered chintz over a quilted petticoat, about 1770	223
220. Elderly man of business in a coat of strong fustian over nankeen breeches, 1770–1790. From a coat lent by Miss Sallie Johnson	223
221. Group of colonial garments, eighteenth century	227

FIGURE	PAGE
222. Calashes, Quaker hats, Quaker bonnet, riding hat, etc., eighteenth century	227
223. Lady in capuchin, with fur trimmings and muff, reign of George III	229
224. Mr. and Mrs. Ralph Izard, 1774	231
225. Portrait of the West family, 1799	231
226, 227. Calashes, 1765	233
228. (In colours) Dress of blue lutestring worn by Mrs. St. Clair, 1760. Lent by Mrs. Rachel St. Clair Miller	235
229. (In colours) Suit of dark satin worn by Robert Livingston of Clermont. Lent by Miss Anna Griffith	235
230. (In colours) White satin wedding gown of Mrs. St. Clair, 1760. Lent by Mrs. Rachel St. Clair Miller	235
231. (In colours) Suit of uncut velvet, waistcoat of quilted satin, worn by Robert Livingston, of Clermont, reign of George III. Lent by Miss Anna Griffith	235
232. Quaker cape and cap, 1780	237
233. Embroidered reticule	239
234. Ladies gloves of doeskin, 1717. Lent by Mrs. William H. Dreer	239
235. Bead reticule and paste buckles. Lent by Mrs. John Biddle	239
236. Bonnet of muslin made over reeds, 1780. Lent by Mrs. John Biddle	239
237. Crêpe shawl with printed figures, late eighteenth century	239
238. Linen pocket embroidered in colours, 1752	239
239. Colonial jewelry and snuff-box. Lent by Mrs. Howard Gardiner	239
240. Lady's slipper of green and white taffeta. Lent by Mrs. William H. Dreer	239
241. Fan painted by Gamble, 1771. Lent by Mrs. Charles Hodge	239
242. Typical dress of a country girl, 1780	246
243. Night-rail, eighteenth century	252
244. Gown of mauve crêpe, end of eighteenth century. Lent by Miss Janethe	253
245. Front view of Watteau gown of fawn-coloured silk, brocaded in flowers	253
246. Gown of white embroidered muslin worn in 1790. Lent by Mrs. George Knorr	253
247. Calico short sacque, late eighteenth century	253
248. Gown of glazed buff chintz, 1795. Lent by Mrs. Cooper Smith	253
249. Riding habit, about 1785	260
250. Mrs. Pennington in Quaker dress, 1780. From a portrait lent by Mrs. Howard Gardiner	261
251. Catharine Schuyler Van Rensselaer, 1795. Lent by Mrs. J. K. Van Rensselaer	261
252. Mrs. Morris in Quaker dress, 1785	261
253. Dutch lady of the New York Colony, 1765. Lent by Mrs. J. K. Van Rensselaer	261

FIGURE   PAGE

254. Summer costume, 1790–1795................................... 264

255. (In colours) Suit worn at the court of France by William West, Esq., of Philadelphia, 1778. Lent by Mr. Hemsley 265

256. (In colours) Lady's costume of the prevailing French fashion, 1777–1779 265

257. (In colours) Gentleman's suit of drab cloth, 1786.................... 265

258. (In colours) Muslin gown with flowing skirt and long sleeved bodice, 1790 265

259. Woman in typical working dress, 1790–1800......................... 268

260. White satin wedding slippers, 1800. Lent by Mrs. Schaeffer.......... 269

261. Cups and saucers, owned by Robert Treat Paine. Lent by Mrs. William H. Dreer 269

262. Group of slippers, 1735–1780..................................... 269

263. Blue brocade wedding slippers, 1771. Lent by Miss Helen Morton.... 269

264. Wine glasses and point lace belonging to Governor Wentworth, 1717–1730. Lent by Mrs. William H. Dreer............................. 269

265. Back of mauve crêpe shown in figure 341........................... 273

266. Silk pelisse with quilted border, 1797. Lent by Frank W. Taylor, Esq. 274

267, 268. Seventeenth century utensils................................... 275

269. (Initial) Boy and girl after Sir Joshua Reynolds, late eighteenth century 283

270. (In colours) Girl in red stuff gown and muslin cap, about 1730......... 285

271. (In colours) Child in printed gown and embroidered cap, about 1710.... 285

272. (In colours) Child in gown of white damask linen, about 1720.......... 285

273. (In colours) Little boy in blue suit, about 1740...................... 285

274. (In colours) Boy in brown velvet suit and cocked hat, about 1760....... 285

275. (In colours) Boy in blue ribbed silk suit worn in Pennsylvania about 1756 285

276. (In colours) Child in buff printed cambric dress, about 1760........... 285

277. (In colours) Child in sheer muslin gown, with cap to match, 1790...... 285

278. (In colours) Little girl in cloak, muff and hat, after Sir Joshua Reynolds, about 1780 285

279. (In colours) Young girl in muslin gown trimmed with embroidery, about 1790 285

280, 281. Child's stays. Lent by Mrs. Gummere........................ 287

282. Portrait of young girl in Philadelphia, about 1760.................... 289

283. Miss Hill of Philadelphia, 1756.................................... 289

284. Portrait of a child in New York, about 1700. Lent by Mrs. J. K. Van Rensselaer 289

285. Christiana Ten Broeck, early eighteenth century.................... 289

286. Baby dress and cap, 1771. Lent by Mrs. George Knorr.............. 291

287. Boy in ordinary dress, 1790....................................... 292

288, 289. Front and back views of a "flying Josie," late eighteenth century. Lent by Mrs. Schaeffer.. 293

FIGURE	PAGE
290. Suit of blue silk worn by a little boy about 1756	293
291. Child's dress of buff chintz worn in Pennsylvania, 1710	293
292. White shift with plaited sleeves	293
293. Child's dress of damask linen worn about 1720	293
294. (Initial) Man in long trousers and riding boots, late eighteenth century	299
295. Kiliaen Van Rensselaer, reign of Queen Anne. Lent by Mrs. J. K. Van Rensselaer	301
296. Jan Baptist Van Rensselaer, reign of George I. Lent by Mrs. J. K. Van Rensselaer	301
297. A genuine Roquelaure, middle of eighteenth century. Lent by Frank W. Taylor, Esq.	303
298, 299, 300. Wigs, 1700–1750	304
301. William Penn, by Benjamin West	305
302. George Washington, by Gilbert Stuart, 1797	305
303. Back view of suit of dark satin worn by Robert Livingston	308
304. Rev. George Whitefield, latter half of eighteenth century	309
305. Rev. Jacob Duché, D.D., late eighteenth century	309
306. Dr. Ezra Stiles, late eighteenth century	309
307. Rt. Rev. Richard Challoner, Vicar Apostolic of the English Colonies in America, 1756	309
308. Jonathan Edwards, second half of eighteenth century	309
309. Rt. Rev. Samuel Provoost, D.D., First Bishop of New York, late eighteenth century	309
310. Back view of coat of light brown velvet, reign of George II	313
311. Front view of same	313
312, 313. Front and back views of coat of brown twilled cotton jean, typical summer garment of a Friend	313
314. Gentleman in banyan and cap, middle of eighteenth century	315
315. John Penn, in fur-trimmed coat	317
316. Thomas Penn as colonial governor	317
317. Patrick Gordon as colonial governor	317
318. James Hamilton, Lieutenant Governor of Pennsylvania, 1783	317
319, 320, 321, 322. Boots, 1702–1784	319
323. James Logan in judicial robe, 1745	321
324. Fisher Ames, middle of eighteenth century	321
325. John Jay in robe, as Chief Justice of the United States	321
326. Nathaniel Appleton of Boston, by Copley	321
327. Henry Laurens, by Copley	321
328. Man in working garb, 1750	323
329. John Hancock, Governor of the Massachusetts Colony, reign of George III	325
330. Samuel Shoemaker, Mayor of Philadelphia, and his son, 1789	325

FIGURE   PAGE

331. Portrait showing the plain but handsome costume of a gentleman in
     Pennsylvania at the outbreak of the Revolution..................... 325
332. Portrait of a Quaker gentleman, 1774.............................. 325
333. Sporting dress, about 1733 327
334. Suit of velvet with raised figures, worn by Robert Livingston about
     1770. Lent by Miss Anna Griffith.................................. 329
335. Pistols with silver mounting, about 1765. Lent by Mrs. John Biddle.. 329
336. Cap worn by Governor Taylor of New York, 1730.................... 329
337. Silk waistcoat, 1780. Lent by Mrs. Krumbhaar..................... 329
338. Double-breasted waistcoat of figured silk, about 1790............. 329
339. Working man, last half of eighteenth century...................... 331
340. (In colours) Brown broadcloth suit worn by Mr. Johnson of German-
     town, 1790. Lent by Miss Sallie Johnson........................... 333
341. (In colours) Mauve crêpe gown worn by Mrs. Sartori of San Domingo.
     Lent by Miss Janethe.. 333
342. (In colours) Dress of fine glazed buff cambric owned by Madame Cheva-
     leir, end of eighteenth century. Lent by Mrs. Cooper Smith......... 333
343. (In colours) Man in short-waisted, high-collared coat and nankeen
     breeches, end of eighteenth century. Lent by Frank W. Taylor, Esq. 333
344. (In colours) Muslin dress trimmed with tambour embroidery worn in
     Philadelphia, 1797.. 333
345. Doctor of Civil Law, end of eighteenth century.................... 336
346. Summer coat of dark blue silk with nankeen breeches, late eighteenth
     century... 337
347. Back view of brown broadcloth coat worn by Mr. Johnson about 1790.
     Lent by Miss Sallie Johnson....................................... 337
348. Front view of same over nankeen waistcoat......................... 337
349. Coat of brown twilled cotton, over white silk embroidered waistcoat
     and brown satin knee breeches, worn in Philadelphia about 1790.
     Lent by Mrs. John Biddle.. 337
350. Judge in scarlet robe, end of eighteenth century.................. 339
351. Dress of ordinary seaman, 1775................................... 341
352. Portrait of Washington, drawn from life by Du Simitière........... 343
353. Henry Laurens, drawn from life by Du Simitière.................... 343
354. W. H. Drayton, Esq., drawn from life by Du Simitière.............. 343
355. Gouverneur Morris, drawn from life by Du Simitière................ 343
356. Silhouette of John Randolph of Roanoke............................ 347
357. Silhouette of Washington, showing fine net over hair and queue.... 347
358. Silhouette of Bishop White, showing knickerbockers................ 347
359. Silhouette of Alexander Hamilton................................. 347
360. Silhouette of James McClellan, of Connecticut.................... 347
361. Uniform of Light Horse Troop of Philadelphia, 1775............... 349

FIGURE   PAGE

362. Commodore Barry of the United States Navy......................... 351
363. Paul Jones of the United States Navy.............................. 351
364. Camp at Valley Forge, showing military cloak and great coat......... 351
365. General Warren in dress of a minute-man........................... 355
366. General Daniel Morgan in buckskin coat of the Virginia Rangers...... 355
367. Comte De Rochambeau in dress of a French officer, 1791.............. 355
368. Uniform recommended by Washington in the early part of the Revolu-
    tion.. 359
369. A minute-man... 359
370. Dress of First Company, Governor's Foot Guard, Connecticut......... 359
371. Dress of First Pennsylvania Infantry.............................. 359
372. Dress of Second Pennsylvania Infantry............................. 359
373. Uniform directed by Minister of War, 1785......................... 359
374. Uniform of the Light Infantry, 1782............................... 359
375. Front view of uniform recommended by Minister of War, 1785......... 359
376. Major General Pinckney in uniform................................. 363
377. Major General St. Clair in uniform................................ 363
378. General O. H. Williams in uniform................................. 363
379. General Andrew Pickens in uniform................................. 363
380. General Montgomery in uniform..................................... 367
381. General Francis Marion in uniform................................. 367
382. General Israel Putnam in uniform of a Continental trooper.......... 367
383. General Philemon Dickinson in uniform............................. 367
384. General John Sullivan in uniform.................................. 367
385. Uniform of an American officer, 1796.............................. 376

RULERS OF THE SETTLEMENTS AND COLONIES IN AMERICA

Spanish. Philip II..1556–1598
Philip III..1598–1621
Philip IV..1621–1665
Charles II..1665–1700
French. Louis XIII..1610–1643
Louis XIV..1643–1715
Swedish. Christina 1633–1654
Charles X..1654–1660
Charles XI 1660–1697
German. Frederick William, Elector of Brandenburg..................1640–1688
Frederick, Elector of Brandenburg, afterwards King Frederick
I of Prussia..1688–1713
Leopold I, Emperor of Germany..........................1658–1705
Dutch. Maurice, Stadtholder..1587–1625
Frederick Henry..1625–1647
William II..1647–1650
United Provinces of the Netherlands 1650–1672
William of Orange, afterwards William III of England.......1672–1702
English. James I 1603–1625
Charles I 1625–1649
Commonwealth under Cromwell 1649–1653
Protectorate under Cromwell 1653–1660
Charles II 1660–1685
James II 1685–1689
William and Mary 1689–1702
Queen Anne 1702–1714
George I 1714–1727
George II 1727–1760
George III 1760–1820

PRESIDENTS OF THE UNITED STATES

George Washington..1789–1797
John Adams..1797–1801

DATES OF THE SPANISH, FRENCH, SWEDISH, AND GERMAN SETTLEMENTS

Florida	1565	Spanish
Acadia	1605	French
Quebec	1608	French
Louisiana	1680	French
Texas (afterwards a part of the Spanish Province of Mexico)	1692	Spanish
Mississippi Valley	1699	French
California	1769	Spanish
Banks of the Delaware	1637	Swedish
Pennsylvania	1683	German

DATES OF THE ENGLISH AND DUTCH COLONIES

Virginia	1607	English
Massachusetts	1620	English
New Amsterdam	1621	Dutch
New York	1664	English
New Hampshire	1623	English
Barbadoes	1625	English
Maryland	1633	English
Connecticut	1635	English
Rhode Island	1636	English
The Carolinas	1655	English
New Jersey	1664	English
Pennsylvania	1682	English
Delaware	1682	English
Georgia	1732	English

INTRODUCTORY CHAPTER

ON DRESS IN THE

SPANISH AND FRENCH SETTLEMENTS

UNDER

PHILIP II AND LOUIS XIV

The Spaniards in Florida and California
1565–1764

"Those were the days of dreams and legends,
Continents were new."

FIGURE 2.
A Spanish Galleon.

HE first settlement in North America was the Spanish post of St. Augustine in Florida, founded by Pedro Menendez de Aviles in August, 1565. Unsuccessful attempts had been made to colonize Florida both by the French and the Spaniards from very early in the sixteenth century, but the hostility of the native Indians had prevented the founding of anything like a colony. Menendez (Figure 7) found a small Huguenot mission when he landed, which he immediately destroyed, putting the people and Jean Ribaut, their leader, to death in the most heartless manner. Horribly cruel, deplorably superstitious, and very short-sighted in their policy were these early Spanish settlers, but their costumes, as represented by the great contemporary painters, Vargas, Roelas, Velasquez, Murillo, Moro and others, must have been strikingly picturesque.

Parkman says: " Month after month, and year after year the adventurers came, a procession of priests and cavaliers, crossbowmen and arquebusiers (Figure 4), and Indian guides laden with baggage." *

They came in search of fabulous riches which, according to some

*Pioneers of France in the New World, by Francis Parkman.

25

Spanish Munchausen, the soil of the interior contained, and also to bathe in the waters of a river of perpetual youth, a fable in which even their leaders believed.

The dress of a Spanish gentleman of this period consisted of a doublet and slashed breeches, with long silken hose and shoes of Cordovan leather slashed on the toe, a ruff of lace at the neck, and a silk hat with high soft crown and narrow brim. The dress of a Spanish soldier is shown in detail in Figure 4.

FIGURE 3.
A Spanish Gentleman, End of Sixteenth Century.

Sir Francis Drake (Figure 8), in 1586, stopped at St. Augustine on his way from the West Indies to join Sir Walter Raleigh in Virginia (Figure 11), and made a reconnoissance of the harbour, but the Spaniards fled at his approach. He destroyed a few houses and outposts in order probably to inspire the inhabitants with a wholesome respect for the English navy, and went on his way rejoicing in the capture of a pay-chest containing £2,000. St. Augustine at that time is described as "a prosperous settlement with a council house, church and handsome gardens." Some traces of the Spanish occupation are yet to be seen and the old castle or fortress built in 1620 is still standing.

It was never the policy of Spain to make her colonies self-supporting; they were not allowed to raise or manufacture even the necessaries of life, everything must be imported from the mother country.

Later in the seventeenth century, settlements were also made in California, where the Spaniards established missionary and military

stations in 1698, and Spain had for a time two flourishing colonies
in the territory now embraced within the limits of the United States.

In Spain and France, as well as in England and the Low Countries, the prevailing types of costume during the seventeenth century
were very much alike, and the people in all the Colonies of America,
following the fashions of their time, wore doublets, farthingales, ruffs,
bands, hoods, riding-masks, etc., full descriptions of which are given
in the glossary and throughout Part I, with many illustrations.

FIGURE 4.

Spanish Soldiers of the Middle of the Sixteenth Century, with Rapiers and Arquebuses
(from a Contemporary Print).

During the reign of Charles II of Spain his kingdom was continually at war with England. The Spanish population of St.
Augustine numbered about three hundred people and fifty Franciscan
friars in 1665, when Captain John Davis, the notorious English
buccaneer, landed and destroyed the town. After this the Spanish
Government established a fort at Pensacola to protect its interests

in Florida, but finally the two kings, Charles II of England and Charles II of Spain, made a treaty for the suppression of buccaneering, causing a marked decline in that lawless but romantic profession which has furnished plots for many an exciting tale. In "The Buccaneers of America" * a portrait of Sir Henry Morgan shows a very rich costume of slashed doublet and embroidered baldrick. Francis Lolonais, a fierce-looking buccaneer of French extraction, is portrayed in a very short doublet trimmed with a row of square tabs round the waist.

The records we find of the Spanish rule in Florida, which lasted until 1763, when that province was ceded to Great Britain in exchange for Havana, captured by the English the preceding year, bear witness to the charms of the women, their lovely expressive black eyes, clear brunette complexion, and carefully arranged hair. "At mass they are always well dressed in black silk basquinas with little mantillas (or black lace veils) over their heads. The men are in military costume." Dancing, as in all the Spanish provinces, was a favourite amusement, and the Posey Dance, now obsolete, was very popular many years ago. It is thus described: †

"The ladies of a household arrange in a room of their dwelling an arbour decked with garlands of flowers and lighted with many candles. This is understood by the gentlemen as an invitation to drop in and admire the decorations. Meanwhile the lady who has prepared it selects a partner from among her visitors and hands him a bouquet of flowers. The gentleman who receives this posey becomes for the nonce the king of the ball, and leads out the fair donor as queen of the dance. The others take partners and the ball thus inaugurated may continue several successive evenings. Should the lady's choice fall upon an unwilling swain, which seldom happened, he could be excused by paying the expenses of the entertainment."

* By John Esquemeling.
† History and Antiquities of St. Augustine, by George R. Fairbanks.

FIGURE 5.

FIGURE 6.

FIGURE 7.

FIGURE 8.

FIGURE 5.—Portrait of Fernando De Soto, showing Spanish armour of the sixteenth century.

FIGURE 6.—Portrait of Sieur de La Salle, showing French costume of his day.

FIGURE 7.—Portrait of Pedro Menendez de Aviles, showing Spanish dress.

FIGURE 8.—Portrait of Sir Francis Drake in the dress of an English sea-captain.

These assemblies were always informal and frequented by all classes, all meeting on a level, but were conducted with the utmost politeness and decorum, for which the Spanish character is so distinguished.

The customs, as well as the costumes, of their native land were followed by these Spanish colonists, and as both California and Florida closely resemble Spain in climate and vegetation, the old modes of life were found particularly appropriate.

With the Spanish colonies, Texas may be included, for although this territory was the subject of numerous political intrigues between the Spanish authorities and the French in Louisiana, in 1692 it became a part of the Spanish province of Mexico.

The French Settlements

in

Louisiana and the Mississippi Valley

1680–1764

———

"A gay and gallant company
Those voyagers of old."

Undeterred by the failures and reverses of previous explorers, the French King Louis XIV sent out an expedition under Robert Cavalier de La Salle (Figure 6) in 1680, to discover if possible a waterway across the continent through which ships might pass to the South Sea, as the Pacific Ocean was called in those days.

La Salle experienced many hardships on the way, but finally reached the Mississippi River and sailed southward to its mouth in the Gulf of Mexico. At this point a wooden column was raised, hymns were sung, and La Salle proclaimed, "In the name of Louis the great King of France and Navarre, fourteenth of that name, I do take possession of this country of Louisiana—from the mouth of the river St. Louis and along the river Colbert, or Mississippi, from its source beyond the country of the Sioux as far as its mouth." A cross was raised by the side of the column and in the ground at its foot was buried a leaden plate bearing the arms of France and the inscription, "Ludovicus Magnus Regnat."

By this discovery La Salle had proved that ships from Europe might sail to the vast interior of the continent. He now hoped to colonize the valley of the Mississippi, and add a new lustre to the crown of France.

Father Hennepin, writing in 1683, says: "Le Sieur de la Salle appeared at Mass very well dress'd in his scarlet cloak trimmed with gold lace."* A picture of the fashionable cloak of that period is given in Figure 3.

Discouraged by many hardships, on their way up the Mississippi River some of La Salle's men mutinied and killed the great explorer, but, despite his failure to found a colony at the outlet of the Mississippi, he stands out in history as the foremost pioneer in North America.

Trading posts and mission stations grew up in many places, and were gradually augmented by bands of emigrants from other parts of the country.

Louis XIV still cherished the ambition to found a Colonial Dominion on the shores of the Gulf of Mexico, so dramatically claimed for him by La Salle,—a colony which in time might rival the flourishing English settlements on the Atlantic coast. Accordingly, in 1698, he sent out to Louisiana a squadron of two frigates and two smaller ships bearing a company of mariners and about two hundred colonists. Among the latter were many ex-soldiers of the French army accompanied by their wives and children. Others were artisans, labourers, and needy adventurers. "They were all supplied with necessary clothing, provisions, and implements for beginning a settlement in the remote solitudes of Louisiana."

In 1704, twenty unmarried women were sent out under the charge of two nuns, and shortly after their arrival in Louisiana were married to bachelor colonists. The same ship brought troops to reinforce the garrison, and four priests.

The costume of these early French settlers was somewhat motley in its composition. The women were dressed in coloured bodices and short gowns of handmade woolen stuffs, or of French goods of finer texture. In summer most of them went without shoes, but in

* Description of Louisiana 1683, translated by J. G. Shee.

winter and on holidays they wore Indian moccasins gaily decorated
with porcupine quills, shells, and coloured beads. Instead of hats
they wore kerchiefs of bright colours interlaced with gay ribbons
or wreathed with flowers.

The men wore long vests drawn over their shirts, leggings of
buckskin or of coarse woolen cloth, and wooden clog shoes or moccasins of heavy leather. In winter they wrapped themselves in long
capotes or overcoats with capes and hoods which could be drawn
over their heads, thus serving for hats. In summer their heads were
covered with blue handkerchiefs
worn turbanlike as a protection from
mosquitoes as well as from the sun.

FIGURE 9.

French Peasant Women (from a Contemporary French Print).

The French settlements were
usually small villages on the edge
of the prairie or in the heart of the
woods. They were always near the
bank of a river, for the watercourses
were the only roads, and the light
canoes, such as the Indians used, the
only means of travel. In these
villages the French settlers lived like
one family, ruled by the village
priests and the elders of the com-
munity. Their houses were built along a single narrow street, and
close enough together for the villagers to carry on a neighbourly
gossip, each from his own doorstep.

Adjoining the village was a large enclosure, or common field,
for the free use of all the villagers. It was divided into allotments,
one for each household, the size proportioned to the number of persons in the family.

The village traders always kept a small stock of French goods,
laces, ribbons and other useful and ornamental articles, which they

exchanged with the settlers for the products of the forest. Some of the young men became voyageurs or boatmen in the service of the traders. When the wood-rangers returned once a year to their village homes, great was the rejoicing, and old and young gathered around them to hear the story of their adventures. These French settlers took characteristic delight in amusement and "had almost as many holidays as working days." *

Indian converts lived in amicable intercourse with the settlers, learning from them to culti-vate the ground, and to manufacture various useful articles from the hair of the buffalo.

FIGURE 10.
Jesuit Missionaries.

Many of the original set-tlers married Indian women; their descendants were called half-breeds or Gumbos, the latter being a nick-name given to them by the French. The language of the Louisiana colonists was a patois, a cor-rupted provincial French.

Among them were a few carpenters, tailors, stone-masons, boat-builders, and blacksmiths, the latter capable of repairing a firelock or a rifle.

The city of New Orleans was founded in 1717 and rapidly grew in size and importance. For many years a "rude semblance of a Court" was maintained and social amusements of various sorts could be engaged in, even duelling and brawling, for some of the Louisiana colonists were of noble birth and many were military officers. "All the people shared alike the harmless merriment and

* Discovery of the Old Northwest and Its Settlement by the French, by James Baldwin.

frolic of the carnival. All, too, observed the self-denying ordinances of the Lenten season which terminated in the festival of Easter."

The treaty of Paris, in 1764, gave to the English Government the Illinois and Louisiana colonies as well as the province of Acadia, in Nova Scotia,* originally peopled by Normandy peasants whose pathetic story Longfellow has made so familiar to us. More than six hundred of the Acadian exiles were sent to Louisiana, where they had at least the comfort of hearing their native language, and where the customs and pursuits were more congenial than in the northern colonies. The quaint costumes and the peculiar head-dresses worn by Normandy peasants at the end of the seventeenth century are minutely described in Mrs. Stothard's "Letters written during a tour through Normandy, Brittany and other parts of France," illustrated in colour by her husband. This book was published in London in 1818, and is the earliest authority on the subject I have found. The descriptions are not quoted here, as there is not any evidence that very elaborate peasant dress was ever worn in the American colonies.†

* Thus named by a company of Scots who planted a settlement there in 1622.

† For Spanish and French costumes, see Racinet's Le Costume Historique and Kretchmer's Trachten der Völker.

PART I

THE SEVENTEENTH CENTURY

THE ENGLISH COLONIES

IN

VIRGINIA, MARYLAND, THE BARBADOES, AND THE CAROLINAS

1607–1700

During the Reigns of
James I, Charles I and II, James II, and
William and Mary

TOBACCO

Tobacco is but an Indian weed,
Grows green in the morn, cut down at eve.
    It shows our decay,
    We are but clay.
Think of this when you smoke tobacco!

The pipe that is so lily white,
Wherein so many take delight,
    It breaks with a touch,
    Man's life is such;
Think of this when you take tobacco!

The pipe that is so foul within,
It shows man's soul is stained with sin;
    It doth require
    To be purged with fire;
Think of this when you smoke tobacco!

The dust that from that pipe doth fall,
It shows we are nothing but dust at all,
    For we came from dust,
    And return we must;
Think of this when you smoke tobacco!

The ashes that are left behind,
Do serve to put us all in mind
    That into dust
    Return we must;
Think of this when you take tobacco!

The smoke that doth so high ascend,
Shows that man's life must have an end;
    The vapour's gone,
    Man's life is done;
Think of this when you take tobacco!

—Thomas D'Urfey, **1719**.

The English in Virginia, Maryland, the Barbadoes, and the Carolinas
1607–1700

SIR·WALTER·RALEGH

FIGURE 11.

JAMESTOWN in Virginia was the first actual settlement of the English people in America. The Virginia Company, of which Sir Edwin Sandys was President, was formed under the patent of King James I. The first ships sent over arrived in 1607, at the mouth of the James River, where a fortified village was built, and trade established with the surrounding Indians. One hundred colonists came in the first expedition, a great number of them being men of quality. As Captain John Smith, in his delightful "History of the Virginia Settlement," puts it:

"We had far too many gentlemen adventurers amongst us, and of a necessity some of these must needs be not quite all we could wish as reliable companions. Out of one hundred colonists there are fifty-two gentlemen adventurers besides Master Robert Hunt, the Preacher, and Masters Thomas Wotton and William Wilkinson, the Chirurgeons. We had four carpenters, twelve labourers, a blacksmith, a sailor, a bricklayer, a mason, a tailor and a drummer, four boys and some others."

The Company in London advised each emigrant to provide himself with the following articles of dress:

A Monmouth cap,	Three falling bands,
Three shirts,	One waistcoat,
One suit of canvas,	One suit of frieze,
One pair of garters,	One suit of broadcloth,
Four pairs of shoes,	Three pairs of silk stockings,

One dozen pairs of points.

From original prints in this book of Captain John Smith's, we get the costume of the gentleman adventurer, similar in style, of course, to the garments worn by men of rank in England during the reign of James I. A portrait of Sir Edwin Sandys, or Sandes as it is sometimes written, is given in Figure 13, showing the prevailing dress of an English gentleman, a brocade doublet, a lace-trimmed ruff, and a pointed beard. The strange fashion which was conspicuous at

FIGURE 12.

King James's Court, of padding and stuffing the breeches, called farthingale breeches on account of the resemblance to that most disfiguring but popular article of fashion worn by women in the reigns of Elizabeth and James I, was probably followed in a modified form by these gentlemen adventurers, as the padding was supposed to be a protection against rapiers and arrows.

Stays were also worn by men in those days beneath long-waisted doublets; and ruffs too were used, although they gradually diminished in size and stiffness (Figures 11, 15, and 21).

FIGURE 13.

FIGURE 14.

FIGURE 15.

FIGURE 16.

FIGURE 13.—Portrait of Sir Edwyn Sandys, showing a turned-down ruff, the predecessor of the Vandyke collar. Reign of James I.

FIGURE 14.—Portrait of George Sandys, Secretary of the Virginia Colony, showing slashed doublet and Vandyke collar. Reign of Charles I.

FIGURE 15.—Portrait of Sir Isaac Pennington, showing the style of hat worn in the Virginia House of Burgesses. Reign of Charles I.

FIGURE 16.—Portrait of Sir John Pennington, showing English armour and Vandyke collar. Reign of Charles I.

In the portraits of the Earl and Countess of Somerset,* so often reproduced, may be seen the costumes worn by the nobility of this time, but there were no radical changes in English costume from 1550, the middle of Eliza-beth's reign, until the accession of Charles I in 1625. If any change of fashion appeared in the early days of life at Jamestown, the tailor of the Company was probably responsible for it, and the old adage, "Cut your coat according to your cloth," was very likely his inspiration.

FIGURE 17.
The Farthingale.

The present of a cloak of raccoon skins from King Powhattan to Captain John Smith must have been very acceptable as, according to Stith, the first winter was very damp and cold.

FIGURE 18.
Ordinary Dress of a Boy at this Period, 1602–1676 (from a Contemporary Print).

The first women to come to Virginia were Mrs. Forrest and her maid Anne Bur-roughs, who, soon after her arrival, married John Laydon. This was the first English wedding on American soil.† Figure 21 represents the style of dress worn by Mrs. Forrest. Her maid's costume was of similar cut, but of linsey-woolsey, with cuffs and falling band of plain linen.

As early as 1621 the Company resolved to establish a free school for children. The costumes of children given in Figures 18 and 23 are taken from a picture of a Dame's School in England by A. de Bosse, 1602–1676.

In 1622 the College, afterward known as "William and Mary," was first talked of, but it was in this year that occurred the horrible

* Fairholt's History of English Costume.

† History of the First Discovery and Settlement of Virginia, by William Stith.

massacre of the English by the Indians which sadly reduced their numbers. However, the survivors struggled valiantly on, and gradually comfortable houses were built, even for the labouring men, while the houses of the people of quality could boast of many conveniences.

In 1624 an attempt was made to produce silk from the mulberry trees which flourished in Virginia, and skilled workmen were sent over by Nicholas Farrar from France to raise silkworms, but the effort was not successful.

King James died in 1625 and the accession of Charles I proved a blessing to the Virginia Colony, for the new king left the affairs of government to Sir Edwin Sandys and the Virginia House of Burgesses which held its meetings in the church at Jamestown. The Representatives coming in barges from their plantations along the river were usually accompanied by their wives and daughters, who embraced these opportunities to show off their fine apparel (Figures 20, 21, 32, 33, 35, 36). Very gay and elaborate the finery of that period seems, even from our twentieth century standpoint.

In the body of the church, facing the choir, sat the Burgesses in their best attire, with starched ruffs or stiff neckbands (Figure 22) and doublets of silk or velvet in bright colours. All sat with their hats on in imitation of the time-honoured custom of the House of Commons (Figures 15, 19, and 22).* These same Burgesses, however, did not approve of too general a display of fine clothing, it seems, for among many astute laws passed by them was the following, to prevent extravagance in dress: "Be it enacted that for all public contributions every unmarried man must be assessed in church according to his own apparel, and every married man must be assessed according to his own and his wife's apparel."

The years from 1625 to 1642 were marked with great prosperity and progress, and when Berkeley was sent over with the title of English

* Old Virginia and her Neighbours.

FIGURE 19.

FIGURE 20.

FIGURE 21.

FIGURE 22.

REIGNS OF JAMES I—CHARLES I
1607-1640

FIGURES 19 and 20 represent a colonial governor and his wife of the time of
Charles I dressed in the fashion of the English Court.

The man has a short-waisted doublet with trimmings of gold braid,
and the breeches are finished with loops of ribbon. The slashed sleeves
show the Holland shirt underneath. The boots are the style called "French
falls" with large buckles on the instep. Hat and plumes are of the recognized Cavalier type, and the collar a Vandyke of rich lace.

His lady (Figure 20) has a low-cut, short-waisted bodice finished with
square tabs. The sleeves are full and reach a little below the elbow. Ruffles
and falling band are of rich lace. No farthingale is worn with this gown
which falls in soft folds on the ground both back and front. The hair is
arranged in short ringlets across the forehead, hangs to the shoulders in
curls, and is coiled in the back.

FIGURE 21 shows a planter's wife in the usual costume of the time of James I.
This lady wears a gown of prunella opening over a brocaded petticoat. The
ruff is of stiffened lace. The coif of white linen is shaped over it in the
back. A modified farthingale supports the dress which hangs in heavy plaits
to the ground. The trimming on the bodice is of silk galloon with a design
in gold thread.

FIGURE 22 represents a gentleman planter in the ordinary costume of James I's
day. The doublet and padded breeches of coloured velvet or cloth are
fastened together with points; long oversleeves hang from the shoulders.
The stiff band is of starched linen. The stockings are of silk fastened with
garters tied in a bow at one side. The hat of felt is ornamented with an
embroidered band and a short plume of feathers.

Governor, the inhabitants of Virginia numbered eighteen 'thousand English and three hundred negroes.

At that time London fashions were strictly followed by the quality, and seem to have been not only the chief amusement of the women, but matter of great moment to both sexes (Figures 13, 14, 19, 20, 32, 33, 35, 36).

The fashionable costume in England during the reign of Charles I, made familiar to us by the magic brush of Vandyke, was picturesque in the extreme.

A gentleman of those days wore a doublet of satin or velvet with large loose sleeves slashed up the front (Figures 45, 46); the collar covered by a falling band of richest point-lace with the peculiar edging now called Vandyke (Figures 14 and 16), and a short cloak worn carelessly over one shoulder. Bands were called "peccadilles" when trimmed with this pointed lace, so fashionable in the middle of the seventeenth century, and it is interesting to read that the fashionable London thoroughfare, Piccadilly, gets its name from a shop where "peccadilles" were made and sold in the reign of Charles I. Under slashed doublets, loose shirts of Holland linen were worn. (See portrait of George Percy [Figure 29], second Governor of the Virginia Colony.) The breeches, fringed or pointed, met the tops of the wide boots (Figures 51, 55), which were ruffled with lace, lawn, or soft leather. A broad-leafed Flemish beaver hat, with a rich hatband and plume of feathers (Figure 19), was set on one side of the head, and a Spanish rapier hung from a most magnificent baldrick or sword-belt worn sash-wise over the right shoulder. In troublous times the doublet of silk or velvet was frequently exchanged for a buff coat (Figures 83, 84, 85, 86, 87) which was richly laced, sometimes embroidered with gold or silver, and enriched by a broad silk or satin scarf tied in a large bow either behind or over the hip, in which case, the short cloak was perhaps dispensed with; in some instances the buff jerkin without sleeves was worn over the doublet

(Figure 87). The beard was worn "very peaked with small up-turned mustaches; the hair long on the neck."

George Sandys, the celebrated traveller, a younger brother of the President of the Company in London, was sent over to Jamestown in the capacity of treasurer. During his stay in the colony, he translated ten books of Ovid. This was the first poetical achievement in America. The portrait of him (Figure 14) shows the slashed doublet and the Vandyke collar of this reign.

FIGURE 23.

Ordinary Dress of a Little Girl of the Period 1602–1676 (from a Contemporary Print).

A gentlewoman of the same time wore a long soft skirt, with a low-cut bodice finished with square tabs about the waist (Figures 20, 32, 49), full sleeves a little below the elbow, with soft ruffles of rich lace, a wide collar of the same lace being worn over the shoulders but allowing the throat and neck to show. Soft breast-knots of ribbon were also much worn. The hair was usually curled over the brow, falling to the shoulders in rather tight ringlets, and arranged in a knot at the back (Figures 20, 73).

Earrings were very popular in England in Vandyke's time, not only for women but for men, as we may see by the numerous specimens in his portraits. In his famous painting of Charles I in the National Gallery in London, the King is represented with a pear-shaped pearl-drop in one ear. This was the most advantageous way of displaying a pearl of more than usual beauty, but the origin of the fashion of piercing the lobe of the ear has been ascribed by many authorities to the common belief that it was a cure for weak eyes. Tradition also associates the fashion with navigators and seamen. Probably it was thought to be a safe way of carrying precious stones found in perilous adventures by land and sea, but there is not any evidence that earrings were at any time a fashion favoured by men in the Colonies of America.

Mr. Bruce, in his "Economic History of Virginia," remarks: "The incongruity of shining apparel with the rude surroundings of new settlements in the wilderness does not seem to have jarred upon the perceptions of the population except so far as it implied an unnecessary expenditure, and this view was only taken when the resources of the Colony were seriously impaired.

"About the middle of the century a law was passed prohibiting the introduction of silk in pieces except for hoods or scarfs, or of silver, gold or bone lace, or of ribbons wrought in gold or silver. All goods of this character brought into the colonies were confiscated and then exported."

The typical workingman's costume of this period consisted of loose breeches and jerkin of canvas or frieze; hose of coarse wool, shoes of tanned leather tied in front; hat of thrums or felt. "The carpenters, the labourers, the blacksmith, the mason, and the bricklayer" of the Virginia Company were in all probability

FIGURE 24.

An English Mariner (from a Contemporary Print).

dressed in this way. The tailor and the drummer may have worn their breeches fastened at the knee with points, and all these useful members of the Company wore aprons of dressed leather when at work. Mariners, according to contemporary authorities, wore a similar costume (Figure 24).

Randle Holmes, another contemporary authority, gives the following picture of a countryman in 1660, showing that the hat, doublet, and short breeches of the reign of James I were worn in country districts of England as late as the Restoration; the short breeches probably being of leather and the hose of stout woolen cloth.

Bishop Coleman tells us that in the Jamestown Settlement "church services, according to the English ritual, were held daily by

FIGURE 25.
Countryman in Doublet (from a print by Randle Holmes, 1660).

the Reverend Robert Hunt, formerly rector of a living in Kent. Soon after the arrival of the Colonists sent over by the Virginia Company, in 1607, an altar was erected under the shade of the forest trees, and the emigrants gladly attended the celebration of the Holy Communion. English churchmen came to Massachusetts in 1623; to Maryland in 1629; Lord Baltimore wrote that four clergymen of the Church of England were in his province with decent maintenance in 1676." Surplices were very expensive in the Colonies; 5000 pounds of tobacco was the price paid for three of them in Virginia, and probably they were not available in every parish. Regular services were held in New England in 1638, in South Carolina in 1660, in New York in 1674, in New Jersey in 1678, and in Pennsylvania in 1694.*

These dates are quoted to show that in the English Colonies, under English rule, the clergy wore, as in England, the customary dress of the period: a black coat (ancestor of the cassock), full breeches to the knee, silk hose fastened with points, a soft brimmed hat, and plain stock or falling band for outdoor wear; the white surplice with bands and a close cap of black silk or velvet in church. Bishops

* History of the American Church.

ordinarily wore the usual full-sleeved white robes with black stoles. Out-of-doors long full cloaks were worn universally for protection from the weather.

FIGURE 26.

Soldier in Cuirass and Morion (from an Old English Print, Seventeenth Century).

Hard, indeed, must have been the lives of the pioneer clergy of every denomination in America before 1700, and in remote parts they were probably constrained to wear whatever they could have made at home. The general outlines of the accepted dress of the times, given here, are based upon careful historical research. Further details will be found in the authorities quoted.

Close-fitting black caps were worn habitually by the clergymen of all denominations. Instead of the white surplice, the black Geneva or preaching gown was adopted by Non-conformists, Presbyterian ministers and Puritan divines in all the Colonies.

The Roman Catholic Church was represented chiefly by the Jesuits, a missionary priesthood, who habitually adopted the dress of the people with whom they sojourned. Maryland was the active centre of Catholicism in the Colonies. When Father Greaton of the Jesuit Order was sent from there to Philadelphia and founded the Parish of St. Joseph in that city, we are told that he entered the Province of Penn in the dress of a Quaker.* But this did not happen until 1731.

Maryland was settled in 1633 by Lord Baltimore, whose ambition was to found a commonwealth in the Colonies where Roman Catholics might escape the oppressive legislation to which they were subjected in England. He brought with him his wife, children, and many servants, and following the English customs of living, naturally brought over the prevailing costumes of his day.

That armour was sometimes worn by the Colonists, ample proof is given in the early records. In the archives of the first colony of Jamestown it is stated, among the proceedings of the Virginia Company, that

Brigandines, alias plate coats........................... 100
Jacks of mail 40
Jerkins or shirts of mail.............................. 400
Skulls 2000
Calivers and other pieces, belts, halberts, swords,

* History of Old St. Joseph's, Philadelphia, by Martin I. J. Griffin.

FIGURE 27.

FIGURE 28.

FIGURE 29

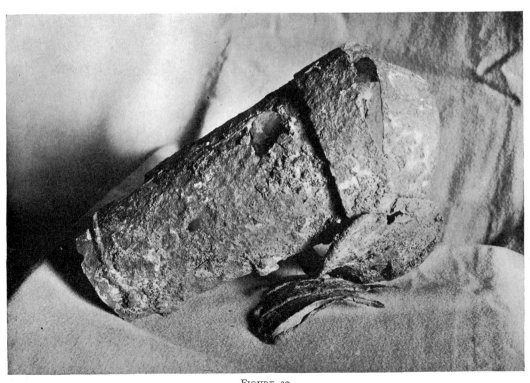

FIGURE 30.

FIGURE 27.—Silver frontlet, bearing the English coat-of-arms, given to the Queen of the Pamunkeys by Charles II.

FIGURE 28.—Silver mace used in the Virginia House of Burgesses.

FIGURE 29.—Portrait of George Percy, second Governor of Virginia, showing the full shirt of Holland linen customarily worn under slashed doublets, and the Vandyke collar and cuffs of Charles I's reign.

FIGURE 30.—Steel vambrace dug up near Jamestown, and preserved by the Historical Society at Richmond, Virginia.

were sent out from London upon request of the Burgesses, July 17, 1622. In the Historical Society at Richmond, portions of a steel vambrace are preserved which were dug up at Jamestown in 1861 (Figure 30).

At the time of the first Colony in America, heavy plate armour had gone out of use, and back and breast plates with overlapping

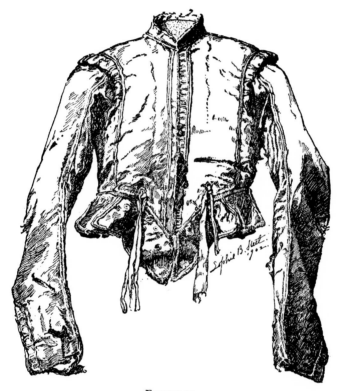

FIGURE 31.

A Doublet of Satin Trimmed with a Narrow Galloon and Points of the Same Colour with Padded Lining, 1600–25 (Reign of James I).

tuilles or tassetts to protect the thighs, and helmets for the head, were generally worn. Whole suits of armour may have been worn on occasions, but so great had been the improvement in firearms that armour was no longer a safeguard, according to Fairholt, and in the time of Charles I, stout buff coats thick enough to resist a sword thrust, under a cuirass and a gorget (Figures 88, 89, and 90) affording special protection for the throat and chest, a helmet of metal, and breeches and boots of tough leather, formed the customary uniform of the soldier. The armour of a mounted officer, judging from effigies on old English tombs and from prints of the day, was more formidable, the arms and legs being encased in steel, at least all that part of the body not hidden by the saddle. Pictures of buff coats (Figures 83, 84, 85, 86, and 87), and drawings of a pikeman and a musketeer are given (Figures 26 and 78).

There is an anonymous pamphlet called "A Perfect Description of Virginia," printed in Force's Tracts, which shows the inducements set forth in England to bring people to the Colony. The great advantages of the country, its resources, agricultural and even educational, are announced in glowing terms, and one citation at least bears directly upon the history of costume. In describing the fine house of one, Sir John Harvey, the author says: "He sows yearly stores of hemp and flax, and causes it to be spun, he keeps weavers, and hath a tan house, causes leather to be dressed, hath eight shoemakers employed in their trade."

After the execution of King Charles I, a great many of the Cavaliers of England sought a haven of refuge in Virginia and Maryland. They were followed by many other representatives of distinguished families who could not brook the rule of Cromwell.

We realize how luxurious life in Virginia had already become for the prosperous, when we read that Governor Berkeley (against whom Bacon rebelled in 1675) retired to his rural estate of "Green Spring" near Jamestown from 1652 to 1660, where he had an orchard of more than two thousand fruit trees—apples, pears, peaches, and apricots— and a stable of seventy fine horses. Here he lived in ease, entertaining Cavalier guests and drinking healths to King Charles, until recalled to Jamestown as Governor. In 1661 he went to London and remained a year. While there he saw the performance of his play,

"The Lost Lady," described by Pepys in his diary. This play contained the following mention of the costumes of the day:

"Observe with me how in that deep band,
Short cloak, and his great boots, he looks
Three stories high, and his head is the
Garret where he keeps nothing but lists of
Horse matches and some designs for his next clothes."

In the first part of the reign of Charles II, doublets were worn much shorter and opened over a Holland shirt, which hung over the waistband of the loose breeches, the latter as well as the large full sleeves were ornamented with points and "ribbands" (Figures 29 and 68). The falling collar was also of lace. With this costume a high-crowned hat with plume of feathers was sometimes worn (Figure 19).

A year or so later the fashion of petticoat breeches, trimmed with "many rows of loops of ribbon overlapping like shingles," came into vogue for a short time (Figure 68). A certain Captain Creedon appeared in the street of Boston with this fantastic garb, much to the astonishment of the pedestrians, we are told. Probably this particular style was more popular with the gayer Colonists in Virginia and the Carolinas, who kept in touch with the Court fashions.

Later in the same reign (Charles II) "the doublet was worn much longer with sleeves to the elbows, finished with hanging ribbands from under which the ruffled sleeves of the shirt hung out." Thus the doublet became transformed into a coat, and in an inventory of apparel provided for the King in 1679, a complete suit of one material is mentioned as "coat and breeches." Neck-cloths were worn toward the close of this reign.

For a few years extending into the reign of James II, a long coat reaching to the knees and closely buttoned down the front came into fashion. Full breeches hanging in full folds over the garters were worn with this style of coat (Figures 137 and 138).

"The gowns of the ladies of the English Court at this period were cut very low, with slashed sleeves, and were trimmed with lace and jewels"* (Figures 20, 32 and 49). Long gloves reaching to the elbow were worn with low cut dresses (Figures 33 and 35).

The fashion of wearing patches came in towards the end of the reign of Charles I, and continued in vogue until George III's day. They are mentioned in 1650. "Our ladies have lately entertained a vain custom of spotting their faces out of affectation of a mole, to set off their beauty such as Venus had; and it is well if one black patch will serve to make their faces remarkable, for some fill their faces full of them, varied into all manner of shapes." Patches are associated with the fashion of powdering the hair (1720–1778), but when Mrs. Pepys was permitted by her husband to wear a patch we have his word for it that she looked "very pretty." It is not likely that the extreme of this fashion, as described in Bulwer's satirical lines, was seen in the Colonies:

> "Her patches are of every cut,
>   For pimples or for scars.
>   Here's all the wandering planets' signs
>   And some of the fixed stars;
>   Already gummed to make them stick
>   They need no other sky."

A seventeenth century author gives the following concise definition of the muff, which figures so frequently in English portraits of the day: "A fur worn in winter in which to put the hands to keep them warm. Muffs were formerly only for women: at the present day they are carried by men. The finest muffs are made of martin, the common of miniver. The country muffs of the cavaliers are made of otter and of tiger. A woman puts her nose in her muff to hide herself. A muff-dog is a little dog which ladies can carry in their muffs." It is not easy to imagine the pioneer men of the Colonies carrying muffs; in fact even a Patroon would have found one sadly

* Book of Costume by a Lady of Rank. (London, 1846.)

inconvenient in the days when "a musket with six shoots of powder" was his constant companion. Towards the end of the century, however, when the peaceful days of William and Mary's reign afforded a life of comparative luxury, the fashion at its height in England was followed in the Colonies by men as well as by women, with whom muffs have ever been deservedly popular (Figure 36).

Mr. Fiske, speaking of Virginia hospitality at that early date, suggests that "in the time of Bacon's Rebellion (1675) your host would have appeared, perhaps, in a coat and breeches of olive plush or dark red broadcloth, richly embroidered waistcoat, shirt of holland, long silk stockings, silver buttons and shoe buckles, lace ruffles about neck and wrists, and his head encumbered with a flowing wig; while the lady of the house might have worn a crimson satin bodice trimmed with point-lace, a black tabby petticoat, and silk hose with shoes of fine leather, galÍooned. Her lace head-dress would be secured with a gold bodkin, and she would be likely to wear earrings, a pearl necklace, finger rings set with rubies or diamonds, and to carry a fan."

This description may be very nearly correct of the man's dress in regard to colour and material, but the style of the coat described is of a later period. To the feminine mind a few items are needed to complete the costume of the lady. For instance, all the pictures of the time show the bodice and skirt of the same material, up to the reign of James II; after that a long skirt still matching the bodice was looped over a gay petticoat sometimes richly trimmed with lace or gimp (Figures 1, 19, 20, 21, 22, 24, 32, 33, 35, and 36).

The Barbadoes and Carolina settlements date from 1650. The Colonists of these Southern ports, being mostly Cavaliers who had seen something of Court life in London, very soon surrounded themselves with comforts and luxuries unknown to the first-comers in Virginia. We read that the Barbadoes Colony resembled a little Court in itself, the planters maintaining large households and many slaves.

* Old Virginia and Her Neighbours.

There was frequent intercourse with the settlements in Virginia and Maryland. The brocade gown in the frontispiece was the property of an English lady who came to Barbadoes when James II was on the throne of England. Figure 104 depicts a gentleman of the same date.

The following description of the articles of dress is quoted from Mr. Bruce's "Economic History of Virginia," but may be reasonably considered typical of all English Colonies in America from 1660 to 1700:

"The shirt was made of holland, blue linen, lockram, dowlas and canvas, according to the quality desired; holland representing the most costly and canvas the least expensive. The buttons used on the shirt were either of silver or pewter, and in many cases were carefully gilded.

"The stockings were either of silk, woolen or cotton thread, worsted or yarn. The shoes worn by men were made of ordinary leather, or they were of the sort known as French Falls (Figures 19, 51, 53, and 55). The shoe buckles were manufactured of brass, steel or silver. There are many references to boots, the popular footwear of the planters, who were accustomed to pass much of their time on horseback (Figures 50, 54, and 57).

"The periwig was worn in the latter part of the century (Figures 134, 135, 140, and 141). In 1689 William Byrd forwarded one to his merchant in London with instructions to have it altered.

"The covering for the heads of men consisted of the Monmouth cap, the felt, the beaver or castor, and the straw hat, occasionally with a steeple crown.

"The neck-cloth, or cravat, was of blue linen, calico, dowlas, muslin or the finest holland. The band or falling collar was made either of linen or lace, in keeping with the character of the suit (Figures 16 and 82).

"The material of the coat ranged from broadcloth, camlet, fustian, drugget, and serge, which became less expensive with the progress of the century, to cotton, kersey, frieze, canvas, and buckskin.

FIGURE 33.
Summer.

FIGURE 32
Spring.

FIGURE 32 represents the fashionable indoor dress of an English gentlewoman, reign of Charles I.

FIGURE 33 shows the usual outdoor summer costume of an English lady, reign of Charles I.

—From Hollar's Sketches of "The Seasons," Spring and Summer.

When of broadcloth, it was lined with calico or coarse linen. There are numerous references to the stuff coat, and the smock, and to the serge or linen jacket (Figure 48).

"The outer garment used in riding was usually a cloak of camlet. The buttons of the coat and waistcoat were made of various materials, from silk thread to brass and pewter, silver, gimp and mohair.

"Over the ordinary coat, a great-coat of frieze was worn in cold weather, or, on special occasions, a substitute was found in a cloak of blue or scarlet silk.

"Waistcoats in 1679 were made of dimity, cotton or drugget, flannel or penistone, of a great variety of colours, white, black, and blue being the most popular.

"The breeches for dress occasions were of plush or broadcloth; for ordinary wear, of linen, common ticking, canvas or leather. There are references in inventories of the period to serge breeches, lined with linen or worsted, with thread buttons, and also to cal-limanco breeches with hair buttons. Occasionally the whole suit was of plush, broadcloth, kersey or canvas, or the coat was made of drugget, and the waistcoat and breeches of stuff cloth. Olive col-oured suits were very popular.

"Handkerchiefs were of silk, lace, or blue linen. Gloves were made of yarn, or of tanned ox-, lamb-, buck-, dog-, or sheepskin, and were of local manufacture. The hands of children were kept warm by mittens."

It was the habit of the wealthy planters to have even their plainest and simplest articles of clothing made in England. Mr. Fitzhugh, of Stafford County, Virginia, instructed his merchant in London, in 1697, to send him two suits of an ordinary character, one for use in winter and the other in summer. The exact measurements for the shoes and stockings needed were to be guessed at, and the only direction given as to the two hats ordered was that they should be of the largest size.

The lists sent out to England show that costly garments were imported for the planters' wives. Many of the gowns worn in Virginia must have been as handsome as those worn by the women of the same class in England. There are numerous allusions to silk and flowered gowns, to bodices of velvet brocade and satin, trimmed with lace (Figures 32 and 49).

Petticoats were of serge, flannel, or tabby, a kind of coloured silk cloth. They were also made of printed linen or dimity and trimmed with silk or silver lace. An outfit of gown, petticoat, and green stockings, composed of woolen materials, is frequently mentioned in the inventories.

FIGURE 34.

Back View of Outdoor Dress (from a Contemporary Print).

For outdoor wear, women of all ranks wore hoods and mantles. The hoods were made of camlet, sarsenet, or velvet, often trimmed with fur (Figures 34, 35, 36, 40, 67, 69, 128, 129, and 144). The mantles of silk (Figure 128) or tippets of fur (Figures 47, 69, and 129) were worn over the shoulders.

Hose varied very much in colour, being white, scarlet, or black. They were held in place by silk garters.

Shoes of the finest quality were either laced or gallooned (Figure 36). Wooden shoes with wooden heels were also worn.

Aprons were of muslin, silk, serge, and blue duffel (Figures 35 and 144). Small fans, many of which were richly ornamented, were favourite items of dress in the toilets of planters' wives (Figure 20), and silver and gilt stomachers were not unknown. Perfumed powders were imported and used in the English Colonies.

FIGURE 36.
Winter.

FIGURE 35.
Autumn.

FIGURE 35 shows an English woman in hood and apron, reign of Charles I.
FIGURE 36.—An outdoor winter costume of an English woman, reign of Charles I.

—*From Hollar's Sketches of "The Seasons," Autumn and Winter.*

About 1661, we are told, a young English lady set out for Virginia, furnished with the following articles of clothing:

"A scarf, white sarsenet and a ducape hood, a white flannel petticoat, two green aprons, three pairs of gloves, a long riding scarf, a mask and a pair of shoes."

"The wardrobe of a rich planter's wife in Virginia, Mrs. Sarah Willoughby, consisted of a red, a blue, and a black silk petticoat, a petticoat of India silk and a worsted prunella, a striped linen and a calico petticoat, a black silk gown, a scarlet waistcoat with silver lace, a white knit waistcoat, a striped stuff jacket, a worsted prunella mantle, a sky-coloured satin bodice, a pair of red paragon bodices, three fine and three coarse holland aprons, seven handkerchiefs, and two hoods. The whole was valued at fourteen pounds and nineteen shillings.

"The wardrobe of another Virginia lady, Mrs. Frances Pritchard, was quite as extensive. It included an olive-coloured silk petticoat, petticoats of silver and flowered tabby, of velvet, and of white striped dimity, a printed calico gown lined with blue silk, a white striped dimity, a black silk waistcoat, a pair of scarlet sleeves, a pair of holland sleeves with ruffles, a Flanders lace band, one cambric and three holland aprons, five cambric handkerchiefs, and several pairs of green stockings."*

Aprons were at least on one occasion conspicuous articles of dress. Although some historians discredit the episode, in a history of costume we can hardly omit the story of Bacon's very ungallant behaviour to the ladies of Jamestown, whom he compelled to stand in a white-aproned row to screen his men while they worked on the entrenchments, as a protection from the Burgesses, who could not shoot without injury to the women. We may at least safely conclude that every woman of consequence was expected to have a white apron in her wardrobe.

* Bruce's Economic History of Virginia.

The favourite ornaments of women at this time were pearl neck-laces, gold pendants and earrings, and rings of various kinds. It was customary to leave mourning rings to a large number of relatives and friends. One lady, Mrs. Elizabeth Digges, in her will desired that eight should be distributed among the members of her intimate circle. A gentleman of Middlesex bequeathed twenty-five pounds sterling for the purchase of rings of the same character; sixteen pounds of this sum were to be expended in such as would cost one guinea apiece.

A rich planter of Lower Norfolk County, at his death, was in possession of "a sapphire set in gold, one ring with a blue stone, another with a green stone, and another still with a yellow stone, two hollow wrought rings, a diamond ring with several sparks, a mourning ring, a beryl set in silver, and an amber necklace."

As real pearls were very costly, a Frenchman, named Jacques, invented a substitute for them in this century (seventeenth). He had observed that the water in which small fish, called "ablettes," had been washed, contained a quantity of silvery particles, and by filling hollow blown glass beads with this sediment, he succeeded in producing an admirable imitation; but about twenty thousand white-bait were required to supply one pound of this essence of pearls.*

Small gold and silver bodkins were used by the wives of the planters for the purpose of keeping the head-dress in place.

Plantation life, even toward the end of the century, gave but few opportunities for display. There were no towns where, as at Wil-liamsburg in the following century, the leading families might gather at certain seasons and show off their fashionable costumes. The church of the parish was the social centre of each community. It was there that fine clothes could be exhibited on Sundays, while at weddings and other festal meetings, the most costly suits and dresses were worn.

* History of Fashion in France.

The store, which every planter of importance maintained on his place, was a notable feature of colonial life. A list of the articles for sale in one of those rural establishments is almost as varied as the advertisement of one of our city department stores to-day. For instance, the Hubbard store in York County in 1667 contained:

Lockram, canvas, dowlas, Scotch cloth, blue linen, oznaburg, cotton, holland serge, kersey and flannel in bales, full suits for adults and youths; bodices, hoods and laces for women; shoes, gloves, hose, cravats, handkerchiefs, hats and other articles of dress. Hammers, hatchets, chisels, augers, locks, staples, nails, sickles, bellows, saws, knives, flesh forks, porringers, saucepans, frying-pans, gridirons, tongs, shovels, hoes, iron-pots, tables, physic, wool-cards, gimlets, compasses, needles, stirrups, looking-glasses, candlesticks, candles, funnels, 25 pounds of raisins, 100 gallons of brandy, 20 gallons of wine, 10 gallons of *aqua vitæ*.

FIGURE 37.
A Peddler (from an Old Print).

The contents of this store was valued at £614 sterling, a sum which represented about $15,000 in our present currency.

Mr. Fiske says: "One can imagine how dazzling to the youthful eyes must have been the miscellaneous variety of desirable things. Not only were the manufactured articles pretty sure to have come from England, but everything else, to be saleable, must be labelled English, insomuch that fanciers used to sell the songsters unknown to England, if they sang particularly well, as English mocking birds."

It was the habit of the early Virginia planters from time to time to purchase silver plate in England. This they looked upon as a sort of wealth which could never lose its value, and pieces of such plate engraved with the crest of the original owner, have in many cases been handed down as family heirlooms, even to the present day. Candlesticks and snuffers, castors for sugar, pepper, and mustard, saltcellars and beakers are frequently mentioned in the wills of the latter part of the seventeenth century.

In one instance dishes weighing eighty and ninety ounces apiece and a case containing a dozen silver-hafted knives and a dozen silver-hafted forks are specified. Mrs. Elizabeth Digges bequeathed two hundred and sixty ounces of silver plate to her friends and relatives. Specimens of old silver, etc., are shown in Figure 159.

FIGURE 37½.
Drawn from an Original Monmouth Cap at the Rolls Hall, Monmouth, Wales.

We read also of the following musical instruments among the household goods of the richer planters: Virginals, hand-lyres, cornets, violins, recorders, flutes, and hautboys.

In the kitchen, various utensils were in use, being made of brass, tin, pewter, wood, clay, and copper.

Another feature of colonial life was the itinerant peddler, who travelled from plantation to plantation carrying the latest fashions and, oftentimes, the latest piece of gossip. He was always sure of a welcome from the people of every class, from the mistress and master at the hall fireside to the maids and men in the servants' quarters, for his pack contained, like that of Autolycus, wares to suit all needs and tastes.

" Lawn as white as driven snow; Bugle-bracelet, necklace-amber,
 Cypress black as e'er was crow; Perfume for a lady's chamber;
 Gloves as sweet as damask roses; Golden quoifs and stomachers,
 Masks for faces and for noses; For my lads to give their dears;
  Pins and poking-sticks of steel;
  What maids lack from head to heel;
  Come buy of me, come; come buy, come buy;
  Buy lads, or else your lasses cry: come, buy."

FIGURE 38.

FIGURE 39.

FIGURE 40.

FIGURE 41.

FIGURE 42.

REIGNS OF JAMES II—WILLIAM AND MARY
1685-1700

FIGURE 38 represents a lady of quality in the fashionable dress of William and Mary's reign. Her gown is of rich silk trimmed with pretintailles, or patterns cut out and laid on in rows across the petticoat. The flounce is edged with gold lace, also the gown which is looped back to show the underskirt. The stomacher is stiff and high; the sleeves loose, ending below the elbow with full ruffles of lace to match the commode head-dress, which has long streamers down the back. The hair is worn low and in soft loose curls on the forehead.

FIGURE 39 is a typical dress of a child of the period. In this case it is of blue Holland, but silk and brocade were much used. Apron with bib is of white linen. Under the loose silken hood is a close-fitting cap of linen which was always worn by little children and sometimes beautifully embroidered.

FIGURE 40 shows the outdoor costume of a tradeswoman late in the seventeenth century. Her gown is of woolen fabric, paragon or linsey-woolsey, made with sleeves short enough to show the undersleeves of white kenting which reach a little below the elbow. Her mantle is of durant trimmed with bands of gimp. The hood is of black ducape and is the popular style of head covering of that period. It is lined and turned back round the face with sarsinet of a contrasting colour.

FIGURE 41.—A man on his way to work about the end of the seventeenth century in leggings of tanned leather and coat of frieze under which is a woolen jerkin. His wide-brimmed hat is of coarse felt.

FIGURE 42 represents a gentleman of William and Mary's day, costumed in dark red broadcloth trimmed with gold braid and gold buttons. He wears a cravat of fine linen with lace ends, and carries his three-cornered hat edged with feathers, rather than crush his voluminous periwig. His shoes have small buckles rather high on the instep.

There is not much to be said about dress among the American Indians. However, the costume of the Queen of the Pamunkeys, who accompanied her husband, Totto Potto Moi, to a conference with the English in Virginia, and who was a lady of some distinction, is worthy of description. She wore a turban made of a wide plait of black and white wampum and her robe was of deerskin, with the hair on the outside, ornamented (from the shoulders to the feet) with a twisted fringe six inches deep. An effective but rather an uncomfortable dress for the season, as this conference took place in May (1677).

The King of the Pamunkeys was afterward killed in fighting with the English under Colonel Edward Hill. His wife, the Queen, made an appeal to the House of Burgesses, whereupon Charles II sent to her, in recognition of her husband's services, a crown consisting of a red velvet cap with a silver plate as a frontlet, to which were attached many chains. During the latter part of the year 1800, the Pamunkeys determined to move westward, and, being under stress of weather, and, also, it is supposed, lacking food, came to Mr. Arthur Morson, who gave them shelter and protection for a time on his plantation. Upon leaving, they expressed their gratitude by presenting their benefactor with this crown, their greatest treasure, which still existed in the original shape. The cap becoming in time moth-eaten, the chains lost and scattered, the Administrator of the Morson Estate sold the frontlet to the Association for the Preservation of Virginia Antiquities, and it was placed in the Historical Society's rooms for safe-keeping (Figure 27).

For descriptions and pictures of the native Indians, the reader is referred to Schoolcraft's exhaustive history, which illustrates the life and customs of the various tribes in North America from the landing of Columbus to the middle of the nineteenth century.*

* History of the Indian Tribes of the United States, by Henry Rowe Schoolcraft, LL.D.

THE ENGLISH COLONIES

IN

MASSACHUSETTS, CONNECTICUT, NEW HAMPSHIRE, MAINE, AND RHODE ISLAND

1620–1700

During the Reigns of
James I, Charles I, Charles II, James II, and
William and Mary

"A Dosen of Points, Sent by a Gentlewoman to Her Lover as a Newe Yeare's Gifte."

As I on a New Yeare's day
  Did walcke amidst the streate,
My restless eyes for you my hart,
  Did seke a fayring mete.
I sercht throughout the faire
  But nothing could I fynde:
No, no, of all ther was not one
  That would content my mynde.
But all the boothes were filled
  With fancyes fond attyre,
And trifling toyes were set to sale,
  For them that would requyre.
Then to myself quoth I,
  What meanes theise childish knacks;
Is all the faire for children made,
  Or fooles that bables lackes?
Are theise the goodly gifts,
  The new yeare to beginne;
Which friends present unto their friends,
  Their fayth and love to winne?
I se I came in vayne,
  My labour all is lost,
I will departe and kepe my purse,
  From making any cost.
But se my happy chaunce,
  Whilest I did hast away;
Dame Vertue doth display her booth,
  My hasty feete to stay.
I joyfull of the sight,
  Did preace unto the place,
To se the tricke and trimmed tent,
  For such a ladye's grace.
And after I had viewed
  Eache thing within her seate,

I found a knotte of peerlesse points
  Beset with posyes neate.
Theise points in number twelve,
  Did shew themselves to be:
The sence whereof by poet's skil,
  I will declare to the.

1. With meate before the set,
    Suffice but nature's scant;
2. Be sure thy tongue at table tyme,
    Noe sober talke doe want.
3. Let word, let thought, and dede,
    In honest wise agree:
4. And loke the pore in tyme of nede,
    Thy helping hand may see.
5. When foes invade the realme,
    Then shew thy might and strength:
6. Tell truth in place wher thou dost come
    For falshed failes at length.
7. Be fast and firm to friende,
    As thou wouldst him to be:
8. Be shamefast there wher shamefull dedes
    Be offred unto the.
9. Weare not suche costly clothes,
    As are not for thy state:
10. Heare eache man's cause as thoh he wer
    In wealth thine equall mate.
11. In place thy maners shewe,
    In right and comly wyse:
12. From the let peace and quietnesse,
    And wars from others ryse.

With these twelve vertuous points,
  Se thou do tye thee round,
And lyke and love this simple gifte,
  Till better may be found.
Yet one point thou dost lacke,
  To tye thy hose before:
Love me as I love the, and shall
  From hence for evermore.—Farwell.

The English in Massachusetts, Connecticut, New Hampshire, Maine, and Rhode Island

1620–1700

FIGURE 43.
A Puritan Dame.

IN 1620 came the first English settlers to Massachusetts—the Pilgrims, or Separatists, as they are sometimes called, in their sombre coloured garments, of the same shapes and fashions, however, as those in vogue at the gay court of Charles I, the superfluous trimmings, knots of bright ribbon, rich laces and feathers, being conspicuously absent.

In this company of one hundred and four Pilgrims, which arrived at Plymouth, December 20, 1620, were the following:

Two carpenters	One wool-carder	Ten adult servants
One fustian worker and silk dyer	One cooper	One lay reader
One lady's maid	One merchant	One hatter
Two printers and publishers	Four seamen	One physician
One tailor	One soldier	One smith
	Two tradesmen	

The Pilgrims, like the Roundheads in England, were minded to discourage extravagance, and made strict laws to control fashions of dress. Three years later they were followed by the Puritans of the Massachusetts Bay Company, who, according to Weedon, settled first at Cape Ann and afterward removed to Salem. This Company was a large and rich organization and provided each man with a suitable outfit:

Four pairs of shoes	A green cotton waistcoat
Four pairs of stockings	A leather belt
A pair of Norwich gaiters	A woolen cap
Four shirts	A black hat
Two suits of doublet and hose of	Two red knit caps
leather lined with oil skin	Two pairs of gloves
A woolen suit lined with leather	A mandillion or cloak lined with cotton
Four bands	and an extra pair of breeches were
Two handkerchiefs	allotted each man (Figure 44).

There were many women in this band of settlers, but no mention is made of their garments.

This outfit was much more liberal than that provided by the Virginia Company, but the climate of Massachusetts was bleak and cold compared with that of Virginia, although the air apparently agreed with Francis Higginson, who wrote the following letter from Boston in 1629:

"But since I came hither on this voyage I thank God I have had perfect health and I, that have not gone without a cap for many years together neither durst leave off the same, have now cast away my cap, and do wear none at all in the day time; and whereas beforetime I clothed myself with double clothes and thick waistcoats to keep me warm even in summer time, I do now go as thin clad as any, only wearing a light stuff cassock upon my shirt and stuff breeches of one thickness without lining."

This company of Puritans, which numbered about two hundred, eventually founded Boston and other places in the neighbourhood: Charlestown, Watertown, Dorchester, Roxbury, Mystic, Lynn, etc. They kept in touch with the Mother Country and imported many comforts, which the Plymouth Bay Company eschewed.

About 1630 a body of this Massachusetts Bay Company, composed chiefly of yeomen of Dorsetshire, England, settled in Connecticut. They were mostly Church of England people of the representative Anglo-Saxon type, and in their laws we find few restrictions concerning dress, although at the dawn of the Revolution the people of Connecticut were among the first of the Colonists to renounce foreign luxuries and augment the use of homemade articles. We read that "master-tailors were paid 12 pence, inferior 8 pence per day, with dyett."

In 1634, the Massachusetts Court forbade the purchase of "Any apparell, either woolen, silke, or lynnen with any lace on it, silver, golde, silk, or thread." They shall not "make or buy slashed clothes, other than one slashe in each sleeve and another in the backe"; there shall be no "cutt works, imbroid'd or needle work'd capps, bands & Rayles; no gold or silver girdles, hatt bands, belts, ruffs, beaver hatts."

In 1636 lace was forbidden; only the binding of a small edging on linen was allowed.

FIGURE 44.

A Puritan Cloak or Mandillion of Black Silk with Small Embroidered Buttons. The original garment from which the drawing is taken is in the South Kensington Museum, London.

Points were the usual fastenings in use during the sixteenth and seventeenth centuries. Sometimes they had metal tags at the ends and were more or less ornamental. Frequent mention is made of them by Shakespeare:

"Their points being broken, down fell their hose;"
"With one that ties his points," etc.

Like their successors, the modern suspenders, they were often very dainty and were appropriately given as love tokens.

Margaret Winthrop, in a letter to England written from Massachusetts, gives a note of daily wear: "I must of a necessity make me a gown to wear every day and would have one bought me of good strong black stuff and Mr. Smith to make it of the civilest fashion now in use. If my sister Downing would please to give him some directions about it, he would make it the better."* Slight as is this note, it proves that Dame Winthrop was not indifferent to the prevailing fashions, and we know that English gentlewomen of that time were dressed as in Figures 21, 32, 33, 35, and 36. The familiar portrait of Governor Winthrop in a ruff and long hair indicates that he had not adopted the dress of the strict Puritans (Figure 93). Unfortunately, no portrait of his wife has been handed down to posterity, and we are left to conjecture that the dress of "good strong black stuff" to "wear every day" was made of durant, something after the fashion of Figure 21, or, perhaps, like that of the Puritan gentlewoman in the initial letter of this chapter, which represents a typical Puritan of the Massachusetts Bay Company.

Abundant evidence of the various styles of dress of English women in the reigns of Charles I and II is preserved in the clever sketches of Hollar. They are invaluable to the historian.

Wenceslaus Hollar (1607–1677) went from Cologne and Antwerp to London in the train of the Earl of Arundel, English Ambassador, in 1635, and was appointed teacher of drawing to the young Prince, afterwards Charles II. A volume of sketches by the royal pupil, to which Hollar had given the finishing touches, may be seen among the Harleian manuscripts at the British Museum. In 1640 appeared his "Ornatus Muliebris Anglicanus, or the Severall Habits of English Women from the Nobilitiee to the Country Women as they are in these times."

* Margaret Winthrop, by Mrs. Earle.

FIGURE 46.

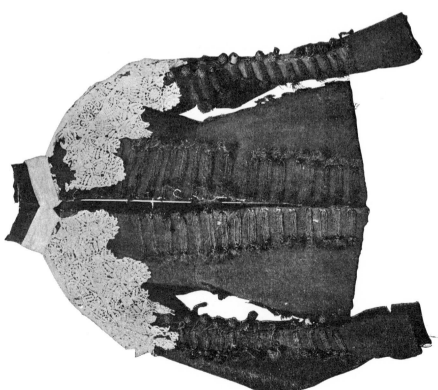

FIGURE 45.

FIGURE 45.—Doublet of black cloth trimmed with silk braid and crochet buttons. The sleeves are slashed. The lace collar is not put on properly. It should turn down over the neck-band and fit close up to the throat, as in Figure 14. Worn in Reign of Charles I. (Photographed from the original garment.)

FIGURE 46.—Doublet of black silk trimmed with points of galloon with silver aiglets. The collar should be turned over the neck-band and fit close to the throat, as in Figure 14. Worn in the reign of James I. (Photographed from the original garment.)

In 1643 appeared a second book, "Theatrum Mulierum," in
which are represented the various styles of dress in the leading
nations of Europe. On the accession of Charles II, Hollar was
appointed His Majesty's Designer.

His books are now very rare. Copies may be seen in the Library
of the British Museum, but I do not know of any in a public library
in this country. The "Theatrum Mulierum" shows the costumes
of the women of Holland in the seventeenth century, specimens of
which are given in Figures 106, 107, 110, 124, and 126.

In the Colony at Plymouth a manifesto against long hair was
published, in which it was called an impious custom and a shameful
practice for any man who had the least care of his soul to wear long
hair. An old song about the Roundhead Puritans runs thus:

> "What creature's this? with his short hair,
> His little band, and huge long ears,
> That this new faith has founded?
> The Puritans were never such,
> The Saints themselves had ne'er so much—
> Oh such a knave's a Roundhead."

The majority of the Puritans, however, were very much in earnest
on the subject of reform in dress, and it has been said they expressed
their piety not only in the choice of sombre hues and simplicity of
cut, but even worked into the garments religious sayings and quota-
tions from Holy Writ. As Fairholt puts it, "they literally moral-
ized dress."

> "Nay Sir, she is a Puritan at her needle too,
>   Indeed,
> She works religious petticoats; for flowers
> She'll make church histories: besides
> My smock sleeves have such holy embroideries,
> And are so learned, that I fear in time
> All my apparel will be quoted by
> Some pure instructor."*

* The Citye Match. Jasper Mayne, L. 1639.

This fashionable custom in England is also mentioned by Ben Jonson. "The linen of men and women was either so worked as to resemble lace or was ornamented by the needle into representations of fruit and flowers, passages of history," etc.*

The inventories of about 1641 show that

3 suits of clothes were valued at £3				
3 coats	"	"	"	2 6s.
1 hat and doublet	"	"	"	3
4 pairs of shoes	"	"	"	9
4 " " stockings	"	"	"	6
1 stuff petticoat was		"	"	6
2 pairs of linen breeches	"		"	1 6s.

In 1652 is found the first mention of shoemaking, at Salem. It was about this time that the General Court of Massachusetts passed sumptuary laws to repress the spending of too large a proportion of income on apparel. Weedon says: "When the Court was not occupied with grave business of State, it devoted itself to correcting morals and regulating dress. The function of dress

FIGURE 47.
Typical Winter Costume of a Lady of the Period, 1640.

in the minds of the anxious Fathers was not only to cover and protect people, but to classify and arrange them. The same conserving prejudice which marked their treatment of labourers and apprentices controlled their notions of dress. Social prestige, rank, caste, and breeding were to be formulated in the garments of the wearer. It was not only that the precious capital of the community was wasted by expensive dressing, but the well ordered ranks of society were

* Every Man out of his Humour.

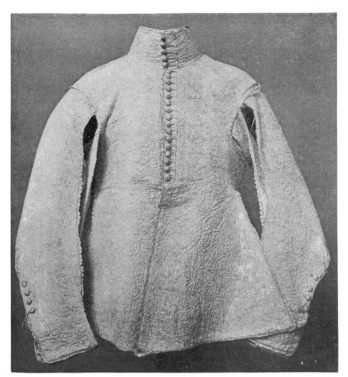

FIGURE 48.

FIGURE 49.

FIGURE 48.—A boy's doublet of white linen quilted, and embroidered with gold-coloured silk. The sleeves are slashed and the whole garment is edged with needle-point lace. Worn in reign of Charles I, 1639. (Photographed from the original garment.)

FIGURE 49.—Bodice of white satin slashed and pinked. A chemisette of silk or embroidery would show in the openings. Worn in reign of Charles I. (Photographed from the original garment.)

jostled and disturbed by the glitter of lace and the show of silken hoods, the tramp of strong boots."

Mrs. Lake, who came over with the Dorsetshire Company in 1635, sent out to England for the following articles for the furnishing of the new household of her daughter, who married John Gallup of the same settlement in 1645. We give the list in full as thoroughly typical of the time:

"A peare of brasse Andirons
A brasse Kittell,
2 grate Chestes, well made,
2 armed Cheares with rushe bottums,
2 carven Caisse for Bottels wch my Cuzzen Cooke has of mine
A Warming Pann,
A Big Iron Pott,
6 Pewter Plates
2 Pewter Platters,
3 Pewter Porringeres
A small Stew Pann of Copper
A peare of Brasse and a peare of Silver Candle-sticks (of goode plate)
A Drippe Panne
A Bedsteede of carven Oake (ye one in wch I sleept in my father's house,
    with ye Vallances and Curtayns and Tapestry Coverlid belongynge
    & ye wch my sister Breadcale hath in charge of Mee)
Duzzen Napekins of fine linen damasque &
    2 table cloathes of ye same. Also 8 fine
Holland Pillowe Beeres and 4 ditto sheetes.
A skellet,
A pestel & mortar
A few Needels of different sizes
A carpet (that is, a table cover; the name was universally applied thus)
    of goodly stuff and colour, aboute 2 Ell longe.
6 Table knifes of ye beste Steal with such handles as may bee.
Also 3 large & 3 smal Silvern Spoones, and 6 of horne."

We are told that Mrs. Lake left a wardrobe of considerable extent and richness, besides a goodly list of linens and other household treasures, with several carved chests to contain them, all of which she bequeathed to friends and relatives: "To my daughter Martha Harris," she says, "I give my tapestry coverlid and all my other apparell which are not disposed of to others particularly, and I give unto her my mantel and after her decease, to all her children as their need is."* This "mantel" was supposed to have been Russian sable, even then as costly as it was rare, and presumably brought from the far East, perhaps China.

We read also in "Colonial Days and Ways" that "all the better class among the Colonists seem to have disproportionately liberal supplies of 'mantels and pettycotes' of velvet or brocade, with other 'garments to consort therewith,' but this was not due so much to vanity as to thrift, the best being literally the cheapest in the days when the fine fabrics were so honestly made as to wear for decades and

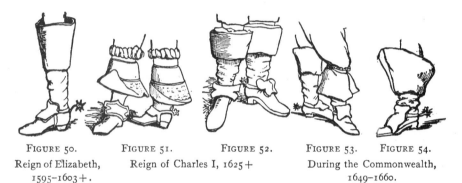

FIGURE 50.   FIGURE 51.   FIGURE 52.   FIGURE 53.   FIGURE 54.

Reign of Elizabeth,   Reign of Charles I, 1625 +   During the Commonwealth,
1595–1603 +.   1649–1660.

the cost of carriage was the same for a coat of frieze as for one of velvet." Mrs. Smith throws a new light on the subject, which also helps us to understand the wills and inventories in which these beautiful old stuffs were handed down as family heirlooms. Fortunately for this book of costume, some Colonial garments have been preserved in their original fashion, while, of course, others bear the marks of many alterations to suit the times.

In 1638 an order was passed by the General Court of Massachusetts:

"No garment shall be made with short sleeves, and such as have garments already made with short sleeves shall not wear the same

* Colonial Days and Ways, by Helen Evertson Smith.

unless they cover the arm to the wrist; and hereafter no person whatever shall make any garment for women with sleeves more than half
an ell wide."

The town records were full of prosecutions, acquittals, and con-
victions for offences against these laws.   In Salem in 1652 "a man
was presented for excess of bootes, ribands, gould and silver laces,
and Ester Jynks for wearing silver lace"; while in Newbury in 1653
"two women were called upon to pay taxes for wearing silken hoods
and scarves, but were discharged on proof that their husbands were
worth two hundred pounds each."

"John Hutchins' wife was also discharged upon testimony of
her being brought up above the
ordinary ranke."   "The latter,"
observes Weedon, "is an interesting
instance showing that rank as well as
property condoned these offences."

Any one of less estate than two
hundred pounds was held to strict
account in dress.   The women
offended especially by wearing silk
and tiffany hoods; but they also

FIGURE 55.   FIGURE 56:   FIGURE 57.
Reign of   Reign of   Reign of
Charles II,   James II,   William III,
1660+.   1685+.   1690+.

wore broad-brimmed hats (Figure 43).   Under the stiff bodice of a
gown a lady wore a petticoat either of woolen stuff or of rich silk
or brocade.   The ruff had given place to a broad collar, plain or
embroidered, falling over the shoulders (Figures 20 and 33).

As leather was much used, a tannery was almost the first industry
started in every settlement.   In 1676 the price of shoes was regulated by law.   "Five pence half penny a size for all pleyne and
wooden heel'd shoes, and above seven pence half penny a size for well
wrought 'French falls.'"   Wooden heels were worn all through
the seventeenth century.   Even at this early date, Lynn, Massachusetts, was the centre for the manufacture of shoes, which were

usually made with broad straps and buckles; women's shoes being of neat leather or woolen cloth and occasionally of silk.

During the seventeenth century leather clothing was much worn, especially by labourers and servants. The excellent brain-tanned deerskin, which the Indians taught the Colonists to prepare, served well for garments. Hampshire kerseys were used for common wear. Monmouth caps and red knit caps are mentioned among the articles used by the lower classes, and the mandillion, or over-garment, fastened with hooks and eyes, is frequently spoken of. Irish stockings, so often mentioned in this century, have been compared to modern socks, but they were of cloth and were very warm. While rich apparel is noted here and there, in spite of statute law, it is evident that the great majority of the people dressed plainly. Their

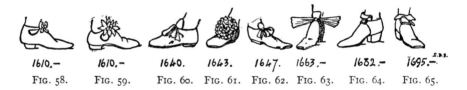

1610.—   1610.—   1640.   1643.   1647.   1663.—   1682.—   1695.—

FIG. 58.   FIG. 59.   FIG. 60.   FIG. 61.   FIG. 62.   FIG. 63.   FIG. 64.   FIG. 65.

frugality and abstinence made a foundation on which sumptuary statutes could be based.

Doublets were worn by both sexes ; they were always lined or padded for extra warmth (Figure 31). The sleeves were often slashed and embroidered extravagantly, as indicated in the "restraining acts" of the Pilgrim Fathers. Falling bands at the neck were very common, and often they were embroidered. A deep linen collar was sometimes preferred in place of the bands.

> "This pretty new fashion indulge him to wear
> There's no law in bands, I may venture to swear,
> But they set off an old fashion face I declare.
> Which nobody can deny, deny, which nobody can deny."

Shoes were ornamented with rosettes (Figures 59 and 61). A beaver or felt hat covered the head. Embroidered gloves were

FIGURE 66.

FIGURE 67.

FIGURE 68.

FIGURE 69.

97

FIGURE 66.—A Puritan Colonist of the Massachusetts Bay Company. Suit of black cloth of the same cut and general make as the Cavalier's costume in Figure 19. Stockings or hose of dark grey or green wool fastened to the breeches by points of black galloon or ribbon. Falling band and cuffs of white Holland. Hat of black felt finished with a narrow band of ribbon and a small silver buckle. The mandillion or cloak is of black cloth lined with drugget or fustian.

FIGURE 67.—A woman of the same Company. Her gown is of cloth, either purple or grey, or perhaps brown; for outdoor wear it is turned under and looped back showing petticoats of homespun or linsey-woolsey. The apron is of white Holland linen. A falling collar or band turns down round the neck of the gown and white linen cuffs are turned back over the sleeves. The kerchief is put on for outdoor wear as well as the hood, which is made of dark coloured silk or camlet and lined with soft silk or fur to match the muff. This was the ordinary dress of a Puritan gentlewoman from 1620 to 1640. In cold weather a cloak and hood of heavy cloth or fur was worn with a velvet mask as a protection from the wind. See Figure 36. Stout shoes with wooden heels and woolen stockings completed the costume. The hair is drawn back under a white linen cap.

FIGURE 68.—The dress of an English gentleman about 1666. Petticoat breeches trimmed with wide ribbon arranged in overlapping loops. Short doublet to match with slashed sleeves opening both back and front and held together by loops of braid and buttons. A collar of linen trimmed with rich lace turns down over the coat, but is much deeper and fuller in front, where it is laid in box-plaits under the chin. The shirt of Holland hangs out from under the doublet. The cloak is of a fine woolen stuff made full and long and gathered into a rolling collar at the neck. The hat is of Flemish beaver with long full plumes of a contrasting colour. The boots are French falls with very wide tops, known as bucket tops. The peruke is long and full without powder.

FIGURE 69.—A lady of the same date (1666) in a walking hood and fur tippet. The gown is of rich silk trimmed with fancy gimp. The bodice is pointed in front and back over a full-gathered skirt and is cut low in the neck and finished by a falling collar of lace under the tippet. Under the short full sleeves of the gown are white puffed sleeves to the wrist. Silken shoes tied with ribbon on the instep match the gown in colour and texture. The hair is worn in curls to the shoulders and held back by a ribbon which is tied in a bow either on top or above the left ear.

always worn with full dress, the flaps of the gauntlets being richly
figured or fringed (Figures 72, 74, 75, 76, and 77). Swords were
suspended from embroidered shoulder-belts. Gold and silver lace
was often used for trimming.

In the Massachusetts Colony, armour was provided for the emigrants. Bandoliers, horn flasks, corselets, and pikes are mentioned
frequently.

In an old book called an "Abridgement of the laws in force and
use in Her Majesty's (Queen Anne) Plantations of Virginia (viz.) of
Jamaica, New England, Barba-
does, New York, Maryland, Carolina, etc., London 1709," will be
found under the heading "Ammunition, Or Laws Concerning the
Colonial Militia": "I. an. 1662.
Every man able to bear arms shall
have in his house a fixed gun, 2 l.
of powder and 8 l. of shot, at
least, to be provided by the Master
of the Family, under the Penalty
of being fined 80 l. of tobacco.
II. an. 1666. Every County shall

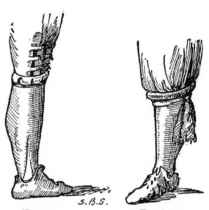

FIGURE 70.   FIGURE 71.
Cannons or Breeches Fastenings (from an
Old Print, 1650).

be empowered by their By-Laws to make such provision of ammunition at the county charges as their several occasions require.
III. Captains of foot and horse shall take a strict account of
what arms are wanting and represent the same to the Colonel,"
etc. This affords valuable proof of the familiarity with firearms
expected of the Colonists in everyday life, also of the early origin
of the American militia. With regard to the latter organization,
we read under the date of 1660 as follows:

"Every person neglecting to appear at the Days of Exercising
the Militia shall be fined 100 l. of Tobacco."

"Ten long guns or muskets with one Barrel of gun powder and Bullets proportionable shall be kept in each garrison as a Reserve and Defence for the same."

"For the better taking alarms upon the approach of Indians the frequent shooting of guns at Drinkings is prohibited."

"Six shoots of powder each man is required to bring with him on Training Days or pay a fine. The latter to be put aside for the purchase of Drums and Colours."

A portrait of Sir John Leverett, Governor of the Massachusetts Colony in 1673, in the Essex Institute at Salem, depicts a buff coat of dressed leather with metal fastenings, like ornamental hooks and eyes, down the front; a falling collar of linen tied with little tassels, and a very magnificent pair of embroidered gloves, which Sir John is holding in one hand, while on a table beside him is a hat ornamented with a long feather (Figure 82). Probably the portrait was taken when he was a Colonial soldier, for history records that he went to England in 1644 and took the side of the Parliament against the King, but after his return to Boston he filled several important offices, and in 1676 was magnanimously knighted by Charles II in acknowledgment of his services to the New England Colonies.

The women of New England in the last quarter of the seventeenth century were well, if not handsomely, dressed. Undoubtedly the gentlewomen of that time had brocades and silks for festive occasions and fur-trimmed cloaks and hoods for the cold season, but the ordinary dress was a short gown of camlet over a homespun petticoat with a long white apron of linen. The sleeves of the gown were supplemented by mittens reaching to the elbows and leaving a part of the fingers and thumbs bare. The cloak worn at that time was short, with a hood to cover the head, which was thrown back in meeting; and those who wore hats took them off. The matrons wore caps habitually and the young women had their hair curled

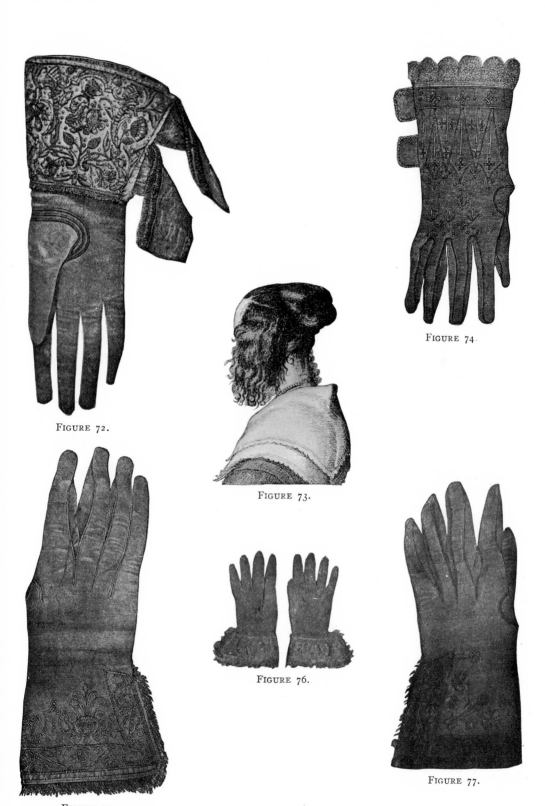

FIGURE 72.

FIGURE 73.

FIGURE 74.

FIGURE 75.

FIGURE 76.

FIGURE 77.

FIGURES 72, 74, 75, and 77 show different specimens of embroidered gloves, made of doeskin, embroidered in coloured silks and gold thread, worn in the seventeenth century.

FIGURE 76.—Gloves worn by Sir John Leverett, Governor of Massachusetts Colony. (From the original gloves in the Essex Museum, Salem, Massachusetts.)

FIGURE 73.—Fashionable style of hair-dressing, reigns of Charles I and II. (By Hollar.)

and tied back with a ribbon or arranged in a soft coil at the back, with short curls on the forehead.

Scarlet robes are said to have been worn by the judges in the

FIGURE 78.
A Man in Buff-coat and Bandolier, 1620–1660.

Massachusetts Colony. Mrs. Earle gives a picture of one stated to have been worn by Judge Curwen, of Salem, during the gruesome witch

trials, but the garment in question is so exactly like the cloaks worn
by the women of the Puritan days that one is tempted to think it was
borrowed from his wife for these solemn occasions.   However, scarlet
was a favourite colour for men in those days, and a very romantic
story has recently been written by Mrs. Austin about the red riding
cloak worn by Governor Bradford, 2d, about the middle of the seventeenth century.

Mourning for the dead was attended by various solemn ceremonies in the Colonies. Judge Sewall, of Mas-
sachusetts (Figure 81), describes minutely the funeral of Lady Andros,
the wife of the Governor (Figure 97), on the 10th of February, 1688, to which
he had been invited by the "Clark of the South Company."   "It took
place between 7 and 8 P. M. probably.   The hearse, surrounded by
torch bearers, was drawn by six horses, and escorted by a guard of

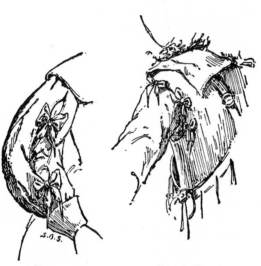

FIGURE 79.
Points with Aiglets
Drawing Together a
Slashed Sleeve.

FIGURE 80.
Points with Aiglets or
Tags Fastening a Buff-coat
and Sleeve Together (from
an Old Print, 1650–1660).

soldiers from the Governour's house to the South Meeting House
where the body was placed before the pulpit, with six mourning women
by it.   There was a great noise and clamour to keep the people out of
the house, which was made light with candles and torches."   He tells
of himself that he went home, and about nine o'clock heard the bell
tolled again for the funeral.   He missed the sermon, whether purposely or not is not told, but knows that the text was "Cry, all flesh

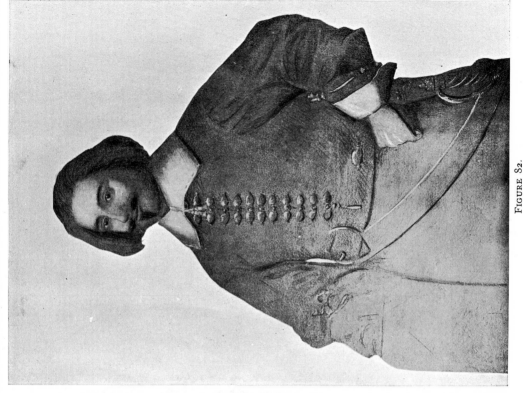

FIGURE 82.

FIGURE 81.

FIGURE 81.—Portrait of Samuel Sewall, Governor and Judge of Massachusetts Colony, showing the periwig and long coat of the reign of James II.

FIGURE 82.—Portrait of Sir John Leverett, Governor of Massachusetts Colony, showing buff coat and plain band of a soldier in reign of Charles I.

is grass." After naming a number of the people who were present, he remarks, "Twas warm thawing weather and the wayes extreame dirty. No volley at placing the body in the tomb." On Saturday, February 11th, another entry in this instructive diary reads: "The next day the mourning cloths of the pulpit is taken off and given to Mr. Willard." Frequent mention is made throughout this diary, and others of the time, of the gloves, scarves, and mourning rings given friends and relatives at funerals, and there is evidence that the general custom of wearing black as a token of sorrow was followed throughout the Colonies, the women wearing gowns and hoods of

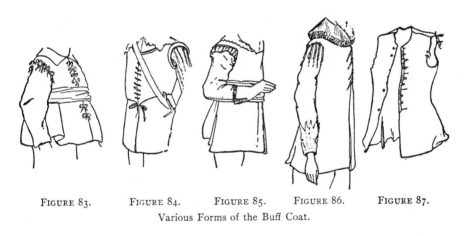

FIGURE 83.   FIGURE 84.   FIGURE 85.   FIGURE 86.   FIGURE 87.

Various Forms of the Buff Coat.

black stuff with trimmings, cuffs, and veils of crêpe, at least such was the "customary woe," but it was observed with less formality by the Non-Conformists than by the Orthodox Church people. Little children were dressed in black and wore black ribbons for a time, and it was not unusual for the servants of a household to be dressed in black when the head of the family died: as in nearly every other respect, English ways and English customs were very closely followed throughout the Colonies in America. In the Philadelphia Library there is preserved, among many other interesting relics of the past, an old hatchment formerly used in the Dickinson family,

—probably brought from England,—which was placed over the doorway when a death occurred in the family. Another specimen is also to be seen at Christ Church, Philadelphia.

The portrait of a widow given in Figure 150 represents Lady Mary Fenwick, in high widow's cap and tippets, black dress and veil, in one hand holding a portrait of her husband, Sir John Fenwick, who by an act of attainder was beheaded 27th of January, 1696, without a trial, for conspiracy in favour of James II. Lady Fenwick made the greatest exertions to save her husband's life and became an object of much interest to the Jacobite Party. The cap is of the shape known as the "commode" in William and Mary's reign (Figure 38).

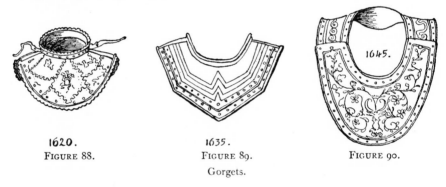

1620.
FIGURE 88.

1635.
FIGURE 89.
Gorgets.

1645.
FIGURE 90.

Though the Massachusetts General Court admonished men against long hair and inveighed against excess in apparel in 1675, the laws in this direction were dropping into disuse in many districts. In the same year the grand jury threatened the selectmen of Dedham with prosecution for their neglect in enforcing the sumptuary statutes. These worthy burghers did not relish the work "of stripping silken hoods and ribbands from irate dames and of arraigning the great boots of dandies. There is no record to show that they heeded the mandate of the grand jury."

The inventories in Boston prove that sumptuous dress was in fashion notwithstanding the written laws against it. Robert Richbell, in 1682, leaves two silver hilted rapiers and a belt worth £12. His wardrobe contained a satin coat with gold flowers, and blue breeches, £4; a stuff suit with lace, several other suits, all accompanied by seven cravats and seven pairs of ruffles and ribbons, valued at £7.

Periwigs came into fashion at the Restoration, 1660. Richbell must have vexed poor Judge Sewall sorely, for he was the possessor of three.

We know that silver buttons were very common in the Colonies in the seventeenth century, and gold ones were also used. Captain Hudson, whose dress was modest in comparison with Richbell's, had two suits equipped with them. In a trading stock, mention is made of 4 gross of silver and gold buttons valued at £3 12s. A curiosity of the time was "Beggars' velvet," 14 yards worth 21s.

The long periwigs introduced into England from France in the latter part of Charles II's reign were promptly assumed by the women of fashion, together with the plumed hats of the same period. Pepys records the fact thus:

"Walking in the gallery of Whitehall, I find the Ladies of Honour dressed in their riding garbs, with coats and doublets with deep skirts, just for all the world like men's, and their doublets buttoned up the breast, with periwigs and hats on, that only for a long petticoat dragging under their men's coats, no body would take them for women on any point whatever, which was an odd sight and a sight that did not please me."

About 1680, the long straight coats, which took the fickle fancy of Charles II for a time, were introduced into New England. They were made without a collar and were worn with a neck-cloth which fastened with a silver buckle under the hair in the back. Specimens of this fashion are given in Figures 137, 138, photographed from the original garments in the South Kensington Museum. They belonged to Sir Thomas Isham (1657–1681), third baronet, who

was born at Lamport in Nottinghamshire.   When still a boy he wrote
a diary in Latin, by the command of his father, which gives a vivid
picture of the everyday doings of a family of the period.   This diary
was translated and privately printed (1875) by the Rev. Robert
Isham, rector of Lamport, where the original is still preserved.   Isham
succeeded to the Baronetcy in 1679.   He is described as a young
gentleman of great expectations.   Figure 137 represents the suit of
light brocade prepared for his wedding, which he never wore, as he
died after a brief illness on the day fixed for the ceremony.

Weedon again records: "In the inventories of women, house-linen
generally formed an important part.   Mistress Anne Hibbins in
1656 had relatively more of the luxuries her sex cherishes in all periods.
A gold wedding ring at 16s., a ring with a diamond at 8s., a 'taffaty'
cloak at £2 10s., a black satin doublet at 10s., a green wrought cup-
board cloth with silk fringe at 15s., 5 painted callico curtains and
valiants at £1 10s., show that Anne loved the things hated by the
Puritans.

"In William Paine's stock in 1660 were silk wares in two boxes
at £31 14s.   These occasional luxuries stand out conspicuously.
Usually the assorted merchandise of the traders is in solid wares
and goods for the everyday use of everyday people.   The women
selected them carefully and conscientiously.   In 1647 one writes:
'She have three peeces of stuf, but I think there is but one of them
yt you would like yrself.   It is pretty sad stuf, but it have a thred of
white in it; it is 3 quarters broad and ye priz is 5s. 6d ye yard.'"*

Towards the close of the seventeenth century we note a tendency
to display in all inventories and descriptions left by the wealthy
colonists of New England, as well as those in the same period in
Virginia, Maryland, and the Carolinas.   It was the reign of William
and Mary in England, and the Colonies were not subject to any form
of oppression.   Intercourse between the two countries was frequent,

* Weedon's Economic History of New England.

FIGURE 91.

FIGURE 92.

FIGURE 93.

FIGURE 94.

FIGURE 91.—Portrait of John Winthrop the second, showing the typical garb of the Puritan in the Massachusetts Colony. 1640+

FIGURE 92.—Picture of Sir John Leverett as Governor of Massachusetts Colony about 1680.

FIGURE 93.—Picture of John Winthrop, Governor of Massachusetts Colony in 1629.

FIGURE 94.—Picture of Edward Winslow, Governor of Plymouth Colony, in Puritan dress, in 1644.

and every ship brought over comforts and luxuries, also fine clothes made by fashionable London tailors, wigs from the popular wig-makers, etc. It is quite safe to conclude that fashions in the Colonies were never more than a year behind those of old England.

Children in the New England Colonies, as elsewhere at that time, were dressed as much like their parents as possible. The baby clothes of the seventeenth century were marvellous specimens of needlework. The earliest garments I have seen are the christening blanket, shirts, and mitts said to have been worn by Governor Bradford, of Plymouth, and now exhibited at Salem in the Essex Institute.

A portrait of Robert Gibbs, aged four and a half, painted in Boston in 1670, also one of John Quincy, at a little more than one year of age, painted in 1690, show the long hanging sleeves usually worn by children under ten years of age (Figure 39). There is also a portrait of Jane Bonner at the age of eight, painted in 1700, which looks almost like a diminutive court lady, with stiff stomacher, ruffles of point-lace, and a necklace of pearls; in one hand a fan, a rose in the other.*

New England by this time included New Hampshire and Maine, settled in 1623 by an English Company in search of gold, and Rhode Island, founded by Roger Williams in 1636.

The attitude of the New England Colonists towards the Mother Church is not clearly outlined in all the authorities of the time; and, in order to prevent anachronisms in costuming a story of that period, it may be well to explain here that the emigrants who came over in 1630 under Governor John Winthrop, and who the day before they embarked sent an address to the "rest of the brethren of the Church of England" calling the Church their "dear mother," had, notwithstanding their dutiful address, when they arrived in America, allowed a sense of freedom to overcome their allegiance, and, following the

* Child Life in Colonial Days, by Mrs. Earle.

example of the Pilgrims of Plymouth and the Puritans of Salem, established separate churches, choosing their own officers. The Plymouth settlers had not openly renounced the authority of the Church of England, but they had laid aside the established ritual. Endicott followed this example and organized the first New England Church at Salem. A few members of that Colony objected, but he had them arrested and sent to England. From that time (1630) Non-Conformist Churches were established in every New England settlement. A simple method of choosing their leaders was adopted. Each member wrote his vote on a piece of paper, stating the Lord moved him to think this man is fit to be pastor, and this one to be teacher. The first pastor thus chosen was Skelton, with Francis Higginson, whose journal is quoted on page 84, for teacher. The choice was confirmed by a number of the leading members of this Company laying their hands on them in prayer.

With the disuse of the English ritual came the abandonment of the white surplice during the service, but the Geneva gown (Figures 148, 149), or preaching gown as it was often called, was worn in the pulpit, not only by the Puritan Non-Conformists, but also by the Presbyterians, who adopted it even before they came to the Colonies. A close-fitting black cap or coif is seen in many of the pictures of New England divines.

From "The Judicial History of Massachusetts" I have gleaned the following account of lawyers in the New England Colonies:

"It was many years after the settlement of the Colony, before anything like a distinct class of Attorneys at Law was known. And it is doubtful if there were any regularly educated Attorneys who practiced in the Courts of the Colony at any time during its existence. Several of the Magistrates, it is true, had been educated as Lawyers at home, but they were almost constantly in the magistracy, nor do we hear of their being ever engaged in the management of cases. If they made use of their legal acquirements, it was in aid

of the great object which they had so much at heart—the establishment of a religious Commonwealth, in which the laws of Moses were
much more regarded as precedents than the decisions of Westminster
Hall, or the pages of the few elementary writers upon the Common-
law which were then cited in the English Courts. It was thus,
therefore, that the clergy were admitted to such a direct participation
in the affairs of the Government, and that to two of their number was
committed the duty of codifying the laws by which the Commonwealth was to be governed thereafter.

"There were Attorneys, it is true, and there were lawyers, and
all the concomitant evils growing out of the bad passions involved
in litigation, and there was a law against barratry, passed in 1641,
because even then there was barratry practiced in the Courts. The
profession seems to have now but little favor in the public mind,
although for the first ten years of the Government there were no fees
allowed to the 'patrons,' as they were called, who defended or aided
parties in their suits."

This statement explains the similarity in the dress of judges,
governors, and clergymen of this period of colonial history, as will
be noticed in the portraits of the day, given in Figures 91, 92, 94,
and 149.

THE DUTCH AND ENGLISH

IN

NEW YORK, LONG ISLAND, THE JERSEYS, DELAWARE, AND PENNSYLVANIA

1621–1700

with brief mention of
the Walloons, Huguenots, and Swedes, as well as of the
Quakers and German Settlers
to which is added an account of the dress of English
Lawyers in the Seventeenth Century

TIME'S ALTERATION;

or

THE OLD MAN'S REHEARSALL, WHAT BRAVE DAYS HE KNEW, A GREAT WHILE AGONE, WHEN HIS OLD CAP WAS NEW.

When this old cap was new,
   'Tis since two hundred yeere;
No malice then we knew,
   But all things plentie were:
All friendship now decayes
   (Beleeve me, this is true),
Which was not in those dayes
   When this old cap was new.

Good hospitalitie
   Was cherisht then of many;
Now poor men starve and die
   And are not helpt by any:
For charitie waxeth cold,
   And love is found in few:
This was not in time of old
   When this old cap was new.

Where-ever you travel'd then,
   You might meet on the way
Brave knights and gentlemen
   Clad in their countrey gray,
That courteous would appeare,
   And kindly welcome you:
No puritans then were
   When this old cap was new.

Our ladies in those dayes
   In civil habit went,
Broad-cloth was then worth prayse,
   And gave the best content;
French fashions then were scorn'd,
   Fond fangles then none knew,
Then modistie women adorn'd
   When this old cap was new.

A man might then behold
  At Christmas, in each hall
Good fires to curbe the cold,
  And meat for great and small;
The neighbours were friendly bidden,
  And all had welcome true;
The poore from the gates were not chidden
  When this old cap was new.

Blacke-jackes to every man
  Were fill'd with wine and beere;
No pewter pot nor kanne
  In those days did appeare:
Good cheare in a noble-man's house
  Was counted a seemely shew;
We wanted no brawne nor sowse
  When this old cap was new.

We took not such delight
  In cups of silver fine;
None under the degree of a knight
  In plate drunke beere or wine:
Now each mechanicall man
  Hath a cup-boord of plate, for a shew,
Which was a true thing then
  When this old cap was new.

The Dutch and English in New York, Long Island, the Jerseys, Delaware, and Pennsylvania

1621–1700

FIGURE 95.
A Dutch Colonist in New Amsterdam.

VEN in a study of costume it is difficult to draw a distinct line between the Dutch and English elements in the Colony of Manhattan.

To an English seaman belongs the honour of discovery in 1609. When Henry Hudson, sometimes called Hendrick (Figure 98), brought the first ship to the mouth of the river which bears his name, he was a navigator of experience, well known to the merchants of Holland, who on this occasion had engaged him to make the voyage, and it is likely that he had under him as many Dutch as English sailors in his ship, "The Half-Moon." After a few weeks spent in exploring the adjacent country, he returned with an enticing report of a great many fur-clad animals near the shore. The trading proclivities of the Dutch merchants were at once aroused and they hastened to send over men to establish trading posts. But the first Colonial settlement was in 1621, when the great West India Company was chartered by the States General of Holland and given the monopoly of the American trade.

Peter Minuit, who was appointed Governor in 1626, arrived with a large number of colonists, men, women, and children, with cattle and household goods. Many of this company were Walloons of French extraction whose forefathers had been driven from their homes in Flanders and Belgium during the Inquisition, and had afterward formed an industrious community in Holland. They were skilled in various trades and were a valuable acquisition to the new colony, but they do not appear to have worn a distinctive dress.

In 1628 an act was passed in Holland giving to every man who raised a company of fifty colonists and brought them to America a large tract of land and the title of Patroon. In fact, many privileges were granted as an inducement to form a settlement in the Colony, and the Patroons became very rich and very powerful. A thousand square miles were included in the estate of Patroon Van Rensselaer (Figure 141). Fine cattle were imported, fruits, wheat, rye, buckwheat, flax, and beans were cultivated. The religious toleration prevailing in this Colony induced men from New England to remove there, and the Huguenots from France also sought shelter from persecution in New Amsterdam, as the town was called under the Dutch supremacy (Figures 145, 146).

In spite of the hardships they had endured before they reached the safe shelter of America, these people were distinguished for a happy, thrifty temperament and gentle manners, and knew many graceful accomplishments in the way of lace-making and embroidery, which they cheerfully taught to their neighbours. They are said to have been the first to weave carpets and hangings of odds and ends of material. They were also versed in the concoction of delicate coloured dyes, which they used for their garments and house decorations.

The Huguenots settled also in Pennsylvania, Massachusetts, the Carolinas, and in Virginia, and their descendants have taken a conspicuous part in the development of our country.

Almost from the outset, Manhattan was a cosmopolitan community, and costumes were as varied as the wonderful tulips in the

FIGURE 96.

FIGURE 97.

FIGURE 98.

FIGURE 99.

FIGURE 96.—Portrait of Peter Stuyvesant, Governor of New York Colony, showing armour and a black skull-cap, 1647.

FIGURE 97.—Portrait of Sir Edmund Andros, Colonial Governor of New York, 1674-1681, and Governor of the Dominion of New England, which included all the English settlements between Maryland and Canada except Pennsylvania, 1686-1690, showing periwig of reign of James II.

FIGURE 98.—Portrait of Henry Hudson, the English navigator, 1609, showing the ruff, reign of James I.

FIGURE 99.—Portrait of Sir William Keith, Governor of the Province of Pennsylvania, showing armour and campaign wig, 1717.

Dutch gardens. As there were neither sumptuary laws nor religious restrictions to control the manner or material of dress, we find the prevailing fashions among the citizens, both Dutch and English, very elaborate. The mercantile spirit ever pervading New York probably stimulated the wearing of fine clothes.

We read of the stalwart Peter Stuyvesant, Governor of New Amsterdam for many years, that "he was never otherwise than faultlessly dressed and always after the most approved European standard. A wide drooping shirt collar fell over a velvet jacket with slashed sleeves displaying full white linen shirt sleeves. His breeches were also slashed, very full and fastened at the knee by a handsome scarf tied in a knot, and his shoes were ornamented with large rosettes."* The leg which he lost in battle was replaced by a wooden one with silver bands, which accounts for the tradition that he wore a silver leg. Mrs. Lamb, in her "History of New York," says of Governor Stuyvesant that "he had sterling excellence of character, but more knowledge than culture," also that "his whole heart and soul became interested in the country of his adoption. In bearing he seems to have been somewhat haughty and exacting. One of his contemporaries recorded that, during his inauguration speech as Governor of New Amsterdam in 1647, he kept the people standing with their heads uncovered for more than an hour while he wore his chapeau, as if he were the Czar of Muscovy. Habitually he wore a close cap of black velvet on his dark hair, which imparted a still deeper shade to his dark complexion, and his stern mouth was not hidden by the slight mustache which he wore" (Figure 96).

From the same authority we learn that Governor Stuyvesant's wife, Judith Bayard, "was a beautiful blonde and followed the French fashions in dress, displaying considerable artistic skill in the perfection and style of her attire." Also that "the purity of morals and decorum of manners for which the Dutch were distinguished

* History of New York, by Mrs. Lamb.

had been ascribed to the happy influence of their women, who mingled in all the active affairs of life and were consulted with deferential respect." As early as 1640 we read of many richly furnished houses with well-kept gardens and choice conservatories in Colonial New York. Governor Schuyler called his town house "White Hall," and he owned a beautiful country-seat in the neighbourhood, for which, it is said, he paid 6400 guilders in 1659.

FIGURE 100.
A Dutch Woman in Working Dress (from a Contemporary Print, Middle of Seventeenth Century).

Markets were held every Saturday in 1656 and after, where laces, flax, linen, linsey-woolsey, duffels, etc., were sold by the farmers' wives.

The annual Fair, or Kermiss, was an occasion of festivity which attracted the people in their holiday garments from the neighbouring villages. It was inaugurated on the 20th of October, 1659, and usually lasted six weeks. The working garb of the Dutch peasant women consisted of a short woolen petticoat with a loose jacket of red cotton or blue Holland, a white kerchief folded around the shoulders, and a close white cap. In Figure 100 a sketch is given in which the long white apron of coarse homespun linen is caught up with the petticoat for convenience.

The Dutch women of the Manhattan Colony were marvellous housewives. They concocted medicines and distilled perfumes from the plants in their flourishing gardens. They instructed the maids in carding and weaving, for the woolen garments worn by the family, as well as the household linen and underwear, were usually made under the home roof. Moreover, they had a shrewd knowledge

FIGURE 101.   FIGURE 102.   FIGURE 103.   FIGURE 104.

REIGNS OF CHARLES I AND II, AND JAMES II
1640-1686

FIGURE 101.—A Dutch lady of New Amsterdam, wife of a patroon, about 1640. Her gown is of crimson silk with a pointed bodice, low neck and full slashed sleeves showing white undersleeves beneath. The ruff and cuffs are of lace starched and wired. A fold of soft lawn edged with lace finishes the bodice in front, held in place by a rosette of ribbon, or a jewelled brooch. An over-garment, the predecessor of the samare, of a woolen fabric, fitting in at the back and confined by a ribbon at the waist, opens down the front. It has full open sleeves tied with ribbons at the elbow. The hair is worn in a knot at the back and in short wavy locks in front with a fringe of short curls across the forehead.

FIGURE 102.—A patroon, about 1640. The baggy breeches and slashed doublet are of cloth or velvet. Woolen hose with a scarf of silk below the points which fasten them to the breeches. The falling ruff (collars were also worn at this time) is of white Holland laid in fine knife-plaits. The hat with a soft flapping brim is of felt trimmed with plumes of two colours. Leather shoes with wooden heels are tied at the instep with large bows of ribbon.

FIGURE 103.—A Dutch lady, about 1660, in a furred samare or jacket of velvet over a gown of amber satin. The arrangement of hair is copied from a portrait of the period; the ends of the side locks are turned under and tied with a ribbon, the rest is taken back and fastened in a coil in which narrow ribbon is twisted.

FIGURE 104.—An English gentleman at the end of Charles II's reign and the first half of James II's. His long coat is of flowered silk, cuffs of rich brocade. The breeches are full and hang over the garters or points which fasten the silk stockings. The shoes are cut rather high and are fastened with a strap of leather through a buckle on the instep. The hat is cocked a little to one side of the front in the fashion called the "Monmouth cock." The periwig is very long and full. An embroidered baldric is worn with the sword and a walking-stick ornamented with a large bow of ribbon is carried in the right hand. The neck-cloth tied in a bow under the chin is the new fashion of this date.

of mercantile pursuits and often carried on business for themselves and invested their savings in trading ventures. Their houses were scrupulously neat; white curtains usually hung in the leaden sashed windows, and pots of flowers stood on the ledges, while a great loom was placed under the sloping roof of the back stoop. Every family in the Colony made a coarse cloth called linsey-woolsey, the warp being of linen and the woof of wool, which they kept ready to be finished off by one of the itinerant weavers. About the middle of the seventeenth century we read of a rattle-watch dressed in a costume of blue cloth with facings of orange, and armed with lanterns, rattles, and long staffs. The duty of this company of watchmen was to patrol the town by day as well as by night. In the early days of the Colony a licensed herdsman was put in charge of all the cattle of the community. The distinctive badge of his office was a twisted cow's horn fitted with a mouth-piece suspended by a green cord across his shoulders. The ordinary working dress of a man was probably of homespun linsey-woolsey with hose of hand-knitted yarn. Monmouth hats of thrums were commonly worn in all the Colonies (Figure 37½).

FIGURE 105.
A Dutchman in Working Dress (from a Contemporary Painting, Middle of Seventeenth Century).

Mrs. Van Rensselaer, in her "Goode Vrow of Mana-ha-ta," aptly describes the quaint costumes of the Dutch people in New York. We will borrow her description of Dutch babies. "Upon the birth of a child, the infant was wrapped in swaddling clothes and put into an elaborately embroidered pocket, which was trimmed with frills of ribbon, the colour indicating the sex of the child. A tiny ruffled cap confined its ears closely to its head, and the baby was wrapped so firmly in its bands that it could move neither hand nor foot, and was laid in its cradle, or hung suspended on a nail in the wall without fear of its stirring from any position in which it might be placed. The birth of an infant was announced to the neighbours by hanging an elaborately trimmed pincushion on the knocker of the front door, the colour of which denoted the sex, blue indicating a boy and white a girl. This cushion was usually provided by the grandmother and was handed down as an heirloom from one generation to another to serve for similar occasions."

All authorities tell us of the many petticoats worn by a bride one over another, and of the bridal crown which in Holland was a token of the wealth of the family. It was made often of silver and adorned with jewels, but when the family was not rich, it was of pasteboard covered with embroidered silk. Only matrons wore coifs, and they varied with the rank and affluence of the wearer (Figures 121, 131).

The inventory of the wife of a respectable and well-to-do Dutch settler in New Netherlands, Vrouentje Ides Stoffelsen, in 1641 contained a gold hoop ring, a silver medal and chain, and a silver under-girdle to hang keys on; a damask furred jacket, two black camlet jackets, two doublets, one iron-gray, the other black; a blue petticoat, a steel-gray lined petticoat, a black coarse camlet-lined petticoat, one of Harlem stuff, a little black vest with two sleeves, a pair of Damask sleeves, a reddish morning gown, not lined, four pairs of pattens, one of Spanish leather; a purple apron and four blue aprons, nineteen cambric caps and four linen ones, a fur cap trimmed with beaver, nine linen handkerchiefs trimmed with lace, two pairs of old stockings and three shifts. Pictures of fur-trimmed jackets and of fur caps are given in Figures 103, 106, 110, 111.

Officials could easily be distinguished by their dress. The leather aprons worn by labourers and craftsmen were often dyed red, and

FIGURE 106.

FIGURE 107.

FIGURE 108.

FIGURE 109.

FIGURE 110.

FIGURE 111.

FIGURE 106.—Dutch girl in fur cap and fur-trimmed jacket, 1641. (By Hollar.)

FIGURE 107.—Dutch lady, hair arranged in puffs at the side, 1645. (By Hollar.)

FIGURE 108.—A little Dutch girl, seventeenth century. (By DeVos.)

FIGURE 109.—A little Dutch boy (from a portrait by Cuyp).

FIGURE 110.—A Dutch lady in fur cap and mantle, 1644. (By Hollar.)

FIGURE 111.—A Swedish lady in pointed fur cap and ruff, 1640. (By Hollar.)

when the wearer was not at work, one corner was usually tucked under his belt.

Different concoctions of bark taught them by the Indian squaws were used by the women to dye their homespun petticoats and short gowns (Figure 100).

The caps, chatelaines, and gowns of the well-to-do matrons were of costly materials and invariably of bright colours. The garments of the men, too, were of satin, velvet, and silk, trimmed with lace and fur. Buttons and buckles were often of gold set with precious stones.

The samare or loose jacket with "side laps" or skirts reaching to the knee, sometimes with elbow sleeves turned back and faced, was worn by the Dutch ladies over a waistcoat and petticoat. A picture of one trimmed with fur is given in Figure 103. The prevailing shapes of coats and hats were not unlike the English. Late in the seventeenth century coats had long wide tails with wide cuffs. Hats were large and low of crown (Figures 42, 104).

Dr. Jacob de Lange and his wife (New York, 1682) left lists of their wardrobes which are documents of great value to a history of costume.

> One under petticoat with a body of red bay,
> One under petticoat, scarlet
> One Petticoat, red cloth with black lace
> One striped stuff petticoat with black lace
> Two coloured drugget petticoats with white linings,
> One coloured drugget petticoat with pointed lace.
> two coloured drugget petticoats with gray linings
> One black silk petticoat with ash gray silk lining,
> One potto-foo silk petticoat with black silk lining,
> One silk potoso-a-samare with lace,
> One tartanel samare with tucker
> One black silk crape samare with tucker
> Three flowered calico samares,
> Three calico nightgowns, one flowered, two red,
> One silk waistcoat, one calico waistcoat
> One pair of bodice,
> Five pairs white cotton stockings,

Three black love hoods,
One white love-hood
Two pair sleeves with great lace
Four cornet caps with lace
One plain black silk rain cloth cap
One black plush mask,
Four yellow lace drowlas
One embroidered purse with silver bugle and chain to the girdle, and silver
    hook and eye.
One pair black pendants, gold nocks
One gold boat, wherein thirteen diamonds & one white coral chain,
One pair gold stucks or pendants each with ten diamonds.
Two diamond rings.
One gold ring with clasp beck
One gold ring or hoop bound round with diamonds

Dr. de Lange's wardrobe was abundant, but not so rich:

One grosgrained cloak lined with silk,
One black broadcloth coat,
One black broadcloth suit,
One coat lined with red serge
One black grosgrained suit
One coloured cloth waistcoat with silver buttons
One coloured serge suit with silver buttons
Three silk breeches
Three calico breeches
Three white breeches
One pair yellow hand gloves with black silk fringe
Five pairs white calico stockings
One pair black worsted stockings
One pair gray worsted stockings
One fine black hat, one old gray hat, one black hat.

When in 1664 the English sailed into the harbour and made
bloodless conquest of the Colony, they introduced but few changes
in the mode of living. In 1675 Manhattan was re-taken by the
Dutch, and affairs of government and life went on as before for another
year.

"The colours in the Dutch gowns were almost uniformly gay—
in keen contrast to the sad coloured garments of New England.
We hear of Madam Corneiia de Vos in a green cloth petticoat, a

red and blue 'Haarlamer' waistcoat, a pair of red and yellow sleeves, and a purple 'Pooyse' apron."

Figure 121 shows a coif or cap worn in New Amsterdam. It is made of gray and white brocade and trimmed with silver lace of an elaborate pattern, put on flat across the top. Around the

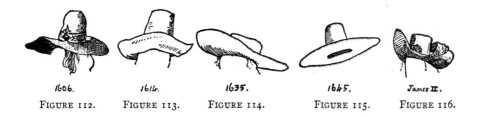

1606.	1614.	1635.	1645.	James II.
FIGURE 112.	FIGURE 113.	FIGURE 114.	FIGURE 115.	FIGURE 116.

face is a plaited ruffle of lace held in place by three rows of silver wire run through the plaits.

The children, too, were gaily dressed, as we can see in the Dutch contemporary portraits (Figures 108, 109, 132, and 133).

A leading man of New Amsterdam, a burgomaster, had at the time of his death, near the end of the Dutch rule, this plentiful num-

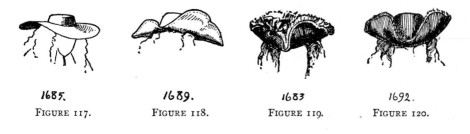

1685.	1689.	1683	1692.
FIGURE 117.	FIGURE 118.	FIGURE 119.	FIGURE 120.

ber of substantial garments: A cloth coat with silver buttons, a stuff coat, cloth breeches, a cloth coat with gimp buttons, a black cloth coat, a silk coat, breeches and doublet, a silver cloth breeches and doublet, a velvet waistcoat with silver lace, a buff coat, with silk sleeves, three grass-green cloaks, several perukes, "tets and fox-tails after the genteelest fashion."

One romantic element in the history of New Amsterdam not found in the other colonies is that of the pirates who carried on a vigorous business at sea and brought into the shops and markets many rich stuffs captured from the ships returning to England and France from the East Indies. The government made no effort to interfere with them, and sometimes, as in the case of Captain Kidd, these maritime marauders finally settled down and became respectable citizens. We are not surprised to read that Captain Kidd started housekeeping in New York with three hundred dollars' worth of plate.

FIGURE 121.

Coif of a Dutch Matron (from the Original Garment, late Seventeenth Century).

The English again conquered New Amsterdam and, under Sir Edward Andros, as Governor (Figure 97), it became an English colony, and was called New York in honour of the Duke of York, brother of Charles II.

There were Dutch and English settlements likewise in Long Island, the Jerseys, and Delaware, more or less under the jurisdiction of the Governor of New York, where doubtless the costumes, like the customs, reflected both nationalities.

THE SWEDES ON THE DELAWARE

In 1638 a colony of Swedes was sent out to America with instructions to settle the land not belonging to the Dutch and English. Selecting a spot on the west shore of the Delaware, they built a fort and called the settlement New Sweden. In 1656 the Dutch sent a company from New Amsterdam to establish a trading post on the Delaware, and they founded the town which is now known as New Castle.

FIGURE 122.

FIGURE 123.

FIGURE 124.

FIGURE 125.

FIGURE 122.—Shows the dress of an English gentlewoman of 1640. (By Hollar.)

FIGURE 123.—Swedish woman in clogs, 1640. (By Hollar.)

FIGURE 124.—A Dutch lady in outdoor dress, 1640. (By Hollar.)

FIGURE 125.—An English lady in house dress, 1640. (By Hollar.)

Frequent skirmishes followed between the Swedish and the Dutch settlers (Figures 95, 106, 111, 123, 124, also 100, 105), and finally the English claimed, by virtue of a patent from Charles II in 1664, all the land from the west side of Connecticut River to the east side of Delaware Bay, which was named for Thomas West, Lord Delaware, one of the early Governors of Virginia; and thus all the colonies of America came under English rule. This was in the latter part of the reign of Charles II.

In Figures 1, 68, and 69 we have the characteristic dress of the English gentleman and gentlewoman of this date, and in Figures 101 and 102 the typical costume of a Dutch Patroon and his wife.

THE QUAKERS IN PENNSYLVANIA

When the Quakers came to Pennsylvania with William Penn, they had not adopted any distinctive style of dress. From choice only were the colours rather grave than gay, for no strict rules had been formulated at this time (1682) prohibiting the use of bright colours or trimmings by the Quakers. The sash of sky-blue silk worn by Penn, either as a badge of office or mark of his rank, is an agreeable note of colour. This sash is described as made of silk network and as being of the size and style of that of a military officer. In an old English publication we read: "This sash is now in the possession of Thomas Kett, Esq., of Seething Hall, near Norwich."*

Shoe and stock buckles were usually of silver, and the ruffles at neck and wrist were of linen, either plainly hemmed or trimmed with rich lace. Heels were rather high, the toes of the shoes square. A gentleman of our day would seem to modern eyes very gaily dressed in such a costume as the first followers of the benign Founder of Philadelphia habitually wore (Figures 143, 144).

However, a certain neatness and staidness distinguished both the men and the women from the earliest days of this Quaker colony,

* Hone's Every Day Book.

although family portraits still in possession of their descendants prove that gowns of blue and red satin were not infrequently worn by members of the Society of Friends previous to 1700. There was nothing of the so-called Quaker simplicity about Penn's household. Pennsbury, his beautiful manor on the banks of the Delaware, was furnished and maintained on a substantial and most liberal scale. Costly silver, fine china, rich curtains and rugs made it a fitting abode for a royal governor. The twelve-oared barge in which Penn usually made his journeys to town was also stately and imposing.

Although the hats of the Quakers (Figures 117, 118, and 143) were of a shape similar to those worn by King Charles and his courtiers, they were put on the head with a certain rigidity, and the fact that they were never doffed in deference to rank or the fair sex may have added a touch of grimness and austerity to the expression of the broad brims in striking contrast to the graceful plumed hats worn by cavaliers and used by them to express every degree of courtesy.

> "The Quaker loves an ample brim,
> A hat that bows to no salaam."

In 1693 Penn, with the welfare of the province always in mind, put into his book, "Some fruits of Solitude," a message of counsel in matters of dress. "Choose thy cloaths by thine own eye, not anothers. The more simple and plain they are, the better. Neither unshapely nor fantastical, and for use and decency, not for Pride."

Mrs. Gummere, who has made an exhaustive study of Quaker dress, says that green aprons were so much worn by Friends at this period as to be regarded "almost as badges of Quakerism"; also that Friends not only called their cloaks by the popish title "Cardinal," but wore them in red and all bright colours.

"Wigs were as generally worn by genteel Friends as by other people" (Figures 134 and 135). This was the more surprising because they religiously professed to exclude all superfluities, and

FIGURE 128.

FIGURE 131.

FIGURE 127.

FIGURE 130.

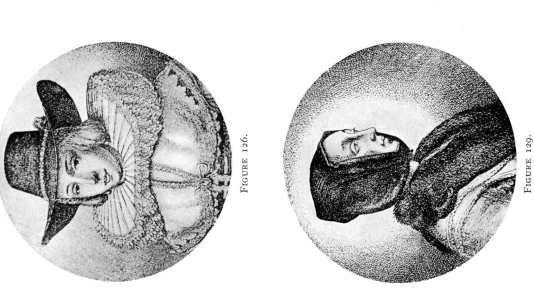

FIGURE 126.

FIGURE 129.

FIGURE 126.—A portrait of a Dutch lady, middle of seventeenth century, showing wide-brimmed hat and ruff. (By Hollar.)

FIGURE 127.—An English lawyer of the seventeenth century. (By Hollar.)

FIGURE 128.—An English woman in silk hood and tippet. (By Hollar.)

FIGURE 129.—A Dutch lady in fur tippet and hood, middle of seventeenth
century. (By Hollar.)

FIGURE 130.—Portrait of a boy in periwig in the Massachusetts Colony, end
of the reign of Charles II.

FIGURE 131.—An English woman in a coif and kerchief trimmed with Vandyke
lace, 1640. (By Hollar.)

yet nothing could have been offered to the mind as so essentially useless."* In the year 1685, William Penn wrote to his steward, James Harrison, requesting him to allow Governor Lloyd, his deputy, the use of his wigs in his absence.

In England there were but few striking changes in the fashionable dress of the upper classes from the end of the reign of Charles II to the end of the reign of William and Mary.

The straight square-cut coats were worn opening over waistcoats of equal length reaching to the knees; the breeches were held in place beneath the knee by long stockings, which were drawn up over them; long neck-cloths of Flanders or Spanish point-lace were used; the shoes, the upper leather of which rose considerably above the instep, were fastened by a small strap over it, passing through a buckle placed rather on one side; the hat was bent up or cocked all round and trimmed with feathers (Figures 118, 119, 120); fringed gloves and monstrous periwigs, which it was the fashion to comb publicly, completed the habit of the beaux of London in the reign of William and Mary.

"The ladies seem to have adopted some of the Dutch fashions," says a contemporary writer. "The stomacher appeared more formally laced. The sleeves of the gown became straight and tight, and terminated with a cuff at the elbow in imitation of those of the male sex. Rows of flounces and furbelows, or falbalas, bordered the petticoat, which was disclosed by the gown being looped completely back. The head-dress was exceeding high in front, being composed of a cap, the lace of which rose in three or more tiers almost to a point above the forehead, the hair being combed up and disposed in rows of wavy curls one above the other (Figure 38). Hair powder was used occasionally, but not generally. Muffs were carried by both sexes. They were very small and ornamented often with large bows of ribands.

* The Quaker: A Study in Costume, by Amelia Mott Gummere.

"The dress of the commonalty underwent no change" (Figures 40, 41).*

We find the same costumes in the colonies. In Tod's "History of New York" is the following description of the fashions about 1695 (reign of William and Mary):

"Broadway on a Sabbath morning, as the bells were ringing for Church, must have presented an animated and even brilliant spectacle far exceeding that which modern beaux and belles present. In these days, however, both ladies and gentlemen shone rich as Emperor moths. These worshippers, whom we imagine ourselves watching, come in groups moving down the wide shaded street, some entering Trinity, others turning into Garden Street and passing into the new Dutch Church on that thoroughfare. Both places of worship are equally fashionable. The Dutch Church is the wealthier, but then Trinity has the Governor's pew, and the prestige that comes of State patronage and emolument. Let us describe, as showing the fashions of the day, the dress of this group bearing down abreast of the church yard. They are Nicholas Bayard and Madam Bayard, William Merritt, Alderman and Madam Merritt, and Isaac de Riemer. Bayard, who has been Secretary of the Province, Mayor, and Colonel of the City Militia, wears a cinnamon coloured cloth coat with skirt reaching quite to the knee, embroidered four or five inches deep with silver lace, and lined with sky-blue silk. His waistcoat is of red satin woven in with gold. His breeches, of the same colour and material as his coat, are trimmed with silver at the pockets and knees. Dove coloured silk stockings and low shoes adorned with large silver buckles cover his nether extremities. His hat, of black felt, has a wide flapping brim and is adorned with a band of gold lace. His full-bottomed wig is plentifully powdered with starch finely ground and sifted, to which burnt alabaster or whiting has been added to give it body, and is scented

* Knight's Pictorial History of England.

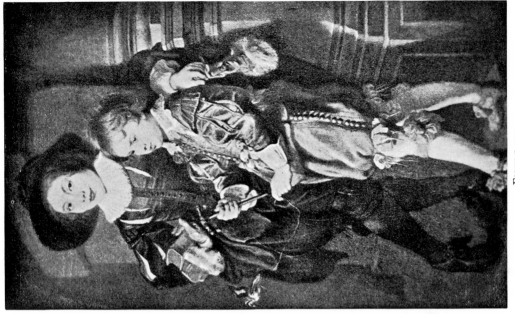

FIGURE 133.

FIGURE 132.

FIGURE 132.—A portrait of Elisabeth and Philadelphia Wharton, showing the
prevailing styles of dress for little girls in reign of Charles I. (By Vandyke.)

FIGURE 133.—A portrait of two Dutch boys, showing the fashionable dress in
the middle of the seventeenth century. (By Rubens.)

with ambergris. A steinkirk of fine muslin encircles his neck, the ends of which are laced and tucked into his expansive shirt bosom. The latter is of fine holland adorned with colebatteen ruffles, the waistcoat being left open to better display them. He carries a cane, too, with a gold head elegantly engraved in cypher and crown, but the sword, with its gay sword knot, then an almost indispensable adjunct to a gentleman's dress, in deference to the day has been left behind. The two other gentlemen are dressed much in the same style except that there is a pleasing variety in style and colour. Merritt, for instance, wears a salmon coloured silk drugget coat, with silver brocade waistcoat and small clothes, while De Riemer has a sagathie cloth coat with waistcoat and breeches of drap du Barre.

FIGURE 134.
Periwig of Charles II,
1660.

FIGURE 135.
Periwig of William III,
1690.

FIGURE 136.
Campaign Wig,
1684.

"But if the gentlemen are thus brilliant, what is to be said of the ladies, who are apt to lead the sterner sex in matters of personal adornment? Instead of a bonnet, Madam Bayard wears a 'front-age' (commode), a sort of head-dress formed of rows of plaited muslin stiffened with wire one above the other, and diminishing in size as they rise. She, too, wears the steinkirk, or neck-cloth. The bodice of her purple and gold atlas gown is laced over very tight stays, and the gown itself is open in front to display the black velvet petticoat edged with two silver orrices and high enough to show the green silk stockings and beautiful embroidered shoes of fine morocco."

"My high commode, my damask gown,
My lac'd shoes of Spanish leather.
A silver bodkin in my head,
And a dainty plume of feather."
—"*Young Maid's Portion.*"

THE DRESS OF ENGLISH LAWYERS IN THE SEVENTEENTH CENTURY

Very little is said by the early authorities on the costumes of lawyers and judges in the Colonies, but there are numerous indications of the fact that scarlet, the judicial colour in England, was worn on the Colonial bench, and Martin, in his "History of the Bench and Bar in Pennsylvania," states that undoubtedly the courts were conducted with much of the state and formality of the Mother Country. It will be interesting in a study of the dress of the day to recall the complicated costumes of the English law courts, although the pomp and display therein detailed were not even possible in the enforced simplicity of the early Colonies. In New England, Virginia, Maryland, the Barbadoes, and the Carolinas, as well as later in New York and even in Pennsylvania, the forms and ceremonies of government were as similar to the English code as circumstances permitted.

In the Southern Colonies especially it is probable that much formality was observed in the dress of lawyers and judges; at all events we do not read of any departure from the English methods of procedure in documents of the Colonies.

In a historical sketch of the English law courts by Inderwick,* we find a description of the gradual changes in legal dress and customs in England during the Colonial period. In the

* The King's Peace, by F. A. Inderwick.

FIGURE 139.

FIGURE 138.

FIGURE 137.

149

FIGURE 137.—Coat and full breeches of buff brocade with flowers and leaves in bright colours scattered over it. Very large cuffs of a richly coloured brocade. A wedding suit of 1681. Reign of Charles II. (Photographed from the original garments.)

FIGURE 138.—Coat and full breeches of dark red flowered silk, 1681. Reign of Charles II. (Photographed from the original garments.)

FIGURE 139.—Coat and breeches of silk trimmed with fancy braid fringed out at the ends and caught with buttons. Worn in reign of James II. (Photographed from the original garments.)

time of Charles I questions relating to the attire of the common-law judges were involved in so much doubt and surrounded with so many contradictory precedents and traditions that the judges resolved to simplify matters by conference. The result of their deliberations was a decree dated June 6, 1635, which, although it could not have direct application to the Colonial courts in every particular, throws important light on the ceremonies and etiquette to which every English lawyer of that date was accustomed. We therefore quote the extract from State Papers given by Mr. Jeffreson: *

"The judges in Term time are to set at Westminster in the Courts, in their black or violet gowns, whether they will, and a hood of the same colour put over their heads, and their mantles above all; the end of the hood hanging over behind; wearing their velvet caps, and coyfes of lawn, and cornered cap. The facing of their gowns, hoods and mantles, is with changeable taffata; which they must begin to wear upon Ascension-day, being the last Thursday in Easter Term, and continue those robes until the feast of Simon and Jude. And Simon and Jude's day, the judges begin to wear their robes faced with white furs of minever; and so continue that facing until Ascension-day again.

"Upon all Holydays, which fall in the Term and are Hall dayes, the judges sit in scarlet faced with Taffata, when Taffata facing is to be worn, and with furs, or minever, when furs or minever are to be worn.

"Upon the day when the Lord Mayor of London comes to Westminster to take his oath, that day the judges come in scarlet, and upon the fifth of November, being Gunpowder Day, unless it be Sunday, the judges go to Westminster Abbey in scarlet to hear the sermon, and after go to sit in Court and the two Lords Chief Justices, and the Lord Chief Baron, have their collars of S.S. above their mantles for those two days.

* A Book about Lawyers, by John Cordy Jeffreson.

"When the Judges go to St. Paul's to the sermon, upon any Sunday in the Term time, or to any other public church, they ought to go in scarlet gownes; the two Lords Chief Justices and the Lord Chief Baron in their velvet and satin tippets; and the hood is to be pinned abroad towards the left shoulder. And if it be upon any grand dayes, as upon the Ascension-day, Mid-summer day, All Hallows-day, or Candlemas-day, then the two Lords Chief Justices and the Lord Chief Baron wear collars of S.S. with long scarlet casting-hoods and velvet and satin tippets.

"At all times when the judges go to the Council-table, or to any assembly of the Lords in the afternoons in Term time, they ought to go in their robes of violet or black, faced with taffata, according as the time of wearing them doth require; and with tippets and scarlet casting-hoods, pinned near the left shoulder, unless it be Sunday or Holyday, and then in scarlet. In the circuit the judges go to church upon Sundays in the fore-noon in scarlet gownes, hoods, and mantles, and sit in their caps. And in the afternoons to the church in scarlet gownes, tippet and scarlet hood, and sit in their cornered caps.

"And the first morning at the reading of the commissions, they sit in scarlet gownes, with hoods and mantles, and in their coyfs and cornered caps. And he that gives the charge, and delivers the gaol, doth, or ought for the most part, to continue all that assizes in the same robes, scarlet gown, hood, and mantle. But the other judge, who sits upon the Nisi Prius, doth commonly (if he will) sit only in his scarlet robe, with tippet and casting-hood; or if it be cold he may sit in gown and hood, and mantle.

"And when the judges in the Circuit go to dine with the shireeve, or to a publick feast, then in scarlet gowns, tippets, and scarlet hoods; or casting off their mantle, they keep on their hood.

"The scarlet casting-hood is to be put above the tippet, on the right side, for Justice Wolmsley and Justice Warburton, and all the judges before, did wear them in that manner, and did declare that

FIGURE 141.

FIGURE 140.

FIGURE 140.—Jeremias Van Rensselaer of the New York Colony, end of the seventeenth century. Reign of William and Mary. (From the original portrait.)

FIGURE 141.—Kiliaen Van Rensselaer, first patroon in New Amsterdam, born 1637. Showing the fashionable coat worn in 1695. Reign of William and Mary. (From the original portrait.)

by wearing the hood on the right side, and above the tippet, was signified more temporal dignity; and by the tippet on the left side only, the judges did resemble priests.

"Whenever the judges or any of them are appointed to attend the king's majesty, they go in scarlet gowns, tippets, and scarlet casting-hoods; either to his own presence, or at the council-table.

"The judges and sergeants when they ride circuit, are to wear a sergeant's coat of good broad-cloth, with sleeves, and faced with velvet. They have used of late to lace the sleeves of the sergeant's coat thick with lace and they are to have a sumpter, and ought to ride with six men at the least.

"Also the first Sunday of every term, and when the judges and sergeants dine at my Lord Mayor's, or the shireeves, they are to wear their scarlets, and to sit at Paul's with caps at the sermon.

"When the judges go to any reader's feast, they go upon the Sunday or Holyday in scarlet; upon other days in violet, and the sergeants go in violet, with scarlet hoods.

"When the judges sit upon Nisi Prius in Westminster, or in London they go in violet gowns, and scarlet casting-hoods, and tippets, upon Holydays in scarlet."

"This order," Jeffreson says, "deserves attentive perusal, for it throws light upon departed manners, exemplifies the obsolete pomp of the law, and recalls the days when the humblest judge of assize was required to ride circuit with an imposing body-guard."

The author of "The King's Peace" records that "in the matter of courts, of officers, and of costumes, the judges of the Commonwealth differed but little from their predecessors, except that the King's Bench was called the Upper Bench, a name by which it also seems to have been occasionally known in previous reigns. The Keepers of the Great Seal wore a robe described by Whitelock, the historian of the epoch, as a 'handsome velvet gown' closely resembling that worn by Lord Bacon in the portrait in Lord Verulam's collection."

The same authority gives the modification of legal dress which followed towards the close of the seventeenth century. "The Common Law judges wore their scarlet, as we know from certain petitions presented to the Protector, praying that the judges who went circuit in their scarlet, and were at times escorted by a troop of horse, should no longer be permitted to 'affright the country with their blood-red robes and their state and pomp.' Sergeants wore their

FIGURE 142.
Sergeant-at-law, Reign of Charles II.

coifs and striped gowns; but the Bar, under the rank of sergeant, wore their own hair trimmed in such device as was prescribed by fashion and not forbidden by the regulations of the Inn to which they belonged. The head-dress of the judges, the sergeants, and the Bar had from the very earliest periods been fixed and determined. The judges wore the coif and velvet cap over their own hair, and with their beards and moustaches as they thought fit. Sergeants wore the coif, while counsel wore a serious dress of the costume of the period. Ruffs were in fashion during the reigns of Elizabeth and James I, when judges and counsel wore them. These were supplanted by a broad lace collar, which was in fashion under Charles I, and by white linen bands under the Commonwealth. In the reign of Charles II the monarch and people of position assumed the periwig, a fashion imported from France, where it was patronized by Louis XIV, and gradually left off wearing beards and moustaches. Some of the judges, but not all, accordingly wore the judicial robes with the

FIGURE 143.

FIGURE 144.

FIGURE 145.

FIGURE 146.

REIGNS OF CHARLES II, JAMES II, WILLIAM AND MARY
1682-1700

FIGURE 143.—A Quaker gentleman in a suit of dark brown or plum-coloured cloth cut according to the English fashion at the end of Charles II's reign. The full shirt-sleeves hang in ruffles over the hand and the neck-cloth, though of the fashionable style and of the finest linen, is untrimmed. The hat is of the shape seen in the portraits of the time. The absence of feathers and lace was the only distinction of Quaker dress before 1700. The hair was occasionally powdered and periwigs were not uncommon, but the hair was usually worn in natural locks parted in the middle and hanging to the shoulders.

FIGURE 144 shows the typical dress of a Quaker lady of the same date—a gown of some soft coloured silk with fine white kerchief and undersleeves. The long full apron is also of silk, probably a dull green. Under the black silk hood for outdoor wear a ruffled cap of sheer lawn is worn. The hair is arranged in a coil at the back and parted in front. With various modifications of material and colour Figures 143 and 144 show the general style of Quaker dress for many years, coats, gowns and hats following very closely the fashions of the time.

FIGURE 145.—A Huguenot lady in the French dress of the period (1686). Mantle of black trimmed with embroidery. Her over-dress is looped up for walking, showing an embroidered underskirt. Under the black hood is worn a high cap of lace over a wire frame called a "commode." The sleeves are finished with plaited ruffles of the material of the gown and she wears long gloves of kid and a muff decorated with a bow and ends of brocaded ribbon. The hair is arranged in curls on the forehead and in a soft knot at the back. Long ear-rings adorn her ears.

FIGURE 146.—A Huguenot gentleman of the same date in a suit of dark blue cloth trimmed with gold braid. His neck-cloth and handkerchief are trimmed with ruffles of lace. The shirt-sleeves end in a ruffle at the wrist and show beneath the wide cuffs of the coat. The hose of dark red or blue are pulled up over the knee and fastened under the breeches. The shoes are cut high on the instep and fastened with a flap of leather through a buckle. The hat is cocked on both sides and worn over a periwig of moderate size without powder.

periwig in place of the coif; and this diversity of head-dress among the judges continued during the reign of James II, when Sir Thomas Street, one of the judges who was in office in 1688, still wore his own hair with the coif and the black velvet cap. The Bar, being younger than the judges, took more generally to the prevailing fashion, and wore first the long and then the short wig. In course of time, under William III, all classes of the community, including bishops and clergymen, wore the long or the short wig, judges and counsel being included in the number; and the sergeants, to indicate their status, wore a black patch on a white silk ground, fastened on to their wigs as a substitute for the black cap and the white coif. The lawyers, however, who followed the public taste in assuming periwigs, failed to follow it in leaving them off. The bishops, who continued to wear their wigs long after the public had ceased to do so, gave up the practice some fifty years ago; but the judges and counsel have continued till to-day the bands of the Commonwealth along with the head-dress of the Restoration, which is no

FIGURE 147.

Sergeant-at-law, Reign of James II.

more any portion of ancient or traditionary legal costume than were the ruffs of Queen Elizabeth or the lace collars of Charles I. And thus it happens that, by a very perversity of conservatism, that head-dress, which in the seventeenth century was worn alike by kings and by courtiers, by clergymen and by soldiers, by Jeffreys on the Bench and by Titus Oates in the dock, has become in the nineteenth century the distinct characteristic of the advocate and the judge. King James I, interfering with the

Inns of Court, as with most other of his subjects' affairs, had ordered that barristers were not to come to the hall of their Inn with their cloaks, boots, swords, spurs, or daggers, showing their ordinary habits were those of the gentlemen of the period, and further that none were to be admitted into the Society who were not gentlemen by descent. These directions were repeated by Charles I, and seem to have been very generally followed, and it was not, I conceive, till the middle of King Charles' reign, if not later, that counsel under the rank of sergeants, when employed in court, took to wearing silk or stuff gowns, and thus became 'gentlemen of the long robe.'"

I feel obliged to quote these items of legal costume and customs in full, not being able to determine with exactness how nearly they were followed in the Colonies in the seventeenth century. In Figure 127 a picture from a contemporary print is given of a lawyer in his wig and parliament. The illustrations (Figures 142 and 147) are also taken from authorities of the time. Much has been said in print of the circuit and the county courts. It is well known that all the pomp and dignity were observed that those occasions permitted in the Colonies, but very grave offences and questions of State were carried before the court in England.

THE GERMAN SETTLERS IN PENNSYLVANIA
1683–1790

The Mennonites, or German Quakers, who settled Germantown in Pennsylvania under the hospitable encouragement of Penn (1683), were speedily followed to America by other German sects from the Palatinate or the low countries on the Rhine. They were the last people to found colonies in the New World, for as a race they had but little of the spirit of adventure in their composition.

Well equipped with implements for farming, the emigrants carefully selected the fertile country near the Blue Mountains, and, once established as colonists, they were joined by large numbers of their

FIGURE 148.

FIGURE 149.

FIGURE 150.

FIGURE 151.

FIGURE 148.—Portrait of Count Zinzendorf in a preacher's robe.

FIGURE 149.—Portrait of Simon Bradstreet, Judge and Governor of the Massachusetts Colony, in gown and cap, 1630-1679.

FIGURE 150.—Portrait of Lady Fenwick, showing widow's mourning, 1695.

FIGURE 151.—Portrait of Mrs. Elisabeth Boehler in the Moravian settlement, Pennsylvania, 1787.

countrymen. In 1703, it is said there were nearly three hundred thousand Germans in Penn's province. At the time of the Revolution they warmly supported the struggle for independence.

Coming chiefly from the low countries along the Rhine, their costumes were not especially picturesque, but they were distinctive in character, and the fashion of them changed less frequently than in some other parts of Germany, so that for many years after their arrival in America they wore the quaint caps and head-dresses, clumsy boots, and odd looking cloaks of an earlier period.*

Not only in Pennsylvania, but in New York, Maryland, New Jersey, Virginia, the Carolinas and Georgia, the Germans also founded pastoral settlements.

The clothing of the new settlers consisted of "home-made cloth, woven from tow, made from flax grown on the virgin soil." Their costume did not admit of much change, and the men were dressed chiefly in shirt, trousers, and coat. In warm weather the shirt and trousers sufficed; in cold weather an additional top coat was worn for protection. The women wore short full skirts with dark bodices laced over coarse white shifts. Shoes were made to last a long time, and were worn only when absolutely necessary. Cobblers travelled through the country among the settlers and mended their shoes, in that way procuring a livelihood.

There were various sects among the German colonists: The Dunkers, whose doctrine was very much the same as the Mennonites, who still wear a peculiar costume; the Schoenkfelders from Silesia, who emigrated to Pennsylvania in 1734; the Moravians, who came to Georgia in 1735 and founded in 1790 a large and important settlement at Bethlehem, Pennsylvania, where they still practice the picturesque rites of their doctrine. The Moravians have many interesting customs, but their costume is decidely conservative, and resembles the accepted Quaker dress in sobriety of colour and simplicity of cut.

* See Trachten der Völker, by A. Kretschmer.

A Moravian community was divided into a number of choirs or bands. One object carefully kept in view was the avoidance of all unnecessary adornment in dress. Among other things, jewelry, lace, parasols, and fans were forbidden. The bonnets worn by the Sisters were usually of white straw with plain ribbon, the colour of which formed the distinction of the choir. White was worn by the widows, blue by the married women, rose colour by the unmar-

FIGURE 152.
Moravian Coif (from an Original Garment).

ried, and red by girls from fourteen to eighteen years of age. The male choirs were not distinguished by any badges, but they all wore very simple clothing, generally gray or brown. Mourning was never worn, as it was thought that death, or "returning to one's native land," as Zinzendorf called it, was not a proper subject for sorrow. Two curiously fashioned palls used for the funerals of children are still preserved with the archives of the Moravians at Lititz. They are made of white damask linen and the inscription:

"Jesus er Mein Heiland lebt
Ich wird auch
Das Leben schauen,"

is embroidered thereon in ribbon gathered in a scallop pattern to form letters. They are bound around the edges with a broader ribbon—pink for the girls and blue for the boys. Similar palls were used for adults. A minute pillow used at infant baptisms is also to be seen. A wedding dress is still preserved of white satin trimmed with gauze roses and ribbon-work like the bag in Figure 153. It has a short waist and little puffed sleeves and was worn about 1790. The lady who wore it had also a white gauze shawl made to wear three-cornered-wise, with only one corner embroidered in an elaborate pattern, which she wore with a black velvet dress. She is

FIGURE 153

FIGURE 154.

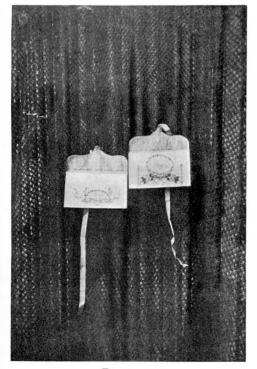

FIGURE 155.

FIGURE 156.

FIGURE 153.—A reticule of white silk embroidered in crêpe flowers.

FIGURE 154.—A waistcoat worn by Count Lemcke.

FIGURES 155 and 156.—Photographs of white silk pocket cases, embroidered in colours.

These relics are preserved in the Moravian archives of Lititz.

described as attending church in this garb, accompanied by a page carrying her train and a foot-stove.

A portrait of Count Zinzendorf and also one of the Countess are in possession of a direct descendant in Philadelphia. The wife wears a close-fitting cap with ribbons of blue (the distinctive trimming for a Moravian matron) (Figure 151) tied under her chin. The unmarried women were called Sisters. They dressed usually in white with a "nice handkerchief" pinned about the shoulders and a close-fitting cap with rose-pink ribbons, the hair all brushed back out of sight.

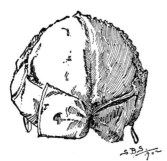
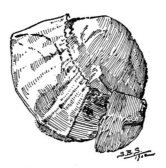

FIGURE 157.   FIGURE 158.
Moravian Cap of Lawn Worn over the Coif.

Before the Revolution, earthenware, paper, and linen were made at the cloister at Ephrata, Pennsylvania. In the Sister-House there may be seen at the present day the blocks of wood used instead of irons for smoothing linen. In Figures 155 and 156 are shown pictures of two white satin note cases, which were worked before 1790 for birthday gifts, each intended to hold a roll of bank-notes. The initials are done in hair and the flowers in silk.

Count Lemcke, the friend of Zinzendorf, brought over the first piano used in America. It was small enough to be carried under the arm, and he is said to have carried it with him when invited to evening parties. This piano may now be seen in the Smithsonian Institute at Washington.

Count Zinzendorf, the promoter and founder of the Pennsylvania settlement of Moravians, lived for a time in Philadelphia, and, according to his portraits, dressed simply in the fashion of his day in Germany. The long coat with many buttons and no collar or flaps, white shirt sleeves gathered into a band at the wrist, and a cravat or stock of plain white linen remind one of the portraits of William Penn about fifty years earlier. A portrait of him in a preaching gown is given in Figure 148.

The dress of the Seventh Day Baptists is peculiar and interesting. It consisted of a sort of cassock over which hung a stole, both back and front, and a close-fitting hood with large capes, or flaps. A picture of one of these hoods may be seen in a scholarly book, "The German Pietists in Provincial Pennsylvania," by Mr. Julius F. Sachse, where the curious customs of the German religious communities before 1700 are graphically described.

FIGURE 159.

FIGURE 160.

Seventeenth Century Silver

FIGURE 159.—Two pomanders
  One snuff-box
  One pair buckles
  Two patch boxes
  One watch fob of Dutch silver
  One porringer
  Travelling case with knife, fork, and spoon
  One sugar basin
  Hot milk jug
  One cream pitcher
  One pair salt cellars
  Two sugar tongs
  One cake basket
  One pap cup.

Other Colonial Utensils

FIGURE 160.—Two Dutch knife-boards
  One flip glass
  Two tinder boxes
  One powder horn
  One pair snuffers
  One pewter pepper pot
  One pewter porringer
  One pewter tankard
  One pewter dish
  One folding pocket-knife and two forks
  One two-pronged table fork.

PART II

THE EIGHTEENTH CENTURY

WOMEN'S DRESS

1700–1800

During the Time of
Queen Anne, George I, II, and III of England,
Presidents Washington and Adams
of the United States

CAPRICES OF FASHION.

"The fickle head-dress sinks, and now aspires
A towery front of lace on branching wires;
The curling hair in tortur'd ringlets flows,
Or round the face in labour'd order grows.
How shall I soar, and on unwearying wing
Trace varying habits upward to their spring?
What force of thought, what numbers can express
The inconstant equipage of female dress?
How the strait stays the slender waist constrain,
How to adjust the mantua's sweeping train?
What fancy can the petticoat surround,
With the capacious hoop of whalebone bound?
But stay presumptuous Muse! nor boldly dare
The toilette's sacred mysteries declare;
Let a just distance be to beauty paid;
None here must enter but the trusty maid.
Should you the wardrobe's magazine rehearse,
And glossy manteaus rustle in thy verse;
Should you the rich brocaded suit unfold,
Where rising flowers grow stiff with frosted gold,
The dazzling Muse would from her subject stray,
And in a maze of fashions lose her way."

—"The Fan."

Women's Dress

1700–1800

"Snuff or the fan supply each pause of chat."

FIGURE 161.
A Sacque, Early Eighteenth Century.

IN THE first half of the eighteenth century, which was the most prosperous and comfortable period of Colonial life in America, fashion was a conspicuous element.

Merchant ships from China and the Indies brought to all the seaport towns rich silks, tissues, and embroidered gauzes, as well as beautiful china and tapestry. These imported stuffs were known by odd sounding names, corruptions of the places of their manufacture. Thus, for instance, we have Nankeen, made in Nankin, China; and calico, originally a silken material first imported from Calicut in India.

Uninterrupted intercourse with England and France enabled the Colonists to keep up with the prevailing fashions in dress, which at that time became most whimsical and capricious. But as there were many people in England who, like Mrs. Hardcastle, "only enjoyed London at second-hand," and depended on the letters of their friends for descriptions of the fashions, so many of the leading families in the Colonies also living remote from seaport towns were content to follow at a distance the bewildering transitions prescribed by *la mode*.

Before the days of fashion plates, jointed dolls were dressed in the latest style and sent from Paris to London every month. Not quite so often, but at regular intervals, similar dolls were sent to the Colonies. The mantua-makers of the day copied them for their fashionable patrons. In "The Spectator," the anxiety caused by the delay in the arrival of one of these dolls in London is described: "I was almost in despair of ever seeing a model from the dear country, when last Sunday I overheard a lady in the next pew to me whisper to another that at the Seven Stars in King Street, Covent Garden, there was a Mademoiselle completely dressed just come from Paris. I was in the utmost impatience during the remaining part of the service, and as soon as ever it was over, having learnt the milliner's address, I went directly to her house in King Street, but was told that the French lady was at a person of quality's in Pall Mall and would not be back again until late that night. I was therefore obliged to renew my visit this morning and had then a full view of the dear puppet from head to foot. You cannot imagine how ridiculously I find we have all been trussed up during the war and how infinitely the French dress excels ours."

This puppet, we are told, was dressed "in a cherry coloured gown and petticoat with a short 'working' apron, her hair was cut and divided very prettily with several ribbons stuck up and down in it. The milliner assured me that her complexion was such as is worn by all the ladies of the best fashion in Paris. Her head was extremely high. Her necklace was of an immoderate length, being tied before in such a manner that the two ends hung down to her girdle." Though the fashion dolls were longer in their voyage to the Colonies, they were apparently expected with the same eagerness described by the London satirist. Could the representative of her tribe whose portrait may be seen in Figures 166 and 167 speak, she would surely tell us that she received a warm welcome and was entertained by the people of "the best fashion in Philadelphia." Her costume

FIGURE 162.

FIGURE 163.

FIGURE 164.

FIGURE 165.

REIGNS OF QUEEN ANNE AND GEORGE I
1702-1725

FIGURE 162.—A Colonial costume of 1711, gown of buff chiné silk with variegated flowers over a blue silk hooped petticoat. The open skirt is pinked at the edges. The elbow sleeves are rather loose with large armholes reaching on to the shoulder, the seams being covered by revers of silk which taper slightly at the waist. The picture is taken from a genuine old gown lent by a direct descendant of the original owner (for back see Figure 174). The hair is arranged in soft curls drawn back loosely from the forehead and fastened to the head with combs. Long loose curls fall on each shoulder.

FIGURE 163.—The typical costume of a gentleman from 1702 to 1720, differing but little from the fashion of William and Mary's reign (Figure 42). The periwig with big curls arranged high on top and hanging in long drop curls to the front is sometimes called the "campaign wig" and it was usually powdered. The square-toed shoes have red heels, according to the fashion introduced in Queen Anne's reign.

FIGURE 164.—A Colonial costume of George I's reign. The original gown is now in the National Museum, Independence Hall, Philadelphia. It is of yellow damask silk and looped back with narrow braid and buttons. The bodice is trimmed with ruchings of the material pinked, and the edges of the skirt are finished in the same way. The hooped petticoat in the picture is of white satin, and the slippers match the gown. The hair is arranged in a low pompadour without powder, which, though occasionally worn with court dress in England, was not in general wear for women until 1750.

FIGURE 165.—Two variations of fashion for men in George I's reign are shown in this figure. These are the fastening of the garters with small buckles below the knee and the wearing of a ramilie wig tied with a large black ribbon bow at the nape of the neck, and powdered white. The style of the coat is not changed, but the tails are stiffened with buckram or wadding and waistcoats were often elaborately trimmed with lace or embroidery. Square-toed shoes were gradually giving way to a more pointed shape, but red heels were still in high favour.

proclaims that she arrived during the reign of George I, probably about 1720. Mrs. Vanderbilt, in her "Social History of Flatbush," says: "We have a vivid remembrance of the old age of one of these fashion-dolls which had been sent from Paris to a fashionable mantua-maker in New York. When the dress was changed as to style, the dressmaker sold the doll to one of her customers, and 'Miss Nancy Dawson' passed into the obscurity of humbler dollies, who had never been sent as ministers plenipotentiary from the Court of Fashion."

REIGN OF QUEEN ANNE

"Tho' stiff with hoop
And armed with ribs of whale.

. . . .

" Invention we bestow,
To change a flounce, or add a furbelow." *

Queen Anne came to the throne of England in 1702, and for the first eight or nine years of her reign, dress differed but little from that introduced under William and Mary (Figures 38, 42), but in 1711 two striking changes are noted. The extravagantly high head-dress and cap, the "tower and commode," so scathingly satirized in "The Spectator," gave way to a simple arrangement of natural hair, noticeable in the portraits by Kneller† of Queen Anne and the ladies of her Court. This change is applauded by Addison, who says: "I remember several ladies who were once near seven feet high, that at present want some inches of five."

We read that these gigantic commodes held their place at Versailles in spite of the disapproval of the old monarch, who protested in vain against towering head-dresses. In 1714, two English ladies with their hair worn low having been presented at the French Court, Louis XIV said to the wives of the courtiers, "If Frenchwomen were reasonable beings they would at once give up their ridiculous

* Rape of the Lock. † Born 1646; died 1723.

head-dresses and wear their hair in the English fashion." How could the court ladies bear to be called "ridiculous," especially by their king? They very soon made their appearance in the king's circle with their hair dressed low.* For once, at least, England set the fashion for France—a pleasing turn of the tables!

The next transformation was the hoop, invented by a mantua-maker named Selby, in 1711, and destined in one form or another to hold its sway over feminine taste for many years. Dresses which had been looped back over contrasting petticoats were hung out over these most awkward inventions. At first they were rather flat in front and in the back (Figure 162), projecting out on each side over the hips to such an extent that the wearer was often obliged to enter a door sideways. Mr. Wingfield, in his "Notes on Civil Costume in England," remarks that "in a sedan chair a lady would some-times pull up her hoop on both sides of her like wings." As sedan chairs were used in all the English colonies of America, fashionable colonial dames probably resorted to the same expedient.

The sacque, the name in use for many years to designate the loose over-dress, at this time hung in wide plaits from the shoulders to the ground over the large hooped petticoat. It was open in front and worn over a petticoat and stomacher of the same material, although a contrast of colour and of material was also popular. This garment was invariably worn by women of fashion in England and France, and in the Colonies for at least half of the century. It survived several generations of change. At first it was long and full as in Figure 161, then short to the knees and very full (Figure 170); later it became a graceful, stately garment, transformed by a few curved lines and worn over a laced stomacher and satin petticoat trimmed with flounces (Figure 204). This charming variety of sacque is usually called a "Watteau." Sacques were made in all materials and worn by all classes until 1777.

* History of Fashion in France, by Challomel.

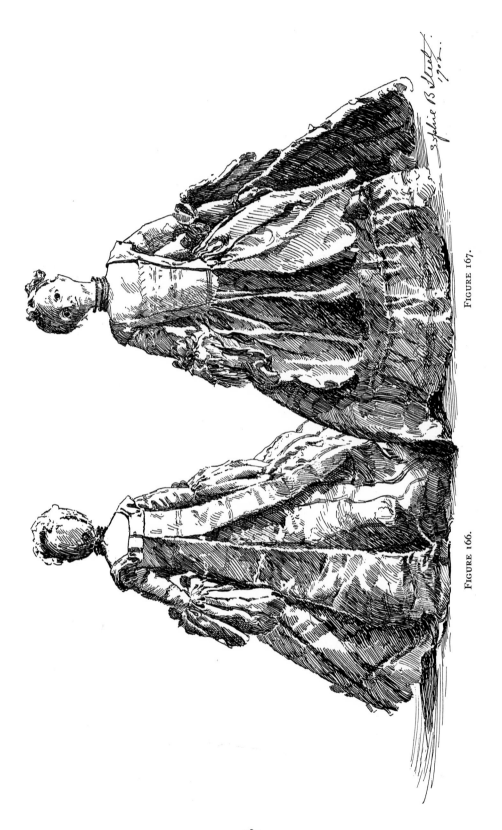

FIGURE 166.

FIGURE 167.

183

FIGURES 166 and 167.—This fashion doll is dressed in a Watteau sacque of taffeta (a white ground with cross-bar lines of red) over a hooped petticoat of the same trimmed with a pinked flounce. The stomacher is plain without a point, but finished by robings of the silk from the shoulder to a little below the waist-line. An apron of soft green silk is worn under the stomacher. The sleeves end at the elbow and are finished with graduated ruffles of the silk pinked, very deep in the back and short in the front; a knot of red, the prevailing colour of the costume, is on each sleeve and also in the hair, which was powdered and worn close to the head, probably in French curls. Red slippers with high heels, a necklace, and bracelets complete this genuine "Fashion-baby's" attire. The original may be seen in the Colonial room of the National Museum at Independence Hall, in Philadelphia.

"Let your gown be a sacque, blue, yellow or green,
    And frizzle your elbows with ruffles sixteen;
    Furl off your lawn apron with flounces in rows,
    Puff and pucker up knots on your arms and your toes;
    Make your petticoat short, that a hoop eight yards wide
    May decently show how your garters are ty'd.
. . . .
But mount on French heels when you go to a ball,
    'Tis the fashion to totter, and show you can fall."*

Figures 168 and 169 show the style of hood in general wear by women of all ranks from 1690 to 1750. The original hood, lent

FIGURE 168.   FIGURE 169.
A Camlet Hood; taken from an Original Garment of about 1702. Reign of Queen **Anne.**

to us for this book, is made of drab camlet and lined with silk to match, for it belonged to a Colonial Quakeress. The fashionable dames of that time made them of gay silk, according to contemporary

* The Beau's Receipt for a Lady's Dress.

authority. The hood, which in the previous reign was commonly of black silk, velvet, or sarsenet, we now find of various colours; and cherry coloured hoods were all the rage in 1712. A group of ladies in coloured silk hoods at the theatre is thus described: "One of them was blue, another yellow and another philomot; the fourth was of a pink colour and the fifth was of a pale green. I looked upon this little parti-coloured assembly as upon a bed of tulips."*

From advertisements of this date (1712) in England, we can form some idea of the garments sent to the Colonies. In one of the papers we read of a black silk petticoat with a red and white calico border, a red and dove coloured damask gown flowered with large trees, a yellow satin apron trimmed with white Persian muslin, and head-cloths with crow-foot edging.

An Isabella coloured kincob gown flowered with green and gold; a dark coloured cloth gown and petticoat with two silver orrices; a purple and gold atlas gown; a scarlet and gold atlas petticoat edged with silver; an underpetticoat edged with gold; a black velvet petticoat; an allejah petticoat striped with green, gold and white; and clogs laced with silver are also mentioned.

In the same year were advertised "a green silk knit waistcoat with gold and silver flowers all over it, and fourteen yards of gold and silver thick lace on it; and a petticoat of rich strong flowered satin, red and white all in great flowers or leaves, and scarlet flowers with black specks brocaded in, raised high like velvet or shag."†

A lady's riding suit of this period is described as consisting of "a coat and waistcoat of blue camlet trimmed and embroidered with silver, with a petticoat of the same stuff, by which alone her sex was recognized, as she wore a smartly cocked beaver hat, edged with silver and rendered more sprightly by a feather, while her hair, curled and powdered, hung to a considerable length down her shoulders, tied like that of a rakish young gentleman, with a long streaming

* The Spectator.   † Pictorial History of England.

FIGURE 170.

FIGURE 170.—Picture of a short Watteau sacque worn over a petticoat to match and trimmed with ruchings of the same. It is taken from a garment in the South Kensington Museum, London, and is of biscuit-coloured taffeta with a damask pattern and scattered flowers and butterflies hand painted in watercolours—a specimen of the fancy-work of some lady of ease in the first half of the Georgian era. It is probable that this style of sacque was often made of Persian or dimity for home wear in the Colonies. The cap of muslin tied under the chin is often seen in contemporary pictures.

scarlet riband."* But powder was not in general use by ladies at this time.

In Queen Anne's day patches meant more than one would suppose; they were not used simply to enhance the beauty of the complexion, but were worn as political badges. The ladies with Whig sympathies wore these patches on the left-hand side of the face, the Tories on the right. Mr. Andrew Lang has suggested that a revival of this fashion in England during the South African War would have greatly facilitated conversation. "If Pro-Boer ladies would only profess their opinion by way of patches, we should know where we are and could make no such mistakes as now occasionally occur in conversation."

Patch boxes (Figure 159) were carried, filled with patches of every shape; under the lid of the box was placed a small glass to assist the fair lady in adjusting them. These boxes were made of silver, ivory, and tortoise shell, and were often, like the snuff-boxes of the same period, very costly.

"That little modish machine," as Addison called the fan, was an indispensable article of fashionable dress. Flory, in his "History of the Fan," says: "We can scarcely imagine the rouged and powdered beauty of the eighteenth century without the fascinating trinket in her hand. Both in England and in France it had gradually become the mirror of the life and pleasure of the time. Political and social events, literature, music, and the fashions and follies of the day, were depicted upon them. Some were covered with words and bars from operas, or with scenes from popular plays, others bore the rules of various games, within decorative borders of playing cards." A picture of a fan painted by Gamble representing a scene from Ovid is given in Figure 241. "There were calendar fans, fortune-telling fans, fans with riddles and charades, political and social caricatures." One is noted representing the separation of America from England.

* The Spectator.

Addison declares there is an infinite variety of motions to be made use of in the flutter of a fan. "There is the angry flutter, the modest flutter, the timorous flutter, the merry flutter, and the amorous flutter. There is scarce any condition in the mind which does not produce a suitable agitation in the fan, insomuch that if I only see the fan of a disciplined lady, I know whether she laughs, frowns or blushes. I have seen a fan so angry that it would have been dangerous for the absent lover who provoked it, to have come within the wind of it; and at other times so languishing, that I have been glad for the lady's sake that the lover was at a certain distance from it."

> "What daring Bard shall e'er attempt to tell
> The powers that in this little engine dwell?
> What verse can e'er explain its various parts,
> Its numerous uses, motions, charms and arts?
> Its shake triumphant, its virtuous clap,
> Its angry flutter, and its wanton tap."

REIGN OF GEORGE I

Black and white beaver hats for ladies were advertised in 1719, faced with coloured silks and trimmed with gold or silver lace. The sacque was still in vogue. The paintings of Watteau, who died in 1721, and of Lancret, who died in 1724, are to a certain extent the authorities for the dress of the preceding reign (Queen Anne).

> "She takes her muff and goes
> To see some one she knows."

In 1720 women's muffs were narrow and long, the crossed hands filled one exactly; afterward they became wider. In various forms they continued in fashion throughout the century.

Stays, or "a paire of bodices," as they were called in the early part of the seventeenth century, were considered a necessary article of woman's dress throughout the eighteenth century, and very, very stiff and straight-laced were these colonial great-grandmothers of our modern corset! (Figure 188.)

FIGURE 171.

FIGURE 172.

FIGURE 173.

FIGURE 174.

FIGURE 171.—Shows a gown of yellow damask brocade worn over a blue quilted satin petticoat. Reign of George I.

FIGURE 172.—Shows a white satin wedding gown worn by Mrs. St. Clair in Philadelphia, 1760.

FIGURE 173.—Picture of a blue lutestring gown worn by the same lady.

FIGURE 174.—Is a very interesting dress of buff chiné silk, with coloured flowers, worn by Lady Stuart in the Barbadoes Colony in the reign of Queen Anne.

(Photographed from original garments.)

About 1720 temple spectacles came into use; afterward "bridge spectacles," without any side supporters and held on solely by nipping the bridge of the nose. Perspective glasses, with long handles of tortoise shell or silver, were carried by gallants in London.

A mask of black velvet (Figure 194) was often worn in winter with a silver mouth-piece to keep it on; green silk masks were used in summer for riding in the sun on horseback, while for young girls in the Colonies they were made of linen and tied on under their hoods.

REIGN OF GEORGE II

At this time hooped petticoats were less exaggerated. Scarlet cloaks with hoods, called "cardinals," were worn out-of-doors (Figure 175). The hair was still worn low and was often covered by a much frilled cap or flat hat of moderate dimensions (Figure 195). During the next decade the caps became smaller, but the hats larger (Figure 216).

The use of powder, according to Mr. Wingfield, was never general in England, although it was worn on all occasions of ceremony in the reigns of George II and George III by both sexes, and was extremely fashionable from 1760 to 1776; but it was not habitually worn in home life with everyday costumes.

In 1735 we notice a change in the shape of the hoop, which was now made to project all around like the wheel farthingale, the petticoat being worn short and the gown without a train (Figure 196).

Lace tippets were now much worn, some having diamond solitaires to hook them together. Very broad laced tuckers, with diamond necklaces and earrings, were popular. Diamond and paste buckles were also very fashionable.

Mrs. Delany, who has been called not only the woman of fashion in her own age, but "the woman of fashion of all ages," records some charming costumes. The following is dated 1738 (when hoops were large):

"After much persuasion and many debates within myself I consented to go with Lady Dysart to the Prince's birthday, humbly dres't in my pink Damask, white and gold handkerchief, plain green ribbon and Lady Sunderland's buckles for my stays." The stays, evidently meaning the stomacher, were on this occasion straps of white silk covered with a lacing through which a handkerchief was passed. This costume is not unlike the yellow damask gown (Figures 164 and 183) worn in Philadelphia in 1740.

FIGURE 175.
Lady in a Cardinal (after Hogarth, Early Eighteenth Century).

Head-dresses at this time were made of three lace ruffles tucked to stand up in front. "Caskades of ribands" and artificial flowers were used as trimming. They were worn over powdered hair pinned up quite short in the back, and sometimes large curls were worn hanging down on the shoulder, as in Figure 198.

In another letter Mrs. Delany says: "I go to-morrow to pay my salutations to their Royal Highnesses at Carlton House in my Irish green Damask and my worked head; on the birthday, which is Tuesday next, in a flowered silk, I bought since I came to town, of a pale deer-coloured ground, the flowers mostly purple, and mixed with white feathers. I think it extremely pretty and very modest." The latter is not unlike the Colonial gown represented in Figures 218, 230. "Ruffles are much the same, large at the elbows and pretty narrow at the bottom. I think they pin their gowns rather closer than before; hoops are as flat as if made of pasteboard, and as stiff, the shape sloping from the hips and spreading at the bottom (Figures 164 and 183), enormous but not so ugly as the square hoops (Figure 162). There are hopes that they will soon be reduced to a very small size. Heads are variously dressed, pompons with some accompaniment of feathers, ribbons or flowers; lappets in all sorts of curli-murlis; long hoods are worn close under the chin, or tied with bows and ends behind."

FIGURE 176.   FIGURE 177.   FIGURE 178.   FIGURE 179.   FIGURE 180.   FIGURE 181.
             Caps, 1744.   Caps, 1745.

Long aprons were worn in 1740, then short ones, and before 1752 long ones again. In the same year (1740) we hear of a successor to the hood under the name of "capuchin."

The description which Mrs. Delany gives of a marvellous toilet worn by the Duchess of Queensbury, in 1741, is worth transcribing as a curious specimen of needle-work. "It was of white satin embroidered, the bottom of the petticoat brown hills covered with all sorts of weeds, and every breadth had an old stump of a tree that ran up almost to the top of the petticoat broken and ragged and worked with brown chenille, round which twined nasturtiums, honeysuckle, periwinkle and all sorts of twining flowers, which spread and covered the petticoat; vines with the leaves variegated as you have seen them by the sun, all rather smaller than nature, which made them look very light. The robings and facings were like green banks covered with all sorts of weeds, and the sleeves and rest of the gown loose twining branches of the same sort as those on the petticoat. Many of the leaves were finished with gold, and part of the stumps of the trees looked like gilding of the sun. I never saw a piece of work so prettily fancied and am quite angry with myself for not having the same thought, for it is infinitely handsomer than mine and could not have cost much more."

French curls (Figure 196), the mode in 1745, were described as looking like eggs strung in order on a wire tied around the head. They were not always false, but could be made of the natural hair. The *crêpe toupée* was also a contemporary fashion. Later came in the Italian curls (Figure 184), which had the effect of scollop shells and were arranged back from the face in several shapes. In the *tête de mouton*, or *tête moutonée*, the hair was curled close all over the back of the head.

In the summer of 1745 Gipsy straw hats appeared, being tied under the chin (Figure 195).

We find that in 1745 the hoop had increased at the sides and diminished in front; and a pamphlet was published in that year entitled "The Enormous Abomination of the Hoop Petticoat as the Fashion now is" (Figure 184). The hoop of this period was a great bell-shaped petticoat or skirt of the dress stiffened by whalebone. The material was placed directly upon it, so that, being a part of the gown itself, it was customary to speak of "a damask hoop" or "a brocade hoop."

Deportment was quite as important as dress in the fashionable world of the eighteenth century. Those were the days of backboards and of most unyielding stays.

The expression "she bridles well," which occurs in letters of this

FIGURE 182. FIGURE 183. FIGURE 184. FIGURE 185.

REIGNS OF QUEEN ANNE AND GEORGE I
1702-1725

FIGURE 182 shows the cloak called a Roquelaure, after the Duke of that name who held the post of Gentleman of the Wardrobe under Louis XIV. It was made of velvet, silk or cloth and was usually lined with a bright coloured silk. Later in the eighteenth century the cloak was worn much longer and became a popular garment for both sexes. It is often mentioned in Colonial letters and papers as a "Roquelo." The cocked hat and campaign wig are typical of Queen Anne's reign, 1702-1714. The use of the muff is worthy of note.

FIGURE 183 represents the back of the yellow damask gown in Figure 164. The small cap, very fashionable in the reign of George I, is of sheer muslin trimmed with lace and has lappets in the back which could be worn hanging down the back or, as in this plate, turned up and fastened on top.

FIGURE 184 is a picture taken from a very handsome gown in the Art Museum of Boston. The ground of the brocade is of green with a pattern in bright colours. It is elaborately made and fitted in at the back like Figure 183. The stomacher is soft and full and held in place by bands of ribbon and rosettes. The hair of this figure is arranged in Italian curls which are fastened close to the head and finished with a small pompon of artificial flowers. It is copied from a contemporary portrait (1720).

FIGURE 185—Back view of costume shown in Figure 165. The plaits in the coat-tail are very full.

time (1747), alludes to a manner of carriage which is now almost unknown. "One of the first lessons in deportment at that period was to hold up the head on entering a room, and to keep the chin in, which is expressed by 'bridling,' and then, having curtseyed at the door, to advance deliberately towards the person who had the first claim to greeting—to sink low gradually—to rise slowly and gracefully."*

The Boston "Evening Post" advertised in November, 1755, "horse hair quilted coats to wear with negligees."

It is difficult to determine the exact limitations of a negligée.

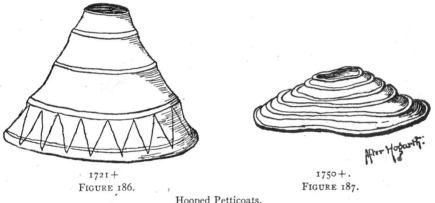

1721+
FIGURE 186.

1750+.
FIGURE 187.

Hooped Petticoats.

It was worn in full dress and was another variety of the sacque. The advertisement quoted suggests an outdoor garment, a quilted coat worn under it for warmth.

"Put on her a sheperdee
A short sack or negligee
Ruffled high to keep her warm
Eight or ten about an arm."†

A garment which became very popular about 1756 was a cloak made of satin or velvet, black or any colour, lined or trimmed with silk, satin, or fur, according to the fancy, with slits for the arms to

* Mrs. Woolsey's Notes to Autobiography of Mrs. Delany.
† Poem printed in New York, 1756.

pass through, and a hood like a capuchin. These cloaks were worn
by everybody and were called pompadours (Figure 216).

Night-gowns or night-rails correspond to our modern dressing-
gowns and were worn without hoops. One is represented in Figure
243 with a short cape over a skirt instead of a sacque.

An historian of Connecticut tells us that "the dress of the middle
period can hardly be praised for its simplicity or economy. In the
upper circles it was rich and extravagant, and among the females

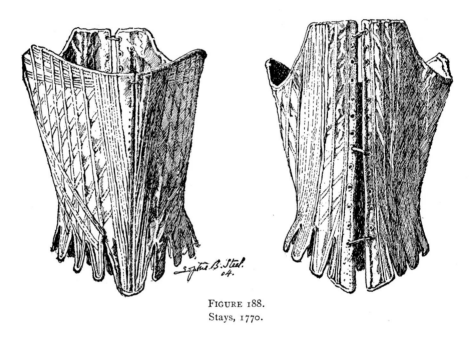

FIGURE 188.
Stays, 1770.

of all classes there was a passion for gathering and hoarding articles
of attire. It was an object of ambition to have a chest full of linen,
a pillow-beer of stockings, and other articles in proportion, laid by."

The inventory of the effects of Mrs. White of Norwich,* taken
August 16, 1757, contained "gowns of brown duroy, striped stuff,
plain stuff, black silk, crape, calico and blue camlet; a scarlet cloak,
blue cloak, satin flowered mantle, and furbelow scarf; a woolen

* History of Norwich, by F. M. Caulkins.

petticoat with calico border, a camlet riding-hood, long silk hood, velvet hood, white hood trimmed with lace, a silk bonnet, and nineteen caps; a cambrick laced handkerchief, silk do, linen do, sixteen handkerchiefs in all; a muslin laced apron, flowered laced apron, green taffety apron, fourteen aprons in all; a silver riband, silver girdle and blue girdle, four pieces of flowered satin, a parcel of crewel, and a woman's fan; a gold necklace, death's head gold ring, plain gold ring, sett of gold sleeve buttons, gold

FIGURE 189.
Clog, Eighteenth Century (from an Old Print).

locket, silver hair peg, silver cloak clasps, and a stone button set in silver; a large silver tankard, a silver cup with two handles, a cup with one handle, and a large silver spoon."

FIGURE 190.
A Patten (from the Original in the Museum at Memorial Hall, Philadelphia).

We know that a salmon-coloured tabby made with a sacque and coat (probably, in this case, waistcoat or stomacher) was the correct thing in 1759, as an order for one for his wife is preserved in Washington's own writing. In the same order we read of "a cap, handkerchief and ruffles of Brussels or Point lace to be worn with the above negligée, to cost £20."

Also two fine flowered aprons
One pair women's white silk hose
Four pairs thread hose
Six pairs women's fine cotton hose
One pair black satin shoes
One pair white satin shoes of smallest 5's
Four pairs calamanco shoes
One fashionable hat or bonnet
Six pairs women's best kid gloves
Eight pairs women's best mits
One dozen round silk laces

One black mask
One dozen most fashionable pocket handkerchiefs
One piece of narrow white satin ribbon with pearl edge
Four pieces of binding tape
Six thousand miniken pins
Six thousand short whites
Six thousand corking pins
One thousand hair pins.

The following note from Washington's manuscripts shows the relationship between a sacque and a night-gown: "Mrs. Washington sends home a green sack to get cleaned, or fresh dyed of the same colour; made into a handsome sack again, would be her choice, but if the cloth wont afford that, then to be thrown into a genteel night-gown."* The latter being the old-fashioned name for a dressing-gown.

REIGN OF GEORGE III

In 1760 gowns began to be worn with a close-fitting bodice ending in a long point in the back (Figures 209, 210, 211, and 213), the

FIGURE 191.

Riding-hat of Fawn-coloured Felt. The original is in the Museum at Memorial Hall, Philadelphia. Reigns of George II and III.

skirt sewn on with a multiplicity of fine gathers, still opening over a petticoat, the latter often beautifully quilted. Aprons were worn, too, according to the dictates of fancy. Occasionally stomacher and apron matched, as in Figure 206. Sleeves were still trimmed with ruffles of lace, but often were edged with narrow cuffs turned back, the lace falling from underneath (Figures 205 and 230).

Every lady of fashion wore an *étui*, or ornamental case, hanging from the waist, intended to hold thimble, scissors, and scent bottle. The snuff-box, the pomander, a box with perforated holes in the lid and used for perfumes, and the pouncet box, of a similar nature, were among the elegant accessories of the toilet of the eighteenth century

* Writings of George Washington, edited by Wm. C. Ford.

FIGURE 193.

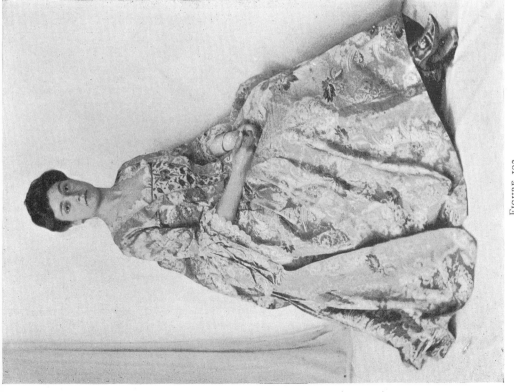

FIGURE 192.

FIGURE 192.—Photograph of a kincob brocade, green figured with flowers in crimson, white, gold and blue, with stomacher in white silk embroidered in colours to match. This dress was owned by a sister of Governor Hancock of Massachusetts, about 1735.

FIGURE 193.—Dress of a young Virginia lady, about 1775.

for both sexes. (See Figure 159.) Physicians made use of the pomanders to carry disinfectants; sometimes they had them inserted in the handle of their canes, and a tap on the floor as they entered a sick-room would scatter the powder through the atmosphere.

The recipe books of the time, written by each housewife for her own use and pleasure, have in many cases been handed down to posterity. Turning over the yellowed leaves of one written in the careful penmanship of the eighteenth century by a notable New York dame, an aroma of agreeable spices seems to emanate from the pages as we read the following:

FIGURE 194.
A Riding-mask, Eighteenth Century.

"Pot Pourri

"Dry your violets in a sunny window. Have ready a quarter of a pound of finely powdered bay salt. When the roses are out, gather all kinds, and dry in the same way. Then add them to the violets, putting layers of salt between each layer.

"Gather a good deal of lavendar, also the leaves of the verbena, and, if possible, myrtle and orange blossoms. After all the flowers and salt have filled the jar, its contents should be constantly stirred for a month."

Here is another recipe from the same book:

"Take a Seville orange, and stick it as full as possible of cloves. Put it in a jar. Pick the rose leaves when full blown. but before they are ready to drop, and spread the petals to dry in the sun. When dry mix them with a little bay salt, some cinnamon, ground cloves, lemon peel, and powdered musk. Stir for some time until well mixed."

Old India jars filled with pot pourri stood in almost every house, and lent a subtle fragrance to the draperies and carpets. This custom was of the same origin as the use of pomanders.

Research on the subject of wedding veils at this period has produced nothing more satisfactory than the following passage from Mr. J. Cordy Jeffreson's "Brides and Bridals":

"The origin of the English bride's veil is one of those disputed questions which will never be settled. What of late years became the most conspicuous feature of her costume may be nothing more than a milliner's substitute for the flowing tresses, which in old times concealed not a few of the bride's personal attractions and covered her face when she knelt at the altar. This opinion is supported by the fact that Elizabeth Stuart, daughter of James I, was not thought to require an artificial veil, since nature had given her such an abundance of circumfluent hair. Heyward says of this wedding:

'At length the blushing bride comes with her
hair disheveled aslant her shoulders.'

"It may be a mere amplification of the coif which medieval brides used to wear between the garland and the hair, of such a coif, for instance, as Margaret Tudor wore under the coronet at her wedding with the King of Scotland."

In the early years of the reign of George III the veil and wreath fell so completely out of vogue that they were for a time seldom seen on brides of the "best ton." Horace Walpole, an earnest social reformer in all trivial matters, was pleased by the neglect of old matrimonial forms. He mentions that his niece Maria had never appeared more lovely than when he watched the alternate blushes and paleness of her unveiled face during her celebration of marriage with the Earl of Waldegrave. The bride wore a hat and a white and silver gown, and when the marriage service had been performed in the drawing-room of a private mansion in Pall Mall by Dr. Keppel, the bridal party sat down to dinner, which was over at eight o'clock in the evening. "It was," wrote Walpole to George Montague, "as sensible a wedding as ever was." This wedding took place in the last year of the reign of George II.

FIGURE 195.

FIGURE 196.

FIGURE 197.

FIGURE 198.

Sophie B. Steel
1903

REIGNS OF GEORGE I AND II
1725-1745

FIGURE 195.—An everyday Colonial costume worn in Massachusetts about 1725. It is made of fawn coloured moiré camlet, and opens over a stiffened petticoat of durant. The ruffle of an under-garment of fine linen with knife-plaited sleeves turns down over the dress at the neck like a falling band. The original gown is exceedingly interesting as a specimen of the ordinary attire of the period. The hat worn over a ruffled cap was the popular style of that time, made familiar to us in the pictures of Hogarth and others.

FIGURE 196.—A Colonial gown of kincob, a very rich brocade imported from China. The original dress was owned by a sister of Governor Hancock of Massachusetts, Mrs. Whittington Allen. It was evidently made to wear over a large hoop (about 1735) and clears the ground. The stomacher is of white silk richly embroidered, the sleeves reach to the elbow and are finished with full pinked ruffles graduated so that they hang long in the back and are short in front. The back of this beautiful old gown is made with two large box plaits which hang out over the hooped skirt. It is of the style popularly termed a Watteau sacque and very fashionable in the Colonies from 1720 to 1776. The front of the skirt is made of two breadths of the kincob tied round the waist over the hooped skirt. The coiffure on this figure, known as French curls, was very fashionable at that time. Shoes match the gown, they have high heels and straps of the brocade pulled through handsome buckles. A strap of wide silver galloon runs up the front of the shoe and at the back from heel to counter; see first pair of slippers in Figure 262.

FIGURE 197.—A young gallant of George II's reign in a full-dress suit and a cocked hat. He wears the latest fashion in ties, 1740.

FIGURE 198.—A Colonial gown of green taffeta worn by Mrs. Wilimina Weemys Moore in Philadelphia about 1740 and lent for this book by a direct descendant. It is trimmed with ruchings and flounces of the material pinked. The bodice is laced in front over a white stomacher and is made without box plaits in the back (see Figure 174). The hair in the picture is copied from a contemporary portrait and is not powdered. As in Figure 196, the front of the skirt is separate and fastens round the waist over a hooped petticoat, evidently with a view to wearing a variety of combinations, for in the case of the kincob gown there was a white satin front to alternate with the kincob front.

In the Colonies the veil does not seem to have been a necessary article of a bride's costume. Several beautiful wedding gowns which have been handed down with care from early in the eighteenth century are of coloured brocade or damask (Figures 184, 213).

Orange-blossoms were not used as wedding flowers until a comparatively modern date, although orange trees were growing in England at the time of Henry VIII.

We read of an English bride * in 1769 who wore "a sacque and petticoat of the most expensive brocaded white silk, resembling network enriched with small flowers, which displayed in the variations of the folds a most delicate shade of pink; a deep and pointed stomacher trimmed with gimp; sleeves closely fitted the elbow, from which hung three point-lace ruffles of great depth; a handkerchief of the same lace covered the shoulders, fastened in front with a large bow of white satin ribbon and a bunch of delicate pink rosebuds. A triple row of pearls tied behind with a narrow white satin ribbon completed

FIGURE 199.

Maid in Sacque, Apron, and Clogs. Middle Eighteenth Century.

* Mrs. Joseph Nollekens, wife of the noted sculptor.

the costume, although I believe a lace apron, previously worn by the bride's mother, was put on, but the fashion of wearing aprons in full dress had gone out at that date.

"The hair was arranged over a high cushion, with large curls on either side, and ornamented by a small cap of point lace with plaited flaps to match the ruffles in the sleeves. The shoes were like the gown and were ornamented with spangles and square buckles with heels three and one-half inches in height."

Lady Susan O'Brien, living in the Colonies, was kept informed by her cousin, Lady Sarah Lennox, of the latest changes in fashion in England. In 1766 she says:*

"I think that by degrees the French dress is coming into fashion, tho' 'tis almost impossible to make the ladies understand that heads bigger than one's body are ugly; it is growing the fashion to have the heads *moutonée*. I have cut off my hair and find it very convenient in the country without powder, because my hair curls naturally. . . . . I wear it very often with three rows of curls behind and the rest smooth with a fringe *toupé* and a cap; that is, *en paresseuse*. Almost every body powders now, and wears a little hoop.

"Hats are mostly left off; the hair down on the forehead belongs to the short waists [waists were apparently very long at the time this letter was written, 1766], and is equally vulgar with poppons [or pompons], trimmings, beads, garnets, flying caps and false hair.

"To be perfectly genteel, you must be dressed thus: *Your* hair must not be cut off, for 'tis much too pretty, but it must be powdered, curled in very small curls and neat, but it must be high before and give your head the look of a sugar loaf a little. The rest of the hair must be drawn up straight and not frizzled at all for half an inch above the rest. You must wear no cap and only little, little flowers dab'd in the left side; the only feather permitted is a black or white *sultane* perched up on the left side and your diamond feather against it (Figure 218).

* Lady Sarah Lennox to Lady Susan O'Brien in America, January 9th, 1766.

FIGURE 200.

FIGURE 201.

FIGURE 202.

FIGURE 203.

FIGURE 200.—Portrait of Mrs. Catharine Van Rensselaer, showing a popular style of cap worn by elderly ladies in the last half of the eighteenth century. (From the original portrait.)

FIGURE 201.—Portrait of Mrs. Nathaniel Appleton in an everyday costume.

FIGURE 202.—Portrait of Mrs. Nathaniel Appleton, Jr., showing a peculiar cap in 1784.

FIGURE 203.—Portrait of Mrs. Mary Faneuil of Boston, reign of George II.

"A broad puffed ribbon *collier* (Figure 206), with a tippet ruff, or only a little black handkerchief very narrow over the shoulders; your stays very high and pretty tight at bottom, your gown trimmed with the same straight down the robings, and a narrow flounce at bottom to button with a *compère* to be loose at the fore part of your robing. The sleeves long and loose, the waist very long, the flounces and ruffles of a decent length not too long, nor so hideously short as they now wear them. No trimming on the sleeve but a ribbon knot tied to hang on the ruffles."

Artificial flowers were worn in full dress. We learn from the newspapers of the day that "the biziness of making flowers" was a thriving one in Boston. Teachers in the art of flower making are often advertised in the Boston papers. We read, too, that Benjamin Franklin's sister and her daughter made a practical use of this accomplishment in the following extract from a letter from Mrs. Mecom, dated Boston, 1766:

"And I have a small request to ask. It is to procure me some fine old linen or cambric dyed into bright colours, such as red and green, a little blue but chiefly red, for with all my art and good old Benjamin's memorandums, I cannot make them good colours. My daughter Jenny, with a little of my assistance, has taken to making flowers for ladies' heads and bosoms with pretty good acceptance, and if I can procure these colours, I am in hope we shall get something by it worth our pains. It is no matter how old the linen is. I am afraid you never had any bad enough."

From a letter of Mrs. Mecom to Mrs. Franklin dated February 27th, 1766, we take the following: "We are now supplied not only with necessary but creditable clothing, for brother has sent each of us a printed cotton gown, a quilted coat, a bonnet, each of the girls a cap and some ribbons. Mine is very suitable for me to wear now, being black and purple cotton, but the girls' are light coloured."*

* Letters to Benjamin Franklin from his Family and Friends, 1751–1790.

The name bonnet, from the French *bonnet*, was often used through-out the eighteenth century in speaking of caps and hoods, but the first actual bonnet was the successor of the Gipsy hat in the latter part of the century, and in 1798 we read that "straw bonnets were in full fashion."

A New England authority tells us that "cushions stuffed with wool and covered with silk, used in dressing the hair, made a calash (Figures 222, 226, 227) necessary instead of a bonnet. This was large and wide, and an awkward article of attire, but often shrouding a health-beaming face in its depths, needing no other ornament than its own good humored smile." *

A gentleman of the courteous old school remarked of this fashion of the calash, "It was like looking down a green lane to see a rose blooming at the end."

From the "History of Norwich" quoted above we give the fol-lowing description: "Women of mature age wore close linen caps (Figure 253). Parasols and umbrellas were unknown or of rare occurrence, but a fan nearly a foot and a half in length, and spread-ing like the train of a peacock, was often carried to keep off the sun as well as to catch the air. At one period feathers were much worn upon the head, surmounting a high turban of gauze or muslin raised on wire and adorned also with ribbon.

"A lady in full dress for great occasions displayed a rich brocade with open skirt and trained petticoat trimmed with lace; an em-broidered stomacher and full ruffles at the elbows. Hood and scarf were of silk. No sumptuary laws restrained the feminine taste for rich attire at this period. When the ladies walked out, they threw the end of the train over the right arm. The foot was dressed in a silk stocking, a sharp-toed slipper, often made of embroidered satin, and with a high heel" (Figure 240). In winter beaver hats were worn over a lace cap, as in Figure 216, or with the brim curved downwards

* History of Norwich, by F. M. Caulkins.

FIGURE 204.

FIGURE 205.

FIGURE 206.

FIGURE 207.

REIGN OF GEORGE II
1735-1760

FIGURE 204 is a picture of a very dainty Colonial gown which in 1752 formed part of the wedding outfit of Mrs. West, *née* Mary Hodge, of Hope Lodge, White Marsh, Pa. The colouring is a soft fawn-coloured ground with nosegays of purple, red, yellow and white flowers scattered over it. The flounce and falbalas are of the silk pinked, the latter graduated as shown in the plate. The train has a graceful sweep in the back. The picture shows a stomacher of lace held in by ribbon tied in bows. The front of the gown and the elbow sleeves are finished with ruffles of lace. The head in this picture is copied from a contemporary portrait, the powdered pompadour being adorned with a string of pearls arranged with pins. Two soft curls hang on the neck in the back.

FIGURE 205 represents a costume worn in the Massachusetts Colony in 1750. It is of very rich crimson brocade over a petticoat of white satin. It belonged to Mrs. Faithful Hubbard, who, in spite of her Puritan name, possessed a very "modish gown." It is made without a Watteau back, like Figure 174, the skirt gathered into the bodice at the waist line. The hair is arranged in the height of fashion in 1759 and is powdered.

FIGURE 206 shows the green kincob gown of Figure 196, arranged over a white satin hooped petticoat with a full-dress apron of white silk embroidered like the stomacher in a bright coloured Chinese pattern. The fichu and sleeve ruffles are of lace and the "collier" of ribbon gathered into a ruche and edged with lace. This neck arrangement as well as the hair without powder are copied from a contemporary portrait.

FIGURE 207 represents the back of the kincob gown. The Watteau hangs out without the curved line shown in Figure 204, as the kincob gown was made some years earlier (about 1735) to wear over a large hoop. The hoop shown in Figure 207 is the fashion of about 1745. The cap is a very popular style of George II's reign, finished with a ribbon and bow at the back. The hair is powdered.

All the gowns in this plate have been lent for this book by direct descendants of the original owners.

by broad ribbon strings tied under the chin (Figure 195). Loose cloaks trimmed with fur were the fashion in the middle of the eighteenth century, also long Roquelaures with short capes or a hood on the shoulders, like those worn by the men.

In Massachusetts, we are told, "ladies wore caps, long stiff stays, and high-heeled shoes. Their bonnets (hoods) were of silk or satin, and usually black. Gowns were extremely long-waisted with tight sleeves. Another fashion was a very short sleeve with an immense frill at the elbow. A large flexible hoop, three or four feet in diameter, was for some time quilted into the hem of the gown, making an immense display of the lower person. A large round cushion, stuffed with cotton or hair and covered with black crape, was laid across the head, over which the hair was combed back and fastened. It was almost the universal custom, also, for women to wear gold beads, thirty-nine little hollow globes, about the size of a pea, strung on a thread and tied round the neck.

FIGURE 208.

A Lady's Shoe, of a Cornflower-blue Serge Silk, Bound with White Ribbon.

"Working women wore petticoats and half gowns, drawn with a cord round the waist, and coarse leather shoes; though they generally had a pair of 'Lynn shoes' for Sunday."*

In Watson's famous "Annals" we read: "The women in Philadelphia wore caps (a bare head was never seen), stiff stays, hoops from six inches to two feet (Figure 184) on each side, so that a full-dressed lady entered a door like a crab. High-heeled shoes of black stuff with white silk or thread stockings, and in the miry times of winter they wore clogs, galoshes, or pattens (Figures 189 and 190).

"Ladies often had their hair tortured for four hours at a sitting, in getting the proper crisped curls of a hair curler. Some who

* History of Lynn, Mass., by Lewis and Newhall.

designed to be inimitably captivating, not knowing they could be sure
of professional services, where so many hours were occupied upon
one gay head, have actually had the operation performed the day
before it was required, then have slept all night in a sitting posture to
prevent the derangement of their frizzles and curls.   This is a real
fact, and we could, if questioned, name cases.   They were of course

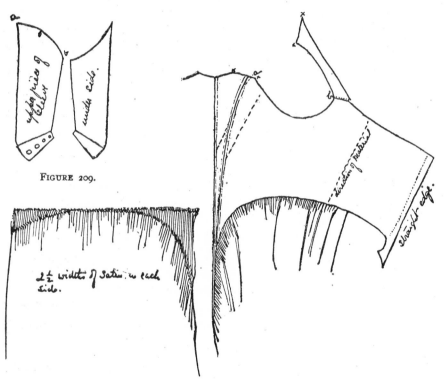

FIGURE 209.

FIGURE 211.   FIGURE 210.
Plan of White Satin Dress shown in Figures 218 and 230.   Reign of George III.

rare occurrences, proceeding from some extra occasions, when there
were several to serve, and but few such refined hair dressers in the
place.

"This formidable head work was succeeded by rollers over which
the hair was combed from the forehead.   These again were superseded by cushions and artificial curled work, which could be sent out

FIGURE 212.

FIGURE 213.

FIGURE 214.

FIGURE 215.

Sophie B Steel
1903.

FIGURE 212.—The wedding gown of Esther Marvel, a New England Quaker lady, married in Salem, Massachusetts, about the middle of the eighteenth century. It is of white satin. The bodice fastens in the back with hooks and eyes, and the upper part of each sleeve is embroidered with a rosebud in white silk. The long sleeves are evidently of a later date and ruffles of sheer lawn like the fichu probably finished the shorter sleeves when the gown was first worn. The reticule carried in the hand is of white lutestring, embroidered like the sleeves in white silk. The cap is of the shape so much worn at that time by women of all classes. The hair is arranged very simply, drawn back softly over the ears and in a knot at the back. The absence of powder and of the fashionable hooped petticoat are the distinguishing marks of this Quaker costume.

FIGURE 213.—A gown of very rich brocade, blue on the surface and green underneath, with a narrow stripe of green at regular intervals and a running vine pattern of small bright flowers and leaves between. It is arranged over a quilted petticoat of blue satin. This gown is made without a Watteau plait, but has the long sweeping train so fashionable in the latter part of George II's reign, 1750-1760. The sleeves are longer than in the earlier part of the reign and reach below the elbows. The style of this gown is copied from one in the Art Museum in Boston, and the colouring from a piece of brocade which was part of a gown worn by Mrs. Michael Gratz, *née* Miriam Simon, of Lancaster, Pennsylvania. The hair is copied from a contemporary portrait.

FIGURE 214.—A suit of uncut velvet worn by Robert Livingston, third Lord of Clermont Manor on the Hudson, New York. Coat and breeches are of the same material covered with a small design in soft shades of red and green, which does not show in the picture but gives a pinkish hue to the costume. The long waistcoat is of corded silk, a shade darker than the coat and embroidered by hand with a very graceful flowered pattern in which the soft red and green of the suit prevail. It is a very beautiful costume in material, colour, and design. The buttons are covered with velvet, and the coat and waistcoat are lined throughout with white corded silk and the knee breeches with heavy swanskin (Canton flannel), while the pockets of the latter are lined with white kid. Small straps of the velvet fasten with buckles below the knee.

FIGURE 215 shows the back of Figure 204, a charming specimen of the fashionable Watteau of George II's reign. Between the nosegays of lilac, yellow, and red flowers, a small brocaded bunch of daisies is seen in the original material, of the same colours as the silk (soft fawn), too small to be reproduced in the picture, but adding to the rich effect of the costume.

to the barber's block like a wig to be dressed, leaving the lady at home to pursue other objects, thus producing a grand reformation

FIGURE 216.

Beaver Hat and Short Cloak, Middle of Eighteenth Century.   Reigns of George II and III.

in the economy of time and an exemption from former durance vile.

"When the ladies first began to lay off their cumbrous hoops, they supplied their place with successive succedaneums, such as these, to wit: First came bishops—a thing stuffed or padded with horse hair; then succeeded a smaller affair under the name of *Cue de Paris*, also padded with horse hair. How it abates our admiration to contemplate the lovely sex as bearing a roll of horse hair or a cut of cork under their garments! Next they supplied their place with silk or calimanco, or russell thickly quilted and inlaid with wool, made into petticoats; then these were supplanted by a substitute of half a dozen petticoats. No wonder such ladies needed fans in a sultry summer, and at a time when parasols were unknown, to keep off the solar rays!"

Other articles of female wear are mentioned: "Once they wore a 'skimmer hat' made of a fabric which shone like silver tinsel; it was of a very small flat crown and big brim, not unlike the late Leghorn flats. Another hat, not unlike it in shape, was made of woven horse hair woven in flowers, and called 'horse hair bonnets,' an article which might again be usefully introduced for children's wear as an enduring hat for long service." Watson had himself seen what was called a "bath bonnet," date unknown, "made of black satin, and so constructed to lie in folds that it could be sat upon like a *chapeau bras*," and observes that "it would be a good article for travelling ladies!" This and the "musk melon bonnet," evidently a modification of the calash, used before the Revolution, had numerous whalebone stiffeners in the crown, set an inch apart in parallel lines and presenting ridges to the eye, between the bones. The "pumpkin hood" was made in the same manner with wadding between the ridges for cold weather.

"A 'calash bonnet,'" according to Watson, "was usually formed of green silk; it was worn abroad covering the head, but when in rooms it could fall back in folds like the springs of a calash or gigtop; to keep it over the head it was drawn up by a cord always held in the

FIGURE 217.

FIGURE 218.

FIGURE 219.

FIGURE 220.

Sophie B. Steel.
pinx.

223

REIGN OF GEORGE III
1760-1776

FIGURE 217.—Back view of the beautiful suit owned by Robert Livingston of Clermont, third Lord of the Manor, of which a front view is given in Figure 231. The powdered hair is tied in a black silk bag under the black ribbon bow—a fashion seen in many portraits of the time.

FIGURE 218.—Back view of the white satin gown in Figure 230. Like the blue lutestring (Figure 228), it is made with deep pointed bodice on to which the skirt is gathered with numerous small plaits. A diagram of this style of bodice is given on page 218. The elaborate powdered coiffure is copied from a contemporary picture. (1760.)

FIGURE 219.—A simple everyday costume of a young lady, 1770-1776, made of flowered chintz or dimity looped over a quilted petticoat. The frilled cap is of the fashion called "palisade," worn over a "fashionable head" too complicated to be arranged every morning.

FIGURE 220 represents an elderly man of business in a coat of strong fustian over nankeen breeches. This is a characteristic suit of the period from 1770 to 1790, and with the exception of the hat, which could be unlooped, was the costume of members of the Society of Friends to the end of the eighteenth century. The picture is taken from a suit worn by Mr. Joseph Johnson of Germantown.

hand of the wearer." When the calash was at the height of popularity, however, it appeared in many varieties of material and colour. I have seen mention of a pink dimity calash and of a flowered Persian worn over high heads, without disturbing the erection, and blue and brown calashes may be seen in the Museums in Philadelphia.

"The wagon bonnet, always of black silk, was an article exclusively in use among the Friends. When on the head it was thought to look not unlike the top of the Jersey wagons, having a pendent piece of the silk hanging from the bonnet and covering the shoulders. The only straw worn was that called the 'straw bee-hive bonnet,' worn generally by old people." Interesting specimens of bonnets may be seen in the Museum of Memorial Hall, Philadelphia, ranging from the calash and the pumpkin hood to the wagon bonnet mentioned by Mr. Watson, but the exact date of the latter is hard to determine.

Mrs. Gummere, in a very brilliant book on a very sombre subject, published recently,* says: "It has been with the Quaker bonnet as with every other garment the Quaker has ever worn—the cut originated in that centre of all ideas of fashion, and the abode of taste, Paris, while the expression of Quakerism lay simply in the absence of any superfluous adornments. In this one idea lies the secret of Quaker dress." Doubtless the author is right, but who can look upon even a picture of a Quaker bonnet without sighing for the superfluous adornments?

Although no rigid laws had been passed by the Quakers forbidding the use of gay colours, members of the sect were recommended to abstain from them, and soft grays, dull drabs, sage greens, and sombre browns were so generally worn by Friends that they were thenceforth associated with them. We read in many instances of the careful pains even the strictest of Friends took to match these solemn colours. Figure 250 is the portrait of a beautiful Quaker lady in a gown of sage silk.

* The Quaker, a Study in Costume.

"The Quaker simplicity of garb was but another name for the finest and costliest raiment that could be produced, the richest sombre coloured silks, the most delicate lawn, the finest broadcloth. A modest splendour which cost more thought and care than the ordinary habili ments which were denounced by the sect as pomps and vanities of the world," says that gentle historian, Mrs. Oliphant. But the use of sheer cambric in caps, handkerchiefs, and aprons gave to the dress of the Quaker maids and matrons a dainty air of unpretentious re finement for which they have ever been distinguished.

The cape in Figure 232 is of pale gray silk lined with white cam bric. It is taken from an original garment of about 1775. The cap is of finest linen cambric sewed with the invisible stitches of early days and worn by that distinguished colonial dame of Pennsylvania, Deborah Norris Logan, at the close of the eighteenth century. The combination may at first seem an anachronism, but in point of fact the Society of Friends followed with reluctant footsteps the changes of fashion, and while caps of the style of Figure 232 were probably worn at the close of the century and even later, the cape is of a shape worn by Quaker dames as early as 1775 and as late as 1800.

A delightful instance of departure from Quaker costume on an especial occasion is thus told by Mrs. Gummere:*

"A Quaker Wedding.

"In the month of May, 1771, Isaac Collins of Burlington, New Jersey, married Rachel Budd, of Philadelphia, at the 'Bank Meeting' in that city. His wedding dress was a coat of peach blossom cloth, the great skirts of which had outside pockets. It was lined through out with quilted white silk. The large waistcoat was of the same material. He wore small clothes, knee buckles, silk stockings, and pumps. A cocked hat surmounted the whole.

"The bride, who is described as 'lovely in mind and person,'

* The Quaker, a Study in Costume.

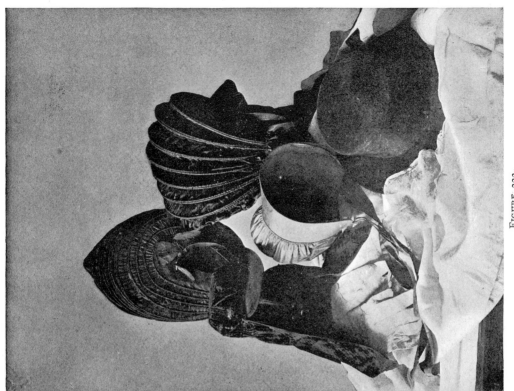

FIGURE 222.

FIGURE 221.

EIGHTEENTH CENTURY.

FIGURE 221.—Two pairs of stays
Corded linen breeches
Leather stock
Bead bag and embroidered purse
Quilted petticoat
Three pairs of spectacles
One silk shoe.
FIGURE 222.—Two silk calashes
One velvet riding-cap with visor
One Quaker bonnet
One beaver hat
Two pairs of men's gloves
Embroidered muslin skirt

wore a light blue brocade, shoes of the same material, with very

high heels, not larger
than a gold dollar, and
sharply pointed at the
toes." In Figure 263 a
photograph of the orig-
inal shoes worn on that
occasion is given. "Her
dress was in the fashion
of the day, consisting of
a robe, long in the back,
with a large hoop. A
short blue bodice, with
a white satin stomacher
embroidered in colours,
had a blue cord laced
from side to side. On
her head she wore a
black mode hood lined
with white silk, the large
cape extending over the
shoulders. Upon her re-
turn from meeting after
the ceremony, she put on
a thin white apron of
ample dimensions, tied in
front with a large blue
bow."

FIGURE 223.
Lady in Capuchin with Fur Trimmings and Muff,
1780. Reign of George III.

Cloaks for outdoor
wear were used with
some changes of form, under the successive names of "pompadours,"
"Roquelaures," "cardinals," and "capuchins," throughout the eight-

eenth century. "Umbrellas to keep off the rain were not known at this time, but a few people used quitasols, which were about the size of the present parasols. They were of oiled muslin, and were of various colours. They must, however, have been but rare, as they never appear in any advertisements," according to Mr. Watson, who is also responsible for the following statement:

"In those days dress was discriminative and appropriate, both as regards the season and the character of the wearer. Ladies never wore the same dress at work as on visits; they sat at home or went out in the morning in chintz, and brocades, satins and mantuas were reserved for evening wear or for dinner parties. Robes or negligées, as they were called (Figures 192, 204, and 207), were often worn in full dress. Muslin gowns were not worn at all."

During the reign of George III, women of fashion began to wear their hair high again. In 1775, it was worn absurdly high, rolled over a framework of wire and surmounted by a large cap, turban, or hat with tall feathers; this fashion was never quite as exaggerated in the Colonies as in England, but many ancestral portraits testify to its popularity. For instance, the portraits of Mrs. Duer and Mrs. Izard in "The Republican Court" show this extreme of fashion.

Virginia was always one of the gayest of the Colonies. In the Diary of Philip Fithian, this description of festivities in 1774 is given:

"A Virginia Ball and Virginia Belles (1774).

"Tuesday, January 18. Mrs. Carter and the young ladies came home last night from the ball, and brought with them Mrs. Lane. They tell us there were upward of seventy at the ball; forty-one ladies; that the company was genteel; and that Colonel Harry Lee, from Dumfries, and his son Harry, who was with me at college, were also there. Mrs. Carter made this an argument, and it was a strong one indeed, that to-day I must dress and go with her to the ball. She added also that she desired my company in the evening when

FIGURE 224.

FIGURE 225.

FIGURE 224.—Portrait of Mr. and Mrs. Ralph Izard of the Carolina Colony. (By Copley, 1774.)

FIGURE 225.—Portrait of the West family.   (By Benjamin West, 1799.)

she should come home, as it would be late. After considering a while, I consented to go, and was dressed.

"We set away from Mr. Carter's at two. Mrs. Carter and the young ladies went in the chariot, Mrs. Lane in a chair, and myself on horseback.

"As soon as I had handed the ladies out I was saluted by Parson Smith. I was introduced into a small room where a number of gentlemen were playing cards (the first game I have seen since I left home)

FIGURE 226.

FIGURE 227.

Calashes, 1765.

to lay off my boots, riding-coat, &c. Next I was directed into the dining-room to see young Mr. Lee. He introduced me to his father.

"With them I conversed till dinner, which came in at half after four. The ladies dined first, when some good order was preserved. When they rose, each nimblest fellow dined first. The dinner was as elegant as could be well expected when so great an assembly were to be kept for so long a time. For drink, there were several sorts of wine, good lemon punch, toddy, cider, porter, &c.

"About seven, the ladies and gentlemen began to dance in the ball-room,—first, minuets, one round; second, jigs; third, reels; and last of all, country-dances. They struck up marches occasionally. The music was a French-horn and two violins.

"The ladies were dressed gay and splendid, and when dancing, their silks and brocades rustled and trailed behind them."

The minuet, from the French *menuet*,—so called from the small steps taken in it,—was invented in France about the middle of the seventeenth century, and throughout the eighteenth century was the favourite dance of all ceremonious occasions in the Colonies as well as in Europe.

The same diary also contains valuable items of contemporary costume and allusions to the fashionable deportment taught to the young ladies of the Colonies and absolutely essential to the proper setting off of the costumes then in vogue.

"Friday, June 24.—To-day Mr. Christian's* dance takes place here. He came before breakfast. Miss Jenny Washington came also, and Miss Priscilla Hale while we were at breakfast. Miss Washington is about seventeen. She has not a handsome face, but is neat in her dress, of an agreeable size, well proportioned, and has an easy winning manner. She is not forward to begin a conversation, yet when spoken to she is extremely affable, without assuming any girlish affectation, or pretending to be overcharged with wit. She has but lately had an opportunity for instruction in dancing yet she moves with propriety when she dances a minuet, and without any flirts or capers when she dances a reel or country-dance. Her dress is rich and well-chosen, but not tawdry, nor yet too plain. She appears to-day in a chintz cotton gown with an elegant blue stamp, a sky-blue silk quilt (Figure 213), and spotted apron. Her hair is a light brown, it was craped up, with two rolls at each side, and on the top was a small cap of beautiful gauze and rich lace, with an artificial flower interwoven. Her person and carriage at a small

* Mr. Christian was evidently a dancing master.

FIGURE 228.

FIGURE 229.

FIGURE 230.

FIGURE 231.

REIGN OF GEORGE III
1760-1776

FIGURE 228.—A house costume of light blue lutestring. The bodice is cut low in front and finished with tabs below the waist. The sleeves fit close to the arm and curve around the elbow; they are finished with a graduated ruffle of lace. This gown was worn by Mrs. St. Clair about 1760. The muslin cap and fichu are taken from a contemporary portrait.

FIGURE 229.—A suit of dark satin with a waistcoat of white satin embroidered in colours, which originally belonged to Robert Livingston of Clermont (third Lord of the Manor). The hair, copied from a contemporary portrait, is powdered and tied with a long black ribbon. The shoe-buckles in the picture are copied from a very beautiful Colonial pair of graduated stones (paste) set in wrought silver; unfortunately, the graceful design cannot be seen in the reproduction. These buckles belonged to Mrs. Jonathan Dickinson Sergeant, of Philadelphia.

FIGURE 230.—The white satin wedding gown of Mrs. St. Clair, who was married in 1760. It is made like the blue lutestring (Figure 228) and trimmed with lace in festooned flounces, or falbalas, edged with silver gimp according to the prevalent fashion. The powdered hair is copied from a contemporary portrait by Copley. A back view of this gown is given in Figure 218. The blue dress is just like it. These gowns are still owned by a direct descendant of Mrs. St. Clair.

FIGURE 231.—A suit of uncut velvet with waistcoat of quilted pale blue satin trimmed with silver galloon. The original costume belonged to Robert Livingston of Clermont, and is of a beautiful soft colour, a sort of warm old rose.

All the costumes on this plate were lent for the purpose of reproduction by descendants of the original owners.

distance resemble not a little my much respected Laura. But on close examination her features are something masculine, while those of Laura are mild and delicate. Mr. Christian very politely requested me to open the dance by stepping a minuet with this amiable girl. I excused myself by assuring him that I never was taught to dance. Miss Hale is about fourteen, and is a slim and silent girl. She has black eyes and black hair and a good set of eyebrows, which are esteemed in Virginia essential to beauty. She looks innocent of every human failing, does not speak five words in a week, and I dare say from her carriage that her modesty is perfect. She is dressed in a white Holland gown, cotton, quilted very fine, a lawn apron, has her hair craped up, and on it a small tuft of ribbon for a cap. She is but just initiated into the school, and only hobbles yet. Once I saw her standing. I rose immediately and begged her to accept my chair. She answered most kindly, 'Sir, I thank you.' That was all I could extract from this wonder of the sex for the two days she staid, and I seemed to have an equal share in the favours of her conversation. So that in describing the mental faculties of Miss

FIGURE 232.
Quaker Cape and Cap, 1780.

Hale, it is sufficient to say that I think she is far removed from most of the foibles of women. Some time after these, came Colonel Lee's chariot with five young misses."

In England, in the first half of the eighteenth century, it was the custom of the noble patrons of the different theatrical companies to bestow their cast-off suits upon their favourite actors.   As national distinction was utterly disregarded in dramatic productions of the day, and histories of costume were unknown, the heroes and heroines of classic lore, as well as of Shakespeare, were dressed in the fashionable garb of the passing hour.   We hear of even Garrick appearing as Othello in a regimental suit of George II's body-guard, with a flowering Ramilie wig; and of Barry in the same rôle (in 1765) dressed in a full suit of gold-laced scarlet, a small cocked hat, and silk stockings.

More striking still must have been the Othello of James Quin in a large powdered major wig and a blackened face.   Fancy Lady Macbeth in a hoop eight yards in circumference, which, as we read, was the costume Mrs. Yates assumed in the part.

Barton Booth, an actor of note in the early part of the century, took pains to encase the soles of his shoes in felt when acting the ghost in Hamlet, but Pope records of his impersonation of Addison's Cato in 1712:

> " Booth enters, hark the universal peal!
> But has he spoken? not a syllable.
> What shook the stage and made the people stare?
> Cato's long wig, flowr'd gown and lacquer'd chair."

Mrs. Cibber as Juliet, in a white satin gown with an enormous hoop, does not seem to have been thought unseemly attired.

Even John Kemble, the author of many reformations in stage effects, appeared as Hamlet in a modern court dress of rich black velvet with deep ruffles, with the pendent riband of an order on his breast, and mourning sword and buckles; his hair was powdered and, in the scenes of feigned distraction, flowed dishevelled in front over his shoulders.*

The first theatre in America was at Williamsburg, Virginia, which was inaugurated by the London Company of Comedians under the management of Mr. Lewis Hallam in 1752.   The play was "The

* Annals of the English Stage, by Dr. Doran.

FIGURE 233.

FIGURE 234.

FIGURE 235.

FIGURE 236.

FIGURE 237.

FIGURE 238.

FIGURE 240.

FIGURE 239.

FIGURE 241.

FIGURE 233.—Reticule made of the court gown worn by Mrs. Carroll of Carrollton, Maryland.

FIGURE 234.—Gloves made of soft doeskin, embroidered with flowers in colour. Worn by Mrs. Wentworth, of New Hampshire, about 1717.

FIGURE 235.—Bead reticule and paste buckles, about 1770.

FIGURE 236.—A bonnet of muslin made over reeds, worn about 1780.

FIGURE 237.—Crêpe shawl with flowers printed in colour, late eighteenth century.

FIGURE 238.—Linen pocket embroidered in colour, worn by Mrs. Wodkind of Massachusetts (1752). (From the original in the Essex Museum, Salem.)

FIGURE 239.—Paste shoe buckles worn by Elisha Lawrence, Esq., New Jersey, in 1720. Silver spoons and steel chatelaine owned by Mrs. Edward Pennington of Philadelphia, in 1754. Snuff-box of conch-shell with the Pennington coat-of-arms engraved on the lid and the date 1777. The lady's snuff-box is also of conch-shell. The monogram E. L. C. (Elizabeth Le Comte) is engraved on the silver cover.

FIGURE 240.—Slipper of green and white striped taffeta, worn by Mrs. Samuel Appleton, of Ipswich, Massachusetts, in 1758.

FIGURE 241.—Fan painted by Gamble, 1771.

Merchant of Venice." The unfortunate Signor Antonio probably dressed in a ruffled shirt, knee buckles, long coat, and buttoned waist-coat, with a powdered wig, after the manner of Mr. Clarke at the Haymarket Theatre in London; while Shylock stood whetting his wicked knife in a very long-tailed coat and a falling band of linen, in imitation of Macklin, who was delighting English audiences with his representation of the part about that time. Opera glasses came into use early in this century (eighteenth).

Miss Sarah Eves, of Philadelphia, remarks in her journal (January 5, 1773): "The poor Doctor thought his clothes were not good enough to wait upon us in, therefore he delays his visit until he gets fitted up in the Macaronia taste I suppose." This was the popular name for a dandy at the time Miss Eves wrote, the Macaronis being a class of fops in London who introduced a particular style of dress in 1772. The name originated in the following manner. A number of young men of fashion who had visited Italy formed an association called "The Macaroni Club," in contradistinction to the "Beefsteak Club" of London. As the fashion of this time was to wear long waistcoats and coats with wide and heavy skirts, they wore theirs exceedingly short, and the whole dress of very close cut. Their wigs were remarkable for an enormous club, or turned-up bunch of hair behind. They had little cocked hats, swords dangling about their heels at the end of long straps, and sticks with large tassels. Their stockings were covered with coloured spots and their dress generally piebald in the same manner.

In 1773 an alteration took place in their dress, consisting chiefly in elevating the hair to an enormous height, with large curls ranging on each side of it, and in wearing immense bunches of flowers at the breast. They attracted much attention during the few years of their existence.*

* Fairholt's English Dress.

"Ye belles and beaus of London town,
   Come listen to my ditty;
The muse, in prancing up and down,
   Has found out something pretty.
With little hat, and hair dress'd high,
   And whip to ride a pony,
If you but take a right survey,
   Denotes a Macaroni.

"Five pounds of hair they wear behind
   The ladies to delight, O!
Their senses give unto the wind,
   To make themselves a fright, O!
Thus fashion who does e'er pursue
   I think a simple tony,
For he's a fool, say what you will,
   Who is a Macaroni."

This ballad was popular in the streets of London at this time, and was probably sung by the English soldiers in the Colonies. It suggests a close connection with the national air, "Yankee Doodle," which so many writers have attempted to explain without, however, settling the vexed question.

"Yankee Doodle came to town
   Riding on a pony
With a feather in his hat,
   Upon a Macaroni"

can be traced to the time of Charles I, and has been ascribed to the pen of a cavalier poet in derision of Cromwell. But this version does not seem any more palpable than other explanations, and "a feather in his hat" is not suggestive of Cromwell.

According to the Century Dictionary, it is said to have been first applied in the Colonies to a Maryland company of militia distinguished for its showy uniform.

The Lydia Fisher jig, sung to the same tune, runs:

"Lucy Locket lost her pocket
   Lydia Fisher found it,
Not a bit of money in it
   Only broidery round it."

We give a picture of a beautifully embroidered linen pocket, made by a colonial lady, which would be well worth finding even as empty as that of Lucy Locket (Figure 238).   This pocket was intended to be worn outside the dress, as the careful needlework proclaims. The original is in the Essex Institute at Salem, Massachusetts.   It was worked and worn by Mrs. Samuel Wodkind about 1750.   A similar pocket made of printed cotton is in the Museum of Memorial Hall, Philadelphia.

According to Fairholt, the Macaroni style of costume was quite the rage with the town (London).   Everything that was fashionable was *à la* Macaroni.   Even the clergy had their wigs combed, their clothes cut, "their delivery refined," *à la* Macaroni.   The shop windows were filled with caricatures and other prints of this tribe; there were portraits of "Turf Macaronis," "Parade Macaronis," "Macaroni Parsons," "Macaroni Scholars," and a variety of other species of this extended genus.   Ladies set up for female Macaronis. Their costume was scarcely so distinctive as that of the men; it was chiefly known by the high head-dress, large bunch of flowers, and an exceedingly wide and spreading sleeve hanging with deep ruffles from the elbow.

> "No ringlets now adorn the face,
>   Dear Nature yields to art,
> A lofty head-dress must take place,
>   Abroad in ev'ry part.
> Patch, paint, perfume, immodest stare,
>   You find is all the fashion.
> Alas, I'm sorry for the fair,
>   Who thus disgrace the nation."*

I have not met with a single notice of a female Macaroni in the Colonies.

The English country people of the eighteenth century were rather picturesque in costume.   When dressed for church or a country fair,

* Fairholt's Satirical Poems on Costume.

the young women wore flowered chintzes with muslin kerchiefs and aprons. The short skirts showed clocked stockings, usually of a bright colour. Their shoes were strong but not clumsy in pattern, and the little muslin caps they wore under their hats were extremely pretty and becoming.

On these occasions the men wore breeches to the knees, coats of homespun, waistcoats usually of some contrasting colour, buckled shoes, and cocked hats.

When at work, the damsels generally wore short skirts of a coarse woolen material tied round the waist over short sacques of calico, with kerchiefs about the neck. (Figures 247 and 259.)

The men wore knit jerkins or blouses of coarse linen, such as oznaburg or dowlas, leather boots pulled up over coarse woolen breeches, and Monmouth caps. Homespun linsey-woolsey was much in use for both sexes.

The domestics of a household were always clothed by their masters. A letter of Mistress Hannah Penn, written in 1700, requests that "ten yards of frieze for seryants and some four or six skirts" be sent by barge from Philadelphia to Pennsbury, where she was preparing for her husband's return. The following items tell us what Washington ordered from England for the servants at Mt. Vernon in 1759:

> 8 doz. pairs of plaid hose sorted,
> 4 " Monmouth caps,
> 25 yds. broadcloth to cost about 7s. 6d.
> 15 " coarse double thick broadcloth,
> 6 " scarlet broadcloth,
> 30 " red shalloon,
> 12 doz. white washed waistcoat buttons,
> 20 " " " coat "
> 40 yds. coarse jean or fustian for summer frocks for negro servants,
> 1½ doz. pairs strong coarse thread hose fit for negro servants,
> 1 " pairs coarse shoes and knee buckles,
> 1 postillion cap,
> 6 castor beavers.

The livery worn by his servants was of scarlet faced with white, the colours of the Washington coat-of-arms.

The following notices from newspapers of 1740 to 1772, show the usual dress of servants and slaves in the Colonies:

"Now in the custody of Thomas Smith, Sheriff of Cape County, a run-away negro man, who goes by the name Jupiter Hazard, is about twenty-seven years of age, but very black, of a middle size and well built. Had on when taken up, a flannel shirt, leather breeches with a fob in the waistband, shoes and stockings, both very good, the stockings of a blue colour, bathmetal buckles, a good felt hat and worsted cap. He speaks English like a country born negro who has lived some time among the Dutch.

"He had a bundle with him which contained two white shirts, a dimity jacket and breeches, a white handkerchief, a linen cap, a pocket-book with four dollars in it, and a pair of silver knee buckles marked N. S."

"Ran away on the 20th from Nathan Watson, of Mount Holly, an Irish servant man, named Christopher Cooney, a short well-set fellow, about twenty-six years of age, of a pale complexion, short brown curled hair, had lost one of his under fore teeth, and has had his right leg broke, and walks with his toe turned outward. Had on when he went away, a new castor hat, a red great coat, a light-coloured fustian coat and jacket, new copper coloured broadcloth breeches, lined with leather, new black and white yarn stockings, old shoes, newly soled. He was some time past a hostler at Jonathan Thomas's, in Burlington. Whoever takes up and secures said servant, so that his master may have him again, shall have forty shillings reward, and reasonable charges, paid by

NATHAN WATSON."

From the "Pennsylvania Gazette," 1773:

"Ran away from the subscriber, an English servant girl named Christina Ball, but calls herself Caty for shortness, about twenty years of age, brown skinned, black eyes, and hair lately cut short, a little stoop-shouldered. Her cloathes are very ordinary, a brown cloth petticoat, other coarse shifts and a striped calico short gown; any other cloathes uncertain. Whosoever takes her up, and confines her in any gaol within twenty miles of this city shall have twenty shillings reward, and three pounds if taken up at any distance further, paid by

HENRY NEILL."

The advertisements in the early newspapers in America are a valuable contribution to the history of costume. I will give a few from the leading papers of different parts of the Colonies early in the eighteenth century.

Among quaint and curious advertisements, we find this one of Thomas Peck's, advertising goods sold by him at the Hatt & Beaver, Merchant's Row, in Boston.

"A fresh assortment of Linen Linings, suitable for Beaver, Beaverett, Castor, and Felt Hatts, Tabby ditto, Mohair Lupings, Silk Braid ditto, flatt and round silk lace and Frogs for Button Lupes, plain and sash Bands,

FIGURE 242.
Typical Dress of English Country Girl, 1780. (End of the Eighteenth Century.)

workt and plain Buttons, black Thread, Gold and Silver Chain, yellow and white Buttons, hard and light Brushes, Velures, Cards, large and small bowstrings, Looping Needles, Verdigrees and Coperas, a good assortment of mens and boys felt Hatts, Castor ditto.—He likewise sells logwood."

From the "New York Gazette" of May 9, 1737, we learn of a thief's stealing "one gray Hair wig, one Horse Hair Wig, not worn five times, marked V. S. E., one brown Natural Wig, one old wig of Goats Hair put in buckle." "Buckle" meant "to curl," and a wig was "in buckle" when it was rolled on papers for curling. Other advertisements tell of the dress-stuffs of the time with the weird names chilloes, betelles, deribands, tapsiels, that were familiar enough over the shop counters in colonial New York.

Here is another curious old advertisement:

"May 11, 1761. Imported by John and Thomas Stevenson and to be sold at their shop at the *Sign of the Stays*, opposite the South Side of the Town-House, Boston, at the very lowest prices, Viz.

"Lawns of all sorts, Strip'd and Flowr'd kenting Handkerchiefs, cotton and linen ditto; silk and gauze ditto; Cambricks, Calicoes and printed Linens—white and coloured Threads; silk, worsted, cotton and thread stockings, Women's silk and worsted Mitts—Broad-Cloths; German Serge—Thicksets; Fustians, Jeans, Pillows and Dimities—Broglios, Dorsateens, Venetian Poplins, flowr'd and plain Damasks, Prussianets, Serpentines, Tammies, strip'd stuff, Camblets, Callimancoes, Shalloons and Buckrams,—Worsted Caps, Garters, Needles and Pins—white brown and strip'd Hollands—white and checked Linnen Diaper, Bed-Ticks, Tartans, Plaids Breeches and Jackets Stocking Patterns, Cotton and silk gowns, Stock Tapes, Leather Breeches, Mens' and Women's Leather Shoes, &c., &c."

The following is also of interest:

"Just imported from London, and to be sold by
"DANIEL BOYER, Jeweller,
"At his Shop opposite the Governor's in Boston.
Best Brilliant and Cypher Earing and Button Stones, Binding

Wire, Brass and Iron ditto, Brilliant and cypher ring stones, Brass stamps, Garnets, Amethysts, and topaz. Buckle and ring brushes, Ring and buckle sparks, Money scales and weights, Locket stones & Cyphers, Small sheers & Plyers, Ruby and white foyle, Screw dividers, Coral beads, Blow pipes, Coral for Whistles, Shoe and knee Chapes, Draw plates, Moulding sand, Rough and smooth files, Crucibles and plack pots, Borax and Salt-Petre, Pommice and Rotten-stone, &c.

Where also may be had, some sorts of Jewellers and Goldsmith work, cheap for cash."

That Paul Revere was at one time a dentist, we learn from the following startling advertisement in the "Boston Gazette," December 19, 1768:

"Whereas many Persons are so unfortunate as to lose their Fore-Teeth by Accident, and otherways, to their great Detriment, not only in looks, but speaking both in Public and Private:—This is to inform all such that they may have them replaced with artificial ones, that looks as well as the Natural, and answers the end of speaking to all Intents, by Paul Revere, Goldsmith, near the head of Dr. Clarke's Wharf, Boston.

"All Persons who have had false teeth fixt by Mr. John Baker, Surgeon-Dentist, and they have got loose (as they will in time) may have them fastened by the above who learnt the Method of fixing them from Mr. Baker."

Here is an invoice of goods imported in 1771:

"Imported in the Neptune (Capt. Binney) and to be sold by Daniel Parker, Goldsmith, At his Shop near the Golden-Ball, Boston,

"An Assortment of Articles in the Goldsmith's and Jewellers Way, viz. brilliant and cypher'd Button and Earing Stones of all Sorts, Locket Stones, cypher'd Ring Stones, Brilliant Ring Sparks, Buckle Stones, Garnetts, Amethysts, Topaz, and Sapphire Ring Stones, neat Stone Rings sett in Gold, some with Diamond Sparks, Stone Buttons in Silver, by the Card, black ditto in Silver, best Sword Blades, Shoe and Knee Chapes of all sizes."

Another invoice by the same ship contains the following list:

"Broad Cloths, German Serges, Bearskins, Beaver Coating, Half Thick, red Shagg, 8 qr. Blankets, Shalloons, Tammies, Durants, Calimancoes, worsted Damasks, strip'd and plain Camblets, strip'd Swanskins, Flannell, Manchester Velvet, Women's ditto, Bombazeen, Allopeen, colour'd Duffels, Hungarians, Dimothy, Crimson and green China, Cotton Check, worsted and Hair Plush, Men's and Women's Hose, worsted caps, mill'd ditto, black Tiffany, Women's and Children's Stays, cotton Romalls, printed Linnen Handkerchiefs, black Gauze ditto, Bandanoes, Silk Lungee Romalls, Cambricks, Lawns, Muslins, Callicoes, Chintz, Buckrams, Gulick Irish and Tandem Holland, Men's and Women's Kid and Lamb Gloves, black and white Bone Lace, Capuchin Silk and Fringe, Gartering, Silk and Cotton Laces, strip't Ginghams, Yellow Canvas, Diaper, Damask Table Cloths and Napkins, Bedtick, Garlix, Soletare necklaces and Earings, Tapes, Women's Russel Shoes, sewing Silk, Looking Glasses, Ticklenburg, English and Russia Duck, English and India Taffety, Grograms, English and India Damask, Padusoys, Lutestrings, black and white Satin, Rich Brocade, Gauze Caps and Ruffles, Shades and handsome Silk Cloakes, &c., &c., &c."

Of interest, too, is this advertisement from the "Pennsylvania Gazette," 1773:

"JOHN MARIE

"Taylor from Paris.

Humbly acquaints the Gentry and Public that he has taken a house in Gray's Alley, between Walnut and Chestnut Streets, the fourth door from Second Street, and has provided good workmen. He has had the pleasure of pleasing some of the most respectable gentlemen in London, and hopes by the strictest attention and most particular punctuality to give general satisfaction.

"N. B. At said Maries', gentlemen's cloaths of all colours cleaned, all spots taken out, and made equal to new, without the tedious and disadvantageous method of ripping or washing them."

The following notice is rather amusing:

"WILLIAM LANG,
"Wig-Maker and Hair Dresser,
Hereby informs the Public, that he has hired a Person from Europe,
by whose assistance he is now enabled, in the several Branches of
his Business, to serve his good customers, and all others, in the most
genteel and polite Tastes that are at present in Fashion in England
and America. In particular, WIGS made in any Mode whatever,
such as may grace and become the most important Heads, whether
those of Judges, Divines, Lawyers, or Physicians, together with
all those of an inferior Kind, so as exactly to suit their Respective
Occupations and Inclinations. HAIR-DRESSING, for Ladies and Gentlemen, performed in the most elegant and newest Taste—Ladies
in a particular Manner, shall be attended to, in the nice, easy, genteel and polite Construction of ROLLS, such as may tend to raise
their Heads to any Pitch they may desire, also French Curls, made
in the neatest Manner. He gives Cash for Hair."

In the Museum at Memorial Hall, Philadelphia, are some jute
braids once worn under nets by women of the Colonies.

The following notices from various newspapers in different parts
of the Colonies, appearing at the dawn of the Revolution, prove
that the people of that day were not wholly given up to the vanities
of the world.

This, from a New England paper about 1768, is a proof of
the patriotic spirit of the dames of colonial days:

"In a large circle of very agreeable ladies in this Town, it was
unanimously agreed to lay aside the Use of Ribbons, &c., &c.,
&c. for which there has been so great a Resort to Milliners in times
past. It is hoped that this resolution will be followed by others
of the Sex throughout the Province—How agreeable they will appear in their native Beauty, stript of these Ornaments from the prevailing Motive of Love to their Country."

Another notice reads:

"We must after all our Efforts, depend greatly upon the Female
Sex for the introduction of Economy among us; and those who

have the Pleasure of an Acquaintance with them assure us that their utmost Aid will not be wanting.

"So strong is the Disposition of the Inhabitants of this Town to take of the Manufacturers that come from the Country Towns, especially Womens and Childrens Winter Apparel, that nothing is wanting but an Advertisement where they may be had in Town, which will be taken in, and published by the printers of this Paper gratis." *

Mrs. Caulkins tells us that "with the prospect of war with the Mother Country before them, many of the inhabitants of Boston decided upon a non-importation system, and a non-consumption of articles on which heavy duties were laid. It was the practice then, as it is at this day, in the Colonies as well as in England, to dress in black clothes on mourning occasions. It was decided to discontinue such dresses, and the custom of wearing black on these occasions was generally laid aside; the only sign made use of was a piece of black crape about the hat, which was in use before, and a piece of the same stuff around the arm.

"An agreement to this effect was drawn up and very generally signed by the inhabitants of the town, also by some members of the Council and Representatives. This would affect the sale of English goods, and none were to be purchased except at fixed prices. At the same time another agreement was very extensively signed to eat no lamb flesh during the year. This was to increase the sheep in the country, and consequently to encourage the manufacture of woolen goods, which were imported from England in large quantities.

"The practice of wearing expensive mourning dresses was soon very generally laid aside. It was further proposed 'to give no other gloves than are of the manufacture of the country in lieu of white ones, that are seldom drawn on a second time.' It was suggested

* The days of the Spinning Wheel in New England. Extracts from Colonial Papers.

to the glovers that, 'it might not be amiss if some peculiar mark were put upon them, as a bow and arrow, or pine tree, instead of the usual stitching on the back,' and a great number of the respectable tradesmen of the Town came into a resolution to wear nothing but leather for their working habits. Instead of the rich cloth Roque-laures, even the magistrate and the colonel were satisfied with cloaks of brown camlet lined with green baize, and the greatest lady in the land had her riding hood also of camlet. As the great struggle for liberty gradually overshadowed the land, and the sacrifices necessary to consummate the Revolution began to be appreciated, a decided change took place in regard to dress, amusements, and display. Women discarded all imported ornaments, and arrayed themselves wholly in domestic goods. Fine wool and choice flax were in higher estimation than silk and laces, and the hearts of the patriots as well as the laudations of the poet were given to beauty in homespun garments. Gentlemen also that had been accustomed to appear in society in the daintiest costume, following the example first set by the women, discarded their shining stocks, their cambric ruffles, silk stockings, silver buckles, and other articles of foreign production, and went back to leather shoestrings, checked handkerchiefs, and brown homespun cloth.

FIGURE 243.
Night-rail.

"The encouragement of home manufactures and the rejection of all imported luxuries were regarded as tests of patriotism. Common discourse grew eloquent in praise of plain apparel and Labrador tea. The music of the spinning wheel was pronounced superior to that of the guitar and harpsichord. Homespun parties were given

FIGURE 244.

FIGURE 245.

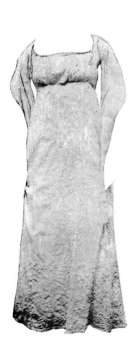

FIGURE 247

FIGURE 246.

FIGURE 248.

FIGURE 244.—A picture of a gown of mauve crêpe, worn about 1795 by Madame Sartori, of New Jersey.

FIGURE 245.—A Watteau sacque, part of the wedding outfit of Mrs. William West, *née* Mary Hodge, of Hope Lodge,. White Marsh, Pennsylvania, in 1752. Fawn-coloured silk, with flowers brocaded in colour.

FIGURE 246.—Picture of a gown of white embroidered muslin, worn in 1790.

FIGURE 247 is a calico short sacque, made without seams on the shoulder, worn in Pennsylvania late in the eighteenth century.

FIGURE 248.—A gown of buff glazed chintz, worn by Madame Chevalier, who came to Philadelphia from Martinique about 1795.

(Photographed from original garments.)

where nothing of foreign importation appeared in the dresses or upon the table. Even wedding festivities were conducted upon patriotic principles."*

After the Battle of Bunker Hill, the colonists everywhere were too seriously engaged to give much attention to the fashions, only the Tories, who persisted in shutting their ears to the spirit of Revolution now rife in the Colonies, and spreading in ever-widening circles about them, continued to import the fashionable novelties from England. On that July morning in 1776 when the Declaration of Independence was read to an eager crowd in the State House yard in Philadelphia, the colonial period of American history came to an end.

AFTER THE REVOLUTION

Philadelphia in the winter of 1777 was the scene of much gaiety. The Tories of the Colony, refusing even then to take a serious view of the situation, amused themselves and the British officers stationed there with Sir William Howe, by a series of dances and routs which had "an appropriate closing" in the famous Mischianza given by Major André and the other members of Howe's staff, probably with the desire to return some of the hospitality received, although Major André himself called it "the most splendid complimentary entertainment ever given by an army to their Commander." The splendour of this ball, preceded by a regatta on the Delaware and the absurd mock tournament, has been so often described that it is not necessary to dwell upon it here. The costumes of the knights and ladies were designed by André as well as the tickets of admission. The original drawing made for the ladies' costumes and one of the tickets for the occasion are in the possession of the Philadelphia Library Company.

During the Revolutionary period (1776–1783), and, in fact, for

* History of Norwich, Connecticut, by Frances Mainwaring Caulkins.

the remaining years of the eighteenth century, patriotic Americans who wished to be very fashionable imported their finery direct from Paris, and French taste prevailed both in furniture and dress.

Depreciation of the currency was one of the many trials entailed by the breach with England.

Speaking of the high prices during the Revolution, Mrs. Bache (Sarah Franklin), in writing to her father, says: "I have been obliged to pay fifteen pounds and fifteen shillings (£15 15s.) for a common calamanco petticoat without quilting, that I once could have got for fifteen shillings. I buy nothing but what I really want, and wore out my silk ones before I got this." (Philadelphia, 1778.)

A few months later she says: "A pair of gloves cost seven dollars. One yard of common gauze twenty-four dollars." *

The hoop skirt, which had held its own for so many years, went out of fashion in 1778.

About this time hair in Paris was worn extravagantly high, but as we do not notice the extreme of this or, in fact, of any of the French styles in the portraits of the day in this country, it seems more than likely that they did not find favour in American eyes.

A letter from Miss Franks, one of the reigning belles in American society, describes a new thing in bonnets to her sister, Mrs. Hamilton, living in the neighbourhood of Philadelphia: "I shall send you a pattern of the newest bonnet; there is no crown, but gauze is raised on wire and punched to a sugar loaf at the top. The lighter the trimming the more fashionable. (Figure 236.)

"Nancy Van Horn and myself employed yesterday morning in trying to dress a rag baby in the fashion, but could not succeed; it shall go, however, as it will in some degree give you an opinion on the subject.

"As to the jacket and the pinning in of the handkerchief, yours you say reaches to the arms. I know it, but it must be pinned up

* Letters to Benjamin Franklin from his Family and Friends.

to the top of the shoulders and quite under the arms as you would a girl's Vandyke (Figure 259).

"The fuller it sets, the handsomer it is thought. Nobody ever sets a handkerchief out in the neck, and a gauze handkerchief is always worn double and the longest that can be got; it is pinned round the throat, as Mrs. Penn always did, and made to set out before like a man's shirt. The ladies here always wear either a pin or a brooch as the men do."*

Chintz gowns were the usual wear for mornings at home, even when admiring British officers were about, for Sally Wister, writing from the country home of her father in 1778, says to Deborah Norris:

"I rose by or near seven, dress'd in my light chintz which is made gown-fashion, Kenton handkerchief and linen apron."† Quilted petticoats were still very fashionable at this time.

Caps of a great variety of shapes were worn on all occasions by the women of this period (Figures 200, 201, 202, and 219). A picture of one of a striking style is given (Figure 202) which was worn by Mrs. Nathaniel Appleton in Massachusetts, in 1784.

Many of the English memoirs and letters mention the "greatcoat," which came into use in 1786, and so pleased Queen Charlotte that she commanded Miss Burney to celebrate it in verse. The result was not remarkable as a poem, but interesting as a note on popular costume.

"The garb of state she inly scorn'd
    Glad from its trappings to be free'd,
She saw thee humble, unadorn'd,
    Quick of attire,—a child of speed.

"Still, then, thrice honour'd Robe! retain
    Thy modest guise, thy decent ease.
Nor let thy favour prove thy bane
    By turning from its fostering breeze."

* Letter written from Long Island to Mrs. Hamilton of Woodlands near Philadelphia.
† Pennsylvania Magazine, vol. vii.

As Miss Burney speaks later of wearing a "white dimity great-coat as usual in the morning," it was probably another form of the negligée, the ancestress of our tea gown (Figure 161). Of the same nature, too, were the gowns which Maria Dickinson mentions; writing of an evening spent at Fairhill, the country-seat of Isaac Norris near Philadelphia, she says:

"It was the custom to disrobe and put on one of the soft warm gowns of green baize provided for each guest," then follows a charming description of innocent gossip over the fire. This letter is dated January 1, 1787.

Quaker dress was at this time noticeable for uniform simplicity of cut and sober colouring, although, as we see by the following extract from a letter, lilac satin was allowed on occasions.

"Phila. 23 Sept. 1783.

"We reached the antiquated building on Front street ere they made their appearance, and being seated very advantageously, we soon had the pleasure of seeing them enter. The bridegroom in a full suit of lead coloured cloth, no powder in his hair, which made him look tolerably plain. The bride was in lilac satin gown and skirt with a white satin cloak and bonnet. It would be needless to enumerate the variety of dresses which made their figures on this occasion. Suffice it to say that all looked much in the smartness especially neighbor G ———, who had procured an enormous large hat which made him the most conspicuous person present" (Figure 220).

For this amusing letter I am indebted to Miss Anne H. Wharton, the author of the delightful biography of Martha Washington, as well as other well-known books on the colonial period.

There are very few portraits of Quakers of this period; two, however, of old ladies in their muslin caps and plain silk gowns are reproduced in Figures 250 and 252. Mrs. Pennington, sister of the Mayor of Philadelphia, wears a dress of sage green under her kerchief. In the original painting the colouring is very attractive. The other portrait is copied from an engraving, but there is great charm in the delicate face. The white sheer cap is fastened with a white ribbon bow and the dress is probably of gray silk (Figure 252).

After the proclamation of peace with Great Britain, while Adams was Minister to the English Court, his wife wrote full accounts of the prevailing styles there for the benefit of her gay friends in the United States. In 1786 she wrote:

"To amuse you then, my dear niece, I will give you an account of the dress of the ladies at the ball of Comte d'Adhemar. There was as great a variety of pretty dresses, borrowed wholly from France, as I have ever seen; and amongst the rest, some with sapphire-blue satin waists, spangled with silver, and laced down the back and seams with silver stripes; white satin petticoats trimmed with black and blue velvet ribbon; an odd kind of head-dress, which they term the 'Helmet of Minerva.' I did not observe the bird of wisdom, however, nor do I know whether those who wore the dress had suitable pretentions to it. 'And pray,' say you 'how were my aunt and cousin dressed?' If it will gratify you to know, you shall hear. Your aunt, then, wore a full-dress court cap without the lappets, in which was a wreath of white flowers, and blue sheafs, two black and blue flat feathers (which cost her half a guinea apiece, but that you need not tell of), three pearl pins, bought for Court, and a pair of pearl earrings, the cost of them—no matter what; less than diamonds, however. A sapphire blue *demi-saison* with a satin stripe, sack and petticoat trimmed with a broad black lace; crape flounce, etc., leaves made of blue ribbon, and trimmed with white floss; wreaths of black velvet ribbon spotted with steel beads, which are much in fashion and brought to such perfection as to resemble diamonds; white ribbon also in the Vandyke style, made up the trimming, which looks very elegant; and a full dress handkerchief, and a bouquet of roses. 'Full gay, I think, for my aunt.' That is true, Lucy, but nobody is old in Europe. I was seated next the Duchess of Bedford, who had a scarlet satin sack and coat, with a cushion full of diamonds, for hair she had none, and is but seventy-six neither. Well now for your cousin: a small white leghorn hat, bound with pink satin ribbon; a steel buckle and band which turned up at the side, and confined a large pink bow; a large bow of the same kind of ribbon behind; a wreath of full blown roses round the crown, and another of buds and roses within-side the hat, which, being placed at the back of the hair, brought the roses to the edge; you see it clearly; one red and black feather with two white ones, completed the head-dress. A gown and coat of Chamberi gauze, with a red satin stripe over a pink waist, and coat flounced with crape, trimmed with broad point and pink ribbon; wreaths of roses across the coat, gauze sleeves and ruffles."

FIGURE 249.
A Riding Habit about 1785 (from a Contemporary Print).

As costumes similar to those described by Mrs. Adams may be

FIGURE 250.

FIGURE 251.

FIGURE 252.

FIGURE 253.

FIGURE 250.—A portrait of Mrs. Pennington, showing the dress of a Quaker lady, 1780.

FIGURE 251.—A portrait of Catharine Schuyler Van Rensselaer, about 1795, showing collarette and cuffs of embroidered muslin. (From the original portrait.)

FIGURE 252.—A portrait of Mrs. Morris, showing the dress of a Quaker lady, 1785.

FIGURE 253.—Portrait of a Dutch lady of the New York Colony about 1765, showing a close-fitting cap and kerchief of sheer lawn edged with lace.

seen in Racinet, Pauquet, and other books of French costume, it is not necessary to give pictures of them here.

The small proportion of the people in America in the latter years of the eighteenth century who could truthfully be called gay lived, of course, in the large towns and cities; the majority lived quietly in the country on their large estates or plantations. The "History of Durham, Connecticut," * describes the home customs as well as the home costumes of rural New England from 1776 to 1800.

"The inhabitants were generally clad in fabrics manufactured, that is made by hand, in the family. There was woolen cloth spun in the house but fulled and dressed at the clothier's shop. There was brown tow cloth, and streaked linen for the males, with bleached linen for shirts. In the summer they generally wore brown tow or linen trowsers and frock; the latter being a kind of over shirt. The fulled cloth worn in the winter time though often coarse was warm. It was sometimes very decent in appearance when made of fine wool, well spun and well dressed. The females were clad in streaked linen or checked linen, on week days, and in chintzes and it may be muslins and silks on the Sabbath. The wedding gowns if not muslin were sometimes brocade or lutestring. Near the close of the last century silk was reeled and woven in Durham. For a considerable time the women wore cloaks of scarlet broadcloth. In the year 1800 women might be seen on the Sabbath riding or walking in the street or sitting at church having on these cloaks; a very comely and comfortable article of dress. Chaises were introduced into Durham about 1775 or '80. For some years there were only three chaises in the town. The people went to meeting on horseback, the women sitting behind the men on pillions. While this fashion continued every house had a horse-block. A characteristic of the houses built in the first half century after the settlement of Durham was the large kitchen fireplace, which in some cases was seven or eight feet in

* By Chauncey Fowler.

width, having sometimes one and sometimes two ovens in it, admitting back logs two or three feet in diameter, and three or four children

FIGURE 254.
A Summer Costume, 1790–1795 (from a Contemporary Portrait).

into the chimney 'corners.' The large and steady fire on the hearth in such a fire-place shone on the faces of many a family circle, gathered together on a winter's evening. To many a large family of eight or ten children the hearth-stone was a load stone to draw them around it. There was knitting for the mother and the elder daughters. There were the slates for the older sons. There were apples and nuts for the younger children, or it may be a lesson in spelling. There were the two volumes from the Town Library for the father and others. There was story telling and song singing. There was the mug of cider enlivened by red pepper against cold. There was the family Bible and there was prayer before retiring to rest. In short, there were family government, family instruction, family amusement, and family religion."

FIGURE 255.

FIGURE 256.

FIGURE 257.

FIGURE 258.

REIGN OF GEORGE III AND FIRST YEARS OF THE REPUBLIC
1778-1790

FIGURE 255.—Copy of a suit worn at the Court of France by William West, Esq., of Philadelphia, in 1778. Coat and breeches are of uncut velvet of a delicate shade of mauve. The waistcoat is of white corded silk with a small embroidered figure scattered over it and a border of flowers in a contrasting colour.

FIGURE 256.—Costume of the prevailing French fashion so popular in the early days of our Republic, 1777-1779. The gown is of flowered silk or lawn looped over paniers; the underskirt of a plain colour, trimmed with a box plaiting of the same. The bodice is pointed sharply in front and laced with a silk cord through eyelet holes. In the back it is cut round about the waist without a point. The hair—still powdered in full dress—in this picture is arranged over a high cushion and finished with an embroidered muslin head-dress arranged like a turban and caught with a bunch of artificial flowers.

FIGURE 257.—Suit of drab cloth lined with green silk; waistcoat of striped silk. From a contemporary print, 1786.

FIGURE 258.—A muslin gown made with flowing skirt and a long-sleeved bodice. Kerchief is very bouffant and tucked into the dress in front. The large hat is of blue silk faced with green and has a soft puffed crown. The hair is powdered lightly after the fashion called "mouse colour," and hangs in the loose curls which were extremely fashionable at the time (1790) both in Europe and America.

On the occasion of the inauguration of Washington as President, in New York, his dress is described as of fine dark brown cloth of American manufacture, with white silk hose, shoes with silver buckles, and a dress sword. The ball which followed brought out all the finery the women of the young Republic could afford. This is the description given in "The Republican Court":

"NEW YORK, 1789. INAUGURATION BALL.

"The costume of the time is very well illustrated by the portraits of the day, of which fortunately there are many, but some readers may be interested in the remarks on the dresses of the women which form a portion of Colonel Stone's description of the First Inauguration Ball. "Few jewels," he says, "were then worn in the United States, but in other respects the dresses were rich and beautiful, according to the fashion of the day. We are not quite sure that we can describe the full dress of a lady of rank in the period under consideration, so as to render it intelligible, but we will make the attempt. One favorite dress was a plain celestial blue satin gown with a white satin petticoat. On the neck was worn a large Italian gauze handkerchief, with border stripes of satin. The head-dress was a pouf of gauze, in the form of a globe, the *creneaux* or head piece of which was composed of white satin, having a double wing, in large plaits, and trimmed with a wreath of artificial roses, falling from the left at the top to the right at the bottom, in front, and the reverse behind. The hair was dressed all over in detached curls, four of which, in two ranks, fell on each side of the neck, and were relieved behind by a floating chignon. Another beautiful dress was a perriot made of gray Indian taffeta, with dark stripes of the same colour, having two collars, the one of yellow, and the other white, both trimmed with a blue silk fringe, and a revere trimmed in the same manner. Under the perriot was worn a yellow corset or bodice, with large cross stripes of blue. Some of the ladies wore hats à *l'Espagnole* of white satin, with a band of the same material placed on the crown, like a wreath of flowers on the head-dress above mentioned. This hat, with a plume, a popular article of dress, was relieved on the left side, having two handsome cockades, one of which was at the top and the other at the bottom. On the neck was worn a very large plain gauze handkerchief, the end of which was hid under the bodice; after the manner represented in Trumbull's and Stuart's portraits of Lady Washington. Round the bosom of the perriot a fall of gauze, *à la Henri IV*, was attached, cut in points around the edge. There was still another dress which was thought to be very simple and pretty. It consisted of a perriot and a petticoat, both composed of the same description of gray striped silk, and trimmed round with gauze, cut points at the edges in the manner of herrisons. The herrisons were indeed nearly the sole trimming used for perriots,

FIGURE 259.

Woman in Typical Working Dress, 1790–1800 (taken from Original Garment at Stenton, Philadelphia).

Figure 261.

Figure 260.

Figure 262.

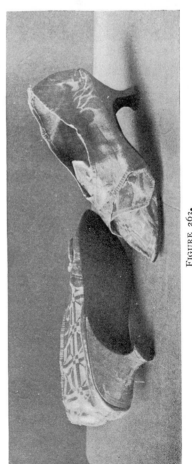

Figure 264.

Figure 263.

FIGURE 260.—White satin wedding slippers, 1800.

FIGURE 261.—Cups and saucers which belonged to Robert Treat Paine, one of the signers of the Declaration.

FIGURE 262.—Group of slippers, 1735, 1770, and 1780.

FIGURE 263.—Slippers of blue brocade worn by a Quaker bride in 1771.

FIGURE 264.—Wine-glasses and a piece of a point-lace ruffle belonging to John Wentworth, Governor of New Hampshire, from 1717 to 1730.

caracos, and petticoats of fashionable ladies, made either of ribbons or Italian gauze. With this dress they wore large gauze handkerchiefs upon their necks, with four satin stripes around the border, two of which were narrow, and the other broad. The head-dress was a plain gauze cap, after the form of the elders and ancients of a nunnery. The shoes were celestial blue, with rose coloured rosettes. Such are descriptions of some of the principal costumes, and although varied in divers unimportant particulars, by several ladies, according to their respective tastes and fancies, yet as with the peculiar fashions of all other times, there was a general correspondence—the *tout ensemble* was the same."

A perriot was evidently an overdress. The name betrays the French influence, and as it is always mentioned in connection with a petticoat it probably opened in front like a polonaise or sacque.

It was so much the custom of the women of that time to write verses, that the following lines by Mrs. Warren * on the frivolities of 1790 have more interest on account of the theme than the literary style could possibly claim:

"WOMAN'S TRIFLING NEEDS.

"An inventory clear
Of all she needs Lamira offers here;
Nor does she fear a rigid Cato's frown
When she lays by the rich embroidered gown,
And modestly compounds for just enough—
Perhaps, some dozens of more flighty stuff;
With lawns and lustrings, blond and Mechlin laces,
Fringes and jewels, fans and tweezer-cases;
Gay cloaks and hats of every shape and size,
Scarfs, cardinals, and ribbons of all dyes;
With ruffles stamped, and aprons of tambour,
Tippets and handkerchiefs, at least three score;
With finest muslins that fair India boasts,
And the choice herbage from Chinesan coasts;
(But while the fragrant Hyson leaf regales,

*Poems Dramatic and Miscellaneous.

Who'll wear the homespun produce of the vales?
For if 'twould save the nation from the curse
Of standing troops; or—name a plague still worse—
Few can this choice, delicious draught give up,
Though all Medea's poisons fill the cup.)
Add feathers, furs, rich satins and ducapes,
And head-dresses in pyramidal shapes;
Sideboards of plate and porcelain profuse,
With fifty dittos that the ladies use;
If my poor treacherous memory has missed,
Ingenious T——— shall complete the list.
So weak Lamira, and her wants so few,
Who can refuse?—they're but the sex's due.
In youth indeed, an antiquated page
Taught us the threatenings of an Hebrew sage
'Gainst wimples, mantles, curls, and crisping-pins,
But rank not these among our modern sins:
For when our manners are well understood,
What in the scale is stomacher or hood?
'Tis true, we love the courtly mien and air,
The pride of dress and all the debonair;
Yet Clara quits the more dressed negligee,
And substitutes the careless polanee;
Untill some fair one from Brittania's court,
Some jaunty dress or newer taste import;
This sweet temptation could not be withstood,
Though for the purchase paid her father's blood.

. . . .

Can the stern patriot Clara's suit deny?
'Tis beauty asks, and reason must comply."

The portrait by Copley of Mercy Warren, reproduced as a frontis-piece to her biography in the popular series "Women of Colonial and Revolutionary Times," represents her in a brocade sacque richly trimmed with lace and a small fly cap, under which the hair is arranged low and without powder.

Mr. Wansey, the English traveller, describes a visit to the theatre in Philadelphia, which he said was "as elegant and convenient and large as Covent Garden. I should have thought myself still in England judging by the appearance of the company around me. The ladies wore small bonnets of the same fashion as those I saw in London—some of chequered straw; many had their hair full dressed, without caps, as with us, and very few had it in the French style. The younger ladies appeared with their hair flowing in ringlets on their shoulders (Figure 254). The gentlemen had round hats, coats with high collars, cut quite in the English fashion, and many coats of striped silk."

In 1795 a very decided change in women's dress is noted. Soft clinging materials superseded the stiff brocades and rustling silks.

Gowns were made with narrow skirts and short bodices with long tight-fitting sleeves; the shoulders were generally uncovered, but muslin or gauze handkerchiefs were sometimes worn in the house, while for outdoor wear, long scarfs were put on around the shoulders and fell to the feet in front. Hair was worn in loose curls, generally caught up with a comb or knot of ribbon. Caps

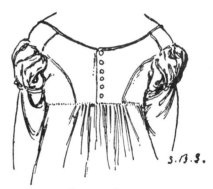

FIGURE 265.
Back of Mauve Crêpe.

for elderly people were made in a variety of styles (Figures 224, 225, 253, 259).

In her memoirs, Elizabeth Bowne takes the trouble to describe just how the gowns of her day were made. In 1798 she writes to her family:

"The gown patterns I shall enclose, the one with a fan back is meant to just meet before and pin in the robings, no strings, belt or anything. The other pattern is a plain waist with strips of the same stitched on, and laced between with bobbin or cord. I have a muslin done so with black silk cord, which looks very handsome, and I have altered my brown silk into one like the other pattern. I was over at Saco yesterday and saw one Mary (King) had made in Boston. It was a separate waist, or rather the breadth did

not go quite up. The waist was plain with one stripe of cording let in behind and the rest of the waist was perfectly plain. The skirt part was plaited in box plaits three of a side, which reached to the shoulder straps and only enough left to meet straight before, and is one of the patterns I have sent."

In Figure 341 the picture of a dress is given which has an interesting story connected with it (Figure 265).

The owner, Mlle. Henrietta Madeline l'Official de Wofoin (afterwards Mrs. Sartori), was a god-daughter of Queen Marie Antoinette, her father being an officer at the Court of Louis XVI, who was sent to San Domingo on official business just before the outbreak of the French Revolution. Soon after occurred the insurrection of the Negroes against the whites in San Domingo. M. de Wofoin

FIGURE 266.
Pelisse of Sage-green Silk with Quilted Border
(from an Original Garment of 1797).

managed to escape to this country, but lost all traces of his daughter in the excitement and knew nothing of her fate. He made his way

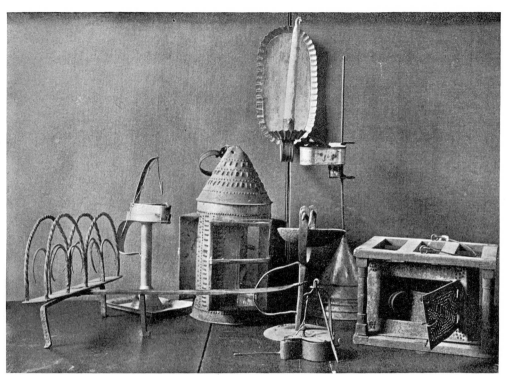

FIGURE 267.

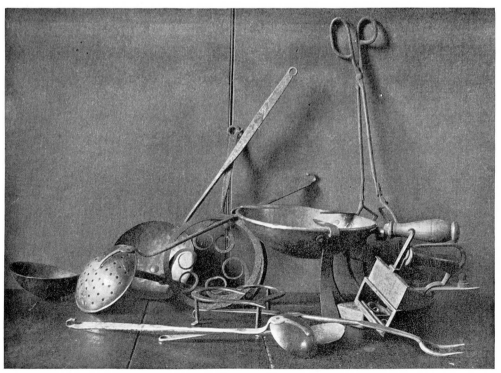

FIGURE 268.

SEVENTEENTH CENTURY UTENSILS

FIGURE 267.—Charcoal foot-warmer
Four fat-oil lamps
One candle sconce
One tin lantern
One toaster.
FIGURE 268.—One sadiron
One charcoal tongs
Ladles, skimmer, and fork
Two trivets
Copper chopping-dish.

to Trenton, New Jersey, and while there wandered one day into the market-place, where he met his daughter's old black nurse. She told him that she had brought "Mademoiselle" to America and also to Trenton. Shortly after young Sartori, who had been sent from Rome by his father to visit this country, arrived at Trenton and fell in love with Mademoiselle. They were married and lived at Lambertville, New Jersey. Mrs. Sartori died at the age of forty, having been the mother of fifteen children. The original gown from which this picture is taken has been most kindly lent to us for this book, by a direct descendant of the heroine of the story.

A dress of a quaint cut and of a fine glazed cotton unknown to-day came from Martinique with Madame Chevalier, who became a pensioner at Christ Church Hospital, Philadelphia, in the last years of the eighteenth century (Figures 248, 342).

This fashion of short waists and narrow skirts for women (Figures 341, 342, 344) and high-collared coats short at the waist for men marked the end of the eighteenth century.

CHILDREN'S GARMENTS
1700–1800

FINERY

In a frock neatly trimmed with beautiful lace,
And hair nicely dressed, hanging over her face,
Thus decked, Harriet went to the house of a friend,
With a large *little* party the evening to spend.

"Ah! how they will all be delighted, I guess,
And stare with surprise at my elegant dress";
Thus said the vain girl, and her little heart beat,
Impatient the happy young party to meet.

But alas! they were all too intent on their fun
To observe the gay clothes this fine lady had on;
And thus all her trouble quite lost its design,
For they saw she was proud, but forgot she was fine.

'T was Lucy, though only in simple white clad
(Nor trimmings, nor laces, nor jewels she had),
Whose cheerful good-nature delighted them more
Than all the fine garments that Harriet wore.

'Tis better to have a sweet smile on one's face
Than to wear a rich frock with an elegant lace,
For the good-natured girl is loved best in the main
If her dress is but decent, though ever so plain.

—J. T.

Children's Garments

1700–1800

FIGURE 269.

HE clothes of the children of the eighteenth century were marvellously made and quaintly resembled the garments of their parents. From many authorities we learn that children wore stays in Colonial times, and one interesting specimen, of which a picture is given in Figures 280 and 281, has been most kindly lent for this book. This particular pair of stays was evidently worn by a child of about two years old. One little gown of which I cannot learn the exact history, although it belonged to the family of James Logan, is made with elbow sleeves and square neck, the bodice evidently to be worn over stays, and the skirt opening over a petticoat. This is made of flowered chintz. (Figure 271.) Another child's dress is made in the same style, but the bodice opens over a sort of stomacher in front, and the material is of heavy damask linen. The sleeves of this gown are finished at the cuffs with three tiny buttons, worked over with linen thread (Figure 272).

Dresses of a little later period, probably 1750, are made with even greater skill, of fine white cambric with low necks and short sleeves fastened up with buttons and loops of narrow tape on the shoulder. They are ornamented with groups of the very tiniest tucks, with cording and tambour embroidery. Caps, which babies wore both by day and night, are also of exquisite needlework. Socks, worked with the initials of the baby, were knitted of fine white silk. One little pair of this kind is owned by the Pennsylvania Society of Colonial Dames, which was worn in babyhood by Isaac Norris, Speaker of the Continental Congress. Little mitts of linen were worn by these babies too. The pictures given here are of mitts worn in Pennsylvania by babies of the Norris and Logan families (Figures 272, 277). One minute pair is marked in red silk with the initials J. L. in monogram. A quaint little gown of buff chintz with flowers in different colours scattered over it is given in Figure 276. This was worn by a child of two years in the West family.

In the Museum of Memorial Hall, Philadelphia, there is a child's quilted hood of about 1760 made of dark blue silk, and some charming little gowns and caps of even earlier date may be seen in the Museum of the Colonial Dames at Stenton, Philadelphia (Figures 271, 272).

Very interesting are the infant dress and cap shown in Figure 286, not only on account of the skilled needlework, but also for the history associated with them. The baby for whom these clothes were made so beautifully grew in time to be a patriotic doctor in New York, and being called upon one day, in 1789, to apply a fly blister to the chest of our great Washington, he mounted the poultice on a piece of white kid and decorated the edges with a pattern in gold leaf. As he was in the act of placing the plaster the illustrious patient startled him by the question, "Will it draw any better for the decoration, young man?" We are told that the doctor finished his work in great confusion, but he lived to be proud of the opportunity which has lent an additional interest even to his baby clothes. It must be confessed that our picture fails to show the exquisite drawn-work where the threads of sheerest muslin have been drawn at intervals to form a stripe of open work and a delicate pattern embroidered

FIGURE 270.   FIGURE 271.   FIGURE 272.   FIGURE 273.   FIGURE 274.

FIGURE 275.   FIGURE 276.   FIGURE 277.   FIGURE 278.   FIGURE 279.

REIGNS OF QUEEN ANNE, GEORGE I, II AND III
1702-1790

FIGURE 270.—A girl in a red stuff gown and muslin cap, about 1730.

FIGURE 271.—Child in a printed gown and embroidered cap taken from a genuine little costume preserved in the Logan family, date about 1710.

FIGURE 272.—Child in a gown of white damask linen with mitts and embroidered cape, date about 1720. This and the costume shown in Figure 271 can be seen at Stenton, Philadelphia.

FIGURE 273.—Little boy in a suit of blue silk, lace ruffles, and powdered wig, date 1740.

FIGURE 274.—Little boy in brown velvet suit and cocked hat, about 1760.

FIGURE 275.—Boy in a blue ribbed silk suit lined with green, which is copied from an original costume now in the Colonial Museum in Independence Hall, Philadelphia. The coat has filigree silver buttons. He has on a waistcoat of flowered dimity. The hair is tied in a queue and is not powdered, date about 1756.

FIGURE 276.—Child in a buff printed cambric dress, with thin muslin kerchief and cap. This is also an original gown, date about 1760.

FIGURE 277.—Child in sheer muslin gown trimmed with tambour embroidery with cap to match, about 1790.

FIGURE 278.—Little girl in cloak, muff, and hat, after Sir Joshua Reynold's picture—1780.

FIGURE 279.—Young girl in a muslin gown trimmed with a very elaborate pattern of embroidery in white cotton. This is from an original garment of 1790.

on the filmy mesh (Figure 286). A simple everyday slip of printed cotton, white ground with a pin dot of red, belonged to the same baby.*

Until the latter part of the eighteenth century it was customary to dress children exactly like their parents. This we learn from old portraits, and very uncomfortable must the powdered wigs and lace stocks have been at a Royal Juvenile Party such as Queen Caroline

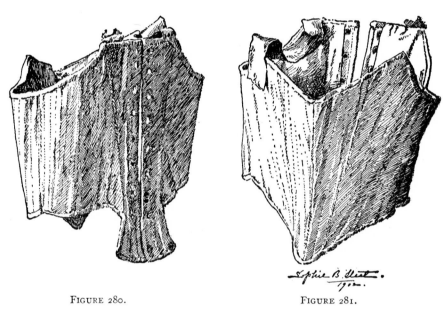

FIGURE 280.   FIGURE 281.

A Child's Stays.

delighted in giving for the diversion of her large family of princelings, where the children were dressed in miniature copies of their parents' court costumes.†

In the Colonies the dress of the children was strangely elaborate.

In the collection of Washington's manuscripts (edited by Ford) are two lists of clothes ordered for the Custis children at the tender ages of four and six, which would startle a modern nursery. Washington

* Samuel Holden Parsons Lee, born in Connecticut, 1771.
† Chronicles of Fashion.

ordered for young Custis, his stepson (aged six), the following outfit from England in 1759:

> One piece Irish Holland at 4s
> Two yards fine cambric at 10s
> Six pocket handkerchiefs small and fine
> Six pairs gloves
> Two laced hats
> Two pieces India Nankeen
> Six pairs fine thread stockings
> Four pairs coarser thread stockings
> Six pairs worsted stockings
> Four pairs pumps
> One summer suit of clothes to be made of something light and thin
> One piece of black hair ribbon
> One pair handsome silver shoe and knee buckles
> One light duffel cloak with silver frogs

And for little Nellie Custis, then at the age of four, the following articles were ordered:

> Eight yards fine printed linen at 3s 6d
> One piece Irish Holland at 4s
> Two ells of fine Holland at 10s
> Eight pairs kid mits
> Four pairs gloves
> Two pairs silk shoes
> Four pairs Calamanco shoes
> Four pairs leather pumps
> Six pairs fine thread stockings
> Four pairs fine worsted stockings
> Two fans
> Two masks
> Two bonnets
> One stiffened coat of fashionable silk made to pack thread stays
> One-half piece of flowered Dimity
> Two yards fine cambric at 10s
> Two caps
> Two pairs ruffles
> Two tucker bibs and aprons, if fashionable.

In addition to this order for suitable clothing and materials, the great man, under whose beneficent care it was the good fortune of the

FIGURE 282.

FIGURE 283

FIGURE 284.

FIGURE 285.

FIGURE 282.—A portrait of a young girl in Philadelphia, about 1760.

FIGURE 283.—A portrait of Miss Hill of Philadelphia, about 1756.

FIGURE 284.—A portrait of a child in the New York Colony, about 1700.

FIGURE 285.—Picture of a girl in New York Colony early in the eighteenth century—Christiana Ten Broeck.

Custis children to come, added 10s. worth of toys, six little books for
children beginning to read, one fashionably dressed baby, 10s. 1d.,
and other toys, 10s.

In New England, too, children were most richly attired; and we
read with amazement of a boarding-school outfit provided for two
maidens of Norwich.

"The daughters of General Huntington were sent successively
at the ages of twelve and fourteen years to finish their education at
a boarding-school in Boston. The lady who kept the establishment
was of high social standing, and made a point of taking her pupils
often into company, that their manners might be formed according
to the prevailing codes of politeness and etiquette. Of course the

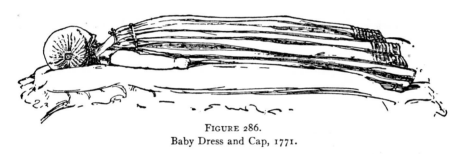

FIGURE 286.
Baby Dress and Cap, 1771.

wardrobe prepared for the young ladies was rich in articles of ornament and display. One of the daughters who had been carefully
fitted out with twelve silk gowns, had been but a short time in Boston when her instructress wrote to her parents requesting that another
dress should be procured for her, made of a certain rich fabric that
had recently been imported, in order that her appearance in society
might be equal to her rank. A thirteenth robe of silk of an exquisite
pattern was therefore immediately procured and forwarded." *

"Little misses at a dancing-school ball (for these were almost
the only *fêtes* that fell to their share in the days of discrimination)
were dressed in frocks of lawn or cambric. Worsted was then thought

* History of Norwich.

dress enough for common days,"* the famous annalist tells us, in speaking of Philadelphia children in the Revolutionary period.

Marie Antoinette was the first mother to disregard the established court fashion. She had a simple suit of jacket and trousers made for the Dauphin, but the Chronicle of Fashion assures us that "even this, probably the most sensible of all the ill-fated Queen's innovations in dress, was reviled as if the paraphernalia of full dress was a moral obligation."

FIGURE 287.
Boy in Ordinary Dress, 1790.

In the portraits of English children in the latter part of the century, we become familiar with costumes at once simple and picturesque, as in Figures 269, 277, 278, 279, 287. Copley's well-known family group, and the picture of his family by Benjamin West (Figure 225), are satisfactory evidence of the adoption of these appropriate fashions for the children of the Colonies.

Figures 284 and 285 are photographed from portraits of two little girls in the New York Colony during the reign of Queen Anne, in gowns so stiff and so unsuitable they would have baffled even the graceful brush of a Reynolds or a Romney.

* Watson's Annals.

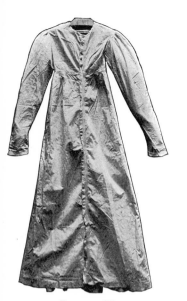

FIGURE 288.

FIGURE 289.

FIGURE 290.

FIGURE 291.

FIGURE 292.

FIGURE 293.

FIGURE 288.—Picture of a garment called a "flying Josie," made of white cambric and worn in Pennsylvania late in the eighteenth century.

FIGURE 289.—Back view of the same.

FIGURE 290.—A suit of blue silk, with buttonholes of silver thread, worn by a little boy in Pennsylvania, about 1756.

FIGURE 291.—Picture of a child's dress, buff chintz with coloured flowers, worn in Pennsylvania about 1710.

FIGURE 292.—Picture of a white shift, the sleeves of which are laid in fine plaits, to be worn under a gown with elbow sleeves and square neck. The ruffle at neck is of very fine linen cambric, and made to turn down over the dress, as in Figure 195.

FIGURE 293.—A child's dress of damask linen, with linen mittens, worn in, Pennsylvania about 1720.

(Photographed from original garments.)

MEN'S APPAREL

1700–1800

During the Time of
Queen Anne, George I, II, and III of England,
Presidents Washington and Adams
of the United States

GOVERNOR WENTWORTH.

"A portly person, with three-cornered hat,
A crimson velvet coat, head high in air,
Gold-headed cane and nicely powdered hair,
And diamond buckles sparkling at his knees,
Dignified, stately, florid, much at ease.
For this was Governor Wentworth, driving down
To Little Harbour, just beyond the town,
Where his great house stood, looking out to sea,
A goodly place, where it was good to be.
It was a pleasant mansion, an abode
Near and yet hidden from the great highroad;
Sequestered among trees, a noble pile,
Baronial and Colonial in its style!

Within, unwonted splendours met the eye,
Panels and floors of oak, and tapestry;
Carved chimney pieces, where, on brazen dogs,
Revelled and roared the Christmas fire of logs;
Doors opening into darkness unawares,
Mysterious passages and flights of stairs;
And on the walls, in heavy gilded frames,
The ancestral Wentworths, with old Scripture names.
Such was the mansion where the great man dwelt.

He gave a splendid banquet served on plate
Such as became the Governor of the State
Who represented England and the King,
And was magnificent in everything."
—"*The Poet's Tale.*"

Men's Apparel

1700–1800

FIGURE 294.

ERIWIGS and cocked hats were the characteristic features of the dress of men in the first half of the eighteenth century.

REIGNS OF QUEEN ANNE AND GEORGE I

Under Queen Anne the hats worn by men were smaller and were regularly cocked on three sides, and the cuffs of the coats were very wide and long, reaching almost to the wrist. The broad sword belt had vanished, and the sword hilt could be seen beneath the stiffened skirt of the square-cut coat (Figure 163). Blue or scarlet silk stockings, with gold or silver clocks, were much worn, as were also shoes with red heels and small buckles (Figure 163); velvet garters were worn over the stockings below the knee, being fastened on one side by small buckles (Figure 163). Campaign wigs imported from France now became popular. They were made very full with long curls hanging towards the front (Figure 163). When human hair was scarce, a little horsehair supplied the place, in the part least in sight.

In 1706 a peculiar cock of the hat came into fashion called the Ramilie, and a long plaited tail to the wig with a great bow at the top and a small one at the bottom known as the Ramilie wig (Figure 299).

Those who did not wear powder and who objected to the

enormous expense or weight of the fashionable wigs, wore their own hair in long curls to resemble them, but the long popularity of the uncomfortable fashion of the periwig is indeed astonishing.

Dr. Granger in his Life of Charles II, speaking of the fashion when it first came into vogue, says: "It was observed that a periwig procured many persons a respect and even veneration which they were strangers to before and to which they had not the least claims from their personal merit," and he quotes the amusing anecdote of a country gentleman who employed a painter to place periwigs upon the heads of several of Vandyke's portraits. Large wigs were worn until the middle of the eighteenth century. A plain peruke imitating a natural head of hair was called a short bob.

A facetious barber in London had the following rhyme painted on the sign over his door:*

"Oh Absolom, Oh Absolom,
Oh Absolom my son,
If thou hadst worn a periwig
Thou hadst not been undone."

The ridiculous long wigs of 1710 were decidedly expensive. One is mentioned in "The Tatler" costing 40 guineas.

We read that in Philadelphia early in the eighteenth century men were wearing "cocked hats, and wigs, coats with large cuffs, big skirts, lined and stiffened with buckram. The coat of a beau had three or four large plaits in the skirt, wadded almost like a coverlet to keep them smooth, cuffs very large up to the elbows, the collars were flat and low, so as readily to expose the close plaited neck-stock of fine linen cambric and the large silver stock-buckle on the back of the neck, shirts with hand ruffles, sleeves finely plaited, breeches close fitted, with silver, stone or paste buckles, shoes or pumps with silver buckles of various sizes and patterns, thread, worsted and silk stockings. The very boys often wore wigs, and their clothing in general was similar to that of the men."

* Hone's Every Day Book.

FIGURE 296.

FIGURE 295.

301

FIGURE 295.—Portrait of Kiliaen Van Rensselaer, Second Patroon and First Lord of the Manor of Rensselaerwyck, 1663-1719, showing coat worn in the reign of Queen Anne. (From the original painting.)

FIGURE 296.—Jan Baptist Van Rensselaer, Director of the Manor of Rensselaerwyck, showing a coat with cuffs reaching above the elbow, in reign of George I. (From the original painting.)

In the year 1719 Jonathan Dickinson, a Friend, in writing to London for his clothes, says, "I want for myself and my three sons, each a wig—good light bobs."

The reign of George I offers no distinctive changes for remark. Wigs held their ground, and in 1720 white hair for the manufacture of them "brought a monstrous price."

Heavy cloaks or Roquelaures were still worn by men and were often trimmed with fur. Mention is made in letters from New England about 1720 of a striped camlet cloak lined with a plain colour. Drugget was also used for the purpose (Figure 297).

The ordinary costume of gentlemen during the reigns of Queen Anne and George I is thus briefly summed up by M. Planché in his "History of British Costume." He says: "Square cut coats and long flapped waistcoats with pockets in them, the latter

FIGURE 297.
Taken from a Genuine Roquelaure, Middle of the Eighteenth Century.

meeting the stockings, still drawn up over the knee so high as entirely to conceal the breeches, but gartered below it; large hanging cuffs and lace ruffles. The skirt of the coat stiffened out with wire or buckram from beneath which peeped the hilt of the sword deprived of the cord and splendid belt in which it swung in the preceding Reigns. Blue or scarlet silk stockings with gold or silver clocks. Lace neck-cloths, square-toed, short quartered shoes, with high red heels and small buckles; very long and formally curled perukes (or periwigs), black riding wigs, and night cap wigs; small three cornered hats laced with gold or silver galloons, and sometimes trimmed with feathers comprised the habit of the noblemen and gentlemen from 1702 to 1724."

As in all ages and all climes, variations of the prevailing style were indulged in by gay young men about town. The pet extravagance at this period was beautiful lace in ruffles and neckties.

FIGURE 298.   FIGURE 299.   FIGURE 300.
Periwig with Tail, 1700.   Ramilie Wig, 1730.   Bag Wig, 1750.

Queen Anne had a zealous care for the English church in America and took personal pleasure in sending beautiful services of silver to parishes in all her colonies. Many of these may be seen to-day with an historic inscription and the Queen's initials engraved in the simple script of her time. In her reign the dress of the English clergyman was inconspicuous but distinctive, and with slight modifications was worn by the majority of clergymen in America. Knee-breeches fitting close, buckled shoes, long black coats, and wigs were the prevailing characteristics in everyday life. In connection with the portrait

FIGURE 302.

FIGURE 301.

FIGURE 301.—Portrait of William Penn, Proprietor and Governor of Pennsylvania Province. (By Benjamin West.)

FIGURE 302.—Portrait of George Washington, First President of the United States. (By Gilbert Stuart, 1797.)

of Bishop White of Pennsylvania given in Figure 358, it is interesting
to recall the story told by himself of his appointment as chaplain to the
Continental Congress. He was riding with a friend when a messenger from Congress overtook him. He hesitated for a few moments,
realizing the danger of enrolling himself with the cause of the patriots,
but after a short deliberation he turned his horse's head and accompanied the emissary to General Washington's headquarters before
Yorktown.* It was a brave step which he never regretted, and his
name has ever been associated with the early sessions of our Congress
in Philadelphia. Bishop White was consecrated at Lambeth Palace
in 1787, and, despite his republican partisanship, amid many tokens
of good will on the part of the king and others.

REIGN OF GEORGE II

There are numerous authorities for the costume of George II's
reign, but the versatile genius of Hogarth † alone has furnished us
with sufficient material for a study of the dress of all classes and conditions of the English men and women of his day. His "Five Orders
of Periwigs" gives us the favorite varieties of that style of head-gear,
which was certainly a very expensive fashion, for in 1734 we read
that in the Colonies periwigs of light gray human hair were four
guineas each. Light grizzle ties were three guineas, and other colours
in proportion, down to twenty-five shillings. Light gray human
hair cue-perukes were from two guineas to fifteen shillings each, and
bob perukes of the same material a little dearer, real gray hair
being most in fashion, and dark of "no estimation."

The court dress of noblemen in 1735 is described as a coat made
of coloured velvet or fine cloth laced with gold or silver, breeches to
match; waistcoat of rich flowered silk of a large pattern on a white
ground. Wigs were still worn with large curls standing up from
the forehead (Figure 296).

* Simpson's Lives of Eminent Philadelphians.   † Born 1697; died 1764.

Fairholt in his "History of English Dress" says: "By the cock of the hat, the man who wore it was known; and they varied from the modest broad brim of the clergy and country-man to the slightly upturned hat of the country gentle-man or citizen, or the more decidedly fash-ionable cock worn by merchantmen, and would - be - fashionable Londoners; while a very pronounced *à la militaire* cock was affected by the gallant about the court." All of these styles may be seen in the pictures of Hogarth. These hats were usually made of soft felt with a large brim caught up by three loops of cord to a button on the top. Being soft, they could be crushed under the arm and each flap could be let down at pleasure in case of wind, or rain, or sun. Mr. Wingfield speaks of a hat "unlooped although it doth not rain," and observes that in one of Cibber's

FIGURE 303.

Back View of Figure 229, Middle Eighteenth Century (from the Original Costume).

FIGURE 304.

FIGURE 305.

FIGURE 306.

FIGURE 307.

FIGURE 308.

FIGURE 309.

FIGURE 304.—Portrait of Rev. George Whitefield, showing the gown and wig worn in New England by a clergyman of the English church in the latter half of the eighteenth century.

FIGURE 305.—Portrait of Rev. Jacob Duché, D.D., showing a gown and close wig worn in Pennsylvania late in the eighteenth century.

FIGURE 306.—Portrait of Dr. Ezra Stiles, in periwig and gown worn in New England late in the eighteenth century.

FIGURE 307.—Portrait of Rt. Rev. Richard Challoner, Vicar Apostolic of the English Colonies in America, 1756, showing that wigs were worn by the priests of the Roman Catholic Church of that date.

FIGURE 308.—Portrait of Jonathan Edwards, showing the plain coat and bands of a Presbyterian minister, second half of the eighteenth century.

FIGURE 309.—Portrait of Rt. Rev. Samuel Provoost, D.D., First Bishop of New York, showing the white wig, full sleeves, and black gown, late eighteenth century.

comedies we find a footman "unlooping his hat to protect his powdered head from the wet."

To use the snuff-box gracefully was an accomplishment considered necessary to the young man of fashion on his entrance into the gay world of the eighteenth century. Made of every sort of metal, adorned with precious stones or costly miniature paintings, the snuff-box was in great demand, and considered as indispensable on occasions of full dress as the fan. Many of these boxes which were used in the Colonies have been preserved. In Figure 239 is given a picture of one owned by Madame Le Comte, for the fashion of using snuff was not confined to men.

A beau of this time is spoken of as "appearing in a different style of wig every day, and thus perplexing the lady to whom he was paying his addresses, by a new face every time they met during the first months of their courtship. Hats could be moulded in so many different cocks as to change the whole appearance of the wearer." *

Hats had broader brims (Figure 197) and "were cocked triangularly, and pulling them off by way of salutation was invariably the fashion for all who had any breeding," according to a famous letterwriter of that day. Boots were worn for riding, with large broad tops which reached half-way up the thigh.

The fashionable costume for men in the Colonies, identical with the prevailing style in England, was not subject to quite as many changes as the dress of the women.

In 1740 a "jockey coat" was ordered from Boston of fine cloth with waistcoat and breeches to match. It is "to be trimmed plain, only with a button of the same sort as that of the waistcoat but proportionately bigger." The same gentleman ordered "as much three pile black velvet as is made for men's wear, and the best that can be had for the money, as much as will make a complete suit." In

* The Spectator.

addition to this he desires a night-gown of a deep crimson Genoa damask lined with the same colour.

About this time there was a slight change in shoes. Square toes went out of fashion and were replaced by pointed toes for both sexes. (See Figures 229, 231.) Buckles became the ambition of all classes, and were worn of every size and shape.

Claret coloured cloth was at that time considered the correct thing for suits, and light blue with silver button-holes and silver garters at the knees, was also very fashionable between 1740 and 1751.

Pigtails came into fashion about the middle of the eighteenth century.

> " ' But pray what's that much like a whip,
>   Which with the air does wav'ring skip
>   From side to side, and hip to hip?'
>   ' Sir, do not look so fierce and big
>   It is a modish pigtail wig.' "

Instead of swords, many of the gay young sparks carried long oak sticks with ugly faces carved on the handles.

One of the marked characteristics of the men of fashion in the eighteenth century was a mincing air. We read of Horace Walpole that " he always entered a room with that style of affected delicacy which fashion had made almost natural; with *chapeau-bras* between his hands as if he wished to compress it, or under his arm; knees bent, and feet on tip-toe as if afraid of a wet floor." *

About 1740 the large cocked hat and full-bottomed wig went out of style, and the lace cravat with long ends, which had been in fashion for about thirty years, gave place to a small black cravat worn with a ruffled shirt front (Figure 197.) There was a change in the coat also. A broad collar which turned back round the neck contrasted strangely with the total want of collar in the earlier style, while the cuffs became very deep, reaching above the elbows and not very wide at the wrists. The coat itself fitted close to the body with skirt reaching to the calf of the leg. This change of style did not

* Miss Hawkins' Memoirs.

FIGURE 310

FIGURE 311.

FIGURE 312.

FIGURE 313.

FIGURE 310.—Back view of a coat of light brown velvet figured in red and green, showing the very full tails of George II's reign.

FIGURE 311.—Front view of the same. Worn by Robert Livingston, Esq., of Clermont Manor, New York Colony.

FIGURES 312 and 313.—Front and back views of a coat of brown twilled cotton jean, typical summer garment of a Friend.

(Photographed from original garments.)

long remain popular even in England.   In prints of 1744 we again notice the wide cuffs and wider hat brims of a few years before.

About 1750 muff-tees, or little woolen muffs of various colours, were used by men in the Colonies. They were "just big enough to admit both hands and long enough to screen the wrists, which were then more exposed than now; for they wore short sleeves to their coats on purpose to display their fine plaited linen shirt sleeves with their gold cuff buttons and on occasions ruffles of lace." (Figures 182, 214.)

In the summer season men often wore calico morning gowns at all times of the day in the street as well as at home. A damask banyan was much the same thing by another name.

We can hardly

FIGURE 314.
Gentleman in Banyan and Cap.

wonder that in Virginia and the southern colonies the hot wigs and cumbrous petticoats prescribed by fashion were often found too uncomfortable for daily wear, and we read with a certain sense of relief, of a negligée costume of banyans and nightcaps adopted by the planters and their wives.

The climate must be remembered as a potent inducement to go without the long curled wigs and wadded coats; and, alas, the discomfort of stiff stays and voluminous petticoats in an American summer!

REIGN OF GEORGE III

In 1760, when wigs were powdered, they were frequently sent for that purpose in a wooden box to the barber to be dressed on his blockhead. "Brown wigs," for which a brown powder was used, were worn, but were less fashionable than "the white disguise."

On ceremonious occasions, if wigs were not worn, the hair was craped, curled, and powdered by barbers.

About 1770, when wigs went out of favour and the natural hair was preferred, it became the fashion to dress it in a queue, or to wear it in a black silk bag tied with a bow of black ribbon (Figures 303, 318, 352, 353, 354, 355).

With the queues belong frizzled sidelocks, and toupées formed of the natural hair, or in the absence of a long tie a splice was added to it (Figures 352, 353, 354, 355). Such was the general passion for the longest possible whip of hair, that sailors and boatmen used to tie theirs in eel skins to aid its growth.

A curious silhouette of Washington by Folwell represents him with what is supposed to be a fine net worn over hair and queue to keep the powder in place (Figure 357).

A colonial item of interest is gleaned from Washington's manuscripts. In 1759 he ordered from England for his own use:

"A New-market great coat with a loose hood (Figure 364) to it, made of Blew Drab or broadcloth with straps before, according to the present taste—let it be made of such cloth as will turn a good shower of rain."

FIGURE 315.

FIGURE 316.

FIGURE 317.

FIGURE 318

FIGURE 315.—Portrait of John Penn, Colonial Governor, showing fur-trimmed coat.

FIGURE 316.—Portrait of Thomas Penn, Colonial Governor.

FIGURE 317.—Portrait of Patrick Gordon, Colonial Governor.

FIGURE 318.—Portrait of James Hamilton, Lieutenant Governor of Pennsylvania, 1783.

"A light summer suit of Duroy by the measure,
Four pieces best India nankeen,
Two best plain beaver hats at 20s.
One piece of black satin ribbon,
1 sword belt, red morocco or buff, no buckles or rings,"

are also ordered on the same date.

In Watson's "Annals of Philadelphia" we read: "Coats of red cloth were considerably worn, even by boys, and plush breeches and plush vests of various colours, were in common use. Everlasting, or durant, made of worsted, was a fabric of great use for breeches, and sometimes for vests which had great depending pocket flaps, and the breeches were very short above the stride because the art of suspending them by suspenders was unknown. It was then the test of a well-formed man, that he could by his natural form readily keep his breeches above his hips, and his stockings without gartering, above the calf of the leg.

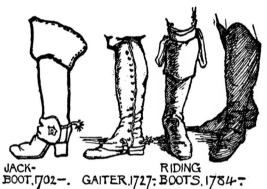

JACK-BOOT, 1702—. GAITER, 1727: RIDING BOOTS, 1784—.
FIGURE 319.   FIGURE 320. FIGURE 321. FIGURE 322.

"In the time of the Revolutionary war many of the American officers introduced the use of Dutch blankets for great coats (Figure 364). Large silver buttons worn on coats and vests were a mark of wealth. Some people had the initials of their names engraved on each button. Sometimes they were made out of real quarter dollars, with the coinage impression still retained; these were used for the coats, and the eleven-penny-bits for vests and breeches. One old gentleman wore an entire suit decorated with conch shell buttons, silver mounted."

In New England before the Revolution, "powdered wigs full and curled were worn by clergymen and other dignitaries (Figures 304,

306, 307, 308, 317, 326, 329). A full-dress suit for a gentleman was usually made of silk, with trimmings of gold and silver lace, the waistcoat often richly embroidered."* Roquelaures and great coats were worn of cloth or camlet in all the colonies.

Mr. Sydney George Fisher, the historian, despite his Quaker ancestry, exclaims with unwonted enthusiasm: "Those were brave days when the judges on the bench wore scarlet robes faced with black; when the tailor shops, instead of the dull-coloured woolens which they now offer, advertised, as in the New York Gazetteer of May 13, 1773, 'scarlet, buff, green, blue, crimson, white, sky blue, and other coloured superfine cloths'; when John Hancock, of penmanship fame, is described in his home in Boston with a red velvet skull-cap lined with white linen which was turned over the edge of the velvet about three inches deep, a blue damask dressing-gown lined with silk, a white stock, satin embroidered waistcoat, black satin breeches, white silk stockings to his knees, and red morocco slippers."†

The first umbrellas to keep off the rain were of oiled linen, very coarse and clumsy, with rattan sticks. Before their time some physicians and ministers used an oiled linen cape hooked round their shoulders, looking not unlike the big coat-capes now in use. They were only used for severe storms, like modern water-proofs.

We believe it was about the year 1771 that the first efforts were made in Philadelphia to introduce the use of umbrellas in summer as a protection from the sun. "They were then scouted in the public 'Gazette' as a ridiculous effeminacy. On the other hand, the physicians recommended them to keep off vertigoes, epilepsies, sore eyes, fevers, etc."

Watches were worn in fob pockets with seals attached by a ribbon, but they were not in common use until the end of the century.‡

* History of Norwich, by F. M. Caulkins.
† Men, Women, and Manners of Colonial Days.
‡ Watson's Annals.

FIGURE 323.

FIGURE 324.

FIGURE 325.

FIGURE 326.

FIGURE 327.

FIGURE 323.—Portrait of James Logan, showing white wig and judicial robe, worn in Pennsylvania, 1745.

FIGURE 324.—Portrait of Fisher Ames, showing a plain costume of the middle of the eighteenth century.

FIGURE 325.—Portrait of John Jay in his robes as First Chief Justice of the United States.

FIGURE 326.—Portrait of Nathaniel Appleton of Boston, showing white wig with puffs at side. (By Copley.)

FIGURE 327.—Portrait of Henry Laurens. (By Copley.)

Of New York in the eighteenth century we read: "Whether it be in the journals of visitors or in private correspondence, we always get the impression of a lively and cheerful town, where people like to come and from which they are sorry to go away. In the old days, indeed, there was a restful sense of leisure which the rapid pace of modern life has ruthlessly destroyed."*

Although the style of living in colonial New York was comfortable, with little display, when we come to the subject of dress, we find the case was very different. Early in the eighteenth century the streets of New York were gorgeous with elaborate costumes.

Gay masculine garments are described in inventories: Green silk breeches, flowered with silver and gold, silver gauze breeches, yellow fringed gloves, lacquered hats, laced shirts and neck-cloths.

From 1760 to 1770, gentlemen in Massachusetts were wearing "hats with broad brims turned up into three corners with loops at the sides; long coats with large pocket-folds and cuffs, and without collars.

FIGURE 328.
Working Garb, Middle Eighteenth Century, 1750.

* Dutch and Quaker Colonies, by Fiske.

(Figures 327 and 334.) The buttons were commonly plated, but sometimes of silver, often as large as a half-dollar. Shirts had bosom and wrist ruffles; and all wore gold or silver shirt-buttons at the wrist united by a link. The waistcoat was long, with large pockets; and the neckcloth or scarf was of fine white linen or figured stuff broidered and the ends hanging loosely on the breast. The breeches fitted close, with silver buckles at the knees. The legs were covered with gray knitted stockings which on holidays were exchanged for black or white silk. Boots with broad white tops, or shoes with straps and large silver buckles, completed the equipment."* It seems strange indeed that, during the eighteenth century when men had so much fighting on hand, they should have paid such attention to dress and fashion, but abundant proof exists in the letters and diaries of the day that every detail, the width of the cuff, the length of the cravat, the size even of the button-holes, was to the masculine mind a matter of grave import. Apparently the sword knot received as much attention as the sword. Even "the greatest American," in his youthful days, paid exact attention to details.

"Memorandum: To have my coat made by the following directions; to be made a frock with the lapel breast, the lapel to contain on each side six button-holes, and to be about five or six inches wide all the way, equal, and to turn as the breast of the coat does, to have it made very long waisted and in length to come down below the bend of the knee. The waist from the arm-pit to the fold to be exactly as long or longer than from thence to the bottom, not to have more than one fold in the skirt and the top to be made to turn in, and three button-holes, the laps at the top to turn as the cape of the coat, and bottom to come parallel with the button-holes, the last button-hole in the breast to be right opposite to the button on the hip."† At this time Washington was only a boy of fifteen.

* History of Lynn, Mass., by Lewis and Newhall.
† The writings of George Washington, edited by W. C. Ford.

FIGURE 329.

FIGURE 330.

FIGURE 331.

FIGURE 332.

FIGURE 329.—Portrait of John Hancock, Governor of the Massachusetts Colony, showing coat with a turned-down collar and double pocket-flaps, reign of George III.

FIGURE 330.—Portrait of Samuel Shoemaker, Mayor of Philadelphia, in a bobwig, and his son, who wears his natural hair long on the shoulders and cut in a straight bang across the forehead (from a portrait painted in 1789).

FIGURE 331.—Showing the plain but handsome costume of a gentleman in Pennsylvania at the outbreak of the Revolution.

FIGURE 332.—Showing a cocked hat worn by a Quaker gentleman of Pennsylvania, 1774.

We learn that English tradesmen were apt to take advantage of their colonial customers, and that Washington had occasion to protest against things being sent to him from London that were unfashionable and inferior in quality. We give his letter of September 28th, 1760:

"And here gentlemen, I cannot forbear ushering in a complaint of the exorbitant prices of my goods this year all of which are to come to hand. For many years I have imported goods from London as well as other ports of Britain, and can truly say I never had such a penny-worth before. It would be a needless task to enumerate every article that I have cause to except against. Let it suffice to say that woolens, linnens, nails, etc., are mean in quality but not in price, for in this they excel indeed, far above any I have ever had.

1733.

FIGURE 333.
Sporting Dress, Middle Eighteenth Century (after Highmore).

"Let us beseech you gentlemen to give the necessary directions for purchasing of them upon the best terms. It is needless for me to particularize, the sorts, quality or taste I would choose to have them in, unless it is observed. And you may believe me when I tell you that instead of getting things good and fashionable in their several kinds, we often have articles sent us that could only have been used by our forefathers in the days of yore. 'tis a custom I have some reason to believe with many shopkeepers and tradesmen in London, when they know goods are bespoke for exportation, to palm sometimes old and sometimes very slight and indifferent goods upon us, taking care at the same time to advance 10, 15 or perhaps 20 per cent. upon them. My packages, per the 'Polly,' Capt. Hooper, are not yet come to hand, and the Lord only knows when they will without more trouble than they are worth."

According to Fairholt, the costume of the ordinary classes during the greater part of the eighteenth century was exceedingly simple, consisting of a plain coat, buttoned up the front, a long waistcoat reaching to the knees, but having capacious pockets with great overlapping flaps, a plain bobwig, a hat slightly turned up, and high quartered shoes.

We read that, in 1746, flat cocked hats were worn by English sailors, and twenty years later, hats of glazed leather or of woolen thrums, closely woven, and looking like rough knap; and their "small clothes," as we would say now, were immense wide petticoat-breeches, open at the knees, and not extending below them. Labouring men wore ticklenberg linen for shirts, and striped ticken breeches, and in winter heavy coats of gray duroy. The leathern breeches worn by men and boys were made without any opening flaps, and, according to Watson, were so full and free in girth that the wearers ordinarily changed the rear to the front if any signs of wear appeared. Aprons of leather were used by all tradesmen and workingmen.

In a paper of 1771, a reward of ten pounds is offered for the arrest of a man named William Davis who robbed the church at Wilmington of its hangings and had a green coat made of them. Green was very fashionable at this period.

AFTER THE REVOLUTION

At his second inauguration, in Philadelphia, 1793, Washington's costume was "a full suit of black velvet," cut in the fashion of Figure 302, "his hair powdered and in a bag; diamond knee buckles and a light sword with gray scabbard. Behind him was Jefferson, gaunt, ungainly, square-shouldered, with foxy hair, dressed in a blue coat,

FIGURE 334.

FIGURE 335.

FIGURE 337.

FIGURE 336.

FIGURE 338.

FIGURE 334.—A suit of velvet with raised figures, worn by Robert Livingston
of Clermont Manor, New York, 1770.
FIGURE 335.—Pistols with silver mounting, about 1765.
FIGURE 336.—Cap worn by Governor Taylor of New York, about 1730.
FIGURE 337.—A waistcoat of buff silk trimmed with shaded brown ribbon, 1780.
FIGURE 338.—A double-breasted waistcoat of figured silk, 1790.
    (Photographed from original garments.)

small clothes, and vest of crimson; near by was pale, reflective Madison and burly, bustling Knox." Unfortunately for us, their dress on that occasion is not described. Adams was clad in a full suit of fine gray cloth.

Powder, worn for a hundred years, went out of fashion in 1794, but the hair was still worn in a queue tied with a black ribbon.

The following list of a gentleman's outfit gives an insight into a fashionable wardrobe at this time:

"A light coloured broadcloth coat, with pearl buttons; breeches of the same cloth; ditto, black satin; vest, swansdown buff striped; ditto, moleskin chequer figure; ditto, satin figured; ditto, Marseilles white; ditto, muslinet figured; undervest, faced with red cassimere; two ditto, flannel; one pair of flannel drawers; one ditto; cotton ditto; one pair black patent silk hose; one ditto; white ditto; one

FIGURE 339.
A Workingman in the Last Half of the Eighteenth Century (from a Contemporary Print).

ditto; striped ditto; ten or a dozen white silk hose; three pair of cotton hose; four pair of gauze ditto; twelve neckerchiefs; six pocket handkerchiefs, one of them a bandanna; a chintz dressing gown; a pair of silk gloves; old kid ditto."

Coats for men became shorter in the waist and all the garments were worn fitting more closely to the figure. The tails of the coats were cut away in front and were quite long in the back. Although a few people might have been seen wearing cocked hats after 1800, a soft, low-crowned straight-brimmed hat came into fashion in 1794. At that time waistcoats were cut low over ruffled shirt fronts. Soft stocks were worn around the neck, finished with a bow and ends under the chin.

Inventory of the wearing apparel of a gentleman in Connecticut at the end of the eighteenth century:

1 Great Coat	3 pr. Old Breeches
1 do do	16 Cotton & Linen Shirts
1 Black Coat	4 pr. Worcested Hose
1 Common do	4 Linen & Cotton do
5 Old Coats	2 pr. plaited do
4 pr. black Breeches	2 pr. black silk do
5 pr. velveteen do	1 Morning Gown
3 worcested waistcoats	3 pr. Cotton breeches
1 velvet do, 1 buff	5 pocket Handkerchiefs
1 Eider down do	1 pr. Gingham Trowsers
1 plaid Gown	7 waistcoats
1 Coatee	3 Neck handkfs.
2 Hats	1 White waistcoat
7 pr. Woolen Hose	3 Under Waistcoats
1 pr. Boots	2 pr. leather mittens
4 pr. Shoes	1 pr. woolen do
1 pr. overalls	1 pr. linen and leather Gloves

A great-coat of blue camlet with several short capes, long of waist and large of button, was the popular garment in severe weather. Trousers of leather and leggings of deer-skin supplemented the coat as a protection against storms. An extra pair of stocking legs well tucked into the low shoes was a homely substitute for leggings, and

FIGURE 340.   FIGURE 341.   FIRURE 342.   FIGURE 343.   FIGURE 344.

Sophie B Steel.

THE REPUBLIC UNDER WASHINGTON AND ADAMS
1790-1800

FIGURE 340.—Man in brown broadcloth, from an original suit worn by Mr. Johnson of Germantown about 1790. The coat is of the cut called shadbelly worn by Friends in Pennsylvania until long after 1800.

FIGURE 341.—A mauve crêpe gown trimmed with groups of tucks and a fold of silk of same colour inserted between. The head-dress is from a contemporary picture. The history of Mrs. Sartori, the owner of this dress, is given on page 274.

FIGURE 342.—A dress of fine glazed cambric made very simply with long sleeves and high waist, owned by Madame Chevalier, end of eighteenth century. The hair is copied from a contemporary portrait of 1797.

FIGURE 343.—Man in style of 1800. High collar and short-waisted coat of changeable plum-coloured silk. Nankeen breeches. Hat of felt with rather high crown.

FIGURE 344.—Muslin dress trimmed with tambour embroidery, worn by Deborah Logan of Philadelphia, 1797. The original dress may be seen at Stenton, Philadelphia.

The pictures on this plate are all from original garments lent for this book.

overshoes of very heavy leather were sometimes worn over the ordinary shoes.

LEGAL DRESS IN THE EIGHTEENTH CENTURY

Martin mentions a portrait of James Logan as Chief Justice of the Province of Pennsylvania which represents him in gown, bands, and wig. The original colour of the gown is hard to determine in the portrait. In shape it represents an academic gown, and may have been worn in more than one capacity, as that distinguished colonist played many parts in his day. The dignified garment in question would equally become the governor and the chief justice. (Figure 323.)

In his diary, under date of 1787, Manasseh Cutler, describing a visit to the State House, says: "In this Hall the Courts are held and as you pass the aisle you have a full view of the Court. The Supreme Court was now sitting. This bench consists of only three judges. Their robes are scarlet, the lawyers' black. The Chief Judge McKean sitting with his hat on, which is the custom, but struck me as being very odd and seemed to derogate from the dignity of a judge."[*]

Among other customs brought over from England by the legal profession is the practice still in use of carrying briefs and papers in bags. "Lawyers' bags," an English authority asserts, "were, until a comparatively recent date, green, but leaders of the chancery and common law bars carried red bags. Chancery juniors, it is stated, were permitted to carry blue bags, etiquette forbidding them to carry bags of the same colour as their leaders."[†]

In those days (latter half of the eighteenth century) it was the custom of the Supreme Court to hold sessions in the various counties. When the Supreme Court came to Harrisburg (1777-78) to hold court, numbers of the citizens of the place—as many as two hundred

[*] Life, Journals and Correspondence of Rev. Manassah Cutler, LL.D.
[†] The King's Peace, by Inderwick.

people at a time—would go out on horseback to meet the judges and escort them to town. The sheriff with his rod of office and other public

FIGURE 345.
A Doctor of Civil Law, End of the Eighteenth Century (from an Old Print).

officers and members of the bar would attend on the occasion, and each morning while the Chief Justice was in town the sheriff and

FIGURE 346.

FIGURE 347.

FIGURE 348.

FIGURE 349.

FIGURE 346.—A summer coat of dark-blue changeable silk with nankeen breeches, worn late in the eighteenth century.

FIGURE 347.—Back view of a brown broad-cloth coat, worn by a Quaker gentleman in Germantown about 1790.

FIGURE 348.—Front view of same suit over a nankeen waistcoat.

FIGURE 349.—A coat of brown twilled cotton worn by a Quaker gentleman of Germantown; a white silk embroidered waistcoat and brown satin knee breeches worn in Philadelphia about 1790.

(Photographed from original garments.)

constables escorted him from his lodgings to the court-room. When on
the bench, he sat with his hat on and was dressed in a scarlet gown.

A "Grand Federal Procession" took place in Philadelphia on
the Fourth of July, 1788, which is described at length in the
"Pennsylvania Gazette," July 9, 1788. A great ship on wheels
represented the Constitution, and in it was seated Chief Justice
McKean in his robes of office, and the judges of the Supreme

after W.H.PYNE. SBS.

FIGURE 350.
A Judge in Scarlet Robe, End of the Eighteenth Century (from an Old Print).

Court in their robes of office. Had there been any decided change
prescribed for the robes of the judges and lawyers in the framing
of the Constitution it would have surely been emphasized in the
procession, but as a matter of fact among the printed articles in
Congress on the subject of the Judiciary, not a word regarding robes
or etiquette is given. The portrait of Chief Justice McKean, which
hangs in the Law School of the University of Pennsylvania, depicts

him in a scarlet gown. It is a recent portrait, but was painted under the direction of the family. The red robe of the English Court was evidently worn throughout the eighteenth century in America.

John Jay, the first Chief Justice of the Supreme Court of the United States, was appointed to that office by Washington in 1789. The full-length portrait of him in his robe is reproduced in Figure 325. According to a contemporary authority, this robe is the black silk gown with facings of salmon-coloured satin with a white edge, given with his degree of Doctor of Laws by Columbia University and worn by the Chief Justice during the term of his high office under the Government.*

UNIFORMS IN AMERICA
1775–1800

The history of the American Navy, according to good authority, dates from the twenty-second of December, 1775, and the history of its uniform from the fifth of September, 1776, when the Marine Committee of the Continental Congress made the following regulations regarding it:

Captains—A blue coat with red lapels, slashed cuffs, a stand-up collar, flat yellow buttons, blue breeches and a red waistcoat with yellow lace.

Lieutenants—A blue coat with red lapels and round cuffs faced, a stand-up collar, yellow buttons, blue breeches, and a plain red waistcoat.

Masters—A blue coat with lapels, round cuffs, blue breeches, and a red waistcoat.

Midshipmen—A blue coat with lapels, round cuffs faced with red, a stand-up collar, red at the buttons and buttonholes, blue breeches, and a red waistcoat.

* Life and Works of Gilbert Stuart.

Marines—A green coat faced with white, round cuffs, slashed sleeves and pockets, with buttons round the cuffs, a silver epaulet on the right shoulder, skirts turned back, buttons to suit the facings, white waistcoat, breeches edged with green, black gaiters and garters.

The men were to have green shirts if they could be procured.

Common sailors and seamen wore loose breeches and short square-cut jackets, according to Watson and other authorities. (Figure 351.)

The British troops established in America had been kept continually on the alert at different points to protect the inhabitants from the dreaded onslaught of the Indians, but a time of comparative quiet gave the commanders an opportunity to observe a certain hostile attitude the citizens had evinced toward the soldiery. This new phase of feeling in the Colonies was duly mentioned in official despatches, but was so little heeded that England felt a slight shock of alarm at the news of the bold measures of the colonists in

FIGURE 351.
Dress of an Ordinary Seaman, 1775.

Boston in 1768, and the spreading discontent which was becoming manifest in all directions. General Gage was ordered in June to send a force "sufficient to assist the magistrates and revenue officers in enforcing the law." Under Colonel Dalrymple the 14th and 29th

Foot* and one company of artillery with five guns arrived at Boston and demanded quarters in the town, which the citizens flatly refused to grant, and Gage, feeling the throbbing pulse of rebellion, withdrew the command and found quarters for the troops at the King's expense. Shortly after this the 64th and 65th regiments were sent as reinforcements, but they were not able to awe the "mob of Boston," which devoted every spare moment to drilling. They found an opportunity to practise the skill thus acquired under their leader, Samuel Adams, in the riots of 1770, which resulted in the withdrawal of both British battalions from the city. The tax on tea and its consequences on the sixteenth of December, 1773, proved a harbinger of the coming trouble. Gage returned from a visit to England, where his chief object had been to explain the tension of affairs in America, with more troops and the title of Governor of the Province of Massachusetts. Ten thousand men were then ordered to America instead of the twenty thousand asked for by Gage.

Meanwhile the Provincial Congress had met at Cambridge and passed resolutions for the collection and manufacture of arms, and General Gage, hearing that a quantity of powder and ammunition had been stored at Concord, sent the flank company of his garrison to seize it. This was the nineteenth of April, 1775, forever memorable in American history.

Paul Revere's gallant ride had not been in vain. The British troops found a body of militia drawn up on the village green at Concord to protect the stores, and after a fierce skirmish the Redcoats were obliged to retreat, followed for about fifteen miles by the Provincials, whose numbers were augmented at every point on the road by "patriots in homespun." This battle of Lexington brings us to the organization of the Continental army, which was strongly urged by the Provincial Congress. The militia troops before Boston had already shown

* For the uniforms of these British regiments, see Her Majesty's Army, by Walter Richards, with coloured plates.

FIGURE 352.

FIGURE 353.

FIGURE 354.

FIGURE 355.

FIGURE 352.—Portrait of Washington, drawn from life, showing hair in pigtail queue.

FIGURE 353.—Portrait of Henry Laurens, Jr., drawn from life, showing hair in side puffs and pigtail queue.

FIGURE 354.—Portrait of W. H. Drayton, Esq., drawn from life, showing hair arranged in puff on top and queue.

FIGURE 355.—Portrait of Gouverneur Morris, drawn from life, showing smooth hair and queue.

good metal in their composition; many of them had fought in the French and Indian War. The Continental army began to drill and manœuvre with redoubled energy, although in the eyes of the British army "their equipment was deficient and their discipline very faulty indeed."

Contemporary letters written from Boston before the Revolution give a vivid picture of the situation.

"The people in England have been taught to believe that five or six thousand regular troops would be sufficient to humble us into the lowest submission to any parliamentary act, however tyrannical. But we are not so ignorant in military affairs and unskilled in the use of arms as they take us to be. A spirit for martial skill has strangely catched from one to another throughout at least the New England colonies. A number of companies in many of our towns are already able to go through the military exercises in all its forms with more dexterity and a better grace than some of the regiments which have been sent to us, and all our men from twenty to sixty years of age are either formed or forming into companies and regiments with officers of their own choosing, to be steadily tutored in the military art. It is not doubted but by next spring one hundred thousand men will be well qualified to come forth for the defense of our liberties and rights should there be a call for it. We have besides in the New England Colonies alone a number of men who, in the last war, were made regulars by their services over your troops now in Boston. I cannot help observing to you here that we have in this town a company of boys from about ten to fourteen years of age who in the opinion of the best judges can go thro' the whole military exercises with more dexterity than a great part of the regulars have been able to do since they have been here."*

An interesting description of the dress and arms of the famous Minute Men is given in the History of Woodbury.†

* Extract from a letter of Charles Chauncey to Richard Price, Boston, January 10, 1775. Massachusetts Historical Society Proceedings, Boston, 1903.

† History of Ancient Woodbury, Connecticut, by William Cothren.

"As the militia rallied on the several calls and detachments, at a minute's or an hour's warning, in whatever clothes they happened to have on, with whatever weapons of war came first to hand, or had descended to them from their fathers, they often presented a very grotesque appearance. They wore small-clothes, coming down and fastening just below the knee, and long stockings with cowhide shoes, ornamented by large buckles, while not a pair of boots graced the company. The coats and waistcoats were loose and of huge dimensions, with colours as various as the barks of the oak, sumach, and other trees of our hills and swamps could make them, and their shirts were all made of flax, and, like every other part of the dress, were homespun. On their heads were worn large round-top and broad-brimmed hats. Their arms were as various as their costumes; here and there an old soldier carried a heavy queen's arm, with which he had done service at the conquest of Canada, twenty years previous, while by his side walked a stripling boy with a Spanish fuzee, not half its weight or calibre, which his grandfather may have taken at Havana, while not a few had old French pieces, that dated back to the reduction of Louisburg. Instead of the cartridge-box, a large powder-horn was slung under the arm, and occasionally a bayonet might be seen bristling in the ranks. Some of the swords of the officers had been made by our province blacksmiths, perhaps from some farming utensil; they looked serviceable, but heavy and uncouth. Such was the appearance of the Continentals, to whom a well-appointed army was soon to lay down their arms."

It is more than likely that the hardest fighting of the war of the Revolution was done by men dressed in hunting shirts of dressed leather, with leather breeches and buckskin shoes. At Bunker Hill the British regiments engaged were the flank companies of the 4th, 10th, 18th, 22nd, 23rd, 35th, 59th, 63rd, and 65th, the entire strength of the 5th, 38th, 42nd, 47th, and 52nd, and two battalions of marines;*

* History of the British Army, by J. W. Fortescue.

FIGURE 356.

FIGURE 357.

FIGURE 358.

FIGURE 359.

FIGURE 360.

FIGURE 356.—Silhouette of John Randolph of Roanoke.

FIGURE 357.—Silhouette of Washington, showing fine net over the hair and queue. (This was reproduced through the kindness of the late Dr. S. Weir Mitchell, who owned one of the few copies of this portrait.)

FIGURE 358.—A silhouette of Bishop White in the knickerbockers worn by English churchmen.

FIGURE 359.—Silhouette of Alexander Hamilton.

FIGURE 360.—A silhouette of James McClellan of Connecticut, showing the queue worn in the last year of the eighteenth century.

these men, in the splendid uniforms of the British regulars, formed a striking contrast to the oddly dressed Continentals. General Washington, who had been chosen unanimously for the Commander-in-Chief of the Continental Army, July 2, 1775, took command of the strangely assorted company before Boston, and later of the three thousand men from Pennsylvania, Virginia, and Maryland.

A few of the provincial regiments were equipped with uniforms, notably the New Jersey Infantry, under Colonel Schuyler, which went by the name of the Jersey Blues, from their coats of blue cloth faced with red; gray stockings and buckskin breeches completed the costume. The Virginia Infantry, of which Washington was colonel, adopted the Whig colours, blue and buff; coats of dark blue faced with buff, with waistcoats and breeches of buff. This was Washington's uniform when he took command of the army at Cambridge. (July, 1775.)

FIGURE 361.
Uniform of the Light-Horse Troop of Philadelphia.

From the "History of the First Troop City Cavalry," which on many occasions had the honour of escorting the Commander-in-Chief, the following account is taken:

"UNIFORM OF THE LIGHT-HORSE OF THE CITY OF PHILA-
DELPHIA. *

"A dark brown short coat, faced and lined with white; white
vest and breeches; high-topped boots; round black hat, bound with
silver cord; a buck's tail; housings brown, edged with white, and
the letters L. H. worked on them." And arms: "A carbine, a pair
of pistols and holsters, with flounces of brown cloth trimmed with
white; a horseman's sword; white belts for the sword and carbine."

In the early part of this year (1775), Captain Markoe presented
to the Troop a handsome silken standard. It is of great historic
interest as being the first flag which bore upon it the thirteen stripes,
symbolizing the thirteen colonies then asserting their rights and
ultimately struggling for their independence. Its first recorded duty
brought the Troop early into the notice of General Washington, who
passed through .Philadelphia June 23, 1775, and was escorted by
the Troop as far as New York, on his journey to the camp at Cambridge, Massachusetts.

In order that reliable descriptions of the uniforms worn by the
soldiers from 1775 to 1800 may be had, extracts from contemporary
official papers, reprinted under the supervision of the Quartermaster-
General of the United States (Washington, 1895), are quoted verbatim.

Resolved. That thirteen thousand coats be provided............
and one thereof be given to each non-commissioned Officer and
Soldier of the Massachusetts forces.

Resolved. That each coat be faced with the same kind of cloth of
which it is made; that the coats be made in the common, plain way,
without lappels, short and with small folds. (Proceedings of Massachusetts Provincial Congress, July 5, 1775.)

Resolved. That the Committee of Supplies...................
are to cause all the coats to be buttoned with pewter buttons, and that
the coats for each Regiment, respectively, have buttons of the same

* Afterwards known as First Troop Philadelphia City Cavalry.

FIGURE 362.

FIGURE 363.

FIGURE 364.

FIGURE 362.—A portrait of Commodore Barry of the United States Navy.

FIGURE 363.—Portrait of Paul Jones, Commodore of the United States Navy.

FIGURE 364.—Picture of the Camp at Valley Forge, showing military cloak and great coat worn by the officers and the Dutch blankets worn by the private soldiers.

number stamped on the face of them.—(*Amer. Archives*, Vol. II, 4th series, p. 1486.)

To prevent mistakes the General Officers and their Aids de Camp will be distinguished in the following manner: The Commander-in-Chief by a light blue ribband, worn across his breast, between his coat and waistcoat; the Majors and Brigadiers General by a pink ribband worn in like manner; the Aids de Camp by a green ribband. (General Orders, Headquarters, Cambridge, July 14, 1775.)—(*Amer. Archives*, Vol. II, 4th series, p. 1662.)

.... every Major of Brigade will be distinguished by a green ribband. .... (General Orders, Headquarters, Cambridge, July 20, 1775.)—(*Amer. Archives*, Vol. II, 4th series, p. 1710.)

As the Continental Army have unfortunately no uniforms, and consequently many inconveniences must arise from not being able always to distinguish the commissioned Officers from the non-commissioned, and, the non-commissioned from the privates, it is desired that some badges of distinction may be immediately provided; for instance, that the field Officers may have red or pink colored cockades in their hats; the Captains yellow or buff, and the subalterns green.

The sergeants may be distinguished by an epaulette or stripe of red cloth sewed upon their right shoulders; the Corporals by one of green. (Gen. Orders, Headquarters, Cambridge, 23 July, 1775.)—(*Amer. Archives*, Vol. II, 4th series, 1775, p. 1738.)

It being thought proper to distinguish the Majors from the Brigadiers General by some particular mark, for the future the Majors General will wear a broad *purple* ribband. (Gen. Orders, Headquarters, Cambridge, 24 July, 1775.)—(*Amer. Archives*, Vol. II, 4th series, 1775, p. 1739.)

The General also recommends it to the Colonels to provide *Indian* boots or leggings for their men, instead of stockings,............

especially as the General has hopes of prevailing with the Continental Congress to give each man a hunting shirt......................... (General Orders, Headquarters, Cambridge, August 7, 1775.)—(*Amer. Archives*, Vol. III, 4th series, p. 248.)

The enlisted men of the 1st Virginia Regiment of Infantry were, however, in the year 1775, uniformed at their own expense in hunting shirts, leggings, and white bindings on their hats.—(*Amer. Archives*, Vol. IV, 4th series, p. 92.)

Resolved. That when the *Green Mountain Boys* are raised, each of them shall be furnished with a coat, and.................be requested to purchase green cloth for that purpose, and red cloth sufficient to face these coats. .... (New York Prov. Congress, Aug. 15, 1775.)—(*Amer. Archives*, Vol. III, 4th series, p 530.)

Resolved. That Clothing be provided for the new Army by the Continent and paid for by stoppages out of the soldiers wages......... That as much as possible of the cloth for this purpose be dyed brown and the distinctions of the Regiments made in the facings.—(Res. Congress, Nov. 4, 1775.)—(*Amer. Archives*, Vol. III, 4th series, p. 1907.)

The Colonels upon the new establishment to settle as soon as possible with the Quartermaster General the uniform of their respective Regiments that the buttons may be properly numbered and the work finished without delay. (General Orders, Headquarters, Cambridge, Nov. 13, 1775.)—(*Amer. Archives*, Vol. III, 4th series.)

It is recommended to those Corps which are not already supplied with uniforms, to provide hunting shirts for their men. (General Orders, Headquarters, New York, May 6, 1776.)—(*Amer. Archives*, Vol. VI, 4th series, p. 426.)

The General being sensible of the difficulty and expense of providing Clothes, of almost any kind, for the Troops, feels an unwillingness to recommend, much more to order, any kind of Uniform; but

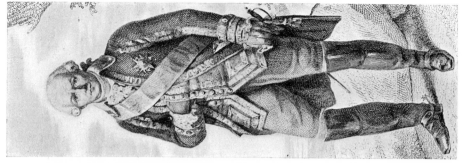

FIGURE 367.

FIGURE 366

FIGURE 365.

FIGURE 365.—General Warren, in the dress of a minute-man.

FIGURE 366.—General Daniel Morgan in a buckskin coat of the Virginia rangers.

FIGURE 367.—Comte de Rochambeau, showing dress of a French officer, 1791.

as it is absolutely necessary that men should have Clothes, and appear decent and tight, he earnestly encourages the use of Hunting Shirts, with long breeches made of the same cloth, gaiter fashion about the legs, to all those yet unprovided. (General Orders, Headquarters, New York, July 24, 1776.)—(*Amer. Archives*, Vol. I, 5th series, p. 677.)

Resolved that, for the further encouragement of the non-commissioned Officers and soldiers who shall engage in service during the war. A suit of Clothes be annually given to each of said officers and soldiers; to consist, for the present year, of two linen hunting shirts, two pairs of overalls, a leathern or woolen waistcoat with sleeves, one pair of breeches, a hat or leather cap, two shirts, two pair of hose and two pair of shoes. (Continental Congress, Oct. 8, 1776.)—(*Amer. Archives*, Vol. II, 5th series, p. 1392.)

.... the Congress of the United States have .... further resolved to give .... annually to each man one complete suit of clothing, which, for the present year, is to consist of two linen hunting shirts, two pair of stockings, two pair of shoes, two pair of overalls, a leathern or woolen jacket with sleeves, one pair of breeches, and one Leathern cap or hat. (General Orders, Headquarters, October 24, 1776.)—(*Amer. Archives*, Vol. III, 5th series, p. 331.)

In 1777, and subsequently, the uniform for the four regular regiments constituting the Corps of Artillery was a blue or black coat reaching to the knee, and full trimmed, lappels fastened back, with ten open-worked button-holes in yellow silk on the breast of each lappel, and ten large regimental yellow buttons, at equal distances, on each side; three large yellow regimental buttons on each cuff, and a like number on each pocket-flap. The skirts to hook back, showing the red lining, bottom of coat cut square, red lappels, cuff linings, and standing capes; single-breasted white waistcoat, with twelve small yellow regimental buttons, white breeches, black half gaiters, white stock, ruffled shirt, and at the wrists, and black cocked hat bound with yellow; red plume and black cockade, gilt-handled small sword and gilt epaulettes.—(*Mag. Amer. Hist.*, Vol. I, p. 473.)

Congress, by resolution of March 23, 1779, "authorized and directed the Commander-in-Chief, according to circumstances of supplies of Clothing, to fix and prescribe the uniform as well with regard to color and facings as the cut or fashion of the Clothes to be worn by the troops of the respective States and regiments, woolen overalls for winter and linen for summer to be substituted for the breeches."

In accordance with the above Resolution, the following General Order, dated Headquarters, Moore's House, 2 Oct., 1779, was promulgated by General Washington:

"The following are the uniforms that have been determined for the troops of these States respectively, so soon as the state of the public supplies will permit of their being furnished accordingly; and, in the meantime, it is recommended to the Officers to endeavor to accommodate their uniforms to the standard, that when the men come to be supplied, there may be a proper uniformity.

NEW HAMPSHIRE, MASSACHUSETTS, RHODE ISLAND and CONNECTICUT.

Blue, faced with white; buttons and linings white.

NEW YORK and NEW JERSEY.

Blue, faced with buff; white linings and buttons.

PENNSYLVANIA, DELAWARE, MARYLAND and VIRGINIA.

Blue, faced with red; buttons and linings white.

NORTH CAROLINA, SOUTH CAROLINA and GEORGIA.

Blue, faced with blue; buttonholes edged with narrow white lace or tape; buttons and linings white.

ARTILLERY and ARTILLERY ARTIFICERS.

Blue, faced with scarlet; scarlet linings; yellow buttons, yellow-bound hats. Coats edged with narrow lace or tape, and buttonholes bound with same.

LIGHT DRAGOONS.

The whole blue, faced with white; white buttons and linings."

FIGURE 368.　　FIGURE 369.　　FIGURE 371.　FIGURE 372.

FIGURE 370.

FIGURE 373.

FIGURE 374.

FIGURE 375.

MILITARY UNIFORMS IN AMERICA
1775-1785

FIGURE 368 shows the uniform recommended by Washington in the early part of the Revolution. A hunting shirt of thick linen cloth or buckskin, according to the season, with ruffled strips of the same material round the neck, on the shoulders, and about the knees; breeches to match and gaiters made of tan cloth steeped in a tan vat until it reached the colour of a dry leaf. Large hat unlooped, black stock, and pigtail queue.

FIGURE 369 represents a minute-man in the ordinary costume of the day. Suit of blue cloth, waistcoat of buff, cocked hat.

FIGURE 370.—A member of the 1st Co. Governor's Foot Guard (Connecticut) in scarlet cloth coat, faced with black, trimmed with gold braid and buttons. Buff cassimere waistcoat and breeches, leggings of brown leather. Bearskin hat with scarlet pompon at one side.

FIGURE 371.—Pennsylvania Regiment of the Continental Line, First Pennsylvania Infantry. Brown coat faced with buff. Overalls instead of breeches and gaiters.

FIGURE 372.—Second Pennsylvania Infantry. Blue coat faced with red, black stock. Cocked hat with tape binding, and buckskin overalls.

FIGURE 373.—Uniform directed by the Minister of War, 1785. Blue faced and lined with white for the infantry, and blue faced and lined with red for the artillery. Buff waistcoat and breeches; half leggings of leather.

FIGURE 374.—Light Infantry in 1782. Blue coat, white facings, white waistcoat and breeches, high leggings, black stock, round hat ferretted, and pigtail queue.

FIGURE 375.—Front view of Figure 373.

Resolved. That the following articles be delivered as a suit of Clothes for the current and every succeeding year of their service to the Officers of the line and staff, entitled by any Resolution of Congress to receive the same, viz: one hat, one watch coat, one body coat, four vests, one for winter and three for summer, four pairs of breeches, two for winter and two for summer, four shirts, six pair of stockings, three pair thereof worsted and three of thread, four pair of Shoes.—(*Journals of Congress*, Nov. 25, 1779.)

As it is at all times of great importance both for the sake of appearance and for the regularities of service that the different military ranks should be distinguished from each other, and more especially at present:—

The Commander-in-Chief has thought proper to establish the following distinctions and strongly recommends it to all the Officers to endeavor to conform to them as speedily as possible.

The Major Generals to wear a blue coat with buff facings, yellow buttons, white or buff underclothes, two epaulettes, with two stars upon each and a black-and-white feather in the hat.

The Brigadier Generals, the same uniform as the Major Generals with the difference of one star instead of two and a white feather.

The Colonels, Lieutenant Colonels, and Majors, the uniform of their regiments, and two epaulettes.

The Captains, the uniforms of their regiments and an epaulette on the right shoulder.

The subalterns, the uniform of their regiment and an epaulette on the left shoulder.

The Aides de Camp, the uniforms of their ranks and Corps, or if they belong to no Corps, of their General Officers.

Those of the Major Generals and Brigadier Generals to have a green feather in their hat. Those of the Commander-in-Chief a white and green.

The Inspectors, as well Sub as Brigade, the uniform of their ranks and Corps, with a blue feather in the hat.

The Corps of Engineers and that of Sappers and Miners, a blue coat with buff facings, red lining, buff undercloaths, and the epaulettes of their respective ranks.

Such of the Staff as have Military rank, to wear the uniform of their ranks and of the Corps to which they belong in the line.　Such as have no military rank to wear plain coats, with a cockade and sword.

All officers, as well warrant as commissioned, to wear a cockade and side arms either a sword or genteel bayonet.　(Headquarters, Short Hills, Sunday, June 18, 1780.)

As it is much wished to establish uniformity in the corps; the officers are directed not to make any changes in the dress of themselves or their men 'till orders are given for a general rule.

The feathers directed to be worn by Major Generals are to have the white below, the black above; it will be best to have one feather the upper part black.　It is recommended to the officers to have black and white cockades, a black ground with a white relief, emblematic of the expected union of the two armies.　(Headquarters, Precaness, July 19, 1780.)

As nothing adds more to the beauty and appearance of a Corps, than exact uniformity of dress, the General recommends it thus early to the "Field Officers" newly arranged to fix upon a fashion for the regimental clothing of the officers of their respective corps (if it is not already done), confining themselves to the ground, facing, linings and buttons already assigned to the States to which they belong.

The General sees with concern the difficulties which the Officers labor under in procuring Cloth.　It is not therefore his wish that those who are already furnished should run themselves to the expense of new uniforms, if their old are not exactly conformable, but that they should in future comply strictly with the regimental fashion and, if possible, get their old clothes altered to it.　It has a very odd appearance especially to Foreigners to see the same corps of officers each differing from the other in fashion of the facings, sleeves and pockets of their coats.

An attention to these minutiæ has been thought proper in all services; it becomes peculiarly so in ours at this time as we shall more than probable take the field next campaign in conjunction with

FIGURE 376.

FIGURE 377.

FIGURE 378.

FIGURE 379.

FIGURE 376.—A portrait of Major-General Pinckney.
FIGURE 377.—A portrait of Major-General St. Clair.
FIGURE 378.—A portrait of General O. H. Williams.
FIGURE 379.—A portrait of General Andrew Pickens.

our Allies, composed of the first troops in Europe, who will receive impressions and form opinions from the first view ....

Strict attention is to be paid to the order of the 18th of June last, distinguishing the rank of officers by their badges. (Headquarters, Totoway, Nov. 15, 1780.)

ORDERS FOR THE MASSACHUSETTS LINE.

January 5th, 1781.

The Committee of Officers appointed to fix upon the fashion of the Massachusetts' uniform, have reported thereupon, and it is as follows:—

The color of the coats, waistcoat, linings and buttons, to be agreeable to the General Orders of the 2nd of October, 1779.

The length of the coat, to the upper part of the knee-pan, and to be cut high in the neck. As 3 is to 5, so is the skirt to the waist of the coat; or divide the whole length of the coat into 8 equal parts, take 5 for the waist and 3 for the skirts.

The lappel, at the top of the breast, to be 3 inches wide, and the bottom $2\frac{3}{10}$ inches; the lappel to be as low as the waist, and its wing to button within an inch of the shoulder seam with a small button on the cape. The epaulette to be worn directly on the top of the shoulder joint on the same button with the wing of the lappel. A round and close cuff, three inches wide, with four close worked buttonholes. The cape to be made with a peak behind, and its width in proportion to the lappels. The pocket flaps to be scollopped, four buttonholes, the two inner close worked, the two outer open worked, and to be set on in a curved line from the bottom of the lappel to the button on the hip. The coat to be cut full behind, with a fold on each back skirt, and two close worked buttonholes on each.

Ten open worked buttonholes on the breast of each lappel, with ten large buttons, at equal distance; four large buttons on each cuff, four on each pocket flap, and four on each fold. Those on the cuffs and pocket flaps to be placed agreeable to the buttonholes; and those on the folds, one on the hip, one at the bottom, and two in the centre, at an equal distance with those on the lappel. The coat is to button or hook as low at the fourth buttonhole on the breast, and is to be fiaunt at the bottom with a genteel and military air. Four hooks and eyes on the breast as low as the coat is allowed to button. The skirts to hook up with a blue heart at each corner, with such device as the Field Officers of each Regiment shall direct. The bottoms of the coat to be cut square. The waistcoat to be single-breasted, with twelve buttons and holes on the breast, with pocket flaps, four close worked buttonholes and four buttons, which shall appear below the flaps. The breeches are to be made with a half fall; four buttons on each knee. The small buttons on the waistcoat to be of the same kind with the large ones on the coat. The number of the Regiment is to be in the centre of the button, with such device at the Field Officers shall direct. The epaulettes to be worn agreeable to his Excellency the Commander-in-Chief's orders of June 18, 1780.

A fashionable military cock'd hat, with a silver button loop, and a small button with the number of the Regiment. To wear a black stock when on duty and on the *parade*.

No edging, vellum lace, or indeed any other ornaments which are not mentioned, to be added to the uniform. No officer is to be permitted, at any time, to wear any other uniform than that of his Regiment.—(*Review Orders*, by H. Whiting, p. 164.)

The clothier is, if practicable, to obtain worsted *shoulder knots*, for the non-commissioned officers; the sergeants are to be distinguished by one on each shoulder; and the corporals by one on the right shoulder; and in the meantime it is proposed that a piece of white cloth should be substituted by way of distinction. (General Orders, Headquarters, Newburgh, May 14, 1782.)

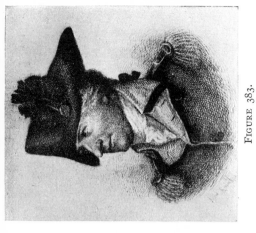

FIGURE 383.

FIGURE 384.

FIGURE 380.

FIGURE 381.

FIGURE 382.

FIGURE 380.—Portrait of General Montgomery, showing a black silk stock, hair in queue.

FIGURE 381.—General Francis Marion, showing coat with high collar and peculiar waistcoat.

FIGURE 382.—General Israel Putnam, showing uniform of a Continental trooper.

FIGURE 383.—General Philemon Dickinson, showing high cut coat.

FIGURE 384.—General John Sullivan, showing cocked hat edged with braid and a gorget.

BRIGADE ORDERS, WEST POINT.

June 17, 1782.

The Honorable Brigadier-General Paterson, having expressed his wish that some honorary mark of distinction should be worn by each Non-commissioned Officer or Private in his Brigade, who has served in the Army of the United States a certain length of time; and has also made a present of materials for that purpose:—

The Commandant thinks proper to direct, that each Non-Commissioned Officer and Private, who has served four years in any Continental Regiment, shall be entitled to wear one stripe of white tape, on the left sleeve of his regimental coat, which shall extend from seam to seam, on the upper part of the sleeve, three inches from and parallel with the shoulder seam, so that the tape may form a herring-bone figure.

That none presume to wear the badge of distinction, but by the immediate permission of the Colonel or Commandant of the Regiment, who, on its being made to appear to his full satisfaction, that the man who applies for the badge has served four years, as above, will please to order this honor publicly conferred on him. The Commandant further directs, that when any Non-Commissioned Officer or Soldier shall complete eight years service, he shall have the addition of another stripe set on one inch below the first.

As emulation is essential to promote discipline, the Commandant wishes, by all laudable measure, to kindle the flame in every breast; and considers that punishment, as well as reward, is absolutely necessary in all government; to promote which design, he directs that these marks of distinction, in the first instance, be for all who have actually served as above, without discrimination of character; but, that after the publication of this order, none who shall commit a crime for which they are punishable by a Court Martial, shall be entitled to this honorary badge for four years from the time they were found punishable; and should any one who is honored with the badge be so lost to a sense of honor, which every soldier ought to possess, as to fall under the sentence of a Court Martial, he is to be divested of this badge of honor at the head of the Regiment, and excluded from wearing it until he shall retrieve his character, by four years' unblemished service. (*Review Orders*, by Henry Whiting, p. 220.)

Honorary Badges of distinction are to be conferred on the veteran non-commissioned officers and soldiers of the Army, who have served more than three years with bravery, fidelity and good conduct, for this purpose a narrow piece of white cloth, of an angular form is to be fixed to the left arm on the uniform coats. Non-commissioned officers and soldiers who have served with equal reputation more than six years, are to be distinguished by two pieces of cloth, set on parallel to each other in a similar form .... whenever any singularly meritorious action is performed, the author of it shall be permitted to wear on his facings, over the left breast, the figure of a heart in purple cloth or silk, edged with narrow lace or binding. (Headquarters, Newburgh, Aug. 7, 1782.)

In order to prevent misapplication of the honorary badges of distinction to be conferred on the non-commissioned officers and soldiers in consequence of long and faithful service, through any mistake or misapprehension of the orders of the 7th inst., the General thinks proper to inform the Army that they are only attainable by an uninterrupted series of faithful and honorable services.

The badges which non-commissioned officers and soldiers are permitted to wear on the left arm as a mark of long and faithful service, are to be of the same color with the facings of the corps they belong to and not white in every instance as directed in the orders of the 7th instant. (General Orders, Headquarters, Newburgh, Aug. 11, 1782.)

The Honorable Secretary of War having been pleased to direct that the uniforms of the American Cavalry and Infantry shall in future be blue ground with red facings and white linings and buttons: The General gives this early notice that provision may be made accordingly before the Army shall receive their clothing for the present year.

The Corps of the Artillery is to retain its present uniform, and the Sappers and Miners will have the same. (Headquarters, Newburgh, Dec. 6, 1782.)

The non arrival of the clothing imported from Europe renders the greatest economy in that article doubly necessary. The Commander-in-Chief therefore recommends that the business of turning and repairing the coats of last year should now be considered as a primary object, in doing which a certain model as to the fashion and length, (for the coats ought to be made something shorter than at present) will be established by the commanding officer of the corps, from which there must be no deviation......................
It is expected scarlet cloth for cuffs, capes and perhaps half facings will be furnished. (Headquarters, Newburgh, Feb. 24, 1783.)

Notwithstanding the proposed alteration in the uniforms of the Infantry and Cavalry it appears necessary from inevitable circumstances that all the Light Infantry companies should be cloathed in blue coats faced with white until further orders. (General Orders, Headquarters, Newburgh, March 3, 1783.)

The regiments which have not turned and repaired their coats are to draw lots for the scarlet cloth which arrived yesterday. (General Orders, Newburgh, April 14, 1783.)

When the Revolutionary War ended, one regular regiment of Infantry .... and two companies of the corps of artillery were retained in service. (General Orders, Headquarters, West Point, 23 Dec., 1783.) The Uniform of the infantry regiment was dark blue, with white facings, white linings, black cocked hats, white hat bindings, white worsted shoulder knots, white buttons, silver epaulettes for Officers, white cross belts, black stocks, white under dress, black gaiters, and black plume. The artillery uniform remained as heretofore; dark blue faced with scarlet, scarlet linings, yellow buttons, yellow binding for black felt cocked hat, and yellow edging of buttonholes; white under dress, gold epaulettes for Officers; and yellow worsted shoulder knots for non-commissioned officers and buff belts, white cravats and black plume, with red top.—(*Mag. Amer. Hist.*, Vol. I, p. 482.)

The coats of the musicians remained red with blue facings, blue waistcoats and breeches, silk epaulettes for Chief Musician. (General Orders, War Dept., N. Y., 30 Jan., 1787.)—(*Mag. Amer. Hist.*, Vol. I, p. 482.)

The Infantry Officers were now required to wear half boots, white pantaloons and white vests, double breasted. (General Orders, Headquarters, Loftus Heights, 19 January, 1791.)

During the period of the confederation the troops retained substantially the revolutionary uniforms. The cavalry had brass helmets with white horsehair. (Secty. War to Q. M. Genl. Saml. Hodgden, 4 Aug., 1792.)—(*Mag. Amer. Hist.*, Vol. I, p. 483.)

Their swords were "long horseman's sword, steel mounted." Officers of Artillery and Infantry had swords of sabre form respectively yellow mounted and steel mounted, two feet six inches in length for each company officer, and three feet in length for each field officer.—(*Mag. Amer. Hist.*, Vol. I, p. 483.)

The officers being arranged to the four sub-legions it now becomes expedient to give those Legions distinctive marks, which are to be as follows, viz:
The first Sub-legion, white binding upon their caps with white plumes and black hair.
The second Sub-legion, red binding to their caps, red plumes with white hair.
The third Sub-legion, yellow binding to their caps, yellow plumes and black hair.
The fourth Sub-legion, green binding to their caps, green plumes and white hair. (General Orders, Headquarters, Pittsburgh, 11 Sept., 1792.)

The Officers will wear plain cocked hats with no other distinctive marks, but the plumes of their respective Sub-legions, except in actual service or action, when they will wear the same caps with the non-commissioned officers and privates of their respective Sub-legions. (Gen. Orders, Headquarters, Pittsburgh, Sept. 12, 1792.)

The following Select Corps shall be immediately drafted from the Legion .... the respective pay-masters will deliver to the Captains or officers commanding companies ....Two pairs linen overalls, two pairs of shoes and two shirts for each non-commissioned officer and private. .... (Gen. Orders, Headquarters, Greenville, June, 30, 1794.)

Paymasters ....will also furnish the commanding officers of each troop of Dragoons with two shirts and two pairs of linen overalls per man ....
The garrison duty men will parade for Review tomorrow...... fresh shaved and well powdered ...... All such as have five months and upwards to serve will be furnished with two pair of linen overalls, two shirts and two pairs of shoes per man. Those whose term of service will expire on or before the 1st of December next with one pair of shoes, one pair of overalls, and one shirt per man .... (Gen. Orders, Headquarters, Greenville, July 1, 1794.)

The Deputy Quartermaster will issue all the bearskins to the Sub-legionary Quartermasters for the use of the Battalion Companies. (Gen. Orders, Headquarters, Greenville, July 9, 1794.)

In 1794 the artillery received helmets, with red plumes. (Secty. War to Quartermaster Genl. Saml. Hodgden, 14 July, 1794.)—(*Mag. Amer. Hist.*, Vol. I, p. 484.)

The commanding officers of the respective Sub-legions, will make out a particular return to the Adjutant General of the number of Non-commissioned officers and soldiers......entitled to summer clothing, and who have not already been furnished........that the whole of the troops may appear in the most soldierly condition. On the 4th July......the Commanding Officers of Corps will cause the uniforms to be repaired, and the Hats and Caps properly decorated. The Acting Quartermaster will procure bearskins for covering the hats and caps. (General Orders, Headquarters, Greenville, June 26, 1795.)

The following uniform for the officers of Infantry is to be observed and adopted until otherwise regulated. Coats reaching to the knee and full trimmed, scarlet lappels, cuffs and standing capes, white buttons and trimmings, lapels and cape two inches, and cuffs three inches wide. Vests and breeches white, the former with short flaps and three buttons. Black stocks or cravats, Cocked Hats, and full boots with black tops. (General Orders, Headquarters, Greenville, 16th Feb., 1796.)

In 1799 the white plume was again prescribed for the Infantry ....(Gen. Orders, Headquarters, Loftus Heights, 2 Jan., 1799.)—(*Mag. Amer. Hist.*, p. 485.)

The uniform of the Commander-in-Chief to be a blue coat, with yellow buttons, and gold epaulettes, each having three silver stars, with lining, cape and cuffs of buff—in winter buff vest and breeches; in summer, a white vest and breeches, of nankeen.

The coat to be without lappels, and embroidered on the cape and cuffs and pockets; a white plume in the hat, to be a further distinction. The Adjutant General, the aids and secretaries of the Commander-in-Chief, to be likewise distinguished by a white plume.

The uniform of the other General Officers to be a blue coat, with yellow buttons, gold epaulettes, linings and facings of buff—the underclothes the same with those of the Commander in Chief.

The Major generals to be distinguished by two silver stars in each epaulet, and except the Inspector General, by a black and white plume, the black below.

The Brigadier to be distinguished by one silver star on each epaulet, and by a red and white plume, the red below.

The Aids, of all general officers, who are taken from regiments, and the officers of inspection, to wear the uniform of the regiments from which they are taken.

"The aids to be severally distinguished by the like plumes, which are worn by the general officers, to whom they are respectively attached.

The uniforms of the aids of the commander in chief when not taken from regiments, to be a blue coat with yellow button, and gold epaulet, buff lining and facings .... the same under-clothes with the commander-in-chief.

The Inspector General, his aids, and the officers of inspection generally, to be distinguished by a blue plume. The Quartermaster General and other military officers in his department, to be distinguished by a green plume.

The uniform of the Infantry and artillery to be a blue coat with white buttons and red facings, white underclothes and cocked hats .... the length of the officers coats to reach the knees, the coats of the Infantry, to be lined with white, of the artillery with red. The uniform of the Cavalry, to be a green coat, with white buttons, linings and facings; white vest and breeches and helmet caps.

Each Colonel to be distinguished by two epaulettes; each Major, by one epaulet on the right shoulder, and a strap on the left. All the Field Officers, (except as above) and the Regimental Staff, to wear red plumes .... the Officers of companies are to wear red plumes.

Captains to be distinguished by an epaulet on the right shoulder; Lieutenants by one on the left shoulder; cadets by a strap on the right shoulder. The epaulets and straps of the regimental officers to be of silver.

Sergeant Majors and Quartermaster Sergeants, to be distinguished by two red worsted epaulets; Sergeants by a like epaulet on the right shoulder; Corporals by a like epaulet on the left shoulder; the flank companies to be distinguished by red wings on the shoulders.

The coats of the Musicians to be of the colors of the facings of the corps to which they severally belong. The Chief Musician to wear two white worsted epaulets. All the Civil staff of the Army, to wear plain blue coats, with yellow buttons, and white underclothes. No gold or silver lace, except in the epaulets and straps to be worn.

The commissioned officers, and cadets to wear swords.

All persons belonging to the Army to wear a black cockade with a small white Eagle in the centre. The cockade of non-commissioned officers, musicians, and privates to be of leather, with Eagles of tin. The regiments to be distinguished from each other, numerically. The number of each regiment to be expressed in the buttons. (War Office, Philadelphia, 9 January, 1799.)

FIGURE 385.
Uniform of an American Officer, 1796.

From "The Uniform of the Army of the United States" (Washington, 1895) is taken the following description of the uniform of an officer from 1776 to 1799: "A blue coat, with red facings and white bindings and white buttons and button-holes, white waistcoat and breeches, white gloves, white epaulettes. Cocked hat bound with white, black pompon. Powdered hair in queue tied with narrow black silk ribbon. High black silk stock, ruffle of white shirt showing at neck and wrists." (Figure 385.)

The short-waisted coats and high collars which marked the end of the eighteenth century were specially noticeable in the uniforms, both military and naval, and form a very striking contrast to the long-waisted garments which characterized the close of the seventeenth century.

For uniforms of the French officers in America during the Revolutionary period see Our French Allies, by Edwin M. Stone. For uniforms of the French troops at this period, see Racinet, Costumes Historiques, vol. v.

The uniforms of a Hessian dragoon and of the Brunswick Troopers in America during the Revolutionary period are given in American History from German Archives, by Mr. J. G. Rosengarten.

GLOSSARY

Glossary

Adonis wigs.—Made of fine white hair, were very fashionable and very expensive in the early part of the eighteenth century.

Aggrapes.—From the French *agrape*, "a clasp or buckle"; also "hooks and eyes."

Aiglet or **Aiguillette.**—A metal tag or point to a lace.

Aigret or **Egret.**—A tuft of feathers worn on the head. Fly caps with egrets were advertised in Boston, 1755.

Alamode.—A plain soft glossy silk often mentioned in advertisements in Colonial newspapers under various spellings—"elamond," "alimod," "olamod," "alemod," "arlimod," "allamode," and "ellimod," are some of the variations. It was used throughout the eighteenth century.

Allapine.—A strong woolen stuff spelled often "ellapine," "allpine," and "alpine," and very popular for men's wear during the first half of the eighteenth century.

Amazeen.—(under various spellings)—A strong corded silk in use from the time of Elizabeth to George III. Often advertised in Colonial papers.

Aprons.—First worn for use by the careful housewife as well as servants and workingmen, the apron became by some unaccountable freak of fashion late in the sixteenth century an article of full dress. In 1659 we read that green aprons went out of fashion. Aprons were worn in 1744 so long that they nearly touched the ground.

Artois.—A long cloak made with several capes and used by men and women in 1790.

Atlas.—A soft silk with satin surface, made in the East.

Baise, Baize, or **Bayes.**—A coarse woolen cloth made at Colchester in the days of Queen Elizabeth. Advertised in Colonial papers in all colours, and used for the clothing of servants and negro slaves.

Balandrans or **Balandranas.**—Cloaks with armholes.

Band.—A collar of lace or linen stiffened with starch or underpropped with wire. When allowed to fall upon the shoulders, it was termed a falling band.

Band-box.—Originally made to hold bands—whence the name.

Bandekyn.—A fabric of silk and gold thread.

Bandileers.—Cases of wood or tin, each containing a charge of powder, strung round the neck of a soldier.

Band-strings.—Were usually of ribbon or of cord finished with tassels; the latter were often decorated with pearls and other jewels.

Banyan.—Originally an Anglo-Indian name for a loose coat. A morning gown or wrapper worn by both sexes, usually of bright-coloured cloth or damask. We read that these garments were much worn in Virginia, and were sometimes lined with a rich material, and thus could be worn either side out.

Barlicorns.—A dress fabric used in the Colonies. "Check'd barlicorns" were advertised in 1755.

Barragon or **Barracan.**—A corded stuff suitable for summer wear. Made originally in the Levant, of camel's-hair.

Barratine.—A stuff, probably of silk, used for petticoats, stomachers, and "forehead clothes" as early as 1697.

Barrow-coat.—A form of swaddling cloth wrapped about an infant's body and turned up and fastened at the bottom to keep the feet warm.

Barry or **Barrie.**—An under-skirt or petticoat.

Barvell.—A coarse leathern apron used by workingmen.

Batts.—Heavy low shoes laced in front. Sent to the New England Colonists in 1636 and after.

Beard-boxes.—Were made of pasteboard and worn at night over a beard to keep it in shape.

Bearer.—A roll of padding placed like a bustle at either hip to raise the skirt.

Bearing cloth.—Old name for a Christening blanket.

Bell-hoops.—Stiffened petticoats in the shape of a bell were fashionable in 1731.

Biggin.—Probably a corruption of *beguine*, "a nun," and sometimes spelled "begin." It was a close cap worn always by young children and sometimes by grown people before 1700.

Binder.—A band of flannel worn by babies under the shirt, sufficiently tight to give some support to the back.

Birdet.—A silk stuff made in China or India. "Strip'd and plain birdet" was advertised in New England in 1737.

Bishop.—A sort of bustle stuffed with horsehair.

Blodins.—(Old English)—Sky-blue.

Bob-wig.—A short close wig worn by men and boys of all classes on ordinary occasions from about 1725 to 1780.

Bodice or **a paire of Boddies.**—A sort of stays, an article of apparel worn often by dandies and in general use by women in the seventeenth century.

Bodkin.—A large pin for the hair, usually of gold or silver.

Bombards.—Padded breeches.

Bombazin, Bomberzeen, or **Bombax.**—A mixture of silk and cotton, frequently advertised in old papers.

Bone-lace.—Usually of linen thread made over bobbins of bone, whence the name.

Bonnet.—We read of silk bonnets as early as 1725 in New England, and in 1760 of satin bonnets, quilted bonnets, and Kitty Fisher bonnets, also of Quebeck and Garrick bonnets, but they do not appear in the portraits of the day, and were probably not as fashionable as hoods and hats until late in the eighteenth century.

Bonnet-paper.—A stiff pasteboard used for the frames of bonnets and hats.

Bosom-bottle.—A small flat glass bottle, sometimes covered with silk to match the gown, concealed in the stomacher of the dress to hold water for flowers, so generally worn by ladies in the last half of the eighteenth century.

Brawls or **Brouls.**—A blue and white striped cotton cloth made in India, advertised in newspapers 1785 to 1795.

Breast Knot or **Bosom Knot.**—A dainty touch of coloured ribbon worn from 1730 and for the remainder of the century.

Breeches.—Were worn by the early Colonists, of dressed leather, but afterward they were made of every material. At first the shape was loose, fastened in at the knee and waist, but before the end of the eighteenth century they were worn skin-tight.

Breeches-hooks.—A device upon which the breeches were hung to keep them in shape, mentioned in the middle of the eighteenth century.

Brigandine.—A plate coat.

Broadcloth.—A fine woolen cloth with a smooth surface, mostly used for men's garments, and always regarded with respect by the lower classes.

> Ye wha are fain to hae your name
> Wrote in the coney Book of Fame
> Let merit nae pretension claim
>   To laurelled wreath!
> But hop ye weel, baith back and wame
>   In gude Braid claith!
> Braid claith lends fock an unco heese!
> Makes many kail-worms butterflies!
> Gives mony a Doctor his degrees
>   For little skaith.
> In short you may be what you please,
>   Wi gude Braid Claith!
>   —*Robert Ferguson.*

Buff-coat.—A leather outer garment made exceedingly strong, sometimes ⅛ of an inch in thickness. Much used in the Civil Wars in England and by the Colonists of that period.

Buffin.—A coarse cloth first made in Elizabeth's reign.

Buffonts.—A piece of gauze or lace worn over or round the neck, and puffed out over the breast like a "pouter pidgeon." In New England papers of 1771 "Gauze Buffons" were advertised.

Bugles.—Glass beads used in trimmings very early in the Colonies.

Burgoigne.—The front part of a headdress next the hair.

Caddis or **Cades.**—A woolen tape, often woven into garters, and in common use in the seventeenth century.

Calash.—From the French *caléche*, a hood made to pull over the head, introduced into England in 1765 by the Duchess of Bedford and very popular in the Colonies. Possibly a revival of the old fashion seen in the recumbent effigies of the sixteenth and seventeenth centuries.

Calico.—Originally Calicut, from the town in India whence it was imported; later the name was applied to a cotton fabric in general wear at the time of the Revolution. Towards the end of the century calico was worn by people of all conditions. The French calicoes imported were very fine and delicate in colouring, and were often used for trimming plain materials.

Calks.—Clogs with spiked soles to keep one from slipping on the ice.

Callimanco.—According to Fairholt, a glazed linen fabric showing a pattern on one side only, but described by some writers as a fashionable woolen material with a fine gloss. It was undoubtedly popular in the Colonies. "Callimanco gounds" are mentioned in America in 1666.

Callot.—A plain cap or coif.

Camlet or **chamlet.**—A fabric made of wool or silk, sometimes of both, much used for cloaks and petticoats in all the Colonies. The name is derived from the place of its manufacture on the banks of the River Camlet in England.

Campaign-wigs.—Were very fashionable at the end of the seventeenth and beginning of the eighteenth centuries. They were full and curled towards the front.

Cannons.—Garters or breeches-fasteners.

Canvas.—A stiff woven cloth of flax or hemp.

Cap.—The general name for a popular head covering of both sexes.

> "Any cap whate'er it be
> Is still the sign of some degree."

Capuchin or **Capucine.**—A cloak with hood like a Capuchin monk's, fashionable in the early part of the eighteenth century.

Carcanet.—A necklace set with stones or strung with pearls.

Cardinal.—Cloak with a hood like the mozetta worn by cardinals which came into use early in the eighteenth century.

Casket-girls.—Name given to the girls sent out by the French Government to Louisiana, each provided with a small trunkful of clothing.

Cassock.—A loose coat, like a jerkin, worn by men.

Catgut.—A cloth woven in cords and used for lining and stiffening garments.

Cathedral Beard.—According to Randle Holmes, this style of beard was worn by dignitaries of the Church.

It was cut square and broad at the ends.

Caul.—A net to confine the hair. The back part of a wig or a woman's cap is sometimes called a caul.

Caushets.—Corsets.

Cherridary.—An Indian cotton stuff like gingham. (1712 and after.)

Chicken-skin.—Chicken skin gloves were worn in bed to keep the hands white as late as the reign of George III.

Chin-band or **chin-cloth.**—A muffler of lace worn by ladies of the time of Charles I.

Chints or **chintz.**—(From the Hindoo "chint," i. e., spotted cloth)—cotton printed in several colours.

Clocks.—The plaits of a ruff, also ornaments on stockings.

Clogs.—Overshoes of various materials worn in the Colonies throughout the eighteenth century.

Cloth of Bodkin.—A rich cloth interwoven of silk and gold. The name is a corruption of Baldach, the ancient name of Bagdad, whence it was brought.

Clout.—A coarse kerchief worn on the head.

Cockers, Cocurs, Cocrez.—Laced high shoes or half-boots; also thick stockings without feet.

Coif or **Quoif.**—A close-fitting cap.

Colbertine, Colberteen, or **Colbatteen.**—A lace resembling network, named for Monsieur Colbert, superintendent of the French King's manufactories. Randle Holmes describes it as "an open lace with a square grounding." It ultimately became cheap and unfashionable.

Swift, in "Cadens and Vanessa," says:

"The difference between
Rich Flanders lace and Colbertine."

Collaret.—A puff made of soft ribbon worn around the throat ending in a bow beneath the chin.

Commode.—A lady's head-dress made on a frame of wire two or three tiers high fitted to the head and covered with tiffany or other thin silk. It came into fashion in England during the reign of William and Mary.

Copatain.—A sugar-loaf hat, "a capped crown hat."

Cordevan.—A leather of goatskin, originally from Cordova, Spain; sometimes spelt "cordewayne," whence "cordwainer" or "cordiner," a shoemaker.

Cornet.—A cap, apparently a Dutch fashion.

Corselet.—A light body armour.

Cote.—In old English was a woman's gown.

Cravat.—A neck-cloth and often a very costly article of dress. Governor Berkeley of Virginia ordered one from England in 1660 which was to cost five pounds.

Cremesyn.—Crimson velvet.

Criardes.—Name given to paniers of stiffened linen, which creaked with every movement.

Crocus.—A coarse stuff worn by slaves and working people.

Crosscloth.—A part of a woman's head-dress worn across the forehead. Worn in Maryland in 1642 and Massachusetts in 1647.

Cue de Paris.—According to Watson, a sort of bustle padded with horse-hair.

Cuirass.—Armour for the breast and back (name derived from *cuir*) made of leather or of metal fastened with leather thongs.

Curch or **Curchef.**—A plain close-fitting cap worn by women in the Colonies.

Curli-murli.—A fantastic curl or twist.

Cypress, Cyprus, Sipers, Sypress, or **Syphus.**—The material, found under all these spellings, is described in 1678 as a fine curled stuff, part silk, part hair, and of a cobweb thinness. It was used like crape for mourning.

Dag-wain.—A rough material used for coverlets for beds, tables, or floors.

Damask or **Damascus.**—A fabric woven in elaborate patterns of silk, wool, or linen. Wool damask was used for curtains and bed hangings in Colonial days.

"Damask white and azure blewe
Well diapered with lilies new."
—"*The Squire of Low Degree.*"

Dauphiness.—A certain style of mantle advertised in Boston in 1755.

Deriband or **Deribund.**—A thin material made in India.

Desoy or **Sergedesoy.**—A coarse silken material used in the eighteenth century for men's clothing.

Dimity, Dimothy, or **Demyt.**—This is a fine ribbed cotton fabric made first in Damietta, used throughout the Colonial period and until the present day.

Dornex.—A heavy coarse linen, like canvas.

Doublet.—A garment usually made of two thicknesses of stuff, whence its name.

Dowlas.—A heavy linen originally from Brittany.

Drawers.—Summer breeches.

Drugget.—A fabric of wool used for heavy coats, etc.

Ducape.—A heavy corded silk of plain colour mentioned in inventories from 1675. It was durable and very popular.

Duck.—A strong linen fabric without a twill.

Duffels or **Duffals.**—A woolen stuff originally made in Flanders, used in the Colonies in 1672 and after.

Durant.—A woolen fabric, sometimes called "everlasting."

Dussens.—A sort of kersey. The Massachusetts Bay Colonists were supplied with "100 sutes of Norden dussens."

Embroidery.—Variegated needlework used for decoration of dress. From the French *broder.*

> "Embroidered was he, as it were a mede
> All of fresh flowers, white and red."
> —"*Canterbury Tales.*"

Engageants.—Deep double ruffles hanging down to the wrist.

> "About her sleeves are engageants."
> —"*Mundus Muliebris,*" 1690.

Eschelles or **Echelles.**—A stomacher laced or ribboned in the form of a ladder.

Face-painting.—Portrait painting.

Falbalas or **Furbelows.**—Rows of plaiting or puffs, fashionable in the time of William and Mary. A puckered flounce.

Falding.—A kind of coarse cloth—like frieze.

Fall.—A falling band, a large collar, worn in the sixteenth and seventeenth centuries.

Fallals.—Full soft ruffles used for trimming.

Farthingale.—The under supporter of the wide gown or petticoat worn in the time of Elizabeth and James I. Made like a circular cushion stuffed with hair, and worn just below the waist-line.

Farthingale Breeches.—Stuffed out like a farthingale, supposed to be a protection from poniard thrusts and for that reason encouraged by James I.

Favourite.—A lock dangling on the temples.

Felt.—A fabric of wool and hair. Felt hats were first made in England in the days of Henry VIII.

Firmament.—An encircling ornament for the head set with gems.

Fly-fringe.—A very popular trimming made of tufts of silk to match or contrast with the gown. In fashion all through the Georgian Era.

Follette.—A very light fichu.

Fontange.—A knot of ribbon worn on the head-dress, so called for Mlle. Fontange, who first wore it. Sometimes confused with the Commode, on top of which it was usually worn.

Fote or **Foot-mantel.**—An outer skirt worn by a woman on horseback to keep her gown clean.

French Fall.—A sort of shoe.

Frieze.—A thick and warm woolen cloth in use since the fourteenth century.

Frilals.—Borders of ornamental ribbon.

Frontlet.—A piece of stuff worn under the hood and projecting beyond it over the forehead.

Furbelows.—An ornamental trimming for women's gowns, described as a puckered flounce.

Fustian.—A species of cloth, originally made at Fusht on the Nile, used for jackets and doublets as early as the fifteenth century. It had a warp of linen thread and a woof of thick cotton.

Fygury.—An old name for silk diapered with figures of flowers and fruit.

Galloon or **Galon.**—A kind of lace made of silk woven with cotton, gold, or silver, or of silk only.

Gamoshes.—High boots worn about 1688.

Garters.—The New England Colonists were furnished with Norwich garters. In the time of James I garters were small sashes of silk tied in a large bow.

Gauze.—A transparent silk texture invented at Gaza in Palestine, whence its name.

Gelofer or **Gillofer.**—The old name for carnation pinks.

Gloves.—Were worn on all occasions of ceremony by both sexes in early Colonial Days. They were often embroidered in gold or silver. We read of perfumed gloves in England in 1631.

> "One gives to me perfumed gloves, the best that he can buy me.
> Live where I will, I will have the loves of all that come nigh me."
> —"*A Fayre Portion for a Fayre Maide.*"

Glove Tightens.—To keep the long gloves in place, were made of plaited hair as well as of ribbon.

Goffering.—The mode of ironing the plaits of a ruff over heated poking or goffering sticks.

Golosh.—A shoe with soles of wood or leather kept on by straps over the instep.

Gorget.—An ornamental neckband which was full and broad in front, worn as early as 1642 in the Colonies. Metal gorgets were worn with armour.

Grain.—Scarlet (a colour).

Grassets or **Grazzets.**—A dress stuff in use from 1712 to 1768.

Greaves.—Armour worn to protect the front part of the legs.

Gridelin.—A soft blue gray colour fashionable in the eighteenth century.

Grogram.—A rough fabric of silk and wool with a diagonal weave. Country women wore gowns of it in the sixteenth and seventeenth centuries in England and it was much used in the Colonies.

Hair-clasps.—Worn to keep the back hair in place, made of various metals, and often set with pearls, etc.

Hair-lace.—A fillet for the hair, much worn in the eighteenth century.

Haling-hands.—Mittens for sailors and workingmen. The palms were often lined with leather.

Hanaper or **Hamper.**—A wicker basket.

Hand-ruffs.—Ruffles for the wrist.

Hanger.—A small sword worn by gentlemen with morning dress in the seventeenth century.

Hatch.—A locker in which clothing was kept and which generally stood at the foot of the bed and was used as a seat.

Hive.—A sort of straw bonnet shaped like a bee-hive.

> "Upon her head a platted hive of straw which fortified her visage from the sun."

Hoods.—(from the Anglo-Saxon *Hood*)—Were worn with great variations of fashion by both sexes from the eleventh to the eighteenth century Replaced by caps and hats in the reign of George II.

Hookers.—The name given to certain sects who eschewed the use of buttons. Mennonites or Dunkers.

Hoops.—In the Colonies followed all the English changes of shape, and were worn by old and young. (1712–1778.)

Hum-Hum.—A coarse cotton fabric brought from India, used for lining coats, etc., 1750–1770.

Inkle.—A woolen tape or braid. Used as a trimming and sewed on in patterns.

Iron-pot.—Familiar name of the iron head-piece worn by Cromwell's soldiers.

Isabella colour.—Dirty white.

Jack-boots.—Were introduced in the seventeenth century.

Jacket.—A popular garment worn in the Colonies from 1641 and after.

Jean.—A twilled cotton cloth used both for underwear and for outer garments. Summer suits for men were often made of jean in the Colonies.

Jerkin.—Another name for jacket or doublet.

Jerkinet.—A similar garment for women.

Joseph.—A lady's riding-habit buttoned down the front. When worn open this garment was popularly called a " flying Josie."

Jumps.—A loose bodice for women, also a loose coat or jacket for men, reaching to the thighs, buttoned down the front, with sleeves to the wrist.

Kendal.—A green woolen cloth or baize first made at Kendal in England.

Kenting.—A fine linen fabric.

Kersey.—(under various spellings)— A fine woolen material.

Kincob or **Kinkhaib.**—A rich Indian stuff of silk, brocaded in flowers and large figures.

Kirtle.—A loose gown or tunic.

Kist.—A chest.

Knop.—A button.

Lace.—A lacing cord (the name came from *lacier*, "to fasten"). In the earlier days, trimming woven with gold and silver thread and put on in flat rows. In its later sense signifying that delicate and beautiful fabric which is one of the most admirable ornaments of costume. Mechlin, a favourite lace in the Colonies, was made in Flanders; point-lace or French point, also much worn, was made in Alençon.

> "Your snowy wrists do Mechlin pendants grace;
> And do the smartest wigs adorn thy face?"
> —" The Test of Love," *Nicholas Amherot.*

Lappets.—The lace pendants of a lady's cap or head-dress. Very fashionable in the last half of the eighteenth century.

Lawn.—A delicate fabric used as early as Elizabeth's day.

Leno.—A thin linen fabric used for caps.

Levite.—Another name for a polonese, and made of dimity and muslin, often bordered with chintz or callimanco.

Linset.—The stool on which a woman sat when spinning.

Linsey-wolsey.—A coarse woolen stuff first made at Linsey in Suffolk, England, and very popular in the Colonies.

Liripipes.—Long streamers of gauze or ribbon attached to a head-dress and often hanging to the feet.

Loo masks.—Half masks covering the face to the nose only.

Loretto.—A silk material used for waistcoats.

Love-lock.—A long ringlet of hair worn on the left side of the head.

Lustring.—A soft silk, plain or flowered, in general wear for many years.

Macaroni.—Nickname for a London fop. Whence arose the use of the word in the contemporary doggerel of Yankee Doodle and its application as a name in the American Revolution to a body of Maryland troops remarkable for showy uniforms. (1770–1775.) (Century Dictionary.)

Mandillion.—An outer garment. The New England Colonists wore them lined with cotton and fastened with hooks and eyes.

Mantee.—A coat with sleeves which hung open from the throat showing the stomacher and petticoat beneath.

Mantua.—A form of sacque for outdoor wear, sometimes name of material for making sacques. We read, for instance, of yellow mantua silk in 1741.

Masks.—As a protection from the sun and wind, were worn by women and children in all the colonies.

Mercury.—The name for a certain kind of cap for women in fashion about 1760 in Boston and elsewhere.

Mittens.—Were made of heavy cloth and of dressed skins as well as knitted of wool.

Mitts.—Fingerless gloves made of kid or silk and often of lace-work for summer wear. Mitts made of cotton or linen like the dress were buttoned to the shoulder of the gown and were in fashion after the Revolution.

Mode.—A contraction of "alamode," a thin silk. A mantle with a hood fashionable in the eighteenth century was also called a "mode."

Modesty-piece.—A piece of lace worn across the upper part of the stays.

Monmouth Cap.—A popular headgear mentioned in the outfits of the Colonists. Made originally in the old parts of the town of Monmouth, which is still known as the Capper's town.

Monteroe or **Mountero Cap.**—Made with a low crown and flap which could be turned down for protection.

Morion.—A head-piece of armour introduced from Spain and worn by English soldiers in the latter half of the sixteenth century.

Mouches.—Black patches were thus called because they looked like flies.

Muffetees or **Wristlets.**—Were worn when the coat sleeves were short, by men and women in the time of William and Mary.

Muffs.—Have been in use from early in the seventeenth century to the present day. For many years they were carried by both men and women and made of woolen stuff, fur, and feathers. We read that Judge Dana of Boston carried one until after the Revolution.

Murry.—Mulberry colour.

Nabob.—A thin East India stuff.

Nankeen.—A cotton cloth of a yellow colour imported from China and named for Nankin, where it was made.

Neck-cloths.—Worn by both men and women in the Colonies.

"Before your glass each morning do you stand
And tie your neck-cloth with a critic's hand."

Neckstock.—A stiffly folded cravat

worn close to the throat, finished with a buckle at the back.

Negligée.—A loose gown or sacque open in front over a handsome petti-coat; and, in spite of its name, was not only in high fashion for many years, but was worn in full dress.

Night-rail.—A dress unconfined at the waist and closed only at the neck—literally night-gowns, which the ladies adopted as a morning costume.

"Three night-gowns of rich Indian stuff."
—"*Mundus Muliebris.*"

None-so-Prettys.—Fancy tapes.

Orange-butter.—A pomade used in the Dutch Colonies.

Orrice.—A lace or gimp trimming woven with gold and silver thread.

Oxford Gown.—The academic gown worn usually on public occasions by men in authority, chiefly as a badge of office in the Colonies.

Oznaburg.—A coarse linen made in Hanover and named for a province of that name.

Paduasoy.—A rich smooth silk made originally at Padua.

Palisade.—A wire sustaining the hair next to the first knot. Part of the commode head-dress.

Paniers.—Were made of hoops of straw, cane, or whalebone fastened together by tapes.

Paragon.—A stuff used for common wear in the seventeenth century.

Patches.—First introduced towards the end of the reign of Charles I and varied into all manner of shapes.

Pattens.—A sole of wood on iron rings fastened to the foot by leather straps.

Pelerine.—A small cape with long ends in front.

Penistone.—(under various spellings)—A coarse woolen stuff made in England in the seventeenth and eighteenth centuries.

Pennache.—A bunch of tassels or narrow ribbons.

Perpetuana, Petuna, or **Perpets.**—A glossy woolen stuff like lasting worn by the Puritans in 1629 and after.

Persian.—A thin silk used for linings of cloaks and hoods or for summer gowns. Sold in New England in the eighteenth century.

Petticoat.—(Originally petty-coet)—A garment worn universally and made of every sort of material. Quilted petticoats were advertised as early as 1720 in the Colonies.

Philomot.—Colour of a dead leaf.

Pig-tail Wig.—Wig with a plaited tail tied with a ribbon, worn very generally in the middle of the eighteenth century.

Pilgrim.—A cape or ruffle fastened to the back of a bonnet to shield the neck; usually made of thin silk.

Pillion.—The extension of a saddle on which a woman rode before the days of side-saddles.

Pinner.—Usually a child's bib or apron and mentioned often in the seventeenth century, but caps fastened on with pins were also called pinners in the eighteenth century.

Pins or **Pinnes.**—Were sold for one shilling and four pence a thousand in the early Colonial days.

Plumpers.—Very thin round and light balls to plump out and fill up hollow cheeks.

Points.—Ties or laces of ribbon or leather decorated with tags and used instead of buttons to fasten garments together. They were in general use until late in the seventeenth century, both for armour and civilian's dress.

Polonese.—A long-sleeved coat-like garment for women opening down the front, finished often with a large hood at the back of the neck.

Pomander.—A perforated ball or box filled with perfumes, used to prevent infection.

Pompadour or **Pompadore.**—Was a word in constant use in the eighteenth century. We read of Pompadore shoes, laces, caps, aprons, sacques, stockings, and head-dresses.

Pompon.—An ornament made of artificial flowers, feathers, tinsel, etc.

Pretintailles.—Large cut-out patterns laid on a dress as trimming. Introduced in the time of William and Mary.

Prunella.—A close woolen stuff like lasting.

Puce Colour.—Colour of a flea. Name given by Louis XVI.

Pug.—A short cape with hood attached and usually made of silk, velvet, or cloth.

Pump.—A shoe with a thin sole and low heel, first mentioned in the sixteenth century.

Purl.—A species of edging used on caps, collars, cuffs, etc.

Qualitie.—A coarse tape for strings or binding, used in all the Colonies between 1700 and 1800.

Rail or **Rayle.**—A loose garment (old English), but later applied only to night-gowns.

Ramall or **Romall.**—A neckerchief or small shawl to be worn over the shoulders.

Ramilie.—A wig bushy at the sides, a braided tail in the back with a large bow at top and small bow at the end. (1708 and after.)

Rash.—A wool fabric of inferior quality.

Ratteen.—A heavy woolen material something like drugget.

Rayonné.—A species of hood.

Robings.—The ornamental part of a gown, such as lapels, reveres, etc.

Rocket or **Rochet.**—A long woolen mantle trimmed with fringe. Brought from Devon or Cornwall.

Roquelaure or **Roquelo.**—A cloak for both men and women, named for the Duke of Roquelaure, mentioned in New England papers of 1730. Made of all heavy materials and generally of bright colours. Often two small capes of the same material finished the garment on the shoulders.

Roses.—Ornaments in the form of roses made of ribbons, lace, and even jewels. One of the pet extravagances of the seventeenth century. Worn on shoes, garters, and hatbands. We read of an English gallant who paid 30 pounds for a pair.

Round-cord Cap.—A cap which was tied on with a fine cord back of the ears.

Ruffles.—Of lawn and lace were worn in the sleeves and in the front of the shirts until after 1800.

Russel or **Russet.**—A twilled woolen stuff like baize, much worn in the Colonies.

> " Our clothing is good sheepskins
> Gray russet for our wives
> 'Tis warmth and not gay clothing
> That doth prolong our lives."
> —" *Coridon's Song*."

Safeguard.—An outside petticoat worn over the dress as a protection from mud or dust in riding by women in the Colonies. (1650 and after.)

Sagathy or **Sagathie.**—A durable woolen stuff.

Samare or **Semnar.**—A lady's jacket. Originally a Dutch garment. "It had a loose body and side flaps, or skirts which extended to the knee, the sleeves short to the elbow, turned back and faced" (Randle Holmes). The samare was often made long and was worn opening over a petticoat and waistcoat very much like the English sacque.

Sarsnet, Sarsenet, or **Sarsinet.**—A thin silk still in use, but dating from the thirteenth century.

Satin Jean.—A thick cotton cloth with a glossy surface used for shoes and similar purposes.

Say or **Soy.**—(from the French *soie*)— Originally a silk and wool material. It is mentioned in Colonial lists from 1629 to 1768.

Serge.—A twilled fabric of either wool or silk, often of both.

Shades.—A head covering, or a stuff suitable for headgear. We read in 1766 of "painted lawns and chequer'd shades."

Shadow.—A sunshade either worn on the head or held in the hand. (1580–1647 and after.)

Shag.—A heavy woolen cloth with a long nap. (1632 and after.)

Shagreen.—An untanned leather with a granular surface often made of sharkskin and dyed green.

Shalloons.—A woolen fabric not unlike the modern challis and made in Chalons, France.

Sherry-vallies.—A sort of legging worn in riding, to protect from mud, buttoned up outside the trousers.

Shift.—A shirt or chemise, usually of fine linen. This undergarment was in Colonial days often made with long sleeves which were laid in fine plaits with a knife when laundered.

Shoepack.—A shoe shaped like a moccasin, without a separate sole, made of tanned leather and much worn during the Revolution.

Skilts.—Short full trousers reaching just below the knee, full half a yard wide at the bottom. Worn during the Revolution by the country people.

Slyders or **Slivers.**—Overalls.

Smock.—A shirt of heavy linen worn by farm labourers and workingmen. Before 1700 a shift was often called a smock. In "Mundus Muliebris" we read:

"Twice twelve day-smocks of Holland fine
Twelve more for night, all Flanders lac'd."

Snuff.—Came into general use in England in 1702.

Snuff-boxes.—Were carried by both men and women for the greater part of the century.

Solitaire.—A broad black ribbon introduced from France in the time of Louis XV worn close around the throat, apparently to protect the coat from the powdered wig. Sometimes it was tied to the back of the wig and brought round and tucked in the shirt ruffle. According to advertisements in the American newspapers, it was much worn in the Colonies.

Sorti.—A knot of small ribbon peeping out between the pinner and bonnet.

Spagnolet.—A gown with narrow sleeves, *à l'Espagnole*.

Spanish Paper.—A red colour with

which the ladies of Spain painted their faces. It was made up into little books and a leaf was torn out and rubbed upon the cheeks, the vermillion powder which covered it being transferred to the face. It was in use at the end of the eighteenth century.

Stamin or **Stammel.**—A heavy cloth like linsey-woolsey.

Startups or **Startop.**—A sort of buskin for ordinary wear worn in the sixteenth and seventeenth centuries by country folk.

Stayhooks.—Small ornamental hooks stuck in the edge of the bodice on which to hang an *étui*.

Steinkirk.—A cravat folded with careless grace. Name given by the French to commemorate the battle in 1692.

Stirrup-hose.—Were worn on horseback to protect the nether garments. They were wide at the back and fastened with straps to the girdle.

Stock.—A stiff neck-cloth buckled at the back of the neck, successor to the cravat.

Stock-buckle.—Buckle which fastened the stock.

"The stock with buckle made of plate
Has put the cravat out of date."

Strap Cap.—A cap which fastened with flaps under the chin.

Sultane.—A gown caught up with buttons and loops.

Swanskin.—A fleecy cloth like Canton flannel, used for linings, etc.

Tabby.—A sort of watered silk.

Tabinet or **Tabaret.**—Another name for poplin, used for petticoats, and also for covering furniture.

Taffeta.—A rich cloth used first in the sixteenth century and considered a luxury in the Colonial days.

Taminy.—A woolen stuff like alpaca, made in Norfolk, 1653 and after.

Tassets.—Splints of steel fastened to the corselet as a protection for the thighs. Worn until late in the seventeenth century.

Thrum.—The extremity of a weaver's warp, often about nine inches long, which cannot be woven. Caps and hats knitted of this material were called thrums.

"And her thrum'd hat and her muffler too."

Tiffany.—A heavy silk fabric. (1792 and after.)

Tippets.—A neck covering made of a variety of materials worn for ornament, of gauze and tissues, and for warmth, of fur.

Tongs.—Overalls of coarse cotton or linen.

Tufftaffeta.—A faffeta with a chenille stripe, worn in New England.

Tuly.—A shade of red.

Turban also **Turbin.**—A head-dress for women made of gauze and trimmed with feathers, very fashionable in the Colonies. (1760 and after.)

Trollopee.—Another name for negligée.

Vambrace.—The piece of armour which protected the forearm from elbow to wrist.

Vampay.—A short hose or sock of wool.

Veil.—One of the most ancient articles of female attire, the *couvre chef* of the Anglo-Saxon ladies and an important part of the conventual costume, but retaining its place in the wardrobes of women to-day.

Whisk.—A collarette or cape to cover the neck and shoulders, usually made of muslin trimmed with lace and worn with low-cut gowns, in the seventeenth and eighteenth centuries. We read of Tiffany whisks in 1660.

Whitney.—A heavy coarse stuff used for coats, cloaks, and petticoats, 1737 and after.

Whittle.—A blanket shawl with fringe, worn in 1665 and after, in the Colonies.

Worsted.—A woolen cloth first made at Worstead in England in the reign of Henry I.

INDEX
Volume One

INDEX
Volume One

ABLETTES, 72
Acadian exiles, 36
Actors in America, 238
Adams's, Mrs. Abigail, letter from England, describing the fashions, 259
Adventurers, 33, 43
Advertisements in colonial newspapers, 245–251
André, Major, 255
Andros, Sir Edward, 136
Aprons, 53, 68, 71, 100, 130, 195, 202
Armour, 56, 59, 60, 99
Arquebusiers, 27
Artificial flowers, 213
Artisans, 33
Attitude of the Colonists in New England towards the English Church, 113, 114

BABY-CLOTHES, 283
Back boards, 196
Bacon's Rebellion, anecdote of, 71
Baize, gowns of, 258
Baldricks, 51
Baltimore, Lord, 56
Bandoliers, 99, 103
Bands, 51, 64
Banyans, 315
Barbadoes, 63
Basquinas, 28
Bath bonnets, 222
Bayard, Nicholas, costume of, 144
Bayard, Madam, costume of, 147
Beards, 44
Beaver hats, 190, 214
Berkeley, Sir Wm., Governor of the Virginia Colony, 48, 60, 61
Bishops, 222
Blacksmith, 53
Boarding-school outfit, 291
Bobs, 300, 303
Bodices, coloured, 33
Bodices, pair of, 190
Bonnets, 202, 214, 222, 225, 256, 273
Boots, 64, 312, 324
Bowne's, Elizabeth, descriptions of dress in 1798, 273
Breeches, 53, 61, 67, 143

Bricklayer, 53
Bridal veil, 206, 209
Bridge spectacles, 193
Bridling, 196
Brigade Orders, West Point, 369
Broad-brimmed hats, 95, 312, 323
Buccaneers, 27, 28
Buckle, 247
Buckles, 311
Buckskin breeches, 346
Buckskin shoes, 346
Buff coats, 59, 60, 107
Burney, Miss, verses on a great-coat by, 257
Burroughs, Anne, 47
Buttons, 64, 67, 109, 324

CALASH, 214, 222, 233
California, 26, 31
Campaign wig, 147, 299
Canes, 205
Cannons or breeches fastenings, 99
Capes, 34
Capotes, 34
Caps for women, 100, 193, 214, 217, 257
Capuchins, 229
Cardinal, 140, 193, 194, 229
Carpenters, 53
Cavalier, Robert, Sieur de La Salle, 32, 33
Cavaliers, 63
Chaises, 263
Chapeau bras, 312
Chatelaines, 133
Chief justice, robe of a, 335
Children, dress of, 17th century, 47, 52, 113, 135
Children, dress of, 18th century, 283, 292
Chintz gowns, 257
Church services, 17th century, 54
City troop, uniform of the, 350
Cleaning establishment, 249
Clergymen, dress of, 17th century, 54, 114, 115
Clergymen, dress of, 18th century, 304, 307
Cloaks, 100, 103, 193, 217, 229, 252, 263
Clogs, 34, 186, 217
Coats, 17th century, 61, 109, 143
Coats, 18th century, 312, 332
Cockades, 376

Cocked hats, 143, 299, 328, 332
Cocking the hat, various forms of, 308, 311
Coif of a Dutch matron, 130, 136
Coifs, men, 152, 156
Coifs, women, 164
Colebatteen ruffles, 147
Colonial militia, 99
Colonial period, end of, 255
Commode, 108, 147, 181
Connecticut settlers, 84, 85
Continental soldiers, uniform of, 359
Cordovan leather, 26
Corselets, 99
Countryman, 17th century, 54
Cravats, 312
Creedon, Captain, 61
Cue de Paris, 222
Cuffs, 143, 202
Cuirass 60
Curli-murlis, 195
Curls, 194
Curtsey, 199
Curwen, Judge, 103
Cushions for the hair, 214, 217
Custis children, clothes ordered for, 288

Dances, 234
Delany, Mrs., 193
Delaware settled, 136
Delaware, Swedes on the, 136
Dentists, 248
Deportment, 196
Dickinson, Maria, letter quoted, 258
Discriminative dress, 230
Domestics, 244, 246
Doublets, 28, 44, 51, 59, 61, 96, 109
Drake, Sir Francis, 26
Drummer, 53
Dutch babies, 129, 130
Dutch bridal crown, 130
Dutch bride, 130
Dutch children, dress of, 135
Dutch merchants, 121
Dutch peasant women, dress of, 126
Dutch settlers, 121
Dutchman, working dress of, 129
Dyes, 122, 133

Earrings, 52
Encouragement of home manufactures, 252
English gentleman, dress of, 17th century, 44, 51, 52, 139, 143
English gentleman, dress of, 18th century, 299
English gentlewoman, dress of, 17th century, 52, 139, 143
English gentlewoman, dress of, 18th century, 177
English rule in all the Colonies, 139
Etui, 202
Eves, Miss Sarah, journal of, 241

Falbalas, 143
Falling bands, 61, 96
Falling collars, 61, 96
Fans, 68, 189, 214
Farthingale, 47, 193
Farthingale breeches, 44
Fashion dolls, 178, 181, 256
Feathers in the hair, 195, 214
Fenwick, Lady Mary, 108
First Troop City Cavalry, uniform of, 349
Fithian, Philip, diary of, 230, 234
Flounces, 143
Fob pockets, 318
Forrest, Mrs., 47
Franks, Miss, 256
French curls, 196
French falls, 64
French settlers, dress of, 33, 34
French taste prevalent in America, 256
Frocks or overshirts, 263
Full dress in New England (middle of 18th century), 214, 217
Funeral of Lady Andros, 107
Furbelows, 143
Fur caps, 130
Fur-trimmed jackets, 130

Galloon, 68
Gauntlets, 99
Geneva gown, 56, 114
George III, dress in the reign of, 202, 316
German settlers, 160, 163
Gipsy hats, 101, 196, 214
Gloves, 67, 96, 99, 100, 256, 323
Gold beads, 217
Gold lace, 99
Gorget, 60
Gray hair fashionable, 307
Great-coats for men, 316, 319, 320, 332
Great-coats for women, 257, 258
Green aprons worn by Quakers, 140
Gumbos, 35
Guns, 99, 100

Hair-dressing, 217, 218, 230, 250
Hair powder, 143, 193, 331
Half-Moon, The, 121
Hampshire kerseys, 96
Hatchments, 107
Hats, 95, 135, 140, 143, 332
Head-dresses, 143, 194
Helmets, 59
Herrisons, 268
Hibbins, Mistress Anne, 110
Higginson, letter from, 84
High heels, 139
High prices during the Revolution, 256
Hogarth, 307
Holland, dress of the women, 89
Holland shirts, 51, 61, 64
Hollar, Wenceslaus, 86
Home Life in New England, 18th century, 263

Homespun parties, 252
Hoods, 34, 68, 100, 108, 152, 185, 186, 214
Hooks and eyes, 96
Hoop, the, 182, 193, 195, 217, 256
Hooped petticoats, 182, 193, 196, 199
Horn flasks, 99
Horse-blocks, 263
Horsehair bonnets, 222
Hose, 68
Household servants, 244
Hubbard store, contents of, 73
Hudson, Captain, 109
Hudson, Henry, 121
Huguenots, the, 122
Hunting shirts, 346, 354

INAUGURATION ball, description of, 267
Inauguration costumes of Washington, 267; 328
Irish stockings, 96
Isham, Sir Thomas, wedding suit of, 110
Italian curls, 196

JACKETS, 130
Jefferson, Thomas, suit worn by, 328
Jersey Blues, uniform of the, 349
Jerseys (the) settled, 136
Jesuit missionaries, 25, 26
Jewelry, 17th century, 72
Jockey coat, 311
Judges, costume of, 152
Jute-braids, 250

KEEPER of the Great Seal, 155
Kerchiefs, 34
Kitchen utensils, 74
Knit caps, 96

LABOURERS, 53, 133, 328
Labrador tea, 252
Lake, Mrs., 93; list of household articles, 93; fur mantle, 93
Lange, Dr. Jacob de, wardrobe of, 134
Lange, Mrs. de, wardrobe of, 133
Lappets, 195
La Salle, Robert Cavalier, Sieur, 32, 33
Law Courts in England, 17th century, 151
Lawyers' bags, 335
Lawyers in the Colonies, 17th century, 114, 115, 148; 18th century, 335
Leather breeches, 328, 332, 346
Legal costumes, 17th century, 148; 18th century, 335
Legal customs, 17th century, 148; 18th century, 335, 336
Leggings, 34, 332
Lemcke, Count, 167
Leverett, Sir John, Governor of the Massachusetts Colony, 100

Light Horse of Philadelphia, uniform of the, 349
Livery at Mt. Vernon, 245
Lolonais, Francis, 28
Long Island settled, 136
Long waistcoats, 303
Lynn, shoes made at, 95; worn by women, 217

MACARONI costume, 241
Macaronis, the, 241, 243
Maine settled in 1623, 113
Mandillion, 84, 85, 96
Manhattan, gay costumes in, 122
Manifesto against long hair, 89
Mantillas, 28
Mantles, 68
Marie Antoinette, Queen, makes a reform in dress of children, 292
Maryland settled, 56
Masks, 193
Mason, 53
Massachusetts Line, Orders for, 365
Massachusetts: Settled in 1620, 83; Order of the General Court of, 94, 95, 108; dress of women, 95; a religious commonwealth, 115
Menendez de Aviles, Pedro de, 25
Mennonites, 160
Militia, dress of the, 346
Mincing air, 312
Minuet, the, 234
Minuit, Peter, 121
Minute-men, dress of the, 346
Mischianza, 255
Mittens, 67, 100
Mitts, children's, 284
Moccasins, 34
Mocking birds, 73
Monmouth caps, 44, 64, 96
Moravian caps, 167
Moravians, 163, 164, 167
Morgan, Sir Henry, 28
Morions, 55
Moro (1500–1778), 25
Mourning dress and customs, 17th century, 104, 107, 108
Mourning dress, 18th century, 251
Mourning rings, 72, 107
Muff-dogs, 62
Muffs, 62, 143, 190
Murillo (1618–1682), 25
Musical instruments, 74
Musk-melon bonnet, 222

NECKCLOTHS, 64, 109, 143, 147, 324
Négligées, 199, 230
Net worn over a queue, 316
New England, 17th century, dress of the women, 100
New Hampshire settled in 1623, 113
New-market coat, 316
New Orleans, 35

Non-conformists, gowns of, 114
Normandy peasants, 36

Oak sticks, 312
Opera glasses, 241
Ordinary people, dress of, 18th century, 328
Ornatus Muliebris Anglicanus, 86
Orrices, 147, 186
Outfit of fashionable man, 331
Outfit of the Massachusetts Bay Colonists, 84
Outfit of the Virginia Colonists, 44
Overalls, 357
Overshoes, 335

Pamunkeys, King of the, 77
Pamunkeys, Queen of the, 77
Parasols, 214
Pastors, choosing, in the Massachusetts Colony, 114
Patch boxes, 189
Patches, 62, 189
Patriotic agreement, 251
Patroons, 122
Pattens, 130, 201, 217
Pearls, 52, 72
Peccadilles, 51
Peddlers, 74
Penn, William, 139; advice on dress, 140; blue sash, 139; wigs, 143
Pennsbury, 140
Pepys, 109
Percy, Sir George, Governor of Virginia Colony, 51
Perfumed powders, 68
Perfumes, 202, 205
Periwigs or wigs, 64, 109, 140, 143, 147, 159, 299, 300, 307, 312, 315, 319
Perriot, 267, 271
Perspective glasses, 193
Petticoat breeches, 61
Petticoats, 68, 130, 193, 202, 217
Pigtails, 312
Pikes, 99
Pillions, 263
Planters' wives, dress of, 17th century, 71
Plymouth pilgrims, 83
Pockets, 242
Points, 53, 54, 59, 85, 104
Political badges, 189
Pomander, 202
Pompadours, 200
Pompons, 195, 210
Posey dance, 28
Potpourri, 205
Pouncet box, 202
Powder, hair, 143, 193, 331
Preaching gown, 56, 114
Presbyterians, gown worn by, 114
Pritchard, Mrs. Frances, wardrobe of, 71
Provincials, uniforms of the, 346
Puritans of the Massachusetts Bay Co., 83, 84

Quaker aprons, 140
Quaker bonnets, 225
Quaker hats, 140
Quaker settlers in Pennsylvania Province, 130
Quaker weddings, description of, 226, 258
Quakers, dress of the, 139, 140, 225, 226, 229, 258
Quakers, portraits of, 258
Queensbury, Duchess of, a wonderful gown of 195
Queues, 316, 331
Quilted petticoats, 202, 257
Quitasols, 230

Ramilie wig, 299, 304
Rapiers, 109
Restraining Acts of the Pilgrims, 96
Revere, Paul, a dentist, 248
Rhode Island settled 1636, 113
Richbell, Robert, 109
Riding dress, 17th century, 109
Riding suit, a lady's, 18th century, 186
Ringlets, 273
Rings, 72, 130
Robings, 196, 273
Roelas, Juan de Las, 1558–1625, 25
Rollers, 218
Roquelaures, 229, 303, 320
Rosettes, 96
Roundhead Puritans (old song), 89
Ruffled shirts, 332
Ruffles, 139, 147, 195, 202
Ruffs, 26, 44, 159
Russell, 222

Sacque, 182, 187, 201, 202
Sailors, dress of, 328
Samare, 133
Sandys, George, 52
Sandys, Sir Edwin, 44
Sartori, Mrs., story of dress worn by, 274
Scarfs, 214
Scarlet cloaks worn by women, 263
Scarlet robes worn by Judges, 103, 152, 335
Scarlet stockings, 299
Scent bottles, 202
Sedan chairs, 182
Sergeant-at-law, reign of Charles II, 156; reign of James II, 159
Servants, 18th century, 244, 246, 268
Seventh Day Baptists, 168
Shoe-buckles, 64, 139
Shoemaking at Salem, 90
Shoes, 64, 68, 95, 96, 139, 143, 217, 328
Shifts, 130
Shirts, 51, 61, 64
Short-waists, 273, 274
Shoulder belts, 99
Silver lace, 99
Silverware (17th century), 74
Skimmer hat, 222
Slashed sleeves, 51, 96

Slaves, dress of, 245, 246
Sleeves, 94, 143, 202, 217
Slippers, 214
Smith, Captain John, 44
Snuff-boxes, 202, 311
Snuff, use of, 311
Spanish gentleman, dress of, 16th century, 26
Spanish painters, 25
Spanish point-lace, 143
Spanish settlers, 25
Spanish soldiers, 16th century, 27
Spanish women, dress of, 28
Spectacles, 193
Square toes, 139, 311
St. Augustine, 25, 26
Stays, 190, 217
Steinkirk, 147
Stock buckles, 300
Stockings, 64, 68, 143, 214, 217, 299
Stocks, 332
Stoffelsen, Vrouentje Ides, inventory of clothing, 130
Stomachers, 143, 182, 202
Store in the Virginia Colony, contents of a, 73
Striped silk, coats of, 273
Stuyvesant, Peter, Governor of New Amsterdam, 125
Sumptuous dress, 109
Surplices, 54

TABBY, 68
Tailors, 53, 249
Tanneries, 95
Tassetts, 59
Temple spectacles, 193
Tête moutonée, 196
Texas, 31
Theatre, first, in America, 238
Theatrical costumes, 238
Theatrum Mulierum, 89
Thrums, 53, 328
Tiffany hoods, 95
Tippets, 155, 193
Tow cloth, 263
Tower and commode, 181
Traders, 34
Tradesmen, dress of, 328
Training Day, 100
Treaty of Paris in 1764, 36
Tuilles, 59
Turbans, 214

UMBRELLAS, 214, 320
Undergirdle, 130
Uniforms, military, 1775–1800, 340
Uniforms, naval, 1775–1800, 340

VANDYKE collar, 52
Vandyke edging, 51
Vargas, Luis de (1502–1568), 25
Velasquez, Diego (1599–1660), 25
Vests, 34
Virginia ball, 230
Virginia Company, 43
Virginia Infantry, uniform of the, 349
Vos, Madame Cornelia de, 134

WAGON bonnet, 225
Waistcoats, 67, 143, 186, 303, 307, 324, 332
Walloons, the, 122
Walpole, Horace, 206
Wansey's, Mr., description of dress at the theatre in Philadelphia, 272, 273
Warren's, Mrs. Mercy, 271; verses on dress, 272
Washington, George, dress of, first inauguration, 267; second inauguration, 328; uniform of, 349
Washington, Mrs., 268
Watches, 320
Waterproof capes, 320
Watteau, the artist, 190
Watteau sacque, 182
West Point, Brigade Orders, 369
Whig colours, 349
White, Bishop, anecdote of, 307
White, Mrs., inventory of, 200
Wig makers, 250
Wigs and periwigs, 64, 109, 140, 143, 147, 159, 299, 300, 303, 307, 312, 315, 319
Willoughby, Mrs. Sarah, wardrobe of, 71
Winthrop, Margaret, 86
Wister, Sally, dress of, 257
Wooden heels, 68, 95
Wooden shoes, 68
Worked head, 194
Workingman, dress of, 17th century, 53, 54
Workingman, dress of, 18th century, 244, 328, 331

YANKEE Doodle, 242

ZINZENDORF, Count, dress of, 168

Authorities Consulted

Calendar of Virginia State Papers, Richmond, 1875.

History of the Virginia Settlement, Captain John Smith, London, 1624.

First Discovery and Settlement of Virginia, William Stith, Williamsburg, 1747.

Virginia Vetusta, Edward D. Neill, Albany, 1885.

Virginia Carolorum, Edward D. Neill, Albany, 1886.

Economic History of Virginia in the Seventeenth Century, Philip Alexander Bruce, New York, 1896.

Old Virginia and Her Neighbors, John Fiske, Boston, 1897.

History of the Barbadoes, John Poyer, London, 1808.

A True and Exact Account of the Island of the Barbadoes, Richard Ligon, London, 1657.

Annals of the Swedes on the Delaware, John C. Clay, Philadelphia, 1835.

Economic and Social History of New England, 1620–1789, William B. Weeden, Boston, 1890.

History of Norwich, Connecticut, Frances Mainwaring Caulkins, Norwich, 1866.

History and Antiquities of Boston, Samuel Drake, Boston, 1856.

History of Lynn, Massachusetts, Alonzo Lewis and James R. Newhall, Boston, 1865.

Life of William Penn, Samuel M. Janney, Philadelphia, 1852.

The Germans in Pennsylvania, William Beidelman, Easton, 1898.

The Story of Louisiana, Maurice Thompson, Boston, 1889.

Colonial Days and Ways, Helen Evertson Smith, New York, 1900.

Dutch and Quaker Colonies in America, John Fiske, Boston, 1899.

New Jersey as a Colony and as a State, Francis Bagley Lee, New York, 1902.

Social History of Flatbush, Mrs. Vanderbilt, New York, 1881.

History of New York, M. J. Lamb, New York, 1877.

A Short History of the English Colonies in America, Henry Cabot Lodge, New York, 1881.

A Story of the City of New York, Charles Burr Todd, New York, 1888.

Goode Vrow of Manahatta, Mrs. John King Van Rensselaer, New York, 1898.

Discovery of the Great Northwest, James Baldwin, New York, 1901.

History of the Antiquities of St. Augustine, Florida, George R. Fairbanks, New York, 1858.

Description of Louisiana in 1683, Father Hennepin, New York, 1888.

Men, Women and Manners in Colonial Times, Sidney G. Fisher, Philadelphia, 1898.

AUTHORITIES CONSULTED

Annals of Philadelphia, John Watson, Philadelphia, 1829.

Annals of New York, John Watson, Philadelphia, 1846.

Letters to Franklin by his Family and Friends, 1751–1790, New York, 1859.

Child Life in Colonial Days, Mrs. Alice Morse Earle, New York, 1899.

Costume of Colonial Times, Mrs. Alice Morse Earle, New York, 1894.

Life of Margaret Winthrop, Mrs. Alice Morse Earle, New York, 1895.

Dolly Madison, Mrs. Goodwin, New York, 1896.

The Writings of George Washington, edited by Wm. Chauncey Ford, New York, 1889.

Martha Washington, Anne Hollingsworth Wharton, New York, 1896.

The Quaker, a Study in Costume, Mrs. Francis Gummere, Philadelphia, 1902.

Colonial Days and Dames, Anne Hollingsworth Wharton, Philadelphia, 1898.

Journal and Correspondence of Abigail Adams, New York, 1841.

Diary of Sally Wister, Philadelphia, 1902.

L'Evantail, Octave Uzanne, Paris, 1882.

L'Ombrelle; le gant; et le Mouchoir, Octave Uzanne, Paris, 1883.

Son Altesse, la Femme, Octave Uzanne, Paris, 1885.

Autobiography and Correspondence of Mrs. Delaney, Boston, 1880.

Diary of Madame D'Arblay, London, 1842.

History of the United States, Thomas Higginson, Boston, 1875.

The Republican Court, Rufus W. Griswold, New York, 1855.

Pioneers of France in the New World, Francis Parkman, Boston, 1865.

Discovery of the Great West, Francis Parkman, Boston, 1869.

The Spectator, London, 1712.

Pepys' Diary, edited by H. B. Wheatley, London, 1896.

Evelyn's Diary, edited by H. B. Wheatley, London, 1879.

Table Talk of Samuel Rogers, New York, 1856.

Nollekins and His Times, John T. Smith, London, 1895.

Trachten der Völker, A. Kretchmer, Leipzig, 1864.

Cyclopædia of Costume, J. R. Planché, London, 1876.

Pictorial History of England, Charles Knight, London, 1841.

History of English Dress, Mrs. Hill, London, 1893.

Annals of Fashion by a Lady of Rank, London, 1847.

Yester-year, Ten Centuries of Toilette, A. Robida, London, 1892.

History of Fashion in France, Augustin Challamel, London, 1882.

Institutions, Usages et Costumes du 17ieme siecle, Paul Lacroix, Paris, 1880.

Institutions, Usages et Costumes du 18ieme siecle, Paul Lacroix, Paris, 1878.

Costume in England, F. W. Fairholt, London, 1846.

England in the Eighteenth Century, William Connor Sydney, New York, 1891.

Notes on Civil Costume in England, Hon. Lewis Wingfield, London, 1889.

Le Costume Historique, A. Racinet, Paris, 1891.

Memoirs of Lady Sarah Lennox, London, 1902.

Civil Costume in England, Charles Martin, London, 1842.

AUTHORITIES CONSULTED

Men, Maidens and Manners a Hundred Years Ago, John Ashton, London, 1888.

Brides and Bridals, John Cordy Jeffreson, London, 1872.

Mundus Muliebris and *The Fop's Dictionary*, Mary Evelyn, edited by her father, London, 1690.

Percy Society Publications, London, 1849.

Their Majesties' Servants, or Annals of the English Stage, Dr. Doran, London, 1865.

Glossary of Words, Phrases, Names and Allusions, Robert Nares, London, 1828.

Chronicles of Fashion, Mrs. Stone, London, 1848.

Gainsborough, Sir Walter Armstrong, London, 1898.

Sir Joshua Reynolds, Sir Walter Armstrong, London, 1900.

Hogarth, John and Joshua Boydell, London, 1798.

Romney, Sir Herbert Maxwell, London, 1902.

The Every Day Book, William Hone, London, 1826.

The King's Peace, a historical sketch of the English Law Courts, F. A. Inderwick, Q. C., London, 1895.

A Book about Lawyers, John Cordy Jeffreson, Barrister at Law, London, 1867.

Bench and Bar of Philadelphia, John Hill Martin, Philadelphia, 1883.

Sketches of the Judicial History of Massachusetts, 1630–1775, Emory Washburn, Boston, 1840.

A History of the American Church, Rt. Rev. Leighton Coleman, D.D., Bishop of Delaware, New York, 1903.

History of the American Episcopal Church, Rt. Rev. William Stevens Perry, D.D., Bishop of Iowa.

A Book about the Clergy, John Cordy Jeffreson, London, 1870.

A Book about Doctors, John Cordy Jeffreson, New York, 1861.

Diary of Samuel Sewall, Massachusetts Historical Collections, Boston, 1878.

Literary Diary of Ezra Stiles, D.D., LL.D., New York, 1901.

Diary of Manasseh Cutler, Cincinnati, 1888.

History of the British Army, Hon. J. W. Fortescue, London, 1902.

History of Our Navy, John R. Spears, New York, 1897.

Uniforms of the United States Army, 1775–1900, Published by the United States Government, Washington, 1900.

HISTORIC DRESS
IN AMERICA
1607=1870

ELISABETH McCLELLAN

Illustrations by
SOPHIE B. STEEL & CECIL W. TROUT

Two volumes in one
Volume Two   1800-1870

about
mid 1804

1804-1

Sophie B. Steel.
1906.

1804

FRONTISPIECE (FIGURE 1).—Picture of an Empire gown worn in Philadelphia, now in the collection at Memorial Hall. The train is of blue satin bordered with a bias fold of white satin embroidered with sprays of roses and leaves in natural colours. Over the short puffed sleeves of white crêpe trimmed with bands of embroidered satin are caps of the white satin with embroidered roses. The same pattern is embroidered above the hem of the white satin under-dress. Around the train and on the hem of the under-dress is a narrow trimming of embroidery in pink and white. The shoulder ruching is made of plaited white crêpe edged with lace. The dress turban of blue satin is embroidered to match the dress and ornamented with two white plumes and one of pink. This beautiful gown is a hundred years old.

MANY books have been written on the houses, the furniture, and the decorations of the century we have so lately seen pass into history, but of the costumes chosen and worn by our immediate ancestors very little has been recorded in print. Yet, as Mr. Calthrop, the English authority on the history of dress has aptly said, " To see our ancestors dressed is to have a shrewd guess as to what they were—as to what they did." The present volume is designed to bring us within the charmed circle of intimacy and to reveal to us the tastes and fancies, the pursuits and pastimes, of our nineteenth century grandparents. It goes to press with many thanks to the friends who have lent me their ancestral treasures. · The scheme of illustration has been to arrange the garments on living models and to copy the hair and accessories from contemporary portraits or old fashion plates. As the first years of the twentieth century have witnessed a revival of the scant and clinging skirts, the turbans and scarf draperies, of a hundred years ago, we are reminded of the old verse :

" Fashions that are now called new
Have been worn by more than you,
Other times have worn the same
Though the new ones get the name."

ELISABETH McCLELLAN.

Philadelphia, November, 1910.

CONTENTS
Volume Two

WOMEN'S DRESS, 1800–1810 23

WOMEN'S DRESS, 1810–1820 87

WOMEN'S DRESS, 1820–1830 141

WOMEN'S DRESS, 1830–1840 182

WOMEN'S DRESS, 1840–1850 213

WOMEN'S DRESS, 1850–1860 245

WOMEN'S DRESS, 1860–1870 263

CHILDREN'S GARMENTS, 1800–1835 295

CHILDREN'S GARMENTS, 1835–1870 311

QUAKER COSTUME, 1800–1870 327

DRESS OF THE SHAKERS 333

MEN'S APPAREL, 1800–1810 347

MEN'S APPAREL, 1810–1830 378

MEN'S APPAREL, 1830–1850 397

MEN'S APPAREL, 1850–1870 414

CLERGYMEN'S DRESS 427

UNIFORMS 430

SPORTING DRESS 431

GLOSSARY 433

INDEX 445

AUTHORITIES CONSULTED 455

ILLUSTRATIONS
Volume Two

Initials

FIGURE   PAGE

1. Working girl and little boy in typical costumes, 1800–1810 . . 23
2. Girl in striped muslin, lent by F. Walter Taylor, Esq., and a letter-carrier in typical costume, 1810–1820 87
3. Embroidered muslin. Lent by Mrs. Samuel Chew, 1820–1830 . 141
4. Walking dress with large sleeves, pelerine and bonnet. Typical styles, 1830–1840 182
5. Lady in flounced dress and small bonnet. Typical dress, 1840–1850 213
6. Lady in hoop-skirt and shawl. Typical costume, 1850–1860 . 245
7. Lady in riding habit, little girl in hoop-skirt. Typical fashions, 1860–1870 263
8. Child in pinafore over a chintz dress, 1800 and after. From a print . 295
9. Child in dress worn over a guimpe; large hat. Typical of styles, 1840–1850 311
10. Quaker gentleman from a pencil sketch. Lent by Miss Anne H. Cresson, 1830–1840 327
11. Gentleman in high-waisted coat and long pantaloons. Typical fashion, 1800–1810 347
12. Gentleman in walking dress. Typical style, 1810–1830 . . . 378
13. Lady and gentleman in riding dress. Typical costumes, 1830–1840 397
14. Military costumes. Typical uniforms of officer and private during the Civil War, 1861–1865 414

Other Illustrations

1. Empire gown worn in Philadelphia, about 1804. Memorial Hall, Philadelphia . . . . Frontispiece
2. Turkish vest and turban. From a plate, 1801 29
3-4-5-6. Progress of the toilet, by Gillray, 1800 29
7. Head-dresses, 1801. From a plate 29
8. Gypsy hat, 1800 +. From a plate 29
9. Cap and locket watch, 1800. From a plate 29
10. Turban and veil, 1801. From a plate 29
11. Outdoor costume, 1801. From a plate 29

FIGURE   PAGE

12. Morning dress, 1801. From a plate   29
13. Walking dress, pelisse and Livinia hat, 1807. From a plate .   . 29
14. Summer outdoor dress, 1806. From a plate 29
15. Fashionable coiffure, 1807. Portrait by Hopner   39
16. Evening head-dress. From a portrait of 1808   39
17. Scarf turban. From a portrait of 1806   39
18. Muslin turban worn by Princess Mary, 1810 39
19. Head-dress of India muslin. From a portrait by Lawrence .   . 39
20. Head-dress, 1805. From a portrait of Mrs. J. Dickinson Sergeant,
        by St. Memin. Lent by George Maurice Abbot, Esq. .   .   . 39
21. Short hair, 1800 +. From a contemporary portrait   .   .   . 39
22. Fashionable coiffure, 1810. From a miniature of the period .   . 39
23. Costume of 1808. Lent by J. Rundle Smith, Esq. 49
24. Hat and veil, 1806. From a plate   49
25. Turban and earrings, 1806. From a plate   49
26. Gown of white muslin, embroidered in "Smyrna work," 1808.
        Lent by J. Rundle Smith, Esq. 49
27. Spencer and hat, 1802. From a plate   49
28. Gown of silver-embroidered muslin, 1808. Lent by J. Rundle
        Smith, Esq. 49
29. Back of pelisse, hat with feather, 1812. Lent by F. Walter
        Taylor, Esq.   49
30. Back view of gown in Figure 56. Lent by J. Rundle Smith, Esq. . 49
31. Hat of 1805. From a plate   49
32. Evening hat of 1808. From a plate   49
33. Muslin gown with stripes of drawn-work, 1808. Lent by J. Rundle
        Smith, Esq. 49
34–39. Head-dresses, 1800–1808. From portraits by St. Memin   .   . 59
40. Silk turban. From a portrait of 1807   59
41. Fringed turban. From a portrait of Mrs. Madison   .   .   . 59
42. Mourning street dress, 1818. From a plate   69
43. Oldenburg bonnet, 1814. From a portrait   69
44. Regency costume, 1813. From a plate   69
45. Regency cap, 1813. From a plate   69
46. Mme. Lavalette. From an engraving of 1815 69
47. Spanish hat and cape, 1811. From a plate   69
48. Walking dress, 1810. From a plate   69
49. Huntley scarf and cap, 1814. From a plate   69
50. Walking dress, 1812. From a plate   69
51. Wedding gown of silver-embroidered muslin in diagonal stripes,
        1800. Lent by Miss Margaret Bullus 79
52. Dress suit, 1803. From a contemporary plate   79
53. Dress of jaconet muslin, 1804. Lent by F. Walter Taylor, Esq.   . 79

FIGURE   PAGE

54. Gown of china crêpe, 1805.   Lent by F. Walter Taylor, Esq. . . 79
55. Man in top coat, 1806.   From a plate 79
56. Wedding costume of white satin, 1808.   Lent by J. Rundle
    Smith, Esq. 79
57. Wedding costume, 1808.   Portrait by Sully 79
58. Dress of yellow gauze, 1808.   Lent by J. Rundle Smith, Esq. . . 79
59. Pelisse, 1805.   Lent by J. Walter Taylor, Esq. 79
60. Angoulême walking dress, 1815.   From a plate. 89
61. Dress of white satin brocade, 1829.   Lent by J. Rundle Smith, Esq. 89
62. White embroidered frock, 1824.   Lent by Miss Cleeman . . 89
63. Dancing frock of white crêpe, 1824.   Lent by Mrs. Samuel Chew . 89
64. Blue silk dress, 1828 89
65. Dancing frock of pink gauze, 1823.   From a plate . . . 89
66. Carriage costume, 1817.   From a portrait by Chalons . . . 99
67. Court dress, 1810.   Portrait by Leslie 99
68. Carriage costume, 1820.   From a portrait 99
69. Street dress, 1818.   From a portrait 99
70. High comb and unique collar, 1824.   From a miniature . . 99
71. Street costume, 1820.   From a portrait 99
72. Wedding dress, 1834.   Lent by Mrs. William Hunt . . . 109
73. Yellow brocade, 1832.   Lent by Miss Anna C. Phillips . . 109
74. Dress of pink satin, 1838.   Lent by Miss Anna C. Phillips . . 109
75. Dress of blue taffeta, 1833.   Lent by Mrs. Talbot M. Rogers . . 109
76. Outdoor costume, 1811 119
77. Empire gown, 1804.   From a portrait by Le Brun 119
78. Court hoop, 1817.   From a fashion plate 119
79. Mourning dress,—mother and child, 1809.   From a plate . . 119
80. Mourning ball dress, 1820.   From a plate 119
81. Kutusoff costume, 1812 119
82. Sleeve cushion, 1830.   Memorial Hall, Philadelphia . . . 129
83. Artificial curls.   Memorial Hall, Philadelphia 129
84. Spencer, 1830.   Lent by Miss Voute 129
85. Bead purse, 1830.   Lent by Mrs. Talbot M. Rogers . . . 129
86. Dress of brown taffeta, 1830.   Lent by Miss Voute 129
87. Dress of sage-green brocade, 1835.   Lent by Miss Anna G. Brinton 129
88. Reticule of 1833 129
89. Satin apron, 1830.   Lent by Mrs. Talbot M. Rogers . . . 129
90. Black lace cape, 1835 129
91. Mouchoir case, 1834 129
92. Scarf drawn through ring, 1833 129
93. Belt buckle of pearl inlaid with gold, 1830.   Lent by Mrs. Talbot M.
    Rogers 129
94. Shoulder cape, 1834 129

FIGURE   PAGE

95. Gentleman's walking costume, 1813 139
96. Outdoor costume, 1814. Lent by F. Walter Taylor, Esq. . . 139
97. White satin dress, with high waist and long sleeves, 1815. Lent
    by J. Rundle Smith, Esq. 139
98. Pelisse of brown satin, 1814. Lent by F. Walter Taylor, Esq. . 139
99. Gentleman in evening dress, 1816. From a print 139
100. Dress of brocaded silk, 1828. Lent by Miss Anna C. Phillips . 139
101. Man in walking suit, 1820. From a print 139
102. Walking dress, 1823. From a plate 139
103. Wedding dress of white satin, 1824. Lent by Miss Cleeman . . 139
104. English gentleman in full dress, 1820 139
105–117. Riding hats and habits, 1800–1842. From contemporary fash-
    ion plates 149
118. Mourning walking dress, 1825. From a plate . . . 159
119. Outdoor costume, 1820. From a plate 159
120. Dinner party dress, 1821 159
121. Extremes of fashion in the thirties. From fashion plates . . 159
122. Wedding dress, 1835. From a portrait 159
123. Extremes of fashion in the thirties. From fashion plates . . 159
124. Satin bonnet, 1847. Courtesy of Miss Dutihl . . . 169
125. Straw bonnet of 1840. From a plate 169
126. Dove-coloured bonnet, 1848. Courtesy of Miss Dutihl . . 169
127. House dress of mousseline de laine, 1845 169
128. Lingerie bodice with Roman scarf, 1840 169
129. Grey satin dress, 1843. Lent by the Misses Stearns, of Boston . 169
130. Velvet bonnet, 1848. Courtesy of Miss Dutihl . . . 169
131. Bonnet of ribbed silk, 1840. Courtesy of Miss Dutihl . . 169
132. Quilted hood, 1845. Memorial Hall, Philadelphia . . 169
133. Hair in bow-knot, 1834 179
134. Evening dress in the forties. From a fashion plate . . 179
135. House dress, 1850 + ... 179
136. Extremes of fashion in the forties 179
137. Street costumes in the forties 179
138. Coiffure of pearls 179
139. Evening dress in the forties 179
140. Fashionable waterfall of 1860 + ... 179
141. Gentleman in court dress, 1824. From a plate . . . 189
142. Dress worn at ball given to La Fayette, 1825. Lent by Miss Bittin-
    ger 189
143. Gentleman in top coat, 1826 189
144. Gauze dress with satin stripes, 1829. Lent by J. Rundle
    Smith, Esq. 189
145. Summer walking dress, 1830 189

FIGURE   PAGE
146. Walking dress of a gentleman, 1835.   From a print   .   .   . 189
147. Figured chintz morning dress, 1833.   From a print   .   .   . 189
148. Walking suit, 1830.   From a fashion plate   189
149. Barége dress, 1850.   Lent by Miss Voute   199
150. Bonnet of 1850.   Lent by Mrs. William Hunt   .   .   . 199
152. Portrait of Mrs. Bloomer, 1851   199
153. Caricature of fashions, 1857.   From Punch   199
154. Hoop-skirt, 1850+.   Lent by Mrs. Talbot M. Rogers   .   .   . 199
155. Basque of pink silk, 1850–1855.   Lent by the Misses Stearns   . 199
156. Back view of peignoir, Figure 271, 1850.   Lent by Mrs. Caspar
        Morris 199
157. Girl in pantalettes, 1813.   From a plate   209
158. Mother and children, 1802.   From a portrait 209
159. Girl in pantalettes, 1837 209
160. Mother and child, 1820.   From an engraving   209
161. Boy in sailor costume, 1850.   From a portrait   209
162. Boys in highland dress, 1854.   From a portrait   209
163. Hat and feathers of 1864.   From a print   219
164. Turban hat, 1860–1870 219
165. Mushroom hat and Garibaldi blouse, 1862   219
166. Croquet costume, 1868   219
167. House-maid, 1860–1870 219
168. Hair in a chenille net, 1860 219
169. Jockey hat and feather, 1860 219
170. Wedding costume, 1836.   Lent by the Misses Mordecai   .   . 229
171. Lace collars, 1850–1870.   Lent by Miss Agnes Repplier   .   . 229
172. Specimens of high combs, 1820–1840   229
173. Bodice of wedding gown, 1854.   Lent by Mrs. William Hunt   . 229
174. Boy in calico suit, 1804.   Lent by Mrs. John Logan   .   .   . 239
175. Girl in red pelisse, 1812.   Lent by Miss Anna C. Phillips   .   . 239
176. Girl in large hat, 1822.   From a print   239
177. Small child in muslin frock, 1800 239
178. Boy in long pantaloons, 1818.   From a plate 239
179. Boy in frock and trousers, 1826   239
180. Girl in gauze dress.   Lent by J. Rundle Smith, Esq.   .   .   . 239
181. Girl in large bonnet, hair in Kenwig plaits, 1831.   From a plate . 239
182. Boy in high hat, 1832.   From a portrait   239
183. Girl in figured lawn dress, 1834.   Lent by Mrs. Wm. F. Dreer   . 239
184. Child in corded muslin, 1837.   Lent by Mrs. Wm. F. Dreer   . 239
185. Boy in coat with frogs, 1838 239
186. Boy in blue waist and white trousers, 1848.   Lent by Mrs. Wm. F.
        Dreer   239
187. Child from fashion plate of 1848   239

FIGURE   PAGE
189. Boy in plaid skirt and velvet jacket, 1856 239
190. Young girl from fashion plate, 1857 239
191. Boy in merino suit and gilt buttons, 1853 239
192. Child in French apron, 1861 239
193. Boy in velvet suit, 1865. From a photograph . . . 239
194. Boy in ankle ruffles, 1806. From a print 249
195. Child in tunic and full trousers,—Mother in mantle, shirred bon-
     net, and pagoda parasol, 1807. From a plate 249
196. Dress of apricot gauze, 1822. Lent by J. Rundle Smith, Esq. . 249
197. Boy's suit, 1833. From a portrait 249
198. Boy in leg-of-mutton trousers, 1833 249
200. Child's turban, 1860. From a photograph 249
201. Dress of checked silk over white guimpe, 1862. From a photo-
     graph 249
202. Tweed suit, 1862. From a photograph 249
203. Child's hat, 1806. School of Industrial Art 249
204. Boy and girl, 1864. From a plate 249
205. Girl in Zouave jacket, 1861 249
206. Boy in brown coat and long trousers, 1865 249
207. Girl from a fashion plate of 1870 249
208. Paper doll, 1829. Lent by Mrs. George Mason Chichester . . 259
209. Doll in wedding dress and veil, 1840. Lent by Mrs. Philip Syng
     Conner 259
210. Doll with patent head, 1855. Lent by Miss Sara Cresson . . 259
211. Doll in bloomer costume, 1851. Lent by Miss Anne H. Cresson . 259
212. Infant's shirt, 1853 269
213. Child's spencer, 1835 269
214. Child's shirt, 1860 269
215. Christening robe, 1855. Lent by Miss Mary Repplier . . 269
216. Child's costume, 1837. Lent by Mrs. Wm. Hunt . . . 269
217. Infant's dress, 1824 269
218. Infant's robe, 1826. Lent by Mrs. Wm. F. Dreer . . . 269
219. Child's shoes, 1860. Lent by Mrs. Wm. F. Dreer . . . 269
220. Baby cloak and bonnet, 1837. Lent by Mrs. Wm. Hunt . . 269
222. Part of the wedding outfit of Miss Lydia Leaming, 1808. Lent by
     J. Rundle Smith, Esq. 279
223–224. Wedding veil, scarf, shawl, etc., 1808. Lent by J. Rundle
     Smith, Esq. 279
225. Baby dress, 1810 ; embroidered pelisse, 1830. Lent by J. Rundle
     Smith, Esq. 279
227. Gentleman in full dress, 1838. Taken from a plate . . 287
228. Wedding dress of 1838. Lent by Miss Anna C. Phillips . 287
229. Tweed suit, 1839 287

FIGURE   PAGE

230. Figured white silk, 1836. Lent by Miss Sara Cresson . . . 287

231. Broadcloth suit, 1837. Lent by Mrs. Caspar Morris . . . 287

232. Silk pelisse of 1847 287

233. Satin gown, 1845. Lent by the Misses Stearns 287

234. Blue coat and white waistcoat, 1845. Lent by Mrs. Caspar Morris 287

235. Coiffure à l' indisposition, 1812 297

236. Dinner cap of 1812 297

237. Hyde Park bonnet, 1812 297

238. Chip bonnet, 1816 297

239. Leghorn hat, 1810–1813 297

240. Straw bonnet, 1817 297

241. Leghorn hat, 1825–1829 297

242. Straw hat of 1818 297

243. Bonapartean hat, 1804 297

244. Bonnet of spotted satin, 1819 297

245. Muslin bonnet, 1816 297

246. Gaiter shoes and slippers, 1820–1860. Lent by the Misses Cresson . 297

247. Velvet evening dress, 1841 307

248. Satin dress with lace flounces, 1843 307

249. Satin ball dress, 1840 307

250. Moiré gown trimmed with lace, 1840 307

251. Waved hair and quaint head-dress, 1850 307

252. Evening dress and wrap, 1851 307

253. Hat from a fashion plate of 1857 317

254. Velvet bonnet of 1856. Courtesy of Miss Dutihl . . . 317

255. Silk dress of 1855. Lent by Miss Agnes Repplier . . . 317

256. Black velvet bonnet, 1859. Courtesy of Miss Dutihl . . 317

257. Velvet wrist band, 1850–1860 317

258. Outdoor costume. From a portrait, 1852 329

259. Quaker dress, 1890. Lent by Ewing Mifflin, Esq. . . . 329

260. House dress of black taffeta. From a photograph . . . 329

261. Portrait showing a dress worn with chemisette and under-sleeves, 1850 329

262. Old lady in Quaker dress. From a photograph lent by Miss Philadore Bell 329

263. Widow's mourning, 1838. From a photograph of Queen Adelaide 329

264. Mantilla trimmed with lace, 1850. Lent by Mrs. Caspar Morris . 337

265. Gentleman in walking dress, 1850 337

266. Muslin gown, embroidered flounces, 1853 337

267. Gentleman in morning dress, 1855 337

268. Silk dress with chiné stripes, 1855. Lent by Miss Agnes Repplier 337

269. Poplin gown with velvet ribbon, 1856. Lent by Mrs. Talbot M. Rogers 337

FIGURE   PAGE

270. Black cloth suit and waistcoat, 1855.   Lent by Mrs. Caspar Morris 337
271. Peignoir of cashmere, 1856. Lent by Mrs. Caspar Morris   .   . 337
272. Bonnet of silk gauze, 1825.   Memorial Hall 349
273. Leghorn hat, 1825–1830 349
274. Taffeta hat, 1829   349
275. Tuscan straw bonnet, 1820   349
276. Bonnet of taffeta, 1830   349
277. Chip bonnet of 1835   349
278. Bonnet of white point d'esprit, 1833.   Courtesy of Miss Dutihl   . 349
279. Bonnet of fancy straw, 1838 349
280. Quilted hood, 1840 349
281. Leghorn bonnet, 1839   349
282. Velvet bonnet, 1860.   Courtesy of Miss Dutihl   .   .   . 349
283. Bonnet of horsehair, 1863.   Courtesy of Miss Dutihl   .   . 349
284. Quaker hat, 1850   357
285. Shaker girl, 1857   357
286. Quaker bonnet and cap, 1860.   Lent by Mrs. Samuel Chew .   . 357
287. Gray beaver hat, 1830   357
288. Pencil sketch of Mary Howitt, 1800   357
289. Quaker costume, 1860.   Lent by Mrs. Samuel Chew   .   . 357
290. Man in Shaker dress, 1857   357
291. Rain cover for bonnet, 1840 357
292. Girl in Shaker bonnet, 1857 357
293. White silk Quaker bonnet, 1830.   Memorial Hall, Philadelphia . 357
294–305. Various styles of hair-dressing and stocks, 1800–1860.   From
        contemporary portraits   365
306–311. Fashionable costumes for men.   From fashion plates of 1828–
        1850   373
312. Lady in fashionable hoop-skirt, 1860.   From a plate   .   . 381
313. Walking costume, 1862.   From a photograph   .   .   . 381
314. Gentleman in frock coat suit, 1864.   From a portrait   .   . 381
315. Lady in dress of Chambéry gauze, 1868.   Head from contemporary
        portrait   381
316. Street dress of 1870.   From a plate   381
317. Ball dress of Chambéry gauze, 1869   381
318. Gentleman in walking suit, 1870.   From a photograph .   . 381
319–325. Fashionable dress from 1830–1840.   From portraits by Maclise 391
326–330. Fashionable stocks and collar, 1829–1840.   From old prints . 401
331. Breadman, 1813.   From a print 401
332. Dustman, 1813.   From a print   401
333. Sailor, 1813.   From a print 401
334. English smock, after old print, 1800–1870   .   .   . 401
335. White satin waistcoat, 1837.   Lent by Miss Sarah Johnson .   . 401

FIGURE   PAGE

336. White linen coat, 1838. Lent by Miss Sarah Johnson . . . 401
337. Linen shirt of 1830 + ... 401
338–339. Military coats, 1825. Lent by Stanley Arthurs, Esq. . . 401
340. *Chapeau Bras*, 1807. From a print 401
341. White beaver hat, 1850 401
342–346. Boots, 1800–1850 401
347. Hat with rolling brim, 1809 401
348. Black high hat, 1850 401
349. Round hat, 1865 401
350. Plaid stock and waistcoat, 1840 + ... 411
351. Quaker gentleman, 1840. From a Daguerreotype, lent by Mrs. Philadore Bell 411
352. Long hair parted in the middle, 1844. From a portrait of J. R. Lowell 411
353. Clerical dress, 1845 411
354. Official robe, 1821 411
355. Clerical dress, 1865 411
356. Frock coat and standing collar, 1869 411
357. Bishop's dress of 1810 411
358. Close-fitting coat with black stock, 1855 411
359. Gentleman in riding dress, 1801. From a print . . . 421
360. Beau Brummell, 1804 421
361. Morning suit, 1806 421
362. English clergyman, 1810 + ... 421
363. Ruffled shirt with long pantaloons buttoned to the knee, 1812 . 421
364. Gentleman in great coat, 1829 421
365. Morning suit of 1830 + ... 421
366. Hunting dress, 1833 421
367. White kerseymere waistcoat, 1830 421
368. Waistcoat and cascade necktie, 1837 421
369. Gentleman in diplomatic dress, 1842. Lent by Mrs. George McClellan 421
370. Hunting costume, 1850–1860 421
371. University student of 1850 + ... 421

Contemporary Rulers

1800–1870

PRESIDENTS OF THE UNITED STATES

John Adams, of Massachusetts	1797–1801
Thomas Jefferson, of Virginia	1801–1809
James Madison, of Virginia	1809–1817
James Monroe, of Virginia	1817–1825
John Quincy Adams, of Massachusetts	1825–1829
Andrew Jackson, of Tennessee	1829–1837
Martin Van Buren, of New York	1837–1841
William Henry Harrison, of Ohio	1841–1845
(Term finished by John Tyler, of Virginia.)	
John Knox Polk, of Tennessee	1845–1849
Zachary Taylor, of Louisiana	1849–1853
(Term finished by Millard Fillmore, of New York.)	
Franklin Pierce, of New Hampshire	1853–1857
James Buchanan, of Pennsylvania	1857–1861
Abraham Lincoln, of Illinois	1861–1869
(Term finished by Andrew Johnson, of Tennessee.)	

KINGS OF ENGLAND

George III and the Regency	1760–1820
George IV	1820–1830
William IV	1830–1837
Victoria	1837–1901

RULERS OF FRANCE

Napoleon, First Consul	1800–1804
Napoleon, Emperor	1804–1814
Louis XVIII, King	1814–1815
Napoleon, Emperor (100 days, March 20–June 22) . .	1815
Louis XVIII, King	1815–1824
Charles X, King	1824–1830
Louis Philippe, King	1830–1848
(Republic proclaimed February 25, 1848.)	
Louis Napoleon, President	1848–1852
Louis Napoleon, Emperor	1852–1870

WOMEN'S DRESS
1800–1870

"The Morning Post may now display unfurl'd
  Four columns of the Fashionable World,
  And not confin'd to tell of war's renown,
  Spread all the news around of all the town.
  While gay gazettes the polish'd Treasury writes
  Of splendid fashions, not of vulgar fights.
  Proud to record the tailor's deeds and name
  And give the milliner to deathless fame
  Who first shall force proud Gallia to confess
  Herself inferior in the art of dress.
  Oh, join to pray and hopes may not be vain
  Commence gay Peace a long and joyous reign.
  May Europe's nations by thy counsels wise
  Learn e'en thy faults to cherish and to prize
  And shunning glory's bright but fatal star
  Prefer thy follies to the woes of war."
                    Prologue to " Fashionable Friends."
                          —Mary Berry.

Women's Dress

1800–1810

AT the beginning of the nineteenth century Fashion reigned supreme over all the civilized countries on both sides of the Atlantic, overcoming geographical and even political restrictions. Monthly magazines with coloured plates of the latest edicts of the invincible tyrant were published in London as well as in Paris,* and were sent regularly to America instead of the fashion dolls of the preceding century. One of the earliest of these fashion books was "The Ladies' European Magazine" edited by a coterie of women of fashion and first published in London in 1798. Another, "La Belle Assemblée," or "Bell's Court and Fashionable Magazine" was issued regularly in London from 1806 to 1832, when a new series was started of which the Hon. Mrs. Norton was editor and the name was changed to "The Court Magazine and Monthly Critic." In addition to the

* " Magazin des Modes" was published in Paris as early as 1785, and "Galleries des Modes" a year or two later.

23

fashions, it contained serial stories, literary reviews, and original
poetry contributed by the distinguished editor. This periodical
was quite as popular in the United States as in England and,
judging from the mutilated plates in the copies I have seen,
probably furnished several generations of American children
with fascinating paper dolls. A letter from Paris every month
kept its readers in touch with the court of the " Great Mogul,"
as Walpole called fashion, and the Calendar of the English
Court, which formed the supplement of the second series, was
evidently read with great interest on both sides of the ocean.

Ackermann's " Repository," published in London in 1809,
was another popular periodical which contained especially tasteful plates of the latest modes. In Philadelphia Mr. Dennie's
" Port Folio," which appeared with the first year of the century
and had great local celebrity from 1801 to 1805, gave a column
or more of its racy pages to the novelties in dress. Under the
heading " Festoon of Fashion " a brief review of the modes
in France and England was given, but " Mr. Oldschool " *
indulged only in pen portraits of the costumes. All these
magazines have been long out of print, but odd volumes of
them may be found in many of our libraries; unlike their
successors of the present day, they are good reading. Moreover,
they are faithful records of the social life of their time.

During the first Consulate and the Empire, France was
possessed with a pseudo-classic mania in women's dress. This
revival of classicism is attributed by Ashton in his " Dawn of
the Nineteenth Century " to the influence of the painter
David. Clinging draperies and Greek and Roman hair-dressing were carried to an extreme which was not noticeable in
England or America, although followed in both countries to
some extent. The simple domestic tastes of George III and

* Pen name of the editor.

Queen Charlotte set an example both in dress and social gayeties which was notably free from extravagance. The English princesses, so loved by Miss Burney, spent much of their time embroidering their own dresses for state functions; while in our own country, President Adams and his wife were living very quietly and, according to the graphic letters of the latter, most uncomfortably in the new home of the government in Washington, indulging in but few entertainments, and going to Philadelphia for most of their shopping. When Madame Recamier visited London in 1802 her "costume à l'antique" caused much comment. She appeared it seems one day in Kensington Gardens, "in a thin muslin dress clinging to her figure like the folds of drapery in a statue, her hair in a coil of braids at the back and arranged in short ringlets round her face; a large veil thrown over her head completed an attire which not unnaturally caused her to be followed and stared at." As early as 1801 Paris fashions had evidently made their way to America, for Mrs. Samuel Harrison Smith writing from the capital in that year observes, "There was a lady here who afforded us great amusement. I titled her Madame Eve and called her dress the fig leaf." *

Letters of the day give us much information on the subject of the prevailing fashions, but the most valuable sources of the history of dress in the nineteenth century are the actual garments which in many cases have been handed down to posterity unaltered, and afford a subtle insight into the character and taste of the wearers. An old writer says, "As the index tells us the contents of stories and directs to the particular chapter, even so does the external habit and superficial order of garments (in men and women) give us a taste of the internal quality of the soul."

* First Forty Years of Washington Society.

The numerous portraits of the day record fashionable costumes and illustrate the customary accessories and styles of hair-
dressing.   In England, Lawrence, Beechey, Hoppner and
Russell achieved some of their best work in the early years of
the nineteenth century.   Raeburn, Hayter, Chalons and
Winterhalter followed in their illustrious footsteps.   David,
Vernet, Ingres, Le Brun, Manet and Fontan-Latour were the
great portrait painters of France between 1800 and 1870; while,
in our own country, Stuart, Sully, St. Memin, Inman and
Healey have also left immortal canvasses which bear abundant
evidence of the transatlantic sovereignty of Fashion.

" Fashion come, on me a while
Deign, fantastic nymph, to smile."

Looking through the old magazines of 1800–1810, " Sacred
to Dress and Beauty's pleasing cares," we see that the short
waists which came into vogue at the close of the eighteenth century were worn for at least ten years of the nineteenth century.
Skirts were very narrow and the ultra-fashionable wore them of
very soft, sheer, clinging materials.   These gowns were the subject of many a satire.   We read of one critic " fond of statistics
who calculated that in one year eighteen ladies caught fire and
eighteen thousand caught cold."   Another wit of the day remarked, " The change in the female dress of late must contribute
very much to domestic bliss; no man can surely now complain
of petticoat government."   In winter, to be sure, warm cloaks
which completely covered the gowns were worn out-of-doors
(Figures 42, 59, 96, 98, 102), but slippers or half-shoes with the
thinnest of soles were worn even for walking and must have prevented the " wrapping cloaks " and big muffs (Figures 11, 102)
from keeping the wearer's body at a comfortable degree of
warmth.

Perhaps the pursuit of fashion is in itself so stimulating an exercise that it acts as a preventive and keeps off the dangers apparently courted by her votaries.

Bodices were exceedingly short in the early years of the nineteenth century. The waist line was entirely obscured (Figures 5, 9, 13, 51, 53, 54, 56, 58, 243). A satirical couplet of the day runs:

> " Shepherds, I have lost my waist
> Have you seen my body ? "

We are all familiar with the portrait of Madame Recamier on an Empire sofa, her Grecian drapery falling around her in graceful lines which could not possibly have been maintained if she stood up, or tried to walk. The mystery of the possibility of this fashion is explained (Figures 3–6) by the famous caricaturist Gillray whose pictures " give us a glimpse," as Ashton says, " of the mysteries of the toilet such as might be sought in vain elsewhere ; and are particularly valuable as they are in no way exaggerated and supply details otherwise unprocurable."

The long and close-fitting stays, though not as stiff and un-yielding as their predecessors of the eighteenth century, pre-vented the untidy negligee appearance the high-waisted gowns would have had without them. As the bodices grew longer, the stays grew shorter until 1819 or 20 when the first French corset in two pieces and laced up the back came into fashion and has retained its popularity ever since. A pair of short stays worn about 1820 may be seen in the Rhode Island His-torical Society's rooms at Newport.

In many old portraits we may notice wigs of short, close curls which were in the height of fashion in the year 1800 (Figures 7, 22), and in a letter of that date, written in Boston by Elizabeth Southgate to her mother, we find that five dollars would buy one of these coveted articles.

1800–1807

FIGURE 2.—1801—A Turkish vest of black velvet. Turban of muslin with a falling end fringed with gold and a bird of paradise feather. Necklace of coral and gold beads.

FIGURES 3, 4, 5, 6.—1800—Progress of the toilet, showing long stays, laced up the back, the dress worn over them, and the maid's costume of the same date.

FIGURE 7.—1801—Afternoon head-dresses.

FIGURE 8.—1801—Gypsy hat, worn from 1800 to 1810.

FIGURE 9.—1800—Cap trimmed with Amaranthus crêpe, locket watch.

FIGURE 10.—1801—A velvet turban with a "banditti" plume and a veil hanging to the shoulders.

FIGURE 11.—1801—Silk bonnet with lace frills, silk spencer with short sleeves and long ends trimmed with lace, large muff and fur.

FIGURE 12.—1801—Morning dress of spotted muslin, cap and neck-frill trimmed with lace.

FIGURE 13.—1807—Summer walking costume, pelisse and dress of Jaconet muslin and a Lavinia hat of straw.

FIGURE 14.—1806—Dress of muslin with a pleated shoulder-cape, straw bonnet with a silk crown to be worn over a cap.

" Now Mamma, what do you think I am going to ask for?— a wig. Eleanor has got a new one just like my hair and only five dollars, Mrs. Mayo one just like it. I must either cut my hair or have one, I cannot dress it at all stylish. Mrs. Coffin bought Eleanor's and says that she will write to Mrs. Sumner to get me one just like it ; how much time it will save—in one year we could save it in pins and paper, besides the trouble. At the Assembly I was quite ashamed of my head, for nobody has long hair. If you will consent to my having one do send me over a five dollar bill by the post immediately after you receive this, for I am in hopes to have it for the next Assembly—do send me word immediately if you can let me have one.

" ELIZA." *

They were still in fashion in 1802, for Martha Jefferson Randolph wrote the following letter to her father just before his inauguration as third President of the United States :

" *Oct. 29, 1802.*

" DEAR PAPA,—We received your letter, and are prepared with all speed to obey its summons. By next Friday I hope we shall be able to fix a day ; and probably the shortest time in which the horses can be sent after receiving our letter will determine it, though as yet it is not certain that we can get off so soon.

" Will you be so good as to send orders to the milliner— Madame Peck, I believe her name is, through Mrs. Madison, who very obligingly offered to execute any little commission for us in Philadelphia, for two wigs of the colour of the hair enclosed, and of the most fashionable shapes (Figures 5, 7 and 22), that they may be in Washington when we arrive? They are universally worn, and will relieve us as to the necessity of dressing our own hair, a business in which neither of us are adepts.

* A Girl's Life Eighty Years Ago.

" I believe Madame Peck is in the habit of doing these things, and they can be procured in a short time from Philadelphia, where she corresponds, much handsomer than elsewhere.

" Adieu, dearest Father."

A rhyme current in the early part of the nineteenth century emphasizes the annoyance of finding a wig necessary in full dress :

" There was an old woman of Gosport
And she was one of the cross sort,
When she dressed for the ball
Her wig was too small,
Which enraged this old woman of Gosport."

Miss Southgate was born in Scarborough, Maine, but spent much of her time in Boston, writing to her mother from there delightfully intimate and chatty letters, which give a charming picture of the social life of the time. The dances, the sleighing parties, etc., are all vividly described, and her remarks about dress are a valuable contribution to our subject.

" *July 17, 1800.*

" I must again trouble my Dear Mother by requesting her to send on my spotted muslin (Figures 12 and 58). A week from next Saturday I set out for Wiscassett, in company with Uncle William and Aunt Porter. Uncle will fetch Ann to meet us there, and as she has some acquaintance there, we shall stay some time and Aunt will leave us and return to Topsham ; so long a visit in Wiscassett will oblige me to muster all my muslins, for I am informed they are so monstrous smart as to take no notice of any lady that can condescend to wear a calico gown. Therefore, Dear Mother, to ensure me a favourable reception, pray send my spotted muslin by the next mail after you receive this, or I shall be on my way to Wiscassett. I shall go on horseback. How I want my habit, I wish it had not been so warm when I left home and I should have worn it (Figure 105). I am in hopes you will find an opportunity to send it by a private conveyance before I go, but my muslin you must certainly send by the mail." *

The sketch of a riding habit of the period is given in Figure 105. The jacket and skirt should be of blue cloth with black velvet collar and double rows of gilt buttons called " Nelson's balls." A close cap of beaver with a gold braid around the crown and a feather in front. Gloves of fine tan leather and half-boots of black Spanish leather.

Another riding dress given in Figure 106 shows the front view of a habit of 1801. It is made of dark blue kersemere and trimmed with three rows of small blue buttons crossed with three rows of blue silk cord. Collar of blue velvet. A white beaver hat with a very narrow brim and two short white feathers.

In a letter from Paris during the First Consulate, Miss Berry, in her " Diary and Letters," describes an assembly at which she was present when Bonaparte addressed each lady with the question : " Do you ride on horseback ? " Evidently it was the correct thing for a lady to do in France as well as in England and America.

Miss Austen mentions the fashionable muslins too. Writing to her sister in 1801, she says :

" . . . I shall want two new coloured gowns for the summer, for my pink one will not do more than clear me from Steventon. I shall not trouble you, however, to get more than one of them, and that is to be a plain brown cambric muslin, for morning wear ; the other, which is to be a very pretty yellow and white cloud, I mean to buy in Bath. Buy two brown

* A Girl's Life Eighty Years Ago.

ones, if you please, not both of a length, but one longer than the other; it is for a tall woman. Seven yards for my mother, seven yards and a half for me; a dark brown, but the kind of brown is left to your own choice, and I had rather they were different, as it will be always something to dispute about which is the prettiest. They must be cambric muslin." *

In another letter written in the same year we read of a new wrap:

" . . . My cloak came on Tuesday, and though I expected a good deal, the beauty of the lace astonished me. It is too handsome to be worn, almost too handsome to be looked at." †

A wrap trimmed with lace is given in Figure 11, from a plate of 1801.

Mrs. Ravenel in her delightful book, " Charleston, the Place and the People," gives us the following description of the ball dresses worn in that picturesque city of the South during the first quarter of the nineteenth century.

" No more the rich brocades and damasks, the plumes and powder; instead the scantiest and shortest of gowns, bodices at most eight inches long and skirts of two or three breadths, according to width of stuff and size of wearer, coming barely to the ankles. The stuff was the softest of satin, India silk, or muslin that could be found; the feet clad in heelless slippers tied with ribbons that crossed about the instep. The hair, descended from the high estate given it by the last and fairest of French queens, hung in loose waves upon the neck until the awful fashion of wigs came in. When that strange mania prevailed, it was hardly thought decent to wear one's own hair. No matter how long, how thick, how beautiful, the ruthless scissors must clip it close and a horrible construction by a hair-

* Letters of Jane Austen. Edited by Lord Brabourne. † *Ibid.*

dresser take its place. The wig fashion did not last long, only a year or two, then came the Grecian bands and plaits with short curls on the forehead, and next turbans."

Turbans, capotes and head-dresses of every possible material were in the height of fashion in the early years of the century. All the young ladies of that time were on the alert to get the newest designs and the following extract from an unpublished letter written by a Miss Smith in Philadelphia to a Miss Yeates of Lancaster, dated September 14, 1800, proves that it was fashionable to decorate turbans with hand painting.

"In the pacquet you will find three ˙painted Tiffany Turbans, of which I beg your acceptance of one, & Betsy & Kitty of the others. They are not as well done as I could wish, but they are as well done as I who never learnt to draw could do them." *

In Figures 2 and 7 specimens of fashionable head-dresses are given taken from the " Ladies' Monthly Museum " for January and March, 1801, which show that feathers and turbans were both worn with short hair.

In the " Festoon of Fashion " for October, 1801, is the following entry :

" A round dress of thick white muslin (Figure 13) ; a pelisse of cambric muslin, trimmed all round ; long sleeves. A bonnet of buff silk, trimmed with purple ribbon.

" A round dress of white muslin, drawn close round the throat with a double frill (Figure 12) ; long sleeves. A green handkerchief tied carelessly round the neck. A straw hat, turned up in front, and trimmed with green ribbons (Figures 27 and 31).

" A black silk hat, turned up in front, with a full crown, and ornamented with black feathers. A white muslin bonnet,

* Extract from letter to Miss M. Yeates, Lancaster.

trimmed and tied under the chin with white ribbon (Figure 23).

"A straw hat, turned up before, and lined with blue; blue ostrich feathers in front.

"A bonnet of dark green silk, two ostrich feathers of the same colour, placed in front, to fall contrary ways, a bow of green, edged with white, on the left side.

"A bonnet of pea-green, or other coloured silk, tied under the chin, and ornamented with white feathers.

"A cap of white and lilac muslin.

"A wreath of oak or laurel through the hair."

We are further informed : "The most fashionable colours are buff, scarlet, and blue for flowers and feathers, but white dresses are the most prevalent."

Two morning costumes of that year are copied from the "Ladies' Monthly Museum" for March, 1801 (Figures 11 and 12).

Bonnets were small and close-fitting and evidently of a variety of materials. We read in this same Philadelphia publication for 1802 of "a bonnet of black velvet trimmed with a deep black lace round the front. A close bonnet of purple, or other coloured silk, trimmed with ribbon of the same colour and ornamented with a flower in front. A bonnet of black velvet, turned up in front, and lined and trimmed with scarlet, a scarlet feather in front. A domestic or undress cap of fine muslin (Figure 12). A bonnet of pink silk, trimmed with black ribbon and a black feather; black lace round the front. A dress hat of white satin, turned up in front, and trimmed with purple velvet. A hat of brown velvet, turned up in front, and trimmed with pink ; bows before and behind."

As shown in Figures 24, 27 and 31, hats were small in the first years of the nineteenth century, but the following extract from " Lady Brownlow's Reminiscences" suggests that it was not the fashion to wear anything on the head in Paris in 1802.

" It was the month of November and cold weather and therefore the walking dress of the majority of the women surprised us not a little. It consisted of a gown *très décolleteé*, and extremely short-waisted, with apparently only one garment under it ; this gown they held up so as to discover one *jambe*, a shawl hung over the shoulders, the feet *chaussées* in their slippers, no bonnet, or cap, and the curls on each side of the face greasy with *huile antique.*" This description recalls the remark of Madame Jerome Bonaparte that dress at that time was chiefly an aid to setting off beauty to advantage ; and her own famous wedding-gown of India muslin and old lace, which one of the guests declared he could have easily put into his pocket. But the fact that this airy costume excited so much comment at the time it was worn proves that it was very unusual even in those days of scanty drapery. It was a caprice of fashion impossible for ordinary mortals to follow.

In February, 1802, a striking walking costume is described : " Round dress of white muslin, under a Hungarian cloak made of scarlet silk trimmed all round with black lace. A bonnet of the same colour as the cloak, trimmed with black lace and ornamented with flowers of the same colour."

Then comes the description of a ball dress : " A short robe of fine muslin with a train of the same : the robe made plain over the bosom, with additional fronts, to fly open from the shoulders. The whole bound with scarlet ribbon, the sleeves and the robe from the shoulders to the bottom ornamented with scarlet ribbon. The bosom trimmed round with deep white lace. A hat of white silk, turned up in front, and lined with scarlet ; a feather of the same colour fixed in front, to fall over the crown."

1800–1810

FIGURE 15.—1807—Fashionable hair arrangement. From a portrait by Hopner.

FIGURE 16.—1808—Evening head-dress. From a contemporary portrait.

FIGURE 17.—1806—A scarf of India muslin worn like a turban. From a portrait of the Princess Amelia.

FIGURE 18.—1810—Muslin turban, with the front hair arranged in bow-knot. From a portrait of the Princess Mary.

FIGURE 19.—1806—Head-dress of India muslin. From a portrait by Lawrence.

FIGURE 20.—1805—Head-dress of white mull. From a portrait by St. Memin.

FIGURE 21.—1800—Arrangement of short hair fashionable in the early years of the century. From a contemporary portrait.

FIGURE 22.—1810—Simple arrangement of hair, fashionable at the period. From a contemporary miniature.

15

22

20

16

17

21

18

19

A letter on London Fashions for the winter season of 1802 also describes evening dresses worn with hats :

" A dancing frock of white muslin ; the train very long, and trimmed round the bottom with black and yellow trimming ; over the train a plain drapery trimmed all round to match the train ; the back plain, and ornamented with alternate bows of black and yellow ; full sleeves of lace and muslin. Small hat of white satin, turned up in front, and ornamented with black and yellow ostrich feathers.

" An opera dress, made of white satin, and trimmed with swansdown. A mantle of the same, trimmed also with swansdown. A hat of black velvet, ornamented with one large ostrich feather." *

During a visit to Paris in 1802 Miss Berry describes a costume of Madame Napoleon Bonaparte : " A smart *demi-parure*, a pink slight silk gown with a pink velvet spot upon it, a small white satin hat with two small feathers, tied under the chin." †
And in England we find fanciful caps were as important an accessory of evening dress as they had been in the time of George I and George II. Some of the descriptions sound very attractive ; for instance : " A cap of white lace with a deep lace border ; bows of white ribbon on the front and left side. A cap of fine muslin, the front finished with white ribbon ; the crown full, and finished on the left side with a long end. A cap of lace, made open behind to show the hair, and ornamented with an ostrich feather. A cap of white satin, ornamented with a small wreath of flowers. A close cap of white satin, trimmed round the front with fancy trimming, and ornamented with flowers. A Parisian cap, made of worked muslin, lined with pink silk ; a deep lace border round the front. A cap of lace, drawn up close behind, and finished with

* Port Folio, 1802, Festoon of Fashion.   † Diary and Letters of Miss Berry.

a lace frill; a coquelicot feather (Figure 10) or flower in front "
(Figure 9).

A novelty of the spring of 1802 was the Bonapartian hat.
We read of one made of " salmon-coloured satin, in the form of
a helmet, surrounded with a wreath of laurel," and in Figure
243 a picture of one is given made of white gauze.

Plain white chip hats in the Gipsy style, without
any ornament whatever, tied carelessly under the chin
with coloured ribbon " were popular for a number of years "
(Figure 8).

Among the London modes we find described the " Archer
dress, a petticoat without any train, with a border of green or
blue; a blue or green sarsnet bodice, vandyked at bottom;
loose chemise sleeves, and no handkerchief. The head-dress, a
small white or blue satin hat, turned up in front." We also
learn that " brown, grey, or olive silk stockings, with yellow
or orange cloaks, are worn by the ladies "; that " feathers and
flowers continue to be much worn, and wreaths of roses
on the hair for full dress, in preference to more cumbrous ornaments " (Figure 160); and that small watches " are worn,
by a few dashing belles, on their bosoms, not bigger than the
round of an half guinea."

These were called locket watches and were suspended by a
gold chain from the neck (Figure 9).

Short pelisses (Figure 27) of black lace or of black silk
lined with scarlet or purple, and trimmed all round with fur or
lace, were very much worn (Figure 11).

A note on Parisian Fashions for the same winter (1802)
gives the information that " buff colour satin hats, with
amaranthus colour drapery, are very fashionable; " as are also
" apricot velvet hats, trimmed with amaranthus colour ribbons
with gold stripes, and feathers of the same colour; " and those

of "capucine colour velvet, with ribbons of the same colour, and some of pale blue velvet with blue feathers."

"The head-dresses in hair (Figure 18), which were entirely out of fashion, are again in favour; some ornamented with a polished steel diadem. The caps worn under turbans are generally made of black velvet instead of poppy-colour.

"Morning caps are of white crape and have bands of Chinese ribbon across them. The ends of the ribbons are left very long, and cut in the form of horns." For illustrations of caps see Figures 16, 18, 20, 21, 34, 35, 36, 37, and 38.

From Paris we hear that "silk stuffs are adopted for full dress for the winter, and muslins for undress. The *robes de bals à la Clotilde, à la Hebe, à la Syrène*, the Swiss, Italian and Spanish dresses are all made of these materials." We also learn of an alluring invention in cloaks called *belles douillettes à la Russiene.*

"These cloaks are of three cuts, and three different sorts of wadding according to the needs of the wearer. They are also adapted to different figures, some for slender persons, some for *en bonpoint,* and some for those who are much encumbered with flesh. They are extremely convenient, and find a ready admittance into fashionable society." Apparently nobody of any size could object to them.

Short pelisses and spencers, garments resembling jackets with the skirt cut off, were very popular in all materials and colours from 1800 to 1820 (Figures 11, 27).

"Nine heads" are described in the "Port Folio" for 1802:

1. "A bonnet of blue satin, trimmed round the front with deep black lace, and ornamented with black feathers.

2. "A bonnet of white satin, made open at top to admit the hair, and trimmed all round with chenille trimming; two white feathers in front.

3. " A hat of brown velvet, turned up in front, and lined with yellow ; brown and yellow feathers in front.

4. " A cap of white velvet, spotted with gold, and with gold trimmings.

5. " A bonnet of white satin, and yellow crape, ornamented with a white flower, and with yellow and white ribbons.

6. " A cap of white muslin, trimmed with gold trimming, three white ostrich feathers fixed on the right side to hang in front.

7. " The hair dressed in the present fashion, and banded with gold.

8. " Round bonnet of velvet and trimmed with steel beads, purple feather in front.

9. " Turban of white satin, with a band of muslin round the front, fastened on the left side with a gold loop ; gold flower in front."

In the same year (1802) mention is made of two very pretty costumes worn by American ladies at the court of St. James.

" In the beginning of April last, at the queen's drawing-room, Mrs. Derby, of Boston, was presented by Mrs. King, and was much admired for her beauty, and the simplicity of her dress, which was of white crape, and tastefully arranged with wreaths of white flowers and beads.

" Miss Bingham, who was likewise presented by Mrs. King, wore a black crape petticoat richly embroidered with black bugles and beads, bodice and train to correspond. Head-dress, tiara of bugles with diamonds and feathers."

Among the London Fashions a quaint walking dress is described : " A dress of white cambric, made close round the neck with a collar. A spencer of lilac silk, trimmed with lace. Large straw hat, looped up in front with a straw button and tied under the chin with ribbon." Also: "A round dress of sprigged muslin, long cloak of cambric muslin, trimmed all round with lace; close bonnet, trimmed and ornamented with lilac."

Reticules were so universally carried during the first part of the nineteenth century that they were popularly called "Indispensables," and a few years later ridicules. Miss Southgate describes one in a letter in 1802 : *

"Martha sent me a most elegant Indispensable, white lutestring spangled with silver, and a beautiful bracelet for the arm made of her hair; she is too good to love me, as she says, more than ever."

Under date of June 18, 1803, the writer speaks of half handkerchiefs as a new fashion :

"I am just going to set off for Long Island and therefore promise but a short letter. I have a mantua maker here making you a gown which I hope to have finished to send by Mrs. Rodman. The fashions are remarkably plain, sleeves much longer than ours and half handkerchiefs are universally worn. At Mrs. Henderson's party there was but one lady except myself without a handkerchief, dressed as plain as possible, the most fashionable women the plainest. I have got you a pretty India spotted muslin, 'tis fashionable here." †

"Mr. Oldschool" is responsible for the following:

"RECEIPT TO MAKE A FASHIONABLE LADY

"Take about eight yards of gingham, or sprig muslin, that is seamed together in the form of a Churchman's pulpit robe. Slip on this easy frock, draw it across the shoulders, girt it round about, and across the middle; and let the end of it sweep

* A Girl's Life Eighty Years Ago, by Eliza Southgate Bowne.
† *Ibid.*

at least a quarter on the ground.   The flowing tresses, which
Nature in her luxuriance designed to adorn and cover the
shoulders, must be stuffed, powdered, knit at the end, and
folded up under the turban *à la mode*, in the exact form of
her refrigerating hand weapon.   To the many other embellish-
ments of the head-dress must be added a quarter and a half of
black or green silk love crape, to defend from the insolence of
the sun-beams and render the inhabitant within mosquito proof.
Place this figure in a pair of red or blue Morocco slippers, and
set her a-walking on the pavement, Phaon by her side, and the
work is complete.

"N. B.   To make her irresistible she must, at every other
step, give her head a toss, smack her lips and turn up her eyes
to her beloved country the Moon : making it evident, that she
is none of the mean-spirited beings that delight in things
below."

The following parody is also from the caustic pen of the
editor of the " Port Folio " :

"An Exercise of the Lips
"Moisten your lips
Bite your lips
Open your lips
Close your lips
Pout your lips
Rest your lips."

From the advertisements of that time one gleans many
amusing notes.   The following is a Philadelphia hair-dresser's
announcement for 1802 :

"Ross respectfully informs the ladies that he has on exhibition a most elegant and whimsical head-dress, calculated either
for mask balls, full dress, or undress, and may be worn instead
of a veil, having the peculiar quality of changing its shape, occa-

sionally covering the whole face, yet capable of being disposed into wandering ringlets; as a mask the disguise is complete without oppression; as a veil it protects without the dull uniformity of drapery, and may be scented to the perfume of any flower; for beauty it cannot be surpassed, and for simplicity it stands unrivalled. The patent was granted by the Goddess of taste, inspired by the spirit of fancy, secured from imitation by the genius of merit, patronized by the votaries of elegance, and exhibited in the temple of fashion."

And this device of a London hair-dresser reminds one very much of the transformation arrangements of the present day:

"Mr. T. Bowman of London, peruke maker, etc., gives a noble specimen of a disinterested spirit, when he tells the ladies that his ' Full dress patent head-dresses are beautifully simple when folded up and fastened with a bodkin; are easily dressed in any style the best head of hair is capable of, and much *superior in beauty.*' Price 6, 8, 10, 12, 15 and *twenty guineas!*"

While on the subject of hair-dressing, it may be well to quote another London advertisement which assuredly promises a great deal:

" To those who are ashamed of red hair, which the Romans thought a beauty, and to those who are ashamed of grey hair, which many think looks venerable, we must recommend the following suggestions by the ingenious Mr. Overton, who seems to contradict the Scripture assertion, ' Thou canst not make one hair white or black ':

"To the nobility, gentry, etc. . . . No. 47, New Bond Street, Mr. Overton's, where may be seen specimens of red or grey hair changed to various beautiful and natural shades of flaxen, brown, or black. As many ladies are compelled from their hair changing grey, at a very early period, to adopt the use of wigs, such ladies are respectfully informed that their own

1806–1812

FIGURE 23.—1808—Dress, mantle and gloves from original costume. Bonnet of white straw with full crown of silk and bows of taffeta ribbon.

FIGURE 24.—1806—Hat of fancy straw, with veil.

FIGURE 25.—1806—Turban and earrings.

FIGURE 26.—1808—Sketch of an original gown made of white muslin, embroidered with "Smyrna work" in red and green. Head with muslin turban.

FIGURE 27.—1802—Spencer of black lace. Hat turned up in front and tied under the chin.

FIGURE 28.—1808—Gown of India muslin, embroidered with silver. Head from a portrait.

FIGURE 29.—1812—Back of sage-green pelisse. Hat with feather.

FIGURE 30.—1808—Back view of white satin gown in Figure 56. Head from a portrait.

FIGURE 31.—1805—Hat of fancy straw, turned up in front.

FIGURE 32.—1808—Evening hat.

FIGURE 33.—1808—Gown of white India muslin with stripes of fine drawn-work. The hair curled under a "half-turban" of white mull trimmed with lace, is from a contemporary portrait.

hair may be changed to any shade they choose, in the course of a few hours, by the use of the never-failing tricosian fluid, and such is its permanency, that neither the application of powder, pomatum, or even washing, will in the least alter the colour. It is easy in application, and may be used at any season of the year, without danger of taking cold, being a composition of the richest aromatics, and highly beneficial in nervous headaches, or weakness of the eyes. To convince the nobility, etc., any lady sending a lock of her hair, post paid (sealed with her arms so as to prevent deception), shall have it returned the next day, changed to any colour shown at the places of sale. Sold in bottles at one pound one shilling by Mr. Golding, perfumer to her majesty, Cornhill; Mr. Overton, No. 47 New Bond Street; Mr. Wright, Wade's Passage, Bath, and nowhere else in the kingdom." *

The following squib on the subject of the scanty draperies worn by the most ardent votaries of Fashion, is taken from a Paris journal:

" THE PIN

" Our neighbours, the English, if we may judge from their marriage contracts, are, or at least were, the greatest consumers of pins in the world. Nothing is more usual than for a lady of fashion to be allowed a thousand pounds sterling a year for the single article of pins. Historians relate that in those days when pin-money was first introduced the English ladies consumed a vast number of pins to fasten their clothes. In process of time, however, the consumption of pins has decreased, and in exact proportion with the diminution of drapery. At Paris, God knows, a husband will not be ruined by the expense of pins. Now-a-days, an *elegante* makes almost as little use of a pin as of a needle." †

* Port Folio, July 3, 1802, Festoon of Fashion.   † *Ibid.*

Although bodices were cut very low and displayed a great deal of neck, tuckers or frills of lace were generally worn as we may notice in contemporary portraits, always more reliable sources of the history of dress than the fashion plates. Fans were small at this period (Figure 56). In the " Port Folio " for 1802 appeared this anecdote :

" A finished coquette at a ball asked a gentleman near her while she adjusted her tucker, whether he could flirt a fan which she held in her hand. ' No, Madam,' answered he, proceeding to use it, ' but I can fan a flirt.' "

As will be seen in the illustrations given, there were not any marked changes in the shape and cut of gowns or wraps during the first decade of the nineteenth century, but on the other hand an endless variety of head-dresses, trimmings and accessories followed with bewildering rapidity, and the names it was the fashion to give each innovation would fill a dictionary.

" Variety is the very spice of life
And lends it half its charm."

These names are worthy of mention, however, as by means of them the current historical events can be traced even in the pages of a " Magazin des Modes." It was an age of sentiment as well as of variety. Young ladies took great delight in the most romantic and fanciful nicknames. A couplet by Coleridge published in a periodical of 1803 runs :

" I asked my fair one happy day,
What I should call her in my lay ;
By what sweet name from Rome or Greece ;
Lalage, Neaera, Chloris,
Sappho, Lesbia or Doris,
Arethusa or Lucrece ?

" ' Ah,' replied my gentle fair,
    ' Beloved, what are names but air ?
        Choose thou whatever suits the line ;
    Call me Sappho, call me Chloris,
    Call me Lalage or Doris,
        Only, only call me thine.' "

Trains and round skirts were both worn, but all the gowns were very scanty, the latter measuring scarcely more than two yards at the bottom. (See Figures 5, 12, 51, 53, 54, 56 and 58.) The waists were made with a little fullness in front and cut very low about the shoulders. Guimpes of muslin with or without sleeves were worn on ordinary occasions (Figure 54), also low-necked dresses with long sleeves which could easily be removed, leaving the little puffs or short sleeves on the shoulders. Pin tucks and heavy cords were very much used for trimming. (See Figures 53 and 54.)

The costume of a French " milliner's assistant " given in the initial at the head of this chapter, is taken from an old print of 1804, and shows a bonnet with a high crown tied at one side of the chin, a kerchief knotted round the throat, a low-necked dress with short sleeves, and a very long apron. An English or an American girl of the same class would probably have worn a cape or a spencer covering the arms and shoulders.

Fur was worn too as trimming, and large muffs (Figure 11) of it were carried, not only in winter when they were needed, but they are often seen in many of the early fashion plates from 1800 to 1810 with straw hats and muslin costumes. In the " Port Folio " for 1803 we read :

" The contest between muffs and muslins is at present very severe among the ladies, most of whom condescend to keep their hands warm, though the cold and thin clothing should dye parts of their sweet persons an imperial purple."

Slippers with astonishingly thin soles and no heels (see Figures 3, 11, 26 and 54) were worn to match or contrast with the dress, and the long gloves as shown in Figures 5, 14, 28 and 51 were made of lace, linen, or kid. Veils were long and usually of very delicate lace. Muffs were large and made of beaver, chinchilla and swansdown. Chintz, lace, cambric, tissue, gauze, silk, satin and brocade were alike fashionable and worn as occasion required.

> " If on her we see display'd
> Pendant gems and rich brocade,
> If her chintz with less expense
> Flows in easy negligence."

It is said that " to encourage commerce, Napoleon bade his wife entertain as much as possible, thus setting an example to all those whose means permitted display. Josephine, who delighted in dress as much as ever, although her charms were somewhat dimmed, was only too glad of any pretext for devising new costumes, upon which she spent much time, and no less than a million francs per year. Her budget of expenses, which is not without interest, included in one year three thousand francs' worth of rouge. She paid her hair-dresser a salary of six thousand francs, and ordered in one year two hundred white muslin dresses costing from five hundred to two thousand francs apiece, five hundred and fifty-eight pairs of white silk stockings, five hundred and twenty pairs of dainty shoes, five hundred lace-trimmed chemises at three hundred francs each, two hundred and fifty-two hats, and, after shawls came into fashion, no less than sixty, which cost from eight to ten thousand francs apiece. Strange to relate, however, her wardrobe included but two flannel petticoats, and two pairs of tights for riding. Warmth was supplied by cloth or velvet gowns, which, as they were low-necked and short-sleeved, were often supplemented by redingotes lined with fur or silk. The fit of gowns in her day precluded the use of many underclothes, and, aside from a chemise and corset, Josephine wore nothing but a slip, even when her upper garment was one of her favourite white muslins. The shoes and slippers made to match her gowns, were for ornament more than use, for it is said that when she once showed her shoemaker some footgear which revealed holes after one day's wear, he gravely examined them, and justified himself by exclaiming : ' Ah ! I see what it is. Madame, you have walked in them !' Josephine also delighted in dainty wrappers, nightgowns, and caps and her husband once declared that her night toilet was as elegant as that used by day, and that she was graceful even in bed." *

The Empire dress was a great favourite in Court circles, not only in France, but in England, where Napoleon was more feared than loved. Some very beautiful specimens of this style may be seen in the South Kensington Museum in London, and one of blue satin richly embroidered in coloured silks and crape is on view in Memorial Hall, Philadelphia, which through the courtesy of Mrs. Harrison we have been permitted to reproduce in the frontispiece of this volume. The long heavy trains of this mode were usually of some thick material, velvet, satin or brocade, while the under-dress was of filmy embroidered gauze, India muslin, or soft finished satin.

The hair was worn in short ringlets over the forehead and generally parted in the middle and coiled at the back. Although it did not require a great deal of hair for this arrangement, wigs still continued in favour, to the evident displeasure of a contributor to the " Evening Fireside," edited in 1804.

* Empress of France, by H. A. Guerber.

" On Seeing S. L. Dressed in a Fashionable Wig

" As Nature to preserve an equipoise,
   Redundant pow'r of principles destroys,
   Blending attractive and repulsive might,
   And mingling shade (to save our eyes) with light,
   So modish dames repell us from the gaze,
   And kindly deaden beauty's ardent blaze,
   When o'er their charms, contrived in pireous gig,
   They spread that monstrous veil y-clep'd a wig—
   Had those famed Syrens whose allurments bland
   Attracted heroes to the fatal strand,
   Had they worn wigs, by modern artists shap'd,
   Others besides Ulysses had escap'd . . .
   Or when in Eden beauty held the bait
   And tempted Adam from his blissful state,
   Had round Eve's brows a shaggy wig been curl'd,
   Her charms less potent had not lost the world."

Mrs. Smith, formerly Miss Bayard of Philadelphia, writing to her sister Mrs. Kirkpatrick, has given us graphic pictures of society in the United States.   In January, 1804, she says :

"Since my last letters, we have been at a large and splendid ball at Mrs. Robert Smith's, a dancing party at Mdm. Pichon's, a card party at Mrs. Galatin's, at Mr. Beckley's and at Mr. Von Ness's, and at the City Assembly.   Mrs. R. Smith's was by far the most agreeable.   Mrs. Merry (wife of the British Minister) was there and her dress attracted great attention ; it was brilliant and fantastic, white satin with a long train, dark blue crape of the same length over it, and white crape drapery down to her knees and open at one side, so thickly covered with silver spangles that it appeared to be a brilliant silver tissue ; a breadth of blue crape about four yards long and in other words, a long shawl, put over her head instead of over her shoulders and hanging down to the floor, her hair bound tight to her head with a diamond crescent before and a diamond comb behind, diamond earrings and necklace displayed on her bare bosom.

"I am half tempted to enter into details of our city affairs and personages, but really I shall have to be so scandalous that I am afraid of amusing you at such a risk. But certainly there is no place in the United States where one hears and sees so many strange things, or where so many odd characters are to be met with. But of Madam ——— I think it is no harm to speak the truth. She has made a great noise here and mobs of boys have crowded round her splendid equipage to see what I hope will not often be seen in this country, an almost naked woman. An elegant and select party was given to her by Mrs. Robert Smith; her appearance was such that it threw all the company into confusion, and no one dared to look at her but by stealth; the window shutters being open a crowd assembled round the windows to get a look at this beautiful little creature, for every one allows that she is extremely beautiful. Her dress was the thinnest sarsnet and white crape without the least stiffening in it, made without a single plait in the skirt, the width at the bottom being made of gores; there was scarcely any waist and her arms were uncovered and the rest of her form visible. She was engaged the next evening at Madam P.'s. Mrs. R. Smith and several other ladies sent her word if she wished to meet them there, she must promise to have more clothes on. I was highly pleased with this becoming spirit in our ladies."

We suspect that the heroine of this scandal was Madame Jerome Bonaparte, whose scanty draperies are mentioned in many contemporary letters, and whose wedding costume has been already described.

From a letter from Paris dated 1806 the following items are gleaned :

"Square shawls are more in favour than long ones. Few feathers or flowers are to be seen; they have almost entirely

1800–1812

Figure 34.—1800—Head-dress of India muslin.   From a portrait by St. Memin.

Figure 35.—1801—Cap of muslin and ribbon.   From a portrait by St. Memin.

Figure 36.—1802—Cap of an elderly lady.   From a portrait by St. Memin.

Figure 37.—1803—Cap tied under the chin.   From a portrait by St. Memin.

Figure 38.—1805—Ruffled mob cap.   From a portrait by St. Memin.

Figure 39.—1808—Cap with bands of ribbon.   From a portrait by St. Memin.

Figure 40.—1807—Turban of soft silk.   From a portrait of Mme. Catalani.

Figure 41.—1812—Fringed turban.   From a portrait of Mrs. Madison, by Wood.

40

38

36

34

39

37

35

41

given place to ribbands of various descriptions. Lavender is a new colour and much worn, dove, fawn, pale-pink and blue are the colours at present most admired."

The last mentioned, blue, appears to have been the most favoured colour of all ages. There is something blue in every list of costumes, calling to mind the popular old rhyme:

> " Green is forsaken
> And yellow forlorn
> But blue is the prettiest colour that's worn."

Thistleton Dyer, however, tells us that blue is considered unlucky for a wedding dress in some parts of England, proving that the time-honoured adage that no bride will be lucky who does not wear

> " Something old and something new,
> Something borrowed and something blue "

is not universal.

In the spring of 1806, " large shawls of silk or mohair were much worn, and of various shapes; some in the form of a long mantle, with a hood; others *à la Turque;* others again square. Loose spencers of pale blue or apple-blossom sarsnet, or of cambric muslin were popular. Pelisses were made of plain nankin and were very appropriate to the season. The most fashionable hats were of yellow straw, with a large rim *à la Pamela,* ornamented with very broad plain ribbon, or a flower; a sort of bonnet with a small brim of straw, and the crown of white silk, was worn with a riding habit. A lace frill was worn with this costume, round the neck, or a coloured hunting neck-handkerchief." The picture of a riding costume of 1806 is given in Figure 107. It is intended to be made of fine broad-cloth, the colour a dark lavender blossom; it has a high rolled collar, lapelled front, deep cape *à la pelèrine,* a broad belt secured in front with a double-clasp of steel, and a high ruff of double-plaited muslin sloped to a point at the bosom. Hat of amber coloured velvet, band of same formed in leaves. Hair in close curls. Light tan gloves; half-shoes of lavender blossom kid. Certainly a very dainty creation for the purpose. Everybody rode on horseback in the first half of the nineteenth century, and every lady had a riding habit, more or less elaborate, as the illustrations in Figures 105–117 show. They are all taken from contemporary prints.

Riding hats were often trimmed with fur, and in a fashion magazine for 1806 we read : " The latest style for these hats is quite novel ; they are made of a fawn-colour, the brims are raised on each side to the height of the shape, and are cut round to resemble a fan."

Pelisses and robes of velvet, cloth and silk were still fashionable. We read of a pelisse " of dove-coloured velvet, worn loose and open before, embroidered in silk of the same colour down the front, with a running foliage of *vine* or *olive* leaves."

Later in the season bonnets and hats were of straw of different shapes, gracefully turned up in front and lined with various coloured velvets and ornamented with artificial flowers.

Fancy-coloured silk, nankin, and jean shoes, and parasols of white cambric were very generally in use.

The following details are from Paris :

" Silk hats à *la Turban* are generally covered with leno, or fine embroidered muslin ; they are popular and have a neat unobtrusive effect. The Gipsy hat and cloak is a most distinguished outdoor covering, but suits only women tall in stature and graceful in carriage. We never recollect a greater variety of fancy cloaks than have been introduced this spring. The Spanish cloak now gives place to the Grecian scarf, which is exceedingly elegant. Lace and work is introduced as much as ever round the bottom, on the sleeves and up the front of dresses." *

In an English magazine of 1806, a new hat is described as of " fancy straw without any trimming, turned up on the left side immediately over the edge, the rest of the rim slouched. A plain lace veil of the scarf form with a narrow border all around is fastened on the top of the crown with a small antique stud, and left open in front." A picture of this is given in Figure 24.

The ruffs which came into vogue at this time are carefully described in the following extract from a letter from Paris :

" Before I bid you good-night I will endeavour to give you a practical description of the new ruff, now almost indispensable in morning and outdoor costume. (And I beg you to remember, dear Julia, that nothing is considered so vulgar and indecorous as to exhibit the bosom, throat or arms with the above mentioned habiliments.) This ruff has about half an ell of broad lace, fulled into a band of narrow raised needlework, a little larger than the size of the throat. A band of muslin is gathered full on the other edge of the work, about an eighth in depth, and finished with a row of similar needlework at the bottom. The lace, which sits high and straight round the chin, is finely crimped ; and the full muslin, confined by the rows of work, sits in hollow gathers round the throat. When the habit shirt is made without a collar, or with the high morning dress, this elegant ruff is particularly convenient and becoming." (For illustrations of ruffs see Figures 7, 11, 29, 31, 41 and 54.)

" Veils are still very prevalent; as head-dresses they are worn either at the back of the head, or flowing on one side, shading the shoulders (Figure 28), which would be otherwise entirely exposed. The gowns are made high in the bosom, and

* La Belle Assemblée.

low in the back. No trains are to be seen with morning
dresses. The bodice of coloured sarsnet, a sort of spencer without sleeves, formed like the plain waist of a gown, with plaited
net all round, has a very pretty effect."

Among the variations of Fashion described in 1806 are:
" A full-dress lace turban, ornamented with gold-spangled net,
an aigrette in front, with a large bow of muslin confining the
whole, and a row of gold, intermixed with spangled net, hanging tastefully on one side of the forehead.

" The Circassian straw hat, which has some resemblance to a
Gipsy hat, but has a fanciful crown, and is ornamented with
lilac, salmon, and other spring coloured ribbands. A half
Gipsy straw hat, tied down with yellow or green ribbands, is
fashionable. A straw hat for mourning wear in the turban
style, embellished in front with primroses, or a bunch of mi-
gnonette and yellow roses, and a loose bow of white ribbands."

A simple but attractive walking dress is shown in Figure 14.
It consists of " a plain muslin frock, walking length, the front
of the bodice and the short sleeves made rather full, the latter
gathered with a band and finished with a bow of ribbon. The
bonnet is of the cottage shape, the front of straw or chip with a
round crown of lavender-blossom silk. A handkerchief of the
same silk crosses the crown and is tied in a bow under the chin.
Under the bonnet a small round cap with a frill of lace is seen.
A sash to match the bonnet trimming is tied in the back under
the pelerine, which is made of three falls of finely crimped or
plaited muslin. The scarf is of pale green with a narrow variegated border. The long gloves and the half-shoes are of buff
kid." With this costume, which is taken from a plate in " La
Belle Assemblée " for the summer of 1806, we read that amber
earrings were worn. Two fashionable straw bonnets in the

summer of 1806 were the conversation (Figure 27) and the cottage (Figure 23) bonnets.

A simple evening dress is described in an English paper: " A French jacket of coloured crape, ornamented with narrow lace, also a trimming of lace round the bottom of the dress; long sash of ribbon tied carelessly on one side, of a colour corresponding with the dress. Front made plain and very high over the bosom, trimmed round with plain double *tulle.* No neckerchief or tucker is necessary with this dress; white kid gloves and shoes." Also a popular walking dress: " A short round frock of nankeen, trimmed round the bottom with sapphire ribbon, binding of the same round the bosom; narrow sash of the same ribbon tied on one side; lace chemissette; nankeen boots or shoes, and a Gipsy hat of silk."

Another letter from Paris says: " Ball dresses, dear Julia, were never more attractive than this spring. Frocks of French net over white satin, painted in natural flowers. Dresses of white Imperial satin, with a silver brocade ribband at the bottom, and French aprons of net or lace, bordered all round, and ornamented at the pocket-holes with Chinese roses. Round train-dresses of Moravian muslin, let in all round with fine footing lace, and fastened up the side with clasps of embossed gold or steel. These dresses, amidst many others, are conspicuous for their taste and elegance. I no longer remark the long sleeve in full dress, except on women who have passed their maturity. I hope, dear Julia, you have never worn the backs of your dresses immoderately low; a correct taste must ever condemn a fashion so disgusting. I am happy to tell you that at the last Opera, and at the Marchioness of D——'s Assembly, the most elegant women wore the backs of their dresses much advanced, or shaded with soft folds of muslin or lace.

" . . . Mary's French coat rivals the primrose hue, while

my Curacoa cloak the violet's shade assumes. Our Gipsy hats, of chip, are decked with wreaths in imitation of these beauteous offspring of the season. We have also hats of satin-straw, for half-dress, with the high tiara front and globe crown, the most novel and elegant article of the kind I have witnessed for many months."

A magazine much used in America makes the announcement for 1806 that "white satin dresses will continue fashionable the whole of the season; ball dresses worked in gold and silver *lamè*, or crape embossed in white or coloured velvets. Silver *chambery* is extremely fashionable and elegant both for turbans and dresses. The most fashionable ornaments are amethyst tiaras and *bandeaux* of velvet. Dove brooches are worn in the front of dresses, with or without other ornaments, and are much admired. Silks of every colour, spotted with white, are prevalent; silk hats and bonnets to correspond are worn with them. An evening dress of *leno*, worked in the Etruscan pattern, is much approved of; the back of this dress is low, drawn full, and is finished with a loose bow of narrow ribband, high in front, and is ornamented with footing lace. Head-dress of white satin, ornamented with flowers. Lace caps are now more universally worn than ever by our most fashionable females; the mob (Figures 35 and 39) has not entirely disappeared, but the small round cap seems to be more admired " (Figure 38).

An English walking costume of 1807 is thus described : " A Polish robe of purple velvet, open in front, rounded gradually from the bottom towards the lappels, which are continued across the shoulder, and finished in regular points on the back. A yoke of the same, with high fur collar; the whole trimmed all around with red fox, mole, leopard-spot or grey squirrel. A rich cord and tassel is attached to the centre of the back, and fastened at the waist in front. The bodice and skirt cut in one and the sleeve fitting close to the arm. Polish cap of the same material, trimmed round the edge and across the crown with fur, a cord and tassels hanging from the right side of the crown. York tan gloves and primrose shoes."

A trimming of spangled velvet is mentioned in the same magazine. " A ball dress of plain crape, over a white satin slip, made dancing length; plain back and sleeves, with quartered front, trimmed round the bottom, on the waist and on the sleeves with a white velvet ribband thickly spangled with gold or lace." In the words of a contemporary authority, " the chemissette, so long and so justly esteemed for its delicacy and utility, is now worn with a double plaiting of Vandyked muslin, forming a very high and stiff frill, which sits close round the throat, and is sloped to a point at the chin ; " and the winged ruff is described as "a dignified and fashionable appendage to the evening dress." For short sleeves we learn a Vandyke trimming was preferred, but the crescent sleeve and the full puffed sleeve, formed in three divisions, with bands of lace, needlework, silver, or gold, were alike fashionable.

" The fronts of dresses are generally cut to fit the form," Mrs. Bell, the famous English authority, remarks, " and where the bust is finely turned, we know not of any fashion that can be more advantageous ; but to a spare figure we recommend a little more embellishment." Specimens of this style are given in Figures 13, 21, 53, and 54. Round gowns were in 1807 arranged with French gores, so as to have no gathers at the bottom of the waist in front.

Veils, both as head-dresses and on bonnets, were much worn ; a figure of one worn with full evening dress is given in Figure 28. The popularity of the veil is proclaimed in the following sonnet :

1810–1818

FIGURE 42.—1818—Mourning street dress, showing a cloak fashionable for the first quarter of the century.

FIGURE 43.—1814—Oldenburg bonnet.   From a portrait.

FIGURE 44.—1813—Regency costume, trimmed with fur.

FIGURE 45.—1813—Regency cap of white satin.

FIGURE 46.—1815—Costume of Mme. Lavalette, in which her husband made his escape from prison.

FIGURE 47.—1811—Spanish hat and ermine cape.

FIGURE 48.—1810—Walking dress with straw hat.

FIGURE 49.—1814—Huntley scarf and cap.

FIGURE 50.—1812—Walking dress with a cottage bonnet.   Roman sandal.

42   C.W.T. 1907 After Print

43   G.W.T. 1907

44   C.W.T. 1907

45   C.W.T. after Pri

46   C.W.T After Portrait

47   G.W.T after Print

48   C.W.T. After Print.

49   G.W.T. after Print

50   C.W.T After Print

" THE VEIL *

"Though to hide a sweet face,
  With a curtain of lace,
Makes oglers of fashion to rail ;
  Though our Fair would shine bright
  Midst a full blaze of light,
My lines I'll devote to the veil.

" Master Cupid we know,
  When he aims a sure blow,
With enchantment of face will assail ;
  Yet his Godship knows too,
  How intense men pursue,
Ev'ry Venus that's deck'd with a veil.

" For the peace of mankind,
  It is both right and kind,
Some fair ones their charms shou'd conceal ;
  Since a pair of bright eyes,
  Will, in spite of disguise,
Inflict a deep wound through a veil.

"Now if one roguish beam,
  From an eye can inflame,
And to do execution not fail ;
  What destruction of hearts,
  Wou'd be found in all parts,
Did Beauty relinquish her veil ! "

Pelisses, usually of cambric and opening down the front,
were called " fugitive coats," a revival of the flying Josies popular for morning wear at the close of the eighteenth century.
A sketch of one of these graceful garments is given in Figure
13, trimmed with Vandyke edging and embroidery, and worn
with a Lavinia hat. The Lavinia hat is a variation of the
Gipsy hat, which had been in favour for several years ; and was
probably named for the rustic heroine in Thomson's " Seasons,"
of whom the poet says :

* La Belle Assemblée, 1807.

" He saw her charming, but he saw not half
   The charms her downcast modesty concealed."

The dress in the illustration is of Jaconet muslin made with a
gored bodice finished with a tucker of fine embroidery. The
cambric pelisse is made with long sleeves which fall over the
hand ; the parasol is of silk to correspond with the hat trimmings and breast knot.

The following verses show that the use of rouge was neither
universal nor unusual in 1807 :

THE FAIR EQUIVOQUE

" As blooming Harriet moved along,
   The fairest of the beauteous throng ;
   We beaux gaz'd on with admiration
   Avow'd by many an exclamation.
   What form ! what naiveté ! what grace !
   What roses decked that Grecian face !
   ' Nay,' Dashwood cries, ' that bloom's not Harriet's ;
   'Twas bought at Reynold's, Moore's, or Mariot's,
   And though you vow her face untainted,
   I swear by Heaven, your beauty's painted.'

" A wager instantly was laid,
   And Ranger sought the lovely maid,
   The pending bet he soon reveal'd
   Nor e'en the impious oath conceal'd.
   Confused, her cheek bore witness true,
   By turns the roses came and flew.
   ' Your bet,' she said, ' you'll win I ween,
   For I am painted, Sir—by Heaven.' "

Although there were not any marked changes in the fashions of 1808, variations in trimmings were innumerable. Imported India muslins embroidered with silver and gold, and
sometimes in small sprigs and figures, finished with a deep
border of a very rich pattern, were in great favour for ball
gowns. The dress in Figure 28 is a very beautiful specimen of

silver embroidery on the sheerest mull and was worn over a slip of white satin. It belonged to Miss Lydia Leaming, whose wedding dress is given in Figure 56. The veil in our illustration is of thread-lace arranged after a contemporary print. The hair is parted on the left side and curls hang down over the left cheek. Drop earrings of Roman pearls finish this costume.

Another evening gown made for the same trousseau is pictured in Figure 26. The material is also India muslin, but in this costume the embroidery is of Smyrna work done with a fine chenille thread in green and red. A turban trimmed to correspond represents the popular head-dress as worn in 1808.

Much prettier, however, is the gown in Figure 23 embroidered by Miss Leaming herself. The material is also India muslin, probably imported, and the gloves which are hand-made of white linen must have been a comfortable fashion for a hot summer outing. The bonnet is copied from a print of 1808. It is of straw with a soft crown of white silk and is trimmed with satin ribbon.

The dainty gown in Figure 33 belonged to the same outfit of 1808. The trimming consists of stripes of drawn-work resembling innumerable rows of hemstitching with embroidered edges. The head is copied from a contemporary portrait, the loose, soft curls confined by a half-turban of thin muslin, the ends of which are trimmed with lace, and tied in a becoming knot. This was a favourite head-dress from 1800 to 1810 and may be noticed in many of the portraits by Russell and Sully (Figure 17). In Figure 30 the back view of Figure 56 is given. The head-dress is of blue velvet embroidered with seed pearls, and is taken from a print of 1808.

Little French caps were worn with morning dress (Figures 18, 19 and 20), shading the ears and covering the hair at the back.   Bonnets followed the same lines and were trimmed with puffings of either lace or ribbon.   (See Figures 23 and 32.) Long sleeves set in at the shoulder were first worn in 1808 ; also ruffs of scalloped lace with gowns cut high in the back.   (See Figure 17.)

"La Belle Assemblée" for November, 1808, gives the following fashions :

"Walking Dress.   A round cambric gown, with high fan ruff; a Polish coat with Carmelite mantle, of bright grass-green, or royal purple velvet, trimmed entirely round with ermine, and clasped up the side of the figure with steel or silver.   A Shepherdess hat of green velvet, or moss straw, with variegated green feather, and a Chinese tassel.   Shoes of black Spanish silk, or pale amber velvet, and gloves of York tan."

"Walking Dress.   A round robe of muslin in white or colours.   A plain French coat (Figure 59) of merino cloth, or shot sarsnet, the colour bright morone, or crimson, trimmed all round with chenille or fur.   A three-quartered Opera tippet of the same.   A Village bonnet (Figure 59) of sarsnet or satin, formed in French flutings in front, ornamented with a full bow of appropriate ribband in the centre and tied under the chin with the same.   Shoes of grass-green, or morone velvet ; and gloves of grey Limerick."

"The cardinal, or rustic mantle, recommends itself also from its convenience and warmth, and from the graceful negligence of its folds, when wrapt round the figure."

A riding habit for 1808 is described as follows in the same periodical :

"A Spanish Habit or Polish Riding Dress, with the Patriotic helmet; formed of superfine Georgian cloth, or thin kerseymere.   Gold buttons and trimmings to correspond. Small French watch, worn on the outside.   Plain high cravat of French cambric; collar of the habit sitting close round the throat. Hair in irregular ringlets. Gloves and shoes of lemon-coloured kid." (See Figure 108.)

Miss Austen, writing to her sister in 1808 on the subject of the mourning considered appropriate on the death of a sister-in-law, says: " . . . I am to be in bombazeen and crape, according to what we were told is universal here, and which agrees with Martha's previous observation. My mourning, however, will not impoverish me, for by having my velvet pelisse fresh lined and made up, I am sure I shall have no occasion this winter for anything new of that sort. I take my cloak for the lining, and shall send yours on the chance of its doing something of the same for you, though I believe your pelisse is in better repair than mine. One Miss Baker makes my gown and the other my bonnet, which is to be silk covered with crape." *

Mourning dress at this time was very elaborate and certain rules of etiquette were observed strictly, with subtle distinctions between half and full mourning as well as between full and demi-toilette (see Figures 79 and 80), which must have been an occupation more or less diverting, and, where the grief was not of the heart, probably worked its own cure. Richter's adage, " the only medicine which does women more good than harm is dress," seems especially applicable to the intricacies of the fashionable mourning in the first half of the nineteenth century. Solace might also have been found in the general becomingness of sombre tints. Johnson described Stella's beauty :

> " But brightened by the sable dress
> As virtue rises in distress."

Bombazine is generally associated with crape and very deep mourning, but it appears to have been popular in colours at this

* Letters of Jane Austen.

time, as we often find mention of dresses of white, blue and red bombazine. According to Pope : " A saint in crape is twice a saint in lawn." It must have required considerable self-restraint to be a saint in bombazine of any colour, so irritating to the touch is the surface of that old-fashioned material. Gossamer satin sounds much more soothing and possibly was worn by Serena when she inspired the following verse :

" SERENA, IN A MOURNING DRESS
" So have I seen behind some sable cloud
    (Its skirts just tinted with a silver hue)
    The queen of planets veiled in lovely gloom,
    Such gloom as o'er the saddening landscape sheds
    The soft and soothing spirit of the sigh,
    Such as the poet courts when fancy's pow'r
    Wakes the loved shade of some departed hour,
    Breathes in regret's dull ear a soothing strain,
    And almost bids past joy be joy again."

Although convention required that only certain materials should be worn in mourning, it was not customary for mourners to seclude themselves, or refrain from social gayeties, for in all the fashion books of the first half of the nineteenth century, plates and descriptions of full dress as well as demi-dress, both in deep mourning and light mourning, are given. From a letter published in an English periodical of 1808, we quote the following elaborate description :

" Amidst the brilliant throng assembled this evening, I was much struck with the beauty and singular appearance of two young women dressed in slight mourning; and who I afterwards found to be the two Misses J——s, who were the reigning belles at Cheltenham and Worthing during the season. Their attire this evening consisted of a round train dress of black gossamer satin, rising to the edge of the throat, where it finished in a kind of neck-band of three rows of fine pearls. A

fine silver filagree net extended over the bust in front, somewhat like the bibs worn by the ancients and it was terminated
at the bottom of the waist with an elastic band, and large acorn
tassels of silver. To these dresses were attached the long bishop
sleeves like those already described as chosen by Mary, except
that these were of plain French lawn, clearer than any I have
ever before seen, and plaited with the utmost delicacy. On
their heads they wore turbans of grey *chambery*, thickly frosted
with silver; these were fancifully disposed, yet much in the
Indian style. But the most attractive part of this interesting
costume was a Jerusalem rosary, formed of the beads called
Virgin's tears."

The following advertisement appeared in 1808 :

" INVISIBLE DRESSES.—Drawers, Petticoats and Waistcoats
made of real Spanish Lamb's Wool.

"Mrs. Morris, late Mrs. Robert Shaw, informs Ladies she
has now ready for their inspection an entire fresh and extensive
Assortment of her patent elastic Spanish Lamb's Wool Petticoats, Drawers and Waistcoats, all in one, and separate. Articles
much approved of for their pleasant elasticity, warmth and delicate colour, will add less to size than a cambric muslin, and
warranted never to shrink in the wash. Children's of every
size, and made to pattern, at the Original Hosiery, Glove and
Welch Flannel Warehouses, No. 400 Oxford Street."

Reading this advertisement now, a hundred years after it
appeared, we find a possible explanation of the most perplexing
problem of the history of dress. The lamb's wool underwear,
like the union suits so universally worn in our day, were invented for warmth, and yet were so close-fitting in shape that
they did not interfere with the slim effect of the scanty gowns
of sheer muslin and transparent gauze or silk tissue then in
vogue.

FIGURE 51.—1800—A wedding gown of sheer India muslin embroidered with silver thread in diagonal stripes. It is very scanty, barely two yards in width and very high in the waist. This dainty little dress was worn by a bride of sixteen, Miss Charlotte J. Rumsey, of Cecil County, Maryland, who married Dr. John Bullus of the United States Navy, in 1800. The head in our picture is copied from a contemporary miniature.

FIGURE 52.—1803—Dress suit. From a contemporary plate.

FIGURE 53.—1804—An afternoon dress of Jaconet muslin. The long sleeves are finished with a puff at the top drawn up by a narrow tape in a casing. The narrow skirt is trimmed with many rows of corded tucks and hemmed in scallops. This very attractive gown was worn in Philadelphia about 1804, but the fashion prevailed for some years. The head is taken from a miniature of the day.

FIGURE 54.—1805—A gown of sage-green China crêpe worn in Philadelphia about 1805. It is brocaded in stripes and has a wide border of the same design on the hem, above which is a group of fine tucks. The head and hat are taken from a print of the same year.

FIGURE 55.—1806—Man in walking dress of 1806. Top-coat of green cloth, showing striped waistcoat, ruffled shirt, folded stock and high collar. A beaver hat with rolling brim, gloves of tan kid and high boots of soft leather complete the costume, which is copied from a contemporary plate.

FIGURE 56.—1808—Taken from an original wedding costume of white satin worn in Philadelphia in 1808. The only trimming is a row of lacing up the front of the bodice, but the dress fastens under the right arm. The reticule is of spangled gauze. The arrangement of the hair is copied from a miniature, being braided and carried in two bandeaux across the head. A photograph of the veil is given in Figure 223, showing the beauty of the lace. The bride was Miss Lydia Leaming, who married Mr. James Smith of Philadelphia.

FIGURE 57.—1808—Dress suit of a gentleman of the period. The blue cloth coat is cut very high at the back. The high rolling collar of the same cloth allows a fine cambric stock and ruffled shirt-front to show above a white satin waistcoat. The short trousers are of buff kerseymere, fastened at one side of the knee with small bows of the same. The stockings are of white silk. The low slippers are of black leather. The hat has a rather wide brim and the gloves are of yellow kid. This costume is taken from a portrait by Sully.

FIGURE 58.—1808—A gown of yellow gauze with a raised spot of velvet which was part of the outfit of Miss Lydia Leaming. The lace scarf, a photograph of which is given in Figure 224, belonged to the same lady. The head is copied from a portrait of 1808.

FIGURE 59.—1805—Back view of a pelisse worn in Philadelphia about 1805. It is of green China silk and lined with pink cambric. The beehive or cottage bonnet is copied from a plate of that year, but was a popular fashion from 1800 to 1812.

1800-51   1803-52   1804-53   1805-54

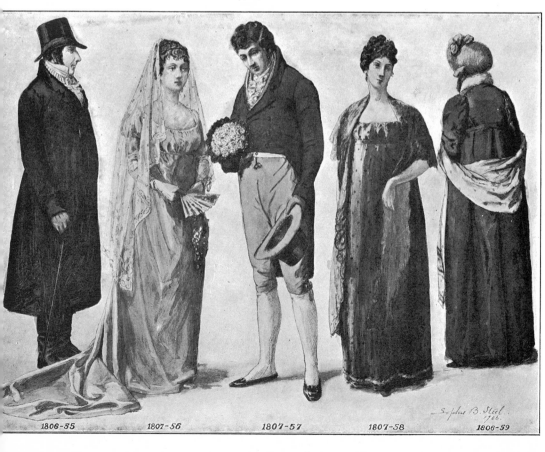

1806-55   1807-56   1807-57   1807-58   1806-59

We do not read, however, of any similar invention to protect the feet, which it was still the fashion to dress in very thin-soled slippers even for the street. As the season advanced, the ingenious Mrs. Robert Shaw offered another novelty for the requirements of spring, union suits much like those in the advertisements of to-day :

"Invisible India Cotton Petticoats, Drawers, Waistcoats and Dresses all in one.

"Mrs. Robert Shaw respectfully informs those Ladies she had the honour to serve for several years, and Ladies in general, that she has manufactured for the Spring a fresh and extensive assortment of the above articles of real India Cotton ; which articles Ladies will find well worthy their notice ; being of a soft, thin, delicate and elastic texture, will add less to size than a cambric muslin, and warranted never to shrink the least in the wash. Children's of every size and made to pattern, at her Hosiery, Glove and Flannel Warehouse, No. 400 Oxford Street."

A quaint ball dress is given in a Philadelphia magazine for 1808 : " A round robe of India muslin, worn over a white sarsnet slip ; tamboured in a small stripe either in white or colours. The dress formed on the most simple construction, plain back and wrap front, sitting close to the figure ; a plain frock sleeve edged with the antique scollop ; a short train, finished round the bottom in a similar style. Hair brought tight from the roots behind, and twisted in a cable knot on one side, the ends formed in falling ringlets on the other ; with full irregular curls. A full red and white rose, or ranunculus placed on the crown of the head towards one side. Emerald necklace linked with dead gold. Earrings and bracelets to correspond. French kid gloves above the elbow. Pea-green slippers of fancy kid."

We read in the same periodical that "no lady of fashion

now appears in public without a ridicule—which contains her handkerchief, fan, card-money and essence-bottle.   They are at this season usually made of rich figured sarsnet, plain satin or silver tissue, with strings and tassels, their colours appropriate to the robes with which they are worn."   (See Figures 48 and 56.)

"La Belle Assemblée" for August, 1808, describes the following costumes : " A round robe of white or jonquille muslin made a walking length, with spencer waist, and deep falling lappels, trimmed with lace and edged at the wrist to correspond. A bonnet of celestial blue crape, with jockey or antique front, edged and ornamented with the shell or honey-comb trimming, formed of the same material.   Gloves and shoes of pale blue or lemon-coloured kid.   Necklace and bracelets of the composition pebble, and earrings of silver filagree of the hoop form. Hair in full irregular curls.   Quilted parasol of shaded silk, lined with white satin."

" A round dress of pea-green or lilac muslin, over a white cambric slip ; a short cottage sleeve, plain back and handkerchief front, fastened in a small tufted bow and ends at the centre of the bosom.   Provincial bonnet of fine split straw, or moss straw, with band and full bow of folded sarsnet the colour of the dress, terminating in a pendant end on the left side, and finished with a corresponding tassel.   A Sardinian mantle, of French net, muslin, or spotted leno, the corners terminating in a full knot.   A double high frill around the throat, edged with scolloped lace, tied in front with a ribband."

The following concoctions for the complexion are taken from a periodical of 1808 :

"Saccharine Alum.—Boil white of eggs and alum in rose-water ; make into a paste and mould into the form of small sugar loaves.   The ladies use this paste to give greater firmness to the skin."

" Eau de Veau.—Take a calf's foot and boil it in four quarts of river water till it is reduced to half the quantity. Add half a pound of rice, and boil it with crumbs of white bread, steeped in milk, a pound of fresh butter and the whites of five fresh eggs, with their shells and membranes. Mix with them a small quantity of camphor and alum and distil the whole. This cosmetic is one that may be strongly recommended."

So accustomed are we to the advertisements of Pear's soap in all the magazines of our day that it is indeed surprising to read it in a periodical of a hundred years ago. It was introduced as a novelty, and made its first appearance in print, in October, 1808. We quote from " La Belle Assemblée " :

" PEAR'S CELEBRATED SOAP. The Proprietor of this excellent composition is proud to offer it to the notice of the Nobility, Gentry and the Public at large. The virtues of this Soap are almost too many to enumerate ; while it possesses the cleansing and purifying properties of other Soap, it is free from those noxious ingredients which are so prejudicial ; on the contrary, while it cleanses the skin, it adds a delicacy and beauty indescribable to the face and hands. The Ladies will find it a most agreeable appendage to the Toilette, and in using they will be convinced that it will render the arms inimitably white, equal, if not superior, to the most celebrated cosmetic. One trial is sufficient to evince its agreeable and salutory effects. Sold in Pots at 3 s."

In 1809 women began to wear their bodices longer. Miss Austen in a letter of that year says: " . . . I can easily suppose that your six weeks here will be fully occupied, were it only in lengthening the waists of your gowns." (See Figure 30.)

The editor of an old fashion magazine, referring to the red cloaks or Cardinals which came into vogue before the American Revolution and were popular in the early years of the nine-

teenth century, remarks : " Red cloaks are at length completely abandoned, and we congratulate our lovely readers on
their emancipation from the most despotic dress that ever was
introduced by the whimsical and arbitrary goddess of fashion.
The writer of this article predicted, on their first appearance,
that a colour so disadvantageous to beauty could never become
prevalent."

In the styles of hats and bonnets for 1809 there were a few
changes. Among them we read in " La Belle Assemblée " of
" the Spanish hat in split straw, with the long white drooping
ostrich feather," and of " the Flushing hat ; it is of the Gipsy
form, in white chip, with a double or second crown supplying
the place of a cap. This is at once novel, elegant, and
convenient ; it is usually worn with a wreath of puffed ribbands
or wild flowers. The Cottage bonnet is still seen, made of
satin, with the crown a little raised and called by some
ingenious milliners the Parisian bonnet. Caps with veils,
ornamented with artificial flowers, are in great favour in morning and evening dress, varying, however, slightly in their form
and texture. Our most matronly belles seem indeed (and we
think very judiciously) to reject the straw bonnet altogether.
Lace and finely embroidered muslin with an intermixture of
satin are unrivalled in the construction of caps, which continue
still to be made close to the head, raised rather more behind
than before."

Among the novelties introduced in 1809 was the Hungarian
wrap. A contemporary description reads : " This graceful garment is usually made of velvet, or brocaded sarsnet, generally
wadded and lined throughout with a corresponding silk ; it has
large loose sleeves ; it hangs loose from the back and shoulders
and is wrapped in folds round the figure."

Long mantles of Devonshire or reddish-brown velvet,

trimmed round with broad leopard skin or chinchilla, and worn with bonnets of the same, were also very fashionable. Sable caps and furs of various qualities are often mentioned ; indeed, skins of every kind were much in request.

Another invention of this period was, " the Grecian sandal in the form of a half-boot, cut out on each side of the lace holes, showing the stocking, made of white kid, bound, laced and embroidered in silver."

In a letter from Paris written in October, 1809, we read : " The newest materials are the striped sarsnets, but imperial bombazines, gossamer gauzes, Italian tiffanies, spotted cambrics and fine embroidered muslins are still much worn in full dress. Shot and figured twill sarsnets remain high in fashionable favour. Scarfs are still popular ; we have noticed several in bright jonquil. The simple pelerine in white tiffany lined with satin and trimmed with swansdown is truly elegant. The round tippet in pink or white satin with handkerchief ends edged with lace or swansdown, crossed over the bosom and tied behind with a bow of ribband, is also very genteel. Mantles of every possible form are still to be seen; the prettiest we have observed has a wrap front attached to the shoulder, and is confined to the figure by a sash passed round the back and brought to tie in a bow before. Morning and walking dresses are still made high in the neck, but with collars of lace meeting in front and trimmed round the throat and wrists with a double row of shell lace. In full or evening dress the backs of gowns are made square and rather high, without lining, let in on the bottom of the waist with an easy fullness ; the bosoms are worn low and shoulders much exposed, the sleeves long and mostly of lace ; trains are still moderate in length ; the favourite sash is of ribband tied on the left side with small bows and long ends.

" Lace caps or combinations of lace and satin have taken the place of straw bonnets." A very striking cap is described in the same letter. " It is of oriental silk fastened under the chin by a Turkish handkerchief caught in a rosette at the right side, ornamented with a demi-tiara of Indian feathers." Another creation is described of " pink satin and lace with a cone-shaped crown, the front of alternate stripes of lace and ribband. It is tied in a careless bow on the right, and a small full wreath of heath is placed under the brim in front."

Another invention in shoes, and a rival to the Grecian sandal, was the " high shoe " in white kid bound and laced with a coloured ribbon. Gloves were made in straw, stone colour, and bloom-pink as well as in white. Necklaces in amber, sapphire, topaz, pearl and gold, with drop earrings to correspond were much worn.

The foreign names which it was the popular fancy to give to each article of apparel as it appeared, were carried to excess about 1809, and in an old paper of that year, we find the following satirical comment :

" Mr. Adair's treaty with the Sublime Port will doubtless introduce amongst our spring fashions a profusion of Turkish turbans, Janizary jackets, mosque slippers, and a thousand similar whimsicalities ; all of which (provided a northern coalition be accomplished) must speedily give way to Russian cloaks, Hussar caps, Cossack mantles, Danish robes, etc., etc., so that by the setting in of the dog-days our ladies will stand a chance of being arrayed in the complete costume of all the shivering nations of the north. Such is the capricious system introduced and acted upon in the empire of the despotic Goddess of Fashion."

Women's Dress

1810–1820

N 1810 we remark a few noticeable changes. According to " La Belle Assemblée," " the dresses of all descriptions are made fuller, which is undoubtedly a great improvement, it gives ease and play to the figure. Coloured muslin pelisses of a very transparent texture are very fashionable, the colours of every kind of dress are of pale and undecided hues, gay colours at this season would appear gaudy. A new kind of hat has just appeared, made in white whalebone, which has all the delicacy of chip and from its transparent quality, has the appearance of being lighter ; we have observed several coloured chips and straws, and have also remarked that they are very unbecoming, as well as inconvenient, being difficult to adapt to every kind of dress ; a mixture of ribband and straw is surely to be preferred " (Figure 48).

The following description of an evening full dress in 1810 is quoted from a popular authority : " A pale blue gossamer silk

1814-1829

FIGURE 60.—1815—Angoulême walking dress, worn at the time of the
    Bourbon Restoration.
FIGURE 61.—1829—Opera dress, cloak and hat, from a print. Dress of
    white satin brocade piped with coral satin, worn in Philadelphia.
FIGURE 62.—1824—White embroidered frock, opening over a white em-
    broidered petticoat, part of the trousseau of Miss Colquhoun, of Virginia.
FIGURE 63.—1824—Dancing frock of white crêpe over white satin, trimmed
    with artificial white roses with tinsel leaves. Head from miniature of
    the day.
FIGURE 64.—1828—Blue silk dress with flounce of gauze, trimmed with
    blue satin ribbon.
FIGURE 65.—1823—Dancing frock of pink gauze over satin.

60   G.W.T. 1907. After Pri

61   G.W.T 1907 After Print.

62   G.W.TROUT 1907

63   C.W.TROUT 1907.

64   G.W.T 1907 After Print.

65   S.B.STEEL.06 after a print.

dress, worn over a white satin slip, made with short train, opening up the front and tied with small bows of white satin ribband; long sleeves of pale blue gossamer net, and the same shade as the gown, caught down on the outside of the arm with small pearl brooches, the tops of the sleeves and bosom of the dress bound with silver edging, and trimmed with Valenciennes lace; the bottom of the skirt and train are trimmed with a silver edging, a little above which is laid a rich Valenciennes lace, on the head is worn a bandeau of pearls, fastened in a knot on the right side, with a Bird of Paradise plume. The hair in rather short full curls over the forehead, and curled in light ringlets on the right side of the neck. A scarf of pale buff silk (ornamented at the ends with white silk tassels) is worn fancifully over the figure and confined in a pearl ring. Pearl earrings, shoes of pale buff satin, yellow kid gloves."

The English fashion books for August, 1810, record the following attractive costumes: "A lemon-coloured sarsnet dress, trimmed with an embroidery of roses: a white lace drapery with train, fastened down the front with topaz snaps; a richly embroidered scarf is thrown carelessly across the shoulders. Topaz necklace and earrings. The hair in loose ringlet curls, divided by an ornamental comb. Gloves and shoes of white or lemon-coloured kid. A bouquet of natural flowers."

"Promenade Walking Dress.—A plain cambric morning dress, made high in the neck, with short train, let in round the bottom with two rows of worked trimming. A pelisse of green sarsnet, made to fit the shape, trimmed round with a narrow fancy trimming fastened with a gold brooch, and confined round the waist with a girdle of the sarsnet with a gold clasp. A Lavinia unbleached chip hat, tied down with a broad white sarsnet ribband, a small white satin cap is worn underneath, with an artificial rose in front. The hair is dressed in full curls. A plaid parasol, with York tan gloves, green silk sandals." A picture of the Lavinia hat is given in Figure 13.

A new fashion in 1810 was the walking shoe of brocaded silk, or embroidered satin. A pair of the latter may be seen in the South Kensington Museum (London) of black satin embroidered in coloured flowers, laced up the front. They have leather soles and no heels. Walking shoes of nankeen and sandals of jean bound with coloured ribbon were popular, while the newest slippers for evening wear were of white satin trimmed with silver or made of silver brocade. Light delicate colours were especially fashionable at that time, the favourites being pale blue, pink, buff, lavender, straw, lilac and yellow. White satin tippets interlined with wadding and edged all round with white swansdown, were popular for chilly days. Later in the season a mantle of white bombazine lined and bound with pale green is mentioned as a novelty, and white satin caps turned up in front with two small ostrich feathers, also lace hoods trimmed with small bunches of flowers and fastened under the chin, were introduced in the autumn of 1810.

In the same year we read of a variation in gowns which sounds very much like the Princess dress so fashionable a year or two ago. " Dresses are made tight to fit the shape without a band, buttoned from the neck to the feet with small raised buttons." A few illustrations may be seen in the fashion plates of that year, and there is a well-known portrait of Marie-Louise arriving at Compèigne in a similar costume, but it does not appear to have been a very popular fashion.

We read with pleasure that " skirts are increased in width ; they must no longer cling but hang lightly on the figure." Morning dresses were made high in the neck and finished with a standing ruffle and with long sleeves. Dinner gowns were worn both high and low according to the taste of the wearer and were usually made with moderate trains. Dancing frocks were invariably short and on entering a ballroom one could tell at a glance which ladies expected to dance that evening.

During Jefferson's two administrations, 1801–1809, life at the capital was marked by a modest simplicity. Under the genial sway of the wife of Mr. Madison, who took up her abode at the White House in March, 1809, her biographer, Mrs. Goodwin, says: "Dress grew gayer, entertainments more elaborate, and when the President's wife took the air it was in a chariot built by Fielding of Philadelphia at a cost of fifteen hundred dollars." In her daily home life, however, we read that this lady wore a "stuff dress protected by a large housewifely apron with a linen kerchief pinned about the neck." At that period ladies of fashion everywhere made use of rouge and pearl powder. Speaking of this practice a contemporary letter mentions: "Mrs. Madison is said to rouge, but it is not evident to my eyes, and I do not think it is true, as I am well assured I saw her colour come and go at the Naval Ball when the Macedonian flag was presented to her by young Hamilton." There are several portraits of Mrs. Madison from which we can judge for ourselves of her style of dress. The most familiar is probably the half length painting by Wood in a turban (Figure 41). Almost equally well known is another, in a simple white muslin gown, with low neck and short sleeves, the hair simply parted and curled on the temples. A very attractive miniature by Peale taken before her marriage to Mr. Madison, is reproduced in Miss Wharton's "Social Life in the Early Republic." The quaint cap with high puffed crown in the portrait is very becoming.

On the occasion of one of the state balls in Washington Mrs. Madison is described as wearing a stately gown with a long train of buff velvet, and a turban of the same colour ornamented with a Bird of Paradise.

The period known as the "Regency" in English history, covered the years from 1810–1819 and was distinguished from the first decade of the century by an almost lavish extravagance in social life and costume. Brighton was the centre of gayety and the famous dinners and suppers of the Prince Regent were notoriously expensive. There are many portraits of the beautiful Mrs. Fitzherbert, who for a time set the fashions for the London world.

The most noticeable changes in 1811 were in the bonnets and hats which were worn much larger than before, the brims being lined with a bright colour to correspond with the trimming. Full frills of lace were worn on the edge of some of the most fashionable bonnets and hung down over the forehead (Figure 75). Lace was used in great profusion at that period and several different kinds of this beautiful trimming were worn on one costume. Mechlin lace was perhaps the favourite, but Brussels, English Point and Valenciennes were all popular. There were many varieties of pelisses in fashion, but the close wrapping kind "was universally adopted for cold weather." They were wadded throughout and lined with a contrasting colour of soft cambric for in the "good old days" silk linings were not considered essential (Figures 96 and 98). Frogs of sewing silk called Brandenburghs were used to fasten the pelisses down the front, and they were very often trimmed with fur. Shoes of white Morocco are mentioned among the novelties of 1811, also Kemble slippers. Roman sandals vied in popularity with the Grecian sandals of the preceding year, but the exact point of difference is hard to discover. Nets, muslins, gauzes, and crapes were still the favourite materials for gowns, but we read also of evening dresses of satin and velvet. Jonquille and amber were the most fashionable colours. Many new hats are mentioned in the magazines of

London and Paris, among them the Comet hat which we are told was considered very stylish for carriage wear. In Figure 47 a sketch is given of a Spanish hat of purple velvet with a white ostrich plume and an ermine tippet, taken from a contemporary print. The Buonapartian hat of gauze trimmed with a wreath of laurel in Figure 243 is from a plate of 1811. The Cavalier's hat trimmed in front with a large ostrich feather and the Pilgrim's hat of Carmelite brown cloth or velvet with an ornament in the shape of a cockle-shell. Dress-caps made of lace or silk and lace combined were worn by young and old with evening dress. A new creation was the Devonshire mob with a point on the forehead and usually made of fine Brussels lace. It was worn very much on one side with the hair in full curls on the exposed side. On ordinary occasions the hair was dressed with great simplicity, generally in soft curls held in place by a comb. For full dress, flowers, feathers, dress-caps and turbans, still in popular favour, were worn. In a September magazine of that year (1811) we read of a new bonnet made of India muslin with a cone-shaped crown and trimmed with a bow of lace on top, around the face a deep frill of Mechlin lace, and the bonnet lined throughout with a bright sea-green sarsnet (Figure 75); but the greatest innovations of fashion were the short kid gloves which suddenly superseded the long gloves so many years considered indispensable with short sleeves. Gowns made with close-fitting fronts were preferred and were cut rather higher in the back than the front. The very short Grecian waists of 1800–1802 were temporarily revived by the ultra-fashionable. The sleeves were usually short and the skirts a trifle wider at the bottom measuring about three yards. In some of the dresses of that date we find the front breadth slightly gored at the waist.

Gold chains were in great vogue and a number of rings and

bracelets in every possible device were worn. A single string of large pearls fastened with a diamond clasp was much admired, but emeralds and garnets were considered especially becoming to the complexion. Watches were still worn in locket fashion, but they were smaller than they had ever been.

"La Belle Assemblée" describes nankeen pelisses with an undervest of blue satin or sarsnet, to be worn at fêtes champêtres. Morning dresses, it seems, were made in the pelisse shape, buttoned down the front with small raised buttons, or with an apron front and stomacher let in and laced across like a peasant's bodice, with coloured ribbons, and others again with a short jacket trimmed with lace. Spencers and mantles edged with lace also and large squares of lace were worn over the shoulders. Dinner dresses were made low in front and high in the back, and in the following description of an evening gown in a London periodical we notice that long sleeves are mentioned : " A gown of plain white India muslin, made loose in the neck, with long sleeves, and short train trimmed with a fancy border of stamped leaves in satin. A white satin cap, ornamented with crimson or morone coloured floss silk trimming. A short Persian scarf of morone coloured silk, with rich border and tassels, is fancifully worn over the shoulders. Amber necklace and earrings. Hair in full curls, divided rather towards the left side. Gloves and shoes of white or morone kid." Another evening costume mentions slippers with very pointed toes and instead of the newest fashion of short gloves, long ones, " à la Mousquetaire, with many wrinkles."

"A gossamer satin robe of French grey or celestial blue, with a demi-train ; stripes of white lace let in the cross way of the skirt, and relieved by a very narrow border of black velvet ; a broad lace Vandyke pattern round the bottom ; short sleeves fastened up in front by a row of pearls. A lace tippet, *à la Duchesse d' Angoulême*, edged with a border of Vandyke lace. The hair in soft curls next the face, *à la Greque;* head-dress composed of plaited braids of hair and pearls, surmounted with a large red cornelian ornament, set round with small pearls; the back hair arranged in a knot and surrounded with a row of pearls; necklace also of pearls in two rows. Drop earrings, each composed of one entire pearl, which should be large. A square cornelian brooch, set in gold, with a drop pendant of pearl to match the earrings. Long tippet of swansdown. White kid gloves, wrinkled so as to cover very little of the arm, below the elbow. Slippers of kid the colour of the gown, the toes more pointed than usual, with small pearl or white bugle rosettes."

A simple every-day costume of 1812 is given at the head of the chapter, taken from a gown of white corded muslin striped with yellow, which was worn in Philadelphia. The bodice and sleeves are cut on the bias of the material and the round skirt is trimmed with two bias ruffles.

In 1812 a Pamona hat of green satin is described as a novelty. It was turned up in front and drooped low on each side of the face, not unlike the hat in Figure 31, which was a shape popular for several years. A new morning dress came into great favour at this time. It is thus described by a contemporary authority: " The most fashionable dishabille is the York morning dress. It is made up to the throat; the body is composed of alternate stripes of muslin and lace, cut in a bias form; round the throat a rich lace ruff, and the sleeves edged with a very fine narrow lace; it is buttoned up the back and has a demi-train without any trimming." Another popular morning dress is announced in an English magazine: " The Russian wrapper, of twilled stuff, is a very neat morning dress, and begins to be a favourite; it is made quite tight to the

1810–1824

FIGURE 66.—1817—Fashionable carriage costume. From a portrait of Princess Charlotte, by Chalons.

FIGURE 67.—1810—Court dress. From a portrait of Mrs. John Quincy Adams, by Leslie.

FIGURE 68.—1820—Carriage costume. From a contemporary portrait.

FIGURE 69.—1818—Street dress. From a portrait of Queen Charlotte.

FIGURE 70.—1824—High comb and turn-over collar. From a miniature.

FIGURE 71.—1820—Street costume. From a portrait of Queen Charlotte.

66

67

68

70

71   69

shape and wraps over on one side very much; it is fastened down the front with small silk buttons to correspond with the dress; a trimming of swansdown goes round the throat, down the side which wraps over, and also round the bottom of the dress, which is made walking length; long sleeves edged also with swansdown."

Figure 111 shows a fashionable riding habit of 1812 of bright green cloth ornamented down the front and on the cuffs *à la Militaire* with black braid. The small riding hat is of black beaver trimmed with a gold cordon and tassels and a long green ostrich feather. The half-boots are black, laced and fringed with green, and the gloves are York tan. As this sketch is taken from the famous English magazine of fashion, it may have been followed by Lady Caroline Lamb, who we are told had just returned from her daily ride in the park, heated and dusty from exercise, when Lord Byron called upon her for the first time. She rushed to her room, " to clean herself " as she expressed it, and returned radiant in a fresh toilet.

The back view of another riding dress is given in Figure 109. It was made of the fashionable Georgian cloth (a light-weight broadcloth) and trimmed with frogs. A hat of green velvet and white fur, buff kid boots and gloves completed the costume.

A series of letters published in the " National Intelligencer " at Washington, during the administration of President Madison, puts us in touch with the fashionable life in America. Under the date, November 12, 1812, we read an enthusiastic description of the President's wife: " . . . I would describe the dignified appearance of Mrs. Madison, but I could not do her justice. 'Tis not her form, 'tis not her face, it is the woman altogether, whom I should wish you to see. She wears a crimson cap that almost hides her forehead, but which becomes her extremely, and reminds one of a crown from its brilliant appearance contrasted with the white satin folds of her dress, and her jet black curls ; but her demeanour is so far removed from the *hauteur* generally attendant on royalty that your fancy can carry the resemblance no further than the head-dress." *

This " crimson cap " was of the shape popularly called a turban. A portrait of Mrs. Madison is given in Figure 41, in a similar coiffure. One of these letters describes a dinner given on board the " Constellation," that famous old war-ship which is still preserved at the training station at Newport, and proves that fashions have changed very much in ships as well as in dress during the last hundred years : " . . . Some days ago invitations were issued to two or three hundred ladies and gentlemen, to dine and spend the day with Colonel Wharton and Captain Steward on board the ' Constellation,' an immense ship of war. This, of all the sights I have ever witnessed, was the most interesting. . . . On reaching the deck we were ushered immediately under the awning composed of many flags, and found ourselves in the presence of hundreds of ladies and gentlemen. The effect was astonishing : every colour of the rainbow, every form and fashion, nature and art ransacked to furnish gay and suitable habiliments for the belles, who with the beaux in their court dresses, were gayly dancing to the inspiring strains of a magnificent band. The ladies had assumed youth and beauty in their persons, taste and splendour in their dress ; thousands of dollars having been expended by dashing fair ones in preparation for this fête. . . . At the upper end of the quarter-deck sat Mrs. Madison, to whom we paid our respects, and then participated in the conversation and amusements with our friends, among whom were Mrs. Munroe, Mrs. Gallatin, etc. I did not dance (though 'twas not for want of asking) being totally unacquainted with the present style of cotillions, which

* By Mrs. Seaton.

were danced in the interstices, that is, on a space four feet square. There was more opportunity to display agility than grace, as an iron ring, a coil of rope, or a gun-carriage would prostrate a beau or belle."

In another letter (January 2, 1813) Mrs. Seaton mentions the gay and youthful dressing of ladies who had reached the advanced age of fifty. Alack ! History sometimes repeats itself !

"The assembly was more numerous at the Secretary of the Treasury's, more select, more elegant, than I have yet seen in the city. Ladies of fifty years of age were decked with lace and ribbons, wreaths of roses and gold leaves in their false hair, wreaths of jasmine across their bosom, and no kerchiefs ! Indeed, dear mother, I cannot reconcile this fashion to myself, and though the splendid dress of these antiquated dames of the *beau monde* adds to the general grandeur, it certainly only tends to make the contrast still more striking between them and the young and beautiful. . . . Madame Bonaparte is a model of fashion, and many of our belles strive to imitate her ; . . . but without equal *éclat*, as Madame Bonaparte has certainly the most transcendently beautiful back and shoulders that ever were seen. . . . It is the fashion for most of the ladies a little advanced in age to rouge and pearl, which is spoken of with as much *sang froid* as putting on their bonnets."

In all the fashion books of that time we find frequent mention of the Regency wrapper, a morning dress which was long and close fitting, and laced up the front with a silk cord. It was richly trimmed with velvet or sealskin, and finished at the throat with a collar cut in points. The sleeves were long and tight and trimmed with epaulets. Another popular garment was the Regency mantle, which was generally of cloth with a small round cape and high collar trimmed with bias folds of velvet or satin edged with a narrow cord. One of these mantles is described in " La Belle Assemblée " (1813) of black cloth trimmed with apple green satin.

The costume in Figure 44 shows the popular Regency hat of velvet trimmed with sealskin. The high crown was large at the top and a long ostrich plume was fastened at the right side, brought across the crown and drooped over the left ear. A gold buckle ornaments the brim in front. Worn with this hat was the Regency jacket of cloth trimmed with narrow bias folds and edged with sealskin and the long sleeves with epaulets which were apparently the chief distinction in the Regency garments. Of course there was a Regency ball dress too. This was a frock of velvet, satin or satin-cloth trimmed around the bottom and up the fronts with a bias fold of satin or velvet edged with narrow silk fringe. Epaulets of satin and fringe were worn on the shoulders, and the long sleeves fastened in front of the arm with three small buttons.

A London correspondent for a contemporary magazine says : " Everything now takes its name from our beloved Regent ; hats, caps, dresses, mantles, in short all the paraphernalia of a well-dressed belle is distinguished by that appellation, and so various are the habiliments which have no other name, that we were not surprised at hearing a young lady from the country inquire the other day of a fashionable dressmaker at the west end of the town, who had been showing her a variety of head-dresses, ' Pray, after all, which of these is the real Regency cap ? ' "

We trust the picture in Figure 45, taken from an unimpeachable authority, may prove satisfactory to our readers : " A Regency cap of white lace, with a small front turned up all round, and what was formerly termed a beef-eater's crown of lace drawn very full ; three ostrich plumes are affixed to the right side of the crown, and a twisted rouleau of satin ornaments the front."

The unfortunate Princess Caroline also had a bonnet named for her. The description is most attractive : It was made of " white satin with a round crown, the front turned up a little on one side; at the other a small white lace cap was just visible. The edge of the front was finished with a rich silk trimming, of the palest pink and a very long pale pink feather fell over to the left side." A contemporary authority says, " Nothing can be more elegant than this bonnet, which is also the most generally becoming thing that we have seen."

The Cossack hat was also very fashionable ; it was made of white satin too, but the shape was a helmet crown and the front, which turned up all round, was sloped a little in the middle, and was edged with pearls; it was finished with a small white feather, placed rather to the side.

For every-day wear cottage bonnets were still in favour, and riding hats which were of plain straw of the same shape as the gentlemen's, were adopted for walking dress also (Figure 113). They were sometimes trimmed with a figured ribband with a bow in front, while the cottage bonnets were appropriately trimmed with flowers. As we notice in the following description of a walking dress in "La Belle Assemblée" for June, 1813, bodices were again worn very low and full, and the skirts were again narrower, a revival of the fashion prevalent from 1800–1810.

" Short dress of jaconet muslin, made rather scantier in the skirt than they have been worn, and cut down as much as possible all round the bosom and back of the neck. The body full, but drawn in at the top of the back, which is ornamented with a white silk button and confined to the waist by a girdle of rich white figured ribband, a jacket of the same materials as

the gown, fastened to the waist by a white silk button.   Over
this our fair pedestrians throw a sky-blue scarf, bonnet of white
willow-shavings, ornamented with a flower and wreath of sky-
blue, and tied under the chin with a ribband to correspond.
Hair dressed in very loose curls on each side of the temple, and
parted in front.   Gloves and sandals of sky-blue," and to complete the colour scheme "a parasol also of sky-blue silk,
trimmed with a deep fringe to match."

In the winter of 1813 we read of a "high dress for walking,
of ruby merino cloth, made very tight to the shape and the
waist rather longer than last season.   Made up to the throat,
without a collar: buttoned in front from the throat to the
waist, and finished at the waist by a broad band of rich
fancy ribband of a very dark bottle green shot with ruby ;
two rows of the same ribband go around the bottom of the dress,
which is made walking length.   A long sleeve, easy but not
very wide, is finished by a cuff of the same ribband.   The
throat was also finished with a binding of ribband and displayed
a rich lace shirt with a collar also of lace put on quite plain.
White satin cap, with a rich broad lace quilling in front, and
tied under the chin by a white lace handkerchief.   A white
lace veil reaching to the shoulders was thrown carelessly over
the cap.   With this costume were worn York tan gloves, and
black kid half-boots."

Another striking garment was the Kutusoff mantle, made of
pale pink or scarlet cloth, trimmed with a broad velvet ribband
to correspond, a spencer of the same material, one sleeve of
which was concealed by the folds of the mantle ; the collar,
which was high and puckered, fastened at the throat with a
broach ; and a long lappel, ending in a point fell over the left
shoulder.   A Kutusoff hat to match turned up in front, with a
little corner to the right side, tied under the chin, and was finished

with a pink or scarlet feather; a full puffing of lace or net was seen underneath * (Figure 81).

The Rutland poke was a popular variation in bonnets; of white satin, edged with swansdown, and wadded and lined with white sarsnet, the front was cut in points, and tied under the chin with a soft white ribband; an ostrich feather of a colour corresponding with the pelisse or mantle was placed very much on one side.

Miss Austen wrote from Bath in 1813, on the subject of caps, to her sister: ". . . Miss Hare had some pretty caps, and is to make me one like one of them, only *white* satin, instead of blue. It will be white satin and lace, and a little white flower perking out of the left ear, like Harriet Byron's feather. I have allowed her to go as far as £1 16 s. My gown is to be trimmed everywhere with white ribbon plaited on somehow or other. She says it will look well. I am not so sanguine. They trim with white very much." † And we read in one of the authorities of the day that " lace caps are universal for full dress, although turbans have not lost their popularity." Among other novelties the " Wellington hood " seems to have been a lace cap made full at the temples and ornamented with a sprig of geranium in front but suggests neither in style nor colour the name of the great warrior. Much more worthy of its name is the Wellington mantle, which is described as follows: " A piece of cloth about three yards in length, and one in breadth, entirely bias, which makes it hang very gracefully, and sloped at each end to a point; the cape is formed like a half handkerchief and the collar which is about an eighth of a yard deep falls a little over it. The mantle is drawn in with a slight fullness to the waist and forming a sort of jacket in the back; it is usually made of slate colour or brown cloth; and

* La Belle Assemblée.   † Letters of Jane Austen.

1832–1838

FIGURE 72.—1834—Wedding dress of white gauze over satin, worn by a Quaker bride in Philadelphia. Head from a portrait of the day.

FIGURE 73.—1832—Yellow brocade trimmed with folds of the same material, worn by Miss Mary Brinton, of Philadelphia. Head from a contemporary portrait.

FIGURE 74.—1838—Dress of pale pink satin, sleeves trimmed with blonde lace, part of the wedding outfit of Miss Mary Brinton, of Philadelphia. Head from portrait of the day.

FIGURE 75.—1833—Dress of blue-green taffeta, with puffed sleeves and cape trimmed with pipings of the silk. Head from a contemporary print.

72

73

74

75

its principal attraction is the trimming which is a very rich embroidery of laurel leaves in coloured silks; the effect is really beautiful."

An attractive half-dress is given for February, 1813:

"Plain frock of amber satin-cloth, shot with white, and ornamented round the bosom and the waist with a rich white silk trimming, called frost work; it is the lightest and most elegant trimming we have seen for some time, and is universally worn; a double row of this trimming crosses the breast. The back, which is plain and very broad, is ornamented with pearl buttons, or small silk ones to correspond with the trimming. White lace sleeves, made very full, fastened about the middle of the arm by a broad band of 'letting in' lace [insertion] and drawn up by two buttons near the shoulder, while the fullness which falls near the bottom is confined by one; plain demi-train." *

In the year 1814, Napoleon having given up the fight for a time and retired to Elba, the English people of fashion hastened to Paris, and a wag of the day expressed his sentiments in this couplet:

"London now is out of town,
  Who in England tarries,
Who can bear to linger there
  While all the world's in Paris?
Mrs. Brills is full of ills,
  Nothing can improve her,
Unless she sees the Tooleries,
  Or waddles thro' the Louvre!"

Later the Emperor of Russia went over to London with his sister the Duchess of Oldenburg who introduced a novelty in bonnets which was immediately named after her. This bonnet was long and narrow, projecting far over the face, and was ridiculed by a contemporary comic singer.

* La Belle Assemblée.

" Then the ladies their dresses are equally queer,
   They wear such large bonnets their face can't appear,
   It put me in mind, don't think I'm a joker,
   Or a coal-scuttle stuck on the head of a poker."

The sketch of the Oldenburg bonnet given in Figure 43 is copied from a portrait of the Duchess at the time of her visit.

Dear Miss Austen gives us some interesting items of the fashions in England, in her letters of 1814. Of an alteration in the shape of stays she says : " I learnt from Mrs. Tickars's young lady, to my high amusement, that the stays now are not made to force the bosom up at all ; *that* was a very unbecoming, unnatural fashion. I was really glad to hear that they are not to be so much off the shoulders as they were."

The fashion of using ribbon for trimming, and the comfortable feeling of having a suitable dress, which has doubtless found an echo within many a pair of stays, are expressed in an extract from another letter of the same year : ". . . I have determined to trim my lilac sarsnet with black satin ribbon just as my China crape is, 6d. width at the bottom, 3d. or 4d. at top. Ribbon trimmings are all the fashion at Bath, and I dare say the fashions of the two places are alike enough in that point to content *me*. With this addition it will be a very useful gown, happy to go anywhere."

The following extract mentions a gown with long sleeves, about which Miss Austen expresses some doubt : ". . . I wear my gauze gown to-day, long sleeves and all. I shall see how they succeed, but as yet I have no reason to suppose long sleeves are allowable. I have lowered the bosom, especially at the corners, and plaited black satin ribbon round the top. . . . Mrs. Tilson had long sleeves too, and she assured me that they are worn in the evening by many. I was glad to hear this."

Mrs. Bell, the celebrated London modiste, made a happy hit when she invented an evening crush hat for ladies. It is eloquently announced in her magazine for January, 1814:

" A Lady's Chapeau Bras.—A most novel and ingenious Ladies' head-dress will make its appearance, *for the first time,* on Thursday, February 3d. It is a *Lady's Chapeau Bras,* an original and unrivalled head-dress of Millinery, and combines the following most important advantages :—*Elegance,* from the originality of its form, and the beauty of its materials. Secondly, *Convenience,* as it is adapted to be worn *over the head-dress of Ladies,* without the hair or any part of the dress being in the least deranged when the *Chapeau Bras* is removed from the head. Thirdly, it is made so that it may be taken off previous to entering a room, or public place of resort, and carried *in the hand* or *under the arm,* with as little inconvenience as a pocket-handkerchief; in truth, with no inconvenience whatever. It has also the additional advantage that a Lady *may walk full dressed along the streets without being conspicuous.* The idea suggested itself to the Inventress from the numberless inconveniences ladies are subjected to when full dressed from the want of a proper covering for the head-dress, in going to routs, operas, plays, etc., etc. By this original and elegant preserver of *Ladies' head-dresses,* the health will be preserved, and the dangerous effects of colds will be prevented. In short the *Ladies' Chapeau Bras* will be found a *desideratum* in Ladies' costumes, and requires only to be seen to be approved. Ladies in the country can be supplied with the *Chapeau Bras,* on commissioning a friend in London ; its form being generally adapted to all complexions and sizes."

This convenient head-covering was made like the calashes of the previous century, on wires run through cases.

The Oldenburg dinner dress, named by Mrs. Bell, in honour

of the distinguished visitor, was a "white satin slip, decorated round the bottom with a rich white lace, and headed with pearl trimming. Over the slip is a short Russian robe of white crape open front, edged with a rich pearl trimming to correspond with the slip; the wreaths which ornament the robe are formed of pearls also, to correspond. The back is made full, and the waist very short. Long sleeves of crape trimmed with pearl bands at regular distances. Small lace cap, decorated with pearls, and finished with tassels to match; a fancy flower is placed to the side." "The form of this cap" we learn "is extremely elegant, exquisitely tasteful, and becoming." Also that "a white satin *Chapeau Bras*, ornamented with a spread eagle on the crown, worked in chenille, is indispensable." With this costume the hair should be worn in loose ringlets in front, and twisted up *à la Greque* on the left side, and there fastened in a full knot. Gloves and slippers of white kid are suggested and an ivory fan.*

Scotch plaid or tartan came into fashion again in 1814. An adaptation of scarf and bonnet for walking costume is shown in Figure 49 called the Huntley costume.

In the pages of the "National Intelligencer," a letter of Mrs. Seaton, wife of the editor, is given describing the New Year's Reception at the White House, and the discomforts of the heat and crush:

"January 2, 1814.

". . . Yesterday being New Year's day, everybody, affected or disaffected towards the government, attended to pay Mrs. Madison the compliments of the season. Between one and two o'clock we drove to the President's where it was with much difficulty we made good our entrance, though all of our

* La Belle Assemblée, July, 1814.

acquaintances endeavoured with the utmost civility to compress themselves as small as they could for our accommodation. The marine band, stationed in the anteroom, continued playing in spite of the crowd pressing on their very heads. But if our pity was excited for these hapless musicians, what must we not have experienced for some members of our own sex, who, not foreseeing the excessive heat of the apartments, had more reason to apprehend the efforts of nature to relieve herself from the effects of the confined atmosphere. You perhaps will not understand that I allude to the rouge which some of our fashionables had unfortunately laid on with an unsparing hand, and which assimilating with the pearl-powder, dust and perspiration, made them altogether unlovely to soul and to eye."

Our ladies of fashion were following the example of their cousins across the sea even in those days. A London wit, parodying the " Maid of Athens," wrote to a suburban damsel:

> " Is thy blush, which roses mocks,
>   Bought at three and six per box?
>   And those lips I seem to taste,
>   Are they pink with cherry paste?
>   Gladly I'd the notion scout,
>   Answer me, ' It is not so'
>   Maid of Clapham, come, no larks,
>   For thy shoulders leave white marks,
>   Tell me, quickly tell to me,
>   What is *really* real in thee?"

The President's wife, as we have already been told by a contemporary, did not use either rouge or pearl-powder, and without the aid of these artificial agents made a very imposing appearance on occasions of state. According to Mrs. Seaton, " Her majesty's appearance was truly regal, dressed in a robe of pink satin, trimmed elaborately with ermine, a white velvet and satin turban, with nodding ostrich plumes and a crescent in front, gold chain and clasps around the waist and wrists. 'Tis here the woman that adorns the dress and not the dress that beautifies the woman. I cannot conceive a female better calculated to dignify the station which she occupies in society than Mrs. Madison. Amiable in private life and affable in public, she is admired and esteemed by the rich and beloved by the poor. You are aware that she snuffs; but in her hands the snuff-box seems only a gracious implement with which to charm. Her frank cordiality to all guests is in contrast to the manner of the President, who is very formal, reserved and precise, yet not wanting in a certain dignity. Being so low of stature he was in imminent danger of being confounded with the plebeian crowd; and was pushed and jostled about like a common citizen, but not so with her ladyship! The towering feathers above the excessive throng distinctly pointed out her station wherever she moved."

Noticeable among the new modes of 1814 were the Cachemire shawls. They were very expensive and therefore very much admired, but a contemporary authority speaks of them as "most graceful and becoming."

Pelerines were still very popular, but they were made longer and fuller, the ends crossed over the bosom and held in by a sash at the waist and hanging down each side. They were especially pretty made of sheer muslin, trimmed with a frill of the same; and of China silk, finished with a puffing of ribbon.

The Bourbon hat and mantle were named to celebrate the return of the Royal family to Paris. The hat was a favourite of the Duchesse d'Angoulême, and was generally made of blue satin trimmed with fleurs-de-lis in pearls; an edging of floss silk and pearls finished the brim and a white ostrich feather was placed on one side. It was said of this hat in the advertisement, that not the least of its recommendations was that it could be "packed in a portmanteau in scarcely any space." Fleurs-de-lis trimmed both the Bourbon dress and mantle. The Angoulême spencer and the Angoulême hat also had temporary popularity. The back of the former was made full and was very becoming to the figure, the front was trimmed with fleurs-de-lis of chenille. This costume is illustrated in Figure 60 from a fashion plate of 1814.

Large Spanish hats and feathers were a pretty fashion which followed the Regency hats in favour, and small slouch hats and feathers are spoken of as "very becoming to a delicate face." Of veils we read : "Nun's veils are now worn as drapery in full dress, but the manner in which they are put on depends entirely on the taste of the wearer. Some ladies bring them round the neck, so as partly to shade it, and one side of the face also ; others have them fastened very far back on the head, and wrap them carelessly round one arm ; but in whatever way they are worn they can be becoming only to tall and graceful figures ; when adopted by undersized belles they are the very reverse of becoming."

The Princess Augusta poke bonnet, named for the king's daughter, was usually made to match the pelisse, both in material and colour.

In her entertaining book, "Social Life in the Early Republic," Miss Wharton says : "Washington was so gay during the winter of 1815 that it would have been difficult to believe it had so recently known war and devastation, had it not been for those silent witnesses, the ruined Capitol and White House, whose charred remains were blots upon the smiling plain." On their return to the capital after the conflagration, Mr. and Mrs. Madison took up their abode in the famous Octagon House, where in the following February the Treaty of Peace was signed.

1804–1820

FIGURE 76.—1811—Fashionable outdoor costume showing scarf drapery and cone-shaped hat. From a fashion plate.

FIGURE 77.—1804—Empire gown and child's dress trimmed with Valenciennes lace. From a portrait of the Queen of Naples, by Le Brun.

FIGURE 78.—1817—Court hoop and feathers,—the regulation costume for English Court functions. From a fashion plate.

FIGURE 79.—1809—Mourning dress of mother and child, of black cashmere with scarf drapery of crêpe; child's cap of white mull with black ribbon. From a fashion plate.

FIGURE 80.—1820—Mourning ball dress of black grosgrain silk, trimmed with crêpe arranged in a shell pattern. From a fashion plate.

FIGURE 81.—1812—Kutusoff costume of pink broadcloth with hat and mantle of the same. From a fashion plate.

76

77

78

80

79

81

In a delightful letter quoted in this book there is a note on costume during the escape from the burning city. " On leaving the city," says the writer, " I wore a bonnet that was considered just the style for a young lady of fifteen beginning to think her personal adornment of some importance ; it was of white satin gayly trimmed with pink ; also as was the fashion a large shell comb."

During the hundred days following Napoleon's dramatic return from Elba, political feelings were outwardly demonstrated in dress. Violets, the Emperor's favourite flower, became the badge of his adherents. After the twentieth of May, 1815, no " Imperialist lady " appeared in public without a large bunch of these flowers on her breast, while " Royalist ladies " wore white jaconet gowns with eighteen tucks in their skirts in honour of Louis XVIII.

Many varieties of Cornettes and Mob caps were worn. For morning dresses they were made of violet cambric trimmed with figured satin ribbon ; for more dressy occasions, fine spotted India muslin was used, trimmed with lace and rose-coloured ribbon.

An unusually attractive riding habit appeared in an English fashion plate of 1815. It was the invention of the famous Mrs. Bell who had the happy faculty of adjusting the extravagant fancies of the Parisian modistes to suit English taste. A copy of the original print is given in Figure 112. This habit was made of " finest pelisse cloth, the body cut in a novel style, with front and cuffs tastefully embroidered. A lace ruff was worn around the neck. The hat was of moss silk and ornamented with feathers to correspond." In the words of the fashion editor of " La Belle Assemblée " : " The *tout ensemble* of this dress is striking and tasteful beyond what our descriptive powers can portray, and we have no doubt that its striking utility as well as elegance will very soon render it a general favourite ; at present it is adopted by some of the most distinguished fashionables of the *haut ton.*"

In 1816 the new creations of fashion were named in honour of the Princess Charlotte, and her marriage to Prince Leopold of Saxe-Coburg ; we hear of the " Coburg walking dress," a round dress of fine cambric under a pelisse of amber shot sarsnet, trimmed with blue satin ribband. "Oatlands" hat to correspond with the pelisse, tied with a chequered ribband of blue or white, and surmounted with a bunch of tuberoses or passion flowers. Morocco shoes or half-boots of light blue the colour of the pelisse trimming. Limerick gloves, and the hair dressed forward in curls. The hat gets its name from the country seat of the Duke of York where the Princess spent her honeymoon.

Feathers striped in two colours and called " Zebra feathers " were a novelty in 1816, and a straw hat or bonnet lined with lilac silk and trimmed with a Zebra plume of lilac and white was a favourite combination. The "Sempstress cap" was of muslin, " the crown drawn in with two rows of narrow pink ribband next the head piece, and bound round with a pink brocaded satin band." An authority of the day says: " White dresses are now becoming general, and several gowns have appeared made of superb India muslin of exquisite texture, with half-sleeves, embroidered in colours, and the border of the robe ornamented in the same manner." The newest wraps were comfortable garments called " Carricks ; " long double capes of cloth lined with silk and fastened down the front with straps which buttoned " like a Canadian hunter's coat." They were worn by both men and women.

The Caledonian caps of black and crimson with a profusion of black feathers, Neapolitan head-dresses made of blue and white striped gauze and trimmed with silver ornaments, and theatre head-dresses of tulle and satin " with a quilling of net next the face and fastening tastefully under the left ear ; " Netherland bonnets with crowns of carmine velvet and brims of white satin edged with the velvet and finished with white plumes, are mentioned in " La Belle Assembleé " for the winter of 1816. The new colours were " Carmine, Burgundy, Nicolas blue, and American or Forrester's green."

Among the novelties we notice : Mrs. Bell's " new invented long corsets : ladies inclined to too much *embonpoint* will derive singular advantage from them : they are equally free from hard substances as the short ones, which for more slender ladies have given such universal satisfaction."

In 1817 a contemporary fashion book describes a new and very expensive wrap, the " Witzchoura." The name suggests a Russian or Polish origin. It was lined throughout with fur and finished with a high standing collar, to which sometimes a pelerine was added, both of fur.

In the entertaining memoirs of the Comtesse de Boigne the changes in customs of dress are amusingly described. " Among other changes, or among changes which I had forgotten during my absence, was the style of ladies' dress in the country. I learnt this change to my cost. I had been somewhat intimate with Lady Liverpool in the days of our youth. She invited me to go to dinner some miles out of London where Lord Liverpool had a house. She asked me to come in good time, that she might show me her garden and spend a pleasant day in the country. I arranged to go with my father, but he was detained by business, and we did not arrive until half-past five. Lady Liverpool scolded us for our late arrival, and then took us round her garden, her greenhouses, her kitchen garden, her farmyard, her fowl-house, her pig-sty, all of which were in somewhat poor repair.

" Lord Liverpool arrived from London ; we left him with

my father and went back towards the house.   I remember that I was wearing a long coat of Tours silk, flounced all round ; I had a white straw hat with flowers, and thought myself very beautiful.   When I came into the house Lady Liverpool said to me:

" ' Will you come into my room to take off your coat and hat?   Have you brought a maid, or would you like to have mine ? '

" I answered with some embarrassment that I had made no arrangements for changing my dress.

" ' Oh, it does not matter in the least,' she replied.   ' Here is a book to look at while I am dressing.'

" I had hardly been alone for one moment when I heard a carriage arrive, and Lady Mulgrave soon entered, in a satin dress with jewels and flowers in her hair.   Then Miss Jenkinson, a niece of the family, appeared in a white dress with white shoes and a garland of flowers.   Then came Lady Liverpool herself: I forget how she was dressed, but she was wearing on her head a veil held back with a golden diadem encrusted with precious stones.   I hardly knew where to hide my head.   I thought that a magnificent diplomatic dinner was on foot, and that we were about to see the arrival of all the fashionable people in London.

" We sat down to dinner, eight in number, and of these five were members of the household.   No other guests were expected.   The custom, however, is to dress for a quiet dinner in the country as for a great public reception.   Henceforward I have never set out for a pleasant day in the country earlier than half-past seven, and never in morning dress.

" While I am on the subject of dress I must speak of that in which I appeared at court.   Possibly in twenty years it will be as ordinary as it seemed extraordinary to me when I wore it. Let us begin with the head.

"My head-dress was surmounted by the obligatory plume. With great trouble I had induced the fashionable plumier, Carberry, to make it only of seven enormous feathers, the smallest number allowed. Plumes of moderate size were composed of twelve or fifteen feathers, and in some cases of as many as twenty-five. Beneath the plume I wore a garland of white roses resting upon a circlet of pearls. The finishing touches were given by diamond buckles, a diamond comb, and tassels of white silk. This mixture of jewels, flowers, and feathers was highly repugnant to our taste, which had remained classical from the time of the Greek costumes.

"That, however, was a trifle. The body of my dress was arranged much as usual. When the bodice was put on, an enormous hooped skirt, three ells long, was laced to my waist. The skirt was made of waxed calico stretched upon whalebone, which made it very wide in front and behind, and very narrow at the sides. Over the satin skirt was placed a second skirt of tulle, ornamented with a large furbelow of silver lace. A third and shorter skirt, also of tulle with silver spangles, ornamented with a garland of flowers, was turned up as a drapery so that the garland surmounted the skirt crosswise. The openings of the tucks were ornamented with silver lace and surmounted with a large bouquet of flowers. I carried another bouquet in front of me, so that I seemed to be emerging from a basket of flowers. I also wore all the jewels for which room could be found upon my person. The bottom of my white satin dress with its silver embroidery was turned up in loops, and did not reach the bottom of the skirt, such being the fashionable etiquette. The Queen alone wore a train, while the skirts of the princesses were not turned up, but hardly touched the ground.

"When I had seen the immense preparations for this toilet,

I was doubtful whether to laugh at their absurdity, which seemed entirely comical, or to be vexed by the necessity of dressing in such ridiculous style. I must admit that when the process was complete I was well pleased, and thought that the costume suited me " * (See Figure 78).

Shoes lined with fur were introduced into England about this time, 1816. They were cut high and were finished with three bows of ribbon on the instep one above the other. They sound very comfortable for a cold winter, and were very picturesque when made of velvet either black, dark green, or mazarin blue.

Figured sarsnet of a white ground, with small sprigs of colour came into fashion at this time, also striped gauzes for ball-gowns.

A spring costume for 1817 is thus described. " Round dress of fine cambric, under a pelisse of emerald-green rep sarsnet, ornamented with flutings of green and white satin, elegantly finished by British silk trimming ; the waist girt by a rich silk cordon of the same manufacture with full tassels. Spring bonnet of green curled silk, the crown and ornaments of white satin and emerald-green, to correspond with the pelisse. Green satin half-boots and Limerick gloves. Berlin ridicule of green and white satin."

The very elaborate mourning of that period is illustrated in Figure 42. It consisted of a " round dress of fine black bombazeen, the trimming of crimped crape, formed into small roses. . . . Over this dress is worn a new and elegant wrapping cloak, made of grey mole skin or fine Bath coating ; it descends to the feet and is wide enough to protect the wearer from the inclemency of the weather ; it is cut out on the shoulders to fit the shape with large military cape and hood,

* Memoirs of the Comtesse de Boigne, 1815–1819, Vol. II.

which folds, being made like the ladies' *chapeau bras*, lined and bound with black sarsnet. Shade bonnet of fine black cane, embroidered with chenille and velvet flowers round the front; the crown, of black satin very full, and high in the back, is made of cane and chenille like the front. The crown is surrounded with a wreath of crape and satin flowers, and tied under the chin with a broad satin ribband. Beaver gloves and shoes."

An extract from the "Memoranda of a Residence at the Court of London" describes the Drawing-room held in celebration of Queen Charlotte's sixty-seventh birthday, and the Court costumes with the prescribed court hoops as they impressed the Envoy Extraordinary and Minister Plenipotentiary from the United States in 1818 : *

"February 27. Yesterday Her Majesty held a Drawing-room. It was in celebration of her birthday. My wife was presented to her, by Lady Castlereagh. Besides being a birthday celebration, it was the first drawing-room of the season and the first since the death of the Princess Charlotte.

"Foreigners agreed that the united capitals of Europe could not match the sight. The glitter of the carriages was heightened by the appearance of the numerous servants in glowing livery, there being generally two and often three footmen behind each carriage. The horses were all in the highest condition, and, under heavy emblazoned harness, seemed like war horses to move proudly. Trumpets were sounding and the Park and Tower guns firing. There were ranks of cavalry in scarlet, with their bright helmets and jet black horses, the same, we were informed, men and horses, that had been at Waterloo. Their appearance was in a high degree martial and splendid. The hands of the men grasped their swords in

* Richard Rush, Minister, 1817–1825.

1830–1835

Figure 82.—1830—Sleeve cushion worn with leg-of-mutton sleeves from 1830 to 1835.

Figure 83.—1835—Artificial curls fastened to a comb.

Figure 84.—1830—Spencer with embroidered collar.

Figure 85.—1830—Bead purse, a fashion in vogue for many years.

Figure 86.—1830—Dress of brown taffeta, worn in Philadelphia. Head from a contemporary portrait.

Figure 87.—1835—Dress of sage-green brocade, worn by Miss Halderman. Bonnet from a plate of the day.

Figure 88.—1833—Reticule of figured velvet.

Figure 89.—1830—Apron of buff satin embroidered with coloured flowers in chenille and crêpe.

Figure 90.—1835—Black lace cape. From a plate.

Figure 91.—1834—Mouchoir case. From a plate.

Figure 92.—1833—Lace scarf drawn through a ring. From a plate.

Figure 93.—1830—Belt buckle of pearl inlaid with gold.

Figure 94.—1834—Shoulder cape of embroidered muslin. From a plate.

82

83

84

85

86

87

88

89

90

91   1834

92

93

94

gloves of white buckskin, the cuffs stiffened and reaching half way to the elbow, a prominent part of the equipment that made up the exact uniformity and military beauty of the whole array.

" We were soon set down and entered the great hall (Buckingham Palace). We were not out of time for by appointment our carriage reached the palace with Lord Castlereagh's; but whilst hundreds were still arriving hundreds were endeavouring to come away. The staircase branched off at the first landing into two arms and was wide enough to admit a partition which had been let in. The company ascending took one channel those descending the other and both channels were full. The openings through the old carved balusters brought all under view at once.

" The hoop dresses of the ladies, their plumes, their tippets, the fanciful attitudes which the hoops occasioned ; the various costumes of the gentlemen, as they stood pinioning their elbows, and holding in their swords ; the common hilarity created by the common dilemma ; the bland recognitions passing between those above and those below, made up altogether an exhibition so picturesque, that a painter might give it as illustrative of the English Court of that era.

" The party to which I was attached reached the summit of the staircase in about three-quarters of an hour. Four rooms were allotted to the ceremony. In the second was the Queen. She sat on a velvet chair and cushion a little raised up. Near her were the Princesses and Ladies-in-waiting. The doors of the rooms were all open. You saw in them a thousand ladies richly dressed. All the colours of nature were heightening their rays under the fairy designs of art.

" It was the first occasion of laying by mourning for the Princess Charlotte and it was like the bursting out of spring.

No lady was without her plume. The room was a waving field of feathers. Some were blue like the sky, some tinged with red, here you saw violet and yellow, there shades of green, but the most were of pure white like a tuft of snow. The diamonds encircling them caught the sun through the windows, and threw dazzling beams around. Then, the hoops! these I cannot describe, they should be seen. To see one is nothing, but to see a thousand, and a thousand wearers, on such a day! Each lady seemed to rise out of a gilded little barricade or one of silvery texture. This topped by the plume, and the 'face divine' interposing, gave to the whole an effect so unique, so fraught with feminine grace and grandeur, that it seemed as if a curtain had risen to show a pageant in another sphere. It was brilliant and gorgeous. The ceremonies of the day being ended as far as myself and suite were concerned, we sought the corridor to come away. Will it be believed that the channels were as full as ever of hoops and plumes. Positively, it came over the eyes like beautiful architecture, the hoops the base, the plume the pinnacle. The parts of this dress may have been incongruous, but the whole was harmony."

This extraordinary fashion of wearing enormous hoops with Court dresses is illustrated in all the fashion books from 1800 to 1820 and, in spite of the eloquent eulogy pronounced by Mr. Rush, strikes us as both hideous and grotesque, but as a matter of history it is not without interest. A specimen of a Court hoop for 1818 is given in Figure 78.

The advance of manufactures in England called forth the eloquence of a contemporary periodical: " Fashion, that motley divinity, now again is seen welcoming the approach of spring, and from the looms of the British manufacturers are dispersed at her command, silks, ribbands, and gauzes, all of so rich, so exquisite a texture and of such various and tasteful patterns, that we may now dispute the palm of excellence and novelty with every other polished nation on this habitable globe."

With both head-dresses and turbans false curls were worn. We read in a letter of 1818, from Washington : " After breakfast I went forth on a shopping expedition and procured most of the winter clothing for the family, self included. One thing I could not get—Curls, French curls, parted on the forehead, you know how. You must get them for me either in New York or Philadelphia. Now remember *Curls!* " *

" La Belle Assemblée " says : " Amongst the novelties in head-dresses are the Caroline, or Como turban, of pale blue crape, ornamented with white beads ; and the turban *à l'antique*, more costly than becoming, of very fine white net, superbly ornamented with gold, with a gold tassel. Flowers in half dress are but little worn, and gold and silver ornaments are more popular at present in full dress than plumes of feathers, which are better suited to the hussar cap. In jewellery, pearls, rubies, and coloured gems, the initials of which form devices or sentimental words, are now in high favour ; and curiously wrought gold ornaments are very much in demand by the British fashionables. The favourite colours are peach-down, emerald-green, Palmetto green, pale tea-leaf, Spanish brown, scarlet and celestial blue."

Many specimens of the acrostic or anagram jewelry have been preserved, coming into fashion, as we learn, from the authority given above in 1817 ; they were worn in a variety of devices until 1830. An interesting " Regard Ring " worn in Baltimore in the twenties, consists of a small hoop of gold into which is set a ruby, an emerald, a garnet, an amethyst, a ruby and a diamond. This ring was owned by Miss Amanda Nace, afterwards Mrs. Forney.

* First Forty Years of Washington Society.

In a popular magazine of 1819 we read: " The acrostic rage
prevails in jewellery. A ring is given with the following expression, *j'aime* (I love). It is accordingly formed of a jacinth,
an amethyst, a ruby, and an emerald. Such gems form all the
rings of the present day." Also, " A curious romantic fashion
is adopted by some young ladies in the ornamenting of their
hats; it is aiming at the sentimental, but I call it acrostical.
Suppose, for instance, the lady wearing the hat is named
MARIA ; she accordingly sports a marshmallows blossom, an
anemone, a rose, an iris and an asphodel, or evening lily : this
forms a mixture of colours, and even of flowers not always in
season together."

A Paris gossip describes the short sleeves in vogue with all
costumes : (1819) " Let Paris be full or empty, scorching under
summer's sun, or freezing under winter's snows, the changes
among the hats still continue to undergo their usual motley
round. I cannot say the same of our other outdoor covering ;
high dresses, with only a *sautoir*, or half handkerchief are still
the prevailing mode, and these are of Cachemire silk, black
lace, or embroidered muslin ; this fashion seems likely to continue till the shivering fair one shall be obliged to resort to the
more appropriate spencer and comfortable pelisse. It is true
that pelerines buttoned before and trimmed round with muslin
or ribbons in cockleshells, are worn by many ladies; the
pelerines are made of muslin richly embroidered, and whether
the gown is plain, striped, or spotted, the sleeves are worked in
a pattern to correspond with that of the pelerine ; but why are
these pelerines adopted ? Because a lady cannot have a dress
made high that has short sleeves and never were short sleeves
so much in favour. Nothing is to be seen but naked arms and
as the gowns fall off the shoulders, the bust would be entirely
exposed if ladies walked out without a pelerine : let me, how-

ever, tell you, as a warning to your fair countrywomen, that never before in Paris were pulmonary and nervous complaints so frequent. This fashion originated in the reign of Louis XIV as may be seen by the portraits of Ninon de l'Enclos, the Duchesse de Fontanges, and that of Madame de Sevigné; whose cousin, Bussy Rabutin, used to say it was only on account of her arm being beautiful that she displayed it. I sincerely hope, however, that next winter will bring along with its rigour, that modesty which can alone render a female desirable; and that as soon as ices and melons cease to be eaten, short sleeves will cease to be worn."

This fashion introduced many dainty styles of pelerines or shoulder capes. The most popular were made of muslin richly embroidered by hand, others were trimmed with rows of lace insertion and edged with lace.

Long sashes tied in the back were all the rage in Paris in 1819. According to a local authority : " At the Tuilleries we see nothing but sashes, and they are generally of Scotch plaid ; young, old, handsome. ugly, straight, crooked, hump-backed, tall, short, squint-eyed, one-eyed, black-eyed, grey-eyed, flaxen-headed, every one had a sash tied in a bow behind, with long ends hanging to her heels, or streaming on the wind. These ribbons are like the *aiguillettes* of the *gens d'armes*, permanent signals for the fate of captives. Your countrywomen have introduced the opera cloaks of grey coating, lined with coloured sarsnet ; and every French lady has followed this useful fashion, and folds herself in one while she waits in the vestibule of the theatre for her carriage. We give credit to Mistress Bell for the invention of a silk mantilla of this kind with its *chapeau bras* hood ; it is truly elegant, as well as *très commode* (we have really no word to express what you call comfortable) and has been worn by a lady of high distinction, here."

Bonnets had for many years been worn by young and old, but the plates of 1819 show a revival in favour of hats, and we read: " Hats have a decided preference over bonnets ; and one of the former of Carmelite-coloured cloth lined with jonquil coloured sarsnet, has been much admired ; this is of the equestrian shape : London smoke is also a favourite colour for this kind of hat. Black beaver hats are sported by many ladies of fashion ; and a purple bonnet trimmed with gauze spotted with velvet of the same colour as the bonnet, is much in requisition. The beaver hats I mentioned above, are ornamented with a broad band, with a metal buckle on one side. Some have three narrower bands, placed at equal distances, with small buckles. Coloured velvet hats have generally a band of very broad ribbon, made in the form of cockleshells."

From a popular English periodical we glean the following, under the date of December, 1819 : " Grey hats too, lined with rose-colour, and ornamented with a plume of six or eight feathers, half of them grey and the other three or four rose-colour, is another favourite head-dress for the carriage.

" The waists of gowns still continue long, and are made low in the back ; the skirts are plaited very full behind, but without any plaits at the hips. Merino dresses are made with a pelerine of the same ; but instead of flounces they are bordered with velvet, of a colour to suit the dress. Worsted fringe trimming for dresses has in it a mixture of silk, and is headed with plaited satin, forming a rich rouleau ; sometimes three or four rouleaux surmount the fringe ; this trimming is very beautiful."

We read of a new and beautiful manufacture of brocaded gauze fashionable for evening dresses for young people, and are glad to be able to give a picture of a dress of this pretty fabric, that was worn by Miss Elizabeth Smith, in Philadelphia, in 1819 (Figure 61).

About this time the fashionable dance in Europe and America was the Waltz, first introduced in Germany. It attracted almost immediately the popularity which it has enjoyed ever since. It was not, however, as interesting to watch as the old time Minuet with its stately bows and courtesies, nor the Quadrille of the beginning of the nineteenth century, with its intricate figures. An onlooker expressed his feelings on the subject in the following verses which were printed in a Philadelphia magazine of 1819 :

" THE WALTZ

" In patent Kaleidoscopes all may discern
A novel attraction at every turn ;
And every movement presents to the sight
A figure more perfect, a colour more bright ;
But waltzing, though charming to those who can do it,
Is rather fatiguing to people who view it :
For though *turns* are incessant, no *changes* you meet,
But giddiness, bustle, embracing and heat.

" At first they move slowly, with caution and grace,
Like horses when just setting out for a race ;
For dancers at balls, just like horses at races,
Must amble a little to show off their paces.
The music plays faster, their raptures begin,
Like lambkins they skip, like tetotums they spin :
Now draperies whirl, and now petticoats fly,
And ankles at least are exposed to the eye.

" O'er the chalk-cover'd ballroom in circles they swim ;
He smiles upon her, and she smiles upon him,
Her arm on his shoulder is tenderly placed,
His hand quite as tenderly circles her waist ;
They still bear in mind, as they're turning each other,
The proverb—' one good turn's deserving another' ;
And these *bodily turns* often end, it is said,
In turning the lady's or gentleman's *head*."

— *Q. in a Corner.*

FIGURE 95.—1813—A gentleman in a fashionable walking costume of plum-coloured cloth, drab trousers and white waistcoat. From a contemporary print.

FIGURE 96.—1814—Back view of an outdoor costume. The wadded pelisse of golden brown satin with a high rolling collar is copied from an original garment worn in Philadelphia. The hat is from a contemporary print.

FIGURE 97.—1815—White satin afternoon dress with high waist and long sleeves falling over the hands. From an original garment worn in Philadelphia about 1815. The Vandyke ruff and embroidered muslin collarette are copied from plates of that date. Head from a contemporary miniature.

FIGURE 98.—1814—Front view of the pelisse in Figure 96. It is fastened with small gilt catches with snap springs, such as are used for necklaces, showing the collar turned down. Ruff and English walking-hat of brown velvet are taken from a plate of 1814.

FIGURE 99.—1816—Evening dress of a gentleman of this date, taken from a contemporary print. Dark blue coat and white kerseymere trousers and waistcoat. White silk stockings and black slippers.

FIGURE 100.—1828—Dress of very rich corded silk with brocaded flowers arranged in stripes, made with a full skirt and plaited bodice, with a broad belt of the silk. Copied from an original gown worn by Miss Mary Brinton in Philadelphia about 1828.

FIGURE 101.—1820—A walking suit. Long-tailed coat of green broadcloth with silver buttons and black velvet collar. Long pantaloons of white kerseymere. Stock of white satin and hat of rough beaver. From a contemporary print.

FIGURE 102.—1823—Brown cloth pelisse trimmed with bias folds of cloth. Velvet bonnet to match with bows of taffeta and a group of brown feathers on the crown. Brim faced with pink taffeta. A double ruffle of white lawn is worn around the throat and an enormous muff of bearskin completes the costume, which is taken from a plate of this year.

FIGURE 103.—1824—White satin wedding gown made with a deep trimming of white gauze held in place by bows of gauze bound with white satin. Three rouleaux of white satin edge the bottom of the skirt and the low-cut neck of the bodice. The sleeves are made of a full puff of the gauze caught down with satin pipings finished with a tassel of sewing silk. This charming costume was worn by a Virginia bride, Miss Colquhoun of Petersburg, in 1824. The head is copied from a portrait and the veil from a plate of that year.

FIGURE 104.—1820—Full dress of an English gentleman in this year. Blue broadcloth coat edged with white satin and adorned with silver buttons. Knee-breeches of brown satin and stockings of white silk. This figure is copied from a plate in the " La Belle Assemblée."

1813-95 1814-96 1817-97 1814-98 1812-99 Cecil W. Trout

1827-1828-100 1818-101 1824-102 1823-103 1820-104 Cecil W. Trout. 1907

Women's Dress
1820–1830

" Fashions change with every changing season
Regardless quite of money, rhyme or reason."

WITH the year 1820 we reach the third decade of the nineteenth century, and note a few striking changes in fashion. The first variation to be commented upon is that black dresses came into favour, and two new materials, plume velvet and levantine satin, were used for evening dresses. The former, plume velvet, was distinguished by narrow satin stripes, and the latter, levantine satin, was very soft and rich. Highland tartans had been worn for the last five years off and on but became a pronounced fashion in 1820, even for evening dresses. We read of Caledonian caps of white satin, and of Ivanhoe caps of black tulle and geranium satin, both of these head-dresses being designed for evening wear, and the latter of course named in honour of Scott's delightful romance just published in Edinburgh.

Two new ball dresses for young ladies are described by Mrs. Bell. "One is of figured satin, a new manufacture, with the figures woven into the satin in such a manner that they are transparent; round the border is a beautiful festoon of artificial

141

roses and their foliage in rich clusters ; they are smaller than nature, but faithfully coloured from it.   The other ball dress is almost equally attractive on account of its chaste simplicity : it is of fine white net over white satin, and is finished by two flounces of net, richly embossed with fancy flowers and foliage in white satin."

In the letters of the Hon. Stratford Canning, English Minister to the United States in 1820, we find mention of a " revolution in court dress " which was being accomplished at that time. He attended a Drawing-room in London just before he started for America, and remarked, " The great event which at present occupies the public mind is the abolition of hoops, announced in Tuesday's ' Gazette ' preparatory to the Drawing-room fixed for the fifteenth of next month at Buckingham House.   I fear we shall regret them in spite of their unbecoming appearance. They have the effect of leaving a little room in the Drawing-room crowds so as to prevent your being squeezed to death." According to Mrs. Bell's magazine, a new style of hoops was introduced for court dress in England in 1817.   In Figure 78 we give the sketch of one designed for the Drawing-room of that year, which is undoubtedly an improvement on court hoops shown in the earlier numbers of " La Belle Assemblée."   Hoops are not mentioned in the descriptions of ball dresses of that time.   They were evidently a court fashion, which lasted until 1820, according to the letter quoted above.

We read of a pelisse of garter blue embroidered in the same colour and lined with white sarsnet, also of black velvet pelisses worn with bonnets of black satin, and as we see by the following extract from " La Belle Assemblée," bonnets were again in the ascendency : " A favourite bonnet for the promenade is of lavender rep silk, with a double quilling of Italian net, edged with narrow satin ribband ; the crown is formed of Italian net and ribbon. On the white lining underneath is a broad layer of pink satin in bias. Another promenade bonnet is of fine black leghorn, trimmed with peach-coloured crape, and crowned with a beautiful bouquet of half-blown roses, lilacs and field flowers ; the trimming at the edge of this bonnet forms a double row of cockle-shells cut in bias. A carriage bonnet of straw gauze is justly admired, the material entirely new ; it is edged with transparent net, embossed with pink ornaments, and is finished with a curtain of blond ; the crown ornamented to correspond with the pattern of the embossed border, and trimmed with a full plume of white uncurled feathers, intermixed with three that are pink. Another carriage bonnet is made of fine net, spangled with straw in small figures, and the crown richly trimmed with flowers."

Turbans which had held the popular fancy from the beginning of the nineteenth century were still worn in every variety of material, Chinese crape and Peruvian gauze being favourites. Many new styles of head-dress had come and gone during the reign of the turban ; among these was the Vevai cap, something like a Tyrolese cap in shape, but less high. It seems to have greatly pleased the fancy of Mrs. Bell, who says of it (1820) : " Nothing can be more chaste or tasteful than this elegant little ornament ; its plumage hangs down like the fantastic fretwork formed by frozen snow ; while here and there seem lodged on it a few Christmas berries, either of the red or white berried holly."

We notice at this time frequent mention of flounces as trimming for ball dresses, but it soon became fashionable to trim everything with flounces. At first there was but little fullness in them, for skirts were still narrow. In the following description we read of fluted flounces : " Evening dress of black crape, over a black satin slip made with a demi-train, and ornamented round the border with three fluted flounces of crape, each flounce headed by an embroidered band of small jet beads and bugles. Corsage à *Louis Quatorze*, ornamented with jet and bugles to correspond. Tucker of white crape in folds." It was the fashion at that time to trim dancing frocks with artificial flowers, for instance: a ball dress of tulle over white satin was ornamented above the hem with full blown roses. The hair was adorned with silver ears of corn, red roses, and rows of pearl. White satin sandal slippers, white kid gloves, and carved ivory fan were the appropriate accessories.

Spencers were still in favour, the latest being made with a little jacket tail, like that of a riding habit, and a sash the colour of the spencer was worn with it. Long mantles of grey or violet sarsnet were also much worn; they reached as far as the heels, and had hoods drawn with ribbon and stiffened with whalebone, "which latter improvement, to be candid with you," writes our authority, "is, I think, an awkward imitation of Mrs. Bell's *Chapeau Bras*."

The following chatty letter from Paris is dated September, 1820:

"My last letter contained lamentations on the continued length of our ladies' waists; thanks to all the powers of taste, they begin to shorten, and I hope soon to see them placed on that standard of beauty, without which there can be no claim to the epithet, when divested of all proportion, by being too long or too ridiculously short. A high dress, that marks more justly the contour of a fine shape, is now a favourite outdoor costume; and no other ornament is worn with it, except a cravat-scarf of Scotch plaid gauze, which is gracefully tied on one side. However, when the mornings are chill, a grey sarsnet pelisse, for early walks, is thought very elegant; this silk pelisse has a beautiful falling collar, which takes from it any

winter-like appearance. If a *sautoir*, or half-handkerchief, is
worn with this pelisse it is of rainbow gauze and is tied close
round the throat, like a cravat. These gauze handkerchiefs are
trimmed round with a broad silk fringe. Black lace shawl
handkerchiefs are very prevalent for the public promenade.

" Leghorn hats are very much worn ; they are often ornamented with a bow of ribbon, with long ends (what our grandmothers used to call streamers) on one side. A bouquet of wild
poppies is placed in front, surmounted by a plume of marabout
feathers. The ribbon is either straw colour or striped. Amongst
the newest ribbons is that of Egyptian-sand colour ; the common
sand sold by stationers, to prevent writing from blots, may give
you some idea of this colour. Straw hats are ornamented with
a large cluster of corn poppies, or with ears of corn, mingled
with marabout feathers. The brims of some hats have a quilling of blond, both above and beneath, or a very full *bouillon*
of gauze : the crown of such hats is simply ornamented with a
bow of ribbon on one side, or a full-blown rose, especially if the
hat is of straw. Lilac linings to hats are popular, but it is not
a becoming colour when placed so near the face unless the complexion is very fair and clear. The flowers are mostly placed in
front of the hat in large bunches, composed generally of wild
poppies and honeysuckles. For the promenade, straw hats are
usually tied under the chin with a plaid ribbon. For the carriage, handkerchiefs of stamped crape are often tastefully disposed on straw hats and bonnets ; the ground of these handkerchiefs is generally white, flowered with lilac. Muslin bonnets
are worn for the *déshabille* morning walk. Rose-coloured hats
are much in favour, with trimmings of the same colour ; lemon-
coloured hats are ornamented with trimmings of lilac, and lilac
hats with lemon-colour. Straw-coloured gauze is much used
in the trimming of straws hats : rainbow gauze is a favourite

trimming for chip hats. Flame-coloured feathers, grouped together so as to resemble flowers, are favourite ornaments on carriage hats; as are all kinds of field flowers, particularly the woodbine and wild poppy. The brims of some hats are entirely covered with honeysuckle. Sometimes the hat is trimmed with either a bouquet of corn poppies or of roses. The semptress bonnet is again revived for the morning promenade. All bonnets are placed far back, and are generally ornamented at the edges with tulle quilled in large plaits, with gauze ribbon *bouillonés,* coxcombs, or ribbons laid on plain. The bouquets placed in the front increase in magnitude, and are spread almost over the whole of the brim: tobacco-plant flowers and others equally spreading are mixed with those most in season. Scotch caps are not so much in favour as formerly, except those that have a kind of gauze drapery depending or a quilling of blond next the face; and with such appendages they are certainly no longer Scotch caps. Transparent bonnets of rose-coloured crape are much admired; they are ornamented round the crown with a wreath formed of bows of ribbon; the bonnets are fluted, and they are trimmed at the edge with a double row of plaited gauze. White gauze hats, chequered with blue, are generally ornamented with blue larkspur arranged in parallel lines on one side, while the other remains bare.

"Cambric gowns are often ornamented round the border with stripes of clear muslin let in full, and as many stripes, alternately, of hemstitched cambric. The corsage is also formed of these alternate stripes in bias: when cambric dresses are flounced, it is always with the same, but the edge of each flounce is hemstitched and each flounce is headed with a letting in of muslin, embroidered in openwork. Silk dresses were never in such favour for evening and half dress as they are now; they are ornamented with separate pieces of quilling, like the frill of

a shirt; and these are placed separately, rather in bias, forming
two rows, which have a very elegant and rich effect.   The jockey
at the top of the sleeve, which we formerly called *mancheron*, is
not quite so full as it was; it is very prettily fancied, and so
slashed as to appear a *mélange* of Spanish, French and English;
its latter similitude, perhaps, obtained for it the title of jockey.
The bodies of the silk dresses are all plaited horizontally.
Frocks which button behind are very fashionable.   A favourite
trimming on violet-coloured silk gowns, which are very prevalent, consists of four flounces placed two and two and laid in
flat whole plaits; between the hem of the gown and the edge of
the lower flounce is a space of about two fingers in breadth and
between the first and second row of flounces is a space much
more considerable.   Metallic gauze still continues in fashion for
dress hats and turbans.   Court head-dresses are much lower
than formerly, the hair is divided in front, but is dressed very
full on each side, in regular small curls.   Parasols are lined and
finished with a very broad fringe from which depend balls the
colour of the lining.   The latest ridicules are woven without
seam: they are made in the English fashion, and are drawn up
and ornamented with Scotch plaid ribbon."

A novelty of short duration was in the form of a head-dress
for home costume.   It was a silk handkerchief, called *mouchoirs
aux bêtes*, from the corners being embroidered with different
animals and scenes from the fables of La Fontaine.   These
handkerchiefs were sold at 720 francs the dozen.   A French
wit made a pun on this head-dress, calling the handkerchiefs
" *mouchoirs affables.*"

A great variety of fancy gauzes came into fashion in 1821.
Each variation had a name.   There was the marbled gauze, the
marabout gauze, the deluge gauze, and the flowered gauze.   The
whys and wherefores of these names it would indeed be difficult

FIGURE 105.—1800—Riding habit of blue cloth, black velvet collar and a double row of gilt buttons called Nelson's balls. Tan gloves and half-boots of black Spanish leather. Round cap of beaver with plume and feathers in front, and band of gold braid around the crown.

FIGURE 106.—1801—Dark blue kerseymere habit with three rows of small blue buttons crossed with blue cord ; collar of blue velvet. White beaver hat with very narrow brim and two short white feathers.

FIGURE 107.—1806—Riding habit of lavender blossom cloth. Hat of amber velvet trimmed with loops of black silk. Ruff of lace and muslin ; tan gloves and tan shoes.

FIGURE 108.—1808—Riding habit of dark green cloth trimmed with black braid and gilt buttons. Cap of the same cloth. Gloves and shoes of lemon-coloured kid.

FIGURE 109.—1810—Habit of Georgian cloth, ornamented with military frogs. Hat of green velvet trimmed with white fur.

FIGURE 110.—1817—Riding dress of light brown trimmed with frogs of dark brown. Dark brown hat with feathers.

FIGURE 111.—1812—Habit of bright green cloth, embroidered down the front and on the cuffs *à la militaire*. Hat of black beaver trimmed with gold cord and tassels and a long ostrich feather. Black shoes and tan gloves.

FIGURE 112.—1815—Riding habit of fine blue cloth, front and cuffs embroidered ; lace ruff. Hat of moss silk trimmed with feathers.

FIGURE 113.—1816—Riding hat of black beaver.

FIGURE 114.—1814—Riding hat of blue brocaded silk. Wetherill collection in Memorial Hall.

FIGURE 115.—1812—Riding costume of Marie Louise blue, trimmed with gimp to match. A small blue cloth hat and feathers of the same colour.

FIGURE 116.—1830—Habit of very dark blue cloth. Top hat of black with a blue veil.

FIGURE 117.—1842—Riding dress of black cloth, top hat of beaver and tan feathers. High black satin stock and bow headed with cambric frill.

105

106

107

108

109

110

111

112

113

114

115

116

117

to define, but the materials were especially designed for bonnets and head-dresses.

White silk parasols with borders of flowers painted round them were among the novelties from Paris in that year, and the newest colours were wall-flower and Apollo's hair; the latter must have been difficult to match, but rose, pistachio-nut colour, ponceau, and roasted coffee, were all popular.

In a letter from Paris (1821) we find this: " Vandyke frills, round the back and shoulders of dress gowns, are now much in vogue. Mary has scarcely an evening dress without them. No ornament gives a more becoming finish to the bust; and while it dresses consistently and elegantly the back and shoulders, it has the effect of lessening the appearance of the waist at the bottom. . . . Caps with long lappets are also much in request; and these lappets confine the cap under the chin; this head-dress, on a pretty woman, gives the countenance a resemblance to the beautiful faces of Isabey's. Turbans richly embroidered, and fastened with gold brooches, are much worn by young married ladies; they are surmounted either by marabouts, esprits, heron's feathers, bird-of-Paradise plumes, or curled ostrich feathers. A long veil is often worn with a turban, the veil floating behind à la Reine. The hair is now divided, in equal bands, on the top of the head. If a lady, however, wishes to appear lovely, she will not follow the disagreeable fashion of showing the skin of the head, which has always an unpleasing appearance.

" Jewelry is made chiefly of polished steel. A brooch of polished steel confines the gown to the bust, and another is placed in the back between the shoulders: these brooches are of immense price and of most beautiful workmanship. A very pretty woman appeared in public last week and all her numerous ornaments were of polished steel: her dress was a marshmallow-blossom colour, which admirably set off the superb brooches she wore in front of her bust, and at her back.

"The white gloves worn with short sleeves are finished by a sharp point above the elbow, that comes up to the middle of the thick part of the arm, which the glove is made exactly to fit: they are therefore so tight that they never fall down or wrinkle.

"The hair is dressed high, and the temples are adorned with locks of hair which are lightly frizzed before they are curled.   At the benefit of Mademoiselle Georges, turbans were very general particularly the Moabitish turban, fastening under the chin. Toques of satin with white marabout feathers, mixed with ears of corn, in gold, are much in favour for *grande costume;* and cornettes of very sheer muslin with broad long ends, are universal in undress.

"The most elegant parasols are of India muslin, embroidered with a beautiful border in feather stitch, instead of fringe ; the edge is finished with broad Mechlin lace, about four inches in breadth ; the parasol is lined with azure blue, shot with white ; the stick and handle are of polished steel, the thick part is beautifully wrought and the handle is formed like the leaf of the acanthus.

"Bouquets are much worn ; they consist of a large bunch of Parma violets, or a full bouquet of roses, jessamine, and helio-tropes.   Flowers are always offered as an homage to beauty ; every gallant gentleman presents them to a pretty woman, and she accepts them as her due.

"Very rich bracelets on the wrists, and rings on every finger, are indispensable ornaments at evening parties.   The clasps of belts in gold, representing two hands locked together, are very fashionable."

Reticules of Morocco leather were considered more fashionable than those of silk or velvet.   We hear, too, of Scotch plaid fringes as a new trimming for gowns and wraps. Bonnets were still large, but they were somewhat flattened on top as in Figures 118 and 119. The newest were transparent and lined with coloured silk to match the trimming. All that could be said on the subject of the latest fashions in hats, will be found in the following extract from a letter by a Parisian correspondent :

" Many carriage hats are made of striped gauze (Figure 272), or crape, of pale straw-colour, and are trimmed with lilac. The hats are somewhat smaller in the brims, though there are some hats which are bent down in the shape of bonnets (Figure 120) : straw hats, of every shape, are now becoming very general for walking ; Leghorn hats have already made their appearance ; the brims much narrower than formerly ; they are ornamented with a narrow scarf of plaid silk, forming a circular drapery. These hats are placed on one side, and the hair that is exposed is arranged in full curls or ringlets. Some of the new carriage hats are of red currant colour, with the strange association of rose-coloured feathers. The most tasteful bonnet for walking is curled plush silk of a beautiful pink ; and grey hats with flowers of the same colour, made of velvet or chenille, are in very great favour. Dress hats for the theatre, or for evening parties, are often seen ornamented with cock's feathers ; and hats of black velvet are trimmed with white marabouts mixed with gold ears of corn. Wreaths of flowers are the chief head-ornament for young ladies ; the flowers with their foliage are thinly scattered in front but very full on the temples ; geraniums and eglantine, with little spiral white flowers from the cups of which issue little tufts of silk, are used for these wreaths. Bandeaux of pearls are worn in the ballroom, and for evening visits bandeaux of white or rose-coloured satin, wreathed round with summer roses.

" Five separate strips of satin form the chief trimming on

the border of merino dresses. On muslin or cachemire there are the same number of full quilled narrow flounces. The dresses for walking are so long that they nearly touch the ground. Black velvet dresses are much worn at evening parties; they are ornamented with beads, with a girdle of rose-coloured or blue velvet; which girdle is adorned with Brandenburghs made of bugles. White cachemire dresses, trimmed at the border with three bands of satin, are much worn at the Parisian tea-parties; those parties, which I recollect so much astonished you when you first beheld them; not only at the sight of the orange flower water mingled with the tea, but at the enormous bowl of punch which made a part of the repast. *Les Thès* are not much improved; and there are none but the British, and more especially the Irish, that know how to make this refreshment a real banquet."

An extract from another letter on French fashions describes the newest designs in fans :

"Two ladies, eminent for fashion, have lately sported at the theatres a kind of fan made of a bunch of feathers like those fans we see in old English pictures; they collect the air, and it is possible that they may become more general. Fans, however, of the last fashion are of sandalwood, mother-of-pearl, horn in imitation of tortoise shell, or of ivory : they are ornamented with garlands of roses, heart's-ease, lilacs, or the little blue flower, forget-me-not. The wreaths are painted at the top very near to the narrow ribbon that confines the mountsticks."

Turning over the fashion plates of 1821, we notice that the dresses are worn decidedly shorter again. Fluted and plaited trimmings of the material are used on the sleeves and also around the bottoms of the skirts (Figure 120). What was called a matted silk trimming was also very popular; six rows

of it were sometimes used, about one inch apart, a little above
the hem. Small caps were very much worn with evening
gowns. Pelisses were still in vogue. A very pretty one is
given in a French magazine of 1821.

"Grey levantine pelisse trimmed down the front, round the
border, and at the *mancherons* with full puffings of the same
colour and material. The pelisse left open in front of the
bust. Marguerite coloured satin bonnet, edged with short
white marabouts; and the bow of satin on the bonnet fastened
with two rows of pearls. Plain fichu of fine India muslin
worn under the pelisse; slippers of grey kid; a ridicule of
small beads beautifully wrought, and lemon-coloured gloves."

We hear of Nile-green as a new colour at this time, and
Marguerite pink is repeatedly mentioned. Broad sashes of
watered, figured, and striped ribbon were now introduced and
became very popular.

From a contemporary letter we take the following: "When
the corner of the white handkerchiefs of fine lawn had only a
little embroidery, then one of these corners served as a purse to
the French ladies; and after tying a knot they fastened their
ring of keys to it. Now these handkerchiefs are so beautifully
embroidered, that they require more management in the display
of them; and those fashionable dames who will not take the
trouble of carrying a little basket or a ridicule have a silver
purse that they fasten to their belt.

"If the *plumassiers* have feathered their own nests, the
flower-makers have also their profits. Young ladies have a
bouquet of flowers on one side of the head, while a wreath is
entwined among their tresses; and every ladies' hat, bonnet, or
cap is almost covered with flowers.

"Expense and luxury of every kind increase; I asked a
young lady yesterday, who I know has very little fortune, but

whose connections often oblige her to mix much with the gay world, which obligation, it must be confessed, she fulfills to the very letter, how much it cost her for every ball she went to, without reckoning her frock and slip, or indeed her jewels, which are most of them presents. She told me that what with hiring a carriage (for her parents do not keep one), the expense of the hair-dresser, added to other trifles, such as ornamented white gloves, white satin shoes, flowers for her hair, ribbons, some slight alteration in the fashion or the trimming of her robe, or a new corsage by way of change, it cost her every night she went to a ball or concert about one hundred and twenty francs."

Café au lait was a new colour in 1822, and the favourite trimming seems to have been wadded *rouleaux* of satin. In Figures 61 and 103, pictures of this trimming are given. It was in favour for several years and was revived about 1870, as is shown in Figure 315. Feather trimming was also popular. We read of "a black dress, trimmed with rows of feathers, much in vogue; the last row terminates at the knee, the spaces between the rows of feathers are not very wide; the gown is made high, with a standing up collar, edged with feathers. Merino is much worn in half dress, with wadded *rouleaux* and braided satin trimmings between."

A note from Paris in the autumn of 1822 says: "Small fichus, tied carelessly round the throat, are also much worn at dress parties; they are of one colour, and often fastened with a golden arrow."

An interesting bonnet of 1823 may be seen in the Wetherill Collection at Memorial Hall, Philadelphia. It is made of pink silk with alternate watered and figured stripes and trimmed with bows of pink ribbon with a satin border and evidently had flowers arranged in the bows at the left side. A sketch of it is given in Figure 272.

Three elaborate bonnets are described in a London magazine of the same date : " Carriage bonnet of pink crape ornamented with *rouleaux* of pink satin, relieved by brocaded crape of the same colour edged with blond lace ; lappets of brocaded crape edged with lace take the place of strings, the back of the bonnet is very richly ornamented with pink satin, and the crown is in the toque form.

" A walking bonnet of white sarsnet, with raised spots, bound and trimmed with Danish blue satin, three bouffont flutings of which material ornament the left side, representing tulip leaves on the edge of the brim ; the other side ornamented with full puffings edged with narrow straw plaiting.

" Park carriage bonnet of white crape over white satin, lined with a fluting of broad blond ; the crown finished by a light gauze puffing, with a leaf end richly trimmed with blond. On the left side a full bunch of Provence roses, surmounted by a marabout plume of feathers."

We read that " a new kind of hat has lately been invented, platted like straw ; but its fabrication is of silk. These were first invented to send out to the United States, where Leghorn hats are prohibited. Leghorn hats, with bands of straw and ripe ears of corn round the crown, are very popular." Why they were not allowed to be imported into America we have not been able to discover.

Chambery gauze, a tough but shimmery material, was popular in 1822, and was much worn also in the seventies. " Broad belts of leather buckled on one side " were preferred by many to the long sashes of ribbon.

The bodices of the gowns were cut square behind and before, and they had a double tucker, one falling, and the other standing up. A great deal of trouble was apparently taken to produce new effects in the trimming of white dresses. Sometimes

1820–1840

FIGURE 118.—1825—Fashionable mourning walking dress.   From a plate.
FIGURE 119.—1820—Outdoor costume.   From a plate.
FIGURE 120.—1821—Dinner party dress.   Drawn from a plate.
FIGURE 121.—Extremes of fashion in the thirties.
FIGURE 122.—1835—A wedding dress.   From a portrait.
FIGURE 123.—Extremes of fashion in the thirties.

118

120

122

119

121

123

the " trimming represented branches of the acacia, the leaves formed by puffs or folds of muslin, the stalks embroidered in cotton, and the branches separated by openwork ; the embroidery at the bottom of the skirt reached up to the knee; the branches of acacia were made to twine round the sleeves, and a falling collar was worn edged with this design."

Other cambric dresses were finished at the bottom by two rows of "letting-in lace." Between these rows was an embroidery on the cambric of muslin leaves, the letting-in lace being six inches wide. An apron of cambric, it seems, was often worn with white dresses, trimmed with two rows of quilled muslin.

Some ladies wore a dozen flounces on their dresses, about three fingers in depth, and scalloped at the edges. On sarsnet dresses narrow flounces caught up in scallops were a favourite ornament ; six of these flounces might be used, placed at "about a finger's length distance" from one another.

Corsages of silk or satin ball dresses were covered with tulle and a tucker of plaited net drapery was fastened with a brooch as a modest covering for the bust. Barege silk dresses were made with long sleeves of embroidered muslin; when the sleeves were short they were very full.

A Paris correspondent recounts a very extravagant costume and other fashions for 1822 : " A wedding dress has lately been made for a very charming young lady of large fortune. It is of tulle embroidered in embossed daisies, which are all of seed pearls. A diadem for her hair is formed of five daisies in pearls ; this diadem is valued at thirty thousand francs. At the last evening's musical performance of M. Massimimo, I remarked a white hat of straw, the brim of which was embroidered in white silk flat embroidery. A very full and high plume of marabout feathers was placed on one side.

" Turbans are of two colours, for example : celestial blue and white; cherry colour and white; or pink and straw colour. Small Leghorn hats, à *l'Arcadie,* are now much worn at balls; the strings hang down as low as the sash.

" The favourite shoes are black satin, with or without sandal ties, according to the taste of the wearer. Lilac kid shoes are also very fashionable. When gaiters and English half shoes are worn for walking the petticoats are always very short.

" The gloves worn with short sleeves do not come up to the elbow : they are very tight, but are so much rusked that they are only two fingers' breadth higher than the bracelet.

" A cross with a little watch in the centre is the newest ornament in the jewelry line. Some other crosses, with a floweret between each branch, conceal a spying-glass. A new kind of seal, called *cachet à la roue,* has lately been invented; it is fixed to a wheel suspended from the watch-chain, and on different kinds of gems are engraved letters, so combined that the initials of these gems form a device. The newest bracelets are of red morocco fastened with a buckle."

The principal change in the fashions for the winter season of 1823 was that bonnets were made of more substantial materials, such as velvet or beaver, the latter being very much in favour. They were lined with coloured satin and trimmed with long feathers hanging down over the shoulder. The latest hats were of black velvet, but there was no marked change in the shapes, except that the brims spread out more like a fan. Hats were faced with a sort of silk plush and the trimming consisted of rosettes, half satin, half plush.

Black velvet dresses were exceedingly fashionable for the winter of 1823, made very short and trimmed with flounces of black lace. A novel combination is described in a French magazine : " The dresses most in favour are of black velvet, made very short, and flounced with black lace; one of these flounces is set on at the edge of the hem, and is of a very rich pattern, which is admirably displayed over a white satin dress worn under the velvet one, and made as much longer than the upper garment, as the lace is broad."

"The materials for turbans this autumn (1823) are of the most effective kind, and well adapted for evening wear. Some are of white gossamer gauze with green and gold stripes, with the white spaces between slightly clouded with gold; others are of a rainbow striped gauze, on a green ground powdered with gold; the stripes are crimson, royal blue, green and yellow; but the most superb material for the full dress turban is pactolus, or golden sand gauze. It combines both lightness and richness, and makes up beautifully; but much care is required in not making it appear heavy, and none but a skillful *Marchande de Modes* can possibly pin up a turban of this material so as to give it a proper effect. It is peculiarly becoming to ladies with dark hair and eyes."

According to all the authorities, pelisse dresses were the favourites for house wear. Made to clear the instep, and opening over a false petticoat trimmed to match the gown, they were both graceful and dignified. In Figure 62 a charming morning frock of this style is shown, made of fine cambric, beautifully embroidered by hand. The hat in the sketch is taken from a contemporary plate. It was worn by a Virginia bride, Miss Colquhoun, of Petersburg, the morning after her wedding in 1823. Evening dresses were made of gauze and trimmed with puffings of satin or net, and caught down with rosettes or knots of the gauze. The wedding dress of Miss Colquhoun, given in Figure 103, was made in this way.

A Paris letter informs us that "at public spectacles and especially at concerts, caps are universally worn; these head-dresses have, however, undergone a change ; they are no longer of the Mary Stuart shape with the point on the forehead. The fashionable cap now is called the Clotilda cap ; it is almost a complete garland of musk roses, white thorn, small daisies and clematis, under a trimming of blond, and this full wreath lies between the blond and the hair and terminates at the ears. Dress hats are made of spotted velvet and are ornamented with three or five plumes, laid round the brim of the hat."

The same correspondent continues : " A dress scarf occasionally thrown over an evening robe is much in favour ; it is of flame-coloured barege silk, each end ornamented with three black stripes and a black fringe ; some of these scarfs have the stripes entwined with rings of gold.

" The fashionable furs are the fox, the white wolf of Siberia, and the chinchilla : the fur tippets have very long ends. The fur trimmed shoes are of violet or dark blue velvet ; they tie up the front and are finished with three large rosettes of satin ribbon, with short ends.   .   .   .

" Half-boots are again very popular for walking ; they are of dark blue, dark green, jean colour, or black ; and made of a new kind of fine morocco leather called Turkish satin.

" A lady has lately arrived here from Louisiana, and has presented some of her friends with very pretty fans, made of feathers, which fans were fabricated in that part of America. They are composed of twenty-five different feathers, each seven inches long, ranged in a half circle, twelve belonging to the left wing, and twelve to the right : these feathers all turn inward ; and it is observed that in fixing one to the other the barbs of the second feather half cover those of the first, and so on to the twelfth. The middle feather inclines neither to one side nor the other, but its barbs half cover the two feathers on each side of it. The stalks of the feathers are all stripped to a certain height ; and it is these which form the sticks of the fan ; above and beneath each stick is a narrow ribbon the two ends of which, before the rosette at the extremity is formed, leave a loop, whereby to hang the fan on the arm, when not in use. The natural colour of the feathers of the different birds from whence they are taken, gives to the fan the appearance of a shell : the bowed-out part of the mount is painted with flowers or devices and the hollow part is held next the face."

A gown of white cashmere embroidered in jonquil-coloured silk with shoes to match, is a costume described in a contemporary letter that sounds very attractive. Sleeves both short and long were made very full.

The chief novelty of the year (1823) were the plaited blouses. In " La Belle Assemblée " is the first mention of the familiar garment, we have found, and we pinch ourselves to see if we can be awake when we read : " The new blouses are many of them made of clear muslin." " Nothing is thought rare that is not new and follow'd, yet we know that what was worn some twenty years ago comes into grace again." * Several times twenty years brought the " too prevailing " blouses into grace again. Parti-coloured feathers were " all the rage " in the last half of this year ; four plumes each of a different colour were often worn on one hat or bonnet.

Although lace has never been manufactured at its best in this country, it is interesting to know that in 1823 a successful effort was made in Massachusetts.

" Medway Lace.—We examined yesterday (says the ' New York Statesman ') at John Nesmith & Co.'s store, Fly-market, two boxes of lace, manufactured at Medway, Mass., by Dean Walker & Co., in a singularly constructed loom, made in this country, from the recollection of a similar machine examined

* Beaumont and Fletcher.

by one of our artists in England, and who, by his genius and
memory has thus obtained what he wished, without violating
the law of England against the exportation of machinery.
. . . The lace is pronounced by good judges to be of a
superior quality, and that it will not suffer in comparison with
the imported, made from the same material, while the price is
stated to be much lower. The widest is very beautiful, and
richly and tastefully wrought. We may add that it is destined
to become very fashionable as we learn that the proprietor, on a
late visit to Washington, was very much gratified to find a
liberal purchaser in the lady of one of the honourable
members of the cabinet." *

The chief social excitement of this year in the United
States was the visit of La Fayette, who came as the guest of the
nation invited by President Monroe by order of Congress. The
coming of the great Frenchman revived the feeling of gratitude
and friendship for France. Our people throughout the country
exerted themselves in every way to show their appreciation of
the aid of the French troops at Yorktown. Balls, fêtes, dinners,
parades, etc., were given in every city. In Philadelphia the
celebration lasted for several days. A local newspaper gives
the following account:

"THE NATION'S GUEST

" On Monday morning, the 4th inst., about three hundred
children of both sexes, from the different schools in Philadelphia, were arranged in the State House yard to receive General
La Fayette: the spectacle was most beautiful and highly interesting.

" In the evening he attended a grand ball at the theatre:
the lobby of which was converted into a magnificent saloon,

* Niles' Weekly Register (1823–1824).

adorned with beautiful rose, orange and lemon trees, in full bearing, and a profusion of shrubbery, pictures, busts, banners with classical inscriptions, etc., all illuminated with a multitude of lamps. For the dancers there were two compartments, the house and the stage; the upper part of the former was hung with scarlet drapery, studded with golden stars, while the great chandelier, with two additional ones, and a row of wax tapers, arranged over the canopy, shed down a blaze of light. The first and second tiers of boxes were crowded with ladies in the richest apparel, as spectators of the dazzling array. Beyond the proscenium the stage division wore the appearance of an Eastern pavillion in a garden, terminating with a view of an extended sea and landscape, irradiated by the setting sun, and meant to typify the Western world. The company began to assemble soon after seven o'clock, and consisted of two thousand or more persons, of whom 600 or 700 were invited strangers. Twenty-two hundred tickets had been issued. No disorder occurred in the streets, with the arrival and departure of the carriages, which formed a line along the adjoining squares.

" General La Fayette appeared at nine o'clock and was received at the door by the managers of the ball. He was conducted the whole length of the apartments through an avenue formed by the ladies to the bottom of the stage, where Mrs. Morris, Governor Shulze, and the Mayor waited to greet him in form: the full band playing an appropriate air during his progress. As soon as he was seated, the dancers were called, and at least four hundred were immediately on the floor. The dancing did not cease until near five o'clock, though the company began to retire about three. At twelve, one of the managers, from an upper box, proclaimed a toast ' to the nation's guest,' which was hailed with enthusiasm and accompanied by the descent

1840–1848

FIGURE 124.—1847—Bonnet of shirred white satin with *panache* of ostrich tips. From the collection of Miss Dutihl, in Memorial Hall, Philadelphia.

FIGURE 125.—1840—Plain straw bonnet trimmed with brown ribbon. From a plate.

FIGURE 126.—1848—Bonnet of dove-coloured satin with pale pink and green-figured ribbon. From Miss Dutihl's collection, in Memorial Hall, Philadelphia.

FIGURE 127.—1845—House dress of *mousseline de laine*. Hair in Polish braids. From a Daguerreotype.

FIGURE 128.—1840—Walking costume showing lingerie bodice and silk scarf with Roman stripes. From a plate.

FIGURE 129.—1843—Dress of grey satin with black lace scarf. Worn in Boston.

FIGURE 130.—1848—Bonnet of pink uncut velvet trimmed with silk fringe and a band of braided velvet of the same colour. Miss Dutihl's collection, in Memorial Hall, Philadelphia.

FIGURE 131.—1840—Bonnet of white ribbed silk. Blond veil with pink ribbons. Small pink flowers inside the brim. Miss Dutihl's collection, Memorial Hall, Philadelphia.

FIGURE 132.—1845—Quilted hood of ruby silk. Memorial Hall, Philadelphia.

124

125

C.W.T.
After Print.

126

S.B.S.

S.B.S.

127

128

J.C.W.TROUT

129

130

S.B.S.

131

S.B.S.

132

S.B.S.

of a banner from the ceiling.   Behind this was suddenly displayed a portrait of the general, with allegorical figures." *

We are told that as each guest was presented to the Marquis de La Fayette, he bowed with much grace of manner and said in very careful English : " How do you do ? "

Speaking of the ball given to General La Fayette in Baltimore a few nights afterwards, the same paper says : " It was the grandest entertainment of the kind ever witnessed in this city, both as regards the style and taste of the decorations and the brilliant and elegant appearance of the company, which was far more numerous than usually assembled here on such occasions. When the music for the dancing ceased, the military band of the first rifle regiment played the most pleasing and fashionable airs. . . . Just before the ladies of the first tables retired, General La Fayette requested permission to give the following toast, which was received in a manner that reflected credit on the fair objects of it : ' The Baltimore ladies—the old gratitude of a young soldier mingles with the respectful sense of new obligation conferred on a veteran.'   The ladies rose and saluted the general, and the sensation and effect is not to be described ; when he sat down there was a burst of applause from all the gentlemen present."

> " See the proud eagle now with folded plume
> The form and temper of the dove assume :
> Now free to soar through his own native skies,
> Nor vengeful beak, nor toiling wing he plies,
> But all his struggles o'er, his wrongs redress'd,
> He bends to greet a friend, his country's guest." †

We are so fortunate as to be able to give a picture in Figure 142 of a ball dress actually worn at this important function by Miss Amanda Nace.   A badge, with the head of the dis-

* Niles' Weekly Register (1824–1825).   † Ibid.

tinguished guest on a white silk ribbon edged with gold fringe, will be seen on the breast. The dress itself is of white chambery gauze and the trimming a deep pink gauze piped with white satin. The costume is complete all but the gloves, about which an interesting anecdote has been related to me by Miss Bittinger, a granddaughter of the owner of the gown, to whom I am also indebted for the picture. The head of La Fayette was stamped on the back of each glove, and as the old courtier bent over the hand of the wearer to imprint thereon a kiss in the old style, he recognized his own likeness, and with a few graceful words to the effect that he did not care to kiss himself, he made a very low bow, and the lady passed on.

As La Fayette went through the streets of Washington on the day of his arrival, a woman dressed to represent Fame recited the following lines :

"Take this wreath, the badge of glory,
　　Which thou hast so nobly won,
La Fayette shall live in story,
　　With the name of WASHINGTON.

"Warriors known by devastation,
　　Who have filled the world with fears,
Never gained my approbation,
　　When their wreaths were stained with tears.

"But thou, a suitor, far more true,
　　Has courted me with winning wiles,
As thy desert, I give to you
　　The crown of laurel, deck'd with smiles."

Less bombastic, but certainly more touching, was the presentation of a ring containing Washington's hair which was made at Mount Vernon with this address : "The ring has ever been an emblem of the union of hearts, from the earliest ages of the world, and this will unite the affections of all the Americans to the person and posterity of La Fayette now and hereafter ; and

when your descendants of a distant day shall behold this valued
relic, it will remind them of the heroic virtues of their illustrious sire, who received it, not in the palaces of princes, or amid
the pomp and vanities of life, but at the laurelled grave of
Washington."

From 1825 to 1835, the leg-of-mutton sleeves were undoubtedly the most striking article of woman's dress. It is not known
who invented these sleeves or gave them the name which so
well describes their shape, but like most popular fashions they
increased in size until they became absolutely grotesque.
Almost as much material was required to make a pair of fashionable sleeves as for the skirt of the gown, although the latter
was more voluminous than it had been for many years. Like
the hooped skirts and panniers of George IV's time, the sleeves
took up so much room that it was necessary for the wearer to
go through an ordinary door sideways. A contemporary says
of this fashion that walking behind a pair of these sleeves one
could always hear a curious creaking sound made as they
rubbed together at the back.

The picture of a large Leghorn hat of this period is given in
Figure 273. The brim is cut at the back and caught up with a
large bow of white ribbon. A rosette is placed over the right
ear, and the strings tie under the chin. This style of hat was
fashionable from 1825 to 1830. Our illustration is copied from
an original hat in the Wetherill Collection at Memorial Hall,
Philadelphia.

Bonnets and hats were very much alike and stood up
around the face. Fur boas and lace scarfs were in great favour,
and the hair was arranged in curls on the temples.

"Fair tresses man's imperial race ensnare."

In a letter of invitation (1827) from Mrs. Mason of Washington to Miss Chew of Philadelphia, which we are courteously permitted to quote, is the following advice about the dresses she should bring with her for the visit :

"Let your dress for the wedding be as simple as you please. The same dress you wore to E. Tucker's wedding will be much handsomer than any you will find here. Virginia will wear a white crape trimmed with large white satin *rouleaux* over white satin, the same dress that she has worn at all the parties she has attended this winter, and T—— will wear a plain bobinet trimmed with a lace flounce she has worked for herself. I shall wear my white satin which is still decent. Nobody here will make dress a matter of moment, and your wardrobe will pass unnoticed and unobserved unless you bring anything very extravagant. The prettiest dress you can wear at the grand occasion will be a white book-muslin trimmed with a wreath of white flowers, or with three rows of plain bobinet quilled double through the middle."

In Figure 63 and in the initial on page 141 pictures of two costumes worn by Miss Chew are given, but the date is earlier than this visit to Washington. One is a short dancing frock of white crape over a slip of white satin, trimmed with white roses with tinsel leaves. The other is a beautifully embroidered India muslin made with a high bodice, long sleeves which fall over the hand, and a very long train.

It is interesting to know that Miss Chew made the journey in her father's coach, travelling from the historic house of Chief Justice Chew, Cliveden, near Philadelphia, to Washington in three days.

A charming little gown of pale blue gauze trimmed with satin of the same shade is given in Figure 64. It is taken from a print of 1828.

Figure 61 shows an opera costume, cloak of silk and hat of

black velvet trimmed with white ostrich plumes. The dress is copied from one of white satin brocade which was worn in Philadelphia in 1829.

Another dress of this period is pictured in Figure 73. It is of a rich yellow brocade and was worn in Philadelphia by Miss Mary Brinton about 1829. The trimming is all made of the material of the gown. The head in the sketch is copied from a contemporary portrait.

Dress does not seem to have been made a matter of moment in the histrionic thought of that time, for we read that Fanny Kemble, the idol of the English stage, on which she made her début in 1829, represented Juliet in a fashionable ball dress of white satin with a long train, short sleeves and low bodice, a girdle of paste brilliants being the only theatrical property of the costume.

At the time of Jackson's election (1829), party spirit ran high in American politics. His lady partisans were to be distinguished by dresses and aprons of calico imprinted in great medallions with the very unhandsome head of their hero. Specimens of the Jackson calico may be seen in the Historical Society at Newport, Rhode Island. This whim of fashion recalls to mind the eighteen tucks in the white dresses of Louis XVIII's adherents in 1815, and the bunches of violets worn by the admirers of Napoleon at the same time.

On the occasion of Jackson's inauguration, we read of a gorgeous costume of scarlet velvet, richly trimmed with gold embroidery, worn by Mrs. Bomford; a "large ruby, for which Colonel Bomford had refused five thousand dollars," in her turban.

It was at this period that Miss Harriet Martineau made her celebrated visit to the United States and was fêted and entertained a great deal in Washington. Having been invited to spend a " sociable day " with a lady who probably thought that form of hospitality would be more enjoyable than a dinner party to the distinguished visitor on account of her deafness, Miss Martineau and her companion, Miss Jeffrey, arrived quite early and were shown to a bedroom to take off their " bonnets and long capes."

" You see," remarked Miss Martineau to her hostess, " we have complied with your request and come sociably to spend the day. We have been walking all the morning and our lodgings are too distant to return there, so we have done as those who have no carriages do in England when they go out to spend the day."

" I offered her," observed her hostess, " combs and brushes, but having one enormous pocket in her French dress, she assured me that they were provided with all that was necessary and pulled out nice little silk shoes, silk stockings, scarf for her neck, lace mits, a gold chain and some other jewelry, and soon without changing her dress was prettily equipped for dinner or evening company." *

This is the first record we find of a pocket in a gown, but we hope it was not without precedent in America.

The hats were almost as remarkable as the sleeves as will be seen in the illustrations of this period. Figure 274 shows a very quaint specimen in the Wetherill collection. It is made of sage green taffeta with a cross-bar of salmon pink, and is corded and bound with pink satin ribbon. The date given is 1829.

The Cabriolet bonnets shown in Figures 240, 241 and 244 were named for the fashionable carriage of the day. Both of these novelties were adopted by the eccentric Lady Morgan in 1829. In a recent memoir we read :

* First Forty Years of Washington Society, by Mrs. Samuel Harrison Smith.

"It was never known where this vehicle was bought, except that Lady Morgan declared it came from the first carriage-builder in London. In shape it was like a grasshopper, as well as in colour. Very high and very springy, with enormous wheels, it was difficult to get into, and dangerous to get out of. Sir Charles, who never in his life before had mounted a coach-box, was persuaded by his wife to drive his own carriage. He was extremely short-sighted, and wore large green spectacles out-of-doors. His costume was a coat much trimmed with fur, and heavily braided. James Grant, the tall Irish footman, in the brightest of red plush, sat beside him, his office being to jump down whenever anybody was knocked down, or run over, for Sir Charles drove as it pleased God. The horse was mercifully a very quiet animal, and much too small for the carriage, or the mischief would have been worse. Lady Morgan, in the large bonnet of the period, and a cloak lined with fur hanging over the back of the carriage, gave, as she conceived, the crowning grace to a neat and elegant turn-out." *

A contributor to the "National Recorder" in 1829 paid a graceful tribute to women, saying :

"The history of woman is the history of the improvements in the world. Some twenty or thirty years ago, when manual labour performed all the drudgery, some five, six or seven yards of silk or muslin or gingham would suffice for the flitting and flirting of the most gay and volatile of the sex. But as soon as the powers of steam are applied, and labour is changed from physical to intellectual, the ladies, in their charitable regard for the operative class of the community, begin to devise means for their continued employment, and as the material is produced with half the labour, the equilibrium must be sustained by con-suming a double quantity."

* Little Memoirs of the Nineteenth Century.

1834–1860

FIGURE 133.—1834—Hair in high bow knot. From a portrait of Miss Lander.

FIGURE 134.—Evening dress in the forties. From a plate.

FIGURE 135.—1850—House dress. From a portrait of Miss Cary.

FIGURE 136.—Extremes of fashion in the forties. From a plate.

FIGURE 137.—Street costumes in the forties.

FIGURE 138.—1850—Graceful arrangement of hair. From a portrait of Empress Eugenie.

FIGURE 139.—Evening dress in the forties. From a plate.

FIGURE 140.—1860—The fashionable "waterfall" of 1860 and after. From a portrait of Miss Lane.

137

139

133

138

140

136

134

135

This is certainly a charitable view to take of the new fashion of very full skirts and leg-of-mutton sleeves. An elaborate style of hair-dressing came in at that time, which met with approval on the same grounds.

"I knew of one lady who, for the same reason, sported a large head of puffs and curls, to prove that she not only encouraged but engaged in the support of domestic productions. It does seem peculiarly hard that, while the ladies are thus carrying their principles into practice, even at the expense of their loveliness, they should have to encounter the sarcasm and the ridicule of the other sex. Let us hope that they will not be discouraged in their endeavours by such mean and inconsiderate abuse. They may be assured that there are those who duly estimate their motives and principles and who respect them accordingly."

We do not notice any marked change in riding habits in the twenties, but riding was still the fashionable exercise and we read that Fanny Kemble in 1829 wore a suit of brown cloth with a red waistcoat.

Women's Dress

1830–1840

HERE were not any very marked changes in 1830 in the style and cut of gowns. Although the skirts were somewhat fuller than they had been, they were still worn short, and elaborately trimmed, and were gathered at the waist into a band, which was hidden under a belt made broader than in the previous year and fastened with a buckle in front (Figure 93).

For house wear the shoulders were usually uncovered, the bodices being finished with a tucker or frill of lace. Out-of-doors little capes or pelerines, either matching the dress or of a contrasting colour, were worn (Figures 90 and 94).

Cushions, which were fastened in the tops of sleeves to produce the desired effect, were made larger and larger. The sketch of a pair of these sleeve-extenders, made of brown cambric and filled with down, is given in Figure 82. They belong to the Museum of the School of Industrial Art in Philadelphia. With this order of dress waists looked proportionately slender. Deep collars, sometimes of plain linen but generally

182

of lace or needlework embroidery turned down round the neck, contributed to the broad effect. Scarfs of cachemire, silk or lace were worn universally.

Hats or bonnets still were of the Cabriolet shape, faced with a contrasting silk, and trimmed with large ribbon bows, and wide strings tying under the chin (Figures 87 and 123). The crowns were high and sloped upwards when on the head. In Memorial Hall, Philadelphia, may be seen a bonnet of 1830 made of white silk gauze straw, trimmed with white gauze ribbon with pale yellow and green figures. A sketch of this bonnet is given in Figure 276 and in Figure 293 a picture of a Quaker bonnet of white silk of about the same date, shows a modest adaptation of the fashion from 1830–1840. This bonnet is also in the valuable collection at Memorial Hall. Feathers were still worn, many bonnets being almost overladen with plumes. A wit of the day said of Lady Cork, then over eighty years old, that she resembled "a shuttlecock, for she was all cork and feathers."

In 1830 fashion dictated that the hair should be worn high, and very high it continued throughout that period. This was undoubtedly the ugliest style of hair-dressing ever introduced and could hardly have been becoming to any one, but the coquettish bow-knots and rosettes all made of hair would have been particularly inappropriate in grey, and the use of hair dye became very popular (Figures 73, 83, 121 and 133). Fur boas were in vogue at this time and low thin slippers still prevailed for all occasions.

A letter written about this time points a moral on the subject of dyeing the hair.

"A young lady, a friend of mine residing in the same house, found, to her utter dismay, that her hair was becoming grizzled. It was a terrible misfortune, as she had really a fine head of hair, and false curls were not, at that time, much worn ; so she had no need or excuse for substituting other hair for her own, except that ugly one, growing grey. . . . She purchased, at a very high price, a bottle of 'Imperial Hair Restorer'—I think it was called, or some such sounding name—'warranted to give the hair a beautiful glossy appearance, and restore it to its pristine colour without failure or danger.' The restorative was plentifully applied and in two days' time the curls of the young lady, where the grey hairs had chiefly obtruded, were changed to an equivocal hue, bearing a near resemblance to the dark changeable green of the peacock's feathers. The only truth of the restorative was its glossy qualities. The hair of the unfortunate young lady was glossy enough, and stiff as bristles. I cannot even now, though several years have passed, think of the ludicrous appearance of that patent coloured hair, and the mirth it created in our little coterie, without laughing heartily."

From the " Lady's Magazine," we give an elaborate full dress : " The skirt is of blond gauze. The sleeves and flounce are richly figured with a pattern in white ; but the bouquets embroidered above the deep flounce are in the most delicate shades of French blond. The corsage is of white satin, made plain and tight to the shape both in the back and front. The short *beret* sleeves, beneath those of white gauze, are of white satin, and exceedingly full. The long sleeves narrow a little towards the wrist, but were never made fuller at the top. The belt is of plain satin, corded at the edges. The hem of the white satin dress appears below the flounce ; it is very much puffed, so as to give a great richness to the finish of the costume. The arrangement of the hair is new and beautiful, braids are wound over one high bow, with two folds. A delicate silver sprig is the sole ornament of the head, excepting a long silk scarf, which is gathered slightly on the top of the bows of the hair and falls on each side nearly as low as the knees. The head-dress is called *en barbe*. Necklace, earrings and bracelets of wrought silver and gold. Bouquet of spring flowers."

This odd arrangement of bow-knots and puffs of hair, which we notice in many of the contemporary portraits, was obviously very difficult to adjust without artificial aid. In Figure 83 we give the picture of a cluster of curls of false hair fastened to a comb, showing an easy way of surmounting the difficulty. It is copied from the original article in the School of Industrial Art, in Philadelphia.

Another fashionable coiffure is given in the following description of a ball dress: "Hair braided with gold beads, in Grecian bands, and a low coronet and large knot, ornamented with plumes or silver barley, *à la* Ceres. Dress of white gauze lisse, gathered in front of the corsage with full loose folds. Underdress of deep rose-coloured satin *à la* Reine. The epaulettes and the bottom of the lisse robe are cut into square dents. The upper dress is looped up on the left side to the knees, *à la* Taglioni, with bouquets of gold barley. The rose-coloured satin skirt is finished with a border of full puffs at the feet. Long white kid gloves, fan embossed with gold ; necklace of gold medallions."

And here is another description of hair arrangement for evening dress : "The hair is banded *à la Greque,* small knot on the crown, from which depend a number of ringlets *à la* Sevigné, and is ornamented with a small crown of field flowers. Dress of crape over a slip of satin *à la* Reine ; corsage *à la* Roxalane, over which fall very pretty reveres and epaulettes of satin. The skirt is ornamented with a wreath of cut ribbands *à la* Taglioni, fastened on the right with a few large satin leaves and ends and a bunch of minute field flowers."

We read of many new materials and colours. A pelisse is described of *gros de Tours* in *bleu de Berry*, embroidered down the front, which opened part way showing the underdress. It was close-fitting and finished with a double pelerine embroidered to match the fronts. The sleeves were finished with a plain tight cuff also embroidered. With this was worn a *gros de Naples* bonnet, the colour "a new shade of *vapeur*," trimmed with knots and bows of pink gauze ribbon. These materials and colours are probably known to-day by different and less fanciful names.

The following dress, which sounds unusually pretty, is described in a contemporary magazine :

"Evening Dress.—A straw-coloured crape dress over a *gros de Naples* slip to match. Corsage cut low and square, and trimmed with a falling tucker of *blonde de Cambray*. *Beret* sleeve, finished *en manchette*, with the same sort of lace ; a *noeud* of gauze ribband, to correspond in colour, is placed in front of the arm. The skirt is trimmed with a flounce of *blonde de Cambray*, headed by a cluster of narrow *rouleaux* of satin to match the dress. The trimming is raised a little on the left side, and finished with a single flower with buds and foliage. With this is worn a crape hat of a darker shade than the dress. The brim faced with gauze ribband. The crown trimmed with white feathers placed in different directions ; some are passed through openings made in the brim, and partially shade it. The jewelry worn with this dress should be a mixture of gold and pearls."

Here is another Evening Dress.—"A changeable *gros de Naples ;* the colours blue shot with white. The corsage is cut very low, fits close to the shape, and is ornamented in front of the bust in the fan style with satin *rouleaux* to correspond with the dress. A trimming of rich fringe, the head of which is composed of beads and the remaining part of chenille, goes round the bust. The *ceinture* fastens behind in a rosette with a richly-wrought gold clasp in the centre. *Beret* sleeves, the shortest we have seen."

Two pretty dresses are described by a contemporary London correspondent in 1830 :

" Ball Dress.—White blond gauze over a pale pink satin slip ; from a blush rose on each shoulder a pink ribbon is draped and caught under another blush rose above the centre of a pink satin belt. The skirt is trimmed with blush roses, joined by a loop of pink satin above the hem. The hair is arranged in large Madonna curls, which are somewhat drawn up and heightened by a wreath of blush roses with leaves.

" Dinner and Carriage Dress.—Hat of rice straw, trimmed with bunches of pink azalea. Ribbons of light green, shaded *à milles rayes*, the stripes very minute, and shot with white. The dress is of soft *gros de Naples* of prismatic rose colour, the lights of which are bright lilac. Many other varieties of colour in shot silk are used, but this is a favourite. The corsage is made with large horizontal plaits, confined up the front with a band. The shoulders are trimmed with three falls of silk, the edges worked in loose floss silk into small points ; these falls are seen one below the other, and narrow until they meet in front under the belt, which is broad and made of the same material as the dress. The sleeves are full at top, and are plaited under a band at the elbow and to correspond at the wrist."

An issue of the " Lady's Book " (1830) announced the following :

" Fashions for October.—A frock of changeable *gros de zane*, the body plain behind and full in front, worn occasionally with a pelerine of the same ; the frill of which is very deep and full

1824-1835

FIGURE 141.—1824—Gentleman in court dress trimmed with gold lace ;— blue coat, white trousers and waistcoat. From a contemporary plate.

FIGURE 142.—1825—Dress of white satin trimmed with cerise gauze, worn at a ball given for La Fayette at Baltimore in 1825. On the back of each glove was painted a head of the distinguished visitor to match the badge worn on the left breast. This interesting costume was worn by Miss Amanda Nace.

FIGURE 143.—1826—Gentleman in top-coat of drab cloth and hat of black beaver. From an old print. Head from a portrait of 1826.

FIGURE 144.—1829—White gauze dress with satin stripes, worn in Philadelphia by Miss Elizabeth Smith in 1829. Head copied from a contemporary portrait.

FIGURE 145.—1830—A summer walking dress of embroidered muslin with trimmings of blue ribbon. Taken from a plate of 1830.

FIGURE 146.—1835—Gentleman in street dress of 1835 ; brown coat and waistcoat and drab trousers. Taken from a print of that date.

FIGURE 147.—1833—Represents a lady in a figured chintz morning dress, from a print of this date. The apron of blue silk was worn in Philadelphia about this time.

FIGURE 148.—1830—Gentleman in walking dress of 1830, with green suit and drab-coloured hat.

1824–141   1825–142   1826–143   1829–144

1830–145   1830–146   1835–147   1835–148

at the shoulders, becoming gradually narrower and plainer as it descends to the belt.   The skirt of this dress is made extremely wide, and is set on the body with five plaits only, one in front, one on each side, and two behind : these plaits are of course very large.   The bottom of the skirt is finished with a thick cord sewed into the hem.   The sleeves are very wide, till they reach the elbow, and fit tightly to the lower part of the arm. The ruffle round the neck and hands is of plain bobinet quill-ing.   Bonnet of Dunstable straw trimmed with a band, and strings of broad pink satin ribbon.   Large scarlet shawl of embroidered Canton crape."

Mrs. Hale, in the "Lady's Magazine," gives advice on the subject of corsets :

"Corsets should be made of smooth soft elastic materials.

"They should be accurately fitted and modified to suit the peculiarities of figure of each wearer.

"No other stiffening should be used but that of quilting, or padding ; the bones, steel, etc., should be left to the deformed and the diseased for whom they were originally intended.

"Corsets should never be drawn so tight as to impede regular natural breathing, as, under all circumstances, the improvement of figure is insufficient to compensate for the air of awkward restraint caused by such lacing.

"They should never be worn, either loose or tight, during the hours appropriate to sleep, as by impeding respiration and accumulating the heat of the system improperly, they invariably injure.

"The corset for young persons should be of the most simple character, and worn in the lightest and easiest manner, allowing their lungs full play, and giving the form its fullest opportunity for expansion."

The extreme of fashion was not always adopted in America.

In Figure 86 we give a sketch of a simple costume of brown taffeta with leg-of-mutton sleeves of modern dimensions which was worn in Philadelphia in 1830. The hair is arranged in a simple but dignified coil of braids copied from a contemporary portrait. An illustration of a bonnet of this period (1830) of moderate size is given in Figure 275. It is made of fancy Tuscan straw and trimmed with white ribbon, and belongs to the Wetherill collection at Memorial Hall, Philadelphia.

Riding has always been a favourite form of exercise in England and considered an essential part of a young lady's education. Undoubtedly it was an Englishman who penned the following tribute:

> " How melts my beating heart as I behold
> Each lovely nymph, our island's boast and pride,
> Push on the generous steed that sweeps along
> O'er rough, o'er smooth, nor heeds the steepy hill,
> Nor falters in the extended vale below."

But it was by no means a lost art on this side of the Atlantic and was probably only less in vogue in the large cities. At this period of the thirties, habits as well as hats were more severe in outline, and rather conspicuous for the absence of trimmings. Not only were they more suitable for their purpose than the equestrian fashions of the early part of the century, but infinitely more becoming with their short jackets outlining the waist. Figure 116 represents a habit from a plate of 1830, in which the effect of the mannish hat is softened by a flowing veil. Perhaps it was the change of fashion which inspired the following lines:

> " Her dress, her shape, her matchless grace
> Were all observed, as well as heavenly face."

In the reign of William IV we read of the Marchioness of Salisbury, a prominent personage of the time, that she was a fearless horsewoman, and hunted with the Hatfield hounds in 1831, riding hard and clearing fences as ardently as any sportsman in the field, clad in " a habit of light blue cloth with a black velvet collar and a jockey cap ; " and that when she was an old lady of eighty years and very feeble, she had herself strapped into her saddle, and ambled up and down Hyde Park in the midst of the moving throng.   Locker, in his verses on " Rotten Row," laments :

> "But where is now the courtly troop
> That once rode laughing by ?
> I miss the curls of Cantilupe
> The smile of Lady Di."

Specimens of the very large bonnets worn in 1830–40 are given in Figures 87, 123, and 276 ; also in the initial on page 182.

Shawls were so much worn at that time, both genuine India cachemire and imitations thereof made in France, that it may be of interest to readers to know something of their manufacture and the origin of the strange names of the different varieties, for like the oriental rugs each design had a symbolic meaning.

> "Not a vanity is given in vain."

According to an article on the manufacture of cachemire shawls, nearly " 5,000 people were employed in making them in 1831.   About three weavers were kept at work in each shop, and when the pattern was especially fine they could not make more than a quarter of an inch a day, so that the most elaborate shawls were made in pieces.   The weaver was seated on a bench and a child placed a little below him with its eyes fixed on the pattern, who every time the frame was turned told the weaver the colours wanted.   The wages of first-rate workmen were from four to five pence, and the child labour it is to be feared counted for nothing. The pattern familiar to us as the palm-leaf is not a palm of the desert, but the cypress, the lover's tree among the orientals, which is sculptured on the ruins of the palace of Persepolis exactly as it is figured on the shawl borders. The cypress adorns the border of a shawl, even as the tree itself overshadows the bank of a stream ; and is considered by the Easterns as the image of religion and moral freedom, as Saadi has expressed in verse:

> " ' Be thou fruitful as the palm, or be
> At least as the dark cypress, high and free,'

because its branches never incline to the earth, but all shoot upward towards heaven.

" The original meaning of the wreaths and bunches of flowers woven in the middle of the square shawl pieces, and which so greatly enhance their value, is full of significance. The Turkish and Persian name of these shawls is Boghdscha ; the origin of the word is, however, neither Turkish nor Persian, but Indian, from Pudscha, which means a flower offering. When the season of the year will not afford the flowers which the Hindoos offer to their gods, the women spread out shawls, in the middle of which the embroidered basket of flowers supplies the place of fresh blossoms ; on this they kneel, as do the Moslems on the little carpets which exhibit a representation of the altar in the holy temple of Mecca, towards which they turn when they pray. The Boghdscha, or square shawl, with the flower-basket in the centre, may here take precedence of the other kinds, from the superiority of its original destination, rather than from its commercial value; for, in this respect, it is usually surpassed by the long scarf shawls, which are commonly denominated Risajii. A third class of shawls are woven without flowers or borders and are generally made into dresses by the

women ; these are called Toulik.   In the shops and warehouses
where the shawls are first sold, they are called Kaschmiri or
Lahori, according as they are the produce of Kaschmire or
Lahor.   The imitations of them, whether they come from Bagdad, Paris, or London, are all called Taklid, *i. e.*, imitations.
The workshops of Kaschmire have very lately produced some
splendid shawls, which are always marked with the word new-
tash, signifying new-fashioned.   The patterns of these represent
banners, pinnacles, chains, peacock's feathers, etc. ; they are denominated in Persian, Alemdar (containing banners) ; Kun-
keredar (containing pinnacles) ; Koeschedar (having corners if
the corners are ornamented) ; Lilsiledar (containing chains) ;
Peri-taus (peacock-winged) ; etc.   These denominations are frequently worked on the shawls with coloured silk ; the name of
the manufacturer is also generally inscribed on them, and very
often the epithets of God ; as, O preserver !   O protector ! be a
blessing granted to us ! and single letters, which form the word
Ahmed, or Mohammed, or some talismanic word with the addition of Allah, Allah, ' the highest, the highest ' (of the best
quality)."

> " I long not for rich silks or satins,
> My mind is contented with the schal and woollen stuff,'

is the illustration given in the Persian Dictionary for the word
shawl.

A decided change in the style of dressing the hair is
noticed in 1832.   " The low Grecian arrangement in the severe
classic taste of the antique, is universally adopted by ladies
whose profile will admit of this often most becoming style.
Coronets of pearls, cameos, or flowers are worn very low on the
brow.   Gold beads or pearls are woven with the braided hair.
The high gallery shell combs are now considered vulgar.   In

place of carved shell combs, gold combs, on which four or
five classic cameos are arranged *en couronne*, are worn in full
dress."

An English contemporary authority says : " The last week
has produced a novelty in evening dress, the adoption of
natural flowers for the hair.   Wires are made to support them
invisibly.   The flowers, which are not wreathed in the hair till
the moment of departure for the ball or *soirée*, are found to
retain their freshness during several hours.   This fashion has
been revived from the last century, when little vases were made
on purpose to contain a few drops of water, and were hid
among the hair, with the stalks of the flowers inserted in
them." *

Another style of hair-dressing which was probably more
generally becoming, as it remained in fashion much longer,
was a Grecian knot worn high in the back, the front hair
parted and arranged in soft curls on the temples.   (See Figures
72 and 230.)

Black velvet came into fashion for trimmings, for belts, and
for wristlets, in 1832, and has been more or less in favour ever
since.   We read, too, of sleeves made plain to the elbow and
very full above.

It was in 1832 that Mrs. Trollope visited the United States
and on her return to England published an ill-natured book
entitled " Domestic Manners of the Americans."   She dwells
at length on the unhappy partiality for false hair, forgetting
that the fashion prescribed in Paris was exceedingly popular
in London.   Her remarks are shrewd, however, and sometimes
amusing, for instance : " Though the expense of the lady's dress
greatly exceeds, in proportion to their general style of living,
that of the ladies of Europe, it is very far (excepting in Phila-

* Royal Lady's Magazine.

delphia) from being in good taste. They do not consult the seasons in the colours or in the style of their costume ; I have often shivered at seeing a young beauty picking her way through the snow with a pale rose-coloured bonnet, set on the very top of her head. I knew one young lady whose pretty little ear was actually frost-bitten from being thus exposed. They never wear muffs or boots, and appear extremely shocked at the sight of comfortable walking shoes and cotton stockings, even when they have to step to their sleighs over ice and snow. They walk in the middle of winter with their poor little toes pinched into a miniature slipper, incapable of excluding as much moisture as might bedew a primrose. I must say in their excuse, however, that they have, almost universally, extremely pretty feet. They do not walk well, nor, in fact, do they ever appear to advantage when in movement. I know not why this should be, for they have abundance of French dancing-masters among them, but somehow or other it is the fact."

In Figure 75 is a specimen of fashion in America in 1832. The original dress from which the sketch was made is a beautiful shade of blue-green taffeta trimmed with folds of itself. The cape and long undersleeves could be taken off indoors, but were always worn in the street. It belonged to a belle of the thirties, noted for her graceful carriage. The bonnet, copied from a print of 1833, is of white chip trimmed with white satin and pale pink daisies. The dress apron in Figure 89 belonged to the same lady and was worn in 1833. It is made of old gold satin, embroidered in flowers of all colours ; roses of pink chiffon, pansies of arasene (or chenille), small roses of chiffon, forget-me-nots (pink and blue) and jonquils of chiffon, green stems and leaves of arasene, and other small flowers of chiffon.

1850-1857

FIGURE 149.—1850—Dress of grey barege with bonnet of fancy straw trimmed with white ribbon.

FIGURE 150.—1850—Back of bonnet in Figure 149.

FIGURE 152.—1851—Mrs. Bloomer in the costume she invented.

FIGURE 153.—1857—Caricature of the fashions from "Punch," showing hoop-skirt made of reeds and muslin.

FIGURE 154.—1855—Hoop-skirt of steel wires covered with webbing. Worn in Philadelphia 1850–1855.

FIGURE 155.—1850—Basque of pink silk with a Chiné stripe of roses, trimmed with pink and white fringe and bows of ribbon to match.

FIGURE 156.—1850—Back view of pink cashmere peignoir in Figure 271. Cap from contemporary print.

149

150

152

153
C.W.T.
After Print.

154
C.W. Trout.
1907.

155
C.W. Trout. 1907.

156
Cecil W. Trout
1907

A charming old bonnet of 1833 is preserved in the Dutihl collection at Memorial Hall, made of white *point d'esprit* over white silk, with trimmings of white ribbon with a satin spot and a loop edge. The crown is stiff and the brim is formed of slender wires and lined with sarsnet. A picture of this bonnet is given in Figure 278.

White satin was still a favourite material for evening dresses in 1834. A lady writes from Washington: "I was gratified by Julia's good looks. She was dressed in plain white satin, and pink and white flowers on her head. Her hair was arranged by a hair-dresser."

Bodices for evening wear were made close fitting to the figure, and generally were trimmed with a bertha of lace or gauze. The sleeves were short and puffed, and gloves were worn reaching to the elbow. As for the hair-dressers' work, specimens of the prevailing styles are given in Figures 72, 73, 86 and 230.

A beautiful wedding dress, worn by a Quaker bride in Philadelphia in 1834, is sketched in Figure 72. It is of white satin with short puffed (melon) sleeves, over which are full long sleeves of white silk gauze, fastening at the wrist.

Pelisses of velvet and satin, closed down the front, and made with double pelerines, completely disguising the figure, were in great favour in the autumn of 1834. Bonnets were even larger and more flaring than before. Some of the latest were made of velvet and trimmed with a single large rosette of ribbon to match. Morning dresses were made of cashmere, and chintz robes printed in colour were popular. They were made with plain high bodices and fastened up the back. Shoulder capes were much worn with low or square cut bodices in the mornings. Large bonnets were a distinctive feature of costume in the thirties; the flaring brim lined with a becoming tint was surely an appropriate frame for a young face, and attractive indeed must have been Miss Wilkins' * heroine in

" HER BONNET

" When meeting bells began to toll
And pious folk began to pass,
She deftly tied her bonnet on,
The little sober meeting lass,
All in her neat white curtained room before her
　　tiny looking glass.

" So nicely round her lady-cheeks
She smoothed her bands of glossy hair,
And innocently wondered if
Her bonnet did not make her fair ;
Then sternly chid her foolish heart for harbour-
　　ing such fancies there.

·" So square she tied the satin strings,
And set the bows beneath her chin ;
Then smiled to see how sweet she looked,
Then thought her vanity a sin,
And she must put such thoughts away before
　　the sermon should begin.

" But sitting 'neath the preacher's word,
Demurely in her father's pew,
She thought about her bonnet still,
Yes, all the parson's sermon through,
About the pretty bows and buds which better
　　than the text she knew.

" Yet sitting there with peaceful face,
The reflex of her simple soul,
She looked to be a very saint
And maybe was one on the whole,
Only that her pretty bonnet kept away the aureole."

The bonnet referred to in the following verse must have been especially attractive :

* Mrs. Mary Wilkins Freeman.

" THE LOVE KNOT

" Tying her bonnet under her chin,
    She tied her raven ringlets in ;
    But not alone in its silken snare
    Did she catch her lovely floating hair,
    For tying her bonnet under her chin,
    She tied a young man's heart within."

Mantles trimmed and lined with fur were very fashionable. Sable, Isabella bear and a delicate fur called Kolinski were all used. A silk cord fastened the mantle at the waist and hung down low in front, finished with a handsome tassel. Olives and Brandenburgs were used as fastenings on velvet pelisses. Sleeves were very wide from the shoulder to the wrist and there finished with a deep cuff. Satin bonnets were trimmed with satin ribbon to match and bordered by curtain veils of rich black lace. The curtains at the back were very shallow and moderately full.

Among the new materials of the year were Persian taffeta with milk white or cream white ground, covered with small bouquets of roses and satin *moyenage* with a dark blue ground and an arabesque pattern in gold, or black with red figures. A new design for bodices was cut high at the throat, the front laid in plaits from the shoulder to the waist, like a fan. Long full sleeves caught in with two bands giving the effect of three puffs. The short puffed sleeves of 1835 were called melon sleeves ; over them long sleeves of blond lace were sometimes worn. In a fashion column of the " Court Magazine" for July, 1835, we read : " Lightness and simplicity are this month's characteristics, but it is a simplicity as expensive as it is tasteful ; the rich satins, velvets and furs of winter costumes were not in reality more costly than the comparatively plain attire of the present month."

Very dainty but costly must have been the *peignoir* described for that month, made of French cambric trimmed down the front with a deep ruffle of Valenciennes lace caught together at intervals by knots of the cambric edged with lace. The pelerine or shoulder cape was also trimmed with Valenciennes. We read about this time of a new Swiss muslin, with rich foulard patterns stamped on it. The bonnets and hats were enormously big in 1835. The brims were wider, the crowns were higher, and the curtains of bonnets were deeper. Veils of blond, illusion, or *dentelle de soie* were fastened to the brims of some of the newest bonnets.

We hear at this time of a new ribbon. It was of six different colours very tastefully mingled, in patterns of a rather bizarre effect, and was called Chinese ribbon. Flowers of all kinds, as well as feathers, were worn in hats. Printed cambrics, figured organdies, *mousseline de laine* and delicate lingerie continued in favour, and fichus of mull and lace were still very popular. One striking novelty is recorded for this year (1835) : gloves of rose-colour and of flesh-colour were preferred to white.

Turbans, although not as generally popular as they had been, were still worn. A new style was called the turban *à la juive*. It was made of white satin covered with tulle and ornamented with bandalettes *à l'antique*, embroidered with gold, and hanging down in the back almost to the neck. Another turban worn in that same year is described as " of the Turkish form " and as made of white net and maize coloured velvet, ornamented with two aigrettes held in place by a gold ornament set with brilliants.

A popular American periodical which first appeared in 1830, and had a wide circulation, was the " Lady's Book," published by Louis Godey in Philadelphia. It was founded on somewhat the same basis as the " Court Magazine " in London, containing serial stories and verses by recognized authors of the day, as well as fashion plates in colour. Two evening costumes for 1835 are described in the September number :

" A printed satin robe, white ground with a pattern in vivid colours of small sprigs in winding columns. The corsage is cut very low and square at the back and front of the bust, but rather higher on the shoulder than they are generally made, and pointed at the waist. It is trimmed round the top with a single row of narrow blond lace laid on flat. Blond lace long sleeves of the usual size at the top, and moderately full from the elbow to the wrist; they are made open from the bend of the arm, but are caught together in three places by gold filagree buttons, and surmounted by *mancherons* of broad blond lace. The hair, parted on the forehead, is arranged on each side in a plaited band, which is doubled and hangs low. The back hair, also arranged in a braid, is twisted round the top of the head. Gold earrings, necklace and bracelets. White kid gloves; white satin slippers.

" A robe of pale rose-coloured *mousseline de soie* over *gros de Naples* to correspond. A low corsage fitting close but with a little fullness at the bottom of the waist; trimmed round the neck with a blond lace ruche. Short undersleeves of white *gros de Naples*, with an oversleeve of blond lace of the Marino Faliero shape confined by a gold agraffe on the shoulder. Armlets and *ceinture* of gold net, with gold clasps. The hair is parted on the forehead and turned up behind ; the ends form a cluster of curls. A band of fancy jewelry and bunches of gold wheat complete the coiffure. White silk net gloves. White *gros de Naples* slippers of the sandal form."

An attractive costume, which was worn in Pennsylvania, is given in Figure 87. The gown is of soft sage satin with brocaded flowers of the same colour made with bias folds of the satin, broad at the shoulder and tapering in at the waist ; the folds are finished with a shell trimming of the satin, the same trimming being used on the caps of the sleeves and on the cuffs. This unusually pretty dress was worn by Miss Haldeman. The style was fashionable in 1838 and the bonnet is copied from a plate of the same date.

Fashion was by no means an unimportant factor in the social life of rural neighbourhoods throughout the United States. Mrs. Gaskell's tea-party at Cranford might easily have taken place in a small community in Virginia or in New England, for instance. We remember the invitation was discussed and then accepted because " Miss Pole possessed a very smart cap which she was anxious to show to an admiring world." The expenditure in dress in Cranford was principally in the article referred to. If the heads were buried in smart caps, the ladies were like ostriches, and cared not what became of their bodies. With old gowns, yellow and venerable collars, any number of brooches (some with dog's eyes painted on them, some that were like small picture-frames with mausoleums and weeping-willows neatly executed in hair inside ; some again with miniatures of ladies and gentlemen sweetly smiling out of a nest of stiff muslin) and new caps to suit the fashion of the day, " the ladies of Cranford always dressed with chaste elegance and propriety," as Miss Barber once fittingly expressed it. " And with these new caps, and a greater array of brooches than had ever been seen together at one time since Cranford was a town, did Miss Forrester, and Miss Matty, and Miss Pole appear on that memorable Tuesday evening. I counted seven brooches myself on Miss Pole's dress. Two were fixed negligently in her cap (one was a butterfly of Scotch pebbles which a vivid imagination might believe to be a real insect) ; one fastened her net neckerchief ; one her collar ; one ornamented the front of her gown between throat and waist ; another adorned the front of her stomacher.   Where the seventh was I have forgotten, but it was somewhere about her, I am sure."

Needlework was still in vogue and was commended in the following verses by a contemporary poet :

'THE NEEDLE

" The gay belles of fashion may boast of excelling
    In waltz or cotillion, at whist or quadrille ;
And seek admiration by vauntingly telling
    Of drawing and painting and musical skill ;
But give me the fair one in country or city
    Whose home and its duties are dear to her heart,
Who cheerfully warbles some rustical ditty,
    While plying the needle with exquisite art.
The bright little needle, the swift flying needle,
    The needle directed by beauty and art.

" If love have a potent, a magical token,
    A talisman ever resistless and true,
A charm that is never evaded or broken,
    A witchery certain the heart to subdue—
'Tis this, and his armoury never has furnished
    So keen and unerring or polished a dart
Let beauty direct it, so pointed and burnished,
    And oh, it is certain of touching the heart.

" Be wise then, ye maidens, nor seek admiration
    By dressing for conquest and flirting with all ;
You never, whate'er be your fortune or station,
    Appear half so lovely at rout or at ball
As gaily convened at a work-covered table,
    Each cheerfully active and playing her part,
Beguiling the task with a song or a fable,
    And plying the needle with exquisite art."

A photograph of the wedding outfit worn by Miss Sarah Hayes who, in 1836, married Major Mordecai, a distinguished officer of the United States Army, in the Synagogue in Philadelphia, is given in Figure 170.   The gown is of the sheerest, filmiest India muslin we have seen, and was imported for the

1802–1854

FIGURE 157.—1813—Little girl in pantalettes.   From a plate.
FIGURE 158.—1802—Mother and children.   From a portrait of Mrs. Hind.
FIGURE 159.—1837—Girl in pantalettes.
FIGURE 160.—1820—Mother and child.
FIGURE 161.—1850—Boy in sailor costume.   From a contemporary portrait.
FIGURE 162.—1854—Boys in Highland dress.   From a portrait.

161

158

157

160

159

162

occasion by the bride's father, one of the leading merchants of the day. The slippers have square toes, the new fashion for 1836, and the short gloves are embroidered and originally were trimmed with blond lace to match the veil. The handkerchief case was the work of the bridesmaids and also the beautifully embroidered handkerchief with "Sarah" in flowered letters in one corner. The fan is an exquisite specimen of carved ivory made in India, with the monogram of the bride in the centre. The marriage certificate is in Hebrew characters, which unfortunately do not show in the photograph. We notice that the sleeves were originally puffed, a very fashionable style in 1836.

About this date the extravagantly large sleeves went out of fashion, and were followed by a more graceful style, fitting close to the arm on top and full at the elbows.

In Figure 230 is shown a gown of cream white figured silk worn in 1837 by a Quaker maiden at a wedding in a Philadelphia Meeting. The sleeves are in the new fashion, which succeeded the leg-of-mutton in popularity. The hair is copied from a contemporary portrait.

Some of the costumes worn by Queen Victoria, her coronation robes as well as some every-day dresses, are exhibited in her rooms at Kensington Palace, and it is surprising to see what a little woman the great queen was. One gown of black poplin, worn on some occasion of court mourning, has very small sleeves, finished with exquisitely neat little cuffs of embroidered muslin.

In 1837, when President Van Buren took up his abode at the White House, Mr. Andrew Stevenson was sent as Minister to Great Britain from the United States, and was of course present at the coronation of Queen Victoria with Mrs. Stevenson, whose portrait was afterwards painted by Healey in the costume she wore when she was presented at the Queen's Drawing-room. This picture is well known and we regret space will not permit us to give a copy of it here.

A Philadelphia bride of 1838 wore the attractive gown shown in Figure 228. It is made of white satin and the trimmings are of blond lace. With this costume short gloves with embroidered tops were worn fastening over the band of the long lace sleeves as shown in the illustration. The veil and arrangement of hair are copied from a portrait of the same year. The dress in Figure 74 belonged to the same bride. The colour is a delicate pink and the sash of soft figured satin ribbon to match ; the lace at the neck and on the sleeves is of white blond which was the favourite of fashion at the time. The hair is copied from an English portrait.

Women's Dress
1840-1850

"Change of Fashion is the tax which industry
imposes on the vanity of the rich."

ITH the new year, 1840, we notice a decided
change in bonnets. The immense flaring
brims which had been worn for the last ten
years were replaced by a new shape somewhat resembling the capotes of the early
years of the nineteenth century. The long
veils of brocaded gauze so fashionable in
the thirties were also superseded by shorter
veils of net or lace, with small figures or
with plain centres of lace with figured borders (Figures 128
and 131).

In a letter from the Paris correspondent to the "Court Magazine" for July, 1840, we find the following description of the
new bonnets: "They are worn rather close to the face and
made of *Paille de riz*, Crêpe lisse, Leghorn and fine straws. The
crowns sit back quite flat and the fronts are rather less open but
very long at the ears." (See Figures 128, 129 and 131.)

"The most elegant bonnets are covered with what we call a
voilette of lace or tulle illusion; this little veil does not fall over
the face, but merely covers the bonnet, being frequently brought
from underneath the front; a long lappet falls as low as the
waist from each side of the front."

213

A bonnet worn in Philadelphia in 1840, of white ribbed silk, trimmed with white satin ribbon and a *voilette* of blond lace hanging in long lappets on each side, and with pale pink flowers inside the brim, belongs to Miss Dutihl's Collection at Memorial Hall. A picture of it is given in Figure 131.

"On coloured silk bonnets these *voilettes* are made of the same shade as the silk. Drawn *capotes* are also *de mode;* some have *voilettes* and others a narrow ruche of white tulle round the edge of the front. Straws and Leghorns are trimmed with velvet, violet or dark green being the favourite colours for this purpose; a *torsade* intermingled with straw goes round the crown, and the brim is edged inside and out with a band of velvet more than an inch in depth. A flat ostrich feather is placed at one side and lies perfectly flat across the bonnet, drooping to the opposite side; this feather may be white or the colour of the velvet, or any colour that contrasts well with the trimming. The younger ladies who do not wear feathers prefer a half wreath of field flowers."

The same correspondent announced that long cachemire shawls were coming in and would take the place of square shawls. They were to be worn as scarfs. "White, black and blue grounds with patterns of palms or rosettes joined with light running patterns," were the most desirable combinations. "Black shawls trimmed with lace or fringe, and black silk scarfs trimmed all round with lace, or only with silk fringe at the ends, are universally worn. Coloured silk scarfs are also in fashion," and it was considered *trés distingué*, we learn, to have your scarf and your dress of the same colour, and with a white dress a scarf of the colour of the bonnet.

Lace was worn extensively in the forties. Brussels and Honiton lace were perhaps the most fashionable. Queen Victoria's wedding dress (February 10, 1840) was of this beautiful fabric made at the picturesque village in Devon from which the lace gets its name.

The first note on crinoline, so soon to be an indispensable adjunct to the fashionable toilet, is given in the same letter from Paris : " Of course you have heard of the *Jupons de Crinoline* ; they are very light and cool, and make the dress sit beautifully, and one perfection in them is that they never crease or get out of form."

Sleeveless jackets, called *Canegous*, came into fashion in 1840. They were open in front, but finished at the neck with small collars, and were either richly embroidered or trimmed with lace. In 1840 we read of white spencers, to be worn like our modern blouses with coloured skirts. Another familiar fashion of to-day seems to be a revival of 1840 ; cuffs and collars on the sleeves and neck are spoken of by a contemporary author as " indispensable." Spencers of black or coloured velvet were a very becoming fashion.

Close-fitting dresses, called Redingotes, were very popular at this time. We read of one in a London magazine, made of white India muslin lined with pale blue silk and trimmed with lace, and another lined with pink and trimmed with hand embroidery. Sleeves were either tight or full according to the fancy of the wearer ; specimens are given in Figures 128 and 136. Bodices were made with a sharp point at the waist in front and round in the back, and were usually open at the throat, and either worn over a chemisette or finished with a ruching of lace for morning or street wear. Evening gowns were cut low and finished with a bertha of lace, or silk to match the dress (Figures 134 and 135).

Very elaborate head-dresses were worn at this date, made of India muslin or organdie, trimmed with lace. Appliqué and English point lace were used instead of the blond lace which had been so fashionable in the thirties. (See Figures 134, 139 and 233.) The front hair was worn either in broad braids, smooth bands, or in long ringlets, while the back hair was braided or coiled very low on the neck. Short gloves were still in fashion and trimmed with lace, swansdown, ribbon, etc. They were either fastened with buttons (two or four) or laced up with a silk cord.

At this period, slender waists being very much admired, the bodices were gradually made with deeper points and worn without belts, and the gathers of the full skirts were distributed at the sides and back to produce that effect. An authority of this time says: "I agree with the doctors in setting my face against tight lacing, the most dangerous practice a lady can persevere in; so have your dress made with a long waist; have your petticoat gathered into a very broad band cut on the cross way, and with a point in front, so as not to have gathers under the point of your dress; let the petticoat be made of crinoline, or of a very thick cotton material with a sort of honeycomb pattern all over; this will make your dress appear sufficiently full and form a proper contrast to the waist, thereby sparing you the necessity and agony as well as injury, of tight lacing."

Wadded cachemire shawls were in vogue, but the newest wrap was a small wadded cape with a pointed hood. We read, too, of the Palatine, a cloak of much the same style made of black satin wadded and lined with blue, rose-colour, or apricot satin trimmed all round with black lace, and reaching to the knees in front, the hood made to be drawn over at pleasure; especially adaptable for an evening wrap.

A walking dress for the winter of 1840 is described in the "Court Magazine": "Made of satin lined and wadded throughout; the corsage close fitting, and with tight sleeves with two seams. Upon the front of the waist is a trimming consisting of four rows of black lace set on in regular fluted plaits, extending from the shoulder to the waist in the form of a V, and is likewise carried across the back in the style of a pelerine; besides this the trimming is carried down each side of the front breadth of the skirt *en tablier*, becoming wider as it goes down and also increasing in distance."

In 1841, we notice that sleeves were worn long and close-fitting for house and street wear, sometimes finished with an epaulet cap called a jockey (Figure 136). Evening dresses were made with voluminous skirts trimmed with flounces; bodices fitted close to the figure and were stiffly boned and finished with a point coming a little below the waist line in front. Berthas of lace or of the same material as the dress were not only in the height of fashion during the forties, but have been a favourite style of trimming ever since.

The numerous Daguerreotypes of that period furnish us with many accurate details of dress. From these we learn that it was still the fashion to wear the hair parted in the middle, and although curls which had been the favourite style for so many years were still worn, the most fashionable arrangement was to draw the front hair down in smooth bands concealing the ears and fasten the ends with the coil at the back. Often the front hair was braided in many strands. The so-called "Polish braid" was in nine strands and was most becoming to a delicate face. When the hair was very long, the braids were often carried across the head, making a sort of coronet. (See Figure 136.) In many of the portraits of Queen Victoria we notice this effect, but it was a favourite style in America too; at that period almost every lady had an abundance of natural hair, and very little false hair was worn.

In 1841 Mrs. Julia Ward Howe made a visit to England and records in her " Reminiscences " some of the costumes worn by

1860–1870

FIGURE 163.—1864—Small hat with rolling brim and feathers. From a print of the time.

FIGURE 164.—1860–70—Turban hat with white feather. From a print of the time.

FIGURE 165.—1862—Mushroom hat and Garibaldi blouse. From a contemporary print.

FIGURE 166.—1868—Croquet costume showing small hat worn over a "waterfall." The ruffled skirt is short and shows the Balmoral boots. From a contemporary picture.

FIGURE 167.—1860–70—House maid in a figured calico and small cap. From an English print.

FIGURE 168.—1860—Hair arranged in a chenille net. From a print.

FIGURE 169.—1860—A jockey hat and feather. From a contemporary print.

163 C.W.T. After Print.

164 C.W.Trout.

165 C.W.Trout. After Print.

166 C.W.Trout.

167 C.W.T. After Print

168

169 C.W.T.

English ladies of note in the early days of Queen Victoria's reign. She met the beautiful Mrs. Norton at a dinner, and says : " Her hair, which was decidedly black, was arranged in flat bandeaux according to the fashion of the time. A diamond chain formed of large links encircled her fine head. Her eyes were dark and full of expression. Her dress was unusually *décolleteé*, but most of the ladies present would in America have been considered extreme in that respect." *

On another occasion Mrs. Howe met the Duchess of Sutherland, and describes her costume as follows :

" She wore a brown gauze or barege over light blue satin with a wreath of brown velvet leaves and blue forget-me-nots in her hair, and on her arm, among other beautiful jewels, a miniature of the Queen set in diamonds." A dress of pink moiré worn by the same lady, with a wreath of velvet leaves interspersed with diamonds, is also mentioned. Wreaths of artificial flowers combined with ribbons or jewels were fashionable from 1840 to 1850. (See Figure 139.)

A letter from Paris, written in 1841, describes an evening costume of pale blue satin trimmed with sable round the bottom of the skirt and up the front *en tablier*, the short plain sleeves also trimmed with the fur. The bodice was made with a deep point. A toque of blue velvet was worn with this dress ornamented with a Henri IV plume fastened with a diamond aigrette. The graceful Pompadour sleeves, with ruffles of lace falling very low at the back of the arm, were revived in 1841, and for evening dress the points of bodices were very deep. But tight sleeves were worn for dinner and house gowns. Much fur was used in trimming. Muffs of moderate size (Figure 137) and round pelerines or capes were made generally of ermine, sable, marten and swansdown. Passementerie, Bran-

* Reminiscences 1819-1899. By Mrs. Julia Ward Howe.

denburghs and bias folds were universally used, but ruffles and flounces were temporarily out of favour. Bonnets were made very long at the sides projecting below the chin in a very unbecoming style which did not long remain in fashion (Figure 137). Three new caps are mentioned: *La Coquette*, a half cap with a deep fancy border trimmed with marabout tips; *La Religieuse*, a nun's cap made of fine materials; Marie Stuart cap, with point in front, made of lace for morning wear and of velvet for evening dress.

Arrows with diamond heads were worn in the hair and large high backed combs again made their appearance, some plain and others again ornamented with gold and inlaid with precious stones. Coral ornaments were very much worn. A single gold bracelet on the right arm above the glove was very fashionable, and a serpent with ruby eyes was said to be " the most splendid thing of that description ever seen." Several novelties in feathers are also mentioned. " There are willow feathers, *panachées*, the ends tipped in shaded colours running one into another, as green into lilac, thence into orange, and ending in shades of blue. We have also marabouts, *sablés d'or* or *d'argent* having the appearance of gold or silver-dust shaken upon them. For dress turbans they are truly splendid." A certain delicate shade of purple called *pensée* was also new in the winter of 1841–1842, and pearl-grey and watered blue were very popular for street wear.

Many costumes were made *en redingote* buttoned all the way down the front with small buttons. Tight plain sleeves were the best suited for this style of dress, although full sleeves were worn finished with plain cuffs. Gold or silver cord and tassels were twisted in and out among the braids of the back hair, and both tassels brought behind the right ear, and allowed to hang loosely. With this coiffure long English curls were usually arranged on each side of the face, but the front hair was very generally worn in smooth bands throughout the forties, as we notice in many portraits of the day, and turbans of every variety were still in vogue. Bows without ends were used extensively in trimmings for turbans and bonnets. Quillings of tulle were worn inside bonnet brims or, instead of the ruche, plaitings of silk or tulle were sometimes placed on the edge of the brim and flowers worn inside.

Morning dresses of wadded cashmere or merino with loose sleeves showing undersleeves of cambric are noticed in the plates of 1842, and were worn for many years (see Figure 156), sometimes with little caps of India muslin trimmed with lace and ribbon.

Revers worn very low on the shoulders were a noticeable feature of walking dresses in 1842, but many costumes were made without any trimming on the corsage. A new fashion was an arrangement of horizontal puffings of the material of the dress across the front of the bodice; this was called *en coulisses*.

Separate bodices of lingerie were also fashionable at that time made of alternate puffings of thin muslin and embroidery. A picture of one is given in Figure 128, which also shows a scarf of Roman striped silk worn in Philadelphia and a bonnet from a plate of 1842.

During this year skirts were still worn very full over petticoats of crinoline. Sometimes they were made perfectly plain without trimmings, but generally bias folds of the material were put on *en tablier* or in groups above the hem. Bodices were made with rounded points at the waist and laced up the back, and they were usually half or three-quarters high. Sleeves were worn in a great variety of shapes. Long and tight, short and close-fitting, puffed to the wrist with fanciful caps at the top, and even bell sleeves with undersleeves of thin white muslin are seen in the fashion plates of this time. The shoulders are very long and sloping. Black varnished leather shoes were a new fashion. Very fanciful caps were worn. Mits and even gloves of lace were very much in vogue. Bonnets still projected over the face and ears, and were trimmed with feathers, ribbon and flowers. Parasols were very small and muffs moderately large.

In 1842, a French periodical, " Le Follet," was combined with the " Court Magazine " and the descriptions of the new fashions were written in French.

For the spring of this year we are told that soutache braid and passementerie were lavishly used in trimming and that the most fashionable materials were batiste, *mousselline de laine*, and *tissue bayadère*. The crape hats of Mr. Leclerc appear to have been " the rage " in Paris at that time. We read that nothing could be " more delicious " than his hats in rose-coloured crape ornamented with a bunch of moss roses at one side ; nothing more dainty than his *capotes* of white crape and Valenciennes insertion trimmed with bias folds of *gros de Naples* in rose-colour. Some of these hats are trimmed with shaded ribbons and marabout feathers shaded to match, producing a very unique effect. Mits of velvet were a Paris novelty described in 1842. They were especially intended to wear with short sleeves and were trimmed with lace and embroidery.

A mourning dress is described in a magazine of 1842 : " Dress of black barege made with a deep hem at the bottom of the skirt, and a fold of the same depth above. Bodice cut three-quarters high and laced up the back. A ruche of the material finishes the neck of the corsage, and the edge of the long tight sleeves. A pelerine of black lace cut low in the neck is worn round the shoulders and fastened with a black ribbon bow. An under-dress which shows through the barege is of grey *gros de Naples*. A drawn bonnet also of grey *gros de Naples*, trimmed round the face with a ruche of black tulle, and small black flowers and a long grey feather surrounds the crown and hangs down on the left side. Gloves of black lace, and slippers of black *panet de soie* completed this costume."

A graceful walking dress is described as follows: " Redingote of Pekin stripe, blue and brown. The corsage is tight and almost high in the neck, tight sleeves trimmed with two bias folds of the silk at the top. The skirt is very full, and trimmed with two bias folds (*en tablier*) down each side of the front. Apricot-coloured gloves and parasol. Black shoes and gaiters. Bonnet of rice straw trimmed with pink ribbon ; a large veil of white gauze, drawn into fullness by a ribbon in a hem, is fastened round the crown, and thrown back over the shoulders. Hair is in full ringlets at the sides."

The following extract is from a letter dated Paris, June 25, 1842 : " Bareges, tarlatans and such light textures are the only things that we can wear here just now, but after all can anything be prettier? The dresses are still very long and the skirts ample though one of our *couturières* has tried to bring in the fashion of not having any fullness in front. Comment! I think I hear you exclaim, ' Can this really be ? ' *Oui, ma chère*, but never mind ; it is an innovation that will not take, so we need give ourselves no trouble about it. In light materials the corsages are invariably made *en coulisses*. They are very becoming to the figure and suitable for muslins and bareges but in anything of a more substantial texture, they do not look well. Corsages with *ceintures* (Figure 127) are a good deal worn in morning negligee ; after all there is something very pretty in seeing the waist neatly supported (the French *soutenue* would suit me better) by a pretty belt and buckle ; it is therefore a fashion not likely to remain long in disuse. We have de-cidedly triumphed over our antipathy to short sleeves and we wear them at all times now."

From Paris comes the following amusing bit of advice : " I must let you into a little secret about the manner of getting up your fine things which will render them more becoming. It is to put an imperceptible tinge of pink into the rinsing water in-stead of blue, which our grandmothers for a hundred genera-tions past have been content to use. But now that the other has been discovered, we wonder how we could have put up with such an unbecoming thing as what is called ' snow-white linen.' But recollect your collars must not be pink ; the tinge must be felt, not seen, if I may so express myself."

In the chronicles of 1843, we notice that in spite of the in-convenience of the fashion, street dresses were still worn ex-tremely long especially in the back. They were a little shorter in the front. Corsages were all made tight fitting. Belts and buckles gained in popularity especially for morning wear. In the spring of this year (1843) we read of a new wrap, a Paletot, generally of silk trimmed with black lace, or with a quilling of ribbon, caught in about the waist with a broad ribbon. Man-tillas were in the height of fashion at that time and were trimmed with frills and quillings innumerable. A slight change in bonnets is mentioned. The brims did not project quite so much over the face, and the crowns were less deep also. In Figure 126 is given the picture of a bonnet in Miss Dutihl's collection, which shows the change in shape. It is made of dove-coloured satin trimmed with pink and green figured ribbon.

Another bonnet of this year (1843) is given in Figure 129, worn with a dress of grey-green satin and a black lace shawl.

The fashion plates of this decade are very attractive. A cer-tain harmony of colour and feminine grace pervades them. But the bonnets must have been most uncomfortable, projecting beyond the face. It must have been a constant temptation to push the brims back to get a good look at something, and they were worn by young girls, in fact by little children as the pictures show. The newest materials were changeable coloured silks, shot silks and Pekin stripes. House gowns of cashmere and *mousseline de laine* were very popular in winter, and of cambric and printed muslin for summer.

We read in an American publication of a new head-dress for 1844. "A most irresistible coiffure is a wreath of periwinkles with pendant sprigs of the flowers mingled with the curls at each side of the face, or if the hair is worn in bands, the wreath may be most becoming, arranged around the head with small bunches of the flowers and leaves hanging from the coil at the back."

The only change in the form of caps was that they were a little smaller, and often made of plain muslin without any ribbon. The crown was very small, and they had broad lappets of muslin falling on each side behind the ears. But another and decidedly more becoming style, was of plain India muslin, trimmed with two rows of Valenciennes, and ornamented with a broad blue ribbon in the front, and shaded with a second row of lace, falling over the ribbon. A rosette of blue silk with long ends, placed on the left side, was also a tasteful trimming. Another pattern had a very small head piece, with lappets of Mechlin lace reaching only to the edge of the ears on both sides, and ornamented with green satin ribbons. Another is trimmed with two rows of embroidered muslin, slightly fulled, and decorated with two small *coques* of plaited white and blue silk ribbon, a twist or roll of the same encircling the crown. The cap in Figure 233 is on this order without lappets and trimmed with *choux* of pink satin.

1820–1870

FIGURE 170.—1836—Wedding costume of Miss Sara Hayes, of Philadelphia.

FIGURE 171.—1850–70—Lace collars and cuffs worn in Philadelphia during this period.

FIGURE 172.—1820-40—Specimens of high combs worn during these years.

FIGURE 173.—1854—Bodice of wedding gown; embroidered net over white satin, trimmed with blond lace. Worn by a Philadelphia bride.

170

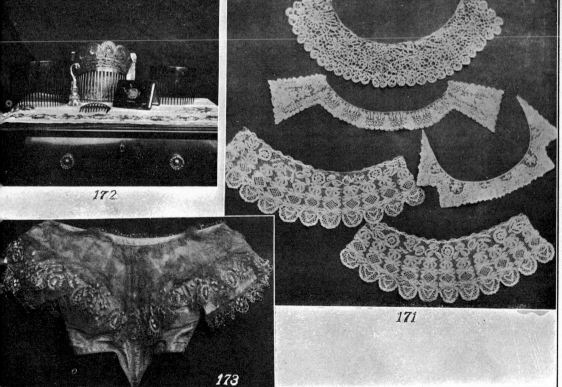

172

171

173

A dainty gown of white cashmere is taken from the same authority : "The front of the skirt is trimmed with a facing of pink ; tight and high corsage, finished with a square collar, full hanging sleeves, bordered and faced to match the skirt. Underdress of muslin, trimmed round the bottom with two rows of embroidery. Cap of light spotted lace, decorated with roses ; this cap is considered the neatest of the season and is universally admired."

Under the heading "Bonnets, etc., in New York," a correspondent of the "Boston Transcript" thus describes the fashions there : "Within the past week an invoice of bonnets has arrived from Paris and on Sunday the congregations of the fashionable churches looked like beds of lilies and roses. The latest style is really very beautiful, or as the ladies say 'sweet.' The one I have been most pleased with is a perfect flower. The material is white figured muslin, delicately trimmed with ribbons and roses, and in form like the cup of a morning glory. If the humming birds and honey-bees don't light upon it on Broadway, I shall think they show a great want of taste. For dresses, chameleon silks are much worn, three distinct colours, by some magic of art, being thrown on a plain ground, looking as if 'Iris dipt the wool.' A new style of evening dress appeared at the last 'Hop' at the 'Astor House,' which attracted the attention of connoisseurs as something quite original and beautiful ; a white muslin with two broad and richly coloured borders, looking like an illuminated title page."

As shown in the initial at the head of this chapter skirts were often trimmed with deep flounces in 1845, and they were worn wider and fuller than ever before in the nineteenth century. Stiffly starched underskirts were worn to keep out the dresses and they were so full over the hips that the waist appeared very small in proportion. The shoulders of bodices were cut long and sloping, and the sleeves continued to be worn almost skin-tight. Shoulder capes of embroidered muslin and lace were very fashionable. (See Figure 233.) Turned-down collars were most popular, but narrow ruchings were also worn at the throat and wrists. (See Figure 127.) A material called delaine, a merino without the twill, with figures or spots stamped in contrasting colours, was popular for house dresses. It was like the fashionable challis of to-day, but delaines are mentioned in old letters and books up to the sixties. In Figure 127, a picture is given of a gown of this material worn in Boston in 1845. Bonnets were now made to flare a little round the face and were often of tulle or gauze shirred over silk of the same colour (Figure 124). A pale pink bonnet of this description worn in Philadelphia in 1846 is preserved at Stenton, Philadelphia.

In 1845 we notice that the berthas on evening gowns were very deep, reaching about to the waist line. Black moiré was a new fashion for evening dress, and in an English magazine of February, 1845, is described a costume of this material which would have suited Lady Dedlock to perfection. " Skirt long and ample, close-fitting pointed bodice reaching to the throat, and tight long sleeves. A passementerie trimming, also black, is arranged at the foot of the skirt, in *bretelles* on the bodice, and also trims the sleeves. A small embroidered collar is fastened with a brooch at the throat, and a dress cap of English Point lace trimmed with pink flowers and ribbons completes the costume."

A style of dress which came into vogue at this time and remained long in fashion was the bodice opening over a chemisette of white muslin and finished with revers.

In 1846 bonnets were noticeably smaller and the fronts were less flaring. This change is shown in Figure 136. Caps and fanciful head-dresses were still in vogue for evening as well as morning dress. Ball dresses were cut quite high in the neck, a very awkward style. House gowns were worn high at the throat and finished with a small flat collar of lace or embroidery, or cut square or surplice and worn over a chemisette with a flat collar; a pretty fashion which afforded an opportunity for the exercise of individual taste, for endless was the variety of dainty lingerie and lace in use at this time. Tarlatan was the most fashionable material for dancing frocks. Parasols were very small in the forties, and in 1846 a new fashion of folding parasols was introduced.

The morning or "undress" costumes of this time were, as we see by the following contemporary verses,* made high neck and long sleeves, and being very comfortable, were adopted both for summer and for winter, and were a great contrast to the full dress for winter balls :

> "She was in fashion's elegant undress,
>   Muffled from throat to ankle ; and her hair
> Was all 'en papillotes,' each auburn tress
>   Prettily pinned apart. You well might swear
> She was no beauty ; yet, when 'made up' ready
> For visitors, 'twas quite another lady.

> "Since that wise pedant, Johnson, was in fashion,
>   Manners have changed as well as moons ; and he
> Would fret himself once more into a passion,
>   Should he return (which Heaven forbid) and see
> How strangely from his standard dictionary
> The meaning of some words is made to vary.

> "For instance, an undress at present means
>   The wearing a pelisse, a shawl, or so ;
> Or anything you please, in short, that screens
>   The face, and hides the form from top to toe ;
> Of power to brave a quizzin-glass, or storm ;
>   'Tis worn in summer, when the weather's warm.

*Fanny, by F. G. Hallack.

"But a full dress is for a winter's night,
    The most genteel is made of 'woven air';
That kind of classic cobweb, soft and light,
    Which Lady Morgan's Ida used to wear.
And ladies, this aerial manner dressed in,
    Look Eve-like, angel-like, and interesting."

In 1848, the date of the second Republic in France, bodices were worn opening in front over white chemisettes, and sleeves were wide at the bottom, showing an undersleeve to match the chemisette. This fashion was very generally adopted in the United States and worn more or less for twenty years. (See Figure 135.) We read of a garment called the Kasaveck imported from Russia at this time. It was a sort of jacket reaching to the waist, close-fitting and with wide braided sleeves, and was usually made of cashmere or satin and wadded. This garment was known under several different names: "*Coin du feu*," "*Casagne*," "*Pardessus*," etc. "Women of fashion," we read, "never wore them out of their own houses in the daytime."

A new wrap called the "Cornelia" was introduced about 1848. "It had no seam on the shoulder, and could be gathered up on the arms like a shawl at the pleasure of the wearer." Mantles of cashmere with double capes edged with braid, and the Josephine mantle with one cape, without shoulder seams, reaching to the waist, were popular favourites. Long chains of beads and cameo brooches without clasps were worn.

When Mr. Bancroft was Minister to England (1844–1848) his wife wrote her impressions of the English people she met to her friends in Boston. From her letters, published a few years ago, we quote the following descriptions:

"And now having given you some idea whom we are seeing here, you will wish to know how I like them and how they differ from our own people. At the smaller dinners and *soirées* at this season I cannot of course receive a full impression of English society, but certainly those persons now in town are charming people. Their manners are perfectly simple and I entirely forget, except their historic names fall upon my ear, that I am with the proud aristocracy of England.

"The forms of society and the standard of dress are very like ours except that a duchess or a countess has more hereditary point lace and diamonds. The general style of dress perhaps is as simply elegant as ours. There is less superiority over us in manners and all social arts than I could have believed possible in a country where a large social class have been set aside for time immemorial to create, as it were, a social standard of high refinement.

"Our simple breakfast dress is unknown in England; you come down in the morning dressed for the day until six or seven in the evening when your dress is low neck and short sleeves for dinner. At this season the morning dress is rich silk or velvet, high body cut close in the throat with handsome collar and cuffs and always a cap. I adhere to a black watered silk with the simple cap I wear at home.

"For the Drawing-room my dress was of black velvet with a very rich bertha. A bouquet in the front of *fleurs-de-lis* like the coiffure, and a cachemire shawl. Head-dress of green leaves and white *fleurs-de-lis* with a white ostrich feather drooping on one side. I wear my hair now plain in front, and the wreath was very flat and classical in its effect. I have had the diamond pin and earrings which your father gave me reset and made into a magnificent brooch and so arranged that I can also wear it as a necklace or bracelet. On this occasion it was a necklace."

Describing a Court dinner at Buckingham Palace, Mrs. Bancroft continues:

" My dress was my currant-coloured or *grossaille* velvet with a wreath of white arum lilies woven into a kind of turban with green leaves, and bouquet to match in the bertha of Brussels lace.

" On the occasion of the Queen's Birthday Drawing-room I went dressed in white mourning. It was a petticoat of white crape flounced to the waist with the edges notched. A train of white glacé trimmed with a ruche of white crape. A wreath and bouquet of white lilacs without any green, as green is not used in mourning.

" My dress for the Queen's Ball was a white crape over white satin with flounces of white satin looped up with pink tuberoses. A wreath of tuberoses and bouquet for the corsage." *

Lady Stuart Wortley made an extensive tour in America and evidently found much to delight and interest her. Arriving in New York in the summer of 1849, she was at once attracted by the fashionable attire of the people and dismayed by the " hot weather."

" We soon saw some evidence of the warmth of a New York summer, in the profusion of light cool bonnets furnished with broad and deeply hanging curtains, shading and covering the throat and part of the shoulders, a very sensible costume for hot weather. The fashion just now seems to be for all the ladies to wear large white shawls. I never beheld such a number of white shawls mustered ; the female part of the population seem all *voueé au blanc.* It is very seldom you see any equestriennes in these Northern cities. Every lady chooses rather to walk or go in a carriage. Crowds of carriages, private and public, are to be seen in Broadway, passing and repassing every

---

* Letters from England, by Mrs. George Bancroft.

moment, filled with ladies beautifully dressed in the most elaborate Parisian toilets." *

A column in the "Lady's Book" (1849) tells of the winter fashions in Philadelphia :

" We will describe three or four of the prettiest costumes of the season, that our lady readers may gather from them some idea of Chestnut Street, and our fashionable concert-room, the Musical Fund Hall :—

" A walking dress of dark green cashmere, with three bias folds upon the skirt, graduating in depth, and edged with a narrow bias velvet binding of the same shade. Corsage and sleeves plain and tight, a velvet fold upon the short cap of the sleeve, and a corresponding trimming also about the throat. White cashmere long shawl folded carelessly. Bonnet of deep green velvet. Marie Stuart brim, edged with blond, and small plume of the same shade as the bonnet.

" A walking dress of rich brocade silk, blue figures upon a fawn-coloured ground. Sacque of fawn-coloured silk, richly embroidered in blue. Bonnet of blue uncut velvet, with folds and bands of the same, mixed with blond.

" Dinner dress of chameleon silk, blue and silver. A small Marie Stuart cap of blond with rosettes of pale blue satin ribbon."

A summer walking costume of 1849 is shown in the initial of this chapter. This dress is of foulard silk trimmed with rows of velvet ribbon at the edge of the flounces. The mantilla is of black lace and the bonnet of white crape trimmed with pink flowers and white satin ribbon.

" Evening Dress.—Crape robe of pale rose-colour, embroidered up the front of the skirt. Girdle of broad brocaded ribbon the same shade, with flowing ends. Hair arranged in

* Travels in the United States, by Lady Stuart Wortley.

FIGURE 174.—1804—Boy in suit of striped calico and ruffled shirt.

FIGURE 175.—1812—Little girl in a scarlet cloth pelisse and bonnet to match. Worn by Mary Brinton, of Philadelphia.

FIGURE 176.—1822—Girl in a buff cashmere gown with long white sleeves. A large hat with brown ribbon. From a contemporary print.

FIGURE 177.—1800—Small child in white muslin gown. From a plate.

FIGURE 178.—1818—Boy in striped duck pantaloons, dark blue jacket and waistcoat. Dark cloth cap with visor. From a contemporary plate.

FIGURE 179.—1826—Little boy in white dress embroidered in blue, over trousers of same material. From a contemporary portrait.

FIGURE 180.—1828—Little girl in pink gauze dress. Worn by Miss Elizabeth S. Smith, of Philadelphia.

FIGURE 181.—1831—Girl in green and white silk gown. Green silk apron. Large white bonnet of *Gros de Naples* with white ribbon. Hair in Kenwig plaits. From a plate.

FIGURE 182.—1832—Boy in high hat, brown kerseymere tunic, and white pantaloons. From a portrait.

FIGURE 183.—1834—Girl in figured lawn dress. Hair in plaits twisted and tied with lilac ribbon.

FIGURE 184.—1837—Little girl of eight in brown and white corded muslin. Bonnet from contemporary plate.

FIGURE 185.—1838—Boy of fourteen. High hat of grey, coat of bottle green, grey trousers.

FIGURE 186.—1848—Little boy of five. The waist is of turquoise blue merino, scalloped with yellow silk and buttoned down the back with gilt buttons. The trousers are of white jean, striped with black.

FIGURE 187.—1848—Little girl from fashion plate of this date. The dress is of pink cashmere trimmed with narrow pink velvet ribbon. Hat of Leghorn trimmed with pink roses and pink ribbon. Pale blue kid shoes.

FIGURE 189.—1856—Boy of three in costume taken from an Ambrotype. The jacket is of black velvet trimmed with black braid and the skirt of plaid poplin ornamented by strips of black velvet ribbon.

FIGURE 190.—1857—Girl of twelve taken from a fashion magazine. Cloak of blue grey cloth trimmed with black velvet. Hat of grey trimmed with blue ribbon and blue feathers. Skirt of old rose. Shoes brown.

FIGURE 191.—1853—Little boy from a Daguerreotype. Suit of brown merino ornamented with gold braid and gilt buttons.

FIGURE 192.—1861—Small child in blue cashmere dress with white apron tied with blue ribbon at the shoulders. From a photograph.

FIGURE 193.—1865—Boy in black velvet suit trimmed with black silk braid. From a photograph.

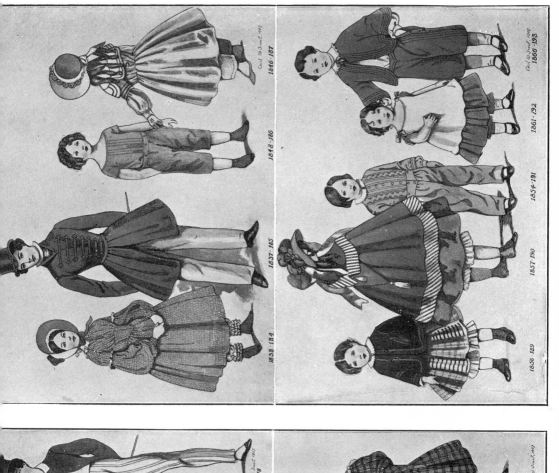

plain bands with a wreath of mingled sweetbrier and lily of the valley. The contrast of the two flowers is very delicate and beautiful. Robe imported by Levy, wreath by Madam Patot.

"The prettiest style of morning dresses are of cashmere."

The following note on caps and capes is taken from an American authority:

"No unmarried lady should wear a morning cap; it is the mark, the badge, if we may so call it, of the young matron. And if the wife cares as much for her husband's admiration after marriage as before it, she will never dispense with this tasteful, coquettish appendage to a morning toilette.

"There has been an attempt this season to make up delicate India muslin with triple embroidered frills of the same. These are quite simple and require only a bow and strings of some bright coloured ribbon to finish them. A pretty cap is composed of Guipure lace (or what is called Guipure), with a bow and band of ribbon and *noeuds* of the same each side of the face. These are all intended for plain house-costumes and may be worn with propriety by older ladies.

"Capes are rarely worn in the morning, and are more particularly suited to dinner or small evening companies. They are worn of all sizes and patterns, as may be seen from Figures 134, 139 and 233. A favourite style is of lace; Brussels or a fine imitation is allowable. The ribbon knot should correspond or contrast in colour with the dress over which the cape is worn."

Leghorn hats and bonnets were very fashionable in 1849. The "Lady's Book" for the summer of that date says:

"In trimming a Leghorn bonnet, the richest ribbon is required and it should be of some pale shade. Dark blue, green, or brown have a bad effect. White is the most suitable, and straw colour looks well. With white ribbon, small ostrich plumes tipped with marabout are often seen. Chip bonnets are next in cost, and perhaps first in beauty. Their purity allows them to be trimmed with almost anything the wearer's complexion will allow. Bouquets of French flowers fastened with knots of ribbon are graceful. Embroidered crape bonnets are the newest. They are both simple and elegant, and were introduced by Miss Wilson, one of the most fashionable Chestnut Street (Philadelphia) milliners, direct from Paris. The material is *crêpe lisse* of some delicate hue, with silk floss embroidery about the front and on the crown piece. The cape embroidered to correspond. Trimming very simple. The prettiest one we have seen was a pale green bonnet, with a bouquet of purple lilies on each side, the ribbon just crossing over the top of the bonnet; there was not a single bow in the whole arrangement. A tulle quilling and a single lily inside the brim. Mourning bonnets are of drawn crape, trimmed with crape ribbon which is a new material."

The following note on new fashions is also from the same authority :

" Slippers, as we have before said, threaten to supersede gaiters for the street. The toes are rounded, and the instep ornamented with a small bow, quite as our grandmothers recollect them.

" The hair is dressed considerably higher than formerly, and puffed, as in old pictures, over a cushion at the back. Combs are principally of shell with round tops, that curve close to the head at the side. They are valued according to the newness of the pattern, those which sold for fourteen dollars in the spring being only eight dollars now.

" A new style of dress is made with a double skirt lined with paper muslin, which has a facing of the silk eight inches in depth. Just over this comes the real skirt, the edge of which is scolloped, and bound; it does not meet at the waist, but opens over a plain breadth faced up the lining. This has exactly the effect of a tunic. Plain waists are still the rage, there being two seams each side the centre. Sleeves are mostly plain, or slightly full, with a band at the wrist. Belts are universally worn; some have them set into the dress."

Looking over the pages of the "Quarterly Review" we came across the following appreciation of the dress of the forties:

"The present dress has some features worth dwelling on more minutely. The gown is a good thing, both in its morning and evening form, and contains all necessary elements for showing off a fine figure and a graceful movement. There is something especially beautiful, too, in the expanse of chest and shoulder, as seen in a tight plain-coloured high dress, merino or silk, like a fair sloping sunny bank, with the long taper arms and the slender waist so tempting and convenient between them, that it is a wonder they are not perpetually embracing it themselves. And then the long full folds of the skirt which lie all close together above, like the flutings of an Ionic column, as if loth to quit that sweet waist, but expand gradually below as if fearing to fetter those fairy feet. And the gentle swinging of the robe from side to side, like a vessel in calmest motion, and the silver whisper of trailing silk. Flounces are a nice question. We like them when they wave and flow as in a very light material, muslin or gauze or barege, when a lady looks like a receding angel, or a dissolving view; but we do not like them in a rich material where they flop, or in a stiff one, where they bristle; and where they break the lines of the petticoat, and throw light and shade where you don't expect them. In short we like the gown that can do without flounces, as Josephine liked a face that could do without whiskers; but in either case it must be a good one. The plain black scarf is come of too graceful a parentage—namely, from the Spanish and Flemish mantilla—not to constitute one of the best features of the present costume. It serves to join the two parts of the figure together, enclosing the back and shoulders in a firm defined outline of their own, and flowing down gracefully in front, or on each side, to mix with that of the skirt. That man must be a monster who would be impertinent to a woman, but especially to a woman in a black scarf. It carries an air of self-respect with it which is in itself a protection. A woman thus attired glides on her way like a small close-reefed vessel, tight and trim, seeking no encounter but prepared for one. Much, however, depends on the wearer ; indeed no article of dress is such a revealer of the wearer's character. Some women will drag it tight up their shoulders, and stick out their elbows (which ought not to be known to exist) in defiance at you, beneath. Others let it hang loose and listless like an idle sail, losing all the beauty of the outline, both moral and physical. Such ladies have usually no opinions at all, but none the less a very obstinate will of their own. Some few of what are nowadays called mantillas, which are the Cardinals and Capuchins of a century ago, are pleasing and blameless. A black velvet one turned up with a broad dull black lace, the bright metal chased with dead, is very good. But whatever piece of dress conceals a woman's figure is bound in justice to do so in a picturesque way. That a shawl can never do with its stiff uniformity of pattern, each shoulder alike, and its stiff three-cornered shape behind with a scroll pattern standing straight up the centre of the back. If a lady sports a shawl at all, and only very falling shoulders should venture, we should recommend it to be always either falling off or putting on, which produces pretty action, or she should wear it up one shoulder and down the other, or in some way drawn irregularly, so as to break the uniformity."

Women's Dress

1850–1860

" Fashions that are now called new
Have been worn by more than you ;
Elder times had worn the same
Though the new ones get the name."
                                   —MIDDLETON.

NOTICEABLE feature of the dress of 1850 was the basque, a bodice with short skirt or tails below the waist line. According to the fashion plates of that period an attempt had been made to introduce this style of dress late in the forties, but it did not become a popular fashion until early in the fifties.

Basques made of velvet of some dark colour were worn with silk skirts of contrasting design. A black velvet basque which could be worn with any skirt was in almost every woman's wardrobe. Even riding habits were made in this popular style, as will be seen in the pages of " Punch " for 1850.

At that time Prince Albert had proposed to have the Industrial Palace built in Hyde Park, which would have spoiled the famous resort of English horsewomen, Rotten Row. The suggestion caused a flutter of indignation which found expression in the following verses :

245

" Then take our lives and spare our ride the only place we know,
  Where ladies pent in London for exercise can go.
  'Tis not with us as with our lords for they, the park beside,
  Have got the House of Commons where their hobbies they can ride.
  The Prince looked grim, it was his whim, humbugged he would not be,
  When lo ! a stately lady is kneeling at his feet
  I too would ride, she sweetly said, so Albert if you please
  Don't there's a darling, for my sake please don't cut down the trees."

India muslins, embroidered in colours, were popular at this period. In Figure 266 is given a picture of a dainty gown of this material which was worn in Philadelphia about 1853.

Chemisettes and undersleeves were still worn and were more or less elaborate for different occasions. Flounces were extremely popular; as many as five were worn at a time, the upper flounce being gathered in with the skirt at the waist.

Early in this decade a novel and very hideous costume was devised by Mrs. Bloomer, editor of a temperance journal in the United States, who went about the country giving lectures in 1851–1852, on Woman's Suffrage, and advertised the new dress henceforth known as the " Bloomer costume." By way of manifesting the independence of her sex she advised the women to adopt a part at least of the customary costume of the men. This was her idea of a reform in woman's dress :

" A skirt reaching to about half-way between the knees and the ankles and not very full. Underneath the skirt trousers moderately full, and in fair weather coming down to the ankle and there gathered in with an elastic band. The shoes or slippers to suit the occasion. For winter or wet weather the trousers should be fastened under the top of a boot reaching three or four inches above the ankle. This boot might be sloped gracefully at the upper edge and trimmed with fur or embroidery according to the taste of the wearer, the material might be cloth or morocco, and waterproof if desired."

The upper part of this costume was left to be determined by the individual fancy of the wearer. Mrs. Bloomer had a picture taken exemplifying her favourite dress, a copy of which is given in Figure 152. " The fashion," we read, " did not fail to make itself apparent in various parts of the United States." The " Washington Telegraph," the " Hartford Times," the " Syracuse Journal " and many other leading papers " noticed the adoption of the costume and generally with commendation." In the autumn of 1851 an American woman dressed in a black satin suit of jacket, skirt and trousers gave lectures in London urging the adoption of the reform dress, but succeeded only in raising a storm of merriment on the subject. Even in America the Bloomer costume soon became a thing of the past. In Figure 211 we give a photograph of a doll dressed in this eccentric fashion, which was the cherished plaything of a little Quaker girl in Pennsylvania.

The invention of Mrs. Bloomer was soon cast into oblivion by the marvellous creations of the beautiful Empress Eugénie, whose dresses became the envied models of the world of fashion in 1853. We read that " a glimpse of the Empress in the drive through the Bois de Boulogne sufficed to set the fair observers to work upon a faithful reproduction of her costume, and her toilette on the occasion of a ball at the Tuileries afforded food for thought during many days to those who had been present." At the civil marriage on the evening of January 29, 1853, which took place in comparative privacy, Eugénie wore a white satin gown trimmed with lace, with two rows of magnificent pearls around her neck, and flowers in her hair, and at the religious ceremony on the following morning, in Notre Dame, she wore a gown of white velvet with a long train covered with lace in a design of violets which is said to have been worth at least 30,000 francs. Around her waist was a belt of diamonds and

1806–1870

FIGURE 194.—1806—Boy in brown suit of kerseymere; collar and ankle ruffles of white cambric. Cap with full soft crown and visor. From a print.

FIGURE 195.—1807—Boy in short sleeved tunic of blue cloth over white full trousers. Black slippers and straw hat. Mother in short dress of jaconet muslin, black silk mantle trimmed with lace. Shirred muslin bonnet. Pagoda parasol. From a print.

FIGURE 196.—1822—Girl in dress of apricot gauze, worn in Philadelphia.

FIGURE 197.—1833—Boy in suit of brown kerseymere, white waistcoat and black tie. From a portrait.

FIGURE 198.—1833—Boy in leg-of-mutton trousers of green kerseymere. From a print.

FIGURE 200.—1860—Child's turban hat and feather. From a photograph.

FIGURE 201.—1862—Girl in a checked silk over a white guimpe. Braids tied at the back with a ribbon and ends. Gaiter boots. From a photograph.

FIGURE 202.—1862—Boy in a grey tweed suit and striped stockings. From a photograph.

FIGURE 203.—1806—Child's hat with straw buttons and strings of white ribbon. School of Industrial Art, Philadelphia.

FIGURE 204.—1864—Boy in a brown suit braided in black. Little girl in pale blue cashmere trimmed with quilled ribbon to match and worn over a white guimpe. From a plate.

FIGURE 205.—1861—Girl in a Zouave jacket and skirt. Hair in a net of chenille. From a photograph.

FIGURE 206.—1865—Boy of sixteen in a short round coat and long trousers. From a photograph.

FIGURE 207.—1870—Little girl of this date. From a fashion plate.

C.W.T. After Tin. 194

S.B.STEEL. 06. after a print 195

C.W. Trout 1907. 196

C.W.Trout 1907. 197

C W. Trout 198

C.W. Trout From Photograph. 200

203

C.W.Trout After Photograph 201

C.W.T. After Photograph 202

C.W. Trout After Photograph 204

C.W.TROUT. After Photograph. 205

C W T After Photograph 206

C.W.T. 1909. 207

she had the same coronet of brilliants which Marie Louise had worn on her wedding day, to which was fastened a long lace veil and a wreath of orange blossoms.

The description of the famous dressing-room of the Empress Eugénie at the Tuileries, with its revolving mirrors, etc., has often been recounted. On the upper floor over this dressing-room, and connected with it by a lift and a speaking tube, were the rooms set apart for her personal attendants and her wardrobe. " Separate rooms," we are told, " were devoted to hats and bonnets, boots and shoes, sunshades, dust cloaks. Each morning a life-sized doll made to resemble the figure of the Empress was carefully dressed in every particular and sent down by the lift and exhibited before her. In spite of the pains taken by the dressmakers and tailors to please her it was a rare occurrence for a gown to satisfy her entirely ; she criticized, altered and rejected incessantly until she succeeded in recomposing the costumes to her satisfaction." The second empire of the hoop-skirt was inaugurated in 1854, and in spite of jeers, jibes and caricatures held its sway over feminine taste to the exclusion of beauty and convenience. We read that " the first form of this invention was a whalebone skirt not unlike a bee-hive ; the largest circumference was around the hips whence the rest of the dress fell in perpendicular lines ; others preferred hoops arranged like those on a barrel." But the most popular form of hoop-skirt was made of graduated steel wires covered with a woven cotton netting held together by perpendicular straps of broad tape. A picture of a genuine skirt of this description is given in Figure 154. It was worn in Pennsylvania about 1856. More unassuming followers of fashion lined the edges of their gowns with horsehair and their flounces with stiff muslin. Petticoats were also made with casings around them at intervals, into which canes were run.

Numerous are the tales of accidents which happened to the wearers of the fashionable hoops. A very thrilling escape is recounted by Lady Neville in her recently published diary. She speaks of the offending garment as "that monstrosity the crinoline, which once came near costing me my life; in fact I only escaped a terrible fate through mercifully retaining my presence of mind. It was in the drawing-room one evening after dinner, before the gentlemen had joined us there, that my dress caught fire. I was showing a lady an engraving of Mr. Cobden which he had just given me and which hung over the fireplace. Somehow or other my voluminous skirt caught fire and in an instant I was in a blaze, but I kept my presence of mind, and rolling myself in the hearth rug by some means or other eventually put out the flames. None of the ladies present could of course come to assist me for their enormous crinolines rendered them almost completely impotent to deal with fire." *

In Watson's "Annals" (1856) a caustic arraignment of this fashion appeared under the heading "Hoops Again":

"We had hoped that our ladies would never again be brought to use such ill-looking, useless and deforming appendages to their dresses. They are, too, so annoying and engrossing of place and room in omnibuses, rail cars, and in church pews and aisles, and why all this; but as spellbound subservients to some foreign spell; one feels scandalized for 'the Land of the Free!' Nor is this all. Ladies who profess to be Christians and communicants too, pledged 'to renounce the vain pomp and vanities of the world, and not to be led thereby,' go up to the sacramental altar, showing before the eyes of all beholders an unseemly vanity!"

The prices current in Philadelphia in 1856 provoked the aged annalist to an outburst of righteous indignation:

* Reminiscences of Lady Dorothy Neville.

"Extravagance in Dress

"At this time a fashionable dry goods store advertises a lace scarf for 1,500 dollars! Another has a bridal dress for 1,200 dollars. Bonnets at 200 dollars are also sold. Cashmeres from 300 dollars and upwards are seen by dozens along Broadway. And 100 dollars is quite a common price for a silk gown. Think of such a scale of prices for 'un-ideaed' American women! Can the pampering of such vanities elevate the character of our women?"

"The Rise and Fall of Crinoline" is delightfully set forth in "Punch." Figure 153 is copied from a cartoon of 1857, and shows, besides the crinoline, the fashionable wrap and bonnet. A glimpse of a head-dress of bows of ribbons, which was also characteristic of the period, is shown on the left side of the picture.

The dress shown in Figures 255 and 268 is made of a rich lustrous silk which stands out by itself, although it was evidently assisted by crinoline in the days of its youth. The prevailing colour is brown, the alternate stripes being a cross-bar pattern of two shades of brown, and a pattern of variegated roses *en chiné*. The trimmings are, according to the fashion of the fifties, made to match the dress, the colours brown and pink being woven into the fringe and the guimpe heading. The lace collar and the brooch are also copied from originals and were worn in Philadelphia in 1855. The hair is taken from a contemporary portrait.

Deep collars were worn at this time (see Figure 255) and bonnets were shallower in the crown and worn back from the face as in Figures 149, 268 and 269.

Cashmere shawls and inexpensive imitations of them were worn very generally throughout the fifties. A very beautiful specimen of the former is shown in the initial to this chapter.

It was worn in Philadelphia by Mrs. Emlen Cresson. Tunisian shawls, manufactured from silk refuse and usually woven in stripes of two colours, were worn in summer, and a very graceful wrap, the Algerian *burnous*, was introduced at this time, and became a favourite garment for theatre wear. The material was a mixture of silk and goat's hair, and the full flowing lines of this Arab mantle with a sort of hood finished with a tassel, were not ungraceful even over the fashionable hooped skirt. Beaver hats with long ostrich feathers were worn by young ladies in 1859. At least one American girl bears witness to this fashion :

"I wonder if my descendants, should they ever read these memoirs, will be shocked at the levity of an ancestress who frankly acknowledges that the most vivid recollection left in her mind is a grey merino pelisse and black beaver hat and plumes, with which her small person was decked during the winter of 1859." *

The fashionable shape for several years was a shallow crown and soft, wide drooping brim like the picture of a fine straw hat trimmed with ribbon copied from a fashion plate of 1857 given in Figure 253 and the soft felt hat in Figure 258.

Mrs. Clay, the wife of the Senator from Alabama, spent many years in Washington at that prosperous and pleasant period of American history, "before the war." In her most entertaining Diary she gives very valuable notes on the fashions of the fifties, although we may not agree with her in pronouncing them "graceful and picturesque."

"In 1858–59 the hair was arranged on the top of the head in heavy braids, wound like a coronet, over the head (Figure 255), and the coiffure was varied now and then with a tiara of velvet and pearls, or jet, or coral. Ruffled dresses gave place to panelled skirts in which two materials, a plain and embossed or

* A Southern Girl in 1861.

brocaded fabric, were combined, and basques with postillion backs became the order of the day. The low-coiled hair, with brow free from frizzes and bangs, was the style adopted by such prominent beauties as Mrs. Pugh and Mrs. Pendleton, who in Lord Napier's opinion had the most classic head he had seen in America. Low necks and lace berthas, made fashionable because of their adoption by Miss Lane,* were worn almost universally, either with open sleeves revealing inner ones of filling lace, or sleeves of the shortest possible form allowing the rounded length of a pretty arm to be seen in all its perfection. Evening gloves were of half length only, or as often reaching half way to the elbow. They were of kid or silk with backs embroidered in delicate silks with now and then a jewel sparkling among the colours. Our gloves and our fans and handkerchiefs and bonnets and the larger part of our dress accessories, as well as such beautiful gown patterns as were purchased ready to be made up by a New York or Washington dressmaker, were all imported directly from foreign houses and the services of our travelling and consular friends were in constant requisition for the selection of fine lace shawls, flounces, undersleeves and other fashionable garnitures. Scarcely a steamer but brought to the Capital dainty boxes of Parisian flowers, bonnets and other foreign novelties despatched by such interested deputies."†

Speaking of shopping in Washington, another gifted woman of the South has recorded her own experiences in a book which we venture to say will always hold a high place among contemporary histories of that unhappy period of our national life. ‡

" . . . There were few shops. But such shops! There was Galt's, where the silver, gems and marbles were less attract-

---

* Niece of President Buchanan.
† A Belle of the Fifties : Memoirs of Mrs. Clay, 1855–56.
‡ Reminiscences of Peace and War, by Mrs. Roger A. Pryor.

ive than the cultivated gentlemen who sold them; Gautier's,
the palace of sweets, with Mrs. Gautier in an armchair before
her counter to tell you the precise social status of every one of
her customers and, what is more, to put you in your own; Harper's, where the dainty, leisurely salesman treated his laces with
respect, drawing up his cuffs lest they touch the ethereal
beauties; and the little corner shop of stern Madame Delarue,
who imported as many (and no more) hats and gloves as she
was willing to sell as a favour to the ladies of the diplomatic
and official circles, and whose dark-eyed daughter, Léonide
(named for her godmother, a Greek lady of rank), was sus-
ceptible of unreasoning friendships and could be coaxed to preserve certain treasures for humbler folk.

"Léonide once awoke me in the middle of the night with a
note bidding me 'come *toute de suite*,' for '*Maman*' was asleep;
the boxes had arrived and she and I could peep at the bonnets
and choose the best one for myself. Thus it was that I once
bore away a 'divine creation' of point lace, crape and shaded
asters before Madame had seen it. Otherwise it would have
been reserved for Miss Harriet Lane or Mrs. Douglas. Madame
had to know later; and Léonide was not much in evidence the
rest of that season. At Madame Delarue's, if one was very
gentil, very *convenable*, one might have the services of François,
the one and only hair-dresser of note, who had adjusted coronets
on noble heads, and who could (if so minded) talk of them
agreeably in Parisian French."

"Le Follet" was the great Parisian authority whose dictates
were published every month not only in England but also in
the United States. At the close of this decade, a tendency
to exaggeration in the prevailing fashions may be noticed
which called forth the following satire from Mr. Punch: *

* Punch, 1859.

"From 'Le Follet' of this month, we have the pleasure of learning that 'the robes are generally made with five or seven flounces, the top one not reaching higher than the knee.' This is extremely moderate, and husbands, with incomes under £300 a year, will be delighted to learn that the number is so limited. For ourselves, we think 'seven flounces' positively absurd, and you might as well have none at all, if they are not to go any higher than the knee. We had hoped to see a lady who was all flounces—a regular muslin *La Scala*, tier upon tier of flounces rising right up to the proscenium. The time was when you could not distinguish the dress from the profusion of the trimmings. If they keep falling off in this way, we shall soon be able to see what the pattern of a lady's dress is like.

"Further on 'Le Follet' tells us confidentially that it 'prefers a skirt completely *bouillonneé*, notwithstanding the inconvenience of its holding the dust.' We do not know what *bouillonnée* exactly means. We are perfectly aware that *bouillon* means broth, but still it is a mystery to us how any one can prefer a skirt that is *bouillonéed* all over, for we have noticed ladies, who at dinner have had a little soup spilt over their dress, look as though they did not altogether like it; nor can we see how 'broth' and 'dust' would go very well together. Supposing they do, the recommendation of this new fashion seems to be that it enables every lady to be her own Dust Carrier. The scavengers ought to be very much obliged to them.

"With regard to bonnets we are informed that 'thin bonnets are usually made with double curtains.' Why not have your bonnet like an old four-post bedstead, with curtains all round it? It would be much cooler, though we have a difficulty in seeing what great use there is in having a bonnet at all, when you have a couple of curtains to hide it! We cannot help star-

1829–1855

FIGURE 208.—1829—Paper doll of this date and her outfit.

FIGURE 209.—1840—Doll in wedding dress and veil.

FIGURE 210.—1855—Patent-headed doll in pantalettes.

FIGURE 211.—1851—Wax doll in Bloomer costume.

208

209

210

211

ing also at the notion of a 'thin bonnet.' The thinness may be in consequence of the weather."

The custom of wearing mourning has always been combated by the masculine mind. Trollope's veiled satire on the conventional costume of an English widow is a touch of nature that awakens an echo of kinship in men the whole world over. We recall Mrs. Greenow in " Can You Forgive Her ":

" The Widow was almost gorgeous in her weeds. I believe that she had not sinned in her dress against any of those canons which the semi-ecclesiastical authorities on widowhood have laid down for outward garments fitted for gentlemen's relicts. The materials were those which are devoted to the deepest conjugal grief. As regarded every item of the written law her *suttee* worship was carried out to the letter. There was the widow's cap, generally so hideous, so well known to the eyes of all men, so odious to womanhood. Let us hope that such head-gear may have some assuaging effect on the departed spirits of husbands. There was the dress of deep, clinging, melancholy crape, of crape which becomes so brown and so rusty, and which makes the six months' widow seem so much more afflicted a creature than she whose husband is just gone, and whose crape is therefore new. There were the trailing weepers, and the widow's kerchief pinned close round her neck, and somewhat tightly over her bosom. But there was that of genius about Mrs. Greenow, that she had turned every seeming disadvantage to some special profit, and had so dressed herself that though she had obeyed the law to the letter, she had thrown the spirit of it to the winds. Her cap sat jauntily on her head, and showed just so much of her rich brown hair as to give her the appearance of youth which she desired. . . . She spent more money, I think, on new crape than she did on her brougham. It never became brown and rusty with her, or formed itself into old lumpy folds, or shaped itself round her like a grave cloth. The written law had not interdicted crinoline, and she loomed as large with weeds, which with her were not sombre, as she would do with her silks when the period of her probation should be over. Her weepers were bright with newness, and she would waft them aside from her shoulder with an air which turned even them into auxiliaries. Her kerchief was fastened close round her neck and close over her bosom; but Jeannette well knew what she was doing as she fastened it, and so did Jeannette's mistress."

In Figure 271, a *peignoir* or house gown of pink cachemire, trimmed with a Persian border, is given. It opens over a white embroidered petticoat. The sleeves are full, showing white undersleeves at the wrist. In Figure 264 a mantilla of black velvet, trimmed with Chantilly lace, pictures a fashionable outdoor garment in the fifties.

Women's Dress
1860-1870

" L'acoutumace nous rend familier
Ce que nous parassait terrible et singulier."

IN the year 1860 Fashion had set its seal on the most exaggerated form of the hoop-skirt. We are told that it was not really ungraceful when first introduced by the Empress Eugénie, but there was no grace whatever about the hoop-skirt of the sixties. From our point of view, accustomed to many years of clinging draperies, it seems almost incredible that women of judgment and taste could ever have adopted this monstrosity of Fashion. Nevertheless there are reams of contemporary evidence to prove that it was universally worn and by women of all classes. A popular song runs thus :

" Now crinoline is all the rage with ladies of whatever age,
A petticoat made like a cage—oh, what a ridiculous fashion !
'Tis formed of hoops and bars of steel, or tubes of air which lighter
    feel,
And worn by girls to be genteel, or if they've figures to conceal.
It makes the dresses stretch far out a dozen yards or so about,
And pleases both the thin and stout—oh, what a ridiculous fashion ! "

The noted historian, McCarthy, in his " Portraits of the Sixties," although not without prejudice in matters of much greater importance, bears such witness to the prodigious spread of the crinoline in circumference and popular esteem as cannot be denied.   We give his animadversion in his own words :

" There is one peculiarity belonging to the early sixties which I cannot leave out of notice, although assuredly it has little claim to association with art or science, with literature or politics.   The early sixties saw in this and most other civilized countries the reign of crinoline.   It is well for the early sixties that they had so many splendid claims to historical recollection, but it may be said of them that if they had bequeathed no other memory to a curious and contemplative posterity, the reign of crinoline would still have secured for them an abiding-place in the records of human eccentricities.   I may say, without fear of contradiction, that no one who was not living at the time can form any adequate idea of the grotesque effect produced on the outer aspects of social life by this article of feminine costume.   The younger generation may turn over as much as it will the pages of ' Punch,' which illustrate the ways and manners of civilization at that time, but with all the undeniable cleverness and humour of ' Punch's' best caricatures, the younger generation can never fully realize what extraordinary exhibitions their polite ancestresses made of themselves during that terrible reign of crinoline.   .   .   .   The fashion of crinoline defied caricature for the actual reality was more full of unpicturesque and burlesque effects than any satirical pencil could realize on a flat outspread sheet of paper.   The fashion of crinoline, too, defied all contemporary ridicule.   A whole new school of satirical humour was devoted in vain to the ridicule of crinoline.   The boys in the streets sang comic songs to make fun of it, but no street bellowings of contempt could incite the wearers of this most inconvenient and hideous article of dress to condemn themselves to clinging draperies.   Crinoline, too, created a new sort of calamity all its own. Every day's papers gave us fresh accounts of what were called crinoline accidents, cases, that is to say, in which a woman was severely burned or burned to death because of some flame of fire or candle catching her distended drapery at some unexpected moment. There were sacrifices made to the prevailing fashion which would have done the sufferers immortal honour if they had been made for the sake of bearing some religious or political emblem condemned by ruling and despotic authorities. Its inconvenience was felt by the male population as well as by the ladies who sported the obnoxious construction. A woman getting out of a carriage, an omnibus, or a train, making her way through a crowded room, or entering into the stalls of a theatre, was a positive nuisance to all with whom she had to struggle for her passage. The hoop-petticoats of an earlier generation were moderate in their dimensions and slight in the inconvenience they caused when compared with the rigid and enormous structure in which our ladies endeavoured to conform to the fashion set up by the Empress of the French. I remember well seeing a great tragic queen of opera going through a thrilling part at one of the lyric theatres. Her crinoline was of ultra-expansion, was rigid and unyielding in its structure as the mail corselet of the Maid of Orleans. The skirt of silk or satin spread over it, so symmetrically and so rigidly conformed to the outlines of the crinoline that it seemed as if it were pasted to the vast arrangement beneath. The thrill and tragedy of the part were wholly lost on me. I could only see the unpicturesque absurdity of the exhibition. I could feel no sympathy with the dramatic sufferings of the melodious heroine thus enclosed. Every movement and rush of passion, of prayer, of wild despair, or distracted love was lost on me, for each change of posture only brought into more striking display the fact that I was looking at a slight and graceful woman boxed up in some sort of solid barrel of preposterous size over which her skirt was artificially spread. To this day I can only think of that glorious singer as of a woman for some reason compelled to exhibit herself on the stage with a barrel fastened round her waist. A lyrical heroine jumping in a sack would have been graceful and reasonable by comparison. Do what we will, we who lived in those days cannot dissociate our memories of the crinoline from our memories of the women of the period." *

The obnoxious hoop-skirt was usually made of graduated rows of steel wire with a woven cotton casing, held together by broad strips of tape running lengthwise. It was collapsible and very easily broken, adding another inconvenience to its use. The earlier form of reeds run into casings made in a petticoat of cotton, proved to be too heavy and clumsy, and was almost entirely abandoned in 1860.

Mrs. Pryor narrates an adventure during the Civil War, of which the derided hoop-skirt was the heroine.

" One day I was in an ambulance, driving on one of the interminable lanes of the region, the only incident being the watery crossing over the ' cosin,' as the driver called the swamps that had been ' Poquosin ' in the Indian tongue. Behind me came a jolting two-wheeled cart, drawn by a mule and driven by a small negro boy, who stood in front with a foot planted firmly upon each of the shafts. Within and completely filling the vehicle, which was nothing more than a box on wheels, sat a dignified-looking woman. The dame of the ambulance at once became fascinated by a small basket of sweet potatoes which the dame of the cart carried on her lap.

" With a view to acquiring these treasures, I essayed a tenta-

* Portraits of the Sixties, by Justin McCarthy.

tive conversation upon the weather, the prospects of a late spring, and finally the scarcity of provisions and consequent sufferings of the soldiers.

"After a keen glance of scrutiny the market woman exclaimed: 'Well, I am doing all I can for them! I know you won't speak of it. Look here!'

"Lifting the edge of her hooped petticoat, she revealed a roll of army cloth, several pairs of cavalry boots, a roll of crimson flannel, packages of gilt braid and sewing silk, cans of preserved meats, and a bag of coffee! She was on her way to our own camp, right under the General's nose! Of course I should not betray her, I promised. I did more. Before we parted she had drawn forth a little memorandum book and had taken a list of my own necessities. She did not 'run the blockade' herself. She had an agent, 'a dear, good Suffolk man,' who would fill my order on his next trip."

Another hoop-skirt story seems worthy of repetition and offers a practical suggestion to the Women's Society for the Prevention of Cruelty to Animals. A young lady in San Francisco dressed in the height of the fashion of the summer of 1865, which of course included a wide-spreading crinoline, was out walking and had with her a pet spaniel, for whose protection she had neglected to take out a license. Suddenly the dog catchers, with their horrible paraphernalia of nets, etc., and followed as usual by a mob of idle boys and men, came into sight, and in a few minutes the officials of the law confronted the young lady and tried to seize her dog. Tilting her hoop-skirt a little to one side, she called the dog who wisely took refuge under the protecting shelter that offered, and with flaming cheeks, the lady held her ground despite the vituperation of the dog catchers. The crowd cheered her with shouts of " Good for you, Lady," " Don't let them have him, Lady," etc., and

1824–1860

FIGURE 212.—1853—Infant's shirt of linen cambric.

FIGURE 213.—1835—Child's spencer of white linen, shirred on the shoulders and with leg-of-mutton sleeves.

FIGURE 214.—1860—Child's shirt of linen cambric.

FIGURE 215.—1855—Christening robe.　Worn in Philadelphia.

FIGURE 216.—1837—Costume of light brown cashmere.　Bonnet to match. Worn in Philadelphia.

FIGURE 217.—1824—Infant's dress of fine cambric trimmed with tiny rows of cording and a ruffle.

FIGURE 218.—1826—Infant's robe trimmed with insertion and edge of English eyelet embroidery.

FIGURE 219.—1860—Child's blue kid shoes with strings.

FIGURE 220.—1837—Baby in a long cloak of fawn-coloured cloth.

212 C.W.TROUT

213 C.W.TROUT

214 C.W.TROUT
1907.

215 C.W.Trout
1907.

216 J.B.Stiel
1906
after a photo.

217 C.W.TROUT
1907.

218

219

220 C.W.Trout
1907.

finally the enemy retreated and the lady took her dog into her arms and fled homeward.

The reign of the hoop-skirt was beginning to decline in 1865, and the change for the better was joyously recorded by " Punch."

" RHYMES TO DECREASING CRINOLINE
" With exceeding satisfaction
A remarkable contraction
Of thy petticoat our eyes have lately seen ;
The expanse of ladies' dress,
Thank its yielding arbitress,
Growing beautifully less,
Crinoline."

A maker in London offered a prize of a hundred guineas for the best poem on the hoop-skirt by way of advertising the garment, and with the purpose of keeping it in favour. This fashion " finally and reluctantly disappeared " about the time that the rule of the beautiful Empress and the Second Empire of France was drawing to a close.

As we will see by the following story, vouched for by a contemporary, the fame of one crinoline outlived its fragile frame.

" Some time after the close of the Civil War, about 1869–70, a story was published by a Northern writer of a somewhat facetious nature, purporting to explain the failure of the Southern cause. The title as well as can be remembered was ' How the Southern Confederacy Was Lost,' and the story was about as follows : In the South during the war it was very hard for the women, shut off as they were, to keep up with the fashions in dress. From time to time an illustrated paper or magazine would get within the lines, showing what was being worn in the outside world. This was quite provoking as many of the things were not to be had in the Confederacy. Among others, the hoop-skirt of the period, made of steel wire woven into a cotton cover, was much coveted and very hard to get.   In a certain part of the South it was the ambition of a young lady to obtain one of these much-wished-for garments, shall we call them? and after much trouble and a large expenditure of paper money, the object was achieved.   Here, as they say on the play bills, 'a period' is supposed to have elapsed and the erstwhile stylish and proud fabric of steel and cotton has suffered the inevitable fate, and, although mended and tied up in places, is at last, sad to say, no longer a sustaining force, but rather a depressed object, and from the amount of cotton casing considered more fit for the rag bag than the metal scrap heap.   Now it happened that a critical time had come in the history of the South.   It was becoming more and more evident that without foreign recognition, the effort to establish a nation would fail. A ray of hope came; it was reported that England would not only recognize them, but would take millions of their bonds, and everything was hurried with the object of getting these bonds out as quickly as possible.   In fact, it was declared that they must be ready on a certain day for shipment on an English ship which could not remain beyond a certain date.   The paper mills were working night and day making the paper for the bonds, then they were to be printed, signed and shipped, but alas, a catastrophe occurred.   Among the rags now being made into paper was what remained of the old hoop-skirt and still sticking to part of the webbing there was a small piece of the steel wire.   Need we tell more?   This, getting into the machinery, soon ruined it; no more machines could be procured, the works stopped, and before matters could be again arranged, the ship for England had to sail and the hopes of the Confederacy were blasted forever."

This period, known in the history of our country by the ambiguous title of the "Civil War," offers for our observation two sides to the question of dress, as well as of politics. With the latter we need not meddle, but the picture of the restricted social life of the South and the economies in dress practised by the once most fashionable element of our people is very interesting.

While pathetic scenes were being enacted in camp, the ladies of Richmond were entertaining, dressing, and dancing by way of keeping up their courage.

"President and Mrs. Davis gave a large reception last week, and the ladies looked positively gorgeous. Mrs. Davis is in mourning for her father." *

During the progress of the war Mrs. Pryor was reduced to finding some means of feeding her household, and, out of a trunkful of "before the war" finery, which had been long stored away, manufactured articles of lingerie, collars, undersleeves, neckties, etc., which brought good prices in the inflated Confederate currency. In her endeavour to keep in the neighbourhood of General Pryor's brigade, she stopped for a while at Petersburg, and describes the ingenuity of the women there.

Mrs. Pryor also mentions the advanced prices during the war times in the Southern states.

Calico of the commonest kind in those days was sold at twenty-five dollars a yard, "and we women of the Confederacy cultivated such an indifference to Paris fashions as would have astonished our former competitors in the Federal capital."

Invention, that clever daughter of Necessity, devised a costume for a Southern belle (for in peace or in war the women of Dixie were always belles) which made such an impression on an English newspaper correspondent, that he sent a description of it to his London paper. This was a gown of unbleached

* Reminiscences of Peace and War.

muslin (made at Macon, Georgia) and trimmed with gourd seed buttons dyed crimson.

" My Petersburg beauties were all wearing hats of their own manufacture, the favourite style being the Alpine with a pointed crown. For trimming, very soft and lovely flowers were made of feathers, the delicate white feather with a tuft of fleecy marabout at its stem. The marabout tuft should be carefully drawn off, to be made into swansdown trimming. A wire was prepared and covered with green paper for a stem, a little ball of wax fastened at the end, and covered with a tiny tuft of the down for a centre, and around this the feathers were stuck, with incurving petals for apple blossoms, and half open roses, and reversed for camelias. Neatly trimmed and suitably tinted, these flowers were handsome enough for anybody, and were in great demand. Cock's plumes were also used on hats, iridescent, and needing no colouring."

The becoming fashion of wearing black velvet around the throat was revived in 1860, a gold locket or a jewel pendant usually being worn on it in the evening. Gold chains and rows of gold beads were also very popular.

A prevalent style of coiffure during the ten years between 1860–1870 was popularly known as the waterfall. A frame of horsehair was attached to the back of the head by an elastic, and the back hair brushed smoothly over it, the ends caught up underneath. A net was usually worn over this " chignon " to keep the hair in place. Often the whole structure was made of false hair and fastened on with hairpins. Augustus Hare tells a good story about a " waterfall " or " chignon " of this kind. " How well I remember the Aumales riding through the green avenues near Ossington ; Mary Boyle was with them. She was a most excellent horsewoman, but a great gust of wind came and the whole edifice of her ' chignon ' was blown off before she could stop it. The little Prince de Condé was very young and he was riding with her. He picked it up and said, 'I will keep it in my pocket and then when we reach Thorsby you can just go quietly away and put it on '—and so she did."

Many illustrations of this arrangement are given in "Punch." In Figure 140 the back hair is done in a "waterfall," and in Figure 168 the hair under the net is arranged over a horsehair rouleau attached to the head by a narrow elastic cord. The latter was generally adopted by schoolgirls, and was very easily adjusted.

"In the arrangement of the hair," says an acknowledged American authority of this period, " regard ought to be paid to the style of the features as well as to the general appearance of the wearer. When the features are large or strongly marked, the hair should be arranged in masses, in large curls or well defined bows, so as to harmonize with the general cast of the countenance. If, on the contrary, the features are small and delicate, the greatest care should be taken not to render too striking the contrast between them and the magnitude of the head-dress. Small and delicately formed curls or ringlets, braids, or light and airy bows are the most pleasing varieties for this style. The features of the greater number of young ladies, however, cannot be classed under either of these extremes. When such is the case, the fancy of the individual is of course allowed greater latitude, but ought to be no less subject to the dictates of taste."

While on the subject of hair, it is interesting to note that " Miss Reed (of Tennessee) was the original girl with a curl in the middle of her forehead," the "coquettish item of coiffure" being speedily imitated by a hundred other girls in Washington.

A new fashion in 1866, introduced by Eugénie, was known as the " Empress peplin." It consisted of a belt with basque tails cut square in front and back and very long at the sides.

A French authority remarked of this innovation : " The peplin marks an epoch in history, and deserves our gratitude, for with it crinoline was decidedly an anomaly and its fall was assured."

Nets for the hair (Figure 168) and the still popular *en tout cas*, between a parasol and an umbrella, were also novelties stamped by the approval of the Empress.   Not the least popular of the fashions adopted by this lady was the arrangement of hair which is still known by her name.   A photograph is given (Figure 138) showing the curls hanging from the coil at the back, etc.   The Empress was a most accomplished equestrienne, and for this exercise preferred an almost masculine costume. The long full skirt was worn over grey cloth trousers and on her feet were patent leather boots with high heels and spurs. The curls were concealed by a trig coil of braids under the long plume of her hat.   It was, we are told, her custom to ride astride and she " despised the side saddle ordinarily used by her sex."

A contemporary American authority speaks of " Foulard," a silk first introduced in 1860 which still retains popular favour.

" In the foulards for ordinary wear, pansies, clusters of berries, fruit, as the cherry and plum, are among the newest designs."

Specimens of the fashions in bonnets of this decade are illustrated in Figures 282 and 283 from originals in the interesting collection of Miss Dutihl in Memorial Hall, Philadelphia.   One of these bonnets (Figure 282) is made of emerald green velvet with a brim of white bengaline, a full trimming next the face of blond lace, green velvet and white roses, and two sets of strings, one of white ribbon and the other of green velvet.   The other (Figure 283) is of brown horsehair braid and brown silk with a quilling of the same.   White tulle, black velvet ribbon and red poppies inside the brim.

These bonnets are much flatter on top and more open at the ears than formerly. A variety of fancy braids, and some delicately fine Dunstables and split French straws were popular. We find the following under the heading " Spring Bonnets " :

" A Neapolitan braid, grey and white, trimmed with Solferino and grey ribbon drawn into rosettes on one side, with straw centres, which give them much the appearance of poppies, a long loop of ribbon and two straw tassels complete the trimming of the left side, and on the other side the ribbon is drawn down perfectly plain. The cape and front of the bonnet are finished with a puffing of Solferino crape.

" An English chip bonnet, with pansy-coloured velvet cape. On the right side of the bonnet are two bows of pansy ribbon worked with gold stars, and on the other a large bunch of scarlet flowers.

" Fine split straw with dark crown, trimmed with a sapphire blue ribbon and a white ribbon. On the right side of the bonnet is a large water-lily with buds and leaves. The inside trimming is a roll of sapphire blue velvet, black tabs, and a small lily on one side.

" A Tuscan braid trimmed on one side with white ribbon bound with black velvet, and black lace rosettes with jet centres, and on the left side are handsome jet tassels fastened by medallions of white gimp. The inside trimming is in a puffing of white illusion, and large black rosettes with jet pendants. This is a beautiful style of bonnet for light mourning." *

Hats were very small in the sixties. The mushroom hat of 1907 is a revival of a style introduced in 1862. Another shape much worn at that time had a round crown and small rolling brim, and was usually trimmed with a drooping ostrich feather. Illustrations of both these fashionable hats are given in

* Godey's Lady's Book (1861).

1808–1830

FIGURE 222.—1808—Specimen of hand-painted trimming, a popular fancy-work in the first quarter of the nineteenth century. Chinese shawl of muslin embroidered in a design of pagodas and trees. White mull shawl. White satin slippers. Part of the wedding outfit of Miss Lydia Leaming, worn in Philadelphia.

FIGURE 223.—1808—Wedding veil, fan and reticule. Linen gloves cut out and sewn by hand.

FIGURE 224.—1808—Black lace scarf.

1820—Three-cornered shawl.

FIGURE 225.—1810—Baby dress.

1830—Embroidered pelisse.

222

225

223

224

Figures 163 and 165 and in Figure 169 will be seen the picture
of a walking hat decorated with a feather which came into
favour in 1865, and was celebrated in the following verses of a
popular song:

"THE JOCKEY HAT AND FEATHER

" As I was walking out, one day,
    Thinking of the weather,
I saw a pair of roguish eyes
    'Neath a hat and feather ;
She looked at me, I looked at her,
    It made my heart pit-pat,
Then, turning round, she said to me,
    How do you like my hat ?

" CHORUS—Oh ! I said ; it's gay and pretty too ;
        They look well together,
        Those glossy curls and Jockey hat,
        With a rooster feather.

" She wore a handsome broadcloth basque,
    Cut in the latest fashion,
And flounces all around her dress
    Made her look quite dashing ;
Her high-heeled boots, as she walk'd on,
    The pavement went pit-pat,
I will ne'er forget the smile I saw,
    Beneath the Jockey hat.

" CHORUS—Oh ! I said," etc.

The pork-pie was the name of another style of hat. It was
not unlike the turban hat in shape, but there was a little space
between the brim and crown. (See Figure 164.)

In the year 1863, the game of croquet was introduced and
became very popular on both sides of the ocean. " Punch " has
described it in the following verses:

"CROQUET

"Aid me, ye playful nymphs that flit around
   The Pegs and Hoops of every Croquet ground !
   Ye gentle spirits do not mock, nor blame
   My humble efforts to describe the Game.
   Eight's the full complement of players : more
   Than six is bad, I think ; let two or four
   Of equal skill for Croquet's laurels fight,
   This the best form of game.   Say, am I right?
   Let Messrs. Robinson and Jones choose sides ;
   Miss Smith, Miss Brown ; perchance their future **brides,**
   Events do happen strange as those we read,
   And Croquet may to Hymen's Altar lead.
   Jones wins the toss, and cunning dog, forthwith,
   Takes for his partner blonde Miss Emmy Smith,
   While Robinson, who'd just begun to frown,
   Looks happy and selects brunette Miss Brown.
   On Emmy, Blue her partner's care bestows,
   And her with Yellow does Brunette oppose ;
   Jones chooses Green ; two laugh : 'he laughs who wins' :
   To Robinson the Red : and Red begins."

A croquet costume is shown in Figure 166 from a fashion book of 1868, in which the dress is made with an apron front and looped up over a gay coloured under petticoat and the high walking boots are finished with a silk tassel at the ankle. A short sacque or loose jacket is worn with this dress, and a small hat with a long ostrich feather falling over the hair.

In Figure 246 illustrations of shoes worn during the sixties are given. Congress gaiters were made of cloth and, instead of opening up the front, were finished with a broad piece of elastic on each side. They were cut rather low, and were made in different colours and tipped with patent leather. Balmoral boots, depicted in Figure 166, were very popular. They laced up the front and were considered very stylish, and were effectively worn in the game of croquet, or with seaside costume. A sketch by Leech in "Punch" has the following squib printed underneath it :

"That the mermaids of our beaches do not end in ugly tails,
　　Nor have homes among the corals, but are shod with neat balmorals,
　　An arrangement no one quarrels with,
　　As many might with seals."

A riding habit of 1865 is given in the initial at the beginning of this chapter. It is taken from a contemporary English print. It is similar to the costume worn by Queen Victoria as represented in the equestrian statue at Liverpool. Several attractive riding habits are described in the magazines of the sixties :

A black cloth with a long basque with revers in front, standing white collar with cherry silk necktie. Black felt hat with dark blue grenadine veil.

A blue cloth habit made with a square coat tail in the back, and point in front. Standing linen collar with necktie of white muslin. Black straw hat with blue feathers.

Habit of grey cloth made with a short point back and front. Standing collar and blue silk necktie. Veil of grey tissue.

Among other innovations introduced in this decade was the Garibaldi blouse, which for a while attained great popularity in America as well as in Europe. Two new colours which mark that dramatic period of Garibaldi's career, "Solferino" and "Magenta," were in favour during the sixties. A costume worn by Eugénie, grey woolen skirt looped in festoons over an under-petticoat of Solferino cashmere with a Garibaldi blouse of the same new colour, small hat with feather, may be considered typical of the middle of that decade. (See Figure 165.)

A popular song of that time describes these prevailing fashions.

"RED PETTICOAT
"You may talk about the fashions,
　　Of bonnets neat and small,
　　Of crinoline and flounces,
　　But the stripes exceed them all.

I'm fond of little bonnets,
  Of skirts quite full and wide,
But they want the striped petticoat
  To show them off beside.

" There's a beauty in the gaiter,
    That defies the clumsy foot,
But the tidy little slipper,
    Looks best upon the foot.
And if you wish to show it,
    Or have it well display'd,
Then with the striped petticoat
    Just take a promenade.

" All women take the fashions
    Of Empress and Queen,
Victoria wears the petticoat,
    And crinoline—Eugene;
Victoria is a model,
    As every woman knows,
And every girl should imitate
    Her virtues, well as clothes."

The Zouave jacket, made either with or without sleeves, rivalled the Garibaldi blouse in popular favour. Like the spencers of an earlier date, these little jackets were made in every colour and combination. Zouave trousers for riding were among the new fashions for women in 1869. A plate of that date, in the collection of the Salmagundi Club of New York, shows a suit of dark green cloth, Zouave jacket and full Turkish trousers fastened at the ankle, and a fez to match with a black tassel hanging over the left side.

Printed calicoes and chintzes were worn by maids, with white aprons and, in many households, white caps with a bow of ribbon, as in Figure 167, which is taken from a contemporary print.

In the winter of 1869–1870 the hoop-skirt, which had been gradually diminishing in circumference since 1865, was superseded by dress improvers or bustles. These articles of attire were made either of horsehair with a series of ruffles across the back, or of cambric with steels run through a casing, their object being to hold the dress skirt out at the back. They were made like a petticoat with a plain breadth in front and the full trimming in the back breadth only, but they gradually grew smaller and smaller.

Overdresses were worn with every costume in 1870, caught up at the sides and decorated with numerous bows or rosettes. Bodices were cut high and sashes to match the dress were very much worn in the street as well as with evening dresses. Very long trains were worn with the latter, but street costumes were made to clear the instep. Bonnets and hats were very small and flat.

At this period (1869–1870) the hair was usually arranged in braids at the back and turned up and pinned close to the head, while the front hair was crimped, parted in the middle and drawn back above the ears, and the ends made into finger-puffs on top of the head. Curls were much worn, sometimes hanging in a soft cluster over the braids, but the favourite style was a long ringlet coming out from the braids at the left side and hanging down over the shoulder. For full dress occasions the coiffure consisted entirely of finger-puffs and small artificial flowers were placed at intervals through them. Bonnets were worn for visiting, etc., by every lady from the age of eighteen upwards.

A *débutante* costume for fashionable street wear in 1870 was usually a dress of black silk trimmed with ruffles of the same, a close-fitting basque coat of black velvet trimmed with fur or with ostrich feather trimming, a bonnet of coloured velvet trimmed with flowers and, instead of strings, a bridle of velvet under the chin. Such a combination would be considered much

FIGURE 227.—1838—A gentleman in full dress. Taken from a plate.

FIGURE 228.—1838—A white satin wedding dress trimmed with blond lace, worn in Philadelphia by Miss Mary Brinton. Head and veil from a contemporary portrait.

FIGURE 229.—1839—Gentleman in morning suit of mixed tweed. From a print of that date.

FIGURE 230.—1836—A soft white figured silk gown worn in Philadelphia. The trimming is of the same material plaited and arranged in a fan-shaped bertha. Head is from a contemporary portrait.

FIGURE 231.—1837—Bottle-green broadcloth coat, white figured silk waistcoat; worn in Philadelphia. Pantaloons, stock, etc., from a print of that date. Head from a portrait.

FIGURE 232.—1847—Blue changeable silk pelisse, wadded and lined with white silk; worn in Boston. Bonnet and gown from a print. Head from a contemporary portrait.

FIGURE 233.—1845—Greenish-gray satin gown, worn in Boston. Embroidered muslin cape from a plate. Head from a portrait of the same date.

FIGURE 234.—1845—Blue coat with gilt buttons and white silk waistcoat; worn in Philadelphia. Stock, hat, etc., from a plate. Head from a contemporary portrait.

1838·227   1838·228   1839·229   1836·230

Cecil Walter Trout, 1907

1837-231   1847-232   1845-233   1845-234

Cecil W. Trout, 1907

1845

too sedate for a grandmother in the present day. Black silk was also worn for evening dresses with sashes and trimmings of a bright colour or with a flat trimming of jet passementerie.

Possibly the popularity of black may be traced to France, which was in great trouble in 1870. During the disastrous siege of Paris, Challomel tells us, " Fashion veiled her face. The ' Magazine des Modes ' was silent and under the melancholy circumstances black was universally worn, but it was not like ordinary mourning, being richly trimmed."

Gloves with one button had been worn throughout the sixties even with short sleeves, but at the end of that decade a pronounced change was introduced. Picturesque Musquetaire gloves of " Suède," reaching almost to the elbow, at once claimed popular favour for evening dress. For street wear from two to six buttons were in vogue. Soft shades of tan and grey were the fashionable colours. The following verses by Locker gracefully express the sentiment attached to the glove at all periods :

> " Slips of a kid-skin deftly sewn,
>   A scent as through her garden blown,
>   The tender hue that clothes her dove,
>   All these, and this is Gerty's glove.

> " A glove but lately dofft, for look
>   It keeps the happy shape it took
>   Warm from her touch ! who gave the glow ?
>   And where's the mould that shaped it so ?" *

                    * London Lyrics.

CHILDREN'S GARMENTS
1800–1870

"NEW DRESSES

" New dresses ? Ay, this is the season
    For ' opening-day ' is close by :
  Already I know the ' Spring fashions '—
    Can tell you, I think, if I try.

" Of colours, the first thing to mention,
    There's a great variety seen ;
  But that which obtains the most favour
    Is surely a very bright green.

" True, the elderly portion are plainer,
    And choose, both in country and town,
  To appear in the shades which are sombre,
    And keep on the garment of brown.

" Miss Snowdrop, the first of the season,
    Comes out in such very good taste—
  Pure white, with her pretty green trimmings ;
    How charming she is, and how chaste !

" Miss Crocus, too, shows very early
    Her greetings of love for the sun,
  And comes in her white, blue or yellow ;
    All dresses of hers are home-spun.

" And who is this handsome young master,
    A friend to Miss Crocus so true ?
  He comes dressed in purple or yellow,
    And sometimes in pink, white and blue.

" In form he is tall and majestic ;
    Ah ! the Spring has just whispered his name :
  ' Hyacinthus '—the beau of the season !
    And sweet and wide-spread is his fame.

" Madame Tulip, a dashing gay lady,
    Appears in a splendid brocade ;
  She courts the bright sunbeams, which give her
    All colours—of every shade.

"She came to us o'er the wide ocean,
    Away from her own native air,
But if she can dress as she chooses
    She can be quite at home anywhere.

"Narcissus, a very vain fellow,
    Has a place in the Spring fashions, too—
Appears in his green, white and yellow,
    In his style, though, there's nothing that's new.

"Miss Daisy wears white, with fine fluting ;
    A sweet little creature is she,
But she loves the broad fields and green meadows,
    And cares not town fashions to see.

"Another style, pretty and tasteful,
    Green, dotted with purple or blue,
Is worn by Miss Myrtle, whose beauty
    In shade and retirement grew.

"I've borrowed these styles from Dame Nature,
    Whose children are always well drest :
In contrast and blending of colours
    She always knows what is the best.

"Already her hand is arranging
    More elaborate trimmings for May ;
In silence, unseen it is working,
    Accomplishing much every day.

"Her 'full dress' and festive occasion
    Will take place quite early in June,
Ushered in by low notes of sweet music,
    Which her song-birds alone can attune."
                                    —S. H. BARKER.

Children's Garments

1800–1835

" Oh, what a silken stocking,
And what a satin shoe;
I wish I was a little toe
To live in there, I do."

THE dressing of babies and little girls in the early part of the nineteenth century was very simple and very pretty. The prevailing fashions for women were in fact more suitable for children than for their mothers, and the numerous portraits of that period show infants and children dressed in soft muslin, made with low necks, short sleeves, high waists, and scanty skirts just reaching to the ankles. Slippers or low shoes made of kid or satin were worn at all seasons, and a sash of ribbon and a necklace of coral or of gold beads were the favourite adornments.

The little shoes sketched in Figure 219 belonged to a baby girl in Philadelphia and recall another rhyme of Kate Greenaway's :

" As I stepped out to hear the news,
I met a lass in socks and shoes,
She'd shoes with strings, and a friend had tied them,
She'd a nice little pair of feet inside them !"

The hair was generally cut short, which is not a becoming fashion even to a pretty face. Curls, however, came into vogue

1804–1860

FIGURE 235.—1812—Morning cap of embroidered muslin, called "coiffure à l'indisposition." From a plate.

FIGURE 236.—1812—Dinner cap of lace and muslin trimmed with white satin. From a plate of the day.

FIGURE 237.—1812—White "Hyde Park" bonnet. After a print.

FIGURE 238.—1816—Bonnet of white chip trimmed with rouleaux of gauze and bunch of white flowers. From a plate.

FIGURE 239.—1810–13—Hat of Leghorn trimmed with pale blue ribbon and straw rosettes around the crown. Wetherill collection.

FIGURE 240.—1817—Straw bonnet trimmed with green ribbon rosette. From a plate.

FIGURE 241.—1825–29—Leghorn hat with blue satin ribbon in a brocade scroll pattern. Wetherill collection.

FIGURE 242.—1818–19—Hat of white straw with gauze ribbon; white flowers and gauze plaits under the brim. Wetherill collection.

FIGURE 243.—1804—Bonaparte hat of white gauze trimmed with wreath of laurel.

FIGURE 244.—1819—Bonnet of white spotted satin trimmed with white satin ribbon. Wetherill collection.

FIGURE 245.—1816—Muslin morning bonnet. From a plate.

FIGURE 246.—1820–60—Pale blue ribbed silk slippers with satin rosettes. Gaiters of drab cloth laced up the side. Bronze kid slipper with red inlaid rosette. White kid slipper.

235 S.B.S. after print

236 after print.

237 S.B.S. after print

238 S.B.S. after print

239 S.B.S.

240 S.B.S. after print

241 S.B.S.

242 S.B.S.

243 G.W.T. 1907

244 S.B.S.

245 S.B.S. after print

246 C.W.TROUT 1907

soon after 1800 and were encouraged and cultivated whenever it was possible. In a few years the fashion became so popular that curl papers were the torment of almost every little girl in the nursery. Caps, which as we have seen were ordinarily worn by grown people, were also worn in the house by children from 1800 to 1825, and will be noticed in many of the portraits by Sully, Stuart, and St. Memin. Over the caps, hats of beaver or straw, according to the season, were worn out-of-doors, demurely tied under the chin, for

> " Little Fanny wears a hat
> Like her ancient Grannie."

Mits of thread and silk, which were fashionable in the latter half of the eighteenth century, were still worn by children from 1800 to 1830.

During the First Empire period the gowns of children were of the plainest. In Figure 77 a picture of the little niece of Napoleon shows a very unpretentious costume of sheer muslin trimmed with Valenciennes lace, which has been selected as a typical specimen of the garb of little girls from 1800 to 1820 in France, England and America. For outdoor wear pelisses or wrapping cloaks, lined or wadded and often trimmed with fur, were fashionable during the first quarter of the century, made as in Figure 175, with a standing collar, high waist and buttoned closely down the front. This particular pelisse is of red cloth and was worn in Philadelphia by little Mary Brinton in 1812. It is not unlike the green pelisses of Kate Greenaway's verses :

> " Five little sisters walking in a row,
> Now isn't that the best way for little girls to go?
> Each had a round hat, each had a muff,
> And each had a new pelisse of soft green stuff."

These outdoor garments were often made with capes, as in the following description taken from a fashion book of 1808 :

" A frock and short trousers of cambric, with Turkish pomposas [slippers] of jonquille kid. A wrapping coat with deep cape, formed of fine scarlet kerseymere. A beaver hat and feathers of dove colour."

The hats of that period, illustrated in Figures 194, 195 and 203, were quaint enough to find favour with Miss Greenaway when she started the picturesque revolution in the dress of children, which is still known by her name. Bonnets much like their elders were worn by small girls from the age of seven up, and remained in fashion all through the century (Figures 157, 175, 181, 184, 187 and 280.)

" Polly's, Peg's and Poppety's
　　Mamma was kind and good,
She gave them each, one happy day,
　　A little scarf and hood.

" A bonnet for each girl she bought,
　　To shield them from the sun ;
They wore them in the snow and rain,
　　And thought it mighty fun."

An infant's dress worn in Boston in 1824 is illustrated in Figure 217. It is very dainty and a beautiful specimen of plain needlework. Another little dress of about the same date (see Figure 218) is trimmed with openwork insertion. A christening frock shown in Figure 215, which is of a much later date, was worn by a Philadelphia baby in 1855.

Long cloaks of merino, wadded and lined with silk and trimmed with embroidery or swansdown fur, were the usual outdoor garments of babies from 1800 to 1870. The picture of one in Figure 220 is taken from a baby cloak of fawn-coloured merino embroidered with silk of the same colour, and lined throughout with silk to match. It was made in England, and was sent to Philadelphia as a present to a little Quaker baby in 1834. The bonnet was made to match the cloak and the ribbon trimmings are all of the exact shade of brown. A coat and bonnet of the same material and colour and made for an elder sister of three years of age are shown in Figure 216. Both of these costumes are beautifully embroidered and nothing but the colour, which is rather sober for babies, suggests that they were especially designed for the children of Quaker parents. In the early part of the century, however, Quakers were much more rigid in their regulations with regard to dress. In the "Autobiography of Mary Howitt" she describes the austerely plain costumes of a little Quaker girl in 1809 as follows :

"How well I remember the garments that were made for us. Our little brown cloth pelisses, cut plain and straight, without plait or fold in them, hooked and eyed down the front so as to avoid buttons, which were regarded by our parents as trimmings, yet fastened at the waist, with a cord. Little drab beaver bonnets furnished us by the Friends' hatter of Stafford, James Nixon, who had blocks made purposely for our little ultra-plain bonnets. They were without a scrap of ribbon or cord, except the strings, which were a necessity, and these were fastened inside. Our frocks were, as usual, of the plainest and most homely fabric and make."

Nothing could be more sad and doleful than the garb in Figure 288, copied from the woodcut in the book.

The love for pretty things is almost an instinct with young children, and it is not easy to imagine the "Sophia" of Jane Taylor's verses entitled :

" Sophia's Fool's Cap

" Sophia was a little child,
  Obliging, good and very mild,
  Yet, lest of dress she should be vain,
  Mamma still dressed her well but plain —
  Her parents, sensible and kind,
  Wished only to adorn her mind ;
  No other dress, when good, had she,
  But useful, neat simplicity.

" Though seldom, yet when she was rude,
  Or even in a naughty mood,
  Her punishment was this disgrace,
  A large fine cap adorned with lace,
  With feathers and with ribbands too ;
  The work was neat, the fashion new,
  Yet, as a fool's cap was its name,
  She dreaded much to wear the same.

" A lady, fashionably gay,
  Did to Mamma a visit pay.
  Sophia stared, then whispering said,
  'Why, dear Mamma, look at her head !
  To be so tall and wicked too,
  The strangest thing I ever knew,
  What naughty tricks, pray, has she done,
  That they have put a fool's cap on ?' "

A story is told of a little Quaker girl whose soul yearned for bright colours. Having made an engagement to take a country walk with a boy neighbour, she stole quietly out of the house and gathered in the orchard some ripe cherries with which she adorned her plain straw hat and drab ribbons, being very careful to throw away the bright cherries on her way home.

Another story of the days of pantalets is told of a little Quaker girl and her sister, who laid a deep scheme to procure a pair of those uncouth garments which, being in the height of fashion among children of the world, were forbidden to the children of Friends, and consequently much coveted by them. Before the grown people were stirring, these two children got up and fashioned for themselves two pairs of pantalets out of one of the sheets from their bed. They were busy plying their needles when the door suddenly opened and their mother appeared. Needless to say, an emphatic demonstration of maternal disapproval ensued and the little Quakeresses never finished the pantalets.

In 1815 great changes in fashion for everybody were introduced. The big hats and full skirts were well enough for little girls, but alack! the pantalets reaching to the ankles spoiled everything. These obnoxious articles must have been very troublesome to make and very uncomfortable to wear, but they held their sway from about 1818 to about 1858. There are several specimens to be seen in the collection at Memorial Hall, Philadelphia. It was the custom of thrifty mothers to make the pantalets for school and every-day wear of stout calico or nankin, but for afternoon and dress occasions they were always of white and often elaborately trimmed with lace and embroidery. Occasionally they were trimmed with deep gathered ruffles, and awkward indeed must have been the wearing of these stiff and starched vanities. Pantalets were usually adjustable and made to button on to the edge of the drawers, but occasionally they were made to full into a band and finished with a ruffle at the ankle, as in Figures 157 and 181.

Old fashion books tell us that when children were dressed in mourning, a general custom on the death of a parent in the first half of the nineteenth century, they had pantalets made of crape; could anything be more hideous?

From 1825 to 1835, leg-of-mutton sleeves figured in the children's corner of Fashion's kingdom, as elsewhere. Broad belts or sashes were universally worn too, and everything was made to stand out about the shoulders. Hats were rather aggressively trimmed with projecting bows of ribbon, etc. In Figure 208 will be seen pictures of a paper doll dressed in the very height of the fashion of 1829. It was owned by a little girl in Philadelphia named Elizabeth Randolph. The costumes are all well preserved, as the photograph shows, but the original doll has been lost in the course of time and the modern representation who now displays the wardrobe wears high heels, which no fashionable doll of 1829 would have thought of doing.

Perhaps the original doll is still lamenting her fate in some obscure closet like the heroine of Eugene Field's pathetic verses :

"LAST YEAR'S DOLL

"I'm only a last year's doll !
    I thought I was lovely and fair —
But alas for the cheeks that were rosy,
    Alas for the once flowing hair !
I'm sure that my back is broken,
    For it hurts me when I rise,
Oh, I'd cry for very sorrow,
    But I've lost out both my eyes.

"In comes my pretty mistress,
    With my rival in her arms,
A fine young miss, most surely,
    Arrayed in her borrowed charms !
My dress and my slippers too,
    But sadder, oh, sadder than all,
She's won the dear love I have lost,
    For I'm only a last year's doll.

"Oh, pity me, hearts that are tender,
    I'm lonely and battered and bruised,
I'm tucked out of sight in the closet,
    Forgotten, despised and abused !
I'm only a last year's doll,
    Alone with my troubled heart,
Sweet mistress, still I love thee,
    Inconstant though thou art."

Fancy aprons were fashionable for little girls in the period of the thirties. They were usually made of silk and were considered very stylish when made with bretelles and trimmed with a ruching of the silk as shown in Figure 181. But fine muslin aprons, trimmed with lace or embroidery, were also worn; and printed calico and white cross-barred cambric, trimmed with narrow frills of the same, were used for the aprons of less fashionable children for many years.

The costumes in fashion for little boys from four to ten were not quite as simple as those for girls. Sometimes, it is true, we notice a short-waisted jacket with low neck and sleeves, like a girl's, but the ruffled shirt collars and close-fitting jacket and trousers devised by Marie Antoinette for the unfortunate Dauphin, were very generally worn by boys upward from the age of four years.

The sketch of a small boy from a print of 1808 is given in Figure 194 showing a cloth cap with a full soft crown and a visor worn with a kerseymere suit.

In Figure 195 a boy in a short-sleeved tunic with full trousers reaching to the ankle, copied from a fashion plate of 1810, is given. The straw hat is turned back in front and is not very unlike the hat shown in Figure 203, which is in the interesting collection at the School of Industrial Art, Philadelphia.

In Figure 174 we give a picture of a suit worn by a little American boy, about four years old, in 1804. The material is a striped brown and white calico, and the pantaloons, which fit close to the leg, are fastened with a fly front like a man's. The short waisted jacket has tight long sleeves and revers at the neck in front, allowing the ruffled collar of the linen shirt to show. It is a fascinating costume and we consider ourselves most fortunate in securing a picture of it for this book. It

1840–1851

FIGURE 247.—1841—Red velvet evening dress. From a portrait by Winterhalter.

FIGURE 248.—1843—White satin dress with black lace flounces. From a portrait by Winterhalter.

FIGURE 249.—1840—White satin ball dress. Portrait by Winterhalter.

FIGURE 250.—1840—Moiré gown trimmed with lace. Portrait by Chalon.

FIGURE 251.—1850—Waved hair and quaint head-dress. From a portrait of Lola Montez.

FIGURE 252.—1851—Evening dress and wrap. From a portrait of the Duchess of Sutherland.

247

250

248

249

252

251

is much too small for a modern boy of four, however; in fact, it was a tight fit for the little fellow of two and a half who posed in it. Evidently this was the style of suit worn by Miss Austen's little nephews in 1801 and mentioned in the following extract from a letter of that date:

"Mary has likewise a message: she will be much obliged to you if you can bring her the pattern of the jacket and trousers, or whatever it is that Elizabeth's boys wear when they are first put into breeches; so if you could bring her an old suit itself, she would be very glad, but that I suppose is hardly done."

Some years later, in 1809, Miss Austen writes of getting black suits for her nephews whose father had just died, establishing for us the fact that it was customary for little boys, as well as girls, to wear mourning for their parents.

"Mrs. J. A. had not time to get them more than one suit of clothes; their others are making here, and though I do not believe Southampton is famous for tailoring, I hope it will prove itself better than Basingstoke. Edward has an old black coat, which will save his having a second new one, but I find that black pantaloons are considered by them as necessary, and of course one would not have them made uncomfortable by the want of what is usual on such occasions."

Before promotion to trousers, an event which usually took place when a boy had reached his fourth year, queer little tunics of merino opening down the front and reaching below the knees were worn over white trousers reaching to the ankle either of material to match or of white linen. (See Figure 179.)

In the thirties exaggerated leg-of-mutton sleeves were worn even by boys. In Figure 197 a suit of dark green merino is shown, copied from a portrait of 1833, in which not only the sleeves are of this shape, but the long pantaloons follow the same

lines, being cut very full from the hip to the knees, and tapering to the ankle. This was worn in England by a boy of
about ten years, while the suit with very pronounced leg-
of-mutton trousers in Figure 198 was worn by a younger brother
of eight.

From 1830 to 1835 the ordinary costume of boys over ten
years of age was a suit of long, rather loose-fitting pantaloons,
a waistcoat cut rather low and showing a white shirt beneath,
and a short jacket reaching to the waist line.

The hats for boys of the early part of the nineteenth century
were extremely ugly. The jockey cap with a round crown and
a visor is seen in many of the prints from 1801 to 1810, a long
tassel hanging down over the left ear being the only decoration.
Then came the stove-pipe hat, made of straw in summer and of
beaver in winter, which was actually worn for several years
even by little boys in frocks. During the Regency period
(1810–1819) caps were worn with crowns of cloth and visors of
enamelled leather as in Figure 178, taken from a drawing of
Boutet de Monvel. From 1820 to 1830 hats worn by small
boys were like that shown in Figure 351, with rather high
crowns and straight brims. In 1830 high hats were worn by
very fashionable boys in trousers (see Figure 182) which looked
like inverted flower pots. Beauty and fitness seem not to have
been considered.

Children's Garments

1835–1870

" Young ladies then wore gowns with sleeves,
 Which would just hold their arms ;
 And did not have as many yards
 As acres in their farms."

HE leg-of-mutton sleeves, which in 1835 had indeed reached extravagant proportions, declined in favour for the gowns of little girls towards the end of that year. In 1836 sleeves were made less full and gathered into three puffs from shoulder to wrist, or the fullness was laid in flat plaits at the top of the arm, hung loose about the elbow and was finished with a cuff at the wrist. A little later straight, close-fitting sleeves trimmed with frills and puffings were popular. In 1840 sleeves to the elbow were introduced. This fashion still retains its popularity and is very appropriate as well as becoming. In the forties sleeves for little girls were often made to reach a little below the elbow, showing undersleeves of white muslin. A small plaited frill of the muslin was worn at the throat. For girls of fifteen pelerines were in vogue. They were fastened at the waist, both front and back, and trimmed with frills of lace or muslin. In the fifties big sleeves with muslin undersleeves were worn by girls from twelve years up.

After the decline of the leg-of-mutton sleeves and trousers,

311

boys wore tight sleeves, but the pantaloons, as we notice in many of the portraits between 1835 and 1850, were usually loose at the ankle. The following extract is from an American book, late in the forties :

"Small jacket, open and rounded in front, of dark velvet, cloth, or cashmere, with buttons of the same. Small square linen collar turned over, a ribbon necktie. Loose trousers of blue and white striped linen. Cap of dark cloth."

From 1835 to 1850 we notice in the fashion plates as well as in portraits that most of the skirts were trimmed with flounces, and until 1846 the pantalets covered the tops of the shoes, but at the end of the forties pantalets were worn shorter and gradually disappeared. In fact in the fifties they were visible only on very small children and under very short skirts. Plaids and graduated stripes were very fashionable for both boys and girls throughout that decade.

Before 1835 the hair was usually worn parted in the middle by girls of all ages. Curls were fashionable and by the help of curling tongs were easily acquired by every one. Maggie Tulliver's short mop of hair was a special vexation, we know, to her mother, who always felt a pang of envy at the sight of Lucy's neatly arranged curls. But for a time between 1835 and 1870 a very popular fashion was to plait the hair in two long braids, like the two eldest Kenwigs who, as we recall, "had flaxen hair tied with blue ribbons in luxuriant pigtails down their backs." Some time in the forties it became fashionable to comb the hair back from the forehead without a part, and springs of steel covered with ribbon or velvet were introduced to keep it in place. Back-combs were another novelty introduced for the same purpose. Older girls arranged the back hair in a net of silk or chenille, as in Figure 205, or fastened the "pigtails" in a coil at the back, as in Figure 201.

Boys wore the hair parted very much to one side at that time, and it was not cropped close to the head as is the fashion of to-day. About 1860 the fashion of parting the hair directly in the middle was introduced and followed for some years by big boys as well as men, although this change was considered effeminate at first, and consequently disliked by little boys ambitious for promotion to long pantaloons.

Bonnets and hats were equally fashionable for girls from 1835 to 1860. Illustrations of the prevailing styles of both are given in Figures 181, 184, 187, and 190. In Miss Whitney's "Stories of New England" a great deal is said about the clothes of girls from 1840 to 1850. We learn that when Augusta Hare, who was almost grown up, appeared to the unsophisticated eyes of Anstiss Dolbeare in mourning for her father, wearing "a black merino shawl and long veil that made her face so sweet and fair, these garments were to my childish fancy the very poetry of bereavement, there seemed a grandeur and solemn distinction in having lost a friend. My openworked straw bonnet with blue gauze ribbons seemed so tawdry, so little girlish."

The adventures of this straw bonnet were very interesting. Anstiss, having seen some scarfs of silk with fringed ends, which Augusta Hare had brought, longed to have one too, but knew that "Aunt Ildy" would never listen to such an extravagance.

The next morning, however, Anstiss saw the pretty face of Miss Augusta smiling at her from the doorway. She was dressed on this occasion "in a clear black muslin with the tiniest dash of white, and a knot of black ribbon in her hair. In her hand, streaming down in brilliant contrast over her dress, was a rich broad bonnet scarf of blue with fringed ends." In a short time the despised bonnet was completely transformed and not until this change was accomplished did Anstiss realize how difficult it would be to gain her aunt's approval. Hastily the bonnet was put away on a shelf in the closet and when finally the aunt discovered the change, the little girl was sent to bed under most aggravating circumstances and the old trimming replaced by the angry fingers of Aunt Ildy, whose displeasure was visibly expressed in the hopelessly flattened bows of the old gauze trimming. And yet the fashion which was new in 1840 was by no means elaborate. A scarf " was passed up from under the chin across the bonnet in the depression between the brim and crown and tied at one side with a careless knot, long ends fluttering down upon the shoulder." According to the simple habits of New England village life, a Dunstable straw was worn by girls until Thanksgiving and then replaced by a bonnet of beaver.

Sunbonnets of calico, stiffened with many rows of cording, were much worn in summer time by little country girls. In winter quilted hoods, like the sketch in Figure 132, were substituted. A specimen of a pink sunbonnet of the above description worn by a little girl in Pennsylvania is shown in Figure 132.

A little girl of twelve " was allowed one clean print gown and two aprons each week, a change and one for best, and if she spilled or tore she went to bed." Calicoes that were well covered and would wash, silk that would wear and turn, and above all, things that were " in the house " and could be made over were usually allotted to little girls. They were undeniably calculated to discourage vanity.

Infant caps were small and close-fitting and were trimmed with ruchings of lace and ribbon from 1835 to 1870. A picture of one trimmed in this way is given in Figure 160. A narrow satin ribbon with a loop edge was used for this purpose up to 1870.

The following description of a costume for a little girl four or five years old is quoted from the " Lady's Book " for 1849 :

"Dress of shaded silk (grey and rose-colour). The skirt very full and edged at the bottom by a broad hem, headed by a row of gimp in tints corresponding with the shades of the silk. The corsage is half high, square in front, and plaited in broad folds, which are confined by a band at the top and at the waist. Short sleeves edged by two bias folds of silk headed by gimp. Under the corsage is worn a spencer chemisette of jaconet muslin drawn on the neck in fullness, and set on a band at the throat. The chemisette has long sleeves, slightly full, and drawn on wrist bands. Loose trousers of cambric muslin, edged at the bottom by a bordering of needlework. The hair divided on the forehead and combed straight to the back of the neck, where it hangs down in long plaits. Boots of black glazed leather, with grey cashmere tops."

For an older girl an English magazine gives the following for the same year:

"Coarse straw bonnet lined and trimmed with blue silk. White openworked muslin waist, and a skirt of some light and delicate material. It may either be a glacé silk, as in the plate, or lawn, French cambric, etc. Pantalettes quite plain and finished by a narrow frill."

In the hoop-skirt days (1855–1865) little girls of seven years and over wore those weird inventions too, but the decline of the pantalets was heralded at the same time. White lingerie blouses were worn very much by young girls and Zouave jackets worn with skirts to match or of a contrasting colour were in vogue from 1860. (See Figure 205.) Garibaldi blouses were the next novelty and they won universal favour. Suits consisting of a grey skirt, trimmed with a broad band of plain colour above the hem, and a Garibaldi blouse, of the same colour as the trimming, were "quite the rage" during the struggle for independence in Italy. Solferino and Magenta were the fa-

1850–1860

FIGURE 253.—1857—Straw hat with drooping brim and streamers of ribbon. From a plate.

FIGURE 254.—1856—Bonnet of pale blue uncut velvet and white blond lace. Miss Dutihl's collection in Memorial Hall, Philadelphia.

FIGURE 255.—1855—Dress of silk with alternate stripes of brown and white plaid and coloured flowers. The basque and bell sleeves are trimmed with fringe and gimp heading of pink and brown. The picture is taken from a dress worn in Philadelphia. Head showing a braided coronet of hair. From a contemporary portrait.

FIGURE 256.—1859—Bonnet of black velvet and corded silk. Has had a bunch of currants and a red feather around on the side. Miss Dutihl's collection.

FIGURE 257.—1850–60—Black velvet wrist-band with mosaic clasp.

253

254

255

256

257

vourite shades of red, named of course for the famous battles. Boys wore these blouses too, with long pantaloons. Later a fancy for plaid materials prevailed over the plain colours. (See Figures 183, 189 and 201.)

It was the fashion in 1840 and after, to make dresses for girls with low or half-low bodices, to be worn over guimpes of white muslin (Figure 201). The skirts were made very full and were often lined with crinoline or worn over petticoats of crinoline like their mothers'. Instead of a bodice an arrangement of bretelles was often worn by little girls, as in the initial at the head of this chapter. Shoes made of morocco or leather, with cloth tops, called gaiter boots or gaiters, were much worn from 1835 to 1870 (Figures 181, 183, 184, 186 and 189). Sashes of ribbon tied at the back with long ends reaching to the end of the skirt were in general vogue.

In the sixties velvet ribbon and braid were the favourite trimmings and were used in a great variety of designs.

Bonnets at last went out of fashion in 1860 and even big girls began to wear hats instead. All the shapes worn by grown people were adopted for children at this time. The mushroom, the turban, and the pork-pie were worn very generally by girls of from ten to eighteen. For little girls under ten hats with low crowns and wide flapping brims were fashionable. They were popularly called "flats," and when simply trimmed with a wreath of small flowers or a band and ends of ribbon were exceedingly pretty and becoming.

The little girl of Austin Dobson's verses, "Little Blue-Ribbons," probably wore a hat of this shape :

> " 'Little Blue-Ribbons.' We call her that
> From the ribbons she wears in her favourite hat;
> For may not a person be only five
> And yet have the neatest of taste alive?

As a matter of fact, this one has views
Of the strictest sort as to frocks and shoes ;
And we never object to a sash or bow,
When ' Little Blue-Ribbons ' prefers it so.''

For dressy occasions in the fifties suits of black velvet or velveteen were worn by little boys under ten and made often with full short trousers to the knee.   Queen Victoria adopted the Highland suit of Scotch tartan for the English Princes on a visit to Balmoral in 1854, and the Highland dress, especially the kilts, soon became popular for boys from five to ten all the world over (Figure 162).

"THE COMING MAN

" A pair of very chubby legs
Encased in scarlet hose :
A pair of little stubby boots
With rather doubtful toes ;
A little kilt, a little coat
Cut as a mother can,
And lo ! before us strides in state
The Future's coming man.''

Another fashion which at once became popular, and which probably had a similar origin, was the sailor costume, which was worn by boys from about seven to fourteen (Figure 161).   Larger boys, of fifteen and upward, at this period wore long pantaloons like their fathers, with round short jackets to match, as in Figure 206.   In England the high hat was still the regulation head-gear for little boys and for young men in the winter, but soft felt and straw hats of the sailor type will be seen in most of the contemporary illustrations.

Although dolls of the nineteenth century were not used as fashion models, they were always dressed according to the prevailing styles, and the few of them that have outlived their generation record the fashions of their time. For instance, the doll in Figure 211 is dressed in the Bloomer costume, which was introduced in 1851. Although it is happily quite out of fashion, this costume has become historic. In Figure 209, a photograph of an interesting doll of the forties with her front hair in (painted) braids in the fashion adopted by Queen Victoria is given. Her wedding gown is of white satin trimmed with silver and her veil and wreath of white flowers are worn in the height of the fashion of 1840, the year of the Queen's marriage. This doll also possesses a stylish bonnet of white tulle and white flowers. Another doll of about 1850 is shown in Figure 210, wearing the fashionable pantalets and an apron with bretelles, which were thought almost indispensable for little girls at that time. The two last mentioned are wooden dolls " with necks so white, and cheeks so red." They have probably outlived more than one waxen rival like the wooden doll of Jane Taylor's verses.

"THE WOODEN DOLL AND THE WAX DOLL

" There were two friends, a charming little pair
Brunette the brown, and Blanchidine the fair :
This child to love Brunette did still incline,
And much Brunette loved sweet Blanchidine.
Brunette in dress was neat yet wond'rous plain,
But Blanchidine of finery was vain.

" Now Blanchidine a new acquaintance made,
A little miss, most splendidly arrayed :
Feathers and laces most beauteous to behold,
And India frock, with spots of shining gold.
Said Blanchidine, a miss so richly dressed,
Most sure by all deserves to be caressed ;
To play with me if she will condescend,
Henceforward she shall be my only friend.
For this new miss, so dressed and so adorned,
Her poor Brunette was slighted, left, and scorned.

" Of Blanchidine's vast stock of pretty toys,
  A wooden Doll her every thought employs ;
  Its neck so white, so smooth, its cheeks so red,
  She'd kiss, she'd hug, she'd take it to her bed.

" Mother now brought her home a Doll of wax,
  Its hair in ringlets white and soft as flax ;
  Its eyes could open, and its eyes could shut,
  And on it with much taste its clothes were put,
  My dear wax doll, sweet Blanchidine would cry :
  Her doll of wood was thrown neglected by.

" One summer's day, 'twas in the month of June,
  The sun blazed out in all the heat of noon,
  My waxen doll, she cried, my dear, my charm,
  You feel quite cold, but you shall soon be warm.
  She placed it in the sun—misfortune dire !
  The wax ran down as if before the fire !
  Each beauteous feature quickly disappeared,
  And melting left a blank all soiled and smeared.

" She stared, she screamed with horror and dismay,
  You odious fright, she then was heard to say ;
  For you my silly heart I have estranged,
  From my sweet wooden Doll, that never changed.
  Just so may change my new acquaintance fine,
  For whom I left Brunette, that friend of mine.
  No more by outside show will I be lured,
  Of such capricious whims I think I'm cured :
  To plain old friends my heart shall still be true,
  Nor change for every face because 'tis new.
  Her slighted wooden doll resumed its charms,
  And wronged Brunette she clasped within her arms."

QUAKER COSTUME

and

Dress of the Shakers

1800–1870

"THE FRIEND

" In patriarchal plainness, lo ! around
  The festive board, a friendly tribe convene ;
  Chaste, simple, neat, and modest in attire,
  And chastely simple in their manners too ;
  To them her gay varieties in vain
  Fashion displays, inconstant as the moon.
  Them to allure, in vain does chymic art
  For human vestments multiply its dyes.
  One mode of dress contents them, and but few
  The colours of their choice—the gaudy shunned
  E'en by the gentle sisterhood.   In youth,
  The rose's vivid hue their cheeks alone
  Wear, dimpling ; shaded by a bonnet plain,
  White as the cygnet's bosom ; jetty black
  As raven's wing : or if a tint it bear,
  'Tis what the harmless dove herself assumes.
  The hardier sex, an unloop'd hat, broad brimm'd,
  Shelters from summer's heat and winter's cold ;
  That from its station high ne'er deigns to stoop,
  Obsequious not to custom nor to king ;
  Yet, though precise, and primitive in speech,
  Restrain they not the smile, the seemly jest,
  Nor e'en the cordial laugh, that cynics grave
  Falsely assert ' bespeaks a vacant mind.'
  Serenely gay, with generous ale they fill
  The temp'rate cup : no want of new-coined toast
  To give it zest ; 'Good fellowship and peace'
  Their sentiment, their object, and their theme."
        —*From " The Evening Fireside."*

Quaker Costume

1800–1870

"While Quaker folks were Quakers still some fifty years ago,
    When coats were drab and gowns were plain and speech was
        staid and slow
Before Dame Fashion dared suggest a single friz or curl."

N the first years of the new century a very distinct costume was worn by the Quakers. Not only were all colours but grey and brown and white eschewed by strict members of the sect, but black was considered worldly. Everything they wore was of the best quality, most durably made and most neatly adjusted. Beaver hats with brims especially broad were worn by Quaker men for the greater part of the century. In the words of an English essayist: " A Quaker's hat is a more formidable thing than a Grandee's," and " Broad Brim " is one of the most familiar soubriquets by which members of the Society of Friends are known.

Short clothes were worn by more than usually conservative Quaker gentlemen throughout the thirties. A picture of Gabriel Middleton, said to have been the last man in Philadelphia to wear knee-breeches, is given in Figure 351. It is copied from a daguerreotype taken in 1840, and shows the dress fashionable in the beginning of the century, and " the hat

327

1838–1866

FIGURE 258.—1852—Outdoor costume; dress of cashmere, cloak of soft English cloth. From a contemporary portrait.

FIGURE 259.—1840—Typical Quaker dress of 1840 and after, with slight variations in the fullness of skirt and sleeves. This costume was worn in Pennsylvania in 1840.

FIGURE 260.—1866—Fashionable indoor gown of black taffeta trimmed with velvet ribbon. From a photograph.

FIGURE 261.—1850—Gown opening over a chemisette of shirred muslin and insertion, with undersleeves to match. From a portrait of the day.

FIGURE 262.—1865—Old lady in Quaker dress. The shawl is of a soft woven fabric called Chenille. The bonnet is a grey silk shirred over small reeds. From a photograph.

FIGURE 263.—1838—Widow's mourning; bombazine dress with trimming of crêpe. Collar and cap trimmed with goffered frills. From a portrait of Queen Adelaide.

258

259

260

261

262

263

which had not yet lost all its original beaver," but was still adhered to by the Friends. The coat is cut high, but is made without a collar and the plain buttoned waistcoat is also high and collarless. In the initial to this chapter the picture of a Quaker gentleman of Philadelphia is given, taken from a pencil sketch made by Dr. Valentine in 1838.

The subject of Quaker costume has been so ably covered by Mrs. Gummere* that it is not necessary to attempt a description in these pages. Only one to the persuasion born could master the subtle differences in the garb of the two factions, the Orthodox and Hicksite Friends. To the worldly eye the most obvious distinction seems to be that the Orthodox Quakers wear unorthodox garments, while the followers of Hicks dress in ordinary apparel. The division of the sect took place in 1827. The Orthodox members were at one time so strict in matters of dress that even buttons were forbidden as unnecessary ornaments. It has been narrated that on one occasion a Friend was publicly rebuked at a Meeting in Philadelphia for a breach of this regulation, whereupon the spirit moved Nicholas Waln, a famous preacher of his day, to remark that "if religion consisted of a button, he did not care a button for religion."

The Friends of the first quarter of the nineteenth century were conservative in customs as well as in costumes. In the diary of William Howitt we read of the observance of mourning in England in the year 1820 :

" A day I have not forgotten was when I was sent on Peter to the Friends' families for some miles round, to invite them to the burial of my paternal grandmother. This was called ' Biddin' to the berrin'.' At all the country funerals then people got their black crape hatband and pair of black gloves, but the Friends not wearing mourning, we gave a pair of drab

* The Quaker, a Study in Costume.

gloves. At the funeral the guests were treated to wine and cake made for the purpose, called 'berrin' cake,' and when the funeral left the house each person received the customary gloves and a square piece of 'berrin' cake' wrapped in white paper and sealed."

The following extract from a letter of Mary Howitt describes the wedding costume of that most gentle poetess:

"On the 16th of Fourth month, 1821, we were married, I wearing my first silk gown, a very pretty dove-colour, with bonnet of the same material, and a soft white silk shawl. Shawls were greatly in vogue, especially amongst Friends, and my attire was thought very appropriate and becoming. For a wedding-tour my husband took me to every spot of beauty or old tradition in his native country, romantic, picturesque Derbyshire."

A very interesting portrait miniature of Miss Woolston, a Hicksite Friend, is given in Figure 70; the hair is arranged in curls and held in place by combs at the side, and a very high comb of the prevailing fashion of 1824 is worn at the back. The very sheer lawn collar is of an unusual design, and the low cut dress is of black which was considered worldly by Orthodox Friends. Another costume of interest is shown in Figure 259. The short waist and the scanty skirt, as well as the little cap with the bridle of ruffled lawn under the chin, will be noticed in portraits of the twenties, although this costume was worn by a Quaker in Pennsylvania until 1840.

The bonnets worn by Quaker ladies were decidedly distinctive. Pictures of them will be seen in Figures 293 and 286. Figure 286 shows the bonnet worn with the costume in Figure 289, which is also of brown satin.

An ingenious device to protect bonnets from the rain was used by the Friends. It consisted of a carefully fitted cover which could be folded into a small parcel and carried in the reticule until needed. In Figure 291 a picture of one of these rain covers is given, drawn from the original in Memorial Hall, Philadelphia. The shape suggests that it was in use during the forties.

The slight changes in Quaker fashion are exemplified in the interesting costume in Figure 289, which resembles with absolute fidelity the dress of Elizabeth Fry in the portrait by Richmond painted in 1824, although it was worn by Mrs. Johnson of Philadelphia about 1860.

DRESS OF THE SHAKERS

Although the belief and rites of the sect called "Shakers" are very different from the tenets and practice of the Quakers, there is a similarity in dress which it seems appropriate to describe at this point in our history. The most flourishing settlement of their community is at New Lebanon, New York.

As this sect is gradually dying out and their ways and ceremonials will before many years have become obsolete, we will give the following account of a visitor to this Shaker village in 1829, describing the costume which still remains unchanged.

"The Elders wear long plain coats and wide brimmed hats, but the Sunday costume of the ordinary man consists of pantaloons of blue linen with a fine white stripe in it, vest of a much deeper blue linsey-woolsey, stout calfskin shoes and grey stockings. Their shirts are made of cotton, the collars fastened with three buttons and turned over. The women wear, on Sunday, some a pure white dress, and others a white dress with a delicate blue stripe in it. Over their necks and bosoms were pure white kerchiefs, and over the left arm of each was carried a large white pocket handkerchief. Their heads were covered with lawn caps, the form of all, for both old and young, being alike. They project so as to fully conceal the cheeks in profile. Their shoes, sharp-toed and high-heeled, according to the fashion of the day when the Society was formed [1747], were made of prunella of a brilliant ultramarine blue. And there were children too, with cheerful faces peering out from their broad hats and deep bonnets, for they were all dressed like old men and women. I marvelled at the sight of children in that isolated world of bachelors and maidens, forgetting that it was a refuge for orphans who are unsheltered in the stormy world without."

Perhaps a brief account of Shaker worship by an eye-witness may be of interest to our readers in connection with their severe costumes.

"As I entered the room, the Shakers were arranging themselves on both sides of it ; the women on the right and the men on the left. Some of the men had taken off their coats, and placed them aside. They formed themselves into figures, leaving an open space in the centre which I afterwards found was for any one who chose to address the society. They stood in this position for some time, without a word being spoken by any one ; and their countenances wore a serenity and fixedness very unusual among any denomination or class of people. The hands of all were pressed together ; and the women had handkerchiefs hanging vertically from their arms, clean from the drawer, and half unfolded. They stood thus nearly ten minutes, with their eyes bent upon the floor, and you might have heard a pin drop, so very still was every one in the building. They forcibly reminded me of the sleeping scene in the Enchanted Castle, if I may not be thought making an irreverent comparison. Presently, a man who seemed the chief among them, broke the silence, by suddenly commencing a tune upon a base key, and ascending suddenly to a sharp one. His next hand neighbour joined and the next, and the next, each a little behind the other; and then by degrees the females, till every voice in the room swelled the fitful chorus; yet they seemed as incapable of motion as statues; except their hands, which were gently lifted to keep time to their voices and of which you would know nothing unless your eyes were turned to them. This tune continued about ten minutes; after which followed a breathing time of several more, during which a death-like silence again prevailed. The man whom I took to be the chief among them, then came forward into the space I have mentioned, and addressed the society, calling the members of it brothers and sisters. His voice was so low that I could only catch a few words; enough, however, to assure me that his speech was directed alone to the Society, and was not intended for others. The burthen of his remarks was, as well as I could hear, the importance of the Gospel to mankind, and the inducements they had to exertion, under the Christian revelation. Then followed another tune, in which all joined with the same devotion as before, after which another member came forward and spoke substantially to the same effect as the former speaker. He was listened to with attention, and though his language was very simple and often unhappy, yet his words were uttered with that kind of solemnity that never fails to carry conviction to the mind. He had no sooner withdrawn to his place, than another hymn followed; which to my ear seemed of a piece with the preceding ones. It was loud, faint, quiet and slow by turns, and the change was very sudden, from one pitch to another. As soon as it was concluded they all bowed and separated in such disorder that I thought the exercises over. Not a man went near a woman, though they all seemed separating in confusion and wild disorder. They

1850–1856

FIGURE 264.—1850—Black velvet mantilla trimmed with Maltese lace, worn in Philadelphia. Head from a portrait.

FIGURE 265.—1850—Gentleman in walking dress. From a portrait of that date. Brown cloth coat and pantaloons of brown and white plaid.

FIGURE 266.—1853—A white muslin gown embroidered in colours, worn in Philadelphia. Head from a contemporary portrait.

FIGURE 267.—1855—Gentleman in morning dress ; black coat, buff nankin pantaloons and white waistcoat. From a contemporary print.

FIGURE 268.—1855—A gown of brown silk with chiné stripes, made with a basque trimmed with fringe to match. Worn in Philadelphia. Bonnet from a plate of that date. Head from a contemporary portrait.

FIGURE 269.—1856—Blue poplin gown trimmed with black velvet ribbon. Bead bag of crochet work. Worn in Philadelphia. Bonnet and head from a Daguerreotype.

FIGURE 270.—1855—A suit of black broadcloth, waistcoat fastened with oblong mosaic buttons. Worn in Philadelphia. Head from a contemporary portrait.

FIGURE 271.—1856—A peignoir of old-rose cashmere with Persian trimming ; worn in Philadelphia. Head from a contemporary portrait.

1850·264   1850·265   1858·266   1855·267   Cecil W. Trout. 1907

1855·268   1856·269   1857·270·   1858·271

came together by degrees and soon arranged themselves into two solid squares, the women composing one and the men the other. This was done by way of preparing for what they call the labour-dance; of which I will endeavour to give some idea.

"After arranging themselves into two squares, with their faces towards the singers, who, about ten in number, male and female, stood in one row at the farther part of the building, they commenced a slow dance, keeping time with the singers not with their voices, but their hands, and feet. They danced two steps forward, then turned suddenly, as before; danced two steps forward again, and so on, till they reached the point from which they started. This they repeated, until the tune ended, which was very long. As soon as it ended, they all bounded and had a short breathing spell, standing in the same spot and attitude they happened to be in when the dance ended; but yet, though one would have supposed them nearly exhausted when they stopped, judging alone from their loud breathing, the chief speaker called upon them to labour on. 'Let us on, brothers and sisters,' said he, throwing his hands forward, suiting the action to the word, 'let us on, and take the kingdom of heaven by violence!' They rested about three minutes after which they commenced the dance again, though with a more lively step, quicker gesticulation, and a brisker voice than before. After this, they scattered in confusion, but came together again in the form of a circle, preparing for what they call the labouring march; they marched round the room in a circle, the singers being in the centre, pouring forth a high and low keyed hymn, to which the rest kept time, as they went round, with a quick rise and fall of their hands. When this was over, and after a sufficient pause, they began a quicker march, which they went through after the same fashion as the last. After about five minutes of deep silence, one of the society arose, came forward into the space between the males and females, and addressed those whom curiosity had brought there to witness their mode of worship. He spoke with fervour and animation, and expatiated, with a fluency that would have shamed many public speakers, upon the happiness attending their mode of life and worship. They then all arose, and joined in a hymn much the same as the one which commenced their exercises. The words of the hymn or psalm accompanying the slow labouring march were these, as well as I could catch them, now and then :

> " So let us live in this world below,
> Serving our God where'er we go,
> That when we quit this frame of clay,
> We may rise to glory's eternal day."

We believe that the Shakers have never had an established community in England, although Mr. Meredith's weird poem, " Jump to Glory Jane," is very suggestive of the vigorous mode of worship we have described above.

> " A Revelation came on Jane,
> The widow of a labouring swain :
> And first her body trembled sharp,
> Then all the woman was a harp
> With winds along the strings ; she heard
> Though there was neither tone nor word.

> " For past our hearing was the air,
> Beyond our speaking what it bare,
> And she within herself had sight
> Of heaven at work to cleanse outright,
> To make of her a mansion fit
> For angel hosts inside to sit.

" They entered, and forthwith entranced
    Her body braced, her members danced ;
    Surprisingly the woman leapt ;
    And countenance composed she kept ;
    As gossip neighbours in the lane
    Declared, who saw and pitied Jane.

" These knew she had been reading books,
    The which was witnessed by her looks
    Of late : she had a mania
    For mad folk in America,
    And said for sure they led the way,
    But meat and beer were meant to stay.

    *   *   *   *   *   *

" It was a scene when man and maid,
    Abandoning all other trade,
    And careless of the call to meals,
    Went jumping at the woman's heels.
    By dozens they were counted soon,
    Without a sound to tell their tune."

MEN'S APPAREL

1800–1870

" May he who writes a skillful tailor seem,
    And like a well made coat his present theme ;
    Tho' close, yet easy, decent but not dull,
    Short but not scanty, without buckram full."
                                —SAMUEL FOOTE.

Men's Apparel
1800–1810

" Be not the first by whom the new is tried
Nor yet the last to lay the old aside."
—POPE.

CCORDING to Mr. Ashton, in his " Dawn of the Nineteenth Century," " there is little to chronicle concerning the dress of the men as the radical changes during the last ten years of the eighteenth century maintained popularity for the first years of the nineteenth." The changes from season to season were trivial, it is true, from 1800 to 1810. A modification of the Jean Debry coat, popular in Paris after the Revolution and of which a copy of Gilray's caricature is given by Ashton, was worn in England and America, the shoulders much padded to give breadth and the coat buttoned at the waist to make the wearer look slender, and cut short enough to show the waistcoat which was usually of a contrasting colour. Sometimes two waistcoats were worn, an undervest of a bright colour showing above and below a drab or brown outer garment. Hessian boots were worn with this style of costume (Figure 345) and a high hat which in the early years of the century was usually very large. (See Figure 361.) Collars were worn extravagantly high, and slippers, according to Mr. Ashton, were preferred by

347

FIGURE 272.—1825—Bonnet of white silk gauze, with crown pattern of white carnations and stripes of yellow straw. Trimmed with white gauze ribbon with pale yellow and green figures. Wetherill collection, Memorial Hall, Philadelphia.

FIGURE 273.—1825–30—Leghorn hat trimmed with white ribbon. Piece of the brim cut away at the back and drawn up to the crown with a large bow. Strings and rosette over right ear. Wetherill collection, Memorial Hall.

FIGURE 274.—1829—Hat of sage green and salmon pink taffeta bound and corded with pink satin ribbon. Wetherill collection, Memorial Hall.

FIGURE 275.—1820—Bonnet of Tuscan straw trimmed with white ribbon. Wetherill collection, Memorial Hall.

FIGURE 276.—1830—Bonnet of white taffeta trimmed with white ribbon with fringed ends. Wetherill collection, Memorial Hall.

FIGURE 277.—1835—Bonnet of chip, brim faced with pale pink silk and trimmed with pink ribbon and white lace. Spray of small white flowers on top. From a plate.

FIGURE 278.—1833—Bonnet of white *point d'esprit* over white silk. Ribbon with satin spots and loop edge. Stiff crown ; brim made over slender wire frame and lined with white sarsenet. Miss Dutihl's collection, Memorial Hall, Philadelphia.

FIGURE 279.—1838—Bonnet of fancy straw trimmed with blue ribbon. From a plate.

FIGURE 280.—1840—Quilted silk hood. Wetherill collection, Memorial Hall.

FIGURE 281.—1839—Leghorn bonnet trimmed with plaid ribbon. Wetherill collection, Memorial Hall.

FIGURE 282.—1860—Bonnet of light velvet with white roses and green velvet leaves ; frills of blond lace inside the face ; two sets of strings—white ribbon and green velvet. Miss Dutihl's collection, Memorial Hall, Philadelphia.

FIGURE 283.—1863—Bonnet of brown horsehair braid ; black velvet ribbon, white tulle and red poppies inside the brim. Miss Dutihl's collection, Memorial Hall, Philadelphia.

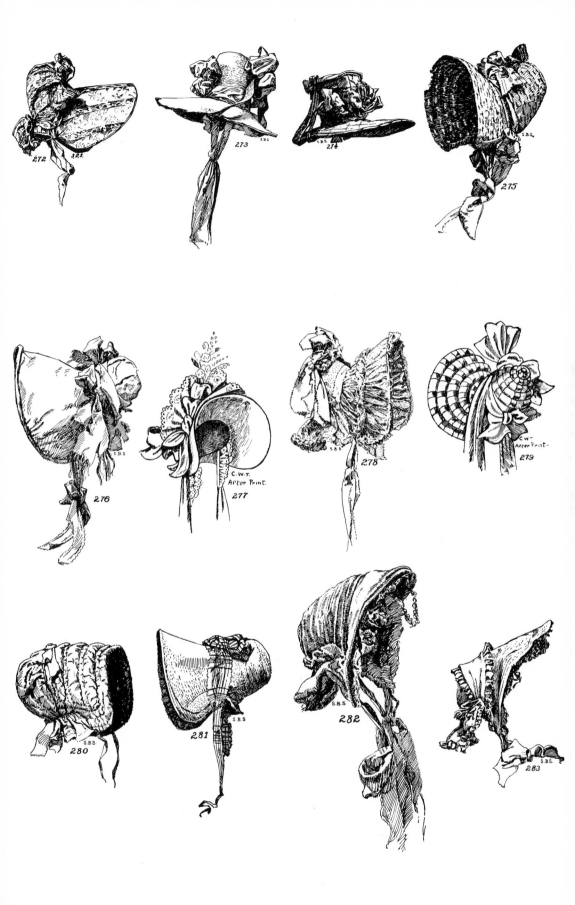

many to boots. Gay gallants still sported short trousers or "shorts," as they were familiarly called, and white waistcoats displaying ruffled shirts and high white stocks. Pantaloons, however, were a new fashion from Paris in 1800, and were chronicled in contemporary English verse:

"The French we conquered once
Now give us laws for pantaloons."

Trousers were not worn with evening dress, however, in the first quarter of the century.

The "Port Folio" for 1801 tells us of the fashions in the United States:

"All our young men of fashion wear frocks of dark blue, dark green, or dark brown cloth, with convex metal buttons, round hats with broad brims, short breeches and white stockings, or pantaloons with Hessian boots."

The frock coat of this period is illustrated in Figure 57 which is copied from a portrait by Sully painted in 1807. It was fashionable from 1800 to 1810, as well as the hat and short breeches for dress occasions which are shown in the same figure. The "Port Folio" is also the authority for the following items of fashion in this country:

"Mixed grey, bottle-green, Vandyke brown, and Spanish blue are the prevailing colours for morning coats, which are made in every respect the same as the dress coats, except that they have gilt basket buttons, sleeves with slits and three buttons, and pockets in the plaits of the skirts. Waistcoats are made of striped marseilles, and light-coloured double-milled cassimere pantaloons are worn with half-boots, or nankeen trousers and gaiters. We must not omit noticing in this place an ingenious article just invented, called Key's travelling waistcoat, which by folding answers the purpose of two waistcoats. It may be made either single or double-breasted, and of any material."

President Jefferson began his administration with an effort to set aside conventionality in dress and shocked the Federalist party by a certainly ill-timed exhibition of his democratic ideas. We are told by an eye-witness of his first inauguration, March, 1801, that " he made no preparation for the ceremony as far as his appearance was concerned. His indifference was ostentatious and evidently intended to cause comment. He wore a blue coat, a thick drab-coloured waistcoat with a red under-waistcoat lapped over it, green velveteen breeches with pearl buttons, yarn stockings, and slippers." Another contemporary says Jefferson's democratic simplicity was affected. " It was part of his political policy to dress badly, although he did not adopt it until he was elected President. While Minister to France he lived in great elegance, not only expending his entire salary, but drawing on his private income to maintain an appearance befitting his position. While a member of Congress and Secretary of State in Philadelphia, he occupied a beautiful place near Gray's Ferry outside the city. He was passionately fond of good horses and owned five beautifully matched bays, four to draw the carriage designed by himself, and one for his man, Burwell, who always rode behind. Two servants rode on horseback each guiding a pair, for he never trusted a driver with the lines." Many anecdotes are told of Mr. Jefferson's unceremonious treatment of the ambassadors from foreign countries during his eight years as President of the United States, but there has been much controversy published on the subject and it is difficult to get at the exact truth. The well-known portrait of Mr. Jefferson reproduced in Figure 296 is certainly not lacking in dignity nor propriety of dress.

In an American periodical of 1802 appeared the following paragraph under the heading " Parisian Fashions " :

" The young men still wear their coats very short, excessively *degagé*, and with the lapels buttoned. . . . Each lapel has now seven buttons instead of six. The three cocked hat is strictly and exclusively for full dress. The cockade is subject to almost daily changes in the combination of the three colours. The cravat is no longer so large. A great many wear frills. They wear at the knee-bands very small plain gold buckles, round or square, with rounded corners ; and in their shoes silver buckles of the same shape " (Figure 52).

The " Port Folio " printed this ridiculous satire in 1802 :

" RECIPE TO MAKE A MODERN BEAU

" Take anything . . . put it into a pair of pantaloons, put a binding on the top of the pantaloons (called a vest) and attach to the bosom of the shirt an oval glass case with a wig on it, pare away the skirts of its coat to the width of a hat-band. If the subject is doomed to pass its time in the house, it will require a heavy pair of round toed jack boots, with a tassel before and behind. Lift up by the cape of the coat, pull its hair over its face, lay a hat on its forehead, and spectacles on its nose.

" N. B. Its hands must, on no occasion, be suffered to escape from the pantaloon pockets, nor the spectacles from its nose."

It will be noticed that the fashionable high collars are often spoken of as capes in the printed descriptions of this period.

In another paper we find under " Fashions for September " (1802) :

" The following is now all the rage with the fashionables in London :

"Blue coat made very scant, with pockets in the skirts; blue velvet cape, high up in the neck; pantaloons of mix'd broadcloth made very loose, with pockets. Suwarrow boots (all the vogue) and black hat with a narrow brim!"

Of this new fashion in boots, which were made without any apparent seam, we read "the artist who has discovered the mode of kneading the leather so as to make solid boots, without any apparent seam, uses for the purpose a glossy gum, which prevents stains."

Hats were extravagantly large in 1802, and the shafts of "Mr. Oldschool's" ridicule are aimed at them in the following paragraph:

"Our High-street loungers sport a hat of an enormous circumference. A small beau is so overshadowed by one of Tiffin's best, that his dimensions to any thick sight are invisible."

The fashionable coat is the next target for his wit:

"I believe it is remarked in 'A Merry Connoisseur' that the winter fashions of London reach this country in sufficient season to be in full bloom at midsummer. Our coats, on this side of the Atlantic, are copied from the London model generally after the original has become quite faded at home. If an early autumnal scheme of dress can be of any use now, let the beau of Philadelphia copy the following, taking especial care, however, to avoid the old hat. Gentlemen's coats are very short and loose, the collars are merely turned over; round, concave middle-sized buttons of yellow metal are put on the facings at each side."

A curious anecdote concerning silk stockings, which were still worn with knee-breeches in Washington, in 1802, is told by Rev. Manasseh Cutler:

"On Thursday evening about ten, Mr. Dayton, going to bed, pulled off a pair of silk stockings, laid his stockings on his slippers at the bedside; he perceived some sparks as he pulled them off. In the morning both stockings were burnt to a cinder, threads appearing to lie in their position in a coil; slippers burnt to a crisp; carpet burnt through and floor to a coal, so as to cause the resin to run. Many gentlemen noted the sparking of their silk stockings as they went to bed. I wore silk stockings that day, but did not notice sparks."

In 1803 coats were made somewhat broader in the waist, and cut lower in the neck, and the collars were less high. Knee-breeches were still in favour and boots with high tops. High shirt collars were worn with stocks, and beaver hats with rolling brims. Mr. Ashton mentions an advertisement of a London firm in 1803, which offered " to make a gentleman's old hat as good as it was when new; gentlemen who prefer silk hats may have them silked and made water-proof." Late in 1803 long coats not cutaway came into fashion, also pantaloons reaching to the ankle, and in 1804 coats were worn much longer in the waist and slightly cutaway. Ruffled shirt fronts were fashionable and low cut waistcoats. High close-fitting boots were worn over long pantaloons (Figure 360). Hats changed a little in 1804, the brims drooped back and front and were rolled slightly at the sides (Figure 347). It became the fashion in this year to carry very short canes and a satirical couplet in the " Port Folio " for December, 1804, proves that the new fashion was in vogue in America also.

"SHORT CANES

" Two bucks, having lost their bamboos in a fray,
Side by side swagger'd into a toy-shop one day,
Each, by a new purchase his loss to repair—
But, lo ! when for payment our heroes prepare,
All the cash in their pockets, together combin'd,
For the purchase of *one* scarce sufficient they find.
In common they buy it ; and, nice to a hair,
In two they divide it, and each takes his share.

1800–1860

FIGURE 284.—1835–50—Quaker hat of black silk beaver. Memorial Hall, Philadelphia.

FIGURE 285.—1857—Shaker girl in costume. From a print.

FIGURE 286.—1860—A Quaker bonnet of brown satin, showing a ruffled cap of sheer lawn underneath.

FIGURE 287.—1830—Grey beaver hat with a broad brim, worn by a Quaker gentleman in Philadelphia.

FIGURE 288.—1800—Pencil sketch of Mary Howitt as a child in Quaker costume.

FIGURE 289.—1860—Quaker dress of brown satin with white kerchief crossed in front and fastened under the belt. White silk shawl and cap of sheer lawn. Typical costume of a Quaker lady for many years. This dress was worn in Philadelphia in 1860.

FIGURE 290.—1857—Costume of a young Shaker. From an old print.

FIGURE 291.—1840—Silk rain-cover for a bonnet. Wetherill collection.

FIGURE 292.—1857—Outdoor dress of a Shaker girl. From an old print.

FIGURE 293.—1830—Quaker bonnet of white silk. Memorial Hall, Philadelphia.

284 S.B.S.

285
C.W.Trout.
After Print.

286 C.W.TROUT.
1907.

287 S.B.S.

288

289 Cecil W. Trout.

290 C.W.TROUT.
After Print.

291 S.B.S.

292 C.W.T. After Print.

293 S.B.S.

Our beaux economic, improving the hint,
The length of their canes have determined to stint :
And when they would buy, a whole company splice
Their pence and their farthings, to make up the price,
Hence, view the smart beau, and you soon ascertain
The depth of his purse, by the length of his cane.''

Coats in 1805 were long and not cutaway, with tails full in
the back. Waistcoats were cut high and single-breasted, and
the long close-fitting trousers were shaped over the instep like
gaiters and fastened under the boot with a strap. Long gaiters
were also in fashion reaching as high as the knee. The newest
hats were very big, having wide brims and high crowns. Top-
coats with three capes were very generally worn.

Many varieties of dress must have been observed in Washington in the first decade of the nineteenth century, when the
foreign legations displayed so many rich colours and such a
wealth of embroidery. A contemporary makes the following
mention of a foreign minister at the President's levee in 1805 :

" We went at twelve. The French Minister, General Tau-
reau, had been in, and was returning. We met him at the door,
covered with lace almost from head to foot, and very much
powdered. Walked with his hat off, though it was rather
misty ; his Secretary, one Aide, and one other with him. When
we went in the number was small, but soon increased, until the
Levee room, which is large, was nearly full. A large number
of ladies, Heads of Departments, Foreign Ministers and Consuls
and the greater part of both Houses of Congress. The British
Minister was in a plain dress, but superb carriage."

But even a civilian's dress could be made gay with one of
the fanciful waistcoats in vogue. At the Historical Society in
Philadelphia is preserved a quilted vest of bright gold-coloured
satin which was once worn by Mr. George Logan of Stenton,

a Quaker gentleman of some renown. It is wadded slightly and lined with heavy linen probably with a view to warmth, but the edge of the brilliant satin evidently showed above an outer waistcoat of a sombre tint. Waistcoats were apparently the most important article of masculine costume at that time, and it is amusing to read that the great English statesman, Fox, and Lord Carlisle " made a journey from Paris to Lyons for the sole purpose of procuring something new in waistcoats, and talked of nothing else by the way."

In 1806 we read of fashionable full dress coats cutaway and made with small rolling collars and revers, the tails reaching to the knee. With these coats very short waistcoats were worn, and knee-breeches fastened with small buttons on the outside of the leg, black pumps and stockings of white silk, ruffled shirts and fine cambric stocks. A cocked hat or a *chapeau bras* completed this full dress costume, which is illustrated in Figure 57. The *chapeau bras*, which is mentioned in many descriptions of court dress, is shown in Figure 340 from a print of 1807.

A walking suit of that time consisted usually of a blue coat with black buttons, buff breeches buttoned a little below the knee, over which boots with turned-down tops of buff kid were worn. High stock of white linen and high hat of beaver as shown in Figure 361.

From " Follies and Fashions of our Grandfathers " we transcribe the following :

" GENERAL OBSERVATIONS ON GENTLEMEN'S DRESS FOR 1807

" The general mourning ordered on account of the death of the venerable Duke of Brunswick has prevented much alteration in gentlemen's dress ; evening parties in the fashionable world have been a mere assemblage of sables ; and as many gentlemen's wardrobes furnished them with what was deemed sufficient for the purpose, the inventors of fashion found themselves completely cramped and disappointed in the great field of taste." *

The short period of court mourning over, a great variety of costumes were announced as follows :

" Morning coats of dark brown mixtures, or dark green mixtures, made either according to the same style as the evening coats, or single breasted and rather short, are still fashionable. These we observe to have generally a moderate-sized metal plated button ; and though collars of the same cloth are much used, a black velvet collar is considered as carrying a greater degree of style. For morning wear : Drab-coloured cloth coat, single-breasted, with pantaloons to match, which for the sake of avoiding the weight or incumbrance of boots, are made with buttoned gaiters attached ; with the addition of a striped waistcoat. This costume has undoubtedly a very genteel appearance."

" A single-breasted coat of a dark green or green " mixture with a collar of the same cloth, and plated buttons ; light coloured striped waistcoat made single-breasted, and light drab-coloured or leather breeches, with brown top boots " is a costume suggested for riding or walking."

We read now for the first time of the " parsley mixture, which is beginning to usurp popular preference ; coats of this colour are worn single-breasted with collars of the same cloth, and almost universally plated buttons ; they are shorter than the evening coats, made without pocket flaps, and rendered as light as possible." Quilted waistcoats are also mentioned " printed in stripes, single-breasted and without binding." " Light coloured kerseymere pantaloons or breeches and gaiters," and " white or nankin trousers with or without

* Follies and Fashions of Our Grandfathers, by Andrew W. Tuer.

gaiters" are fashionable details announced for 1807, but worn for several years afterwards.

"We have noticed many gentlemen in plain buff kersey-mere waistcoats of a very pale colour, which certainly have a neat appearance; others of a sort of pearl colour, and also some of scarlet kerseymere, which after being rejected for several years seem to be again coming into notice; but as they do not correspond with the coats usually worn, nor afford a pleasant contrast, they are not likely to become by any means general; indeed, blue or dark brown or corbeau colour coats are the only ones that can well be worn with a scarlet waist-coat. Brown top boots seem to be more worn than they have been for some time past, and with kerseymere breeches, in preference to leather. We have also observed that many gentle-men in their morning walks have attempted to introduce a sort of shooting dress, a short coat of any light colour, and with drab colour cloth or kerseymere gaiters to come up to the knees; but, however well such a dress may suit a watering place or a walk over the grounds of an estate, we do not think it adapted to the promenade of Bond Street. There is also a new article in the waistcoat fashion, which is a sort of silky shag well adapted to the season; and has a good appearance in riding dress, but we think does not seem perfectly in char-acter, unless accompanied with brown top boots and a riding whip."

For September, 1807, we read: "Morning coats of various mixtures are worn; the parsley mixture is decidedly the most fashionable, and that made single-breasted, with a collar of the same cloth, large size plated buttons, and without pocket flaps. Striped marseilles waistcoats single-breasted, or plain buff kerseymere waistcoats, of a pale colour, single-breasted, but not bound. Drab colour kerseymere pantaloons with Hessian boots, or India nankin trousers and gaiters. Dark olive cloth mixtures with covered buttons vie with dark forest green in favour, but blue cloth with gilt buttons is likely to retain popularity. White marseilles waistcoats, single-breasted, and light drab cloth or nankin breeches are still considered the most genteel."

Mixed cloths apparently gained in favour, for another morning dress for gentlemen of this material is given: "A coat, single-breasted, cut off in the front, and made of pepper and salt mixture, with covered or plated buttons, and collar of the same cloth; the skirt rather shorter than the dress coats, and the pockets in the plaits behind. Waistcoats of printed marseilles made single-breasted are most popular and are made without any binding. Light drab kerseymere pantaloons are still worn; as also drab kerseymere breeches with gilt buttons and brown top boots. Nankin pantaloons and trousers are becoming very prevalent as well as nankin gaiters."

In November of the same year, we are told: "Morning coats are still popular of greenish-olive or mixtures, and are worn both double-breasted and single; they are seen with plain plated buttons and collars of the same cloth, and made without pocket flaps, the pocket being put in the plaits behind. Striped toilinet waistcoats of clear distinct stripes, bound with silk binding. Drab kerseymere breeches to come down over the knee with gilt buttons, and brown top boots, or pantaloons of the same colour and Hussar boots. The great coats are generally made of olive browns, single-breasted, with collars of the same cloth, and covered buttons; the skirts lined with silk of the same colour. Many gentlemen who wish to appear in the height of the fashion have the front lined with silk, and if the weather permits the coat to be worn open, this has certainly a very dashing appearance."

1800–1860

FIGURE 294.—1800—Natural hair and high stock. Portrait of Charles Carroll, by St. Memin.

FIGURE 295.—1800—Powdered hair and queue. Portrait of Mr. Brumaud, by St. Memin.

FIGURE 296.—1801—Natural hair and ruffled shirt. Portrait of Thomas Jefferson.

FIGURE 297.—1802—Powdered hair and queue. Portrait of Dr. Rush, by St. Memin.

FIGURE 298.—1802—Powdered hair and queue. Portrait of DuBarry, by St. Memin.

FIGURE 299.—1804—Natural hair and side whiskers. Portrait of Nathaniel Williams, by St. Memin.

FIGURE 300.—1809—Natural hair and clerical stock. Portrait of Rev. Dr. Simons, by St. Memin.

FIGURE 301.—1809—Hair in queue. Portrait of James Madison.

FIGURE 302.—1821—Natural hair parted in the middle. Portrait of James Monroe.

FIGURE 303.—1845—White hair and judge's robe. Portrait of Judge Story.

FIGURE 304.—1840—Black stock and standing collar. Portrait of Franklin Pierce.

FIGURE 305.—1860—Low white stock and high collar. Portrait of James Buchanan.

The colours and combinations for evening dress for gentlemen in 1807 long remained in fashion, as will be seen from the illustrations given for the first half of the century.

"Dark blues with flat gilt buttons, with collars of the same, or of black velvet, according to the fancy of the wearer. The buttons on green coats are guided by fancy. White waistcoats are universal. Breeches are generally of nankin, or light drabs and pearl-coloured kerseymeres."

There were many changes in cut and design from time to time. An evening suit is described in 1809 consisting of a "double breasted dark blue coat with large yellow double gilt buttons; white marseilles waistcoat; light brown kerseymere breeches, with strings to the knees; white silk stockings; shoes with buckles," and at that date we learn "the collar though made to rise well up in the neck, is, however, not so extremely high as it was formerly. It is now made to admit of a small portion of the neck cloth being seen above it; it then descends gradually on the sides of the neck, so as to fall open and rather low in front; the waistcoats are worn both double and single-breasted with collars of moderate heights, and as they are buttoned only half way up, and only two or three of the lower buttons of the coat fastened, they show the drapery of the shirt to much advantage. The breeches come tolerably high up on the hip, and end two or three inches below the bend of the knee, where they sit perfectly close. We notice that waistcoats and small clothes of kerseymere are much more fashionable than silk, which has been gradually declining in favour for many years, and satin which was considered essential to complete the dress of a gentleman, a few years back, has gone out utterly; a pair of satin breeches would attract the observation of every beholder almost as much as a maroon coloured coat."

The following paragraph appeared in a fashion book of 1808:

"Evening dress is invariably black. The coats have constantly collars of the same cloth, and covered buttons : black kerseymere waistcoat and breeches are considered genteel : black silk stockings are necessary in dress parties." Research convinces us, however, that if black was ever recognized as the fashionable colour for evening costume at that period, it had but a brief popularity, light trousers and blue coats gaining ascendency again in the course of the same year.

James Madison succeeded President Jefferson in 1809. He was not only an intimate friend of his predecessor, but to some extent his disciple, and represented the Whigs in opposition to the Federalists. It was said that the barbers were all adherents of the latter party because the leaders of the Federalists wore long queues and powder and thus gave them constant employment, whereas the Whigs wore short hair or small queues tied carelessly with a ribbon (Figure 301). The following anecdote is told by Mrs. Wilder Goodwin in her " Life of Dolly Madison " :

"On the nomination of Madison, a barber burst out : 'The country is doomed ; what Presidents we might have, sir ! Just look at Dagget of Connecticut, or Stockton of New Jersey ! what queues they have got, sir ! as big as your fist and powdered every day, sir, like the real gentlemen they are. Such men, sir, would confer dignity upon the chief magistracy ; but this little Jim Madison, with a queue no bigger than a pipe-stem ! Sir, it is enough to make a man forswear his country.' "

Judging from the numerous portraits painted in 1809, we doubt if the barbers had a good business outlook in any country, for fashion then decreed short hair and no powder, and although a few elderly beaux appear to have worn both until 1810, they illustrated the exception rather than the rule. Another contemporary relates that President Madison " never altered his style of dress. He always wore a plain black cloth coat and knee-breeches with buckles, the hair powdered and worn in a queue behind; the daily task of dressing it devolved upon his wife who did not think his body servant capable of doing it justice." *

This practice probably gave fresh displeasure to the barbers, but it is not a little surprising to read of the use of powder, which actually went out of fashion in 1794, and according to several authorities was regarded almost as a badge of the Federalists in 1809. The following account of Madison's appearance at his first inauguration is from a contemporary pen :

" Arrived at the Capitol, Madison descended from his carriage and entered the Hall of Representatives, where, until the inauguration of Monroe, the newly elected President took the oath of office. Madison was attended by the Attorney-General and other Cabinet officers. One who saw him describes him as looking unusually well, the excitement of the occasion lending colour to his pale studious face, and dignity to his small slender figure. He was dressed in a suit of clothes wholly of American manufacture, made of the wool from merino sheep bred and reared in this country. His coat was from the manufactory of Colonel Humphreys, and his waistcoat and small clothes from that of Chancellor Livingston, both being gifts offered in token of respect by those gentlemen. At twelve o'clock, with marked dignity and composure of manner, he took the oath of office, administered by Chief-Justice Marshall and, amid deafening cheers, as President of the United States began his inaugural address." †

No history of dress in the nineteenth century would be complete without mention of the celebrated " Beau Brummell."

* Mrs. Seaton's Letters.   † First Forty Years of Washington Society.

> "In Brummell's day of buckle shoes,
> Starch cravats and roll collars,
> They'd fight and war and bet and lose,
> Like gentlemen and scholars." *

His figure, which he always dressed so carefully, is described by Captain Jesse as unusually well proportioned. " Brummell," he says, " was about the height of the Apollo," a rather startling comparison, for it is as difficult to think of one in connection with clothes as of the other without them, " and the just proportions of his form were remarkable; his hand was particularly well shaped. His face was rather long and his complexion fair ; his whiskers inclined to sandy and hair light brown. His features were neither plain nor handsome, but his head was well shaped, the forehead being unusually high."

According to another authority, the early part of his career was signalized by the famous pair of gloves to insure the perfection of which two glovers were employed, " one charged with the working of the thumbs and the other the fingers and the rest of the hands, and three coiffeurs were engaged to dress his hair, one for the temples, one for the front, and the third for his occiput. His boots were *cirés au vin de champagne*, and his ties designed by a portrait painter of note."

> " But my beautiful taste (as indeed you will guess)
> Is manifest most in my toilet and dress.
> My neck-cloth, of course, forms my principal care,
> For by that we criterions of elegance swear,
> And costs me each morning some hours of flurry,
> To make it appear to be tied in a hurry ;
> My top-boots—those unerring marks of a blade—
> With champagne are polished, and peach marmalade.
> And a violet coat, closely copied from Byng ;
> And a cluster of seals and a large diamond ring ;
> And *trosièmes* of buckskin, bewitchingly large,
> Give the finishing strokes to the *parfait ouvrage.*" †

* London Lyrics.   † Pursuit of Fashion.

Brummell is accredited with the revival of taste in dress among gentlemen which had been conspicuously lacking at the end of the eighteenth century. His first innovation was in the arrangement of neck-cloths. " His collars were always fixed to his shirt and so large that before being folded down they completely hid his face and head ; the neck-cloth was almost a foot in height ; the collar was fastened down to its proper size and Brummell, standing before the glass, by the gradual declension of his lower jaw creased the cravat to reasonable dimensions."

> " All is unprofitable, flat,
> And stale, without a smart *Cravat*
> Muslined enough to hold its starch—
> That last keystone of Fashion's arch ! "

In his dress he was distinguished for great neatness and perfection of fit, but never for singularity or striking combinations.

For morning wear he appeared in Hessians and pantaloons, or top-boots and buckskins, with a blue coat and a light or buff coloured waistcoat, so that his ordinary costume was similar to that of any other gentleman in Europe or America ; but, we are told by contemporary authority, it fitted " to admiration the best figure in England." His favourite evening dress was a blue coat and white waistcoat; black pantaloons, which fastened tight to the ankle; striped silk stockings and an opera hat. " He was always carefully dressed, but never the slave of fashion." We need not follow the checkered fortunes of this, for many years, cynosure of style, to their pathetic ending at Caen in 1840. The biographer already quoted says, " Brummell and Bonaparte, who had hitherto divided the attention of the world, fell together." A portrait of Beau Brummell (about 1804) is given in Figure 360.

1828–1850

FIGURE 306.—1828—Walking costume.   From a plate.

FIGURE 307.—1830—Walking costume.   From a plate.

FIGURE 308.—1837—Walking costume, showing Aspic cloak.   From a plate.

FIGURE 309.—1839—Two walking costumes.   From a plate.

FIGURE 310.—1840–50—Three costumes of this period.   From a plate.

FIGURE 311.—1845–50—Three costumes of this period.   From a plate.

306

307

308

309

310

311

In the early part of the nineteenth century, Doctors of Medicine were distinguished by long black coats and gold-headed canes. Edmund Yates makes the following statement on this subject in his "Reminiscences": "There are Brightonians yet alive who talk to me of my uncle, Dr. Yates, remembering him with his white hair, snowy shirt frill, Hessian boots, or black gaiters, long black coat and gold-headed cane; a man of importance in the town, physician to the Sussex County Hospital, etc., etc." * Mr. Ashton declares also that during the Regency (1810–1819) "Doctors still clung to their wigs."

Shirts trimmed down the front with ruffles of the finest linen cambric, finished with minute rolled hems, were worn by young and old. The following epigram was printed about 1808, in " La Belle Assemblée":

"SHIRTS AND SHIFTS

"Old Musty had married a modish young flirt,
Who, calling one holiday morn for her shirt,
'Why, how now,' quoth Musty, 'what say you,' quoth he,
'What, do you wear a shirt, Moll?'—'Be sure, Sir,' quoth she,
'All women wear shirts'—'Nay,' quoth he, 'then I trow
What has long been a riddle is plain enough now;
For when women wear shirts, it can lack no great gifts
To discern why their husbands are put to their shifts.'"

Marvels of needlework and feminine patience were the shirts of the first half of the nineteenth century, all made by hand, of course, and with innumerable three-cornered gussets put in to strengthen the seams, and with ruffles of finest linen cambric. Let us hope they were appreciated by the lords of creation who wore them. In the letters of Miss Southgate, the writer speaks of completing a dozen shirts for her father in 1812. A picture of a shirt of 1812 and one of 1830 are given in Figures 337 and

* Reminiscences of Fifty Years.

363.   Happily this painful episode in the history of dress is cast into oblivion by the universal use of the sewing-machine, but the pathetic verses in the " Song of the Shirt " were founded on the true story of many an overworked sempstress in the first half of the nineteenth century :

> " Oh, men with sisters dear!
>   Oh, men with mothers and wives,
> It is not linen you're wearing out
> But human creatures' lives!" *

The following amusing advertisements appeared in " La Belle Assemblée " for 1809 :

" Patent Travelling Hair Caps.—Perfectly unique.—This very useful Invention is entirely new, and particularly well adapted for Officers in the Army and Navy, and Travellers in general, who are obliged to wear either a Welsh Wig or Night-cap, which, from their unhandsome or awkward appearance, persons are under the necessity of throwing off when alighting from the carriage, etc.

" The traveller's hair cap, now recommended to the attention of the Public, possesses every comfort of the former, with the appearance of a curled head of hair, and, from its peculiar elasticity, sits perfectly close to the head without any sort of springs whatever, and cannot be put out of order.   The Hair Caps are equally convenient for the Ladies.   They may be had of the Inventors, Robinson and Holmes, No. 1, Essex-street, Strand, Peruke-Makers to their Royal Highnesses the Prince of Wales, Duke of Clarence, and to the Theatre Royal, Covent Garden. Price one Guinea each.   Considerable allowance made to Retailers.   Sailors and Travellers by Sea, will find incredible ad-

* Hood's Song of the Shirt.   First published in Punch, 1843.

vantage from the use of the Hair Caps ; and Judges and Gentlemen of the Bar.

"Head-dresses, by the King's Royal Letters Patent, lately
granted for a recent discovery in the art of making Head-dresses,
etc., similar to nature, being so ingeniously wrought as to
imitate the skin of the head and the hair as if implanted
therein.

"Sold only by Vickery, No. 6, Tavistock-street, Covent
Garden."

Men's Apparel
1810–1830

"And he the hero of the night was there,
In breeches of light drab, and coat of blue."

 IN the second and third decades of the nineteenth century, we notice that "coats of blue" were still the favoured fashion for both full dress and street costume. In 1810 the tails of coats were rather shorter than in the preceding year, and "did not come lower than within four inches of the knee," according to an acknowledged authority on the subject, "The Repository of Arts." Coats were made, we gather from the same source, with long lappels ending on a line with the hip buttons. The waists were longer too, and the collars, which were cut very high, were slightly padded to make them fit smoothly and were set back about two inches from the neck. Buttons of gilt or silver were worn on both dress and morning coats. Sleeves were made very long. The full dress coat had round cuffs without buttons, and pockets with flaps on the hips. In morning coats the sleeves were slit at the wrist and finished with three large buttons.

Breeches of light drab, made tight-fitting at the hips, and rather long, were in general favour. Pantaloons were made of a material called "double milled-stocking," something like the stockinette of to-day; and a striped kerseymere, adopted by the Prince of Wales, whose taste in matters of masculine attire was rivalled only by Beau Brummell, became very fashionable in 1810.

Waistcoats were gay at this time. They were made single-breasted and with short regimental skirts, the collar fitting under the coat collar. The favourite material was striped marseilles of various colours.

Green was a popular colour, especially for top-coats which were made double-breasted and trimmed with covered buttons. The tails were wonderfully full and had pockets in the plaits at the back. The shape of the coat shown in Figure 55 was fashionable for many years.

In 1811, hats with low crowns and curved brims were introduced, but not to the exclusion of high hats, which have been unaccountably popular ever since the end of the seventeenth century. Walking coats were not cut away, but buttoned up the front. Light pantaloons reaching to the ankle were a characteristic fashion of that year, and black shoes were universally worn.

The next year, 1812, is noticeable for a change in the shape of the high hats. Brims were made very narrow and drooped very much both back and front, while the crowns were narrow at the top like the sugar-loaf crowns worn in 1850. (See Figure 347.) There was a change in the waistcoats too. They were cut high and close up to the chin, allowing only a small bow-necktie to show. Coats were again short-waisted and cut away, showing the waistcoats. Long pantaloons of cloth were worn with high boots (Figure 95). Pictures of this date show long, close-fitting pantaloons finished with a row of small buttons above the ankle. An illustration is given in Figure 363 of a pair made of buff-coloured duck which were worn in Boston about 1812.

Though, as we know now, pantaloons had come to stay,

1860–1870

FIGURE 312.—1860—Lady in white worked muslin dress over a fashionable hoop-skirt. The dress is made with seven graduated flounces and full bell sleeves. From a plate. Head from a contemporary portrait.

FIGURE 313.—1862—Walking costume of this date. A black velvet pelisse over black silk gown. Black bonnet faced with pink. Muff of chinchilla. From a contemporary photograph.

FIGURE 314.—1864—Gentleman in frock coat suit. From a portrait of this date.

FIGURE 315.—1868—Young lady in a dress of blue Chambéry gauze. Head from a contemporary portrait.

FIGURE 316.—1870—Street dress of dull green silk. Mantilla trimmed with black lace. Small bonnet trimmed with roses. From a plate of this date.

FIGURE 317.—1869—Ball dress of white Chambéry gauze trimmed with white satin folds and blond lace. Worn in this year. Head from a contemporary print.

FIGURE 318.—1870—Gentleman in walking suit of dark blue coat, drab pantaloons, white waistcoat, and grey beaver hat. From a photograph of this date.

1860-312   1862-313   1864-314

C W Trout. 1907.

1868-315   1870-316   1869-317   1870-318

Cecil Whittier Trout. 1907.

much hostility was at first shown towards them.   Taken from the military dress introduced into the army by the Duke of Wellington during the Peninsular war, and at first known as " Wellington trousers," they came into more or less general use at the beginning of the nineteenth century, when the clergy and the fashionable world combined to oppose the innovation. An original trust deed, executed in 1820, of a Non-conformist chapel contains a clause providing that " under no circumstances shall a preacher be allowed to occupy the pulpit who wears long trousers " ; * and we are also informed that Almack's would not admit any one so attired.   The universities were equally firm in their opposition, and in 1812 the authorities of Trinity and St. John's Colleges, Cambridge, decreed that students appearing in hall or chapel in pantaloons or long trousers should be considered absent. †

Whiskers came into vogue in 1800 and were extremely fashionable in 1812.   They are commemorated in the following verses published in a magazine of that year :

> " With whiskers thick upon my face,
>   I went my fair to see ;
>   She told me she could never love
>   A bear-faced chap like me.
>
> " I shaved them clean and called again,
>   And thought my troubles o'er ;
>   She laughed outright and said I was
>   More bare-faced than before."

A fashion plate of 1814 shows a close-fitting top-coat of green cloth with cuffs and collar of fur.   The back seams of the coat are trimmed with a flat black braid, the tails plaited

* Early Hostility to Trousers, by William Andrews.
† Cooper's Annals of Cambridge.

full and the sleeves long and tight-fitting. With this coat was worn a small chimney-pot hat with drooping brim.

The new king, Louis XVIII, sent M. de Neuville to represent France in the United States and, in the letters of Mrs. Samuel Harrison Smith which have already furnished us with many valuable facts in the History of Dress of her time, we find a description of the costumes of the French delegation.

" M. de Neuville and suite were at Mrs. Monroe's Drawing-room in the most splendid costumes, not their court dress however. Blue coats covered with gold embroidery. The collar and back literally covered with wreaths of *fleurs-de-lys*. With white underclothes and huge chapeaux with feathers. The Minister's feather was white, the Secretaries' black and their dress, tho' in the same style, was not so superb as his."

At the same time Mrs. Seaton wrote the following account of the gorgeous equipage and liveries of the French Minister on the occasion of a reception at the President's house :

" After partaking of some ice-creams and a glass of Madeira, shaking hands with the President and tendering our good wishes, we were preparing to leave the rooms, when our attention was attracted through the window towards what we conceived to be a rolling ball of burnished gold, carried with swiftness through the air by two gilt wings. Our anxiety increased the nearer it approached, until it actually stopped before the door ; and from it alighted, weighted with gold lace, the French Minister and suite. We now also perceived that what we had supposed to be wings, were nothing more than gorgeous footmen with *chapeaux bras*, gilt braided skirts and splendid swords. Nothing ever was witnessed in Washington so brilliant and dazzling, a meridian sun blazing full on this carriage filled with diamonds and glittering orders, and gilt to the edge of the wheels,—you may well imagine

how the natives stared and rubbed their eyes to be convinced
'twas no fairy dream."

President Monroe endeavoured to restore some of the stately
formalities which had distinguished official life in the capital
during the administrations of Washington and Adams.   When
he sent Mr. Pinckney as Minister to France, the diplomatic
dress of our legations at all the foreign courts was very rich
and dignified.   A portrait of Richard Rush of Philadelphia,
who was Minister at the Court of St. James from 1817 to 1825,
in the possession of his granddaughter, shows a blue coat
richly embroidered with gold.   It was lined with white silk
and worn with white waistcoat, ruffled shirt, knee-breeches
and white silk stockings.   A dress sword and *chapeau bras* completed this costume.

The formal tea-drinkings, solemn weekly dinners at the
White House, and the " infrequent receptions " of Mrs. Monroe
were relieved by numerous card parties and conversation parties.   These, we learn, were " very elegant " at the British Minister's, and " very gay " at the French Embassy.   M. de Neuville it seems " used to puzzle and astound the plain-living
Yankees by serving dishes of turkeys without bones and pud-
dings in the form of fowls, fresh cod dressed as salad, celery like
oysters ; further he scandalized some and demoralized others by
having dancing parties on Saturday evenings, which the New
England ladies had been educated to consider as holy time."

During the last years of the Regency a marvellous variety of
cravats were introduced.

" A book on the intricate subject of cravats was published at
London in 1818 entitled ' Neckclothitania, or Titania : being an
Essay on Starchers, By One of the Cloth.'   The fashionable
varieties of neck-wear at that time appear to have been the Napoleon, American, Mail-Coach, Osbaldestan and Irish ties ; and

another called the Mathematical tie from its triangular form is described as being only one degree less severe than the Oriental tie, which was so high that the wearer could not see where he was going and so stiff that he could not turn his head."

One article of men's attire which has the distinction of an illustrious name and was very popular both in England and America from 1815 to 1850 was the Wellington boot. It was perhaps the most fashionable foot-wear for gentlemen in the first half of the nineteenth century and was popularly supposed to have been designed by the Duke of Wellington, for whom it was undoubtedly named. These boots were made of calfskin and fitted close to the leg as far as the knee and were worn under long trousers fastened with a strap beneath the sole of the boot. (See Figure 343.)

Mr. Richard Rush of Philadelphia was still Minister at the Court of Great Britain at the time of the accession of George IV. In his Memoirs (1817–1825) he describes the gorgeous celebration of the coronation on July 19, 1820. Speaking of the diplomatic corps on that occasion he observes that the box prepared for the Foreign Ambassadors and Ministers was at the south end of the building (Westminster Abbey) opposite the space fitted up for the Royal Family. It was near the throne, affording a good view of the imposing ceremony. The gorgeous costumes worn by the participants in the drama were afterwards reproduced in colour by order of his Majesty and published in a portfolio volume by Sir George Nayler. These costumes must have been very handsome and very hot for a July day. The mantles were of velvet lined and trimmed with fur, and the hats were heavy with groups of ostrich plumes.

In the Memoirs of Lester Wallack, the renowned actor, we find the later history of these same costumes. He says:

" George IV was a most theatrical man in all he did, and

when his coronation took place he dressed all his courtiers and everybody about him in peculiarly dramatic costumes. Dresses of Queen Elizabeth's time. It was all slashed trunks and side cloaks, etc. Of course the dukes, earls and barons were particularly disgusted at the way they had to exhibit themselves and as soon as the coronation ceremonies were over these things were thrown aside and sold, and Elliston bought an enormous number of them. He was then the lessee of the Surrey Theatre where he got up a great pageant and presented the Coronation of George IV."

In the spring of 1820 the Honourable Stratford Canning came to the United States as Minister from Great Britain. In his Memoirs there is an interesting description of the onerous preparations the post entailed. It was considered essential to bring furniture, servants, and all the household equipment he required from England, and it took three days to get his effects on board the ship. He brought over eleven servants, including a French cook. A cabriolet too was brought, but we hear nothing of horses and infer that America was thought capable of supplying suitable steeds for his distinguished use. As he was one of the greatest men England has ever sent to this country, he deserved to be made comfortable, even if his remarks on the manners and customs of the people he met were not always flattering.

He came in a friendly spirit; to use his own words : " The duty imposed upon me by the authorities in Downing Street was principally to keep the peace between Mother and Daughter. It was not easy to keep the peace when the daughter was as vain and sensitive as new fledged independence could make her." Landing at Baltimore, he says : " Fair accommodations awaited me at the Inn, and such native luxuries as soft crabs and cakes made of Indian corn opened a new field to the curious appetite." Of Washington, which he reached the following day, he seems to have received a rather dismal impression. " I know not what appearance the grand seat of government with its Capitol and the celebrated White House present at this period, but when I first saw it forty-eight years ago the Pennsylvania Avenue, extending from one to the other, or nearly so, was the only thing approaching our notion of a street and that for the most part rather prospectively than in actual existence. A low flat space of considerable extent formed the site of the embryo metropolis of the Union."

On the subject of dress he remarks: " Breeches and silk stockings are not infrequently worn of an evening, but these innovations are perhaps confined to the regions of Washington. Even here the true republican virtues have found refuge. At the Foreign Office, trousers, worsted stockings and gaiters for winter. In summer a white roundabout, *i. e.*, cotton jacket, *sans* neck-cloth, *sans* stockings and sometimes *sans* waistcoat. The Speaker of the House in the United States sits in his chair of office wigless and ungowned. I observed several of the members of Congress quite as well dressed as Martin Pitt. The Quakers struck me as being particularly attentive to their persons, their chins close shaved and their hats of the best beaver. Monday, March 9th, when all attended the President's Inauguration in lace coats and silk stockings, was a most wretched day, but as Talleyrand said, ' Nothing is settled in America, not even the climate.' I might be tempted to describe the costume which I assumed since the summer set in, not omitting my white cotton jacket, my umbrella and brimmed hat of Leghorn."

This is Mr. Canning's picture; now let us look on that of Mrs. Seaton from whose entertaining letters we quote as follows :

"The city is unusually gay, and crowded with agreeable and distinguished visitors. Mr. Canning's initiatory ball seemed to rouse the emulation of his neighbours, and we have had a succession of *fêtes*. The British Minister's route was unique. The English are half a century before us in style. Handsome pictures, books, and all sorts of elegant litter distinguish his rooms, the mansion being decorated with peculiar taste and propriety. Mr. Canning is himself a most unpretending man in appearance and manners; modesty appears to be his peculiar characteristic, which for a foreign minister is no negative praise. The birthnight * ball was brilliant. The contrast between the plain attire of President Monroe and Mr. Adams and the splendid uniforms of the diplomatic corps, was very striking, the gold, silver and jewels donned by the foreigners in compliment to the anniversary festival of our patriot and hero certainly adding splendour to the scene. The captivating D'Aprament made his *début* in brilliant crimson indispensables laced with gold, an embroidered coat, stars and orders, golden scabbard and golden spurs. Poor girls! Perfectly irresistible in person, he besieged their hearts and not content with his triumphs there, his sword entangled their gowns, his spurs demolished their flounces, in the most attractive manner possible; altogether he was proclaimed invincibly charming. M. de Neuville has adopted a new course since his return. Formerly, his secretaries were remarkably small and insignificant in appearance, but he now appears to have selected his legation by their inches. The most cultivated Frenchman whom I have ever met is in M. de Neuville's family, the Chevalier du Menu. He has resided ten years in America, and is a poet, orator, and scientific man, though still young."

* Washington's birthday.

1830–1840

FIGURE 319.—Evening dress.   Portrait of Disraeli, by Maclise.

FIGURE 320.—Street dress.   Portrait of Leigh Hunt, by Maclise.

FIGURE 321.—Street dress.   Portrait of Count d'Orsay, by Maclise.

FIGURE 322.—Dressing gown.   Portrait of Count d'Orsay, by Maclise.

FIGURE 323.—Travelling cloak.   Portrait of William Bowls, by Maclise.

FIGURE 324.—Street dress.   Portrait of Lord Lyndhurst, by Maclise.

FIGURE 325.—Travelling shawl.   Portrait of James Hogg, by Maclise.

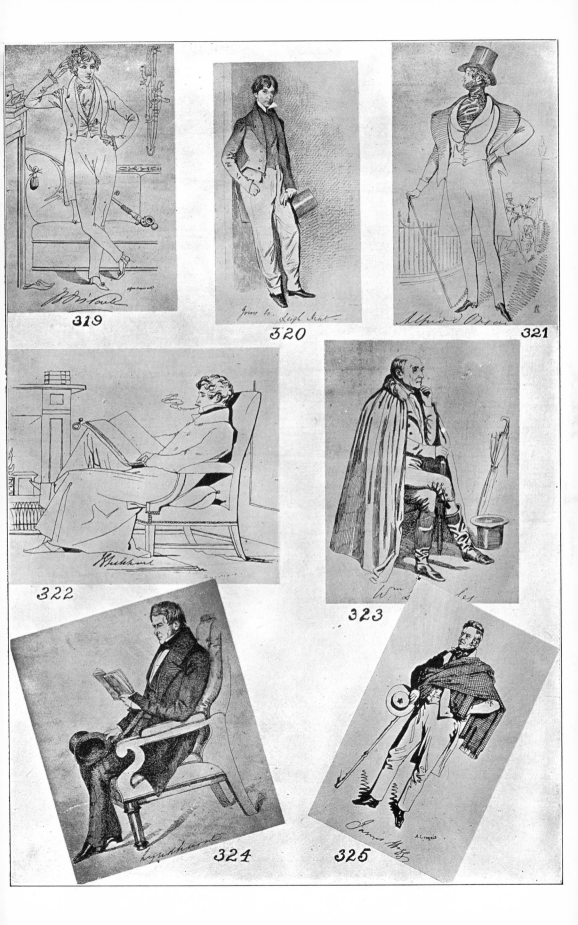

319

320

321

322

323

324

325

In 1820 we notice dark pantaloons were very fashionable, and gaiters, cutaway coats, high stocks and ruffled shirts. There was a slight change in the high hats. They were wider at the top and narrower at the crown, as in Figure 101. Long cloaks were popular. They had a military air and were picturesque when lined with red and ornamented with frogs. Watches were worn with fobs and seals throughout the twenties as will be seen in the portraits of that time. According to the following foolish verses published in "La Belle Assemblée" for December, 1820, pantaloons were worn loose-fitting and shoes with high heels were fashionable :

"MODERN MALE FASHIONS

" Crops, like hedge-hogs, small white hands,
    Whiskers, like Jew Moses ;
  Collars padded, stiff cravats,
    And cheeks as red as roses.

" Faces painted deepest brown,
    Waistcoats striped and gaudy ;
  Sleeves, thrice doubled, thick with down,
    And stays to brace the body.

" Short great coats that reach the knees,
    Boots like French postillion ;
  Meant the lifty race to please,
    But laughed at by the million.

" High-heeled shoes, with silken strings,
    Pantaloons loose fitting ;
  Fingers deck'd with golden rings,
    And small-clothes made of knitting.

" Bludgeons, like a pilgrim's staff,
    Or canes, as slight as osiers ;
  Doubled hose, to shew the calf,
    And swell the bill of hosiers.

*   *   *   *   *

" Such is giddy Fashion's son,
    Such a modern lover ;
Oh ! would their reign had ne'er begun,
    And may it soon be over ! ''

"Small clothes made of knitting" evidently referred to stock-inette.

The inauguration of President Monroe in 1821 (his second term) offers a striking contrast to the coronation of the English King in the previous year. We quote the following description from a letter of Judge Story to his wife in Boston :

"It was, according to arrangement, to be performed in the chamber of the House of Representatives. This is a splendid and most magnificent hall in the shape of a horseshoe, having a colonnade of marble pillars round the whole circular sweep which ascend to and support the lofty dome. The galleries for spectators were about midway the pillars and the seats gradually rise as they recede. The hall was thronged with ladies and gentlemen of the neighbouring cities to witness the ceremony. About 12 o'clock the President came into the hall dressed in a plain suit of black broadcloth with a single-breasted coat and waistcoat with flaps, in the old fashion. He also wore small clothes with silk stockings, and shoes with gold buckles in them. He placed himself in a chair usually occupied by the Clerk of the House of Representatives, facing the whole audi-ence. On his right was the President of the Senate, on his left the Speaker of the House. The Secretaries of all the de-partments sat in a row on the right, and on the left all the foreign Ministers and their suites dressed out in all their most splendid court dresses and arranged according to their rank. Immediately in front of the President at a small distance were placed seven chairs for the Judges who, upon notice of the arrival of the President, went into the hall in their judicial robes attended by the Marshal. The Chief-Justice was immediately requested to take the chair on the left of the President, who soon afterwards rose, and the Chief-Justice administered the oath of office. The President then delivered his inaugural speech, the Justices, the foreign Ministers, the President of the Senate and the Speaker of the House remaining standing. Altogether the scene was truly striking and grand. There was a simple dignity which excited very pleasing sensations. The fine collection of beautiful and interesting women dressed with great elegance, and the presence of so many men of talents, character and public services, civil and military. I do not know that I was ever more impressed by a public spectacle."

John Marshall was Chief-Justice of the United States on the occasion described above. A portrait of him in his official robes is given in Figure 354, and one of Judge Story in his robes in Figure 303, as specimens of typical legal dress in America. Some idea of the splendour of the costumes worn by the foreign embassies on the same occasion may be gleaned from the descriptions given in pages 384 and 388. The embroidered *fleurs-de-lys*, etc., must have stood out in strong relief against the black robes of the judges and the black clothes of the chief actors in the scene.

In 1825 the court dress of ambassadors is described in a fashion book as a cutaway coat trimmed with gold lace over a white waistcoat and knee-breeches and white stockings. Ruffled shirt and high white stock. A dress sword, white gloves and *chapeau bras* similar to the costume worn by Mr. Rush at the Court of St. James. (See Figure 141.)

Long overcoats with full tails and a deep cape, and finished with a broad collar either of the same cloth or of black velvet, were worn from 1825 to 1830. An illustration of one of these coats is shown in Figure 143 and another in Figure 364, taken from a plate of 1829. The pantaloons reaching to the ankle, but strapped under the stocking, are also shown in the latter picture. They were in the extreme of fashion in 1829. Specimens of the high stocks which were worn at this time are given in Figures 326 and 329. The " stock sentimentale " truly merits its name, and the " stock l'Orientale " evidently derived its designation from the crescent shaped tie beneath the chin.

Men's Apparel
1830–1850

"According to the fashion and the time."

THE period of the thirties was distinguished for a rather effeminate and extremely unpicturesque style of costume for men. Coats were made to fit tight, the shoulders were padded and they were drawn in at the waist line without a wrinkle. The sleeves were very tight and put in at the armhole without any fullness whatever. In fact, the coats of this period which have been lent for our illustrations were all so small in the armhole and tight in the sleeves that a full-grown man could not possibly put them on, and in every instance we have had to make use of young boys for models.

> "My love is all that is polite,
> He looks so pale and thin;
> He wears his boots so very tight,
> And pulls so closely in.
>
> "Oh! what a deal in hats and gloves,
> In vests and coats he spends;
> I call the heart that truly loves,
> The tailor's best of friends."

The trousers also were quite tight and produced a slim, genteel effect which seems to have been the beau ideal of masculine perfection at that date.

The hair was worn in loose waved locks over the forehead, and side whiskers were affected by most young gallants of the time (Figures 148 and 307).

We note the description of a suit for summer wear of a dark slate-coloured cloth, made with a collar of black velvet in an American magazine of fashion for 1830, and also the statement that the backs of coats are cut wide across the shoulders and narrow at the waist, the "hip-buttons" being placed about three inches apart. This would naturally contribute to the slender-waisted effect mentioned above. The "latest" in waist-coats, according to the same authority, was white marseilles with large black spots, bound with black galloon and made with a deep rolling collar. The newest trousers were of moleskin, buttoned up the front with a fly, made rather full about the hips, tight from knee to ankle, and cut out on the instep to fit the boot.

The high stocks, which were still universally worn, are illus-trated in Figures 330, 367, and 368, Figure 330 being copied from a wedding stock worn in Philadelphia by Dr. William Hunt in 1834. A specimen of the high shirt collars worn in the thirties is given in Figure 327.

A fashion plate for 1833 * shows the extreme of the lady-like dressing of gentlemen at that time. A tight-fitting overcoat tapering at the waist with a broad rolling collar opening wide to show the waistcoat and shirt bosom, a voluminous skirt reaching to the instep. A chimney-pot hat with scarcely any brim. With this peculiar costume, chin whiskers were worn and the general effect is very foolish (Figures 307 and 309).

> "They've made him a dandy;
> A thing, you know, whisker'd, great-coated, and lac'd;
> Like an hour-glass, exceedingly small in the waist:
> Quite a new sort of creature unknown yet to scholars,
> With heads so immovably stuck in shirt collars,
> That seats like our music-stools soon must be found them,
> To twirl when the creatures wish to look round them." †

* In the valuable collection of the Salmagundi Club, New York.
† Fudge Family in Paris, Thomas Moore.

Palm leaf hats were introduced about 1826 and became so popular in the protracted heat of an American summer that they are often mentioned as typical articles of costume (Figure 371). The following description is taken from " The New England Magazine " of 1831 :

" Palm Leaf Hats are manufactured to a surprising extent in New England, but principally in Massachusetts. The manufacturing of them commenced in 1826, in consequence of the encouragement afforded by the duty laid on imported Leghorn, straw and grass hats. It is believed that in this year alone upwards of two millions of hats will be made, the average value of which is about three dollars a dozen, amounting to a half million of dollars. In Worcester County it is supposed half the quantity above stated will be made. The leaf is imported from the island of Cuba; last year six hundred tons, worth fifty thousand dollars, was received. The hats are all made at the dwellings of the inhabitants, by girls from fourteen years old and upwards, are then sold to the country merchants, who collect them together and send them to Boston, New York and other markets. They are made of every quality, varying from 25 cents to $2 each, and suited to the man of fashion or the labourer."

The high hats of 1830 were still of beaver, but not always of black. Grey and white beavers were equally fashionable from 1830 to 1835 ; the popular shape of that time is illustrated in Figures 148, 307 and 309. Grey hats were worn in the daytime, and black beaver hats in the evening.

In 1830 we read of a new surtout called a Casauba, made with a rouleau of cloth instead of a collar. Dressing gowns of printed cachemire were fashionable too at that time, and a peculiar garment called a redingote vest made of merino reaching almost to

1807–1870

FIGURE 326.—1829—Stock l'Oriental.   From a print.

FIGURE 327.—1830—Shirt collar, 1830 and after.   From a print.

FIGURE 328.—1840—Stock of black satin of this date.

FIGURE 329.—1829—Stock sentimentale.   From a print.

FIGURE 330.—1834—White satin stock worn at this time.   (Back and front views.)

FIGURE 331.—1813—Breadman.

FIGURE 332.—1813—Dustman.

FIGURE 333.—1813—Sailor.

FIGURE 334.—1800–70—English workman in smock.

FIGURE 335.—1837—White satin waistcoat.

FIGURE 336.—1838—Old coat of white linen.

FIGURE 337.—1830—White linen shirt worn in Philadelphia at this date.

FIGURE 338.—1825—Militia coat of red cloth faced with brown velvet.

FIGURE 339.—1825—Military coat of dark blue cloth faced with scarlet.

FIGURE 340.—1807—Chapeau bras.   From a print.

FIGURE 341.—1850—White beaver hat.   Memorial Hall, Philadelphia.

FIGURE 342.—1815–50—Dress boots.

FIGURE 343.—1815–50—Wellington boots.

FIGURE 344.—1800–50—Blucher boots.

FIGURE 345.—1800–40—Hessian boots.

FIGURE 346.—1800–50—Top boots.

FIGURE 347.—1809—Hat with rolling brim.

FIGURE 348.—1850—A black silk high hat.   Memorial Hall, Philadelphia.

FIGURE 349.—1865—Picture of a round hat worn by an old man in this year.   From a contemporary print.

326 327 328 329

330

331 332 333 334

335 336 337 338 339

340 342 343 344 345 346 347

341 348 349

the knees and fastened with buttons of jet or of white metal, for morning wear.

The following remarks on the various expressions of which a coat is capable were found in an old magazine of the thirties:

"Old coats are the indices by which a man's peculiar turn of mind may be pointed out. So tenaciously do I hold this opinion, that, in passing down a crowded thoroughfare, the Strand, for instance, I would wager odds that, in seven out of ten cases, I would tell you a stranger's character and calling by the mere cut of his every-day coat. Who can mistake the staid, formal gravity of the orthodox divine, in the corresponding weight, fullness and healthy condition of his familiar easy-natured flaps? Who sees not the necessities, the habitual eccentricities of the poet, significantly developed in his haggard, shapeless old apologies for skirts, original in their genius as 'Christabel,' uncouth in their build as the New Palace at Pimlico? Who can misapprehend the motions of the spirit, as it slyly flutters beneath the Quaker's drab? Thus, too, the sable hue of the lawyer's working coat corresponds with the colour of his conscience: while his thrift, dandyism and close attention to appearances, tell their own tale in the half-pay officer's smart, but somewhat faded exterior."

The close relationship between the coat and the wearer has been touchingly expressed by an American poet as follows:

"Old coat, for some three or four seasons
    We've been jolly comrades, but now
We part, old companion, forever ;
    To fate and to fashion I bow.
You'd look well enough at a dinner,
    I'd wear you with pride at a ball,
But I'm dressing to-night for a wedding
    My own, and you'd not do at all.

"There's a reprobate looseness about you
Should I wear you to-night I believe
As I came with my bride from the altar
You'd laugh in your wicked old sleeve.

*   *   *   *   *   *

'Tis time to put on your successor,
It's made in a fashion that's new ;
Old coat, I'm afraid it will never
Sit as easily on me as you." *

An English traveller visiting Washington in 1832 was apparently much interested in the appearance and dress of a deputation of Indians which was quartered for a short time in the hotel where he was staying. Several of these, he remarks, " wore only a blanket fastened in front by a skewer, and their hair was adorned with feathers. There were two ladies and several children attached to the deputation, and I desired the waiter if possible to induce some of the latter to pay me a visit. One evening he brought in two, a boy and a girl. The girl's costume consisted of a sort of printed bed-gown without sleeves, fastened close up to the throat; trousers, moccasins or leggins of deerskin, worn generally by the Indians, and the whole covered by a blanket, the drapery of which she really managed with a good deal of grace. In each ear she wore two large ear-rings. Fastened to the crown of her head was a piece of blue ribband, which hung down not unbecomingly on one side of the face. The boy was apparently younger by two or three years, and a fine manly little fellow. He also wore a blanket by way of Benjamin, but instead of a bed-gown rejoiced in a long coat, the tails of which reached almost to his heels, and which, being made for some one of form and dimensions very

* G. A. Baker, Jr.

different, was not remarkable for felicity of adaptation. Neither could speak English, but the boy evidently was the leading person, the girl only following his example. Having a bottle of claret on the table, I filled each of them a glass, but the flavour did not seem to meet with their approbation. I then gave them cigars which they appeared to enjoy ; indeed I never saw any one blow a cloud with greater zest than the young lady. The failure of the claret then induced me to try the effect of stronger potations, and I brought a bottle of Eau de Cologne from my dressing table, the contents of which they finished without difficulty or apparent inconvenience from the strength of the spirit. They remained with me about half an hour, during the whole of which time they maintained the sober gravity of demeanour which the Indians consider to be inseparable from true dignity. Nothing seemed to excite surprise, and the only symptom of animation they displayed was on catching a view of their own countenances in a mirror, when they both laughed. At length the boy rose to take leave followed by the young lady, and shaking hands with me they strode out of the apartment with a sort of barbaric grace which well became these children of the wilderness. Before quitting the subject of the Indians whose wild appearance had excited in my imagination a thousand fantastic associations, I must mention one circumstance which I found sadly hostile to their poetical interest. One morning I observed my diplomatic friends lounging and walking about as usual in the gallery of the hotel, but alas, how miserably transmogrified ! Their 'Great Father,' the President, had, it appeared, preparatory to their departure, presented each person attached to the Mission with a new coat, in shape something like that worn by a coachman, and of blue cloth turned up at the collar and cuffs with scarlet. The women wore cloaks of the same colours and materials and my two little friends, whose barbaric appearance had been delightful, now strutted about in their new finery with a grand air."

From this strictly American costume let us turn to matters of dress in England, and read the graphic descriptions of the apparel worn by different types in the mother country from 1836 to 1846, given by Edmund Yates in his "Recollections and Experiences."

"Dandies wore high collared coats and roll collared waist-coats, short in the waist; round their necks were high stiff stocks with 'an avalanche of satin' falling over the chest, and ornamented with a large pin and a small pin connected with a thin chain, and high sharp-pointed, almost Gladstonian, shirt collars. No gentleman could wear anything in the daytime but Wellington boots (Figure 343), high up in the leg, over which the trousers fitted tightly, covering most of the foot, and secured underneath by a broad strap. The great coats of those days were no misnomers; they were really enormous garments adorned with capes and deep pockets (Figure 364). They were Chesterfields, Petershams, Taglionis, Sylphides, and well I recollect some splendid driving-coats ornamented with enor-mous mother-of-pearl buttons as big as crown-pieces, with pic-tures on them of mail coaches going full speed, which were ex-hibited to admiring crowds in the tailor's windows in Regent Street. Afterwards came the neat paletot, the blanket-like poncho, the blue pilot, and the comfortable Inverness. Some old gentlemen wore cloaks, too, in my youth, and I have a dim recollection of one kind properly, I believe, called 'roquelaure' (Figure 323), but known to the London public as a 'rockelow.'" The latter garment was a survival of the eighteenth century, il-lustrations of which are given in the earlier volume of "His-toric Dress."

The dress of the men of this time (1836–1846) can be studied in the illustrations in " Nicholas Nickleby " and other contemporary publications.

Mr. Yates gives an interesting glimpse of personages once familiar in the streets of London : " The dustman with his call ' Dust O ! ' and his ever-ringing bell ; the buy-a-broom girl, with her Swiss garb and jödling voice ; the thin Turk, turban-topped, and vending rhubarb from a tray suspended from his neck ; the Jew boys who hung about the coach-offices with their nets of lemons and oranges, and were closely elbowed by the peripatetic cutler, whose knives were always open and constantly being polished and sharpened on a tattered leather glove. Gone is the bag-bearing Jew with his never-ceasing cry of ' Old clo ! clo ! ' Gone are the Quakers, the men broad-brimmed, shovel-hatted, stiff-collared and gaitered ; the women generally pretty with hideous bonnets and pretty dove-coloured raiment. Well do I recollect the introduction, simultaneously I imagine, of the handsome cab, then called ' patent-safety,' and the four-wheeler. People nowadays will smile to hear that for years after their first introduction it was considered ' fast ' to ride in a handsome, and its use was tabooed to ladies. Clean-shaven faces were uncommon ; a pair of ' mutton chop ' whisk-ers was *de rigeur ;* but a ' pair of Moustachios,' as they were called, was never seen, save on a cavalry officer, a dancing master, or a ' snob,' and the cultivation of a beard was wholly confined to foreigners."

The costume of the policeman, introduced by Sir Robert Peel in 1850, is described in the same volume as follows : " They wore swallow-tail blue coats with bright metal buttons, and in summer white duck trousers and white Berlin gloves. In lieu of helmet they had an ordinary chimney-pot hat, only of extra strength and stiffness and with a glazed oilskin top." Further details are not given by Mr. Yates, but we are left to infer that in winter the English guardians of the peace wore blue cloth trousers, and in summer the same coat was worn with the duck trousers. We are left quite in the dark about the style of gloves they patronized in winter, but are told very decidedly that policemen were not allowed "to grow either moustache or beard."

Another valuable item of English costume is given in the same book. "The general or country postman wore a scarlet swallow-tail coat; the 'two penny' or London district man a blue uniform; a collection for the night mails was made at five P. M. by men who paraded the streets, each armed with a bell, which he rang lustily; many of the despatches and letters from the head office to the various sub-offices were sent by horse-post, the letters being enclosed in leather valises which were strapped behind in post-bags."

Speaking of the familiar characters in the streets of London about 1846, Mr. Yates says: "There in a hooded cabriolet, the fashionable vehicle for men-about-town, with an enormous champing horse and the trimmest of tiny grooms, 'tigers' as they were called, half standing on the foot-board, half swinging in the air, clinging to the straps, would be Count d'Orsay, with clear-cut features and raven hair, the king of the dandies, the cynosure of all eyes, the greatest swell of the day. He was an admirable whip and always drove in faultless white kid gloves with his shirt wrist-bands turned back over his coat cuffs and his whole 'turn-out' was perfection. By his side was occasionally seen Prince Louis Napoleon, an exile too, after his escape from Ham residing in lodgings in King Street."

The white waistcoat affected by Count d'Orsay and other men of fashion soon became very popular. "Punch's" Muse immortalized them in the following parody on the "Roast Beef of Old England":

"Oh! the vests of young England are perfectly white,
   And they're cut very neatly and sit very tight,
   And they serve to distinguish our young Englishmen
   From the juvenile Manners and Coningsby Ben ;
      Sing Oh! the white vests of young England
      And Oh! the young English white vests.

"Now the old English vest was some two yards about,
   For old England was rather inclined to be stout ;
   But the young English waist is extremely compress'd,
   By the very close fit of the young English vest.
      Sing Oh! etc.

"The young English white vest upon one little score,
   May perhaps be considered a bit of a bore,
   For it makes the resemblance exceedingly near
   Twixt the young English waiter and young English Peer.
      Sing Oh! etc.

"But what are the odds as concerning the vest,
   So long as felicity reigns in the breast ?
   And young England to wear what it pleases may claim
   Let us hope all the tailors are paid for the same.
      Sing Oh! etc."

Count d'Orsay, of whom Mr. Yates has given us such a vivid description, was an artist by profession, and is said to have painted the last portrait of the Duke of Wellington. He settled in England in 1821 and assisted the Countess of Blessington to establish a fashionable coterie in London in that year. Bernard Osborne describes him riding in Hyde Park :

"Patting the crest of his well-managed steed,
   Proud of his action, D'Orsay vaunts the breed ;
   A coat of chocolate, a vest of snow,
   Well brushed his whiskers, as his boots below,
   A short-napped beaver, prodigal in brim,
   With trousers tighten'd to a well-turned limb." *

A manual of etiquette published by him about that time contains the following precepts for the guidance of men of fashion :

* The Chaunt of Achilles.

1810–1869

FIGURE 350.—1840—Plaid stock and waistcoat.   Portrait of Baron Stock-
mar.

FIGURE 351.—1840—Quaker gentleman.   From a Daguerreotype.

FIGURE 352.—1844—Hair parted in the middle; plaid waistcoat.   Daguerreotype of James Russell Lowell.

FIGURE 353.—1845—Clerical dress.   Portrait of Rev. William Chalmers.

FIGURE 354.—1821—Robes of a chief justice of the U. S.   Portrait of John
Marshall.

FIGURE 355.—1865—Clerical dress.   Portrait of Rev. Henry J. Morton.

FIGURE 356.—1869—Frock coat and standing collar.

FIGURE 357.—1810—Bishop's dress.

FIGURE 358.—1855—Close-fitting coat.

350

357

358

353

351

352

355

354

356

"It is bad taste to dress in the extreme of fashion and in general those only do so who have no other claim to distinction; leave it in these times to shopmen and pickpockets. There are certain occasions, however, when you may dress as gayly as you please, observing the axiom of the ancient poet to be 'great on great occasions.' The great points are well made shoes, clean gloves, a white pocket handkerchief, and above all an easy and graceful deportment. Never affect the ruffianly style of dress unless as some excuse you hold a brilliant position in society. Always wear gloves in church or in a theatre. Avoid wearing jewelry unless it be in very good taste and then only at proper occasions. Never leave your hat in the hall when you pay a morning visit, it makes you look too much at home, take it with you into the room." Hints on the art of dancing, card playing and every form of social amusement are given in this little pamphlet which is now almost forgotten. A picture of the author will be seen in Figure 321, copied from Maclise's portrait gallery.

On the subject of hats the following anecdote appeared in the columns of "Blackwood's Magazine" in 1841:

"There is a great deal in the build and wearing of hats, a great deal more than at first meets the eye. I know a man who in a particular hat looked so extraordinarily like a man of property that no tradesman on earth could refuse to give him credit. It was one of Andre's, and cost a guinea and a half in ready money, but the person in question was frightened at the enormous charge and afterwards purchased beavers in the city at the cost of seventeen-and-sixpence, and what was the consequence? He fell off in public estimation, and very soon after he came out in his city hat it began to be whispered abroad that he was a ruined man." It is a good story although the moral is hardly commendable.

Men's Apparel
1850–1870

"The coat is the expression of the man."

 "IT is all nonsense to undervalue dress; I'm no more the same man in my dark green paletot, trimmed with astrakan, that I was a month ago in my fustian shooting-jacket, than a well plumed eagle is like a half moulted turkey. There is an indescribable connection between your coat and your character; and few things so react on the morality of a man as the cut of his trousers," wrote James Dodd, according to Lever, to his friend Robert Doolan during his travels abroad, which were published early in the fifties, a period characterized by rather gay attire in the masculine world.

An American writer mentions that "jewels were conspicuous in men's dressing and gentlemen of fashion were rare who did not have varieties of sparkling studs and scarf pins to add to the brightness of their vari-coloured vests. The latter not infrequently were of the richest satin and velvet, brocaded or embroidered. They lent a desirable note of colour by means inconspicuous to the swallow-tailed evening dress of that time, a note by the by which was supplemented by a tie of bright soft silk and of ample proportions. President Buchanan was remarkable for his undeviating choice of pure white cravats." But we are anticipating; the administration of Buchanan began in 1857.

414

From the letters of our great historian, Prescott, written during his visit to England in 1850, we glean many interesting items of dress. Although a private citizen and not connected in any way with the Embassy, he was constrained to wear a regulation costume at the Court of Queen Victoria. He describes his presentation in a letter to his wife :

"I was at Lawrence's * at one, in my costume, a *chapeau* with gold lace, blue coat and white trousers, begilded with buttons and metal (the coat buttons up single-breasted to the throat), a sword and patent leather boots. I was a figure indeed, but I had enough to keep me in countenance." This costume is not unlike the suit of an attaché of legation in 1840 shown in Figure 369 which is taken from a coat worn by Robert H. Hale, Esq., of Philadelphia, when he accompanied the Minister of the United States to St. Petersburg.

In another letter, to Mr. Ticknor, Mr. Prescott says : " Do you know I have become a courtier and affect the Royal Presence? I wish you could see my gallant costume, gold laced coat, white inexpressibles, silk hose, gold buckled patent leather slippers." This letter is dated June 26th, and the knee-breeches were probably *de rigeur* for a ball. Later in the same season he writes to Mr. Ticknor of the degree bestowed on him at Oxford.

"On Monday morning our party at the Bishop's went to Oxford where Lord Northampton and I were Doctorized in due form. We were both dressed in flaming red robes (it was the hottest day I have felt here) and then marched out in solemn procession with the Faculty, etc., in black and red gowns through the street, looking, that is, we, like the victims of an *auto da fé;* though I believe on second thoughts the San Benito was yellow."

* Amos Lawrence, Minister from the United States to England.

To Mrs. Prescott (August 24, 1850) he writes of his visit to Lord Carlisle at Naworth Castle.

"This is a fine old place of the feudal times indeed. In the afternoon we arrived and saw the banners of the Howards and Dacres flying from its battlements, telling us that its lord was there. He came out to greet us, dressed in his travelling garb, for he had just arrived, with his Scotch shawl twisted about him."

A travelling shawl of this description is shown in Figure 325. It was a favourite garment in the fifties, being worn in place of a top-coat.

A few days later, while a guest of Lord Carlisle at Castle Naworth, Mr. Prescott described to Mrs. Prescott the visit of Queen Victoria and Prince Albert:

"August 28th, Wednesday. The Queen, etc., arrived yesterday in a pelting rain, with an escort of cavalry, a pretty sight to those under cover. Crowds of loyal subjects were in the park in front of the house to greet her. They must have come miles in the rain. She came into the hall in a plain travelling dress, bowing very gracefully to all there, and then to her apartments, which occupy the front of the building. At eight we went to dinner, all in full dress, but mourning for the Duke of Cambridge; I, of course, for President Taylor! All wore breeches or tight pantaloons. It was a brilliant show, I assure you, that immense table, with its fruits and flowers and lights glancing over beautiful plate in that superb gallery. I was as near the Queen as at our own family table. She has a good appetite, and laughs merrily. She has fine eyes and teeth, but is short. She was dressed in black silk and lace with the blue scarf of the Order of the Garter across her bosom. Her only ornaments were of jet. The Prince, who is certainly a handsome and very well made man, wore the Garter with its brilliant buckle round his knee, a showy star on his breast, and the collar of a foreign order round his neck. Dinner went off very well, except that we had no music, a tribute to Louis Philippe at the Queen's request."

During the administration of President Pierce, William Marcy was Secretary of State, and unfortunately assumed charge of the department with the intention of enforcing his plain democratic ideas upon the representatives of our country at foreign courts. Almost the first question he took up, we are told in Rhodes' " History of the United States," was that of diplomatic costumes. From the time of our mission to Ghent until President Jackson's day, " the dress informally or officially recommended was a blue coat lined with white silk ; straight standing cape embroidered with gold, buttons plain or if they can be had with an eagle stamped upon them, cuffs embroidered in the manner of the cape, white cassimere breeches with gold knee buckles and white silk stockings and gold or gilt shoe buckles. A three-cornered *chapeau bras*, a black cockade to which an eagle had been attached. Sword, etc. On gala days the uniforms should be made more splendid with embroidery and hat decorated with a white ostrich feather." Under the strictly democratic administration of President Jackson some changes were suggested in the diplomatic dress in the line of cheapness and adaptability to the simplicity of our institutions. A black coat without a cape and a gold star affixed on each side of the collar, either black or white breeches, *chapeau bras* with cockade and sword were retained.

Mrs. Clay, who was living in Washington at this time, says : " The consequences of Mr. Marcy's meddling were far-reaching. On June 1, 1853, he issued a circular recommending that our representatives abroad should, in order to show their devotion to republican institutions, appear whenever practicable in the simple dress of an American citizen. Our Minister at Berne found the Court of Switzerland quite willing to receive him in his citizen's dress. The Ministers at Turin and Brussels reported they would have no difficulty in carrying out the instructions of the State Department. The representative at Berlin was at once informed that such action would be considered disrespectful. The King of Sweden insisted on court dress at social functions. Mr. August Belmont, at the Hague, received a cold permission from the king to dress as he pleased, and it is recorded (as matter for gratitude on the part of the American Minister) that after all, and notwithstanding, the queen actually danced with him in his citizen's dress, and the king condescended to shake him by the hand and to talk with him! Mr. Mason, at the French Court, could not face the music! He consulted his wife, and together they agreed upon a compromise. He appeared in an embroidered coat, sword, and cocked hat, and had the misfortune to receive from Mr. Marcy a severe rebuke. Mr. Buchanan, at the Court of St. James, having no wife to consult, thought long and anxiously on the subject. The question was still unsettled at the opening of Parliament in February, 1854. Our Minister did not attend—he had ' nothing to wear,' whereupon ' there was quite a sensation in the House of Lords.' ' Indeed,' he wrote to Mr. Marcy, ' I have found difficulty in preventing this incident from becoming a subject of inquiry and remark in the House of Commons.' Think of that! At a time when England was on the eve of war with Russia, all the newspapers, court officials, House of Commons, exercised about the dress of the American Minister! The London 'Times' stated that on a diplomatic occasion ' the American Minister sate unpleasantly conscious of his singularity.' Poor Mr. Buchanan, sorely pressed, conceived the idea of costuming himself like General Washington, and to that end examined Stuart's portrait. He may even have gone so far as to indulge in a private rehearsal, queue, powdered wig, and all; but he seems to have perceived he would only make himself ridiculous; so he took his life in his hands, and, brave gentleman as he was, appeared at the queen's levee in the dress of an American citizen; and she, true lady as she was, settled the matter, for her court at least, by receiving him as she did all others. Mr. Buchanan wrote to his niece, Miss Harriet Lane, ' I wore a sword to gratify those who yielded so much, and to distinguish me from the upper court servants.' Mr. Soulé, at the Court of Madrid, adopted the costume of Benjamin Franklin at the Court of Louis XVI, sword, *chapeau*, black velvet, and much embroidery, looking ' with his black eyes, black looks and pale complexion, less like the philosopher whose costume he imitated, than the master of Ravenswood.' There had been a lively discussion among the Austrian and Mexican Ministers and the Countess of Montijo, the mother of the Empress Eugenia and of the Duchess of Alba, whether or no he should be rejected; but Mr. Soulé did not know this. The queen received him, he wrote to Mr. Marcy, ' with marked attention and courtesy.' "

As we shall see later the reformed diplomatic costume was dropped when a new Secretary of State came into office, who wisely considered it a matter of courtesy, not of state.

From " Things as They Are in America," an interesting book of travel in 1854, we quote the following description of a visit to Congress.

" The House was full. Representatives from California and other distant states were already present—the whole assemblage forming a body of well-dressed persons, such as you would see any day on ' 'Change.' There was little diversity of costume. A black dress coat, black satin waistcoat, and black stock, constitute the general attire—ready for court, dinner, ball, public

1801–1860

FIGURE 359.—1801—Gentleman in riding costume.   From a print.

FIGURE 360.—1804—Picture of Beau Brummell in his youth.   From Jesse's Biography.

FIGURE 361.—1806—Gentleman in fashionable morning suit.   From a contemporary print.

FIGURE 362.—1810—An English clergyman of 1810 and after.   From a contemporary print.

FIGURE 363.—1812—Ruffled shirt and linen pantaloons buttoned up to the knee.

FIGURE 364.—1829—Gentleman in great coat.   From a print.

FIGURE 365.—1830—A fashionable morning suit of 1830 and after.

FIGURE 366.—1833—Hunting dress.   From a print.

FIGURE 367.—1830—White kerseymere waistcoat, plaited shirt, white stock and blue coat.   From a plate.

FIGURE 368.—1837—Waistcoat of cream coloured cashmere ; coat of dark blue cloth ; white cascade necktie.

FIGURE 369.—1842—Gentleman in diplomatic dress.

FIGURE 370.—1850–60—Gentleman in hunting costume.   From a contemporary print.

FIGURE 371.—1850—A university student in 1850, showing panama hat. From a contemporary print.

meeting, or anything. A few wore beards, but clean shaving was the rule. Standing, sitting, lounging, talking, according to fancy, they spent the time till noon. The moment the hands of the clock point to twelve, said my friend, 'Business will commence.' A clerk, seated in advance, and a little below the vacant chair of the Speaker, kept his eye fixed on a clock over the doorway, and accordingly rang the bell when the hour of noon was indicated."

Cutaway coats were known by various names, such as swallow-tail, claw-hammer, and steel-pen. Before 1860 they were worn in morning as well as evening dress, and always had large pockets in the tails. A story is told of a Pennsylvania architect who went to Philadelphia on business carrying in his tail pocket a packet of plans and specifications. He had occasion to cross the river in a ferry-boat from Camden, and on arriving at his destination put his hand in the place where his pocket should have been to take out the plans, but alas, papers, pocket and even the coat tail had been cut off by a venturesome thief in the crowd on the ferry landing. The first lesson in the art of pocket-picking, as taught by Fagan in "Oliver Twist," was to snatch the handkerchiefs and snuff-boxes from the tail pockets of unwary gentlemen in the street. It was even an easier accomplishment than carrying off reticules from the ladies.

White and cream-coloured waistcoats were very fashionable in the fifties. One of cream-coloured silk, wadded and lined with white and fastened with gilt buttons, worn in Philadelphia in 1857, is illustrated in Figure 335.

It was in 1860 that the Prince of Wales, afterwards King Edward VII, visited the United States and was fêted and entertained in all the large cities. At the ball given in his honour in New York an alarming accident happened : a part of the dancing floor gave way. No one was hurt, however, and the progress of his Royal Highness through the country was enthusiastically hailed on every side, and the popular feeling of attachment to the mother country was strengthened thereby.

> "While the manners, while the arts,
>   That mould a nation's soul,
>   Still cling around our hearts,
>   Between let ocean roll,
>   Our joint communion breaking with the sun,
>   Yet still from either breach,
>   The voice of blood shall reach,
>   More audible than speech :
>   'We are one.' " *

The fashions of the sixties are familiar to every one through the medium of photography. The small *cartes de visites*, as they were called, which were very popular in 1860 to 1870, show long black shiny broadcloth frock coats, rather loose pantaloons and careless neckties. The colours were universally sober. The hair was worn rather short than long and beards and whiskers and moustaches were all popular. In Washington of course, as in all the capitals of Europe, with military and naval uniforms and the costumes of the foreign diplomats, a variety and contrast was noticeable. A diplomatic costume was considered necessary for the representatives of the United States government in 1861.

In Carl Schurz's " Reminiscences " he narrates the embarrassing position he was placed in at the Court of Spain, where he arrived without the diplomatic dress which he had ordered in Paris. By special concession of the Queen, he was permitted to present his credentials in ordinary evening dress, but was stopped at the foot of the staircase by two halberdiers in gorgeous mediæval costume who were guarding the passage to

* W. Allston.

the rooms of state. Evidently fearing the dignity of the Spanish throne was at stake, they crossed their halberds and refused to let him pass. Finally a high official at the Court was appealed to and through his intercession admission was gained to the Queen's presence. The delayed uniform consisted of "a richly embroidered dress-coat, with correspondingly ornamented trousers, a cocked hat and a dress sword."

Ugly as men's clothes of this period were, a great deal of attention was bestowed on them everywhere. Poole, the celebrated English tailor, is said to have been accidentally discovered by King Edward VII while he was Prince of Wales. One night when the French actor, Fechter, was playing "Robert Macaire" in a coat apparently of rents and patches, the Prince was looking on and we are told "his keen eye quickly noted that the garment was singularly well cut. After the play, the Prince sent for Fechter and asked him the name of his tailor, and the next day sent for Mr. Poole who from that hour was a made man."

Looking backward at the pictures of the thirties and forties we must at least acknowledge that there was something wholesomely virile about these later day fashions for men. The small waists, the tight sleeves and close-fitting pantaloons were effeminate in comparison.

Like his predecessor, George IV, when Prince of Wales, King Edward was called the best dressed man in Europe, and although he is universally acknowledged to have been the greatest statesman of his day, he never lost his earlier prestige as the "glass of fashion and the mould of form" for men of English birth. We learn on the best authority that it was etiquette in England for men of fashion to follow the Prince's lead in the matter of hats at race meetings and "until his Majesty one year appeared at Goodwood in a round hat, no one ever dreamed even in the hottest weather of attending these races save in a silk hat and a frock coat. But luckily for the world at large the Prince's popularity and good sense broke through old-world prejudices and now a hot summer afternoon sees Goodwood Park dotted with men in blue serge, white duck, and flannel suits, and the lightest and shadiest of straw hats."

Suitable summer costumes have become a necessity in America, and are certainly much more becoming than the thick winter-like clothing of the sixties.

In the first half of the nineteenth century stage traditions were strongly adhered to in costume. We have already mentioned Mrs. Kemble's dress when she made her *début* in "Juliet." In the Memoirs of Lester Wallack we find an amusing instance of the strong prejudice cherished by stage-managers at that date against what they termed innovations.

" My father was cast for the part of Tressel in Cibber's version of ' Richard III.' Tressel is the youthful messenger who conveys to the King Henry VI the news of the murder of his son after the battle of Tewkesbury. My father, a young ambitious actor, came on with the feather hanging from his cap all wet, his hair dishevelled, one boot torn nearly off, one spur broken, the other gone entirely, his gauntlet stained with blood and his sword snapped in twain, at which old Wewitzer, who was the manager and had been a manager before my father was born, was perfectly shocked. It was too late to do anything, but the next morning Wewitzer sent for him to come to his office and addressed him thus : ' Young man, how do you hope to get on in your profession by deliberately breaking all precedent? What will become of the profession if mere boys are allowed to take these liberties? Why, sir, you should have entered in a suit of decent black with silk stockings on and with a white handkerchief in your hand.' ' What, after defeat and flight in battle?' interrupted my father.   'That has nothing at all to do with it,' was the reply, 'the proprieties, Sir! the proprieties!'   Some of the papers spoke very highly of the innovation, and the audience was satisfied if the management was not."

The hero of this anecdote, James Wallack, was a noted actor in London from 1804 to 1845, after which date he settled in New York and became known as the manager of Wallack's theatre from 1852 to 1864.

The colour harmonies and stage pictures to which we are nowadays accustomed came in with the æsthetic movement in 1860.   The success of a modern play depends greatly upon the artistic taste of the stage-manager, who is chiefly responsible for the subtle effects of light and the combinations of colour which contribute largely to the pleasure of the audiences and render them less critical of the histrionic achievements of the actors. In the earlier days, however, very little mention is made in the press criticisms of the scenery or costumes, while every word and gesture of the actors is ardently described.

> " Brief as 'tis brilliant, the Actor's fame
>   With the spectator's memory lives and dies ;
>   Out of the witness of men's ears and eyes,
> The Actor is a name.

> " Yet some so much have stirred the common heart
>   That, when they long have past from sight, we find
>   Memories, which seem undying, left behind
> Of their so potent art." *

CLERGYMEN'S DRESS

Before 1830 a Clergyman of the English Church dressed usually in a suit of black broadcloth and wore a black or white

* To the Memory of Charles Kemble, Punch, 1854.

stock according to his preference. His costume betokened the college graduate of genial disposition and liberal views. His profession did not forbid his mingling in the pleasures of the world when opportunity offered, but a simple domestic life in a rural parish, where but little thought was given to discussions of dogma, was generally his lot. In the pulpit he wore the black academic gown as his predecessors of the eighteenth century had done before him, and read the service in a white surplice, which is still customary. The black gown was worn in the pulpit in some remote parts of the country as late as 1870. A Clergyman of the English Church is illustrated in Figure 362, copied from a print of 1810, when knee-breeches were still worn. It will be noticed that the coat is made with comparatively short tails and is not cut away in front.

The Ritualistic movement in the Church of England effected a revival of the vestments worn during the reign of Edward VI. The change, however, was not noticed in America before 1860. Until that date the black Geneva gown had been worn in the pulpit by Episcopalians, and the white surplice with a black stole and bands of sheerest lawn were considered indispensable adjuncts to clerical dress. The High Church party had been very much in the minority up to that date and the changes were very gradually introduced on this side of the ocean.

Bishops wore then, as they do now, the white linen rochet resembling the surplice, but with less full sleeves, the black satin chimere or outer robe, with lawn sleeves, and black stole. There is a picture of the General Convention of 1859 assembled at Richmond, Virginia, which contains portraits of forty-one bishops of the Church in America. In this group Bishop Hopkinson is a noticeable figure, on account of his independence of established custom. Instead of the usual Bishop's sleeves held in at the wrist by a black band of ribbon, he adopted the open sleeves of a priest's surplice. He was also the only member of the Episcopal Bench who wore a moustache and a flowing beard, although many of his brother bishops wore side whiskers.

Other Protestant denominations, Lutherans, Methodists and Presbyterians, all wore the black gown throughout the entire church service.

It is not necessary to describe the vestments worn in the Roman Catholic Church, as they have never changed, and have often been depicted.

In the street, clergymen of all ranks and denominations wore nothing more distinctive than an ordinary frock suit of black broadcloth and a white or black necktie. Trollope says of Mr. Harding, " He always wears a black frock coat, black knee-breeches and black gaiters, and somewhat scandalizes some of his more hyper-clerical brethren by a black neck-hand-kerchief; " and of that imposing dignitary, the Church Arch-deacon, Grantly, " 'Tis only when he has exchanged that ever-new shovel-hat for a tasselled nightcap and those shining black habiliments for his accustomed *robe de nuit* that Dr. Grantly talks and looks and thinks like an ordinary man. A dean or archbishop in the garb of his order is sure of our reverence ; and a well-got-up bishop fills our very souls with awe. But how can this feeling be perpetuated in the bosom of those who see the bishops without their aprons and the archdeacons even in a lower state of dishabille."

Trollope's graphic pictures of English churchmen in the fifties are undoubtedly drawn from life, and numerous illustra-tions of the bishops' aprons, the shovel hats, the gaiters, and other articles of clerical attire of that period will be seen in the pages of " Punch." " The Warden," etc., was published in 1855, and we venture to say that clerical breeches and gaiters were quite unknown in the United States at that time.

Figure 355, the portrait of a distinguished clergyman of the Episcopal Church in America, the Rev. Henry Morton, of Philadelphia, gives the street garb worn by him in 1865. The surpliced choirs were introduced into America in the seventies. Before that time the church choirs were composed of four trained voices who sang in ordinary costume and usually behind a curtain. Illustrations of the different vestments worn not only by the clergymen of the Anglican Church, but also of the Roman Catholic Church, may be found in the "Encyclopedia of Religious Knowledge." *

UNIFORMS

The Military and Naval uniforms of our own country, from 1800 to 1870, are fully illustrated and described in the government publication of 1889, which may be seen at any public library. For the uniforms of Great Britain the reader is referred to "Her Majesty's Army," † while Lepan's "Armée Francaise ‡ is an excellent authority for the military costumes of France. The illustration of a coat worn in the time of Jackson's famous rescue of New Orleans is given in Figure 339, and a coat which formed part of a militia uniform worn in the United States about 1825 is given in Figure 338.

A unique and most interesting collection of plates showing the uniforms of all nations at different historic periods is in the possession of the Salmagundi Club in New York. It is probably the most complete in this country.

---

* By Abbott and Conant.
† Her Majesty's Army by Walter Richards, London, 1870.
‡ L' Armée Francaise by Lepan, Paris, 1857.

SPORTING DRESS

"Fox Hunting in England

"Pastime for princes !—prime sport of our nation !
  Strength in their sinew and bloom on their cheek ;
Health to the old, to the young recreation ;
  All for enjoyment the hunting field seek.

"Eager and emulous only, not spiteful :
  Grudging no friend, though ourselves he may beat ;
Just enough danger to make sport delightful !
  Toil just sufficient to make slumber sweet."

Figure 361 illustrates the riding-dress of a gentleman in
1800–1810, with slight variations in the coat and the hat. It
was probably in fashion for at least twenty-five years of the
nineteenth century.

The red hunting coats worn in the field by Englishmen
throughout the nineteenth century were not noticeable in
America, where gentlemen of leisure have ever been in the
minority.

"We are off once more !—for the summer's o'er,
  And gaily we take our stand
By the covert-side, in our might and pride,
  A gallant and fearless band !
Again we hear our Huntsman's cheer,
  The thrilling Tally-ho !
And the blast of the horn, through the woodlands borne,
  As merrily onward we go !
              Tally-ho !
  As merrily onward we go !"

Although fox hunting has never been a national pastime in
the United States, other species of sport have always been
popular. The shooting of birds, especially of ducks, woodcocks,

partridges and reed birds, is pursued with great zest and regularity at certain seasons.   In England we read of some changes in guns and in hunting costume about 1830.   From a book on sport in the mother country, we quote the following :

" Gradually welcome improvements were introduced in the muzzle-loading apparatus, as in shooting costume.   For it was astonishing how the gentlemen of the ancient school had stuck to the most inconvenient and uncompromising of garments. We see the heroes of many episodes scrambling over the rocks and worming themselves along the beds of the hill streams in high chimney-pot hats and tight-clinging cutaways.   Their sons, however, discarded blue evening swallow-tails with brilliant brass buttons, and crimson under-waistcoats, and betook themselves to sensible shooting suits of loose-fitting tweeds and homespuns, and the clever mechanism soon came to the front, going forward hand in hand with the rational tailor."

In Figure 366 a shooting dress of 1832 from an old print is given and another of 1860 is shown in Figure 376.

GLOSSARY

Glossary

Agatha robe.—A semi-classical dress (1800) usually of soft muslin fastened with clasps on the shoulder, open at the left side over a full skirt, close-fitting short sleeves.

Amaranthus colour.—A soft pinkish shade of purple, very fashionable in 1802 and popular for many years.

Angoulême hat.—With a very narrow brim and high fluted crown, named for the daughter of Marie Antoinette in 1815. (See Figure 60.)

Angoulême tippet.—Made of satin trimmed with swansdown; worn in 1815.

Angoulême spencer.—A new spencer in 1815. Illustrated in Figure 60.

Anne Boleyn mob.—Name given to a fashionable dress cap in 1807.

Arched collar.—A high collar (1814) curved to fit the throat and finished with a slightly flaring turnover.

Armenian toque.—Small turban of tulle and satin trimmed with feathers and spangled with silver, new in 1817.

Balmoral petticoat.—(1860) A woolen underskirt, originally red with black stripes, worn under a long dress looped up for walking.

Balmorals, or Balmoral boots.—(1860) Shoes which lace up the front, worn by both men and women. First introduced for outdoor wear by Queen Victoria at Balmoral, Scotland. Figure 166.

Bands (clerical).—An adjunct of clerical dress worn by Episcopalians and Presbyterians until 1870. Made of sheer linen cambric, worn around the neck with flat ends hanging down in front. Figures 300 and 357.

Beehive bonnet.—(1806) A shape resembling a hive usually made of plaited straw simply trimmed with ribbon and tied under the chin. Figure 59.

Bishop's blue.—A purplish shade of blue, new in 1809.

Blouse.—A loose-fitting bodice worn by women and children in 1820 and after.

Bluchers. — (1814–1850) Popular style of riding boot named for the famous Prussian General who visited London in 1814. It was

435

heavier than the Wellington boot and better adapted for riding and rough weather.   Figure 344.

Bonaparte hat.—Shaped like a helmet and decorated with a wreath of laurel ; sometimes worn on one side.   Fashionable from 1802 to 1806.   (See Figure 243.)

Boot-hooks.—Used to pull on the long boots worn from 1800 to 1870.

Bottle-green.—A dark bluish green worn from 1800 to 1860.

Bouilloné.—Puffed ; 1800 and after.

Brandenburgs.—Ornamental fastenings made of crocheted silk ; 1812 and after.

Brandenburg fringe. — Made of twisted sewing silk ; 1812 and after.

Buckskin. — Popular name for a riding gaiter made of tan-coloured leather ; 1800 and after.

Burnous or Burnouse.—A fashionable cloak worn since 1850, first introduced in France in imitation of the Moorish mantles worn by the Arabs and usually made of an eastern fabric woven of silk and goat's hair.

Bushel.—(Used only in the United States)—To mend or repair a tailor-made garment.

Busheller or Busheler.—A tailor's assistant whose business it is to repair garments.

Cabriolet.—A carriage with two wheels for one horse ; (ancestor of the cab) 1830 and after.

Cabriolet bonnet. — Large bonnet with flaring brim, named for the two-wheeled carriage introduced in 1830.   Figures 123, 244 and 279.

Caledonian cap.—A small hat fitting close to the head, trimmed with a profusion of black feathers, worn in 1817.

Caledonian silk.—A new material in 1819.   It was very strong and usually of a white ground with a small chequer of colour.

Capot.—An evening hood made of a cardinal silk handkerchief, considered very becoming ; 1816.

Capote or Capotte (same as the Poke bonnet).—A small bonnet with a projecting brim worn by women and children ; 1800 and after. Figure 11.

Capuchin.—A cape with hood, a survival of the seventeenth century ; much worn in 1807.

Capucine colour.—Dark orange or nasturtium colour, fashionable in 1806 and after.

Carmine.—A bright shade of red popular in 1817.

Carrick.—A long loose cloak fashionable in 1817 and after.

Caroline spencer.—Made of white kerseymere with a pelerine cape and trimmed with light blue satin cut bias ; 1818.

Cassock.—A long clerical coat, buttoned in front and reaching to the feet.

Cazenou.—A short sleeveless jacket ; 1855.

Chapeau bras (for gentlemen).—A crush hat of the nineteenth century; quite large when opened but flat when closed. (See Figure 340.)

Chapeau bras (for ladies).—A crush bonnet invented by Mrs. Bell, the foremost London dressmaker; very convenient for concert or opera wear; 1814.

Circassian hat.—Introduced in 1806; something like the Gipsy hat but with a fanciful crown.

Circassian sleeve.—A short sleeve looped up in front; worn by children in 1807.

Clarence.—A closed four-wheeled carriage with curved glass front, and seats for four people inside; 1811.

Clarence blue.—A new shade in 1811, similar to the Cambridge blue.

Coal-scuttle bonnet.—Popular name for the large flaring bonnet, sometimes called Cabriolet, worn in 1830 and after. Figure 272.

Coatee.—A short coat or spencer worn in 1802.

Coburg bonnet.—Bonnet with a soft crown tied under the chin; 1816.

Coburg cap.—Named in honour of the Duke of Saxe-Coburg in 1816. Made with a high crown of silver tissue; fashionable for the opera.

Coburg walking dress.—Named in honour of the Princess Charlotte.

Coiffure à l' indisposition.—Dressy cap made of lace and muslin; worn in 1812 and after. (See Figure 235.)

Conversation bonnet.—Made of chip, with flaring brim; usually lined with soft silk to match the ribbon trimming which was passed around the crown and tied in a bow on top; fashionable in 1807. Figure 23.

Coquillicot feathers.—A stiff little bunch of cock's feathers, fashionable in 1802 and after. Figure 10.

Cornette or French cap.—Fashionable in 1816; like the French bonnet in shape, completely covering the hair and ears; usually made of net or lace. It was tied under the chin with a small bow of ribbon to match the trimming on the top of the high crown. Figure 245.

Cornette à la Diane.—A small bonnet with crescent-shaped front; 1815.

Corset-frock.—Frock with a bodice shaped like a short corset with three gores on each side of the bosom and laced up the back with a white silk cord, short sleeves and short skirt.

Cossack hat.—Hat with a helmet-shaped crown, front turned back and edged with pearls; small feathers at one side; 1812.

Cottage cloak.—Cloak with a hood or cape and tied under the chin; a popular garment throughout the nineteenth century.

Curled silk.—A new material in 1814 used for bonnets.

Curls à la Greque.—Waving locks close to the face; 1802 and after. Figures 9 and 31.

Dandyess or Dandizette.—Popular names for the female dandy in the time of the Regency.

Demi-turban.—Soft scarf of muslin or gauze worn around the head and tied in a bow at the right side; 1800-1812. (See Figures 17 and 33.)

Devonshire brown.—A rich reddish brown like the soil in Devonshire; introduced in 1813.

Dinner cap.—Made of white satin and lace; popular in 1812. Figure 236.

Douillette à la Russienne.—Cloak with a warm lining, usually wadded. Fashionable in 1802 and after.

Dutch bonnet.—A straw bonnet turned up front and back. Fashionable in 1802. (See Figure 31.)

Eau de Veau.—A cosmetic used in 1808.

Egyptian amulet.—A favourite ornament in 1807.

En beret.—An arrangement of the hair with a cap; 1840 and after.

En coulisse.—An arrangement of puffs; 1840 and after.

En manche.—Made with cuffs; 1840 and after.

En ravanche.—An arrangement of flowers and ribbon worn over the left eye.

En tablier.—In apron effect; 1840 and after.

En tout cas.—A small umbrella used for both sun and rain; 1860 and after.

Esprits.—Stiff little plumes worn in hats; 1802 and after. Figure 10.

Eton jacket.—The short coat worn by the boys at Eton; fashionable for women in 1862 and after.

Fatima robe.—Short overgown; sleeves to the elbow; slashed up the front and caught together at intervals with buttons; worn over a muslin gown; fashionable in 1800.

Florence satin.—A thin soft variety of satin much used in 1802 and after.

Flushing hat.—Something like a Gipsy hat in shape, but with a double or under crown supplying the place of a cap; 1809.

Forester's or American green.—A bright green popular in 1817.

French bonnet.—Described in the books of 1811 as made of India muslin with a cone-shaped crown and a deep frill of Mechlin lace around the face and lined with sea-green sarsnet; a large lace bow on top. Figure 76.

French hat.—Another name for the cornet bonnet fashionable in 1815; crown very high and small flaring brim, often trimmed with a group of ostrich plumes.

French net.—A new material for evening frocks in 1807, similar to Brussels net.

Fugitive coat.—A sort of pelisse opening down the front introduced in 1807, a survival of the flying Josie of the preceding century. (See Figure 13.)

Garibaldi blouse.—Loose bodices named in 1859 for the Italian hero. Figure 165.

Georgian cloth.—A light weight broadcloth fashionable in 1806 and after.

Gipsy cloak.—A plain circular wrap, finished with a hood of the material.

Gipsy hat.—A plain hat of straw or chip tied carelessly under the chin with a ribbon; fashionable from 1800 to 1820. Figure 8.

Gossamer feathers.—Downy feathers found under the wings of the goose.

Gossamer satin. — A thin soft-finished satin similar to the Liberty satin of to-day; used for evening gowns in 1813 and after.

Graham turban.—A bonnet of plaid silk with a plume of black feathers; introduced in 1811.

Grecian robe. — A pseudo-classic garment fashionable for evening dress; 1800–1805.

Grecian sandal.—A novelty in footwear in 1812; for evening and street attire. (See Figure 50.)

Grecian scarf.—A graceful adjunct of the toilet illustrated in Figures 48 and 50.

Half boot.—A low shoe for women similar to our Oxford tie; worn in 1812 and after. Figure 48.

Half handkerchief. — A kerchief worn à la Marie Stuart with a point in front; made of net embroidered in gold or silver; very fashionable in 1807.

Hair à la Recamier.—Drawn back from the left eyebrow; 1802.

Hair à la Romaine.—Arranged in coils or braids crossing the head like a coronet.

Head à la Titus.—Name given to the short hair fashionable from 1800 to 1806.

Hessian.—A soft leather boot worn outside the trousers and curved under the knee; usually finished with a tassel at the top; 1800–1850. (See Figure 345.)

Hibernian vest.—A short jacket or spencer of velvet trimmed with fur; 1807.

High-low.—Popular name for a shoe reaching to the ankle; 1810 and after.

Hungarian vest.—A sort of jacket made with a high collar and long sleeves, a scarf hanging from the left shoulder and crossing in the back was caught into a belt; 1807.

Hungarian wrap.—A fashionable loose cloak in 1809, usually made of velvet and lined throughout with a corresponding shade of silk; it was wrapped in folds about the figure.

Huntley bonnet.—A cap of black velvet with silk plumes worn in 1813. (See Figure 49.)

Huntley scarf.—Scarf of Scotch tartan either in silk or wool, the ends fastened on the left shoulder. (See Figure 49.)

Hyde Park bonnet.—Made of white satin and trimmed with four white ostrich plumes. Very fashionable in 1812. Figure 237.

Italian slipper.—A flat slipper without a heel and cut low; worn in 1812.

Ivanhoe cap.—A cap named in honour of Scott's novel which was published in 1820.

Jaconet or Jaconette.—A thin variety of cambric used for dresses, neckhandkerchiefs, etc., originally made in India; fashionable in 1800 and after.

Jockey bonnet.—A bonnet with full crown and visor turned back from the face; 1806 and after.

Jockey hat.—Several varieties of hat are known by this name. In 1806 the fashionable jockey hat was turned up in front to show a contrasting colour and trimmed with fur. In 1820 and after a jockey hat had a peak or visor in front and was trimmed with a tassel or small ostrich feather; while in the sixties the jockey hat, celebrated in a popular song and very fashionable in America, had a small curved brim and round crown and was adorned with a rooster's feather. Figure 169.

Jonquille.—A fashionable shade of yellow; 1811 and after.

Kilt or Kilted skirt.—A short skirt laid in deep plaits; a fashion adopted from the Highland costume which became very popular for little boys in 1870. Figure 162.

Knickerbockers. — Loose kneebreeches worn by boys and sportsmen in 1860 and after. Figure 370.

Kutusoff hat.—Named in 1813 for the Russian General who commanded the Allies against Napoleon. Made of cloth and turned up in front with a little corner to the right side; tied under the chin and finished with a feather; a full puffing of lace under the brim. Figure 81.

Kutusoff mantle.—Made of cloth to match the hat, with a high puckered collar and a long lappel falling over the left shoulder; fastened at the throat with a brooch. Figure 81.

Lavinia hat.—A variety of the Gipsy shape, fashionable in 1807. (See Figure 13.)

Levantine.—A very soft velvet with a satin finish used in 1820 and after.

Limerick gloves.—Gloves made of rough kid; 1807 and after.

Magenta.—A purplish shade of red named for the battle of Magenta in 1859.

Mameluke.—An eastern wrap fashionable in 1806, hanging from the shoulder in full folds down the back.

Mameluke robe.—A full loose gown hanging from the shoulders with a train; 1806 and after.

Mancheron.—A cap-like trimming at the top of sleeves, often slashed; 1810 and after.

Manilla brown.—A soft light shade, new in 1811 ; name derived from Manilla hemp.

Marabout feathers.—Soft and downy feathers found under the wings and tail of the marabout stork ; much used for trimming in 1800 and after.

Marie-Louise blue.—A new shade of bright light blue named for the Empress ; still fashionable.

Marie Stuart bonnet.—Large in the brim, depressed in front over the brow, and flaring at the sides. For dress occasions it was made of white satin trimmed with lace and coloured ribbons. Figure 32.

Metallic gauze.—A new material in 1820. Gauze with a peculiar lustre and made in all colours to resemble precious gems ; emerald, topaz, amethyst, etc.

Minerva bonnet.—Shaped like a helmet with a long ostrich feather across the front ; fashionable in 1812.

Moorish boot.—Shoe of coloured kid laced in front ; 1807.

Mosaic gauze.—A new variety of gauze popular in 1820.

Nakara colour.—Pearl colour, fashionable in 1812 and after.

Neapolitan head-dress.—Worn for full dress in 1817, made of striped gauze and trimmed with silver.

Nicholas blue.—A new shade in 1817.

Oatlands hat.—Named in honour of the place where the Princess Charlotte passed her honeymoon in 1816.

Oldenburgh bonnet.—Named for the Duchess of Oldenburgh, who visited England in 1814. (See Figure 43.)

Over-alls. — Water - proof leggins worn in 1800 and after.

Pagoda or Chinese.—A parasol fashionable in 1818.

Palatine.—A wrap of black satin made with a hood, and lined with coloured silk.

Paletot.—A semi-loose overcoat fashionable in the second half of the nineteenth century.

Pamela bonnet or hat.—Made of straw, trimmed with a simple band of ribbon and tied under the chin. (See Figure 50.)

Panachée.—Variegated.

Panache.—A bunch of feathers.

Paysanne bonnet.—Another name for the cottage bonnet worn in 1800 and after.

Pea-green.—Very fashionable in 1809 and after.

Pea jacket.—A short heavy coat originally made of pilot cloth and worn by seamen, but copied in finer cloth for small boys ; 1850 and after.

Pekin satin.—A heavy satin with a stripe of the same colour ; 1802 and after.

Pelisse or Pelice.—A long coat-like garment usually made to fit the figure ; in general use with slight variations from 1800 to 1870.

Pensée or Pansy colour.—A delicate shade of purple new in 1841.

Percale.—A soft closely-woven cambric first mentioned in 1812 and still in use.

Persian cap.—A fashionable riding hat in 1811.

Persian scarf.—A Cashmere or silk scarf with a Persian border, a fashionable accessory in 1812.

Pilgrim's hat.—Of Carmelite brown with an ornament in front in the form of a cockle shell ; 1811.

Pistache or Pistachio colour.—A soft light shade of green very fashionable in 1819.

Platoff costume.—Named in 1813 for the daughter of Count Platoff who is said to have offered his daughter's hand to any soldier who would bring him Napoleon's head.

Plume velvet.—Velvet with a narrow stripe of satin of the same colour ; 1820.

Poke bonnet.—Popular name for the capote or close-fitting bonnet which projected or poked over the face. Worn in the early part of the nineteenth century. Figures 11 and 288.

Poland mantle.—New in 1806 ; made generally of light silk and fastened with an antique clasp or brooch on the right shoulder.

Pomona green.—A new shade in 1812 similar to apple green.

Pomposa.—A high-cut slipper laced up the front, worn by children in 1807 and after.

Poussière de Paris.—A shade of light brown known by this name in 1819. It was probably like the Bismarck brown of the present day.

Princess Augusta poke. — Usually of white satin with a feather to match, falling to the left side ; tied under the right cheek with a large bow of soft ribbon ; 1813.

Princess of Wales bonnet.—Made with a round crown and turned up at one side of the front. Named for Princess Caroline in 1812.

Provincial bonnet.—Made of fine straw, fitting closely to the head and flat on top ; trimmed simply with ribbon arranged in a flat bow on top ; 1808.

Redingote.—An outer garment or coat fashionable in 1848.

Regency ball-dress.—A plain round frock trimmed with a bias fold of satin up each side of the front edged with fringe ; an epaulet sleeve edged with fringe and fastened in front of the arm with small satin buttons ; new in 1813.

Regency cap.—Made of white satin trimmed with a rouleau of satin and a bunch of ostrich feathers ; new in 1813. (See Figure 45.)

Regency hat.—Crown made to fit the head and gradually widened to the top ; trimmed with cord and tassel and a feather ; new in 1813. (See Figure 44.)

Regency mantle.—Made of cloth, usually black ; about a yard and a half in length, with a small cape and high collar finished with silk tassels ; a wide band of silk cut bias edged with cord trimmed the garment round the bottom and up the fronts. New in 1813.

Regency wrapper.—New in 1813. Made with a train and long sleeves; was laced up the front with a silk cord, trimmed with a flat band of velvet or sealskin, and finished at the throat with a collar cut in points.

Ridicule.—Popular name for the reticule in general use from 1800 to 1850.

Robe à la Joconde.—A long gown opening over a short petticoat, fastened on the left shoulder with a full blown rose; 1817.

Roman sandal.—Fashionable footwear in 1817 and after.

Rutland poke.—A small bonnet of wadded satin edged with swansdown and tied under the chin with a soft ribbon; an ostrich feather was used as trimming placed very much to one side; 1813.

Saccharine alum.—A popular cosmetic in 1808.

Sardinian mantle.—A scarf made of thin stuff such as net, muslin, or spotted leno. The ends were usually caught into a full knot or rosette and hung down to the knee in front; worn in 1808.

Scoop bonnet.—Popular name for the long narrow bonnet worn in 1840. Figures 125, 131.

Sempstress bonnet.—Made of fine muslin, the crown drawn in with two rows of ribbon and fastened under the chin; 1812 and after.

Sleeve à la Minerva.—A full short sleeve caught up in front with a jeweled clasp.

Snap.—A fastening with a snap clasp used on pelisses and dresses in 1810 and after.

Solferino.—A shade of red named for the battle of Solferino in 1859.

Spa bonnet.—Made of a curiously wrought fancy straw sometimes of two colours, worn without any other trimming; 1819.

Spanish blue.—A favourite shade of dark blue for gentlemen's morning coats in 1809.

Spanish cloak.—Short and full mantle, one end of which was usually thrown over the shoulder.

Spanish coat.—Fashionable in 1814; pelisse with standing collar and epaulettes on the shoulders.

Spanish fly.—A rich shade of dark green new in 1809.

Spanish hat.—A felt hat with soft brim and trimmed with a drooping plume; much worn from 1802 to 1807.

Spencer.—A short jacket with or without tails; 1800 and after. Figure 27.

Surtout à la Sultane.—An overdress with a train worn over a white frock; a new fashion in 1802.

Suarrow boots.—Named for the Polish General; went out of fashion in 1802.

Swiss mountain hat.—Hat with a soft brim drooping over the face and trimmed with ostrich plumes; 1819.

Taglioni.—A short overcoat introduced in the days of the celebrated dancer's triumph; 1830 and after.

Tippet.—A flat collar with long ends hanging down in-front. Made of silk, velvet and fur, very popular in the first half of the nineteenth century.

Top boots. — Commonly called "Tops"; fashionable for hunting. They were carefully fitted to the foot and leg and were finished below the knee with buff or white leather tops, whence their name. They came into vogue at the time of the Regency and were worn until the end of the nineteenth century. (See Figures 346, 359 and 361.)

Torsade.—A twisted fringe trimming used in 1840.

Trafalgar dress.—Evening gown of white satin trimmed with silver, named for the battle of Trafalgar in 1806.

Treble or Triple ruff.—Made of three very full rows of pointed lace or of sheer muslin edged with lace, and fastened at the back of the neck; worn in 1813 and after.

Turbans.—Were the most popular head-dresses for women during the first half of the nineteenth century. Many illustrations are given of the different varieties throughout this book.

Turkish turban.—A turban made of folds of silk and gauze; in vogue in 1808.

Vevai cap.—A close-fitting cap of black velvet ornamented with a heron's plume; 1820.

Wallachian cap.—A round cap usually made of dark sable and worn with a tippet to match; 1812.

Washing leather gloves.—Fashionable in 1817 and after.

Wellington boots.—Named for the great General and worn in 1815 and many years after. Figure 343.

Wheel trimming.—Made in 1824 of soft puffings of silk formed into wheel-like circles, each overlapping the other.

Willow green.—Delicate shade of green, fashionable in 1811 and after.

Wraprascal.—Popular name for a loose overcoat used in the first half of the nineteenth century.

Wurtemburg frock.—A frock or dress of 1813, fastened in front under the trimming, which formed a little jacket effect; very long sleeves of lace.

Yeoman's hat.—Felt hat made with triangular points.

York tan gloves.—Made of rough undressed kid without any particular fit; 1807 and after.

Zebra feathers.—Striped in two different colours, fashionable in 1816.

Zephyr cloak.—Long over-garment of lace or net falling in long points to the feet and tied in at the waist by a sash of ribbon.

INDEX
Volume Two

INDEX

Volume Two

ACKERMAN'S "Repository," 24
Acrostic hats, 134
Acrostic jewelry, 133, 134
Algerian burnous, 254
Ambassadors, Court dress of, 395
American manufacture, clothes of, worn by President Madison, 369
Anagram jewelry, 133, 134
Angoulême hat, 117
Angoulême spencer, 117
Appliqué lace, 215
Aprons, 33, 65, 67, 161, 197, 305
Archer dress, 42
Artificial flowers, 36, 37, 44, 62, 66, 81, 141, 142, 143, 144, 155, 164, 187, 204
Austen, Jane, dress worn in her day described in letters of, 107, 112

BACK-COMBS, 312
Balmoral boots, 282
Bancroft, Mrs. George, her descriptions of dress in England, 234, 235, 236
Basques, 245
Bead chains, 234
Beards, 424
Bell sleeves, 224
Belts, 157, 196, 226
Berthas, 217, 232, 236
Bingham, Miss, dress worn by her at the Queen's Drawing-room (1802), 44
Bird of Paradise plumes, 91, 93
Bishop's dress, 428, 429
Bishop sleeves, 77
Black evening dress for men, 368
Black lace gloves, 225
Black moiré, 232
Blond gauze, 184
Blond lace, 212
Bloomer costume, 246, 247, 321
Blouses, 165, 319
Bodices, Corsages, Waists, 27, 51, 64, 65, 83, 85, 95, 96, 111, 187, 201,

205, 223, 226, 231, 233, 235, 237, 245, 319
Boigne, Comtesse de, Court dress and other fashions described by, 123, 124
Bombazine, 75, 85
Bonaparte, ball dress of Madame Jerome, 57 ; wedding dress, 37
Bonapartian hat, 42, 95
Bonnets, 34, 35, 36, 44, 53, 62, 67, 74, 75, 84, 94, 135, 142, 143, 145, 146, 153, 155, 156, 157, 162, 165, 173, 174, 176, 177, 183, 191, 192, 193, 197, 201, 202, 203, 204, 206, 213, 214, 222, 223, 224, 225, 226, 227, 231, 232, 236, 237, 241, 276, 277, 285, 300, 301, 309, 313, 314, 315, 332, 334
Bonnets (children's), 313, 314, 315
Boots, Shoes, 56, 62, 67, 74, 75, 76, 91, 92, 101, 106, 126, 156, 162, 164, 228, 282, 295, 315, 319, 333, 334, 335, 360, 362, 370, 394
Bourbon dress, 110
Bourbon hat, 110
Bracelets, 45, 222
Brandenburghs, 94, 203
Breeches, Trousers, Pantaloons, 361, 363, 367, 368, 378
Bretelles, 232, 319
Brinton, Miss Mary, dresses worn by in Philadelphia, 176
Broad brims, 327
Brownlow, Lady, fashions in Paris (1802), described in the "Reminiscences" of, 37
Brummell, Beau, 369, 370, 371
Brussels lace, 94, 95, 214, 235
Buckles, 136, 182, 226, 367, 369, 394, 415
Buckskins, 371
Bustles, 285

CABRIOLET bonnets, 176
Cachemire shawls, 116, 193

Café au lait (a new colour), 156
Caledonian caps, 123
Cameo brooches, 234
Canegous, 215
Canes, 355
Canning, Hon. Stratford, impressions of dress in America, 142, 388
Capes, 201, 232, 234, 241
Capotes, 35, 224
Caps, 36, 41, 42, 43, 44, 73, 84, 86, 141, 151, 153, 155, 163, 164, 222, 223, 225, 227, 231, 232, 235, 241, 334
Caps (boys'), 305, 310, 312
Caps (children's), 299, 314
Carmelite mantle, 74
Caroline, Princess, bonnet, 105
Caroline turban, 133
Carricks, 122
Cartes de visites, 424
Casagne, 234
Casauba, 399
Cashmere shawls, 116, 193
Cavalier's hat, 95
Ceres, à la (style of hair-dressing), 185
Chambéry gauze, 157
Chameleon silks, 231, 237
Chantilly lace, 262
Chapeau bras (ladies'), 113
Chapeau bras (men's), 360, 385, 395, 415
Chemisettes, 67, 231, 232, 233, 234, 246
Chemisettes (children's), 315
Chew, Miss, dresses worn in 1823 by, 174
Chignon, 274
Classic dress, 25
Clerical dress, 428, 429
Cloaks, 34, 62, 300, 301, 393
Clotilda cap, 164
Coat, varied expressions of a, 403
Coats, 331, 347, 351, 353, 354, 355, 359, 360, 361, 362, 363, 369, 371, 375, 378, 379, 385, 393, 394, 395, 396, 415, 419, 424
Coburg walking-dress, 122
Cocked hats, 353, 360
Coiffure (hair-dressing), 35, 47, 55, 81, 91, 144, 147, 151, 152, 153, 155, 161, 183, 184, 185, 187, 192, 195, 196, 205, 216, 217, 223, 225, 227, 233, 235, 236, 242, 254, 274, 276, 285, 332

Coin du feu, 234
Collars, 182, 183, 231, 232, 233, 235, 332
Collars (men's), 347, 354, 367, 371
Combs, 91, 222
Comet hat, 95
Congress, dress of members of in 1854, 419, 423
Congress gaiters, 282
"Constellation," costumes worn at a dinner on board the, 102
Coquette, La (cap), 222
Coral ornaments, 222
Cord and tassels, 222
Cornelia wrap, 234
Cornelian ornaments, 97
Cornettes, 121
Coronet braids, 217
Corsages, Bodices, Waists, 27, 51, 64, 65, 83, 85, 95, 96, 111, 186, 187, 201, 205, 223, 226, 231, 233, 235, 237, 245, 319
Corsets, Stays, 27, 112, 123, 191
Cosmetics, 82, 83
Cossack hat, 105
Cossack mantle, 86
Costume à l'antique, 25
Costumes worn by Jane Austen, 107, 112.
Cottage bonnet, 84
Court dress in England, 124, 125, 131, 132, 236
Court hoops, 124, 131, 132
Court mourning, 236
Cravats, Neckties, 370, 371, 379, 385, 386, 396, 414, 424
Crinoline, 215, 216. 319
Croquet costume, 282
Curl on the forehead, girl with a, 275
Curls, 35, 55, 91, 133, 187, 312
Cutaway coats, 423

Daguerreotypes, 217
Danish robes, 86
Debry, Jean, coat, 347
Delaine, 232
Derby (Mrs.), dress worn by her at the Queen's Drawing-room (1802), 44
Devonshire mob, 95
Diplomatic dress, American, 417, 418, 419, 424
Diplomatic dress, foreign, 384, 389

Doctors of Medicine, dress of, 375
Dolls, 320, 321
Double skirts, 242, 243
Drawn work, 73
Dress improvers, 285
Dress of American ladies at the Queen's Drawing-room (1802), 44
Dress worn at the ball given for La Fayette in Baltimore, 172
Dressing gowns, 399
Dunstable straw, 277

Ear-rings, 73, 81, 86, 91, 96, 97
Eau de veau (cosmetic), 83
Egyptian sand (colour), 145
Empire dress, 55
Empress peplin, 275
En barbe style of hair-dressing, 184, 185
En chiné, 253
En coulisses, 223
English curls, 223
English Point lace, 94
En redingote, 222, 225
En tout cas, 276
Epaulets, 104, 185
Etruscan pattern (trimming), 66
Eugénie, Empress, coiffure adopted by, 251; famous dressing-room of, 281; inaugurates the reign of the hoop-skirt, 251; riding habit of, 276; wedding dress of, 247

False curls, 133
Fans, 154, 164, 165, 185, 255
Fashion magazines, 23
Feathers, 33, 35, 36, 104, 153, 183, 214, 222, 235, 277
Feather trimming, 156
Fichus, 155, 156
Figured satin, 141
Fitzherbert, Mrs., arbiter of fashion in England, 94
Flats, 319
Flounces, 143, 146, 147, 161, 162, 163, 174, 184, 186, 231, 243, 257
Flushing hat, 84
Fluted trimming, 154
Follet, Le (Fashion Magazine), 224
Foreign Diplomatic Corps, dress of in Washington, 384, 389
Foreign names, 86

Foulard silks, 276
French aprons, 65
French coat, 74
French lawn, 77
French Legation, costumes of, 384
Fringe, 136, 147, 186
Frock coats, 351, 424
Full dress patent head-dresses, 47
Full skirts, 223
Fur, 53, 54, 66, 164, 183, 203, 221, 224, 246
Fur boas, 183
Fur trimmed shoes, 164

Gaiters, 162, 319
Gaiters (men's), 359, 361, 362, 375, 393, 429
Garibaldi blouse, 283
George IV, costumes worn at the coronation of, 387
Gillray, "Progress of the Toilet" by, 27
Gilt buttons, 363, 367, 423
Gipsy cloak, 62
Gipsy hat, 62, 65
Girdles, 237
Gloves, 67, 73, 74, 86, 91, 92, 95, 96, 97, 101, 106, 127, 144, 152, 162, 172, 185, 204, 205, 225, 255, 289
Gloves (men's), 370, 395
Godey's "Lady's Book," 204
Gold embroidery, 384
Gold lace, 384
Gores, 57
Gossamer satin, 76
Great Coats, Top Coats, Overcoats, 359, 363, 368, 383, 395, 399
Grecian bands, 35
Grecian knot, 196
Grecian sandals, 84
Grecian waists, 95
Greque, à la, hair dressed, 185
Guimpes, 53, 319
Guipure lace, 241

Hair caps, 376
Hair-dresser's announcement, 46
Hair-dressing (coiffure), 35, 47, 55, 81, 91, 144, 151, 152, 153, 155, 161, 183, 184, 185, 187, 192, 195, 196, 205, 216, 217, 223, 225, 227, 233, 235, 236, 242, 254, 274, 276, 285, 332

Hair dye, 47
Hair dyeing, 183
Half-boots, 164
Half handkerchiefs, 45
Half-shoes, 62
Half-turbans, 73
Handkerchiefs used as purses, 155
Hats, 35, 36, 37, 41, 42, 44, 62, 63, 84, 87, 94, 95, 104, 105, 134, 136, 173, 176, 183, 187, 195, 196, 204, 205, 241, 254, 277, 285
Hats (children's), 299, 300, 313, 320
Hats (men's), 327, 333, 353, 354, 355, 359, 360, 371, 395, 399, 417, 426, 429, 431
Hayes, Miss Sarah, wedding outfit of, 210, 211
Head-dresses, 35, 46, 47, 73, 163, 164, 215, 227
Head-dresses in hair, 46
Henri IV plume, 221
Hessian boots, 347, 371, 375
High combs, 195, 332
High hats, 320
Highland suits, 320
Honey-comb trimming, 82
Honiton lace, 214
Hoop-skirts, 142, 251, 252, 253, 263, 264, 265, 266, 267, 271, 272
Hoop-skirts, anecdotes of, 252, 266, 267, 271, 272
Howe, Julia Ward, descriptions of dress in England from her "Reminiscences," 217
Huile antiques, 37
Hungarian wrap, 84
Hunting dress, 431
Hussar boots, 363
Hussar caps, 86

Imperial hair restorer, advertisement of, 184
India cotton underwear, 81
Indian costumes (1832), 404
Indian feathers, demi-tiara of, 86
Indispensables, 45
Infant's dresses, 300
Invisible dresses, 77
Ivanhoe caps, 141

Jackets (boys') 320

Jackson calico, 175
Janizary jackets, 86
Jean Debry coat, 347
Jefferson, President, costume worn by him at his inauguration (1801), 352
Jet trimmings, 277
Jewelry (women's), 42, 45, 56, 86, 91, 124, 125, 133, 151, 152, 161, 162, 175, 185, 222, 235, 252, 254, 274
Jewelry (men's), 414
Jockey, 147
Jockey caps, 193, 310, 312
Josephine mantle, 234
Josephine, Empress, extravagance in dress of, 54; slippers of, 55

Kasaveck, 234
Kemble slippers, 94
Kenwig braids, 312
Kerchiefs, 53, 333
Key's travelling waistcoats, 351
Kilts, 320
Knee-breeches, Short Clothes, Small Clothes, 327, 351, 354, 355, 360, 369, 385, 395
Kutusoff hat, 106
Kutusoff mantle, 106

Lace, 54, 165, 166, 214, 215, 225, 227, 256, 262
Lace gloves, 225
Lace made in Massachusetts, 165, 166
La Fayette badge, 171, 172
La Fayette, dress worn at the ball given for him in Baltimore, 171, 172
Lamb, Lady Caroline, in a riding habit, 101
Lamb's wool underwear, 77
Lappets, 151, 213
Lavinia hat, 71, 91
Lawyer's gowns, 395
Leghorn hats, 143, 145, 162, 173
Leg-of-mutton sleeves, 173, 192, 309, 311
Leg-of-mutton trousers, 309
Levantine, 141
Lingerie blouses, 315
Locket watches, 42

Madison's, Mrs., costumes described, 93, 102

Madison's, President, customary dress, 368
Madonna curls, 187
Magenta colour, 283
Maid's costume in the early part of the 19th century, 28
Maid's costume 1850–70, 284
Mancheron, 147
Mantillas, 135, 237, 262
Mantles, 41, 43, 85, 144, 203, 234
Marabout feathers, 145, 222
Marguerite pink, 155
Marshall, John, official robes as Chief-Justice, 395
Martineau, Harriet, costume worn by her during her visit in Washington, 176
Mathematical tie, 386
Matted silk trimmings, 154, 158
Mechlin lace, 94, 95, 152, 227
Medway lace, 165, 166
Merry, Mrs., striking costume of in 1804, 56
Metallic gauze, 147
Mits, 224, 299
Mob caps, 66, 121
Morgan, Lady, description of her cabriolet and bonnet named after it, 177
Mouchoirs aux bêtes, 147
Mourning, 75, 76, 126, 224, 242, 261, 331
Mourning worn by children, 309
Mousquetaire gloves, 96, 289
Muffs, 53, 224
Mushroom hat, 277

NACE, MISS AMANDA, dress worn by her at the ball given for La Fayette in Baltimore, 172
Narrow skirts, 26
"National Intelligencer," letters of Mrs. Seaton on Society in Washington quoted from, 101
Natural flowers, 196
Necklaces, 81, 185, 204
Neckties, Cravats, 370, 371, 379, 385, 386, 396, 414, 424
Nets, 276
Neville, Lady Dorothy, hoop-skirt anecdote quoted from her "Reminiscences," 252
Night gowns, 55
Nile green, 155

Norton, Hon. Mrs., dress of described by Julia Ward Howe, 221

OLDENBURG bonnet, 112
Oldenburg dinner dress, 113, 114
Olives, 203
Oriental ties, 386, 396
Orsay, D' Count, costumes of, 408, 409; "Manual of Etiquette," 413
Overcoats, Great Coats, Top Coats, 359, 363, 368, 395, 399
Overdresses, 285

PALATINE (cloak), 216
Palm leaf hats, 399
Palm leaf pattern, 194
Pamona hat, 97
Pantalets, 303, 312, 315
Pantaloons (boys'), 310, 312, 320
Pantaloons (men's) 351, 362, 371, 378, 379, 393, 415
Parasols, 82, 92, 147, 151, 152
Pardessus, 234
Parisian tea parties, 154
Parti-coloured feathers, 165
Passementerie, 221, 224, 232
Patent leather boots, 415
Patent leather slippers, 415
Patent travelling hair caps, 376
Pear's soap, first advertisement of in "La Belle Assemblée," 1808, 83
Peck, Madame, fashionable milliner, Philadelphia, 1800, 31
Peignoir, 262
Pekin stripes, 225, 227
Pelerines, 85, 116, 134, 135, 182, 224
Pelerines (children's), 311
Pelisses, 144, 155, 186, 201, 254
Pelisses (children's), 299, 301
Pensée or Pansy (colour), 222
Persian border, 264
Persian taffeta, 203
Pigtails, 312
Pilgrim hats, 95
Pin tucks, 53
Plaid ribbon, 145, 147
Plaids, 319
Plume velvet, 141
Point d'esprit, 201
Pointed bodices, 232
Pointed toes, 96

Poke (bonnet), 117
Polish braid, 217
Polish cap, 67
Polish coat, 74
Polish riding dress, 74
Pompadour sleeves, 221
Poole, the English tailor, 425
Portrait painters of the 19th century, 26'
"Port Folio," 24
Postillion backs, 255
Powdered hair, 368, 369
Prescott, William H., dress worn at Court by, 415; red gown worn at Oxford, 416
Princess Augusta poke, 117
Princess Caroline bonnet, 105
Princess dress, 92
Printed satin, 205
Prismatic coloured silk, 187
"Progress of the toilet," by Gillray, 27
Provincial bonnet, 82
Pseudo-classic mania in dress, 24
Pumps, 360

QUAKER bonnets, 332
Quaker children, dress of, 301, 302
Quaker dress, 332
Quaker mourning, 331
Queues, 368, 369
Quilted parasols, 82
Quilted vests, 359
Quilted waistcoats, 361

RAINBOW gauze, 145
Rain cover for bonnets, 332
Ravenel, Mrs., description of dress in Charleston, 1800–1825, 34
Redingotes, 215
Redingote vest, 399, 400
Reed, Miss, the original girl with a curl on her forehead, 275
Regard ring, 133
Regency ball dress, 104
Regency cap, 104
Regency hat, 104
Regency jacket, 104
Regency mantle, 104
Regency wrapper, 103
Religieuse, La (cap), 222
Reticules or Ridicules, 45, 82, 147, 152, 162

Revers, 223
Ridicules—See Reticules
Riding dress (men's), 362, 431
Riding habits, 33, 61, 62, 74, 101, 121, 192, 193, 276, 283
Riding hats, 62
Ringlets, 55, 75, 225
Rocket, 428
Roman sandals, 94
Roman scarf, 223
Romantic nicknames, 51
Rouge, 72, 115
Rouleaux (trimming), 156
Round dresses, 53, 67, 74, 76
Round toes, 242
Ruffs, 63, 67, 74, 97
Ruffled shirts, 351, 355, 375, 385, 393
Rush, Hon. Richard, his description of Court dresses in London, 127
Rush, Hon. Richard, diplomatic costume worn by, 385
Russian cloaks, 86
Russian wrapper, 97
Rustic mantle, 74
Rutland poke, 107

SACCHARINE alum, 82
Sailor costume, 320
St. Memin's portraits, 58
Salmagundi Club in New York, 431
Sandals, 84, 94, 144
Sardinian mantle, 82
Sashes, 85, 135, 155, 319
Scalloped lace, 74
Scanty draperies, 37, 51, 53, 57
Scarf pins, 414
Scarfs, 164, 214
Scotch caps, 146
Scotch plaids, 135, 144, 320
Seaton, Mrs., extract from letters of, 103, 115
Seed pearls, 73, 161
Shaker dress, 333
Shaker worship, 334
Shaw, Mrs. Robert, inventions of, 77, 81
Shawls, 61, 193, 194, 214, 236, 237, 253, 254, 332
Shell combs, 242
Shell trimmings, 82, 142, 206
Shepherdess hat, 74
Shirts, 310, 375, 393, 395
Shoes, Boots, 56, 62, 67, 74, 75, 76, 91,

92, 101, 106, 126, 156, 162, 164, 228, 282
Shoes, Boots (children's), 295, 315, 319
Shoes, Boots (men's), 333, 334, 335, 360, 362, 370, 394
Shooting dress, 432
Shopping in Washington in 1850–60, 256
Short canes, 355
Short clothes—*See* Knee-breeches.
Short gloves, 96
Short skirts, 67
Short trousers—*See* Knee-breeches.
Short waists, 26
Shorts—*See* Short Clothes
Silk net gloves, 205
Silk stockings worn by men, 354, 367, 371, 385, 394
Silver filagree jewelry, 82
Sleeve cushions, 182
Sleeve extenders, 182
Sleeves, 43, 44, 53, 67, 72, 74, 134, 144, 165, 182, 186, 187, 191, 192, 201, 203, 205, 211, 215, 222, 223, 224, 226, 231, 232, 234, 235, 237, 243, 262, 311
Slender waists, 216
Slippers (women's), 34, 46, 54, 81, 94, 96, 97, 144, 183, 211, 225, 242, 295, 300
Slippers (men's), 347
Sloping shoulders, 232
Small clothes—*See* Short Clothes
Smith, Mrs. Samuel Harrison, descriptions of dress in America quoted from her book, 56
Smyrna work, 73
Snaps (fastenings), 91
Solferino (colour), 283
Southgate, Elizabeth, descriptions of dress in 1800, 27, 31, 32, 33, 45
Soutache braid, 224
Spangled velvet, 67
Spanish habit, 74
Spanish hat, 95
Spencers, 43, 44, 144, 215
Spotted muslin, 31, 32, 45
Spying glass, 162
Square toes, 211
Stage traditions in costume, 426
Starched underskirts, 231
Stays or Corsets, 27, 112, 123
Steel ornaments, 151

Steel pen coats, 423
Stock sentimentale, 396
Stocks, Neck-cloths, 360, 393, 395, 396, 419
Stockinette or Stocking, 378
Suède gloves, 289
Sunbonnets, 314
Surtouts, 399
Suwarrow boots, 354
Swallow tail coats, 423
Swords (dress), 395

TAGLIONI, À LA (trimming), 185
Tartans, 141, 142
Tippets, 85, 164
Tissue, 54
Top Coats, Great Coats, Overcoats, 355, 359, 362, 363, 368, 371, 383, 395, 399
Toques, 221
Trains, 53, 76, 85
Tricosian fluid, 51
Trollope, Mrs., extract from her book, "Domestic Manners of the Americans," 196
Trousers, Pantaloons, Breeches, 310, 312, 320, 351, 362, 371, 378, 379, 383, 393, 396
Tuckers, 144, 157, 161, 182, 186
Tunics, 305, 309
Turbans, 35, 44, 73, 77, 133, 143, 151, 152, 162, 163, 204, 220, 223

UNCUT feathers, 145
Uncut velvet, 237
Underclothes, 77, 81
Underdress, 225, 231
Undersleeves, 224, 246, 262
Union suits, 77

VALENCIENNES lace, 94, 204, 227
Vandyke frills, 151
Veils, 54, 63, 67, 73, 151, 203, 204, 213
Velvet ribbon, 237
Vests—*See* Waistcoats
Vevai cap, 143
Victoria, Queen, wedding dress of, 214
Village bonnet, 74
Violets, 121

454 INDEX

____riptt.

Virgin's tears, 77
Voilettes, 213, 214

WADDED capes, 216
Wadded rouleaux, 156
Wadded shawls, 216
Wadded waistcoats, 423
Wadded walking dresses, 216
Waistcoats, Vests, 310, 331, 333, 351, 352, 355, 359, 360, 361, 362, 363, 367, 368, 369, 371, 379, 385, 395, 408, 409, 414, 419, 423
Waists, Bodices, Corsages, 27, 64, 65, 83, 85, 95, 96, 111, 187, 201, 205, 223, 231, 233
Waltz, the, 137
Waterfall, 274
Wellington boots, 383
Wellington hood, 107
Wellington mantle, 107
Wellington trousers, 383

White mourning, 236
Whiskers, 369, 383, 424
Wide skirts, 191
Wigs, 27, 31, 32, 34, 35, 55, 56, 375
Wigs, worn by Doctors of Medicine, 375
Willow feathers, 222
Winged ruffs, 67
Witzchoura, 123
Wrappers, 55
Wrapping cloaks, **26, 299**
Wristlets, 196

YATES, EDMUND, dress of a Doctor of Medicine described by, 375; different types of dress worn in England in 1836–1846, 406, 407, 408
York morning dress, 97

ZOUAVE jacket, 284, 315
Zouave trousers, 284

AUTHORITIES CONSULTED

Authorities Consulted

The Port Folio, Oliver Oldschool, Philadelphia, 1801–5.

La Belle Assemblée, 1806–24, London.

Letters of Eliza Southgate Bowne; or, A Girl's Life Eighty Years Ago, New York, 1887.

Our Grandmothers' Gowns, Mrs. Alfred Hunt, London, 1895.

The Dawn of the Nineteenth Century in England, John Ashton, London, 1886.

Follies and Fashions of our Grandfathers, A. W. Tuer, London, 1887.

Forgotten Children's Books, A. W. Tuer, London, 1898.

Old-Fashioned Children's Books, A. W. Tuer, London, 1899.

Diary of Rev. Manasseh Cutler, New York, 1886.

La Vie Parisienne, 1800–1870, Paris.

Letters of William Winston Seaton, Boston, 1871.

Jane Austen and her Friends, G. E. Mitton, London, 1906.

Jane Austen's Letters, edited by Lord Brabourne, London, 1884.

Travels in the United States, 1849–50, Lady Emeline Stuart Wortley.

Court Magazine, 1830–47, London.

American Ladies' Magazine, edited by Mrs. Hale, Boston, 1831.

Evening Fireside, Philadelphia, 1805–6.

Eugénie, Empress of the French, Clara M. Tschudi, New York, 1899.

Private Life of Edward VII (Prince of Wales 1841-1901), by a Member of the Royal Household.

Memoranda of a Residence at the Court of London, 1819–1825, Richard Rush, Philadelphia, 1848.

In Peace and War, Mrs. Pryor, New York, 1904.

Dixie after the War, Mrs. Avery, New York, 1906.

Punch, 1840–1870, London.

Lady's Monthly Museum, 1799–1824, London.

Beau Brummell and his Times, Roger Boutet de Monvel, London, 1908.

Life of Beau Brummell, Captain William Jesse, London, 1886.

Recits d'une Tante, Memoires de la Comtesse de Boigne, Paris, 1907.

Leaves from the Note-Book of Lady Dorothy Neville, London, 1907.

Extracts from the Journal and Correspondence of Miss Berry, London, 1865.

Social Life in the Early Republic, Anne H. Wharton, Philadelphia, 1902.

Fifty Years of London Life, Edmund Yates, New York, 1885.

Things as They Are in America, Wm. Chambers, Philadelphia, 1854.

History of the United States, James F. Rhodes, New York, 1904–6.

Memoirs and Private Correspondence of the Right Hon. Stratford Canning, London, 1888.

Portraits of the Sixties, Justin McCarthy, New York, 1903.

A Belle of the Fifties, Mrs. Clay, New York, 1904.

A Southern Girl in '61, D. G. Wright, New York, 1905.

Latrobe's Journal, New York, 1905.

First Forty Years in Washington Society, Mrs. S. Harrison Smith, New York, 1906.

Slight Reminiscences of a Septuagenarian, Countess Brownlow, London, 1867.

Memoirs of Lady Dorothy Neville, London, 1908.

Ladies' Magazine, Boston, 1829–1834.

Harper's Magazine (Vol. 15), New York, 1857.

Sartain's Magazine, Boston, 1849.

Moniteur des Dames et des Demoiselles, Paris, 1855.

Little Memoirs of the Nineteenth Century, London, 1902.

Letters from England, Mrs. Bancroft, New York, 1904.

Diary of a Lady in Waiting, Lady Charlotte Bury, London, 1908.

Mrs. Fitzherbert and George IV, W. H. Wilkins, New York, 1905.

Memoirs of Fifty Years, Lester Wallack, New York, 1889.

Memories of Seventy Years, edited by Mrs. Herbert Martin, London, 1883.

Reminiscences, 1819–1899, Mrs. Julia Ward Howe, New York, 1899.

Two Centuries of Costume, Alice Morse Earle, New York, 1903.

Directoire, Consulat et Empire, Paul Lacroix, Paris, 1884.

Dix-neuvieme Siecle en France, J. Grand-Carteret, Paris, 1893.

Le Costume Historique, A. Racinet, Paris, 1888.

The Quaker, a Study in Costume, Mrs. Francis B. Gummere, Philadelphia, 1902.

The History of Fashion, G. A. Challamel, London, 1882.

Modes and Manners of the Nineteenth Century, from the German of Max von Boehm, 3 Vols., London, 1910.

Chats on Costume, G. Woolliscroft Rhead, New York, 1906.

Collection of Fashion Plates, 7 Vols., 1810–1890.

Godey's Lady's Book, 1830–1870, Philadelphia.